T0376825

AFRICAN ETHNOGRAPHIC STUDIES
OF THE 20TH CENTURY

Volume 39

THE REALM OF A RAIN QUEEN

THE REALM OF A RAIN QUEEN
A Study of the Pattern of Lovedu Society

E. JENSEN KRIGE AND J. D. KRIGE

LONDON AND NEW YORK

First published in 1943 by Oxford University Press for the International African Institute.

This edition first published in 2018
by Routledge
2 Park Square, Milton Park, Abingdon, Oxon OX14 4RN

and by Routledge
711 Third Avenue, New York, NY 10017

Routledge is an imprint of the Taylor & Francis Group, an informa business

© 1943 International African Institute

All rights reserved. No part of this book may be reprinted or reproduced or utilised in any form or by any electronic, mechanical, or other means, now known or hereafter invented, including photocopying and recording, or in any information storage or retrieval system, without permission in writing from the publishers.

Trademark notice: Product or corporate names may be trademarks or registered trademarks, and are used only for identification and explanation without intent to infringe.

British Library Cataloguing in Publication Data
A catalogue record for this book is available from the British Library

ISBN: 978-0-8153-8713-8 (Set)
ISBN: 978-0-429-48813-9 (Set) (ebk)
ISBN: 978-1-138-58974-2 (Volume 39) (hbk)
ISBN: 978-0-429-49143-6 (Volume 39) (ebk)

Publisher's Note
The publisher has gone to great lengths to ensure the quality of this reprint but points out that some imperfections in the original copies may be apparent.

Disclaimer
The publisher has made every effort to trace copyright holders and would welcome correspondence from those they have been unable to trace.

Due to modern production methods, it has not been possible to reproduce the fold-out maps within the book. Please visit www.routledge.com to view them.

THE REALM OF A RAIN-QUEEN

A STUDY OF THE PATTERN OF LOVEDU SOCIETY

By

E. JENSEN KRIGE, D.LITT.(RAND), M.A.

Author of *The Social System of the Zulus*

and

J. D. KRIGE, B.A., LL.B.

Advocate of the Transvaal Supreme Court; Lecturer in Bantu Studies at Rhodes University College, Grahamstown

With a Foreword by

THE RT. HON. FIELD-MARSHAL

J. C. SMUTS

P.C., C.H.

Published for the
INTERNATIONAL INSTITUTE OF AFRICAN LANGUAGES & CULTURES
by the OXFORD UNIVERSITY PRESS
LONDON NEW YORK TORONTO
1943

OXFORD UNIVERSITY PRESS
AMEN HOUSE, E.C.4
London Edinburgh Glasgow New York
Toronto Melbourne Capetown Bombay
Calcutta Madras

HUMPHREY MILFORD
PUBLISHER TO THE UNIVERSITY

THE TYPOGRAPHY AND BINDING
OF THIS BOOK CONFORM TO THE
AUTHORIZED ECONOMY STANDARD

Printed in Great Britain

CONTENTS

FOREWORD
    by the Rt. Hon. Field-Marshal J. C. Smuts, P.C., C.H. .   PAGE vii

PREFACE xii

CHAPTER I. PAGEANTS OF THE PAST . . . 1
    Fame of Mujaji, transformer of the clouds—the cycle of the kings—the cycle of the queens—from the pageants to the people.

CHAPTER II. A PICTURE OF EVERYDAY THINGS . 17
    A visitor's impressions of the manners and interests of the people—a glimpse of a village and its huts, of the preparation of food and etiquette in eating, and of the decorum of drinking beer—the evening scene with its hearth fires, riddles and stories—the seasonal calendar of activities.

CHAPTER III. BASES OF SUBSISTENCE   34
    The agricultural complex of activities—culture-change adjustments, and problems of malnutrition, education, and division of labour in agriculture—the place in the society, and present-day problems, of animal husbandry—modern threats to the interest in the vegetation as a basis of subsistence.

CHAPTER IV. CO-OPERATION AND EXCHANGE . 52
    Arrangements of and changes in the work party, partnerships, and solitary occupations—relative roles of economic and goodwill exchanges—beer, dances and bride-price as vehicles of reciprocal exchanges—aversion from business.

CHAPTER V. FAMILY TIES 70
    Personal relations within the polygynous household—the sister as the centre of the social system—behaviour patterns and avoidances between potential and actual relatives-in-law and their modification by personality and adjustment—the position of orphans.

CHAPTER VI. SOME SOCIAL GROUPINGS . . . 85
    Groups in the tribe—analysis of the groups of a district—character, divisions, and subdivisions of groups—the patrilineal lineage as the core of co-residence—marriage groups, age sets and regimentation.

CHAPTER VII. EARLY TRAINING 102
Nursing and growing up—herdboy gang life and the learning of veldlore—an institutionalized play-school—'crossing' rites and the significance of ordeals and obscene language—opportunities and satisfactions of old age—the task of the modern school.

CHAPTER VIII. FERTILITY AND THE DRUM CULT 126
The setting of the sacred drums in a mystical cult—initiation into the secrets of the whistling ancestors—calendric observances connected with fecundity, masks, and mummeries.

CHAPTER IX. MARRIAGE AND THE SOCIAL STRUCTURE 141
Mate selection and marriage exchanges as reflections of the social structure—social and psychological aspects of nuptial rites—the handling of the themes of sex and concubinage, of barrenness and premature death in the marriage situation.

CHAPTER X. COGS IN THE POLITICAL MACHINERY 164
Ritual suicide, divine selection, the fire rite, and celibacy as aspects of the royal complex of institutions—links in the political system forged by the wives of the queen—the part women play in politics—structure and individuality of the districts.

CHAPTER XI. THE GENIUS OF JURIDICAL ADJUSTMENTS 186
Conciliation machinery at the capital—quasi-judicial systems of appeasement—reliance in full-dress trials and sanctions upon agreement and compromise—procedure in 'blood' cases—appeals to ordeals and diviners.

CHAPTER XII. THE PURSUIT OF HEALTH . . 211
Anatomical conceptions in relation to the science of drugs and of healing—cardinal categories of the causation of disease—training for the medical profession—divinatory dice as a method of diagnosis.

CHAPTER XIII. THE ROLE OF THE ANCESTORS . 231
Ancestral caprices and complaints and rites to appease them—the universe of the ancestors a replica of the everyday world—relations of magic, morality, and religion—possession by spirits as a religion and socio-psychological phenomenon.

CHAPTER XIV. WITCHCRAFT AND SORCERY . . 250
Techniques and manifestations of day and night witchcraft—distinctions between witchcraft and magic—smelling out of witches by the forensic physician—social incidence and psychological aspects of witchcraft.

CONTENTS

CHAPTER XV. THE RAIN CULT 271
The rain-queen in her sphere of safeguarding the seasons—technique of transforming the clouds—evils that cause 'heat' and act as impediments to rain—'cooling' rites counteracting the 'heat' of the earth.

CHAPTER XVI. TRIBAL TRAITS AND ATTITUDES . 282
Harmonizing the bases of social security with outlets for personal expression—the role of beer—moderation as an ideal and in the spheres of sex and authority—preoccupation with the quest for health—attitudinal reaction to the Western world.

CHAPTER XVII. CULTURE CONTACT AND CULTURE CHANGE 299
The relativistic approach: value of comparative and historical study—*interpenetration of the tribes*: ethnogenesis of the Lovedu and evolution of some of their cultural patterns—*the iconoclasm of Christianity*: breaking down and building up among converts, repercussions among pagans—*the challenge of Western conquest*: the indirect responses of the culture and its undisturbed foundations.

GENERAL INDEX 329
INDEX OF TRIBES, CLANS AND RACES . . . 336

LIST OF MAPS

PAGE
SUB-DISTRICT OF THE CAPITAL 16
LOVEDU LOCATION 176
ETHNOGENESIS OF THE LOVEDU 302
POSITION OF LOVEDU AMONG N. TRANSVAAL TRIBES *Facing page* 336

LIST OF ILLUSTRATIONS

PLATE
- I. THE LOVEDU LANDSCAPE . . *Facing page* 16
  - (a) The Hill of Cycads
  - (b) Fields and Villages on the Foothills
- II. A GLIMPSE OF VILLAGE LIFE . . ,, 17
  - (a) Courtyard Scene in March
  - (b) Stamping Mealies
- III. ARTS AND CRAFTS . . . . ,, 32
  - (a) Carving a Porridge Bowl
  - (b) Fashioning a Skin Shirt
- IV. CO-OPERATION IN AGRICULTURE . ,, 33
  - (a) Work-party de-cobbing Mealies
  - (b) Work-party carrying Home the Mealie Crop
- V. THE LOVEDU BABY . . . . ,, 96
  - (a) Feeding Baby
  - (b) Bathing Baby
- VI. HOUSEWIVES, YOUNG AND OLD . ,, 97
  - (a) The Watched Pot
  - (b) Water and Vegetables for her Home
- VII. ADOLESCENCE . . . . . ,, 112
  - (a) Realistic Play-cooking in the *Mandwane*
  - (b) A Troupe of youthful Dancers
- VIII. GIRLS' INITIATION INTO WOMANHOOD ,, 113
  - (a) Coming forth from her Puberty Seclusion
  - (b) Girls in the Vyali
- IX. MASKED DANCERS OF RAVOTHATA . ,, 128
- X. MASQUERADE OF THE *VUHWERA* . ,, 129
  - (a) Strutting of the *Vuhwera* Dance
  - (b) Dance of the Duiker
- XI. DOMESTIC DUTIES . . . . ,, 144
  - (a) Dishing up requires great Skill
  - (b) Straining the precious Beer Brew
- XII. THE BRIDE BECOMES A WIFE . . ,, 145
  - (a) 'Little Bride of Ochre, seek Shelter'
  - (b) Still in her Finery, the Bride begins working
- XIII. AT THE CAPITAL . . . . . ,, 208
  - (a) Re-building the Courtyard of the Capital
  - (b) The Courtyard (*Khɔrɔ*), with a Case in progress
- XIV. THE PURSUIT OF HEALTH . . . ,, 209
  - (a) Diagnosing the Cause of Illness
  - (b) The *Khadi* pours Beer to appease the Ancestors
- XV. BEER AS A SOCIAL STIMULANT . ,, 288
  - (a) Beer being carried to the Queen
  - (b) A Beer Party
- XVI. RELIGIOUS PRACTICES . . . . ,, 289
  - (a) At the Lily Shrine
  - (b) A typical Lovedu Shrine

FOREWORD

I AM interested in this book for two reasons. The first is that the authors are my nephew and his wife—both devoted anthropologists, to whom this painstaking research into the least known of our South African native tribes has been a real labour of love. While earth's foundations were shaking in the convulsion of our times they were absorbedly probing into the mysteries of the Rain-Queen and her 'timeless' society. To me this seemed an almost unnatural devotion to science—until I came to read the MS. of this book and found it a fascinating distraction to the war problems which form my daily life. Perhaps the curious reader may find it no less entertaining.

The second reason is that for at least half a century the Rain-Queen and her people and the curious stories about them have interested me. She was said to be very light coloured: was she a descendant of one of a couple of Boer girls who were said to have been spared by those natives, when early in the nineteenth century they massacred the Van Rensburg party without leaving a trace behind? What was the mystery about her which made it almost impossible for Europeans to catch a glimpse of her? Had the Natives adopted a white queen as something divine? Even if these were mere baseless fancies, other points of personal interest attracted me to the subject of the queen. Long ago one of my daughters, when a college girl, visited the country of the queen with a company of friends in the hope that they might be able to see her. In that mountainous, almost roadless country the party was overtaken by a violent rainstorm and late at night arrived at her headquarters drenched, exhausted, and more dead than alive. The queen ordered a hut to be cleaned and prepared for them where they stayed the night; and next day, having probably heard that she was the Prime Minister's daughter, gave a personal audience to her. Imagine the thrill! That established a personal bond between the queen and my wife, suitably recognized in the customary South African way. Then many years after, my nephew and his wife were staying at the headquarters of the queen in order to gather the material for this book. From time to time they informed me of the most interesting anthropological finds they were making. I also learnt that near her headquarters was a forest of cycads (*Encephalartos transvenosus Burtt-Davy*), one of the most unique botanical features in South Africa. This decided me at last to spend a holiday in the queen's country, and, with my relatives as guides, I had a most interesting experience. I saw how they had, through simple humanness, overcome the fears and the shyness of the people and were on most familiar terms both with the queen and her subjects. I saw my cycad forest. Best of all, I saw that wonderful woman, well over sixty, but strong in body and character—every inch a queen. We exchanged information and gifts in the traditional style, and I could thank her for her kindness to my daughter in the distant past. She was much taken up with all the useful domestic articles my wife had sent her. A couple of years afterwards I was once more Prime Minister, and I received a most charming letter from her, expressing her pleasure that she had met and personally knew the man who was 'wearing the crown of South Africa'. Accepting the complimentary expression so kindly meant, I was equally pleased to have met a woman who so impressed me with her force of character and intangible air of authority—a woman who really was a queen. No wonder her subjects look upon her as the embodiment of their divine order. And yet that woman is the centre—in the ritual of her tribe—of a great tragedy which awaits her, as it has awaited her predecessors. That ritual carries us back to the most dim and distant past of the human race, and the interested reader will find it in this book. Mujaji is one of the high lights of anthropology, and, looking at her calm, strong face, I wondered what she thought of the fate in store for her. Here are the tears in things mortal.

This book is interesting from another point of view. It paints the picture of a Native society in which the pattern or plan of the whole determines the character of all the main lines of detail. Religion, law, ethics, social institutions, all fit naturally and almost logically into the scheme as a whole—they appear to be products of the central pattern which has stamped its character on all the details. The social sanctions in law, religion, ethics, &c., are not external and superimposed on the social practice, but flow from the fundamental social system itself as its natural outcome. All are in one degree or another internal to the system. The writers of this study have succeeded in penetrating to this inner core of this particular type of Native society, and in showing the balance and harmony of the system as a whole. This gives, in my opinion, a very special anthropological value to this study.

They have no doubt been able to probe thus deeply into this Native society because of the sympathetic relations they have been able to establish with the Natives. The first task of the anthropological field-worker, that of gaining the confidence of the Native, is more difficult than is generally supposed. As those who know the Native mind realize, it requires qualities of tact, patience, and sympathy of the highest order. This task presents unusual difficulties among the people of Mujaji, whose suave and accommodating manners can be most effectively used to frustrate the quest of the field-worker. And if there is one thing about which they are persistent, it is the safeguarding of their secrets. The tenacity with which they keep these secrets is intelligible, for they attach as great importance to the mystery supporting the powers of their queen as an army commander to the strategy which will ensure the success of his campaign. The queen is rain-maker *par excellence* of South Africa, and to maintain that position her secret weapon must never be divulged. Moreover, intimately linked with the preservation of her powers are many of the constituent parts of the whole tribal structure. All the major institutional arrangements in some way subserve the grand purpose of making her the divine 'transformer of the clouds'. Since the foundations as well as the superstructure of the culture are interlocked with this purpose and are psychologically necessary, as the authors show, for sustaining men's faith in the Rain-Queen's role, investigations even into

FOREWORD BY FIELD-MARSHAL J. C. SMUTS

the most everyday occurrences arouse suspicion and are met with evasions. In these circumstances, penetration into the innermost life and values in the society is an outstanding achievement. The acid test of the investigator's understanding of the primitive people he studies is whether or not he makes sense of what appears to the ordinary observer as a mass of vices, follies, and superstitions. That is the test that the authors have satisfied. In this book, customs and an outlook so different from ours as to be regarded from our point of view as irrational and perverted emerge as perfectly natural and coherent—nay, inevitable in the total context of the culture.

Another reason for ranking this book high among monographs on the Bantu is that it deals with a people whose ethnic affinities give them an important place in future comparative studies. They occupy a country which has been subjected to influences emanating from three major clusters of the Southern Bantu: the Sotho of the central plateau, the Nguni of the south-east coastal regions, and the Shona to the north of the Limpopo. Migrating southward some centuries ago from the disrupted empire of Monomotapa, the land of our enigmatic Zimbabwe ruins, they have absorbed into their original culture many diverse elements from tribes in the south. The composite nature of their culture, which has none the less been welded into a remarkably coherent whole, and the feasibility of studying the character of its constitutional parts in other tribes are of great significance for the comparative study of tribal institutions. I believe that the time has arrived for such a study, at least of those sections of the Bantu of whom we have some considerable knowledge. In a limited sphere, that of the tribes of the Northern Transvaal, the authors, who have tested the value of comparative field-work, point out the perspective they have gained from this method and the clues for interpreting custom that it has given them.

Of the specific contributions in this book to our knowledge of Bantu custom and thought, I need refer merely to a few. The authors are concerned mainly with presenting a balanced analysis of the great dynamic forces in the social system, of the mentality and outlook of the people, and of the tendencies due to culture contact. It is therefore all the more significant that they have found room to emphasize the place in the lives of the people of the practical, everyday business of making a living. Not even a primitive people, however magic-ridden their culture, can afford to give less time and energy to provide for their material needs than to what we call their superstitions. What must strike every reader is the extent of their knowledge and use of the vegetation. We ought to know more of these things in Bantu life, not merely because of their intrinsic interest and the light they throw upon how far empirical relations are recognized by primitive peoples, but also it is upon knowledge of this kind that we can most profitably graft our own scientific conceptions, our measures for their material progress. This is not to say that we should not also know their philosophy of life, for fundamental values cannot be disregarded in the handling of human situations. But it is clear that the vast, only slightly explored field of the Native's knowledge of plants, their properties and uses, awaits intensive investigation. The authors are justified in their admiration for the Native's knowledge of the vegetation. Recent chemical analysis of several Native relishes shows that their protective and nutritional value is not inferior to that of our vegetables and greens. We know very little of the therapeutic value of roots and barks used in Native medicine, but, since close observation of nature and a real capacity for understanding empirical relations is evident in all their practical activities, there is ample justification for research in these matters, even though Native medicine is largely dominated by magical conceptions.

In the complex of social institutions, women have an unusually exalted position, higher even than among the Venda. It is evident that the claims of women to achievement are given special recognition. The maintenance of their status in a patrilineal society is not merely a survival; it is closely connected with the distinctive pattern imparted to the culture by a queen, who, besides being the religious head, is the nucleus of a network of political alliances. Social links in the society have ingeniously been co-ordinated with its predominant pattern. The special link between brother and sister has, for instance, been coupled to the chain of the bride-price cattle exchanges, and in the result a web of influences radiates from the sister to the various parts of the social system. Women thus become the nucleus of a system which holds together the intermarrying groups, the district organizations and, to a large extent, the whole political structure. It is not to be expected that this power of women, in a society which accords legal precedence to men, will always go unchallenged. For that reason, among others, many conflicts as regards succession to important positions and other institutional stresses and strains arise.

The method of settling differences is discussed in an illuminating chapter appropriately headed 'The Genius of Juridical Adjustments'. This chapter throws new light upon, just as it makes an outstanding contribution to, Bantu jurisprudence. Law emerges as an extremely flexible body of rules, enforced chiefly by the complex interconnexions within the institutions of which they form part and administered by a body of men concerned not so much with the superficial issues presented by the parties as with the fundamental causes of friction between them. As contrasted with our legal system, in which law decides between issues, their method is to reconcile persons. The arbitrational machinery in the service of their system ramifies through the whole society. Like the genius of the complex royal institutions, its genius is directed towards appeasement and the maintenance of a well-balanced equilibrium. The emphasis upon these things, coupled with other arrangements in the society, has brought about a system which functions without involving, or at least without relying for its validity upon, sanctions of physical force. The effective sanctions are to be found in the interplay of a network of reciprocal rights and obligations: if the reciprocities are respected life is worth living, if they are neglected life is difficult, often impossible.

Besides these contributions to the working of the society, the book contains a series of chapters on the philosophy of life of the people and their mentality. They do not, of course, speculate about final causes, but their conceptions of the causation of disease and death—the great evils they recognize—and of the interrelations of the worlds of natural and supernatural forces provide evidence of their outlook upon final causes. It is an outlook very different from our own, but nevertheless coherent. If we start from their premisses and the small measure of control they have over the forces of nature, we may come to conclusions not unlike theirs. Their conclusions are, in other words, neither absurd nor the inferences of irrational beings with minds operating differently from ours. This difference in outlook upon final causes is found also in the sphere of what we may call 'moral qualities', such as honesty, industry, moderation. It is in this sphere, as the authors show, that grave misunderstandings are liable to arise between Europeans and Natives in their practical relations with one another. In the timeless society of the Native the need there is among us for intensive striving, precision, and punctuality does not exist; and as a result friction is liable to arise in the employment situation. This is but one of the many instances in which incongruities in the two cultures may cause conflicts when they are brought into contact with one another. The merit of the discussion of this subject lies both in that Lovedu traits and attitudes are shown to be inevitable consequences of the cultural pattern and in the appreciation of the reality of the difficulties encountered by the European in the contact situation. This is the kind of realism that will go far towards making the conclusions of social anthropology more acceptable to practical men and more useful to the administrator.

These are only a few of the many interesting and remarkable features of this study. Other readers may be attracted by other features in it. I commend the book as a whole as one of the most honest and penetrating researches into Native life that I have come across. And I am aware of the hard work and loving care that have gone to the making of it.

J. C. SMUTS.

CAPETOWN.
March, 1941.

PREFACE

THIS book presents the life and culture of the Lovedu, a Bantu tribe in South Africa. Its central figure is a sacred queen. Against the background of our world, she no doubt appears unreal in some respects, like the baseless fabric of a dream, but in others she is real enough. We can, for instance, readily visualize her, without official husband to cramp her authority, bearing her successor by a secret consort; or maintaining her strategic position at the centre of the tribe by re-distributing as favours the wives she receives as tribute. But it is a different and far more difficult matter to depict as real what we regard as mysterious; for, hallowed by a heritage of incest, she is chosen for her role by the ghost of her predecessor, and her destined end is death by her own hands, in order that she may rule by divine right. We have tried to show that these mysteries become realities when we see them as means to the supreme end of consecrating her power to make rain, and when we realize that this power implies control of half the cosmic forces and gives men faith to do their daily tasks.

Our main object has been to describe the culture of the Lovedu. We have set ourselves the task of showing the nature of its parts and their relation to one another. Some space is devoted to the royal institutions; the network of links woven by kinship, marriage and marriage cattle; the legal procedure of compromise and appeasement; and various aspects of magic, witchcraft, and religion. Considered as a whole, the culture emerges as a structure supporting and in turn supported by the Rain-Queen. We may think of the royal institutions as the foundations upon which men build for safety against famines and foes; the culture dispenses with reliance upon garden magic for success of the crops and upon a military system for national defence. Marriage cattle and the kin can be regarded as forging a frame which firmly holds the society together, binding its families, foreign groups and territorial units to one another and to the queen. Stresses and strains are taken by flexible devices for adjusting disputes by conciliation. A cult of masks and man-made mysteries appears to surmount the edifice like spires and pinnacles; we may envisage it as the cultural handling of those enigmas of nature, the exalted themes of growth and fertility.

Next, we have tried to outline the attitudes and interests of the people. They appear as carriers of the culture oriented toward the central figure and helping one another to bear the burden of a timeless society. Our chief concern has been to show how their ideals and motives have been moulded by the culture; why, for instance, they frown upon competition and appraise moderation, and how it is that they are not troubled by sex-guilt or inferiority complexes. We have finally turned to consider some aspects of culture contact, such as the fear and distrust of the agents of an acquisitive society against whom the carriers of the culture have no weapons save secrecy and deception.

In describing these lineaments of Lovedu society, as its stands facing the onslaught of Western civilization, we have set forth the general principles, but eschewed the details. Upon a limited canvas we have striven to draw the main outlines in such a way as both to maintain the proportions of the culture and to interest the general reader as well as the student. Much is left unsaid about such aspects of the culture as the manner in which men try to harness the powers of nature and to condition the individual to his social function, the basic assumptions of the magico-religious world and the elements imparted to the culture by contact with other peoples, both African and European. We have not touched upon many aspects usually dealt with in the larger anthropological monographs. In view of our general object, we have omitted not only whole subjects of interest to the anthropologist, such as birth and death ceremonial, arts and crafts, village organization and kinship terminology, but also details on practices of importance to specialists, such as care of cattle, cultivation, diet and diseases, land tenure and medicine. While we believe that the many omissions do not detract from the essential balance and unity of the whole, it is our intention to fill in the gaps with articles on specialized aspects of the culture, and with additional books on larger topics such as law and judicial arrangements, marriage and social organization, magic, and religion. Too much must not be expected in the present volume.

Our contacts with the Lovedu began more than ten years ago with short visits of a month each in 1928, 1930, and 1932. These visits served as an introduction, but sustained field investigation was rendered possible only when, between 1936 and 1938, we held a Fellowship of the International Institute of African Languages and Cultures. During this period we were in the field sixteen and a half months in all: April to July, 1936, November, 1936, to July, 1937, September and October, 1937, and May to August, 1938. In some of the intervening periods, while one of us was ill, the other as far as possible maintained personal touch with the Lovedu and, in order to verify some of our observations and to investigate a ceremony not held since 1905, we also paid some visits of a few days each in 1939.

Except to mention two points, we shall refrain from expounding our methods of investigation. The principles we adopted were, on the one hand, personal and intensive local observation, and, on the other, comparative investigation over a large area. Personal observation is essential because, though verbal accounts given by reliable informants may serve as useful starting-points, they generally not only are unconsciously idealized, but assume a background unknown to the investigator and often entirely escaping his attention. Accounts may reflect theory and ideals, but often give a very wrong impression of practice and real life; they never convey atmosphere and personal relationships. By comparative study, we obtained a mass of valuable clues as to lines of inquiry or interpretation which we could follow up and check by further local and intensive as well as extensive observation.

Personal observation is tiring, slow to yield results, and usually objectionable to the Lovedu; but in the end the rewards are great. After a long day's work, it is distasteful, but often essential, to keep awake all night sitting in the stifling atmosphere of a hut crowded with dancing, sweating humanity. After an exhausting walk of ten miles or more over difficult country, in order to witness a ceremony, it is discouraging to be refused admittance to the performance or to find it postponed until the European leaves; but occasional success amply repays perseverance. In the timeless Lovedu society, even if the investigator is welcomed, he may have to wait hours for a performance to begin; but the time need never be wholly wasted. Personal observation brings to light bewildering variations in the culture. There is no such thing as rigid conformity, and rules are made for man, not man for rules. Until the observer's own cultural conditioning is re-conditioned by intimate touch with the society, he cannot hope to penetrate its meaning.

In this book we are concerned to describe custom and life as they are to-day, after fifty years of European contact. Every custom, every ceremony, every case in it, has been personally seen except in those instances, always clear from the context, in which the event, such as the death of a Lovedu chief, did not occur during the period of investigation. We have written about everyday things as they are enacted in the tribe to-day, not as they were in the past. For obvious reasons, names mentioned in illustrative cases are all fictitious, save only where they are essential for the subject matter, as in the chapters on tribal history, social groupings, and political organization.

At the outset of our investigation we planned a rough division of work. One of us, E. J. Krige, concentrated upon magic and religion, family life, and women's activities; the other, J. D. Krige, upon laws and political organization, history, and man's activities. But our method of studying human situations as and where we found them, and of recording things as and when they occurred, precluded any rigid division, and each obtained information upon all aspects of culture. Each of us independently studied many institutions, such as marriage, economic life, and medical practices, and the diversity of our information and impressions—often reflections of our personal differences of outlook—provided useful clues to further observation and interpretation, besides showing that in field work the temperament of the investigator is a vital factor. In the preparation of this book E. J. Krige is responsible for Chapters II, V, VII, VIII, XII to XV, and J. D. Krige for Chapters I, III, IV, VI, IX to XI, XVI, XVII and the maps; but each has carefully gone through the work of the other and the whole is the result of the fullest co-operation between us. It does not seem necessary to mention in detail which of us took the photographs reproduced.

As regards the language of the Lovedu, we found that, difficult as it was to acquire, a working knowledge was absolutely essential, because implicit in it is a vast background of associations which can never be recaptured in translation. Khilovedu is now practically a dialect of Sotho, yet it cannot be adequately written in Sotho orthography. It approximates to Venda in much of its vocabulary, falls midway between Sotho and Venda in grammatical structure, and is Sothoized in phonology, but many of its sounds are unknown in Sotho. Generally speaking, we have adopted the orthography recommended by the International Institute with some modifications. For dental *d* and *t* we have used *ḓ* and *ṱ* as in Venda, and now commonly used in Northern Sotho, where these sounds also occur, but, as in Sotho, the semi-flapped alveolar lateral fricative, a phoneme of *d*, has not been distinguished from ordinary *d*; and we have deemed it unnecessary to have a special letter for the sound of English *sh*, or *ts* or *c* for the sound *ch* in English 'church', which we write *tsh*. Many variations are evident in Khilovedu in its movement towards Sotho, the language taught in the schools: there are differences in vocabulary and sounds used by women and young children, on the one hand, and by those who go to town, on the other, and by the young as compared with the old. The old sound of English *z* in *azure* becomes in the mouth of the younger generation the English *j* as in 'John'; *z* as in 'prize' alternates with *dz*, which is more common among the young people; and an old prefixal form, *lu*, is generally now *le*, except among the oldest people. We have used, *j*, *dz* more often than *z*, and *le* not *lu*, in accordance with modern trends. The *u* tends to become the closed *o*, and it is often very difficult to distinguish between these sounds; but here again we have kept as close as possible to the most prevalent pronunciation and have adopted *mu*, not *mo*, as the noun prefix.

We desire to thank the International Institute for publication and for the grants which enabled us to undertake this work, the Rev. W. and Mrs. Krause for hospitality while we were on their mission station, and numerous Lovedu friends, who must remain anonymous, for their co-operation. We desire also to express our gratitude to Dr. A. I. Richards for her invaluable assistance in seeing the book through the Press, and to Miss D. G. Brackett, the Secretary of the International Institute, for additional help in this connexion. But it is to Mrs. A. W. Hoernlé that we are most deeply indebted. When one of us was a student of economics and the other practising at the Johannesburg Bar, she, as lecturer at the University of the Witwatersrand, awakened our interest in social anthropology, made us realize its paramount importance as the basis of policies and national welfare in this southern sub-continent of Africa, and gave us that invaluable background, both of knowledge and ideals, from which our work has since then been oriented. Later, as adviser and friend, she was to us the source of unfailing encouragement, stimulating suggestion, and inspired guidance. For these roles there is no one better equipped than she by knowledge and experience of the Bantu. It is due to her that we have devoted ourselves, not to the professions with which we originally began our careers, but to social anthropology and to the ideal of putting it in the service of the practical problems of black and white in Africa.

E. JENSEN KRIGE.
J. D. KRIGE.

PRETORIA.
November, 1939.

To
A. W. HOERNLÉ
The mother of Social Anthropology
in South Africa

CHAPTER I

PAGEANTS OF THE PAST

Fame of Mujaji transformer of the clouds—the cycle of the kings—the cycle of the queens—from the pageants to the people.

FAME OF MUJAJI, TRANSFORMER OF THE CLOUDS

THE Lovedu are not numerous and, from a military point of view, they are insignificant. Yet among their neighbours and among tribes as far away as the Zulu they have a great reputation. The fame of their queen, Mujaji, is spoken of even by white men as if it were the fame of the monarch of a mighty empire. That is doubly curious. For, on the one hand, the nineteenth century in the southern sub-continent of Africa opens with the Napoleonic career of Chaka, king of the Zulu, whose exploits, followed by great displacements of peoples and spectacular reconstructions of tribes, overshadow everything else. On the other hand, the Lovedu, at the end of the century, ignominiously surrendered to the European without a shot being fired.

Upon what basis has Mujaji, queen of an obscure tribe in the far north-eastern corner of the Transvaal, built her fame? By 1800 the kingdom of the Lovedu had already existed for two centuries in the seclusion of the sheltering foothills of the Drakensberg. It was undistinguished among its far mightier neighbours, the Venda, the Pedi, and even the Dokwa. A mere glance at the map shows their insignificance beside the overwhelming masses of Shangana-Tonga, now almost completely encircling them. They were too microscopic even to be seen on the stage of the sub-continent, when mighty empires succumbed and new nations were born. Nevertheless, it was amid these convulsions, even as a challenge to them, that the kingdom of the Mujajis arose to prominence. The Lovedu kings had always been sacred kings; they had a reputation for rain-making, but it was no unique reputation, shared as it was by several of their neighbours. Among the Lilliputian tribes who had penetrated the geographical barriers isolating the Lovedu lowveld—the tsetse-fly belt east and north along the enveloping curve of the Limpopo, the Drakensberg on the south and the escarpment on the west—the Lovedu could claim precedence and ascendancy. But if the Zulu legions or any one of the pillaging hordes which their ravages had set into motion had violated the sanctuary of Vulovedu, little would have survived of the Mujajis.

To the Zulu, so we are told by Bryant, their historian, Mujaji was the greatest magician of the north. Queen of locusts and of drought, a four-breasted marvel, her name struck terror in the hearts of would-be enemies, and her fame surpassed that even of Mantatisi, the ferocious female tyrant who was leading the Kololo (Tlokwa) and laid the foundations of the Rotse empire. Mujaji also it was who magically smote to death dread Zwide, fleeing from Chaka, when he came too near Vulovedu, even though it was appeasement, not conquest, that he sought. According to

Bryant, Mujaji was conceived to be immortal, inaccessible, mysterious. That is a fair reflection of the opinion held both by her neighbours and by peoples living far from her domain. Even to her own people she was practically inaccessible, appearing but seldom before them; but she was not immortal, and her mystery, if what is natural and inevitable be mysterious, was the mystic power of transforming the clouds into rain. To this central conception the name Ʋulovedu (or Lovedu) bears witness. It is interpreted to mean the country where the cattle and the wealth, even the sisters and the daughters, of foreign chiefs are utterly lost (*hu lova*); they are the offerings for rain which, by accruing to Mujaji, 'waste' the substance of the suppliants. That is the simple secret, out of which the colourful phantasy of the mystery of Mujaji has been elaborated. But it is more than a simple matter. The ancestors of Mujaji also were rain-makers; but they were kings, not queens. If it was the feminine attributes of the ruler which made Mujaji famous among her neighbours, it was, however, the fairness of her skin which captured the imagination of the early European pioneers.

There was enough in the environment itself to lend colour to the picture. The mist-covered mountains are an appropriate setting for the mysterious Mujaji, 'Transformer of the Clouds' (*Khifidula-maru-a-Daja*), for such is her great praise. You can watch from afar how those vapour-laden clouds roll over the hills, constrained, as it were, to pour out their life-giving rain. You can easily imagine the 'huckster in her hut' (*mishava-ndoni*) where it nestles, secreted in the bush, on the edge of a precipice, and from which she sells her rain-making magic. It is well known that there are others who claim the power to constrain the heavens, and it is curious that the greatest among them are or have been women; but by comparison with Mujaji they are mere amateurs, even dabblers and quacks, trespassing upon her prerogative. They can raise storms and send hurricanes, but they do not have the power to withhold rain from the undeserving or to drop it gently upon the deserving with mathematical precision.

If these things appealed to the Native mind, the European was not unimpressed by the babbling of the streams mingling with the sounding of the drums, by the forest-clad ravines that are sanctuaries of ancestral spirits, and by the grotesque kopjes standing out as sentinels guarding the seclusion of savage men. The gateway to Ʋulovedu is the Valley of the Devils (Duivelskloof), a name which reflects the reaction of the pioneers to what was regarded as uncanny. But it was particularly the observances and ceremonial requiring the seclusion of the queen, thereby shielding her from the public eye, restraining her movements and preserving unsullied the secrets of her power, which fired the imagination. No European had seen the predecessor of the present queen; and the fairness of her complexion easily became the subject of rumour and phantasy.

That Mujaji II, who died in 1894, was fair cannot be disputed. Fairness is a feature of many Lovedu; it is a highly prized quality. There are tales among Europeans of the adventures of a Portuguese Don Juan in the bad old days; and undoubtedly, by Lovedu legend, a Portuguese trader visited the royal court. But if he had designs upon the queen, as is alleged, they were frustrated by the beer which was pressed upon him and rendered him powerless. We cannot attribute the sagacity of the queens, as did Rider Haggard, in his story of *She-who-must-be-obeyed*, to her pure Arabian ancestry. There may be Arab blood in her veins, as there probably is in the veins of all her people; certainly it was not by virtue of any foreign blood that 'She' ruled the tribe, and there is nothing that suggests that the Lovedu owe their organization of culture to an alien conqueror. They are among the politically weakly organized rather than highly centralized Bantu. Haggard's book, which appeared in 1886, correctly emphasizes the high status of women, the pride in female ancestry, the inaccessibility of the queen; and it is upon her immortality that the plot turns. There are also mysterious caves, but people never lived in them.

A more recent picture of the Rain-Queen, based upon local rumour, has been given by Dicke in his *The Bush Speaks* (1936). There she is represented as a crafty woman of mixed white extraction who came with her people from West Africa, and with diabolic cunning induced among her people the belief that she was endowed with the supernatural power that created the clouds so often resting upon her mountains. The rain-priestess soon acquired fame, which she used to found a great kingdom, without, however, relying upon force of arms. To account more adequately for her Machiavellian intrigues, he supposes that her female ancestors were white women, sold to the Arabs on the slave markets of West Africa, who enchanted their masters with their sexual attractions; hence the device of ruling her councillors by remaining unmarried; hence also the many girls, wives of the queen, whose duty was to captivate foreign chiefs, to spy, 'to induce their new masters to attend the festivities, dances, beer drinks, orgies, licentious debaucheries continuously held at the rain-priestess' capital'. Thus we get from Dicke's book a picture of intrigue and debauchery at the capital, supported by assassinations and poisonings, of a kingdom 'built up on immorality, deceit and crime, with no effective striking force to support it'. Her councillors preferred to be ruled by a woman, so that sons of the queen always died before reaching maturity.

There is much else that may be gleaned from local gossip. People are incredulous if one says that one has seen the queen. They remember how Mujaji II deceived Joubert, the Boer general, who, after subjugating the tribe in 1894, was shown, not the true Mujaji, but some one who impersonated her. Forgetting the signal service of the missionary, the Rev. F. Reuter, who intervened on her behalf, they attribute to the cunning of the queen her acquittal of complicity in the rebellion which brought Joubert upon the scene and which led to the defeat and wholesale transportation of several tribes in the lowveld. The diplomacy of the queen had overcome the white man. These are the beliefs that have contributed to the fame of the Lovedu. Whatever basis in reality there may be for them, there is one thing we must note. Mujaji lives no more than twenty-one miles from Duivelskloof. There are flourishing European farms, particularly all along the west and south of her country. Yet the Lovedu have maintained intact their culture and their institutions, even the royal constellation of institutions, curious and incongruous with modern conditions though they might be.

And it is to a brief history of the royal institutions, as providing the key to an understanding of the Lovedu, that we shall now proceed. But let us say this: truth is ever stranger than fiction, yet it is also more complex and elusive. The truth that obtains in a strange world, made up of beliefs and values very different from our own, is not easy to recapture; there is no basis, no framework, in our lives for it. We are continuously confounded by inconsistencies and paradoxes, try as we would to turn our conceptions and theories this way and that and even upside down to fit the facts into them. What we shall try to do is to give a visual representation of a few historical events, by way of a series of pageants passing in review. A complete account of the background of the past is far beyond our purpose. It will be sufficient to represent the spirit of these events, leaving for another occasion the question of how far they have a true basis in fact.

The pageants are not arranged into groups by the tribal historian, but we may present them as if they were colossal cycles, the cycle of the kings and the cycle of the queens. Each cycle opens in mystery, the mystery of an incestuous conception that, instead of corrupting the world, crowns the sinner; it is the ritual vindication of revolutionary change. In the first cycle, which starts just before 1600 and ends two centuries later, the change signalizes the birth of the tribe; then follow wanderings and the settlement of an infant community, which slowly develops to the splendid stature of manhood; and, finally, corruption and dissensions lead to a downfall. But in the midst of the ruins of the catastrophic civil war, which ends the first cycle, a new conception is born and we are at the beginning of the second cycle. The first cycle is handled with simple power; but no single doctrine in it runs its full course. Yet it cannot be mere coincidence that the mystery which marks the birth of the tribe should also be invoked to account for the momentous change from kings to queens.

The cycle of the queens has not yet been completed; it began about 1800 and rapidly ran to the height of its splendour; and its crisis, prematurely brought to a head, has also been indefinitely lengthened by the intervention of a new order of things, ushered in by the advent of the European. We cannot predict when the crisis will end or what the outcome of so prolonged a suspense will be, for the response to the challenge of this new order is now only taking shape and direction. But of this we can be certain, that in a world ordained by the white man there is less room for the vast sweep of the legendary mysteries. The tribal historian is unequal to the task of harmonizing the play of new, intractable forces with the theme of his exalted design.

The history of Lovedu kings and queens is not unlike the legends of the saints. The tribal historian is, of course, not troubled by a sacred theme, by the eternal struggle between Good and Evil; but he must justify historical events, he must bring them into relation with the grand purposes of the tribe. He never consciously tampers with essential facts; he uncritically accepts tradition that has been handed down to him.

There is no direct falsification, but the way in which all distinctions of place and time are ignored leads to strange distortions. The tribal historian pictures man and events, not in the shape of their setting in the past, but in the colours of the values of the present. This involves inevitable selection and rearrangement. Again, legend without dramatic appeal is liable to be lost in oblivion; and so the historian, telling his story by the fireside, must be a dramatist. He groups his material, centres them upon important events and colours them to harmonize with the total picture of the society he has in mind. It is not always easy to reproduce either the whole picture or that touch here and those lines there, which give it its distinctive character and meaning. There are delineations of what in the society are regarded as we regard original sin, but they effect the salvation, not the damnation of man. A treacherous deed assumes the form of a glorious achievement. A usurper is turned into a hero. Royal incest, instead of threatening the security of the society, strengthens the divine right to rule. These are some of the critical moments in the history of Lovedu kings and queens that we wish to present by a series of pageants.

THE CYCLE OF THE KINGS

The First Pageant (*c.* 1500). The sons of Monomotapa, mighty monarch of the Vakaranga, quarrel and each sets himself up as an independent *mambo*, or chief, dividing Vukhalaga, the empire of their father, among themselves. One of these chiefs has his capital at the mountain of Maulwi, somewhere in Rhodesia. His people, prostrating themselves in his presence, call him *mulozwi* or *murozwi*, but he has merely taken that name as a praise title to mark the link between him and the king of the Rozwi. Perhaps it is only a political link, not implying kinship of any kind. We do not know. Mambo rules his people, not by force, but through his supernatural prerogatives, for he is a sacred king. Tradition dictates that he should end his reign by ritual suicide. He is appointed, not in accordance with man-made rules, but by the spirit of his predecessor, who holds the door of the hut in which he died against all but the true heir; and it is only through that doorway that his successor can ascend the throne.

This *mambo* has a daughter, Dzugudini, and, though she is unmarried, she has an infant son, Makaphimo. Mambo wishes to punish the seducer of his daughter, but Dzugudini and her mother refuse to disclose the identity of the culprit, saying, 'The father of the child of a king's daughter is not to be known.' Mambo becomes more and more suspicious. Dzugudini's mother steals the rain charms and the sacred beads, and feverishly teaches her daughter their virtues and their use; and before Mambo can take action, Dzugudini and her infant son flee to the south.

After a long and eventful journey, the fugitives, accompanied by a handful of followers, arrive in Vulovedu, where they settle and found the tribe of the Lovedu. We do not know whether Mambo ever discovered who had seduced his daughter; but Lovedu tradition records that Makaphimo was the issue of the incestuous union of uterine brother and sister. The brother remains as *mambo*, successor to his father; the sister, Dzugudini, by virtue of her incest, justifies the creation of a new people.

The Second Pageant (c. 1650). Both Dzugudini and Makaphimo have died, the first in Nareni, the second at Khumeloni. One of the nobles, remaining on the highveld, is moving southwards from near Munnik, later to establish the chiefdom of Mamavolo; two brothers of Makaphimo tarry on the way down the escarpment, and we see the one, Mahasha, sowing his seeds (*hu hasha*) to test the agricultural possibilities, the other, Mudiga, struggling to drive off the lions which surround (*hu diga*) his settlement. Muhale, son of Makaphimo, is ruling at Khumeloni. He is the acknowledged founder of the greatness of the Lovedu during the cycle. He successfully appeals to Mahasha and Mudiga to rejoin him; they give him their daughters as wives and he makes them his great headmen.

But Muhale's reign stands out boldly because of his subjugation of the Khiɔga, primitive denizens of the forest of Ḍaja. They have no fire, and live like wild animals, eating raw meat; their huts are badly constructed and dirty; they till the soil with sharpened sticks instead of hoes; and they have neither chief nor any visible form of government. The fair-skinned, cultured Lovedu set about educating these Calibans of savage humanity, teaching them the uses of fire. The Khiɔga find a new contentment in the sweetness of cooked food and in warming themselves by the hearth fires. Savage pupil and cultured tutor become close friends, so close that the savage unsuspectingly shows his benefactor the qualities of 'the place of the gods' (*vadimoni*) in the forest at Ḍaja. They envisage a brave new world, but they do not know that they are being deceived For in reality the Lovedu, coveting 'the place of the gods', are planning their destruction, They do not disclose the knowledge that fire can burn the veld; for they intend that 'their spears shall be fire'. And presently they set the grass alight and the fire scatters some Khiɔga, but burns most of them to death.

A moment later we see the Lovedu praying at the shrines at Ḍaja. When Muhale dies they bury him there; the Lovedu no longer fear the ancestral spirits of the Khiɔga. (For the fire, we may suppose, is here, as in the great transition ceremonies, a sacred rite. It effects the transition from danger to safety, from defilement to sanctity; the power for evil of foreign spirits it converts to a power for good in the service of the usurper; it cleanses the alien past and welds it firmly into the present.) As the pageant passes we see the ruins of another strange people, the Ḍgɔna. The Lovedu dread these ruins; they build far from them; avenging spirits, who have never been assimilated, contaminate the soil; the fire which purified and aggregated the sacred places of the Khiɔga was not used against them.

The Third Pageant (c. 1700). At Ḍaja, beside the grave of Muhale, we see another, that of Malaji. 'He who makes the country sleep', for that is what his name means, has left behind him peace and plenty. The little colony, sheltered in the fastnesses of its seclusion, is busy working out its salvation. The Lovedu have ample living space, for the lowveld is still almost devoid of inhabitants. Beyond it there are great nations, kept at a distance by geographical obstacles. The Lovedu are not only secure in their mountain fastnesses, but also protected by those far-off barriers—the massive mountains towering over the Olifants River in the south, stretching forth a gigantic limb to the north, and the deep, tsetse-fly infested Limpopo Valley circling the west as a moat defensive of their home.

Men are discussing to whom Malaji has entrusted the rain charms, to Pheduli, 'the Drainer of the Rivers,' or to his eldest son, Madaji, whose nickname, 'the Filler of the Rivers,' is much more auspicious. Madaji settles their doubts by driving off Pheduli and seizing the throne. But in the sequel we see drought and famine in Uulovedu, while at Khivela, where Pheduli rules, copious rains bring plenteous crops. Year after year Madaji's magic sweeps up gales that scatter the clouds hanging over Daja, whereas Pheduli constrains them to drop their gentle rain at Khivela.

The contrast is especially evident to the headmen living near Tzaneen. They secretly ally themselves with Pheduli; they spread rumours of a mighty army marching upon the capital. At length their strategy succeeds. Madaji flees to the forest, unsuspectingly entrusting his defence to the traitors; and when they report defeat and persuade him to rally his forces in the north, he is trapped into crossing the Madazwi River. It is a river which, even to-day, kings cross at the price of their crown; it drains the source of their power to rule. Madaji thus forfeits his right to the throne, and Pheduli, safely installed, becomes the mighty Transformer of the Clouds.

Faith in the sanctity of a system which may exclude the elder in favour of the younger son is restored; man-made rules, which usurp the function of the spirit presiding over the choice of a successor, are discredited. There is no room in this pageant (nor is there in tradition) for the defection, probably at this time, of a considerable section of the tribe, who later become the people of Mamaila.

The Fourth Pageant (*c.* 1750–1800). Pheduli's grave stands beside those of his forefathers. The scene discloses Khiali, the fair-faced king, reclining in a seat hewn out of the rock on the summit of a mountain amid immense walls of stone. In the spirit in which the scene is portrayed, with its mounds of masonry and its structures of stone, the impression conveyed is one of Zimbabwic splendour. (The ruins are still there, phallic stones projecting from rough stone walls some 8 ft. high, and the sculptured seat is merely two rocks in their natural position. But it is with the spirit, not the reality of the scene that we are concerned.)

Khiali does not notice those faint figures of foreigners crowding into the background. They are the Sotho invaders of the lowveld, pressing over the mountains in the south, clambering down the escarpment in the west, and in far-off Phalavorwa settling in an unfavourable environment, whence some would soon leave to encroach upon Uulovedu. On his magnificent material foundations Khiali is concerned to build a strong spiritual edifice. His predecessors were content to entrust the welfare of the divine prince, he who should ascend the throne, to the care of the gods. But he, Khiali, by strengthening the hands of the gods, would secure for ever the succession of the sacred heir.

As Khiali sits there, a youth, obviously concerned to avoid detection, appears in the shadows of an opening in the fence. He slinks away when he sees others beside Khiali in the courtyard. A moment later he reappears, only to be driven back by Khiali, showering curses upon his head. But later we see Khiali and the youth whispering together in the king's private hut; the king is secretly teaching him the use of the rain charms. The youth is Mugɔdɔ the Outcast, youngest son of Khiali His father stints him of everything, makes him dwell far from the capital, treats him like a thief, and refuses him entry into his village except when he comes alone and unobserved by a secret pathway through the undergrowth. These things he does to deceive the people and safeguard Mugɔdɔ's title to the throne. But they also develop a supersensitiveness in the Outcast.

Thwarted in his youth, Mugɔdɔ suffers irreparable damage to his self-respect; he is obsessed by suspicions; he imagines that every man's hand is against him. His councillors are adulterers and sorcerers, corrupting his wives, plotting to usurp his position. Scandal and dissension sap the strength of the kingdom. His elder brother, Khashani, rises against him; he is driven off, but the tribe splits into two; and more than a century later, in the second cycle, a descendant of Khashani challenges Mujaji with a foreign creed. Mugɔdɔ answers his detractors with wholesale executions, but he is concerned to vindicate himself rather than to regain order in the land. In a civil strife between two of his headmen, he makes no move until he feels himself insulted by 'the rusty arrows fit for the rubbish heap' that cause the blood of a kinsman to flow. The crowning catastrophe that embitters his soul is the conduct of his wayward sons. They enter the huts of his younger wives; they slaughter his cattle to gain popularity at their father's expense; they send him the dregs after draining the tributary beer.

And Mugɔdɔ's reign ends in chaos and confusion. Royal kinsmen massacre one another; internecine strife is followed by unparalleled famine; ravenous wild beasts terrorize the villages; Malegudu, one of Mugɔdɔ's sons, gains control for a time, but he has eventually to flee before Mujaji, his sister, and is assassinated in Vendaland; Khiɛbɛ, another son, seeks refuge in Thɔʋɔlɔland, where he dies an unnatural death; Sephumulo, a powerful noble, unable to stomach subjection to Mujaji, who is gaining the ascendancy, severs his allegiance and establishes the twin tribes of Rakwadu and Sekhɔpɔ. And as these disasters befall the tribe, the first cycle completes its course.

THE CYCLE OF THE QUEENS

The Fifth Pageant (*c*. 1800). As the second cycle opens, the disasters which appear to be the Nemesis upon the vice of an uncertain succession (for it was Khiali's attempt to readjust the machinery of succession which maladjusted Mugɔdɔ for the task of a king) are reconstructed to form a chain of triumph for Mujaji. The most dramatic moments are not the disasters, but two interconnected events: Mugɔdɔ's prophecy and Mugɔdɔ's sin.

At the end of the civil strife, into which the insult of the rusty arrows goads Mugɔdɔ to throw his decisive weight, he orders the war horns to be sounded; and as he begins a solitary, spectacular dance (*hu pɛbɛla*), his people, prostrating themselves, solemnly intone his praises: 'Mugɔdɔ of the neck-with-great-folds-of-fat, wherein do rest both goods and men, who hurls his challenge with the rain-horn; Mugɔdɔ of Pheduli, Transformer of the Clouds, he kills as he lists and spares whom he likes.' Pointing in the four directions, he raises his voice in prophecy: 'I am going away to creep into the horn of a cow (i.e. to die). I do not like to sleep in the open, vainly counting the stars. I go to unloose the black ants in the east. They will bite you and kill you, but in the end you will overcome them. Thereafter I shall unleash the red ants in the west; you will fight them, but you will fight them in vain. Further, I say this country will be ruled by a frontal skirt.'

It is Mugɔdɔ's farewell message just before he dies. But the prophecy epitomises the three great moments in the cycle of queens: the accession of a woman, the raids of Ŋguni hordes (black ants), and the conquest by the European (red ants).

The Sixth Pageant (c. 1800). Mugɔdɔ is the instrument of an inexorable fate. His faith in his fellow men, in his councillors, even in his sons, has been shattered. He muses that women also are faithless. But their faith, however unfaithful, keeps them falsely true; they intrigue against him as their husband, but they are loyal to him as their king. Above all, their mystery is allied to a power, not to blast the tribe to fragments, but to subdue men and turn their passions to the service of the state. That is the vision given to Mugɔdɔ, and the guarantee of its divine origin is the far-off past in which Dzugudini originated the tribe. That past also suggests how the vision can be realized. And in the scene before us these mighty issues are handled with a simplicity and a directness which it is impossible to reproduce.

Mugɔdɔ betakes himself to his favourite daughter at Maulwi, sacred reminder of the mountain in Rhodesia. Simply he tells her of his purpose, but she doubts its divine source: 'It cannot be, my father,' she says; 'these things are too difficult.' Mugɔdɔ goes again to her, but she remains mystified that a sin that defiles can be a rite that sanctifies.

Then Mugɔdɔ goes to Lekhwareni, the despised place of stones and of slothful people (for, according to their praise song, they burn their nails roasting the maize that they should have stamped). There lives Mujaji, daughter of his wife, Mamujaji. To her also he confides his vision; he tells her she will be queen if, though celibate, she will bear the heir to the throne. He is not speaking of a virgin birth, for she understands that he, her father, will be the father of her issue. 'You are all-wise, O father,' she replies. 'I am the servant of your will.' A secret hut is built; an inquisitive intruder, the favourite wife of Mugɔdɔ, suffers the extreme penalty; and in due course a son, not a daughter, is born.

But Fate tricks Mugɔdɔ in vain. The son is strangled and a little later there is a daughter. She is to become Mujaji II.

The Seventh Pageant (c. 1850). Mujaji I has already been on her resplendent throne for half a century; she has turned the chaos of her predecessor's reign to peace and prosperity; and, surrounded by restrictions which forced her into seclusion and fostered the idea of her sagacity and immortality, she has won the fame and attraction which drew so many foreigners to her capital. She is 'the white-faced Mankhadeni, radiant as the setting sun'. 'Huckster in her hut', perched like an eagle's eyrie on the fringe of a forest, she dispenses as she wishes the life-giving rain. 'She casts away some; others she shares with the vultures.'

Hosts of foreign ambassadors and potentates gather at her court. Some bring cattle, others their daughters or sisters; these are the gifts with which they show their homage or supplicate for rain. In the company we see messengers from Manukuza, dread monarch of Gasaland, supplicating with mighty gifts from their master; ambassadors of Zwide, challenger of Chaka himself, seeking to ward off the chastisement of locusts and drought, but smitten to death for his presumption in coming so near Uulovedu; and also an envoy from Moshesh in far-off Basutoland. Less pretentious are the men from Malevɔxɔ, whose Loredu wife had taught him the elements of the magic of rain-making; from Vendaland, where they call Mujaji 'the wife who brings them water to wash their face'; from Phalavorwa, upon whose internal struggles Mujaji arbitrates. From Chopiland and Uunyai, from the Uirwa and Tswana, from the very ends of the world, there are suppliants. Sekwati, the great Pedi king, is seeking a matrimonial alliance, hence that herd of cattle in the courtyard; Mali of the Khaha and Magaepia of the Letswalo, queens crowned in their own countries in imitation of the immortal Mujaji, come to be strengthened and fitted for their task. But the mightiest tribute of all is the gift from the Zulu king, who, disappointed by the failure of his mission to the great Swazi rain-maker, supplicates the rain-maker of rain-makers.[1]

The pageant is incomplete without its background, the armed hordes of Chaka and Moselekatse, of Soshangane and Mantatisi, of Thulare and Mafefe, laying waste and massacring, and in the wake of the trail of desolation, the smaller tribes and those miserable remnants, the guerrilla bands of cannibals, completing the destruction. They all are mightier than Mujaji, who is unarmed yet invincible. And, as the pageant passes by, we see innumerable refugees flocking from all points of the compass to seek sanctuary in the inviolable land.

The Eighth Pageant (1894). The sceptre, secretly entrusted to Mujaji II on her accession forty years and more before this pageant passes, is

---

[1] A Zulu author, M. J. Mpanza, in his *UGuqabadele* (1930), p. 53, confirms this. He says that if there was excessive drought, the Zulu king would send black cattle to the Swazi king with a request for rain; and, if there was still no rain, he would send to Mujaji.

the symbol of forces that swayed a bygone world. People are uncertain of their bearings in the new world, their sense of security has been shaken. The black ants from Swaziland have left a scar, though they were chastened when the legions of Ludongo were defeated. Now the red ants are brought upon the scene as the aftermath of the exploits of Albasini, self-appointed chief of the Magwamba (Shangana-Tonga) and Native Commissioner of the Boer Republic. The sceptre only weakly shows the force of spiritual power. The tribute Mujaji sends to Albasini, it is true, smites him with drought; upon General Joubert, curious to behold the royal majesty, a far-off sister of the queen, who was also her 'wife', is palmed off as the mysterious 'She-who-must-be-obeyed'; the Transformer of the Clouds still is the 'huckster in her hut'.

But to the workers and warriors of the 'red ants', the sceptre is like a broken reed rather than a magic wand. Some of them with impunity appropriate the country, enlisting in their service the denizens of the soil; others are collecting taxes, exacting tribute and redrawing age-old boundary lines; still others invade the sacred places, even desecrating the drums at Maulwi. The princes still come, but they supplicate surreptitiously.

The temporary triumphs cannot offset the disastrous defeats, and Mujaji, bewildered by the turn of events, does not know how to adjust her weapons and her diplomacy to the needs of the new situation. She circumvents the curiosity of Joubert, but she fails to save her subjects from serfdom. When the grave of Khashani, the Christian kinsman whom she martyred, becomes the rallying point of a disloyal creed, when the conspiracy to expel the European intruder ends in the disaster of the deportation of her neighbours, she loses her faith in the gods of her ancestors and adjures her followers to trust the apostle of a creed that was uprooting these gods. Pathetically she presses the poison cup to her lips, conforming to the letter, not to the spirit, of the ritual end ordained by her ancestors. In a world indifferent to the eternal verities, that cup is like an empty sham and that end like a vain sacrifice.

The pageant passes on. A cheerless panorama unfolds before us as Mujaji III ascends the throne. To submission is added humiliation. When the white man, coming to arrange for the recognition of the new queen, sees old Mathogani, who had impersonated Mujaji II, the proceedings are stopped. The Lovedu are made to pay for their presumption by being denied a ruler until the old woman dies. They retaliate by dubbing her the 'Chief of the white men' and by accelerating her end.

But it is a fruitless revenge. They are faced with the problem of reconciling the claims of two incongruous worlds: is the authority of the queen to be derived from the alien conqueror and his ceremonies or from the spirit of the deceased and the rite of the door? The reality of the old rite is the sham of the new order; it is a mere coincidence upon which no title can be based. But also in all spheres of culture and of life these dualistic forces clash with one another; they are in a death grapple which lasts throughout the reign of Mujaji III.

The conflict is epitomized in the conflict between Shalala and the royal house. The commoner, using the weapons of the European lawyer, ranges himself against royalty, who invoke the powers of their ancestors When Magɔma, daughter of the queen, illicitly allies herself to the commoner and anarchy threatens disruption of the tribe, the royal house reluctantly invites intervention of the white man, submitting, however, only the superficial issues. Ostensibly Shalala suffers defeat, but in reality the struggle continues; and in this conflict, as in the wider conflict of the warring worlds, we are left in doubt where the victory lies.

FROM THE PAGEANTS TO THE PEOPLE

Only a few of the great figures of the royal family paraded before us in these pageants. We must regard them as expressions of some of the themes which the outlook of the society has emphasized. The twice-invoked incest theme is brought into relation with revolutionary national changes, like a transition rite in the life of an individual. Incest precedes and validates first the birth of the tribe, then the accession of a woman and her elevation to a mystical pedestal. Is it a case of the greater the sin the greater the saint, of the polluted and the sacred converging at infinity? We cannot say for certain. We saw the Lovedu pictured as a Prospero teaching the Calibans of Khiɔga. But primitive and unorganized though these Khiɔga were, they undoubtedly knew fire, and the use of fire against a fireless foe who has become a friend is unnecessarily treacherous, though it is, for the end in view, dramatically and, we may suppose, ritually effective. When internal dissension arises, the conflict is posed as one between the chief son and the 'chosen' son. The victory of the 'chosen' son vindicates the divine right of the rain-priest against mere legal precedence. This theme is once more dramatically thrown into relief by the device of naming the chief son 'the Filler' and the 'chosen' son 'the Drainer of the Rivers'. The contrasts are handled with consummate skill. Notice also the psychological insight that marks the manner in which we are led up to the climax of the change from kings to queens. The Outcast thwarted in his youth is over-sensitive and suspicious; he seeks compensation in revenge; and he is the paranoic who utters the fatal prophecy. The prophecy is not merely a vain delusion; it has a purpose and was put into the mouth of the Outcast after the event; and as such it is a magnificent piece of stagecraft. Yet it is not considered to be equal to the task of sufficiently magnifying the mysticism of Mujaji I; that task is finally achieved by a repetition of the incest theme. Those were dangerous times; drastic handling of their dramatic moments was called for. The culminating point of Mujaji's power stands out prominently amid the surrounding turmoil. It also challenges it. The drama suddenly ends; it has run its course. In the sequel, the problem of the death-grapple of dualistic worlds has developed too suddenly, too disturbingly, for the powers of the tribal historian.

These are some of the conceptions handled in the pageants. They reflect ultimate values, the philosophy of the society. They are on a different plane from the ordinary lives and interests of the people. To re-orientate ourselves, we must bear in mind three things: firstly, the royal pageants are but one of a large series, for besides the nuclear ruling group there are many other groups, each with its own historical background, subtly linked up though it be with the royal background; secondly, great as the glory of the queens is, we must not fail to see their people in their true perspective against the masses of foreign tribes and against the stature of the European Colossus; and, thirdly, however greatly men rely for their sense of security upon ultimate values, their lives are immediately and predominantly concerned with very simple matters, with tilling the soil and caring for their cattle, with getting and preparing food, with securing shelter and warmth, with gossip at beer drinks and with petty domestic squabbles.

The Lovedu to-day are predominant in an area of some 5,000 square miles, the area of the Lovedu lowveld which is bounded by the Game Reserve, the escarpment, the Klein Letaba and the Olifants Rivers. On all sides of this area there are mightier peoples. Shangana-Tonga to the east, Pedi to the south, Venda to the north and several highveld tribes to the west—all these overshadow the people of Mujaji in numbers, in organization, and in power. But within the Lovedu lowveld, if we count all branches of the Lovedu, the subjects under them (about 50,000) outnumber the rest of the Sotho-speaking tribes put together (some 40,000). There are in addition many people (perhaps 25,000) under Shangana-Tonga chiefs, and in the eyes of the European one of them has far greater stature than Mujaji.

The Lovedu live in a location marked out in the early 1890's, immediately after the advent of European settlers and the conflicts that resulted. The original location, just short of seventy square miles, was enlarged during the 1930's by the purchase of tribal farms, and now the whole reserve is about 150 square miles in extent. This falls far short of the 600 square miles within which Mujaji used to exercise effective jurisdiction. She held the area between the Moketsi, the Great Letaba and the Mulodozi Rivers, from where the latter joins the Great Letaba at its northernmost bend, and from there westwards to the Moketsi; beyond it for another 400 square miles, but rather indefinitely towards the north, north-east, and east, where the population was sparse, Mujaji's writ ran, through uncertainly and spasmodically.

The population of the reserve we estimate at 33,000, which is considerably in excess of the official census figure for 1936.[1] The average

---

[1] Official census figures for 1936 are available, not for the Lovedu reserve, but only for two separate units of areas: (*a*) the Lovedu location and (*b*) an area to the north of it, about half of which falls within the Lovedu reserve. For (*a*) the figures are 11,636 and for (*b*) 7,205. If we assume that half of the population of (*b*) falls within the Lovedu reserve, its total population would be 15,238, or only about 46 per cent of our estimate of 33,000. We arrive at our figure from three sources: (1) Kraal-to-kraal countings in three sample districts with a total area of 14·5 square miles and a total population of 3,500. These districts represent different localities, some valley, some hill, and constitute a fair sample. On the basis of the average density of population in them, the total figure for the Lovedu reserve of 150 square miles should be 150 ÷ 14·5 × 3,500, or 36,207. (2) The proportion of people who, according to Native accounts, our own impressions, and independent European eye-witnesses, escaped official enumeration. Despite instructions that the people of each district should collect in their respective districts, the enumerators, finding the districts inaccessible by road

density, though as high as 220 to the square mile, cannot be an over-estimate; it is below the average of the sample areas and much below the 450 found in one of them, which is by no means the densest in the reserve.

The geographical features vary from mountains to flat country. The rainfall, which coincides with the hot months, October to March, is very good on the hills. In the flat country to the north it is rather uncertain. The mountains have many springs, but neither of the two main rivers is navigable and there is little life in them. The people do not eat fish and have no river craft, though they speak of a bark canoe (*legugwa*) used in the old days. On the slopes of the hills there are forests and one is of magnificent cycads (Mujaji palms). The people have an intimate knowledge of the names, the qualities, and the uses of the flora. Their dependence upon trees, shrubs, and grasses for food, economic purposes, and medicine is one of the most impressive aspects of their culture. The soil is a reddish, fairly fertile loam. At present there is hardly any game; but in any case the Lovedu were never great hunters, and knowledge of the fauna is now of small use. The temperature is never excessive; the summer rains cool the hot air and the cold winds are easily subdued by bright sunshine. Summer merges into winter and winter overlaps summer; there is no well-marked spring or autumn. The people are agriculturists rather than pastoralists; the few cattle they have and the more numerous goats are not considered so much as food but rather as pivots of social relationship.

The people of the royal group, the nucleus of the tribe, live mostly on the mountains; the valleys and flats are occupied by Shangana-Ṭonga, recent-comers who are despised by the Sotho, and by the Rɔka, residents of the flats, looked upon as somewhat inferior though of diverse Sotho ancestry. The nuclear group or Lovedu proper are not numerous. Their group name, *kwevo*, is what we may call the surname of one in every ten people in the reserve. Other *kwevo*, 'brothers' of the Lovedu, rule such tribes as those of Sekhɔpɔ, Mamaila and Rakwadu, but many are scattered among dozens of alien tribes. In the whole Lovedu lowveld the *kwevo* are much less than 10 per cent. of the population.

The non-nuclear groups in the reserve are accretions from outside (if we except the Khigɔa, the Ŋgɔna and some Lions and Elephants who either were in the country or came with the Lovedu). They have been

---

and the country mountainous, stationed themselves in a body at a single spot in the valley to which the people were then called. The new arrangements caused confusion and many of those who had collected in their districts dispersed to their homes and never presented themselves for enumeration. In addition, large numbers, as is their habit in the face of European intervention, secreted themselves in the bush. European eye-witnesses estimate that only 33 to 40 per cent, say 36·5 per cent, were actually enumerated, but Natives place the figure as high as 50 per cent. Taking the average of 43·25 per cent, we arrive at a total population for the reserve of 15,238 × 100 ÷ 43·25, or 35,232. (3) The number of taxpayers in the Lovedu location, which is about 4,000. On the accepted basis of calculation, the location population would be 4,000 × 5, or 20,000—that is 1·72 times that of the census figure of 11,636, and the total for the reserve may be calculated as 15,238 × 1·72 or 26,209. Finally, averaging the three figures, 36,207, 35,232 and 26,209, we get 32,549 or, to the nearest thousand, 33,000, which is the figure we adopt.

entering from the first quarter of the eighteenth century until to-day, and are all segments of other tribes, themselves composed of very diverse elements. To-day the task of unravelling the confusion and complexity is beyond the wit of man. It is a complexity which everywhere antedates the nineteenth-century disturbances, probably even the movements and unrest recorded by the Portuguese for the sixteenth century. Not all the groups are equally closely linked with the royal nucleus. The most alien are the Shangana-Tonga. This is because intermarriage with them is frowned upon and because, in the incorporation of a foreign group into the tribe, the most effective instrument is the alignments effected by the bride-price of the marriage system. The process of incorporation is dealt with elsewhere. It depends upon the obligation of the immigrant group to send one of its daughters as a wife to the queen. These are handed out to nobles of the nuclear group and thereby the whole complicated machinery of intermarrying lineages is set into motion. Thus, through the links created by giving brides and in return receiving cattle, loyalties are built up in the foreign groups and they become closely knit into the texture of the tribe and of its social structure, the centre of which from this point of view is the nuclear ruling group.

We have to remember, in considering the pageants of the past, that each of the constituent groups also has a background of history. There are scores of subsidiary pageants, some almost as impressive as the royal pageant. Neither the historical background nor all that it implies as to the meaning of the present culture can be properly interpreted without taking into account the subsidiary pageants. Some of them are almost self-contained side-shows, some have become submerged in the main pageant; but all have contributed something to the total culture of the Lovedu. It is always instructive to observe what the contribution has been and how it has been reshaped to harmonize with the predominant conceptions in the society. The selection of traits that are congenial, the rejection of elements that do not fit, the manner in which the assimilation has altered the details as well as the meaning of borrowed institutions, all throw light upon the values and working of the society. But in this book we are concerned only with the final result; and for that reason also we have omitted the histories and pageants of the constituent groups.

So far we have referred to the background of the royal group and to the great diversity of peoples that make up the Lovedu. It is time that, instead of viewing the tribe in broad perspective, we should turn to the ordinary mundane activities of the people. They do not live by the spirit of the past alone, and we cannot remain on the hilltops looking at them from afar. We must descend into their villages, attend their beer drinks, take a hand in the stamping and cooking, listen to the scandal at beer drinks and join them in their recreation. The contrast between the rarefied atmosphere of their philosophical contemplation, as it emerges in the pageants, and their everyday avocations, as we shall see them when we move in their midst, is very great. But so is the contrast between our philosophy and our everyday life.

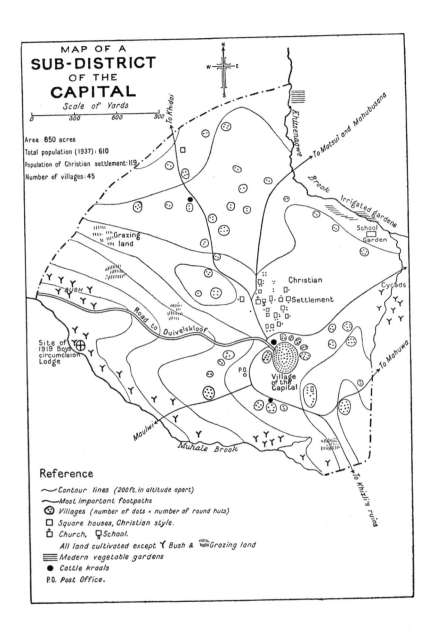

I. THE LOVEDU LANDSCAPE
(a) THE HILL OF CYCADS
(b) FIELDS AND VILLAGES ON THE FOOTHILLS

II. A GLIMPSE OF VILLAGE LIFE

(*a*) COURTYARD SCENE IN MARCH

(*b*) STAMPING MEALIES

CHAPTER II

A PICTURE OF EVERYDAY THINGS

A visitor's impressions of the manners and interests of the people—a glimpse of a village and its huts, of the preparation of food and etiquette in eating, and of the decorum of drinking beer—the evening scene, with its hearth fires, riddles, and stories—the seasonal calendar of activities.

As you drive along the winding road on a visit to Mujaji's reserve, you find yourself in a narrow valley between the two ranges of Uulovedu mountains, where flows the Mulodozi River, fed by countless streams from the bush-covered slopes above. It is the month of March. The mealies in the fields, visible on all sides through the bushy vegetation, stand dark green and high, appearing to grow right to the very doorsteps of the villages you pass. At first and to the untrained eye the country seems relatively empty, so well do the dwellings merge into the general view. On looking more closely, however, you see cluster after cluster of conical, thatched roofs peeping out from the bush on the hillsides, some of them perched on ledges like eagles' eyries. For the reserve is in reality very thickly populated. The villages are small, five to fifteen huts being the average size; a few large villages of from forty to eighty huts represent the old order of things, just as those of only two huts do the new. But the Lovedu village was never very large and never could compare, either in size or arrangement, with the great towns of the Tswana and of some Sotho.

As you go down a steep dip to cross a stream, a sullen-looking woman balancing a wide-mouthed basket on her head, her legs heavy with leg rings which reach almost up to the knee, suspiciously turns her back on you. She wears a cloth of red salampore behind and before, knotted on the shoulders; while from her neck dangles the ubiquitous snuff box on a necklet of plaited string, black with dirt, but holding three or four treasured heirlooms, large deep-blue or white beads and perhaps some small blue, red, and yellow ones of the kind that were brought from Rhodesia long before the European had come. A little further on you hear a shout, '*Makhuwa, Makhuwa*' (Europeans, Europeans), as a group of herdboys runs towards the road. The younger ones among them, mere toddlers playing outside their village, scurry away crying to their mothers, and scatter the chickens from the ash-heap as they do so. A herdboy, wearing nothing but his loin covering and an old tattered coat which was once his father's, shouts 'More Baas,' European words he has picked up from his elders; but the rest run joyfully after the car, rending the air with their shrieks.

The road begins to ascend steeply up the hill to the capital, but here, if you wish to visit headman Raselaka, you must get out and walk. As you go in single file along the narrow footpath, bounded on either side by creeper-covered bush or long grass higher than your shoulders, you become aware of a strong smell somewhat reminiscent of turpentine. In a few moments you discover its cause—the ripening fruits of the morula tree (*Sclerocarya caffra*), from which such delightful cider is made. In the distance you hear the hoarse note of a *phalafala* horn, then the shrill ululations of women. They come nearer. You can hear them shout the words, '*Malematsha wee, Malamatsha wee; budi ga dzwala ga dzwala ga fɔlɔja, ga vuɛla vuphabaleni*' (Malematsha, Malematsha, the goat I bore, I bore and miscarried, as a goatling I returned)—the praise song of a district in Uulovedu. Then at a bend in the road you come upon a picturesque procession: in front walks a man, blower of the horn, followed by twenty women each with a calabash of beer placed in a basket on her head, a gift to the queen from the area of Malematsha. Perspiration runs down their faces; but they do not lose courage, for before they arrive at at their destination they will sit down by the roadside to quench their thirst from one or two of the calabashes they carry. Any one who then happens to pass will beg for a little, and he will not beg in vain.

You continue your way. A pigsty and an ash heap mark the approach to a village. A passer-by, spying a woman about her household duties, shouts her greetings, '*Re fithuleleni*' ('Still our hunger') to which comes the reply, '*Fithulelani zenu*,' a conventional refusal, but equivalent to 'Be hungry nicely' or 'Still your own hunger.' A second woman supplements it with the information, 'We have only just put on the pot.' If the food had been ready or the woman had wished to give the passer-by a tit-bit, the reply would have been, 'Here is food. We are eating.' That one of the ways of greeting should be associated with the begging of food is typical of the Lovedu. Some one returning from a visit to another area is greeted with, 'What are they eating over there,' or 'What are they stinting us of,' and the reply invariably is, 'They are being killed by hunger,' even if there is plenty and you have been royally entertained. There are greetings associated with activities: if you pass a man or woman working in the fields, you say, 'Workers,' and the modest reply is, 'We are hardly working at all'; to a woman carrying wood, you say, '*A di voyi dikhunye*' ('Let the wood return') and the reply is, '*Di voyile*' (It has returned). In fact, learning to greet people politely in the Lovedu language is not at all the simple thing it is in English.

At last you find yourself before the village of Raselaka, larger than any of those you have passed on the way and, unlike many of them, surrounded by a thick hedge of thorny *lenɛdwa* bush (*Pterolobium exosum*). At the entrance you trip over a slate-coloured river-stone, jutting out a few inches above ground. This is a charm, laid when the village was built, to keep out the witches; it makes them cool, causing them to forget their evil designs. It is part of a more comprehensive scheme for the protection of the village: the gate posts are of special wood (*khirale* or *modutu*, *Celtis Kraussiana*) smeared with medicines on the day they were set up; round the circumference are medicated pegs (*diphaba*) of *khirale*, the whole being completed by the magic circle drawn by the sister or father's sister, if she is still alive, who drags a 'doctored' branch of thorny *mukhalo* (*Zizyphus mucronata*) round the circumference. If this is not done by her before the doctor begins his work, it must be done subsequently, when the precaution of smearing the soles of her feet with medicine is taken lest by entering she 'opens up a way for witches'. The methods of various doctors are not the same. Sometimes a goat is killed and very often one finds at the entrance to a village a stick, 3–4 ft. long, on which are the roots of a *ṯiṯigwani* lily (*Hypoxis villosa*) or pieces of skin of the goat that was killed. This 'medicine of the village', some of which is always kept by the owner, is important for curing certain illnesses caused by witches and may be eaten with the firstfruits. Every year the village needs to be 'awakened' (*hu dzosa mutse*) by the renewal of these protective medicines, a process which Rapaka carries out naked at dead of night by sprinkling round the hedge certain medicine, an ingredient of which is river or sea sand. The river sand has the property of making the village appear as an expanse of water before the eyes of the sorcerer, who thereupon concludes that he has come to the wrong place. A village may have no visible hedge, but the invisible, charmed enclosure is never absent.

On passing through the gate you find yourself in the *khɔrɔ*, an open space, in which there is a hearth. Hardly have you seated yourself on one of the sprawling, spider-like stools of forked branches that are ranged around it than Raselaka himself, who has been expecting you, comes forward. He sits down and, inclining his body to the left, claps his hands, saying, '*Ndau dona*' ('Male lion'). He asks after your health, politely inquires about the journey, and pleasantries are exchanged. According to strict etiquette, he ought to have taken his visitors straight to the chief hut, where guests are received, but he knows you wish to be shown over the village, and perhaps that is why he lingers with you in the *khɔrɔ*. A woman passes, bends both knees in a curtsy and inclines the head, passing one palm slowly over the other, a manner of greeting usual to women; then goes slowly on her way. Soon afterwards, you are overpowered by a most offensive smell. You turn round and discover that she has opened up a grain pit, from the roomy interior of which a small boy, who has let himself in through the narrow neck, is handing out dishfuls of brownish-coloured mealies. Dampness has entered and spoilt the mealies, but the process has not gone far enough to make them uneatable. They are called *maduni* and, though the smell may be unpleasant, there are many who, at least as a change of diet, prefer food made of them to that of ordinary mealies. Many people are already inquiring whether the owner is willing to exchange them. Dotted about the *khɔrɔ* are other pits which can be located by means of a stick, for each is covered with a large, flat stone sealed down with mud. The *khɔrɔ* is the place where the men and boys of the village sit, and where cases may be heard; but it is also the playground of the children. Often when children worry their mothers by shouting or playing in the courtyards, they are told, 'Run away and play in the *khɔrɔ*; this is not your playground.' Many villages to-day have no *khɔrɔ*; they are too small to need one or, where there is a much-neglected space for it, it is not used at all, especially when the men are away at work in town.

To the left of the *khɔrɔ* are a small cattle kraal with wire fence, an enclosure for goats, and another with a roof for donkeys. Only a few villages have cattle at all; but, for most of those that have, a kraal outside the village made of rough poles serves now that there is no longer any fear of preying animals or raiding enemies. Old Raselaka complains that herdboys of to-day no longer tend cattle as they should. Cattle used to be taken to graze just after sunrise, at least when there was no summer dew, for the early dew in summer, though not in winter, is dangerous to man and beast. They were brought home to be milked at about 11 o'clock, when the boys would eat their breakfast, and were driven out again till sunset. To-day the boys like having their breakfast first, and it is not unusual in some areas to find cattle still in their kraals at midday, especially where the herdboys are attending school, a practice that seriously decreases their grazing time. Not one of the ten head of cattle in Raselaka's village is in milk. In fact, the cattle in Loveduland give hardly any milk at all, owing largely to over-population (over 75 per cent. of the land is under cultivation and certain areas are under forest) but also because of the poor quality of the cattle. But milk has never played an important part in Lovedu diet and many people find it nauseating.

You are eager to be shown the lay-out of the village and to watch some of the activities. As you pass through a gateway leading from the *khɔrɔ* to the huts, you hear Raselaka giving orders to the boys that a fowl is to be caught and killed for the visitors. The huts stand in two curved rows facing one another, sixteen in all. In a large old-style village like the royal kraal, they would surround the *khɔrɔ*, but here there are too few for that. A complete circle of huts still haunts the dreams of the ambitious doyen of a district. To one side of the line of huts is a tobacco garden, while at the back is the *marala*, or storage enclosure, made of branches with a gate that can be closed against wandering goats. Here stand the large receptacles made of wood interwoven with grass in which mealies are stored after reaping, till dry enough for decobbing. But they are empty now and some are in need of repair. To one side stands a roughly made, unplastered hut full of beer-pots. Here beer is left to ferment and sometimes also served. A number of large green and yellow pumpkins, the sweet kind cultivated by Natives, have been placed beside the beer-pots, while a heap of golden, plumlike *morula* fruits with a cloud of midges above it testifies to the desire of some woman to make a little cider at home. But it is seldom that such cider is made at home; the place for it is in the open under the shade of the trees.

As you look along the space between the two rows of huts, a pleasant and busy scene meets the eyes. It is ten o'clock and cooking operations are at their height. Some are cooking outside in the courtyard; others prefer to cook in the kitchen hut. An old woman is spreading out her newly lifted monkey nuts, together with a few cobs of mealies which had fallen to the ground, to be sun-dried in her courtyard. Some freshly stamped mealie meal on mats and in baskets is also set out in the sun. On an old piece of corrugated iron are lumps of a dark green substance. This is relish, cooked pumpkin and bean leaves, being dried and preserved for use in winter, when greens are hard to obtain. Apparently too much had been cooked for the corrugated iron, so the residue has been plastered on to the thatch of a hut. Roofs are useful also for other purposes; on one is a newly washed salampore cloth spread out to dry.

Each pair of opposing huts forms a separate household, its courtyard, the space between the huts, neatly smeared with dung, separated off from the next by a low wall, sometimes less than a foot high, or the remains of what was once a wall. Not all villages give an appearance of neatness. Sometimes, especially after a rainy season, the huts are dilapidated and greatly in need of repair; courtyards may be untidy-looking and only partially smeared, while often in summer flies are a veritable pest. It is considered unlucky to kill them. Native ideas of cleanliness also differ from those of Europeans: it is considered nothing for a baby to urinate on the hut floor, while hours spent in smoky huts give the cloths and blankets worn by women an unpleasant odour. Each household, the domain of a married woman, is independent, having its own fields and granaries. The household of the chief wife is opposite the main entrance; on either side of her in Raselaka's village are her two fellow wives; further to her left are the households of an orphaned sister's son to the village head, married to one of his daughters, and of his eldest son, whose wife is still cooking for her mother-in-law and has as yet no cooking hut. To the right, beyond the third wife of Raselaka, lives a stranger, Leṭavula, with his wife and mother. There is an extra hut for the young boys of the village and one behind the rest belonging to a woman 'married' to the second wife of Raselaka. The Lovedu have no ranking of wives apart from the chief wife (the mother's brother's daughter) and there is no division of the village into right- and left-hand sides as among Zulu.

There are well marked differences even on the outside between cooking and sleeping or reception huts. The latter all face the *khɔrɔ* and have a wooden door; they are well plastered, many having a veranda all round. The former have their backs to the *khɔrɔ*, a framework of reeds as a door, and are more roughly made, very often unplastered on the outside, so that the framework of wooden posts is clearly visible. On entering a sleeping hut, you find yourself in a pleasing apartment. The floor, the greater portion of which is generally to the level of a foot higher than that of the entrance, is well smeared, while beside the wall are one or two raised platforms used to place things on and sometimes also as seats. The well-plastered walls merge into the roof, forming a white dome. This dome has circular rims marking the cross-laths which, beneath the plaster, hold together the framework of closely packed rafters. Sometimes there are mural decorations and at intervals an outjutting shelf of clay or a peg. The floor of the hut of Raselaka is empty except for a double or waisted basket (*khirudwana*), a wooden platter of food, a lantern, and two smart suitcases. But on the shelves are blankets, a rolled-up sleeping-mat, some clothes and beadwork of the wife, and on the walls a calendar and a coloured picture of the King and Queen of England. You must not expect to find this latter sophistication in many villages, but likewise the smooth, plastered dome is now uncommon. New Government regulations against the cutting of trees for wood, and the men's general disinclination to put much work into a building they will inhabit only at intervals, between periods of service in the towns, are combining with other factors to doom to extinction these beautifully made huts. That of Letavula, newer than the others, is an ordinary *rondavel* with unplastered roof and supporting beams. He had a European bed, but has discarded it as too cold in winter. The veranda of the sleeping hut is used for storage. Here are pots of all sizes, many with lids glued down with dung, calabashes, sacks of corn on stands, medicinal roots, perhaps an old plough, a small grain basket on an inverted tripod of sticks, and a bag of reed pipes for dancing.

The contrast between sleeping and cooking huts is marked: whereas the former is relatively empty, cool and clean, the kitchen hut is generally rather untidy and, when a fire is burning, full of smoke. This is the domain of the housewife. Here are her cooking utensils—pots, baskets, wooden dishes, dishes of white enamel. At first the smoke deters you from entering, but the woman and her children sitting there appear to be quite at ease, so you summon up courage and go in. You splutter at first and your eyes water, but soon you grow accustomed to the atmosphere. You glance up at the unplastered roof and find it black from the smoke of many years. It is the home of countless cockroaches. Stuck in it are ears of corn and mealie cobs kept for seed, and many other articles, such as a cupping horn, some medicinal roots, some old arrows, and axe and spear of Sotho-worked iron kept as religious objects. On a platform of wood, out of the reach of white termites, are several bags of nuts and mealies, while a handbroom of asparagus fern lying near the hearth in the centre comes in useful from time to time for sweeping all the dirt into the fireplace. In this hut women sit at night; grandmothers sleep here with the children; here children are born and here they are often fed; here people lie when ill and here too they die.

A chair, native-made but after the European fashion, with seat of strips of thong, has been placed for you in a shady spot in the chief wife's courtyard. To be perched so high above ground when every one else sits on the floor is distinctly uncomfortable and out of place, but, in deference to the hospitality of your host in according you the honour of a chair, you feel you must occupy it. Four or five small, pot-bellied urchins with dirty noses range themselves near you to watch more closely the features and clothes of the European. One softly points out your peculiar nose to a companion, another comments on your shoes; altogether they find you and your ways absorbing. One small child holds aloof, screaming with fear when the rest try to force him to come near. With her back to the sun, a woman kneels beside a large pot of boiling water, deftly twirling a wooden twirler between her palms. Every now and then she stops to add a little of the fine, white mealie meal beside her by means of a ladle of calabash, for this is the first stage in the making of *vuswa*, cakes of thick meal, their staple food. The twirling prevents the formation of lumps. When the mixture becomes too thick for the twirler, a large, flat, wooden spoon is used with both hands. An aged and wrinkled old woman, mother-in-law of the one who is cooking, arrives from her garden with a basket on her head filled with the young leaves and male flowers of the pumpkin and three or four fresh cobs of mealies. The leaves and flowers are for relish for the meal; the cobs of maize she roasts in the fire for her grandchildren. She sits down, feet straight before her, and begins slowly to pull off the rough outer covering from the stalk of each leaf; it is then broken into two or three pieces and placed in a small, wide-mouthed pot.

Cooking the morning meal is a long-drawn-out process, requiring from two to three hours, for not only does water take a long time to boil in those earthen pots over a slow fire, but everything is done in a leisurely manner. While the meal is being cooked, the children and the women themselves roast mealies or monkey nuts, or sit about the courtyard eating sugar cane, for it is summer, the time when there is plenty. The old woman is now roasting some shelled monkey nuts on a potsherd; these she will stamp fine and add to the relish to give it additional flavouring.

A comely girl of about fourteen enters with a large gourd of water on her head, which a friend helps her to put down. '*Mukhadi wee*,' calls out her mother. '*Mulemya*,' says the girl, a polite reply or formal answering phrase by which you know at once that she belongs to the royal group, for each group has its own distinguishing answering praise-title. 'Get ready the plates. I shall be dishing up soon.' Mukhadi goes into the huts and collects five dishes—three gourds and two wooden plates—in which are the remains of the previous meal. The remains are carefully set aside to be used for making light beer (*mabudu*), for food is never wasted; then the dishes are scoured by means of powdered sandstone and stood in a row in the sun to dry.

In a neighbouring courtyard a grandmother begins feeding a two-months-old baby with thick gruel of sprouted corn. She begins by washing its face, then, cupping her left hand filled with gruel before its mouth, she pushes in the food with a finger of the right hand. Splutterings and gurglings are of no avail till Granny has decided it has had enough. This novel procedure is followed from the day of birth as a supplement to mother's milk. After its meal comes its daily bath. The baby is held over a large potsherd of warm water and washed with a little soap, special care being taken to clean the head and eyes. The baby wriggles and cries; the sherd has jagged edges; the European onlooker fears that at any moment the child may slip out of the woman's hands; but she is skilled and experienced in the handling of infants, and nothing untoward occurs. After being air-dried, the baby's body is anointed with vaseline, an easy substitute for the butter fat of old. In the meantime two boys arrive, one with a large cock under his arm. They are sorry to have taken so long, but, when they looked for a fowl, only the fowls of their neighbours could be seen; their own were nowhere to be found. Your hostess is about to have it killed, but you decide you would prefer to taste native relish, so you give instructions that it is to be left on the hut veranda with legs tied together.

The woman of the *musha* has lifted her pot off the fire and is beginning to dish up. Smoothing down the porridge with her wooden spoon, she skilfully scoops out a spoonful, which she carefully lays on one of the platters. The result is a neat cake of porridge over which a smooth, outer skin very rapidly forms. A cake is placed in each of the dishes before a second is added, till there are four or five on each. A Lovedu housewife is very particular about the manner in which she dishes up food, for untidy-looking cakes with jagged edges give one the reputation of slovenliness. The Lovedu pride themselves on their cleanliness with food; porridge must be white, with no suspicion of a foreign object. When a woman has finished dishing up, she very often wipes out the pot with her fingers before setting it aside, for utensils are washed just before they are needed—not after use. To prepare the relish a little water is placed in a wide-mouthed cooking dish, the pumpkin leaves and flowers are added and then put on the fire. Within a few minutes the spinach is sufficiently cooked. A handful of salt is put in, the ground monkey nuts are added, the mixture stirred once or twice, when it is ready to be dished up into small black earthen basins.

Serving food to guests is a ceremonious affair. The sleeping or reception hut is carefully swept out; the food is placed in it, often before the dust has properly settled, a mat is unrolled and the guests are called to eat. To your surprise, you discover that the host does not dine with honoured guests. A wooden dish of food has been placed in a double basket with a lid. Beside it stands the relish. Mukhadi approaches on her knees with a white enamel basin of water for the guests to wash their hands, then crawls away again, leaving the water to be used again after the meal. Before beginning to eat, the youngest of the visitors claps his hands saying, '*Ndau.*' The rest reply, '*Morɛna*,' and the meal is begun. Each one, using his fingers, breaks a piece of a mealie meal cake, dips it in the dish of relish and eats it. There is no salt in the porridge, to make up for which the relish is very salt indeed. All eat from one bowl but there is nothing unhygienic in this. When finished you again wash your hands. Light beer, if there is any, may round off the meal.

There is no communal meal and no proper mealtime. Each wife places food for the husband in the reception hut of his chief wife and here he comes to eat any time he wishes. Later the remains will be fetched back to the hut whence it came. Food is not sent from one hut to another, except when special luxury dishes are made, known in general as *madzaga* and usually prepared outside of cooking hours. These are always shared. The younger children sit down to eat with the mother in the courtyard, but the herdboys, in a hurry to take out the cattle, seize several cakes, place some relish on them, and walk off. Metiane, aged four, does not want vegetable relish. He has seen meat prepared in the courtyard of his friend Nagambi and so he refuses spinach. When his mother tries to coax him, he merely sets up a dismal howl; but he is neither severely scolded nor beaten as a European child in such a situation might be. Instead they try to pacify him, till at last the mother of Nagambi, seeing the fuss, brings him a small piece of meat, telling him to be quiet.

The cooking done, a general migration takes place, and the village, a hive of industry in the morning, becomes almost if not quite deserted. During the agricultural season one seldom finds people at home in the afternoons. They are all out in the fields. One woman, securing the reed door of her kitchen by means of a wooden stamper balanced against it on the outside, takes a hoe and is off to mound her *njugo* beans. Another is still busy with her weeding. A third, taking a calabash of food with her, goes to join her daughter, who left shortly after sunrise, to make *morula* cider under the trees in their field. It is a process involving considerable labour. Mamadomi is not going to the fields to-day. She wants to smear a fresh coating of dung over her courtyard and to go on with a basket she has begun making. Her small daughter under puberty has, however, to fetch the dung, as their cattle kraal has not been doctored to make it safe for women to enter without harming the cattle. The old mother of the village head sits basking in the sun in the courtyard, guarding the drying nuts and mealies from the fowls that wander freely about the huts now that the people are away. She wields a long stick and every time a fowl approaches whacks at it to chase it off.

The only sound that can now be heard in the village is the thud of three stampers. A woman and two girls are finishing off their stamping begun two hours before. They pound with long, wooden stampers into large, hour-glass-shaped blocks of wood with brisk up-and-down movements from the waist. It is hard work requiring a fair amount of skill. The first stage in stamping is the *hu thovola* process; hard mealie grains are placed in the stamping block, a little water added, and stamping begins. When the outer husks are loose the grains are placed in a flat winnowing basket, where, with an up-and-down movement, the husks are separated out and allowed to fall on the ground. These will later on be used for feeding pigs. The de-husked grains are put back into the block to be further pounded. After a time this is winnowed again in the basket, the lighter husks being made to fall on top of the rough husks of the first winnowing. The husks of the second winnowing are used for making light beer (*mabudu*) and could in time of scarcity be used for porridge. After being stamped a third time, the maize is generally winnowed into a basket, for the third winnowings are used to make *vuthithi*, a coarsish porridge darker in colour than *vuswa*. What is now left of the mealie grains looks like rather rounded grains of very white rice. This ends the first stage in stamping. Boiling water is poured over these grains, which are soaked for about two hours, then taken out and placed on a roughly made or old winnowing basket to allow the water to drain off. At dawn next morning the second main process (*hu seḓa*)—stamping into fine meal—takes place. The result is a very fine, snowy white flour very much like maizena, the pride of the Lovedu housewife. To supply the needs of an ordinary household, it is necessary to stamp two or three times a week, a process involving from four and a half to six hours of work each time. Kaffir corn and millet is subjected to one stamping in the wooden block to get rid of the husks, then ground fine on a flat grindstone. But porridge of kaffir corn or millet is very seldom eaten, most of it being used for beer.

Two boys come home from school and forage in the kitchen hut for their food, as their mothers have gone to the fields; of the twenty-five children in the village, they are the only ones who go to school. The midday heat is intense; the quiet air quivers under the sun's fierce rays. Some small girls sitting under a nearby tree outside the village seize hold of an empty paraffin tin and begin to sing and dance. Two of them are looking after babies, which they have strapped to their backs, but this in no way disturbs their enjoyment. Later on they will set out with old empty jam tins of various sizes to collect grasshoppers, which they catch by beating them with branches. In winter they are sent to collect wild relish for their mothers or to catch *mahoru* (*Macrotermes bellicositermes Swaziae*), which they entice out of their holes by means of a long piece of *leṭaṭe* (*Mariscus sp.*) or *lejɛkɛjɛkɛ* (*Cyperus immensus*), rush-grasses which the ants seize with their antennae. The girls who have been stamping now set out with some friends from a neighbouring village, all armed with axes, to collect firewood. The girls of this company are age-mates; they share their labours, confide their love affairs, bathe together, and, in the late afternoon, when they go to the bush, they sit together elongating their *labia minora* (*hu kwɛva*). Meanwhile the village lies basking and dreaming in the afternoon sun; except for the pecking fowls there is hardly a stir. '*Uu gae*' ('Where is it—beer'), says Raselaka to his son Sekware, as he returns with some poles on his shoulder for repairing his wife's granary. 'There is beer of *lejema* [work-party] over at Mudziri's,' is the reply; and the men, accompanied by the visitors, set out for the beer drink, knowing they will be allowed to partake even though they have done no work.

The hum of voices as you near a certain kraal leaves you in no doubt that this must be Mudziri's village. A fair crowd has gathered in the courtyard of the woman who is holding the *lejema* and a typical beer-drinking scene meets the eye. The centre of the picture is a large pot of beer placed in a rounded depression made for it in the courtyard. Beside it stands a flat winnowing basket containing long-handled calabash cups from which the beer is drunk. Beside the pot sits a man who serves the beer, using a beer-cup as ladle; he gives each cup to a young man of about twenty, who hands it round. The guests have ranged themselves on either side of the beer pot, women on one side, men on the other. As each calabash is emptied, it is brought back by the young man who is doing the waiting, to be filled. There is no hurry. Each one drinks at his leisure and conversation flows freely. Every one knows he will be given in his turn and, if one man is handed a second cup, he will pass it on to any one who has not yet been served, till all have had four or five. It is a pleasant social gathering and all the latest gossip is discussed. Small children toddle about in between the drinkers and may even be given a little of the beer. Ominously Pheduli remarks, 'Madume has seen police near Medingen. There appear to be four of them. What can they be wanting?' 'Oh,' replies Ɖwagu, 'they are no doubt raiding for tax defaulters!' There is general uneasiness, for about a fifth of the gathering are in arrears. Muhale is six years in arrears and, as he never goes to town to work, he has not once been caught. 'They won't catch me napping in my home to-night,' volunteers Mathɛkha. 'I shall go into the bush again. Are they Shangana-Ṭonga or Sotho, those police Madume saw?' a very relevant question, because the Shangana-Ṭonga, more likely than not recruited from outside the reserve, will not know these hiding places in the forests and caves. Here Pɛkɛla describes how his friend Setimɛla, who had himself always been in default and knew all the best hiding places, had joined the police the previous year. Consequently, at the very next raid the police made a most successful scoop, catching ninety-six defaulters, whom they marched to Duivelskloof.

The beer-pot is almost empty and people are merely sitting talking when the host calls Raselaka and his European guest aside into his reception hut, together with a few other intimates. A woman brings in a small pot of beer, decorated in a red chevron pattern, brimming with shining white bubbles at the mouth. A well-scoured basket with four beer-cups is placed beside it. The woman crawls on her knees in the presence of the guests, as is the custom. Turning to his neighbour, the host says, 'Here is a little water in honour of my good friend, headman Raselaka, and his visitor.' The man, turning to his neighbour, says, 'You heard the words of your host?' and he in turn repeats the message to Raselaka himself, who returns thanks for the honour. His thanks are similarly repeated (*hu suma*) till they reach the host, and the dishing-up begins. The host is given the first cup to drink, in accordance with Native etiquette, then Raselaka and his friend are served, the European, as an honour, being given a rounded calabash placed in a small flat basket. The group in the hut is small, so no waiter is needed. Two women form part of the select company. When the beer has sunk to the last dregs, the server says, 'The beer is finished,' whereupon all present *lɔsha* (greet) with a long-drawn-out '*Ndaaaaaaaau*.' The pot is turned upside down and emptied of the dregs, which are drunk by some one in the company. Such are the formalities of beer-drinking.

The sun has sunk low in the western horizon when you wend your way back to the village. The herdboys, with whistles and cries, are bringing home the cattle, goats, and donkeys. Two of them, one on an ox, one on a donkey, are having a race on the last level piece of ground near home. Others carry bundles of wood under their arms for the *khɔrɔ* fire. Suddenly you hear the ululations of beer carriers as a party of ten women carrying calabashes, resting in baskets half-filled with grain, comes towards you. What beer is this? Are these not the in-laws of Pɛkɛla, who lives in the village next to yours? True enough, they are bringing *khirula* beer to their *tsɛzi* (bridegroom), who married their daughter. When the women in the village see them, they, too, begin their cries of joy, accompanied by a few dancing steps (*hu pɛbɛla*); one of them even relieves a carrier of her burden and carries it for her to the hut of the son-in-law. Having set down their pots, the carriers begin dancing about, singing, '*Mushiji khi le; gi y'ɔ sheva ga nama*' (I don't eat blackjacks; I'm going to have relish of meat), in anticipation of the goat that the receiver is by custom bound to kill for them on such an occasion. He has in addition to give them a goat and 10s. to take back in recognition of their gift. If he has no goat, he may give them £1 in all instead. Hence the beer which the relatives of a woman send to their son-in-law each year or every few years, when they are short of corn, is really an exchange of gifts to maintain good relations. In addition, when the in-laws need anything, such as cattle or food, they may make beer and ask their *tsɛzi*, who cannot easily refuse. Immediately after their arrival, the carriers are given a pot of beer from that which they have brought. But, since your capacity for beer is more limited than that of your host, you decide you must go back to the village, as it is getting late.

Every one is converging homewards. Some women are coming with paraffin tins or pots of water on their heads; these four-gallon tins are much liked for their lightness, but the dampness of the climate soon rusts holes into them. Those coming from the fields bring with them baskets of pumpkins and green mealies for the evening meal. One woman, carrying a bundle of sugar-cane, is being tormented by two men who, despite her obvious unwillingness to give them any of it, are helping themselves; for people are thought to have a sort of right to picked sugar-cane, which is not a food, but like sweets among ourselves, something pleasing to the palate, to be shared with others. Last of all, and panting heavily, come the young girls who went to fetch wood, each with a heavy load on the head.

In the village some of the fires are already lit. One woman is cooking pumpkins for the evening meal. She cuts them into convenient pieces, removes the pips but not the outer skin, then packs them one above the other in a large pot, at the bottom of which there is a little water. A second pot, wide-mouthed and shallow, is inverted over the top, smeared down with a little of the red substance covering the seeds, and the whole allowed to steam over the fire. Green mealies for the evening meal are cooked in the same manner. Though pumpkin and mealies cooked in this way are very pleasant to eat, the European misses the salt, which is never added. Another woman is preparing some relish to eat with porridge from the morning. It grows darker and darker. The fires, some in the courtyard, some in the huts, but each the centre of a little family group, become a deeper crimson, their cheerful flickering giving one a sense of homeliness and quiet joy. At the courtyard fire where you are sitting, a small girl is cooking her tin of 'food', consisting of five treasured grasshoppers mixed with tomato, which she found growing in the kraal hedge. Every now and then she stirs this brew with a stick. The others are roasting mealies and nuts. A herdboy comes in and lays down beside his grandmother a bird he has killed. She is pleased with the gift, thanks him warmly and praises him by the praise of his name, 'You have done well, Ḍwagu, you who eat birds and take the heads to give your play-mates' ('*U shumile Ḍwagu wa hu la dinɔnyana ajia dithɔhɔ a fa vasimana*'). If his name had been Boga, the praise would have run, 'Boga, it falls upon people, that thick bush of Mujaji of Muhale' (*Boga le wala vathu lewai la Mujaji a Muhale*); for almost every Lovedu name has its praise, whoever might bear it. Boys are always told by their grandmothers to bring them birds; this they like doing, for there are so many ways in which grandmothers can return the gesture—boiled *njugo* beans, monkey nuts, or sugar-cane being always welcome.

In the *khɔrɔ*, the three men of the village are sitting by their fire; the herdboys sit at another. The boys are listening to a spirited account of the ways of European farmers given by a boy of fourteen whose good clothes and white sandshoes testify to his having just returned from work. A boy, who has just been called to supper, comes back with a cake of porridge and some relish in his hands to eat it in male company in the *khɔrɔ*. Another goes home to eat, but returns later on. The conversation has veered round to the hunting of cane rats with wooden traps, the prevalent sport of this time of the year, when one of the boys comes with some monkey nuts which he has begged from an old woman. These are roasted in their shells in the fire and eaten by the company. Another has managed to obtain some mealies to roast. 'Let's ask riddles,' intervenes Khiebe. 'Here's one: Riddle-me-riddle-me-ree (*thaiii*), the witches are dancing on the thorns.' 'Stupid,' scornfully rejoins Mudumi. 'We all know that one. Hailstones, of course, for they bounce as they fall on the grass.' After pondering a moment he challenges: '*Thaiii*, the ox of my father has entered the pool, I remain holding its tail.' Roars of derision issue from the rest, 'A porridge-twirler,' they answer almost all together. The spiked head of a twirler is like the horns of an ox; it is thrust into the pot of water, while one holds it by its handle. 'Here's something you don't know,' comes from Mudumpani. '*Thaiii*, the nest of the water bird hangs down over the pool.' The company is silent, then there are some guesses, but it is beyond them, and they give it up. 'The eyelashes, of course,' says Mudumpani, 'because they hang over one's eyes.' Once the ball starts rolling, riddles follow one another in rapid succession. 'The babbling of a brook' turns out to be a calabash cup, for down its long handle beer gurgles as you drink; 'They always stand looking at each other' are the doorposts of a hut; and 'The chief entering the crimson (muddy) pool' is sunset. It is impossible to capture the poetry of these riddles; you cannot render their alliteration or play upon words in English. But it is clear that these youngsters are well versed in them. The time when riddles are most popular is, however, when a wedding party is present and the young people have to entertain them in their hut. On such an occasion riddles provide a mild form of competition between the two parties, that of the bride and that of the groom.

The men have retired to their huts, whence they will not reappear. The women have eaten the evening meal informally round the fires and are just chatting. In a hut three girls are sitting by candlelight, one of them, who has been to school, writing a love-letter for her friend to her lover in town. 'Why are you throwing me over?' she asks. 'Why don't you write? Please send me a nice cloth and a blanket, but not one like that which you gave your wife!' In another hut some children have persuaded Mamujaji, an elderly woman, to tell them tales. She begins, '*Ŋgano-Ŋgano* (a story, a story).' They reply, '*Ŋgano*.' 'Once upon a time,' she continues, but before she gets further they again interject, '*Ŋgano*.' Then she goes on, 'There lived a boy who had sores all over his body.' '*Ŋgano*,' they repeat whenever the speaker hesitates or takes breath. 'One day when the girls went to fetch grass. . . .' This is the beginning of a story about a bird who gives away the girls who kill the boy. A marked characteristic is the frequent occurrence of a song and refrain, during the telling of the tale, in this case, '*Phogu, Phogu ya Uorwa*, &c. ('Bird, bird of the south'), so that what with the interjections and singing of the chorus of the refrain, the listeners appear to take as active a part in the story as the narrator herself. At the end of each tale there is a long-drawn-out '*Ŋgaaano*' and all spit into the fire. In the small villages of to-day story-telling has almost completely died out. Where there are only one or two present a story loses most of its charm, and there are many young men and women who know practically no stories, more particularly among Christians, whose parents prefer them to learn their lessons rather than tell them stories.

By eight o'clock most of the people have already retired. The bigger boys, now lustily singing a song, stay up latest; but soon all is quiet. On moonlight nights, however, the boys and girls dance and play in the *khɔrɔ* or outside the village until a late hour. Similarly, if there is beer in the village, there will be noise well into the night and very often quarrels and fights as well. When the spirit of a possessed woman comes upon her, there may be drumming and singing for her to dance to all night; then no one gets much sleep.

You yourself retire into the hut set aside for you, your mind full of the new impressions received during the day. How long you have been asleep you do not know, but suddenly you are aware of a dull, thudding noise. Can it be a drum in the distance? No. It is too regular. Again you hear thud, thud, thud. You look at the time. It is 2 a.m. You try to go to sleep; but the unknown beat is too disturbing, so you go outside to investigate. Some shadowy figures are moving at one end of the village. Women stamping! It is the women you watched in the morning, finishing the last process in their stamping. You wonder how they can see; but the night is, after all, not so dark and the meal is very white. Moreover, soon the moon will be up. The meal is stamped, then, by means of a circular movement of a flat basket, the finer grains are separated from the coarser again and again till the flour is fine enough to pass through the fine mesh of a European sieve, though in a few kraals one still finds even the last process being done by means of a basket. Later, when the sun becomes hot, the meal will be spread out to dry on mats or rocks, if any are conveniently near, or in baskets. If the women finish their stamping before dawn, they may go back to bed, as you have decided to do.

Such is the everyday life in a Lovedu village. There are, however, important differences from one season to another, for Lovedu life is in much closer harmony with nature than ours. The Native himself divides the seasons into three: *khilemo*, the time of hoeing, which is reckoned from about September to January; *leṭavula*, or summer, from about February to the end of May, the time when foods are plentiful; and *maria*, or winter, from June to the end of August. With the introduction of the plough, the planting season has been curtailed and the season of reaping prolonged. Whereas in the old days hoeing and the planting of advance crops in wet places began as early as September, to-day, even if the rains come early, nothing is done until November, more particularly because crops planted earlier are more prone to be attacked by the stalkborer. Consequently we shall consider November as the opening of the seasonal calendar. It must, however, be remembered that division of the year into seasonal activities is somewhat artificial, for activities overlap and life is never directed to one single object. Individuals often pursue their own ends, despite the general activities prevailing, and at all times there is great diversity.

During the ploughing and planting season, November to February, there are not many people, other than children and the aged, to be found in the villages. Workers set out early to begin work in the fields, their food as often as not being brought to them there. Sometimes the women take with them cobs of mealies preserved by being cooked and dried in the summer months, which they have softened by boiling again before use. In stony places and along steep hillsides, where ploughing is impossible, hoeing is to-day still done by hand. Here one can generally see mealie meal spread out to dry near at hand, out of reach of the fowls and goats that would play havoc with it at home, where there is no one to watch it. For it is chiefly the women that hoe while the men plough. Bushes or branches that have grown out from tree stumps in the fields are cut in readiness for planting, and a typical feature of this time of the year is the small fires in the fields every day towards sunset, when dry mealie stalks that have been collected in heaps are burned. Relishes have been reduced to a minimum, blackjacks (*Bidens pilosa*), thɛɛbɛ (*Amaranthus Thunbergi*) and *mufye* (*Solanum nigrum*) being the mainstay, and cooking is done only once a day. There are no nuts or mealies to roast or eat casually, and in years of scarcity this is the time when the pinch of hunger is felt. At night people retire early to bed, tired from the hard work of planting and, later, weeding during the day. Dancing is rare; there is no time for social activities, all energy being directed towards getting the crops planted. Beer parties there are, chiefly work parties for weeding, but they are not as frequent now as in winter. As yet few cases of malaria will have come to light; it is rather the season of dysentery and of cuts and bruises received in hoeing. As the season advances, the first termites make their appearance to relieve the monotony of relish of blackjack leaves, the grass grows longer and weeding becomes imperative.

As a relief to the dullness of the planting season comes the *morula* season, which marks the first two months of 'summer' (February and March) and which from the point of view of seasonal activities can be looked upon as a distinctive period. Everything is green; the grass stands high and weeding is the order of the day, for rain is plentiful. Masses of golden *morula* fruits are falling to the ground. Green mealies from the first-planted fields are beginning to be eaten, spinach of male pumpkin flowers and, later, leaves, make porridge cakes more interesting; and there are sugar-cane and dishes of unripe monkey nuts. People have looked forward eagerly to this time. They are tired of their work and, though much weeding and mounding of *njugo* beans has still to be done, the exultation grows as the cider begins to appear. To those whose granaries are empty, the *morula* season brings a blessed relief from the pangs of hunger, and they drink it as if it were the elixir of life. Much of the day is spent in the fields where the cider is prepared, and from under the trees there is a mighty hubbub of voices. At nightfall, when they return as from a bacchanalian festival, there are opportunities for romantic intrigues, the result rather of exhilaration than of the reputed aphrodisiac effects of the cider. Soon the air is rent by songs and drumming of the possessed, who at this season receive medicine to eat with the *morula* and other green foods of summer. And as the *morula* season draws to a close, the green foods of summer become more plentiful and the beginning of reaping activities ushers in the rich abundance of late summer.

Men have begun to suffer the penalty of reckless exposure to mosquitoes, especially after nightfall in the valleys where *morula* cider was drunk. Leaky huts and damp clothes have brought coughs, rheumatism and perhaps pneumonia. There is disease even among the cattle, which are attacked by the ticks that abound in the high grass. But these things cannot outweigh the pleasures of abundant relishes and summer fruits. April (*Thuduntoli*—the month when women ask you to help them lift (*hu rula*) the load from their heads) is indeed worthy of its name. Each afternoon the women come home with basketfuls of pumpkins, green mealies, nuts and relish. Careful housewives are drying relishes for winter while those whose weeding or mounding is up to date make tasty cakes of ground corn, monkey nuts, or the date-like fruits of the *muukhoma* tree (*Berchemia discolor*). The receptacles for storing have to be renewed for the reception of the new harvest, storage enclosures strengthened and sledges repaired. Men are to be seen daily going out to cut poles or grass, which the women carry home in enormous bundles on their heads. Soon reaping begins. The sesamum is first pulled up, then the groundnuts. Millet and kaffir corn are reaped next, lest the birds create too much havoc in the ripening fields; and, before this has ended, the mealies are garnered, stripped of their sheaths in the fields and carried home in baskets or on sledges. By the end of May, reaping and the threshing of kaffir corn and eleusine, usually done in prepared places in the fields, are in full swing. But in summer people do not, as in the planting season, work much in the mornings, except in working parties. Cooking is first finished and only after about eleven o'clock do the people go out to their fields. The men, especially those lucky enough to have no huts to renew or repair, have more leisure now, and there are daily orgies of beer-drinking. The abundance and variety of food make people forget that there might be a shortage later in the year, coming as a climax to reckless consumption and social activity. This is the time that people begin to compete in great friendly *gɔsha*-dancing displays and carry beer to relatives-in-law. Towards the end of July, when the herdboys turn the cattle to graze on the mealie stalks, there are echoing calls of joy, for soon they will not be herding at all. Grazing near home marks the beginning of the play-housekeeping of boys and girls in the reaped fields at the end of the season.

In contrast to the planting season, when the problem is to put in one's seeds betimes, reaping-time allows of a variety of other activities. From May, therefore, there are not only dances and much beer-drinking, but there is time for the plying of crafts, such as pottery, mat-making, basket-making. For the specialist in any craft is always primarily an agriculturalist who plies his craft only when he has time, and it is in vain that anyone approaches even the most skilled craftsman for an object during the planting or weeding season. Once the summer rains have stopped, courtyard walls are re-plastered and hut-building is possible. The period from August to the end of October when the fields are bare and the grass has dried is *madulahae* ('the time of sitting at home'), three months of leisure so dear to the Lovedu. Though many people are still winding up the work of the year, building and thatching, threshing and

III. ARTS AND CRAFTS
(a) CARVING A PORRIDGE-BOWL
(b) FASHIONING A SKIN SHIRT

IV. CO-OPERATION IN AGRICULTURE
(a) WORK-PARTY DE-COBBING MEALIES
(b) WORK-PARTY CARRYING HOME THE MEALIE CROP

storing, the majority no longer go to the fields and cattle are no longer herded. True, mealies have to be de-cobbed, but this is work done at home to the strains of wagging tongues and friendly gossip. Many visits are being paid to relatives and friends; people are re-establishing contacts with one another. But if it is a time of leisure, it is also a period of monotonous diet, for relishes are scarce and resort is had to dried relishes, roasted pumpkin pips, and *mahoru* ants, for even blackjacks are scarce before the spring rains. This is the season of the year when European vegetables are welcomed and many people, more particularly Christians, specially cultivate them for these months to be sold as relish. Those, like cabbage and lettuce and tomatoes, which can be cooked in the manner of spinach, are preferred. Where beetroots, radishes, turnips, or carrots are grown, it is the leaves that are sold to be cooked and eaten with porridge. More often than not the roots are thrown away or eaten in desperation by the owner himself. Many people willingly hire their services for a day to a farmer in return for a basket of tomatoes.

Changes have and are taking place in village life, but they have as yet been neither very great nor of a fundamental nature. Even the absence of 37 per cent.[1] of the male population over fifteen years of age in European service on farms and in towns, has been more than offset by the use of the plough. There is a growing spirit of independence among younger people of to-day which makes them impatient of control by their elders, and modern conditions of safety and peace make it possible for people to move away from their parents and establish their own small villages after any quarrel or suspicion of witchcraft.

[1] This figure was obtained by a detailed census of three different areas. Women in this tribe do not leave home to any extent to work for Europeans.

CHAPTER III

BASES OF SUBSISTENCE

The agricultural complex of activities—culture-change adjustments, and problems of malnutrition, education, and division of labour in agriculture—the place in the society, and present-day problems, of animal husbandry—modern threats to the interest in the vegetation as a basis of subsistence.

THE Lovedu are great agriculturalists and poor pastoralists. They have a vast knowledge of the vegetation, which constitutes the best example of a science among them. It is a science closely related to their everyday lives and upon which they rely, even more than upon their cattle, goats, pigs, and fowls, for their subsistence. They eat the fruits and roots of the plants, depend for their relishes upon leaves and soft stems, and in dozens of other ways nourish themselves upon the natural products of the soil. Not agriculture and animal husbandry alone, but these, together with wild fruits, woods, and other products of nature, are the bases of subsistence.

These bases are all fundamental, but they have different value in different aspects of the culture. Agriculture is most important as a source of the substantial foods; natural fruits provide relishes and variety, and as a means of nutrition are much more prominent than domestic animals. Cattle and goats are primarily not food at all; their great role lies in supporting the social structure. In considering the sources of the primary needs of man, we should get a wholly distorted picture if we omitted the natural vegetation, the use of which as food, in economic pursuits, and in medicine is one of the most impressive features of Lovedu culture. Tillage and animal husbandry presume an extensive practical knowledge of soils, crops, and grasses; but this body of knowledge takes second place beside the imposing science at the basis of handicrafts, natural foods—indeed, the whole medical, nutritional, and economic structure of the society.

Nature is not merely a physical fact; it is a living reality, an integral part of the culture. Environment is not something apart from man and his needs; it is the medium in which he lives and breathes. And it is their direct reliance on nature that makes the Lovedu so strikingly different from us, just as their everyday knowledge of the names, qualities, and uses of trees, bushes, and all kinds of plants so greatly overshadows the corresponding knowledge of ordinary men among us. We, who live in a world in which nature satisfies our primary needs in a roundabout manner, cannot easily realize how different conditions are in a world where the satisfaction is direct. We are often inclined to picture primitive man as engrossed in ritual pageant unrelated to, and unserviceable for, the major ends of human existence. It is very necessary to correct this view. It is often thought that sex, magic, and witchcraft absorb most of the time, activities, and interests of primitive man. But, at all events among the Lovedu, more time and energy is spent, more interest centred, on getting food, shelter, and the material comforts—in short, on a pragmatic adjustment to nature by the application of empirical knowledge—than on any other aspect of their culture.

The agricultural complex of activities is the end to which the major portion of the people's resources in land, labour, power, capital, and economic energies are directed. For success, practical knowledge of the environment is of the first importance. A feeling of security is attained in agricultural activities, not so much by magical as by empirical means. Skill, experience, close observation, hard work—these are the primary requisites. The struggle to make the soil yield up its fruit is not conceived to be waged or determined by mysterious forces. This does not mean that a European will be impressed by their methods of tillage. Their conditions of life, their technology, their control over nature are different from ours. The manner in which people invest their energies and draw out their rewards does not conform to our ideas of efficiency. We deplore the poor tillage, wonder at the wastefulness during periods of plenty, inveigh against thoughtless improvidence. Lack of intelligence, we say, is the reason for their lack of systematic planning against recurrent famine. But we forget, among other things, that practices based on shifting cultivation, though unsuitable in the new, crowded environment, are still alive; that the problems of storage against the ravages of termites and weevils have not been solved and, with the materials at the disposal of the Native, cannot be solved even by our experts; and that, in the absence of organized exchange and marketing facilities, there is no incentive to produce more than for the annual needs of the household plus the surplus for beer-making necessary to maintain social relations and one's reputation for generosity. Practices which ramify into the cultural structure cannot be changed, costly new materials for combating pests cannot be acquired, nor can a whole superstructure of economic distribution be built up at a moment's notice. While the old values that gave men confidence and sustained the society continue to survive as they do, it is they which will regulate the application of knowledge and resources. A man may wish to increase his food supply, but not at the price of giving up too many of the things valued in the society; a surplus beyond a certain limit means nothing and suggestions for an improvement in methods may thus fall on deaf ears.

We can here refer only cursorily to a few aspects of Lovedu agriculture. There are, firstly, the various crops. In modern times, mealies are considered the most important and are the staple crop on the hills, where they also have the first claim on the best soils. It is eleusine, however, the oldest of the Lovedu grains, that is given to the gods. But no one, so say the old men, must neglect kaffir corn (*Sorghum caffrorum*) and millet (*Pennisetum typhoides*), for upon them greater reliance can be placed in times of drought. In the valleys, despite their vulnerability to the ravages of birds, more of these latter two crops are planted than mealies, largely because they do not answer on the hills. Cereals are cultivated by both men and women; and, in addition, every woman plants also *njugo* beans (*Voandezia subterranea*), peanuts (*Arachis hypogea*), pumpkins, native beans (*Vigna sinensis*) and *mung* beans

(*Phaseolus aureus*). Several varieties of sugar-cane (sweet sorghums) are planted on the boundaries of fields or between the other crops.

Njugo beans are ancient groundnuts which require a good deal of attention by way of mounding, restrictive taboos and careful pulling up, although they are very welcome as a change of diet. In this respect they resemble peanuts, which were popularized by the Shangana-Tonga not so long ago. These nuts sometimes answer well where other crops have failed; in certain years they may flourish while the cereals wither in the sun. Then you may hear people say, but it is only by way of joking among the Lovedu, that the Shangana-Tonga witches have called the cereals to undergo circumcision (*hu ɛba*). Some people in the valleys are half-inclined to believe the claims that the Shangana-Tonga make for their witches, because it is undoubtedly uncanny that, when the nuts succeed the cereals fail, and vice versa. But usually the claim is ascribed to the desire of these outcast people to assert their importance—the Lovedu know nothing of inferiority complexes, but they are shrewd judges of human nature.

Sesamum used to be popular in the valleys and is said to be an old crop of the Rɔka. But peanuts have ousted this wholesome, albeit very troublesome, crop. You will be told that the reason lies in the growing laziness of people; this is a reason given for the neglect of many other old crops, but in truth we have here merely a shift in the application of the available resources. A delightful commentary on some of the values of the society, though we must warn the reader not to judge them from our standpoint, is the name *lenɔnya-vadimo*, 'sesamum of the gods'. It is a wild variety, unsuitable for human consumption, but good enough for the gods. It is not given to the gods, yet it reminds one of the sprouted eleusine merely mixed with water that is offered to the gods with the words, 'This is not water. Truly it is beer.'

There are other crops and the variety furnishes a well-balanced diet. But that is not considered to be the virtue of variety. A food is good if it fills. That is why they prefer their hard cakes of porridge to our watery oatmeal. They are inured to that feeling of fullness since the day of their birth, when Grandmother rammed porridge down their throats. But there is comfortable fullness and uncomfortable fullness—that after a good porridge meal and that after eating too much *njugo* bean. The stomach is not insensible to certain distinctions, though they are not our distinctions. Filling is not the only virtue of a food. Some foods relieve the monotony of the round of porridge and blackjacks, and some are tasty dishes or rare delicacies. But no one thinks of the virtues of a balanced diet, for nutritive and protective qualities of foods are not recognized. The old diet, simple though it might be from our point of view, was sufficiently varied to maintain people in good health; but it is not realized that, precisely because it was so simple, even a small change might eliminate essential ingredients. That change has not yet come among the Lovedu, but it is near at hand. Subsidiary crops are becoming less popular. You still see cowpeas, *mung* beans, water melons, even *baroe*, sweet potatoes, and native beans. Yet, on the whole, what is most impressive is the growing reliance upon cereals and pumpkins, and the neglect of many of the old crops. The balance may be restored by European vegetables, such as tomatoes, cabbage, onions, and carrots. They are planted in irrigated gardens; these, however, are not numerous and could never supply the needs of the whole population. The parsimonious peasant, well-filled with porridge, is hardly likely to spend much time on what are looked upon as luxuries rather than as necessities.

People know that to have many crops in the same field places a great strain on the soil and lowers the productivity of each crop. Yet as a measure of economy, dictated by conditions, every one to-day plants side by side as many different crops as possible. Eleusine is an exception and mealies are spared the worst mixtures, though it is rare indeed that in between the mealies you will not find pumpkins and nuts. Millet and kaffir corn, however, stand alongside sweet sorghums—in the old days planted only on the boundaries of fields—beans and groundnuts, pumpkins, and calabashes. There is no more virgin soil on which the old incipient ideas of rotation of crops can be practised. If by chance new soil is turned, its rich content of ash will no longer be placed at the service of eleusine, as was the old rule; mealies, which followed eleusine as a second crop, are now so much more important that the old priority of eleusine gives way to a mixed crop of mealies and eleusine, though mealies alone are preferred. When mealies, after two or three years, begin to answer badly, millet is planted, in accordance with the old rotation. To-day there is some idea that beans revitalize the soil.

But we must not exaggerate the scientific value of these principles. Rotation was essentially a method of draining from the soil, with more and more hardy crops, the last ounce of energy; a crop was not thought to recondition the soil. On soil that is too poor or unsuitable for any of the cereals, groundnuts are often successful; but usually it is left to lie fallow for many years. In the old days it might have been wholly abandoned; but to-day lands that have lain fallow for thirty years and more are being recultivated, at least if they are not along the steep or stony slopes of hills where ploughing is difficult. The shifting cultivation of the past is no longer possible; there are less men available for clearing, which, moreover, has for long been discouraged by the tribe itself and to-day is forbidden by Governmental regulation. Plough culture also has introduced new practices. These and other changes have had far-reaching results. Time and space for single-crop gardens are lacking. It is convenient and the most economic utilization of the available resources to put into the soil behind the plough a mixture of all kinds of seeds. Some of them will be smothered by the others and that will be a calamity if the staple crops suffer unduly; for that reason the problem now is to determine, with reference to soil and weather conditions, which crops will significantly lessen the productivity of those to which priority is accorded. Everything that requires to be planted separately is as far as possible left aside. Crops specially planted by women tend to fall behind in the race. Women do most of the hoeing to-day, and their labour, valuable as it is on the steep slopes and among the stones, cannot keep pace with the plough. Moreover, men make the modern gardens by the sides of streams, and the *mung* beans, groundnuts, and native potatoes, which the women planted, disappear before the advance of European vegetables. This is as yet not a great change, because there are very few of these gardens, and it is far beyond present resources to construct irrigation furrows.

The balance is also upset by other tendencies. Agriculture is still a vital interest, but others are beginning to compete with it, and the various cultural devices by which interests were massed behind the various stages of agriculture are no longer as effective as formerly. Mobilization of energies by the seasonal calendar and their concentration at the strategic points of time and place are only partially effective. The unfolding of nature, the increasing signs of the coming spring, the more and more auspicious banking up of the thunder-clouds used to be like the culmination of intensive propaganda playing upon the emotions of the people. As the first rains fell and the scent of the veld rose to men's nostrils, they seemed to liberate internal secretions which drove men to action; and the example of the first workers in the fields made the impulse irresistible. But to-day, though much of this is in evidence and one still sees an impulsive restlessness canalized into productive activity, the reactions are, according to Native accounts, much weaker. Neither internal secretions, if such there are, nor suggestion in a tense situation have their old overpowering effect.

Translation of the impulses aroused into useful action is to some extent inhibited by enervating listlessness, at least among a proportion of the people. They are people puzzled by the changes around them or caught in the vicious circle of malnutrition and weakened incentives. They seek solutions in smaller exertions, lotus-like inactivity, and excessive beer-drinking; and in the hierarchy of ideals, these values are beginning to become unduly prominent. It would be disastrous if they created a cultural pattern, as the tendency suggests, in which agricultural work is mere drudgery and people concentrate upon easy crops, thus oversimplifying a wholesome simplicity in food and, as a cumulative result, not fulfilling, but draining the joys of life. Even to-day, weakened by unbalanced nutrition, many more people succumb to tuberculosis, bilharzia, tape-worm, even dysentery and malaria; as disease spreads and shakes the sense of security, sorcery and witchcraft become more common interpretations, and men must rely upon magic to restore their confidence. It is in agricultural practices that some of the greatest changes have occurred in the society. But, as will be seen, the changes are not of a simple nature.

These are the tendencies; but we must remember that the foundations of the society are deeply laid and the tensions are evident only in the upper superstructure. The people have a remarkable capacity for making adjustments, at least when no profound social arrangements are affected. They have adopted new crops, changed from hoe to plough cultivation, and adjusted themselves from unlimited to limited land. Unfortunately, they do not as yet have faith in manure. They have seen, they say, that manure raises an excess of weeds and that for *njugo* beans it is useless, even dangerous. One cannot appeal to the value of medicine, because only witches 'doctor' their fields, not indeed to fertilize them, but to steal the crops of their neighbours. Garden magic is never legitimate, for men rely upon their labours and place their faith in the rain, the making of which is the prerogative of the queen.

Failure of one's crops is attributed, not to witchcraft, but in a bad year to the heat of the sun and in normal seasons to indolence or bad soil. In the last resort, however, when every one suffers equally, or when there is a major drought, the calamity is regarded as a punishment by the gods, who 'hold the arms of the queen', or by the queen herself, who is displeased in her heart. Diseases and pests are not magical visitations. Though called 'the witch of the mealies' because it saps their strength, witchweed (*Wormskioldia longipedunculata*) is neither sent by witches nor combated by supernatural means. Destructive insects and parasites, such as stalkborers, weevils, and caterpillars, are regarded, not as being 'sent', but as perfectly natural results of untimely planting or unseasonal rain. Birds, monkeys, rats, and mice are, generally speaking, combated by the practical means at the disposal of man, such as trapping or scaring. Numerous other precautions are taken: one does not plant millet unless one's neighbours do likewise, because when there are many fields, all, not merely one, will be at the mercy of predatory birds; people favour bird-proof corns, though they are harder to thresh; late-maturing crops, whatever their productivity, are discarded in favour of those ripening early, because they cannot be reaped before the cattle start their unrestricted grazing; and a much-favoured peanut, which is also easy to reap, is liable to sprout unless special precautions are taken. In short, the problems of agriculture are tackled in a practical manner.

This does not mean that a practical demonstration of the superiority of new methods will always have the desired effect. Agricultural demonstrators have made very little impression. It is often thought that this is due to the improvidence, lack of ambition, and innate conservatism of the 'savage'. A farmer will tell you that, after years of experience on his farm, his Native labourers go home to practise their primitive, wasteful methods. The trouble is not savage incapacity, but the incongruity of our ways, our technology, and our ideals with theirs. The demonstrator is like a teacher speaking a foreign language and working with material and concepts which do not exist in the society. He often is wholly ignorant of the background of belief. His education makes him unduly scornful of savage superstitions, instead of using them to advantage. In agriculture, among the Lovedu, there is one practice we might call superstition. It is *hu upa*, a method of safeguarding crops with medicine against the depredations of birds and monkeys. It is quite harmless, absorbs little of the time or energy of the few children who scatter the medicine, and does not preclude the use of other, more empirical methods. There is no need to waste eloquence upon eradicating a practice which strengthens the interest of the children in agriculture, causes no slackening in their scaring activities from the platforms erected in the fields, and, in the last resort, is an effective psychological device; for it equalizes the struggle of man against nature and maintains at the requisite intensity the confidence which enables him to strive hopefully against his difficulties.

Practical knowledge is undoubtedly the weapon with which demonstrators should combat progressive degeneration in agriculture; but it is not practical knowledge applied from our point of view; it must be from their point of view. Instruction must be articulated with their practices and techniques; it must take into account their arrangements and their rhythm of life. The knowledge imparted must be applicable to their conditions and be linked with the instruments at their disposal. For the dietician to extol the virtues of a new crop, for the doctor to show that bacteria more readily enter where resistance is lowered by deficiencies in food, even for the agricultural demonstrator using his superior implements to demonstrate the practicability of the crop—all this is very nearly fruitless. These things will have their value when they can be fitted into the Native's world of thought and technology. In the meanwhile, the execution of our plans, sound though they be in theory, is merely causing irritation and resistance.

All the old Lovedu cultivation was on the hills or along their slopes and, generally speaking, close relatives, not necessarily relatives through males, had all or some of their fields in large blocks (*demo*). Unlike the Tswana custom, these blocks stood in no relation to the social organization; the land was not pointed out by the chief and its size was not predetermined, but depended upon the energy of the individual cultivators. The *demo* was a matter of convenience and utility: the concentration facilitated co-operation in clearing the fields, economized the labour necessary for protecting the gardens, and made mutual assistance in hoeing and weeding much easier. No doubt the arrangements also mobilized incentives and added to the joys of life. There is to-day nothing left of these blocks. The old ones have inevitably fallen into the hands of more and more scattered people and no new ones can be created because large blocks of land are no longer available. The tendency towards dispersal and fragmentation was still further emphasized when Shangana-Tonga cultivation proved the fertility of the valleys. To-day a man must take land where he can find it, and though the Lovedu still live on the hills, they have their lands scattered all over the country. Indeed, since it is easier to plough on level ground, the hills are liable to be neglected, though wisdom dictates that it is best to have fields in two different environments. The result is that a man's fields are widely separated, sometimes being as far as ten miles apart.

The old division of labour in agriculture between the sexes was not uneven; both men and women hoed, weeded, and reaped. Only men cleared the forest, but against that only women cultivated certain crops, such as groundnuts. The old pattern is still more or less maintained, at least in principle. But cultivation by the plough has changed matters. Men look upon hoeing as the work of women, although the old ideal so much survives that they despise the Shangana-Tonga because their menfolk neither hoed nor weeded in the past. To-day hoeing and weeding among the Lovedu fall largely upon the women, and ploughing almost exclusively upon the men. This is not a fair division of labour; it might be fairer if the other activities of men, such as hunting and public life, had not become greatly attenuated. For the women are always busy, and their work is more monotonous than that of the men, who, despite the labour migration to the towns, have much more leisure than women.

More thorough ploughing and a revival of the interest men used to have in agriculture would make the balance swing evenly. A man should not feel, as he tends to do to-day, that he pulls his full weight if he goes out periodically to earn wages, ploughs the fields, discusses cases, and builds huts. He has plenty of time to take a larger part in agriculture, as he did in the old days and as many of the older men still do.

Ploughing has brought about many other changes. It has necessitated clearing of the stumps and stones, and broken down to a large extent the old contour-terracing. This has accelerated erosion, which was in any case inevitable owing to the overstocking, just as overstocking is inevitable, not because men keep many cattle, but because of the density of the population. Erosion impoverishes the soil and over-use exhausts it. The result is that the initial benefits of the plough, which made larger gardens and better cultivation possible, are gradually being turned into liabilities. Every one will tell you that crops are more abundant to-day than in the old days; but the price is already heavy, and as the quality of the soil gets worse it will be increasingly heavier. Variety, the single-crop field, rotation of crops have gone. The planting season is much later and less concentrated in the months of October to December than in the old days, for ploughing is a rapid process as compared with hoeing, and one can avail oneself of good rains even as late as the middle of February. Late ploughing is not always deliberate; the small number of available ploughs and, more serious, the inadequacy of the draught animals, are equally responsible. The distribution of these resources is effected by various forms of co-operation, mostly partnerships in which one supplies labour, another the plough, and still another the cattle or donkeys. These partnerships, though patterned upon old forms of co-operation, have to take account of new factors, economic rather than social, and lead to new alinements in the society. Overstocking and ploughing have contributed to the silting up with useless sand of the old riverside gardens. Their original purpose, which was to tide men over the scarcity in the months November to February, partly fell away when ploughing brought a measure of abundance, but now that the old needs are reasserting themselves these gardens are destroyed. In their place the new Europeanized gardens, irrigated by furrows along the upper stretches of the smaller streams, have arisen, but the incentives that stimulate this new experiment are somewhat different: the gardens are for profit, not for providing an advance crop. The effects of ploughing may be pursued in many directions: it has emphasized the economic as against the purely social value of cattle, at the same time eliminating milk from the diet of adults; it has to some extent militated against husbanding the food resources; it has stimulated excessive drinking of beer; and it has released a large amount of energy for which there is little creative outlet.

For the present, agriculture is in unstable equilibrium. Every adult still has his own field, but the extreme limit of land available for cultivation has been reached. Limitation of stock can no longer ease the situation, as the chief evil is not overstocking but over-population. About 80 per cent. of the entire soil is arable land, at present or in the near past put under cultivation; as much as 80 per cent. of this land is annually tilled, though the actual extent varies considerably according to the vagaries of the weather, the surplus in the granaries, the availability of implements and animals, and other factors. We do not think that in present conditions the absence of man-power in the towns is a material factor. On the contrary the man-power available is more than sufficient as long as present methods are employed. The introduction of the plough has liberated more energy than is absorbed by work among Europeans; the number of inactive men has increased rather than decreased. It is the shortage of animals and implements, rather than of men, that is most impressive. Even European labour and European ploughs and cattle are employed by the Natives; they come from the neighbouring farms and can do the work more economically than the Native with his inadequate resources. But it is not lack of human material, it is the impossibility of making the ploughs and animals go round, that necessitates such expedients. In the companies and partnerships, those who contribute the essentials, the cattle or the ploughs, are the dominant partners, and the others must often wait until late in the season before their needs can be attended to. The partnerships thus lead to tensions and strife, and hiring of services is becoming more popular. Yet on the whole the system works with remarkable smoothness. If it worked perfectly, the Natives would realize much more forcibly that it is not lack of industry that, as they think, is at the bottom of their troubles, but the inadequacy of the land and of their material resources.

Although animal husbandry ranks as a very poor second economic activity, it is still of sufficient importance to warrant a few remarks even in such a general account as this. Pastoral activities are not arduous; in the old days they were worthy of the metal of adult men who went armed to herd the cattle and supervised the milking. But to-day children herd and there are practically no cows to be milked. Cattle are individually owned both by men and women, but the kind of ownership, except in the case of some 15 per cent., is entirely different from what we understand by the word. For the vast majority of cattle are linked to the chain of *munywalo* (bride-price) exchanges and as such the individual's rights over them are subject to many restrictions. The primary value to the Natives of cattle is not economic, but social; he regards cattle as food only in the last resort, though there is no taboo against killing them. Cattle are not killed as sacrifices. Ownership of cattle is not the chief or even a very important method of reckoning status. A man will complain, not because he has no cattle, but because he cannot brew beer to maintain his prestige. The dung of cattle is used for smearing, cattle that die are eaten, and cattle are killed in time of starvation so that the meat can be exchanged for mealies. But cattle are, generally speaking, much too large units of value to be of use in economic exchanges. Finally, the needs of cattle do not determine the routine of the day. They are taken out late, after the dew has dried and the herdboys have had their morning meal; and they come back almost unnoticed without disturbing the arrangements of the village. In a sense, however, their needs set limits to the harvesting season; crops which are not reaped by the beginning of July are practically at their mercy. Yet, despite all this, cattle are regarded with an emotion which, though wholly unlike our humanitarian attitude, finds expression in exaggerated praises. These can be understood only in relation to their immense importance in the social organization.

Lovedu cattle are a blend, it is said, of four different strains: the large, humped Lovedu with backward-curving horns, the small, sturdy long-horned Rhodesian, the small Swazi with incurving horns, and the recent rather nondescript European breeds. In the present environment the mixture has led to inferior scrub cattle, resistent to tick-borne diseases and hardened by the stony hills. There are more cattle to-day than formerly and the distribution is far more equal, but no one believes that dipping has contributed to this result; on the contrary, dipping is regarded as a device to keep down their numbers, to subject the Native to irritating interference, behind which there are sinister motives. Recent attempts by the Administration to improve the breed by introducing thoroughbred Afrikander bulls failed because of these suspicions; the bulls were neglected and no camp was provided for them, and eventually they had to be removed. Cattle of individual owners are listed on so-called cattle lists, which primarily serve as a check upon the efficiency of the dipping; but the lists do not reflect real ownership, for they contain the cattle in a man's kraal, most of which may be merely in his care (*hu fisa*). These lists have considerably altered the incidents of the *hu fisa* contract and other aspects of Native life: they are often illegitimately used as evidence of ownership; orders of Native courts involving payments of cattle are sometimes nullified by the refusal of the owner of the list to authorize the transfer of cattle from his list to that of another; dipping and grazing fees imposed in some parts induce men, on the one hand, to distribute their cattle among different owners so as to keep down the number on any single list and, on the other, to make a charge, unauthorized by custom, for caring for the cattle of others. In short, European intervention has produced as serious changes in pastoral as in agricultural activities. Yet fundamentally the changes have left untouched the real significance and role of cattle in the society.

Cattle are not subject to as many taboos as elsewhere in Southern Africa. Women do not usually herd cattle, but the reason given is that not long ago the dangers from raids and wild animals necessitated herding by armed men; it was regarded as a purely practical measure. Girls or women may herd when the boys are in the circumcision school, and sometimes to-day young girls who have no brothers are seen looking after the cattle. What women may do or may not do varies almost from one kraal to another. Sometimes women of any age may go into the kraals; sometimes the doctor has protected the kraal in such a way that certain classes of women (not necessarily young women) are excluded. There is a fairly uniform fear that the blood of women or a woman who has had an abortion might cause the cattle harm. But the measures to combat these dangers vary very considerably. Kraals are doctored rather than cattle; and they are protected against various dangers, one of them being the danger of women. But elaborate magical practices, elsewhere associated with increasing the fertility of the cattle or safeguarding them against misfortune and disease, are not necessary when a new kraal is built or when the medicated pegs are hammered around the fence as a protection against witches. Some confine their doctoring to the kraals; others, in addition, give the cattle medicine. Bulls are never magically rendered more virile, nor are cows made more attractive by such means. There are to-day hardly any special cattle doctors, and very few cattle diseases are known or subjected to treatment. This is not the result of the breakdown of the cattle cult; it is evidence of the weakness of the cult among the Lovedu. If one were to detail all the magical practices that are to be found, the volume of which would be doubly formidable owing to their diversity, an overwhelming impression might be given; but in true perspective, regarding them against the total background they are almost too insignificant to be noticed.

Far more important from every point of view is the adjustment that Natives are making to modern conditions. On this point we can offer merely a few very general suggestions. Foremost is the problem of better co-operation between the Natives and the Administration. The objections to dipping are a symptom of misunderstanding one another's point of view. The Natives regard the restrictions as a punitive and arbitrary imposition. It is useless merely to urge that, by destroying the ticks that cause cattle diseases, dipping promotes both the increase and the welfare of the cattle. No one believes what is regarded as demonstrably false. Any one can see that cattle often die when they come back from the dip; that the rate of calving has decreased, that there are now no milch cows, that stock have degenerated, and so on. These evils are attributed to dipping, not to the hard driving to the dip, poor grazing, and inadequate care. What is more, it is believed that Europeans do not dip and that tribes that are sufficiently cunning escape the dipping regulations. Not a few advance the theory that dipping is a punishment for attachment to and preservation of old customs—surely an ironical comment upon the execution of a policy that aims at segregation and development on the lines of racial genius. The psychological aspects of these problems are no less important than their other aspects; and they are far more difficult and require delicate handling. It is easy to envisage the immediate effects, for instance, of limitation of stock, such as the starvation that will result from insufficient cultivation and the overburdening of the women with agricultural work; but when it is realized that the cattle are barely sufficient to maintain the *munywalo* exchanges upon which the social organization rests, one cannot venture to predict what the ultimate effect of limitation will be.

Goats are the animals *par excellence* of ritual and religious importance. They also feature prominently in exchanges which promote social inter-relations, such as marriage exchanges and the goodwill gifts between relatives-in-law. Second only to beer in re-establishing relations that have become strained, they are used very largely in the procedure of reconciliation, of righting wrongs by begging pardon, and in the payment of judgement debts. When a distinguished guest visits you, you honour him by killing a goat for him; when you bring beer to your *vaḍuhulu*, the people to whom the daughters of your lineage are married, or even to a friend, they return the compliment by giving you a goat; it is the 'walking-stick' of the old women who brought the beer to her son-in-law, enabling her to go home safely. Goats are dedicated to the gods more frequently than any other animals. A goat is killed at a burial, and its unsalted flesh is eaten. People pay goats to their doctors; they exchange them for mealies. Their skins are still used for making skirts for women and cradles for their babies, whereas cattle hides have no use except for the thongs used in inspanning cattle. Goat's milk, which is never drunk by adults because of its unpleasant odour, is the food of herdboys and girls. All in all, goats play a not inconsiderable part in economic and goodwill exchanges, in legal adjustments, in ritual and religion.

By contrast, sheep, though in the bones of a diviner they represent the men of consequence and goats merely ordinary people, are of no importance whatever. They are very rarely seen on the hills and difficulties connected with dipping have reduced them to a negligible number in the valleys. Fowls are conspicuous everywhere, but only their meat, not their eggs, are eaten. They have recently been introduced by the Shangana-Tonga and even to-day, if found in the capital, are killed and thrown over the hedge. They are never, as among the Shangana-Tonga, used in religious rites. Donkeys, introduced in considerable numbers some thirty years ago, are used in ploughing and for transport, while pigs, also a recent acquisition, figure largely in trading transactions. Pork is not eaten except by men who have worked among Europeans, but the reason is that it nauseates, not so much that it is related to the totem of the tribe. Finally, hunting, as it is to-day, can be dismissed with a reference to the activities of herdboys, who shoot birds with wooden-headed arrows, use birdlime obtained from certain trees, and set various kinds of traps to catch rats, dwarf mongooses, and squirrels.

It is a different matter when we turn to the exploitation of the vegetation. The role that this source of subsistence plays is evident in a thousand ways. It is indeed difficult to give an adequate picture of the manner in which the vegetation enters into all aspects of life and culture. Perhaps, by way of illustration, we may take half a dozen names in order from an alphabetical list of over 500 plants—a small proportion of the flora—which we collected, and note merely a few of the ordinary, well-known uses:

Muvidividi (*Ekebergia capensis*). The wood, which is very white and hence much liked, is used for making spoons and bowls; being soft wood, it is also used for milk pails and door boards. To ensure that it will resist weevils to some extent, it is not cut when very young.

Muvidisa-vyalwa (*Trichodesma zeylanicum*). In winter, when beer is slow to ferment, the leaves are put into the pot to accelerate the process. The roots, chewed or crushed, are put on wounds to relieve the pain and to heal.

Muvilo (*Vangueria floribunda*). Two varieties are distinguished. The primary use is medical and magical, e.g. a branch, first presented to termites and then medicated, is beaten on the temples for migraine; a medicated pole of *muvilo* is placed across gate entrances to keep out witches. For the latter reason, this wood may not be used as firewood; it would reveal the protective medicines (*diphaba*) of the village. The fruits are eaten by herdboys, January to March. The first appearance of its flowers (October) indicates the time when chickens must not be hatched or bought, because of the danger of sand fleas (*madzɛdzɛ*). There are, incidentally, many other plants which indicate the approach of the seasons or the correct time for certain activities, e.g. when *musoso* (*Terminalia serecea*) blossoms, edible termites get their wings and children go out to catch them.

Muvizi (*Colocasia antiquorum*). Planted at home—in the old days also in river gardens—to provide relish from August to November. The leaves take only a few minutes to cook, compared with an hour or more for many other relishes. The bulb is cooked separately, like sweet potatoes.

Muvɔbyani (*Lanna edulis*). A soft wood used for milk pails and bowls. The fruit, which is eaten by children and adults, ripens in November-December. The wood is not suitable for hut rafters, as it is attacked by weevils, but the bark serves as a rough, unworked string for tying together the poles of such structures as pig pens. Water in which the leaves are crushed is used as an eye lotion.

Muvola (*Parinarium curatellifolium*). The fruit, called *grysappel* (grey apple) in Afrikaans, is liked and of very great value in times of starvation. It is said to have saved the people in the years 1894–6, when drought, locusts, and cattle diseases overwhelmed the country. At such times the fruit is prepared, like *morula*, in the form of a cider (*vureba*), which is yellowish and sweet. It also has economic uses.

We have in our list over a hundred different kinds of wild edible fruits and berries, many of them, it is true, eaten chiefly by herdboys. But numerous wild fruits are relished by adults, such as wild figs (of which there are seven different kinds), *muukhoma* (*Burchemia discolor*), of which a tasty, if heavy, cake is made, *mudomma* (*Diospyros mespiliformis*), *muṭazwa* (*Pouzolzia hypoleuca*), *munnthu* (*Syzygium cordatum*), *muɛbɛ* (*Anona senegalensis*), and many others. The *morula* is, as we have seen, an important national beverage with valuable anti-scorbutic properties. There are also wild bananas (*muɔva*), long ago brought from the north, but now practically eradicated by animals. Not much reliance is placed upon cultivated fruits, but there are oranges, some pawpaws, and mangoes, planted by the early Christians; these have not subsequently been added to to any extent and they are very much neglected.

For relishes, without which porridge cannot be eaten, people rely largely upon nature. Apart from the leaves of pumpkins and beans, which are available from February to June, they use a great variety of wild spinaches, chief among which are blackjack (*Bidens pilosa*), *mufye* (*Solanum nigrum*), and *thɛɛbɛ* (*Amoranthus Thunbergi*). In our list we have forty-five greens or relishes. But not only plants provide relishes. In September and in the winter months, when greens are scarce, *mahoru* (*Macrotermes bellicositermes Swaziae*), fatty black male termites, are a great standby. The female of the same species (*dinnṭwa*), which swarm from December to March, the rainy season, are so important in the national diet that they must be ritually 'bitten' (*hu luma*) and sent to the queen from every district. They are roasted, winnowed, and eaten as relish, the winnowing being mixed with salt and pressed into a cake used as spinach or eaten alone. Children eat *dinntwa makhura* (flying ants) and grasshoppers; *maida*, a large red grasshopper and a few other kinds of grasshoppers, as well as swarming locusts, form part of the diet of adults. Indeed, during a famine in the 1850's, Mujaji, it is said, sent locusts, not to plague, but to succour her subjects, the Shangana-Tonga. Honey—not only of the honey bee but also of other insects, such as the *muga*—adds, though only occasionally, to the variety of the foods directly supplied by nature.

For nutritional purposes, a considerable body of knowledge of the vegetation is necessary. This body of knowledge expands to a veritable science when we consider its application to the arts and crafts. It is used continuously in all daily activities, such as building, fencing, renewing hoe handles, yokes, and storehouses, extracting oil or fat, and so on. In the old days it was not merely woodwork that was important; iron-making was one of the great industries. To-day, though many implements of Native ironwork are still to be found, the industry has disappeared, partly because the sources of the ore have been appropriated by Europeans and partly because of the cheapness of European-made iron objects. The smith was a specialist, but also an agriculturist and a student of the vegetation. In his industry he used, not only special ores, but also special woods. Similarly, for each of the crafts—hut-building, fencing, making stamping blocks, sledges, hoe handles, milk pails, spoons, platters, winnowing baskets, drums, and many others—different qualities in the wood are regarded as important. There are half a dozen different kinds of plants that yield fibre from which string can be made, each involving a somewhat different process. The value of certain grasses for thatching and making mats, baskets, and beer-sieves is ritualized in the taboo on cutting grass before the queen eats the first fruits; i.e. thatching grass must be left untouched until it is quite ripe in May and June. The elaborate working up of skin, though now restricted to the purpose of making skin cradles and a few women's skirts, involves considerable skill as well as knowledge of the value of oils and repellents to drive off destructive insects and even dogs. Pottery is still a live industry involving a knowledge of the qualities of clays, and what we call 'herbalism', the use of the medicinal qualities of plants, is not confined to doctors, but is to a large extent common knowledge.

A whole volume could be written on the interest of the average man or woman in the flora alone. He knows a great deal about almost every plant. Even a herdboy, as we found in discussing our list of names of plants, could mention one or two practical uses of more than half of them. Young men could add several medical or magical uses, while old men could bring the names into relation with a bewildering number of ritual, religious, and other occasions, and many had specialized knowledge, according to the nature of their occupations or interests. Speaking generally, and in terms of what is commonly known, we find that of the 500 plants we have listed, 200 have mainly economic uses. They are daily applied to such activities as building huts, thatching, making spoons. Some 20 are specially useful for making string; another 20 for manufacturing baskets, sieves and mats; and still another 25 in the hunting activities of boys (arrows, bows, traps, glue.) Over 100 are known more particularly for their edible fruits or roots and 45 are greens or relishes; 230 are well-known in the everyday medical pharmacopœia, and of these 60 are magical. Among other well-known uses are those of the grasses and sedges (15) from which dancing or initiation costumes are made and those (12) connected with games. Some 5 were considered noxious weeds and 8 had certain taboos attached to them. Plants with conspicuous flowers are not specially observed, and one asks the ordinary man in vain as to the name and uses of the more delicate flowering plants; on the whole, he is far better acquainted with trees than with shrubs and grasses, unless used as relishes.

What is striking is that the ordinary man regards the flora from a most practical point of view. Only a small proportion of the well-known plants have uses which are mainly magical, and knowledge based upon empirical observation overshadows that derived from mystical conceptions. One does not 'doctor' wood to strengthen it against the attacks of termites or woodborers; one selects the proper tree. In 90 out of 100 cases the quality of the wood, not any magical manipulation, is important for the purpose to which it is put, especially if the purpose is economic; and it is in this sense that empirical knowledge is highly developed. Even in the medical sphere, which is predominantly magical, the ordinary man places his faith in the observed action of the herb he uses. The cure may be merely violent internal disturbances, which, in view of the supposed nature of the illness, may be regarded as necessary. The use is not for that reason magical. Many diseases are conceived to have their seat in the stomach; they are to be thrown out by a purgative; and for them purgatives are used with a vengeance. Among doctors, of course, all sorts of magical remedies are added; but that is the sphere of the specialist. The ordinary man uses remedies of which the visible effects are empirically related to the disturbances which he conceives to be the causes of the disease.

From close observation of the qualities of plants, the Lovedu have arrived at some classification of the flora. They recognize the similarity of plants of the same genus and, if external likeness is a matter of practical interest, there is often a similarity of the word used to designate the various species of the genus. This does not mean that they proceed upon genetic principles; to anatomical similarities in flowers, for instance, they are quite indifferent. If the qualities of two plants of the same genus are to their way of thinking significantly similar, the plants might receive names that are similar; if the qualities are dissimilar, they often know that the two plants are related, though they have different names. The same species modified in its external features by different environments is often given the same name. Species of the same genus are likewise sometimes distinguished by qualifications of the generic name. *Khiphadwa* of the plateau (*kha naha*) is, for instance, *Gymnosporia senegalensis*; *Khiphadwa* of stony places (*kha makhwareni*) is *Gymnosporia buxifolia*. Again, *muduvo, muduvatsi, muduvatisbi,* and *muduvolisiga,* all containing the root *duv-*, are all species of *Combretum*. On the other hand, *mugavi, mukwidi,* and *muhahela thudu* are also species of *Combretum*, but there are good reasons for the different names; the anatomical similarities are known, but the uses and other aspects are more important and determine the name. Anatomical differences, clearly recognized, do not stand in the way of designating very different epiphytic plants which secrete 'birdlime' (*vulebo*) by the one name, *khilebo*. What determines nomenclature are not only striking physical features, such as peculiar leaves and seeds, but also a significant relationship with natural phenomena or, most usually, an important use. The variety of unconnected principles used upsets the symmetry, from our point of view, of the classification. But it must not lead us to think that there has been no close observation of the forms and venation of leaves, the taste and smell of the wood, and so on. The details of the flower, except for colour, general shape and size, are regarded as unimportant for purposes of identification. Yet they can name the poorest specimens and wonder why we want flowers and fruit before we can name a plant. The use of many cross classifications is not a burden to the memory, because the names link the plants to their practical uses.

The subject is much too large for adequate treatment here. Yet a few examples, illustrating the general outlook, might be of value. Because of its broad, flat leaves, *Inulata glomerata* is called *zɛvɛ ya ḍou* (the ear of an elephant). The flower of *Wormskioldia longipedunculata*, which is small and crimson and peers through the grass, suggests the name *leiṭɔ la dau* (the eye of a lion). The baobab is *khivuyu*, something inordinately fat and squat; the root *vu-* also occurs in the names of those fat caterpillars that attack mealies, of the hippopotamus, and of the enormous termite queen. Apt as well as picturesque are such names as *khivede kha muri* (the liver of the tree), for all fungi; *leada la khithii* (the egg of the sunbird), for a variety of the groundnut; *Voandezia subterranea*, *moŋkhakhilemo* (scent of spring) for *Phyllanthus reticulatus*, the flowers of which fragrantly herald the spring, and many others. One might think that those who named the plants were poets. Perhaps they were, because there is no lack of exquisite poetry in the beautiful praise songs that are the real literature of the people.

But their interests are many-sided and they do not scorn to have more mundane names. Here are a few that bear upon economic uses. For weaving (*hu loha*) baskets they use the *muloha* plant, *Acacia ataxacantha*; *mulɛde-muloha-ṭhɔḍɔ*, our *Sida cordifolia*, is pliable (*hu leda*), like other *mulɛde* plants, all of which are of the genus *Triumfetta*, and for that reason specially suitable for weaving beer sieves (*hu loha ṭhɔḍɔ*). Mukhaṭisa, our *Indigofera eriocarpa*, is their herdboys' milk-curdler (*hu khaṭisa*, to cause milk to curdle). The sap of *muilantshe*, which we call *Asclepias stellifera*, they use to repel flies (*hu ila ntshe*) from the open wounds of cattle. With the branches of *Ʋasimana-va-a khaḍa*, a stinging weed which we appropriately dignify with the name *Achyranthus aspera*, youngsters (*vasimana*) playfully fight one another.

Consider also, lest we think that the genius for giving apt names has been lost, the following few recently introduced plants. The pineapple, because of its prickly, xerophytic bracts, gets the same name as the aloes, *khiṭuzi*. The scent of the khaki weed calls to mind hemp, *baja*, and so is called the small hemp, *khibajabajani*. The large pods of *legamasi*, a peanut of the *masaimlika* variety, are likened to leggings, for which they use a corruption of the Afrikaans word *kamasters*. *Khiṭhava-misisi* in scientific nomenclature is *Amaranthus spinous* but, for all that, it pricks the 'missus' (*hu ṭhava misisi*). We link the sunflower with the sun, but they call it *munɔntshakhuhu*, fattener of the fowls, because the unaccountable European, instead of leaving fowls to their own devices, fattens them (*hu nɔntsha*) with its seeds. It would be tedious to give more of these interesting names. Suffice it to say that, upon whatever principle they are given, they furnish examples of close observation, of humour and poetry, and of practical sense.

In the command that the Lovedu have over the material supplied by vegetation, knowledge of the suitability of the plant to be used is by far the most impressive aspect. By contrast, preparation of the material, by seasoning or otherwise, and skilful or artistic manipulation to produce the required result lag far behind. Utility rather than artistic beauty is the main consideration; a carelessly made article, generally speaking, serves its purpose as well as one well executed. There is not much specialization and a high standard of workmanship is not aimed at; most men know what wood to select and how to make a great variety of ordinary household articles. Special skill is needed for making wooden dishes, drums, and milk pails. The most skilled work is perhaps the making of baskets (*zwirudwana*), which is done by men. This is not the place to describe the technique of the arts and crafts; all we need insist upon is the widespread knowledge of the virtues and defects of the plants that can be used.

Modern conditions have brought about a serious decline in craftsmanship and in familiarity with the vegetation. Schoolboys no longer have the extensive opportunities of learning veld-lore which herding provided. Herding is to them hardly an institutionalized induction into nature study; instead of being a part of life itself, it assumes the aspect of distasteful labour. The introduction of European articles also lessens the interest in the qualities of the vegetation. Yet these influences are in their infancy. They have made some impression upon the material elements of the culture, but they have tended to impoverish rather than to replace the old. You see petrol tins side by side with water pots, ugly sacks ousting the picturesque granaries, patched pieces of boxwood replacing reed doors, cast-off European clothes instead of graceful coverings of skin, machine-made blankets beside hand-woven grass mats, and axes and knives, no longer from the smithy, but only from the stores.

More serious is the threat to the traditional outlook. Christianity stresses the virtue of being different from the pagan, but the status of Europeanized Natives is precarious both in and outside the tribe, and there is no co-ordinated view of life that can successfully combat the subtle economic onslaught of European culture. And, since 1938, the legislative prohibition of cutting down trees, except after permission having been obtained and a fee paid, threatens a change of which the results cannot be foreseen. Many trees, and among them some essential for the crafts, may not be cut down at all. The inconvenience of walking twenty miles or more, quite apart from the fee, when wood is required for so small an article as a hoe handle, a spoon or a basket, encourages general evasion of the law. Destruction of forests is never wanton; it was necessary to relieve the pressure on the land, and to supply the needs of shelter and warmth. The arts and crafts did not lead to any significant encroachment. Blue-gum plantations can meet some needs, but not any of the specialized needs, and sun-dried bricks, already much in evidence, can extensively replace poles in building. But if we are anxious to lessen the sense of frustration, which the clash of Western culture makes inevitable, we should encourage, not destroy, the arts and crafts. Reclamation of the reserves is essential, both in our interests and in order to implement a policy of segregation, but if it is at the price of those things that give meaning to life, it might well ruin the spiritual foundation of the segregational structure.

CHAPTER IV

CO-OPERATION AND EXCHANGE

Arrangements of and changes in the work-party, partnerships, and solitary occupations—relative roles of economic and goodwill exchanges—beer, dances and bride-price as vehicles of reciprocal exchanges—aversion from business.

To convert to his use the material resources upon which man relies for subsistence, some organization of labour is necessary; man must co-ordinate his energies with those of his fellow man. He must co-operate with some and he may consider himself as a competitor of others. The Lovedu is an individualist, but life is hardly regarded as a competitive struggle, even in respect of the things that are limited in supply. Men aim, not so much at achievement and riches, as at maturity and self-sufficiency. There is no single scale of attainments by which men measure themselves against one another. Moderate success is credited to industry, but immoderate success may be suspect; he who reaps much more than his neighbours is in danger of being looked upon as an enemy in league with anti-social forces. The Lovedu do not display either their emotions or their possessions; ostentation is appropriate only to states of exhilaration. Self-expression finds its legitimate scope, not in worsting a rival, but in a gradually expanding responsibility and prestige. The society has a hierarchical framework so constructed that rank and age interpose themselves between possible competitors This does not mean that there is no competition, but the great emphasis is upon co-operation.

The two methods by which men pool their resources in order to provide for their primary needs are working together in mutual helpfulness and exchanging the products of their labour. Co-operative working together arises chiefly in agricultural and building activities, where its main purpose is easily intelligible; exchanges are not felt to bear such a direct relation to the differentiated needs and activities of men. Yet fundamentally co-operation and exchange are part of the same system of values. Mutual helpfulness is highly esteemed and aggressive exploitation deeply despised. In the co-operative situation these values are intrinsically present; but the exchange situation must be reconstituted to bring it into harmony with them. The problem in co-operative situations is to harmonize with them the individualism of the peasant; the problem of exchange situations is to eliminate the idea of a commercial transaction; and in both types of situations this is done by the stress upon reciprocity. The purely economic aspect tends to become wholly obscured, except in modern forms of co-operation and exchange. In them the helper becomes a servant and exchanges become 'bizmis' (business). Service and 'bizmis' are tolerated only so far as they conform to the old pattern and values.

The *lejema*, which is the most distinctive form of co-operative work, consists of a more or less casual group of workers. Neighbours, relatives, and friends—indeed anyone—may join the group and help in the task, usually agricultural, which is being performed. But the group that collects for the occasion is not wholly fortuitous; relatives and neighbours always predominate. There is no elaborate pre-arrangement. The *lejema*-giver usually announces his *lejema* beforehand and invites some people to come. Women, who brew the beer, usually organize more than men, some of whom rely on those they can collect on their way down to the field that is to be hoed or weeded or reaped. People who are invited are not bound to give an excuse for not coming; it is far more usual to promise to come and not to come than to give an excuse which, whatever it is, can hardly be valid in a society where people are not considered to be bound by time or by their previous engagements. Moreover, the beer for the *lejema* may not yet have matured on the day fixed by the *lejema*-giver. People may have come from long distances, but they will not be annoyed; there is sure to be a beer party in progress quite near. On the other hand, the *lejema*-giver will not complain if those who promised to come do not put in an appearance, for he knows that since 'the far-off well causes thirst', it is better to drink by the way.

Often, though the beer may be ready, no work is possible on the day. The weather may be unpropitious, some important event may require rearrangement of the activities of the day, or sometimes work may be taboo because of a death or hail or the first rain after a period of drought. In these circumstances, the beer must nevertheless be consumed; it is not something that can await the convenience of man. And to those who partake, it is announced that the *lejema* has been converted into a *phɔdwa*—that is to say, the drinkers are not mere drinkers, but a potential labour force that may be expected to do a day's work at some future date. The arrangement is so vague that we cannot fit it into any of our conceptions, such as a promise to perform or a right to demand the labour. The *lejema*-giver may, if he has a good supply of corn, give beer again when he calls those who previously drank of the *phɔdwa*. A *phɔdwa* is essentially a pre-arranged *lejema* which has miscarried; but it may be fortuitous—for instance, when one has to kill a pig against which neighbours have complained. A social occasion at which one gives beer cannot be converted into a *phɔdwa*. Sometimes, when supplies are low or for other reasons no beer can be provided, a man invites a group of people to work for him in anticipation of a beer party, also called a *phɔdwa*, at a future date. But only very special circumstances justify these departures from the *lejema*.

According to our standards, activities at a *lejema* appear to be very haphazard and unorganized. Each member of the group contributes to one end, the execution of the task which is to benefit the *lejema*-giver; but the effort of each worker is not individually assessed; some may turn up when the work begins, others join in much later, even perhaps just before the workers prepare to go home. The work proceeds in a leisurely manner, without undue exertion; no special achievement is expected from any one and the organization is such that the most inexperienced and dilatory can keep pace with the most efficient. Efficiency is as little a matter for comment as inefficiency. There is no rivalry, no spirit of calculation, no supervision. The adjustments in the situation rely upon no pre-organization; there is practically no leadership or direction; and yet an effective interaction is attained. The total pattern is a part of the social system; it is not as if two or more people have casually encountered one another and have by trial and error to discover how to co-operate effectively in performing the task. Christians, whose standards of organization, performance, and efficiency are derived from those of the white man, attempt to submit the workers to discipline. They sometimes constitute themselves as foremen, they attempt to apply the available energy systematically, they have a system of rewards and penalties. The result is, not co-operation, but service; there are few, if any, songs and the occasion is no longer a gala social event.

The workers at a *lejema* usually adjourn after one and a half or two hours to refresh themselves at about 11 a.m., when a pot of beer, euphemistically called 'the knife-sharpener', is brought to the field. The interval is of indefinite duration and is so much out of harmony with modern ideas, that 'the knife-sharpener' is often regarded with disfavour; instead of sharpening, it blunts the edge of activity in the modern situation, in which the *lejema*-giver thinks of himself as an employer and the workers are concerned to avoid being exploited. Neither employer nor employee is equipped by his background of culture and training to achieve success in these new roles; and the result is that tensions arise. Fortunately, however, the *lejema* is still overwhelmingly a collective social event. There is as yet no need to buoy up labour with dignity and moral worth; it is sufficient to submerge it in the sociability of beer. For the real nature of the *lejema* appears when the workers go to the home of the *lejema*-giver. The situation there instantly dispels any preconception we may have of special rewards for the workers. There are visitors, dubbed *vahobedi* (solicitants) and as such are distinguished from the *vashumi* (workers). In our society they would be called 'gate-crashers' or 'beggars', but they are not in needy circumstances and do not ask for favours; they are entitled to join in. Individually they not only imbibe calabash for calabash with the workers, but far outnumber them, not unusually by as much as four or five to one.

To judge the situation correctly, we must remember that begging, one of the traits of the Lovedu we might regard as most irritating, is not socially disapproved. He who has and does not give is the offender, not he who asks for what he needs. The case is different, however, when the beggar is a loafer and sponger, roaming about in search of beer without doing any work; and if, as is not unlikely, he is disliked, his presence during the exhilaration caused by the beer is liable to cause a breach of the peace and he might be turned away. Generally speaking, *vashumi* are not given special beer; the beer is not a reward for their services, but a feast transforming work into recreation and reflecting the emphasis upon liberality. To-day the *vahobedi* are sometimes looked upon as parasitic beggars, and measures are taken to reconstitute the *lejema* so as to make it a more economical method of co-operation. Fundamentally, all the arduous work is still done by *lejema*, though every one knows that, for, say, 4s. worth of salt, more workers could be obtained and better work accomplished than if one had beer made at the cost of 10s. worth of corn, not to mention the time, labour, and firewood that is consumed in preparing the beer. The motive is, however, not economic but social. *Majema* are used, not for long and difficult tasks only, but also for light work, which a man can easily do himself without help. The aim in these cases is not so much to complete the work quickly—time is rarely a matter of importance—as to be credited with generous impulses and to have a pleasant social event. Christians, with their more Europeanized outlook, averse from the waste entailed, and fearing excommunication by the Church, which prohibits beer, nevertheless find it hard not to conform to this custom.

Another form of co-operation is the *khilɛbɛ* (*jɛbɛ*, a hoe). Uncommon to-day in its original form, it has its essentials preserved in ploughing partnerships, the so-called 'stock fair' in towns and particularly in the collective agricultural work of young girls. The co-operating group, defined by convenience and proximity of domicile, is largely a local one and consists mainly of close relatives, both on the mother's and on the father's side. The group is still comparatively stable, as it was in the old days, when it had its basis in common interests and common needs. Its members collectively reaped or weeded or hoed one another's fields, completing one field and then going to the next, and each arranged about his own food. Kin or neighbours had their lands closer together and less split up than to-day; they started their various tasks at much the same time; there was safety in concentration, and economy in co-operation. The great distinction between *khilɛbɛ* and *lejema* was and still is that no beer is provided; but, as in the *lejema*, the *khilɛbɛ* partnership lessened the monotony of arduous work and mobilized energies and incentives. As the group was smaller and more closely knit, relied more tangibly upon reciprocity and had more elements of continuity, the stimulus of beer was not necessary to hold it together. Each partner remained an individualist, for the crops were not shared; but each realized the value of mutual helpfulness and the necessity of minimizing the self in relation to the ends of others.

To-day the conditions of the operation of the *khilɛbɛ* no longer exist in their old form. Fields have become split up; the old dangers are no more; the plough has vastly decreased man's dependence upon the help of his kin or his neighbour. Though it was perhaps the most potent agent of destruction of the old *khilɛbɛ*, the plough has become the centre of the new. The household, which is the economic unit, hardly ever has ploughs, animals, and workers all available at the same time; only 30 per cent. of such units possess ploughs and only 15 per cent. have cattle or donkeys. Thus cultivation calls for some form of co-operation, and the form which was familiar was the *khilɛbɛ*. There are new elements in the situation, but their co-ordination was effected by drawing upon pre-existing patterns of co-operation. Typically the *khilɛbɛ* in ploughing consists of four partners, representing four economic units: one supplies the animals, a second the plough, the third some of the workers, and the fourth the herdboy, who looks after the cattle during the year and might wield the whip or plant behind the plough. The emphasis is upon the sharing of tools rather than upon that sharing of services which characterized the old *khilɛbɛ*. But in the old institution hoes were borrowed from one another and the differentiation of to-day was not unknown, though it took a different form. The organization implies a person-to-person adjustment rather than institutionalized leadership, except that he who provides the animals sometimes tends to dictate whose lands have first to be ploughed. No payment passes, however unequal the contributions or needs of the partners, and sometimes an old widow is a partner who can contribute nothing at all. The essence of the whole institution is a complete disregard of the exact equivalences of the contributions or of the services.

This form of co-operation, in which mutual helpfulness and reciprocity and not economic advantage are stressed, finds expression in many activities. Among Christians there are potters who club together; usually they are kin who live in the same settlement. The only work they share is the excavation of the clay; each works quite independently of the other, though advice is exchanged. Men often build *ga khilɛbɛ* instead of *ga lejema*, but in this case the association is a very loose one, consisting merely of the available friends or relatives in or near the village; and though some small gift is given by the owner of the hut built, the main feature of the co-operation is a sense of mutuality and reciprocity. The conception of mutual helpfulness recedes before that of profit when, as is becoming more common, the person for whom the work is done pays a reward in money. Curious anomalies occur, because sometimes less, sometimes more, consideration is given to the exact money equivalence of the services rendered. Where a man considers that he is paying wages for services, he usually models his behaviour upon his conception of the European employer and the whole pattern of reciprocity falls to the ground. But this model is very unpopular, though for the employer it has distinct advantages; as he contracts for the labour, he can requisition it when he wants it and can control its execution. He is no longer an equal partner, but a foreman.

One development of the *khilɛbɛ* which is seen in townships is the 'stock fair'. It is practicable only where each of the partners periodically receives cash wages. Every month one of the partners, taken in rotation, is entitled to a fixed amount from each of the others, the purpose being to make available to every one in turn a fairly large sum of money. Though the partners wear some distinctive dress, the association is very unstable and many as a result suffer loss. The 'stock fair', far though it be removed from the *khilɛbɛ*, is thus based on a generalization from past experience in which social ends are attained by the application of rule-of-thumb principles, with little resort to trial and error and little dependence on organizing ability or on individual leadership.

With the various forms of co-operation, we may briefly contrast solitary occupations and services. It is somewhat unusual for any one alone to undertake a large task, and among heathens it is rarer still for an individual to hire out his services. There is no real domestic service; even in the royal household, *vulada* is very different from service in our sense of the term. The *mulada*, usually an orphan, is the ward of his guardian rather than the servant of a master. He is, like a member of the family, fed and clothed, but never remunerated; his position is not a derogatory one. He owns his own property, but his taxes may be paid for him, and he receives cattle as *munywalo* (bride-price). His services are essentially voluntary; he participates in all social activities and has no political disabilities.

Rather like the *mulada* was the *muruiwa* (*hu rua*, to rear cattle or other animals). He was a poor man taken in by the family as a hanger-on, was given land, and was helped just as if he were a member of the family. If he was an orphan bachelor, related to the family, he usually married one of its daughters; but he was not bound to the family and could leave whenever he wished. This institution is practically extinct to-day, as is also *hu ṭuḍa* (or *hu sigela*), to work for food. In the old days, a man or woman, short of maize towards the end of the year, would hire out his services; but the work was considered irksome and the worker 'a fool who feeds himself by his labours'. The work is difficult for, 'tired though he be, he must work until the owner of the field is also tired'. *Hu sigela* is spoken of especially when a bachelor, with no sister from whose marriage he could expect the cattle for his marriage, sold his services for hoes and cattle; usually his mother assisted him; and often he carried iron ore from the north to the local smiths, so that it used to be said 'the great road helps bachelors (who have no sisters) to marry the sisters of young men'.

Hu hira (from the Afrikaans *huur*, hire), the hiring out of one's services or implements, is practically confined to Christians; it is a new conception. But pagans who have money or dislike the unreliability of a *khilɛbɛ* arrangement sometimes engage the services or hire the implements or cattle of others. The standard payment is 10s. per acre ploughed. The advantages are that one can insist upon a certain degree of thoroughness in the work and dictate the time of ploughing. In the old days implements were borrowed (*hu adima*); but even *hu adima*, if it is of things falling definitely within the European pattern, nowadays involves the passing of some consideration, especially among Christians. The typical instance is the loan of a boar, which must be returned with one of the litter. But the loan of animals or implements of the traditional economy, such as cattle, goats, or pots, is always gratuitous; even when a herdboy is lent, one must expect only 'thanks', which is generally sent with some beer. Only the utmost care of the thing, not payment, is expected of the borrower, for 'when I, who am a borrower, turn round (to face the lender), I fear to be caught in the thorn tree'. There is an ill-defined custom whereby, when a relative, usually the mother's mother or the mother's brother, cares for (*hu lɛla*) a child for many years, he is given a head of cattle, called the *maledi*. This is hardly a reward for services; it is a gesture of goodwill, is entirely voluntary, and is rarely paid.

When cattle are placed in the care of another (*hu fisa*) no consideration passes; the person to whom the cattle are entrusted, the *mufiswa*, uses the cattle and their milk; but his use is precarious, for 'he scans the road even as he milks' since the owner may at any moment come to take back his cattle. Occasionally when goats are cared for, the herdboy is given a young goat, 'the payment of the herding', to-day, even if the goats have not prospered, because herdboys are no longer willing to work for nothing. Moreover, the *mufiswa* of cattle is nowadays asked to help the owner with his ploughing and he often (illegally, by traditional standards) charges herding and grazing fees. This charge is levied on the model of European farmers and is exacted even in areas within the reserve, where grazing fees are unknown. *Hu fisa* differs from *hu disɛja* (to cause to graze), an arrangement whereby one man allows another's cattle to run with his own, usually because he has no herdboy; for this no consideration passes.

Service, just like the various forms of co-operation, thus hardly ever implies subservience. Where it does, as in the old *hu ṭuḍa* or in the various modern forms of service, its incidents are regarded as derogatory, because they are incongruent with the emphasis on reciprocity. Even *vuthobya* (slavery), which arises from captivity and was practically unknown, implies no real bondage. There is to-day still one 'slave', an old Shangana-Ṭonga woman captured, not by the Lovedu, but by the Shangana-Ṭonga, who sent her as tribute for rain to Mujaji. The institution of slavery is unknown among the Lovedu; so she, just like other wives of the queen, was handed over to one of the nobles, who accepted her as a daughter. As we have mentioned, there is a tendency to adopt European patterns of labour, both in the more or less solitary and in the co-operative activities.

The most important change is the migration to towns and farms in search of cash wages. The cash amount that enters the tribe, as compared with the total income of an average family, is small, not more than 7 per cent. The effects of the migration itself are proportionately small. It is not so much the absence in town of the men nor even the ideas that they bring back with them that are of the first importance. More men, not less, are idle to-day, and more crops, not less, are reaped than in the old days. Moreover, what the men have learnt in the towns is on the whole so different from the practice at home that it has to be laid aside. The greatest changes are not the direct introductions by these men, but the indirect reactions to the rule and the economy of the white man. Many of these reactions are unintelligible in relation to local conditions; they have spread from the highveld. We are concerned at present only with changes in the outlook towards economic arrangements. At first sight they appear to be very great, but the longer one looks the more superficial they appear and the firmer the old foundations stand out. The Christians are a notable exception, not because they migrate more to the towns (on the whole the difference is negligible), but because, orientating themselves from an anti-tribal angle, they have eagerly accepted whatever differentiates them from their heathen brothers. They are competitive and money-conscious; they exploit their brothers.

For purposes of comparison, we may briefly consider two areas: A, with a population of 822, and B, with a population of 610. The census in A was taken in April, 1936, of B in April, 1937, the seasons 1936 and 1937 not being significantly different. A is 40 per cent. Christian and on the whole Christian standards of living prevail; B is 16 per cent. Christian and heathen standards prevail. The main differences between A and B are that in A tribal life is at a minimum and economic obligations are slightly heavier than in B upon both Christians and pagans; and in B, where tribal life is at a maximum, Christians have far better opportunities of economically exploiting their heathen neighbours. The extent of the migration to towns turns out to be a function mainly of economic considerations, but social factors play an important differentiating role, as the following figures will illustrate. The figures refer to males only, as there were no females absent in towns, and they are expressed as the approximate percentage of males absent for each of the age groups that are enumerated.

PERCENTAGE OF MALES WORKING IN TOWNS DURING APRIL (A, 1936; B, 1937)

Age Group	Pagans and Christians			Pagans		Christians	
	A & B	A	B	A	B	A	B
6–14	2	2	1	3	0	0	5
15–19	25	31	11	42	13	16	8
6–19	10	14	4	17	4	7	6
20–25	60	55	68	47	71	58	17
26–49	43	53	33	52	33	55	33
20–49	50	54	40	49	44	56	29
50–	1	2	0	0	0	5	0
All ages, 6 upwards	25	28	21	27	22	31	18

As one would expect, the total exodus in A exceeds that in B, but while the proportion of Christians who migrate is comparatively large in A, it is small in B. On the whole the Christians rely for cash income chiefly upon wages earned in town in A, but not in B, where there are far better opportunities of trade. There are, however, striking differences in the relative numbers of Christians and pagans who migrate in the two areas, especially for the age groups 6–19 and 20–25. This is not the place to give a full explanation; it will be sufficient to note the significance of the fact that for the first-mentioned age group four times larger a percentage of pagans migrate in A than in B, though for Christians there is no marked difference, and, on the other hand, the corresponding percentages in the second-mentioned age group are so strikingly different as to suggest the operation of entirely different factors. Whereas in A it is the pagans, in B it is the Christians who start migrating at an early age. There are many complicated factors that account for these differences, but mainly they are due to the less realistic adjustment of adolescents among pagans in A and among Christians in B, for among them there is little scope for recreational and other activities; and upon young men the burden of providing for the older men, whose social duties and inclinations keep them at home, falls heavily, especially among pagans in B, where tribal life is still in full force. Above all, the figures indicate that the more closely we examine the situation, the more necessary does it become to interpret economic forces as operating, not *in vacuo*, but against the whole background of social life.

It is likewise not economic forces alone, but the diffusion of a new outlook that has caused the major changes in the old co-operative system. Individual achievement was of little account; no one was penalized because he attained only a very indifferent standard of efficiency or industry; people were devoted to a non-material ideal. A man's whole upbringing and training conditioned him to the ideal of reciprocity and helpfulness. Yet in the modern world, where personal achievement is important and rivalries must necessarily arise, the life-adjustment value of this ideal is doubtful. To some extent, the individual adapts himself by accepting European standards when he is in town and relaxing from the strain when he has returned home. He comes back mentally tired, and it is recognized that he is entitled to take a long holiday, even though there is pressing work to be done. His failures in town are attributed, not to causes within himself, but to the operation of external forces. His dismissal is ascribed to the jealousy and witchcraft of a competitor for the same position, and the success of his rival to magic. Rivalry is an unfamiliar situation in economic activities at home, and the competitive, individualistic struggle in the towns is never phrased as being between members of the tribe; the magic that is used to oust him from competitive positions or to cause an employer to favour another is always magic used by members of another tribe, such as the Zulu or Xhosa. The Lovedu traditionally regard luck magic with some suspicion, at least as applied in economic situations. But it has become increasingly necessary in order to re-establish their sense of security; a whole new technique of charms, burning medicines to attract custom, chewing roots to give confidence (what the European might call 'effrontery'), and the like has developed. Many invoke, as before a dangerous enterprise in the old days, the blessing of the gods. Even within the tribal economy itself the spread of ideas of competition has been accompanied by the extension of magic and sorcery to new spheres of activity.

That this answer to contact with the new economy may not always suffice, we see among many neighbouring tribes—for instance, the people of Sekhɔpɔ, 'brothers' of the Lovedu. Among them beer, the quintessence of situations of reciprocity and co-operation, is converted into an article of sale. Beer is provided, even at *majema*, as wages, and hence only to the workers; visitors may join the beer-party, but must pay for each calabash they have. This commercialization is deplored by the Lovedu; it is regarded in the same light as charging strangers for board and lodging, a practice that prevails among highveld tribes; and it is almost as bad as what the Lovedu imagine to be the European custom of making relatives who come on a holiday pay their hosts. 'Our hotels are our relatives', said a Lovedu man to us; but while he was prepared to justify the commercial pattern in which salt, meat, tobacco, European vegetables, even money, oust beer in the *lejema*, the sale of beer seemed to him intolerable. This view fairly reflects the general opinion, as well as the attempt to harmonize the two patterns, among the Lovedu. Rewards are sometimes given to individual *lejema* workers, who are paid in salt and the other commodities mentioned. But the practice is, except for payment in meat, largely confined to Christians. As far as it exists, it completely alters the old long-run reciprocity pattern. There is no social feast. Collective replaces co-operative activity; for personal profit, not sociability, is the prime motive; the social gala is converted into a labour situation, and the interests of employer and employee begin to diverge. Room for roundabout recipocity is narrowed; instead of the indefinite mutuality upon which a man who helps others to-day may rely in the future, he receives an immediate and individual reward; faith in long-range equivalence of services and obligations gives way to a desire for direct personal satisfaction.

To the new situation, in which the *lejema*-giver corrects and directs and the worker obeys and submits, imperfect adjustments have been made. Direction, hitherto unknown in the economic relations of equals, degenerates to exploitation; the answer to unwilling submission is resentment; and the employer is regarded as a renegade and cheat. He is known to buy a bag of salt for 7*s*.—and to distribute it so that each worker receives only one-sixth of the accepted value (1*s*.) of a day's work. The conflict, in which the worker retaliates by calling the employer 'unscrupulous', is only beginning. It may resolve itself by new adjustments, even though an aggravating feature is the fact that it is the Christian who is the budding capitalist and the pagan who is the dependent labourer. From the point of view of progress in agriculture, the danger is that employers are usually progressive, and progress thus comes to stand for anti-social methods. This hampers the work of agricultural demonstrators. It is clear that lasting solutions, even of apparently simple agricultural problems, not to speak of the complicated problems of administration or of wider spheres of culture contact, can be attained only by studying both the forms of the old institutions and psychological reactions among the people to the changes.

Turning to exchanges in the society—that is, purchases and sales, whether cash or kind is transferred—we may consider external and internal trade from the standpoint of whether it falls within a money, money-barter, barter, or gift-barter economy. We use these terms to designate the distinctions mentioned below. *External trade* refers to transactions with people belonging to groups outside or alien to the tribe, such as stores, farmers, and individuals of other tribes. *Internal trade* is largely local, but it may be interlocal when it occurs across the boundaries of the reserve, but between members of the tribe. *Gift barter* is reciprocal gift exchange. There is no exact economic equivalence. Mutuality, goodwill, and reciprocity are the primary considerations, but it is not the same as a gift, for a gift implies no return gift, but merely one-sided donations, such as presents to children. Out-and-out gift is *mpho* (from *hu fa*) and, while such gifts imply indirect mutuality, there is no expectation of a return gift. For our present purposes and in the table given below, they are left out of consideration; it would, for instance, be impracticable to distinguish between feeding one's household and giving them presents. From gift barter must be distinguished *pure barter*, in which the aim is an interchange of goods of equivalent value rather than of goodwill; the goods exchanged are primary and the relations between the parties, though not unimportant, are secondary. In *money barter* it is not the objective value of the goods exchanged against one another, but their value as compared with certain common measures that is in the forefront—for instance, such measures as hoes or goats or certain denominations of money. When a man says he has bought 1s. worth of maize, he may mean, not that he has paid cash, but that he has bought a 4-gallon tinful (which is regarded as the equivalent of 1s. worth) and has paid some goods which are considered to have the value of 1s. What he has in mind is the common standard, which some think of as 1s., while others regard it as a tinful of maize. Finally, in *money exchange*, goods are exchanged for money, not against other goods; yet for our purposes, not all money transactions are included in money exchange, but only those payments in money which are business transactions. Many money exchanges fall under gift barter. For instance, A brings beer to her son-in-law, who, not having the two goats that he should return, hands over £1 to A; he is not paying for the beer, but he is exchanging his goodwill.

The following table approximately reflects the volume of exchanges during the course of a normal year in an average family of five (two adults and three children). It would be impracticable to give the source of our figures, except for the general remark that they have been worked out from mass statistics of a population of about 2,000 people, supplemented by budgets and personal observations, and are expressed in £ s. d.

Medium of payment	External Trade			Internal Trade				
	Money	Money barter	Total	Money	Money barter	Barter	Gift barter	Total
Cash	£ s. d. 1 2 3	s. d. —	£ s. d. 1 2 3	s. d. 5 0	s. d. —	s. d. —	£ s. d. 8 3	£ s. d. 13 3
Agricultural produce and beer	6 2 0		2 6	1 9	1 6	7 0	1 1 6	1 11 9
Livestock, &c.	6	—	6	4 0	2 0	4 6	2 19 6	3 10 0
Total	1 3 3	2 0	1 5 3	10 9	3 6	11 6	4 9 3	5 15 0

It will be seen that money exchange accounts for £1 14s., or 24 per cent. of the total exchanges, money barter for 5s. 6d., or under 4 per cent., barter for 11s. 6d., or just under 8 per cent., and gift barter for £4 9s. 3d., or just under 64 per cent. By far the largest single exchange is brideprice (*munywalo*), which falls under gift barter. The proportion of goodwill or reciprocal exchanges would be considerably enlarged if we included unilateral gifts (*mpho*), such as delicacies given by the mother's mother to a grandchild, goats to important visitors, money or clothes to wives or in-laws, soap and cloth to lovers or concubines, and so on. We have excluded them, but they all arise out of institutionalized situations; to lavish donations or gifts of goodwill upon anyone but relatives is very unusual. So much is needed to maintain reciprocity between relatives that this kind of generosity to strangers is mere lack of balance. The society specially insists that people should direct their energies towards building up firm friendship between those kin whose relationship to one another is subject to strains. There are endless sources of quarrel between relatives-in-law; hence sons-in-law must always help parents-in-law, while the latter must perpetually be bringing beer to their sons-in-law. The gifts that pass, by anticipation smooth out the differences or relieve the strains arising from structural arrangements; mainly they are not what we would call 'friendship gifts'. The clue to a man's behaviour is not to be found chiefly in personality choices; there are no defined occasions, such as marriages or Christmas among us, when friends can show their goodwill or when the whole world is supposed to be well-disposed. Kinship is the scheme in which reciprocity is most appropriate, at least in exchange transactions.

Among the gift-barter exchanges the most distinctive are certain institutionalized gifts, such as *khirula* beer, the *gɔsha*, and *munywalo*. Essentially they do not belong to a trading context at all; they are not economically motivated and do not result from any objective diversification of needs; yet the attitudes appropriate to them are reflected back upon the trading situation. *Khirula* (*hu rula*, to lift off the head) is beer carried to a relative or occasionally a friend, the most impressive occasion being when relatives-in-law bring beer to the *tsɛzi*, son-in-law. As many as twelve calabashes (35–40 gallons), equivalent to one head of cattle, may be carried. One calabash is usually consumed on the way, a second is given to the carriers on their arrival, and the rest is partaken of by any one, including the carriers, who attend the beer-drink. The recipient is expected to return a gift, generally two goats, one slaughtered immediately for the carriers as relish, the second taken home by them and often called 'the walking stick of the in-laws'. The situation is one of good fellowship and friendliness; there are no displays of suspicion and no mutual recriminations as in some other tribes; the givers and the receivers meet one another with joyful shouts and leave one another mutually exhilarated.

There are no special occasions to which *khirula* beer is appropriate, though it is usually stated to be brought for some, usually a fictitious, reason, such as 'to cause us to see the young grandchild', who, in fact, has been seen often before. An old man sometimes asks a distant relative or even a non-relative who has just returned from town for a jacket or pair of trousers perhaps. Some time later his wives brew beer and he 'gives' the beer to the young man, praising him for his generosity and announcing to all that he was indebted to the young man. This is the beginning of a never-ending series of exchanges, for the young man must some day reciprocate and the old man again 'thanks' him with beer given in his honour. And this is an essential aspect of these gift exchanges. The most striking illustration is in respect of *munywalo* (bride-price). The *tsεzi*, it is said, never completes *munywalo* payments (*munywalo a u fεle*); even in his old age he must still respond to the call for assistance from his relatives-in-law; and they in turn never cease bringing him beer. But whatever he gives falls into the *munywalo* and must be returned should the marriage be dissolved; the chain linking the parties into relations of reciprocity has snapped.

The *gɔsha*, essentially a dance performed by the young men of one or more areas, provides the setting of an interesting interchange of goodwill and of commodities. The main object is undoubtedly recreational, and the main participators are not kin, but members of a territorial unit. The district head is not necessarily involved, except as far as he must know what goes on in his district. The old Lovedu word *luεbo*, a musical entertainment, emphasizes its salient features: youths, blowing on reed flutes, dance round in a circle to the accompaniment of four drums beaten by girls. There is much preliminary practising under the leadership of the dance-master (*malogwani*), but in the actual performances leadership is not marked and changes continually as one performer after the other takes his stand in the centre of the ring of dancers. The artistic aspect, the making of the sets of reeds, their tone compass, the rhythmic counterpoints and the various melodic and harmonic sequences of sound may be dismissed in a sentence: close by, one is reminded of the pealing of bells thrown into ever new combinations by complex steps and movements; at a distance one listens as if to an *ensemble* of brass instruments strongly supported by drums. We are concerned with the socio-economic aspects only.

A slight comparison with the Venda *matangwa*, a word also used by the Lovedu (*matagwa*), is instructive. A Venda creditor wishing to collect a debt calls the dancers, gives them some work (such as the building of a hut or the repairing of a fence), and sends them to the recalcitrant debtor. There they stay feeding at the expense of the debtor and of his neighbours until the debtor pays. But the beast that the debtor pays is slaughtered and consumed by the performers, the creditor receiving only a small part. Apart from using the *matangwa* to enforce payment by debtors, the Venda also send such dancers to express sympathy when there has been a death and in that case there is a return visit to get back the beast slaughtered. It has also other uses not relevant to our present purpose.

Among the Lovedu the *gɔsha* is somewhat different. Private individuals send it to friends or relatives to express sympathy or to notify a death as well as to celebrate the occasion of the latter's marriage or setting up a new home; and there are special rules for each kind of *gɔsha*. The *gɔsha* of condolence, for instance, lasts one day, drums are not allowed if the deceased is of a foreign tribe, and refusal of the entertainment is impossible. Generally speaking, a *gɔsha* entails special food and lodging arrangements, food for the visitors being collected from households in the district which also provides sleeping quarters. The old rules designed to prevent promiscuity among young boys and girls are no longer in evidence, and complications are liable to arise where there is a *gɔsha*. The economic aspect of the *gɔsha*, except where it originates in a visit of condolence or is sent to supplicate for rain, is that the host, whether he himself originally invited the dancers or not, may send back a 'revenge' *gɔsha* to get back the beast he killed for the performers. He gets back very little, only the *musumo*, perhaps a leg of the beast, and the performers do not work for him to compensate him for what they have eaten. The *gɔsha* is not conceived of as a debt-collecting institution, it never originates in a debt, and once it is set into motion, its real function is to maintain reciprocal relations. A man may start the chain of reciprocity by inviting a *gɔsha* from elsewhere; on the other hand, a party of dancers out for merriment sometimes descend upon any one they like, but he may refuse the entertainment as too costly or for other reasons. To notify the host that a *gɔsha* is coming is usual; but a man whose *gɔsha* has been accepted by another may stop (*hu thiva*) the latter from returning the compliment (and getting back his beast) by sending *khirula* beer; he will do so, for instance, when he has no beast to kill or is reluctant to part with one.

The *gɔsha* may be a cumbrous instrument to effect exchanges of commodities, but it throws the social concomitants of these exchanges boldly into relief, magnifying them to such an extent that the gift exchange is completely obscured. This is in accordance with Lovedu conceptions, for they have a great dislike of anything that is clearly and primarily a commercial transaction. The *gɔsha* stresses the interchange of goodwill; the guests, drawn perhaps from three or four areas, come to display their skill for the delectation of their hosts; and the latter, hurriedly collecting their dancers, come forth with their drummers and *ensemble* of flute-players to challenge their guests. First the one party, then the next give their performances; it is a social gala occasion and the competition is carried on in the friendliest spirit. The spectators are the judges: an old man passing gives his verdict, perhaps after having heard only one set of performers; an old woman, after a dance of ecstasy (*hu pɛbɛla*), sets the crown, be it merely a leg-ring or necklace, upon the head of her favourite performer; and when the next party dances, the verdicts are reversed and the honours paid anew. In the end neither party is victor or vanquished. The object has been self-expression, without stress upon individual performance, and entertainment in which the competitive element is present merely to heighten the enjoyment. The boys and girls of the competing areas intermingle and there are many lovers' intrigues; the girls give their favourites cloths to wear as if they were knights; it is truly an occasion for the renewal of the ties of friendship, ties between relatives and ties between districts. The reciprocity is generally at long range, for distant districts are brought into relationship. Resting upon a relationship between two individuals, it draws into its sphere, through the dancing, food, and sleeping arrangements, whole territorial units.

The most impressive of all the gift exchanges, however, involves the two groups of people between whom, by reason of a marriage, brides are exchanged against cattle (*munywalo*). This exchange is as far from a commercial transaction as is an engagement ring among us from buying a bride. It constitutes almost 54 per cent. of the total gift-barter economy, but also over 34 per cent. of the total exchanges in the tribe. In order to understand the Lovedu *munywalo* ring—we might almost borrow the name *kula* ring from Melanesia—we have to imagine a number of groups of people arranged in a circle. We have described the institution elsewhere[1] and merely repeat here what is necessary to understand its working. Each group consists of patrilineal relatives and, in the very simplest configuration, each is doubly linked to two other groups. Thus A is linked to both B and F: to B it owes brides and from

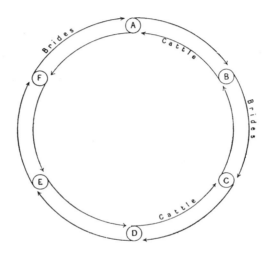

B it receives cattle; from F it receives brides and to F it owes cattle. B is cattle-obligated to A; A is bride-obligated to B. In the figure, brides pass clockwise round an outer circle and cattle move anti-clockwise along an inner concentric circle; the two circles cut through the groups A, B, C, D, E, and F, which are all both cattle-linked and bride-linked. In real life there are no concentric circles and so simple an arrangement is never found; even the general configuration of the groups is obscured by a hundred complications. A polygynist—and about one-third of the men have more than one wife—does not take all his wives from the same group. A man who uses his sister's marriage cattle must return a daughter to be the daughter-in-law of the sister or, in other words, the wife of the man's son; if he had used the cattle of two sisters whose husbands belong to different groups, his sons marry into these different groups. Endless new linkages and complications arise in this and in other ways. Essentially, however, the exchange pattern remains: one kind of valuable (cattle)

[1] Chap. ix. See also J. D. Krige, 'The Significance of Cattle Exchange in Lovedu Social Structure' *Africa*, vol. xii, no. 4.

travels in one direction, another (brides) in the opposite direction. Usually so many groups are involved that the circular reciprocity cannot be seen. But what is clear is that each man has a link (we may say a partner) in each direction; on the one hand, a cattle-linked sister, to whose son he must give his daughter if he is offered *munywalo*; on the other hand, his wife's cattle-linked brother, from whom his wife may demand a daughter-in-law.

The partners are primarily cattle-linked brothers and sisters, but secondarily also the lineage of the brother and the lineage into which the sister has married; for the primary obligations readily extend to descendants and even collaterals in the groups concerned. But the partnership is not conceived as part of an economic scheme. Partners do not bargain for advantages: the transaction is institutionalized, and the values and equivalences are fixed. There is no need to use love-charms, magically to dispose one's partner to favour one's suit; the structure of the society stresses the need for reciprocity and harmonious exchanges. There is no way of manipulating the exchange to one's personal benefit or of making it serve a commercial purpose. If a man has more daughters than sons, he will not be enriched; nor will he be impoverished if he has more sons than daughters. In the first instance, the cattle coming in must be used to 'build houses' where the sons of the daughters may find wives, and in the second a variety of arrangements within the group and between it and other groups that are cattle-obligated to it meets the situation. The system of exchanges, like the working of the social structure itself, relies upon reciprocity and not upon commercial incentives and motives.

In such a society it is not surprising that the Lovedu, unlike the Shangana-Tonga in their midst, have no aptitude for barter and that frankly commercial exchanges are insignificant. Where the scale of values against which people exchange commodities is familiar and standardized, money barter is looked upon much as is barter; but where it is not, as in the case of the 6*d*. tins used for exchanging salt, money barter is as suspect as money exchange. The comparatively large proportion of money exchange (24 per cent.) is due not to inclination, but to necessity. People must buy cloths, dress material, and men's wear from the stores. One of the main causes of tension and even divorce between spouses is the burden of dressing a wife. Likewise, only money can buy the poles and planks, the nails and wire, that are needed for building; even for grass, headmen are beginning to exact a fee. It is true that European contact has touched but lightly the equipment of the Lovedu home and articles of Western manufacture are relatively scarce; nevertheless, people have to buy petrol tins, axes, basins, lanterns, and blankets, not to mention soap and matches; and towards the end of the season much of the maize improvidently sold to stores has to be bought back. Perhaps the most important purchases with money are agricultural implements, sacks, and donkeys. There is a very distinct aversion from all transactions of a commercial nature; and the aversion is minimized only where the trading situation has been institutionalized.

Trade is, however, of no great consequence: it is not the basis of wealth; and the rewards of the society do not go to those who can manipulate the trading situation. Land cannot be traded, and cattle, the only other recognizable form of wealth, are completely absorbed in the *munywalo* exchanges. For the rest, the economic unit is as nearly as possible self-sufficient. There are occasional shortages, but usually they affect everybody more or less equally. The volume of internal trade, apart from gift exchange, was and still is insignificant. There are no markets, and skilled workers do not usually produce articles in anticipation of the needs of others. Hoes were, and pots still are, exchanged for agricultural products. The small interchange of agricultural products in normal times never unduly benefited one man at the expense of another. Animals constantly died, but only those people who had little consideration for their relatives—for elaborate rules exist as to the distribution of the various parts of an animal—thought of selling the meat. In abnormal times people sold and still sell cattle: the instinct of self-preservation overrides the sentiments against tampering with one of the main pillars of the social structure.

The Lovedu are in this respect wholly unlike their neighbours, the Shangana-Tonga, who undertook commercial journeys and had companies of carriers with elaborate organization and sharing of profits. The earliest Europeans constantly mention the begging propensities and topsy-turvy economic conceptions of the Lovedu. And even now it is useless to attempt to buy a valuable thing from them. You may succeed in getting it by begging or appealing to sentiment or showing how much you need it. With a Shangana-Tonga you may bargain; with a Lovedu bargaining arouses suspicion, the suspicion that you are making a profit out of his ignorance, and it is considered better to give than to sell. Begging is not socially disapproved; it is contrasted, not with self-reliance, but with theft; and a man, it is said, should always ask for, not steal, the things of another. Begging is really the counterpart of mutual helpfulness, of the feeling of dependence on one another. Where such sentiments have a right of existence, even in royalty itself, the only consideration that evokes a sympathetic response in the trading situation is the need of the person who wishes to transact the exchange. A man does not sell for his personal gain and the price is not a matter of great moment; either goods have their fixed price or they have no price at all. The situation is always an embarrassing one. The Lovedu, in short, have no commercial instincts; they have been conditioned to mutual helpfulness and non-competitive trading.

They distinguish sharply between trade carried on in the traditional manner and what they call 'bizmis' (business), which generally involves money transactions and is associated with subterfuge and personal gain. 'Bizmis' is beyond the pale of decency; it is specially debased in the hands of those upstarts who hold initiation schools for their own personal profit. The most depraved people are the few Christians, who, in league with Europeans or on their own account, constitute themselves as middlemen and exploit their fellow men. They are *dibava*, deceivers and breakers of promises, comparable only with prostitutes who 'are eaten on the road'. The Christian Church, with its fees and collections, falls, to the Lovedu manner of thinking, within the 'bizmis' scheme: one buys baptism and confirmation; at communion one pays for the flesh and blood of Christ. How different is the institution of *munywalo*. No wonder the work of the Church is infinitely difficult.

CHAPTER V
FAMILY TIES

Personal relations within the polygynous household—the sister as the centre of the social system—behaviour patterns and avoidances between potential and actual relatives-in-law and their modification by personality and adjustment—the position of orphans.

At every turn we seem to be stumbling upon the kin. It cannot be otherwise, because they are very important in the everyday life and contacts of the Lovedu man or woman. The village is a group of relatives, chiefly on the father's side, but sometimes including one or two people from the side of the mother or wife, and even the district consists largely of kin. The modern tendency towards smaller and smaller villages has, in contrast to what one might have expected, hardly acted as a counteracting force, for so often a cluster of small villages, each with no more than two or three huts, turns out on closer inspection to represent what once was a single village. They have moved apart in space, but the ties are still recognized, sometimes even to the extent of acknowledging one man as their 'village' head. In our discussion of the district as a political unit, we refer to the manner in which kin and locality coincide. Suffice it here to say that in one district, with a large element of foreigners, 56 per cent. of the people are relatives of the district head. Of these, 36 per cent. are close relatives—that is, brothers, sisters, uncles—who would be recognized in modern European society, and 20 per cent. classificatory relations.[1] In many areas the percentage of relatives to the headman is much higher.

The Lovedu thus grows up in a circle of kin. As a child, his playmates are relatives; his boyish fights, loves, and hatreds involve his kin; and he grows old along with them. But blood-relationship does not act alone in binding people together. It does not determine the nature and strength of the contacts, the degrees of reciprocity that are to prevail. Here it is that other elements in the social structure step in, strengthening one type of link, perhaps at the expense of another just as close in degree, binding ever more closely certain of the kin and allowing others to drift apart. By means of complicated rights and duties between the individuals, these other elements tend, in different societies, to mould social relationships into different patterns, so that a father in one society has functions very different from those of a father in another, and a maternal uncle, in one society a man with authority over you, in another is perhaps a kind elderly playmate.

An important moulding force in Lovedu family relationships is polygyny. Each wife has her own household, her own fields and grain stores, but polygyny cannot stop at making plural wives independent in these ways; it must create special interrelations within its structure,

[1] The classificatory system of relationship, in which the terms 'brother' and 'sister' are extended to children of father's brothers and mother's sisters as well as other more distant relatives, and in which one has many 'fathers' and 'mothers', is too well known to require attention here.

between husband and wives, between children of different wives, and between fellow wives. Polygyny, reinforced by the segregation of the sexes in everyday life and interests, renders the personal bond between husband and wife much less intimate than is the European ideal. Men are unwilling to spend much time in the company of women, and women prefer the company of their own sex. The polygynist must be most circumspect in his relations with his wives. He must treat them all with strict impartiality. Should he wish to give one a present, all must receive similar gifts. If he spends more time with one than another, this may be the cause of serious domestic discord. He must always be weighing and balancing lest preference shown to one should lead to trouble and unpleasantness. With such considerations uppermost, there is little chance of the development of companionship and communion between husband and wife, although there may be a high degree of co-operation and sympathy. It is generally only in his old age, when his wives have their own daughters-in-law and are already grandmothers, that a man allows himself the privilege of attaching himself openly to one of his wives, the one who has always treated him well. At this stage there is but little jealousy between the fellow wives, and a polygynous husband and one of his wives may sometimes in old age become a regular Darby and Joan. Where a man has one wife only and stays in his own small village without male companionship at home, their relationship becomes noticeably closer. This gain in intimacy is counterbalanced by a loss of independence on the part of the wife. Since there is now no need carefully to distinguish what belongs to the wife, the husband tends to take over most of the control, and the monogamous marriage of Christians, with its greater community of property between husband and wife, has thus its disadvantages as well as its merits.

A wife is expected to obey her husband, who may beat her if she does not; yet he may not interfere in her domestic arrangements. When a woman is busy (and she alone is the judge in this matter), her husband may have to wait till well after midday before receiving his first meal. She uses her own discretion in exchanging the produce of her fields, although she will generally not sell at a store without consulting her husband. Wife-beating is not uncommon, but it takes place usually when a man is drunk or suspects his wife of unfaithfulness. For an angry woman to attack her husband is not unusual and once considerable amusement was caused at a district head's court we attended when a man complained of being beaten by his wife.

It is the duty of a husband to make or buy clothes for his wife, build and repair her huts, provide her every year with storage receptacles and an enclosure for her harvest, and nowadays also to plough for her. Most men have one field of their own which they cultivate and, though they may ask their wives to help them with weeding and reaping, the produce is their own, used for beer-making or, in bad years, distributed among their wives. If his wife or any of his children is ill, a man must be unfailing in his efforts to find medicines or doctors that will provide a cure.

The position of a wife in her husband's home changes with the changing years. For the first few years of her married life she is strictly controlled by her mother-in-law, has a great deal of work to do, and finds little time to attend dances and beer-drinks. Nowhere was the position of a bride more forcefully brought to our notice than in the case of Anna. We met Anna first as an unmarried girl in her own home, a noisy, untidy, empty-headed girl never stirring a finger to help her brother's wife, who, though hampered by a peevish child of two, did all the housework. A year later when we met her again, this time as a bride of six months' standing, we could hardly believe the transformation that had taken place. Here was Anna, quietly doing all the work, waiting on us as guests, smearing the courtyard in the intervals between her other duties, and generally comporting herself in a manner which a year previously we should have thought impossible. Strictly speaking, there is no limit to the length of time a wife should cook for her mother-in-law. If she has married an only or the youngest son, she will continue doing so all her life; otherwise she is generally given her own hearth when the next brother marries and a new bride enters the household. If a bride does not get on well with her mother-in-law, she may, even if there is no other bride, be given her own hearth after a year or so, but in a family where all work harmoniously together, two daughters-in-law may be seen cooking in common for their husband's mother. Every woman can, however, look forward to an old age when she, too, will have her daughter-in-law to relieve her of the hard work she is unable to do.

A married woman moves about freely and goes to beer-drinks when she likes, but she would not go on a visit to her own people without consulting her husband or her mother-in-law. She may, if she is a doctor, own considerable property of her own in goats and cattle and, when her daughter gets married, she has a great deal to say in the disposal of the bride-price. Normally, the cattle coming in for a girl are used to obtain a wife for her uterine brother. If, however, there are more girls than boys, it is seldom that the mother will consent to its being used by the son of a fellow wife. In such a case it is usually given to the mother's brother, who, by using it, establishes a 'house' where the son of his niece will find a wife. Should the husband himself wish to obtain another wife with the cattle he will first have to come to an agreement with his wife, otherwise there may be a lot of trouble. Since a wife so obtained will have to cook for the wife whose daughter's cattle were used to obtain her, ill-feeling would lead to considerable disharmony and might end in breaking up the new marriage by causing the bride to run away.

The term for fellow wives, *vahadigani*, which the Lovedu translate as 'people who roast one another', is said to denote the state of tension and sometimes conflict that one finds between them. So bad does this become occasionally that one may find different wives of the same man living in different villages. Fellow wives may be jealous, yet they help one another in beer-making, lend each other utensils, work at each other's work-parties; and it is seldom that a woman gives her own child a tit-bit without also giving to other children that may be present. The chief wife, always the mother's brother's daughter, has no control over other wives. Where the chief wife is married only late in life, she is in practice often of less importance than the wife married first, and there is sometimes quite a conflict between the principles of age and legality.

Various factors, such as the household arrangements of the polygynous system, tend to make the tie between a mother and her own children, and more especially between mother and son, very strong and lasting. It is often possible to distinguish between the brothers in a polygynous household by the degree of resemblance in general nature and character to their mother. Children share any stigma that may be attached to their mother, and according as a man likes a wife so he likes her children. There is thus a high degree of solidarity between uterine brothers and sisters, who always like each other more than siblings by other wives. The attachment between Lovedu mother and child rests upon the firm foundations of a suckling period of several years, during which the child spends much of its time snugly strapped to her back. It is in many ways also an easier relationship than that among Europeans, with fewer prohibitions, fewer punishments and fewer of the petty grounds of conflict associated with such refinements as keeping hands or clothes clean.

The Lovedu girl is much with her mother, but she leaves home to get married soon after puberty and it is the boy in whose later life the mother plays the greatest role. During his boyhood the mother is the champion of her son. If he has been bullied by another, it is she who will take up the cudgels for him, and many of the worst quarrels between women arise in defence of their children. A boy of fifteen was pulling about and beating a boy of ten because he had not gone out to herd. Two men, in passing, called on him to desist, but to no avail till one of them said to a child standing near, 'Run and tell his mother Dwagu is killing her child.' The mother arrived and harangued Dwagu, who left off, but stoutly defended himself against her scolding tongue, and there the matter ended. When a young man marries, his mother is the dominating figure in his household. She controls his relations with his wife, telling him how to conduct himself while she is pregnant or during the suckling period, giving permission (indirectly through other old women) for their first sexual intercourse. When Masilu, a young man from town, came home ill, it was his mother who took him to a doctor. Ramano, after eight years absence in town, came home because his mother called him back; and Madume, a married man with two children, succeeded in avoiding a dangerous ritual office largely because his mother did not want him to undertake it. Even though he may be head of the village with authority over all its inmates, a man will still be constantly appealing to his mother's greater age and experience for guidance in matters that fall outside his own experience, more especially if his father is dead. Yet the mother, who so greatly controls her son, will never dare to have dealings with a stranger in the absence of the men nor presume to show him over the village. The son is the natural guardian of his mother. Should it be decided that she should move away from her husband's village, even if the cause be witchcraft, her sons will accompany her. Upon the youngest son, more particularly, falls the duty of caring for his parents in their old age.

Within this general pattern, however, there can be infinite variations. Mulata beats his mother whenever he loses his temper and on one occasion severely wounded her with an axe. He is admittedly a bad lot and the talk of the neighbourhood, but such things do occur. Batamedi, who moved away from his brother's village and, as the youngest son, took his mother with him, did not provide her with blankets for the winter nor interfere when his wife shamefully neglected the old woman by visiting for months at her own home. So his mother betook herself back to her elder son, where she was accustomed to receiving better treatment.

The husband's mother, the grandmother of his children, is then an important person, an essential member of the individual household. She has much to do with the children; she it is who, for the first few months, feeds and baths the new baby. Having little to do, she tends the child while its mother is busy, and very often the young baby spends as much time strapped to its grandmother's back as to its mother's. Being old, the grandmother is mild in her treatment of the children, her policy being to pacify and placate rather than to force.

It is not easy to define the relationship between father and children. Because he spends most of his time with the men, there is little personal contact between father and young children, who in their turn are mostly in the company of those of their own age. A Lovedu child who lives in a large kraal may not see his father for days or speak to him for weeks. A girl has little to do with her father, but the boy finds that his father admonishes him or shows displeasure when he cries and on occasion inculcates manly values. The father keeps his distance, yet he becomes the personification of manly ideals, and a boy tries to be like his father. The father has authority, but his authority is never oppressive like that of European fathers, whose children live in much closer contact with them. If a boy has done wrong or let the cattle stray, he will avoid his father by not making an appearance at home till after dark. Dumedi spent two nights curled up in a sledge, afraid to appear at home lest his father should beat him for letting the goats stray. Fathers who wish to punish their sons are very often forced to resort to the plan of appearing at the entrance of the boys' sleeping hut long before dawn, there to round them up and beat them soundly before they have a chance of disappearing for the day! The father represents the polygynous family. Through him brothers by different mothers are linked and, not more than a few years back, fathers used sometimes to call their sons to sit with them at night. Then they would exhort the sons not to quarrel among themselves, to live together in peace, to be mutually helpful, and to behave as men. To-day, however, with the long absence of men in towns, this active education on the part of the father is rapidly disappearing.

Brothers by the same father, though not as closely linked as uterine brothers, nevertheless have certain responsibilities towards one another. They stand by each other in disputes and act in unison against outsiders. In claiming back bride-price for a deserting wife, a man will never act alone; he and his brothers will go together, showing a united front. If a man has to pay a fine and has no goat, his brothers will be expected to help him. When he dies, it is his brothers who will care for his widow and children. Sometimes, in the absence of his brother in town, a man may be consulted by his brother's wife, but he has no real right over her. For a man to beat his brother's wife or order her about, as is said to be the case among Pondo, is quite unheard of. There is nothing special in the relationship between sisters, except that they may marry the same husband, for, quite apart from considerations of the sororate, it is thought at all times good to marry sisters, who will be less liable to make quarrelsome fellow-wives than unrelated girls. Obligations towards classificatory sisters and brothers, children of the mother's sister or father's brother, are not the same as those to brothers by the same father, and the tie is not nearly so close.

Lovedu society is characterized by a very special relationship between brother and sister, a relationship that is given shape to and maintained by the Lovedu pattern of bride-price involving marriage with the mother's brother's daughter and supplemented by the role of women in the religious system. With this are also bound up the close links between two groups of people, the *vamakhulu* and *vaḍuhulu*—a man's own people and those of his mother or wife. The linking of uterine brothers and sisters in pairs, in order that the brother may obtain a wife with the cattle received for the sister, creates this special relationship between them and obliges the man to send his daughter to marry at his sister's place. No man will accept a suitor for his daughter until he has ascertained whether his linked sister wants the girl or not, for though in general it is the sister's son who marries the girl, it is the sister who receives a bride to stamp for her and lessen the labours of her old age. The sister has, in fact, a legal right to the girl. If the girl were to run away or be married to some one else, the court would support the father's sister's claim to the girl or the return of the cattle her brother used. Legally, it is even possible for the sister to dissolve the marriage of her brother by demanding back these cattle, but in practice this is rarely found. It is a common custom for a bridal party to call in at the village of the sister, by means of whose cattle the bride has been obtained, 'to show her the girl who is to bear a bride for her son'. A goat will then be slaughtered by her husband for the bridal party to show their pleasure in the marriage. A value that is constantly being expressed in Lovedu society is that it is fitting and desirable for a girl to 'cook for' her father's sister.

The house of the brother is thought to have been created by the sister whose cattle made the marriage possible. That is why, when he builds a new village, it is the sister who has to draw the magic circle of protection which renders it safe from witches. When the sister visits her old home, it is in the house of this wife that she will 'put her things' and make herself at home and, when she is called to beer, she will be given a special pot in the house of this wife. The sister even wields a certain amount of authority in the house of her brother, as was well illustrated at a gathering we attended where the man of the house was quarrelling with his wife about an uninvited guest. In the midst of the uproar a voice was heard: 'This is my village which I have built. I will have no unseemly behaviour here.' It was the sister rebuking her brother, who subsided immediately and went on with the ceremonial as if nothing had happened. So strong is the interest of a sister in the house established by her cattle that she may on occasion even exercise some control in her brother's choice of a wife. Dwagu wanted to marry Mabula, who was already married. His sister's husband then said, 'We shall not allow you to use my cattle to marry that woman. She will bring nothing but trouble.' If the wife obtained by means of the sister's cattle is badly treated by her husband, she may run to his sister, who will intervene on her behalf, or even in extreme cases arrange for her to live permanently away from her husband, who could then never claim a return of the bride-price from his wife's parents. Muhale, whom we knew well, had, under the influence of his second wife, chased away his chief wife, who ran to his sister. She advised the wife to make some pardon beer and take it as a peace-offering, but when he refused this his sister arranged for the woman to live with a widow in the village next door to her. Now, when Muhale's second wife quarrels and refuses to cook for him, he takes refuge with the wife he chased away till the storm is over!

The influence of a sister is reinforced by her religious position. At the annual harvest offering to the gods, it is always the eldest sister in the family who has to officiate. She is the one best able to intercede with the spirits. Any displeasure or secret grievance against her brother on her part may have the effect of stirring up the spirits to cause illness in his household, especially among his children (certain other relatives also have this power, but one hears most often of the sister). Hence it is said, 'The sister should roast pips; if she roasts the village [is angry] it will go up in flames' (*khadi e hadiga dithaga; ya hadiga mutse u ya swa*). Sometimes a sister may threaten her brother, saying, 'If I complain, nothing will be good in your village.' On the death of the father, it is the eldest sister who, together with the father's brother, divides out the inheritance, and, at the only installation of a district head that we were able to witness, the emblems of office were handed over to the young heir's sister for him, though he was already in his twenties. In view of all these facts, a man's sister has great influence over him and may be called to remonstrate with him, more especially in matters affecting his own household when even his parents have been unsuccessful. But she has no right to interfere without just cause and, if she were to make needless trouble, her brother would very soon ask her to leave his village in peace.

Not all sisters play the role that has been ascribed in general terms to a man's sister. Though every sister is potentially priestess and guardian of her brother's household, in practice all these offices are seldom combined in one person. In religious ceremonies affecting the family as a whole, the eldest daughter of the chief wife would officiate; in case of illness, a man's uterine sister might be asked to officiate. If the sister whose cattle has been used is younger than her brother, she may have little influence as compared with her elder sister; furthermore, where the sister is a woman of no personality, her influence may be negligible. It is a man's uterine sisters that play the biggest part in his life, for in this, as in everything, the individual family is always asserting itself as against the larger, polygynous family group. A classificatory sister, one by the mother's sister or father's brother, or one by a wife of the father other than the chief wife, plays little part in a man's life; she is merely a female relative to whom a certain amount of respect and attachment is due. Often a woman's son marries daughters of several of her brothers. It is, however, only to the daughter of that brother who used her cattle that she has a right—has, as the Lovedu put it, an 'entrance' to his village.

In view of the position of sisters and brothers later in life, one would not expect great familiarity or freedom between them during their childhood. Brother and sister may talk freely to each other, but if they rollick together their parents will stop them. Hence the riddle, 'What is it that is at hand and yet beyond reach?' (*Kha ntsita khi e ma?*) The answer, 'The breast of my sister,' refers to the playful catching hold of the breasts of girls by young boys, which is taboo in case of a sister. In strong contrast to the free, yet proper, relationship between brother and sister stands the joking relationship between cross-cousins. Derived from the brother-sister relationship is that of the father's sister, who is accorded honour and respect by the children of the house she has established. The term *khadi* is used loosely to denote either father's sister or eldest sister, for it is the eldest sister who will take over the religious functions of the father's sister after her death.

A well-marked characteristic of Lovedu society, one that clearly distinguishes it from the strictly patrilineal Zulu, Xhosa, and Pondo, is the importance of the mother's side of the family. Nothing of interest or importance takes place without their presence; even at the annual harvest beer offerings given to the gods on the father's side, relatives on the mother's side, who are not concerned in the religious aspect of the ceremony, will be present for the beer and social amenities. Important in maintaining close links between a man and his mother's relatives are the bonds of interdependence between the families of a brother, and the sister whose cattle he used. The sister's son is a potential son-in-law, who will be accorded great honour in the household of his mother's brother. A man's mother may also be the *khadi* who has to go and make offerings in the mother's brother's household, and in her absence her son might officiate for her. Later, when a man is engaged to his mother's brother's daughter, there will be gifts of beer from the girl's family. They are thus bound together by a variety of links.

But the greatest of all bonds between a man and his mother's side of the family is conceived by the Lovedu to be one of love. There is a saying, usually quoted by women, '*Wa mma u sme; wa rare gi mabakataka,*' which, freely translated, means, 'Love lies on the mother's side of the family; ownership on the father's'. One's relationship with the mother's side of the family is modelled on that towards a mother and is much influenced by the petting and spoiling received at the hands of the maternal grandmother, with whom most children spend a few years of their life, generally soon after the birth of a younger brother or sister. Every child recalls with delight the good time he had when at his mother's brother's village with his mother's mother; how she treated him to tit-bits, how she scolded or beat only her son's children if her grandchildren quarrelled and fought. For, it is said, a woman loves her daughter's children (who only come on visits) far more than those of her son (whom she has always with her). The mother's side of the family, no doubt because of this love, are thought to be peculiarly suited to the rearing of a child whose mother has died. Such a child is, in Lovedu society, never left in the hands of a fellow wife of its mother, but goes to its mother's mother, if she is alive, or its mother's brother or even a mother's sister—any one, in fact, an the mother's side who is kind-hearted enough to wish to rear an orphan.

In constrast to Shangana-Tonga, there is in Lovedu society no joking relationship between a man and his mother's brother. Your mother's brother may be kind to you, but you have to show him respect: if he asks you to go on a message or to help him in the fields you cannot refuse; while, if he needs you, you may be sent to herd for him or help nurse his small children. Moreover, he may one day be your father-in-law and his wife your mother-in-law. The people whom one is privileged to tease to one's heart's content, and with whom one may exchange ribald jokes, are one's cross-cousins, the children of one's mother's brother and father's sister or their children, cross-cousins once-removed, a generation below. When very young, a child may be conditioned to this type of easy relationship by being given a stick and told, 'Go and beat your cross-cousin. Show him your cousinhood,' whereupon he is expected playfully to beat his cousin. If the cousin cries, they will pacify him, saying, 'Gracious! How can you cry? Don't you know it's your cousin? You too can beat him some other time.' Or they will give him a stick and say, 'Go and avenge yourself.' Whenever one finds people behaving uproariously in each other's company or calling out vulgar jokes, one can be quite sure they are cross-cousins. Cross-cousins marry each other; but while cases of a man marrying his father's sister's daughter sometimes occur, specially in the royal family, they are regarded as not quite regular and mother's brother's daughter marriage is by far the most usual. When a man tries to make love to his father's sister's daughter, she may tease him, saying, 'Away with you. We marry you, not you us. We are the husbands who find wives in your family.' The joking relationship between a man and his cousin gives place, immediately marriage negotiations are begun, to one of strict avoidance between prospective bride and groom and a certain amount of respect even between the boys in the two families. Men say they can often tell by the attitude of their cross-cousin that there is an understanding between him and their sister even before negotiations have begun.

Relatives-in-law are quite as important as relatives by blood. Where marriage with the mother's brother's daughter has taken place, the marriage strengthens an existing blood link, giving far greater meaning and intimacy to the bond. The importance of relatives-in-law lies in the fact that there is conceived to be a lasting bond between the two families for generations to come, since where a man has married there his son will find a wife. The bond is kept alive by various social usages, not least among which is the beer that is always passing (about once a year, unless the harvest is bad) from the village of the wife's family to that of their son-in-law. Moreover, a man's relatives-in-law become to his children the mother's side of the family, which plays so important a part in their lives and, where a man marries his mother's brother's daughter, his relatives-in-law are his mother's people. The term *tsɛzi* (bridegroom) has in Lovedu society a very special connotation. The *tsɛzi* is greatly honoured by his wife's people. He is given the best of everything. When he visits, he is brought a rush mat to sit upon and beer in a special small calabash or pot as his own. Christians invite the 'bridegroom' or his people to all meat feasts connected with confirmation, baptism, and other ceremonies (heathens have practically no meat feasts), while a mother-in-law never visits at her son-in-law's place without bringing some gift. One day, when Mudiga's wife was on the point of leaving on a visit with beer she had specially brewed to take with her, a *tsɛzi* (her husband's sister's husband) unexpectedly turned up. So, much to her disgust, her visit had to be put off, 'for one cannot take beer from a *tsɛzi*'. The honour accorded a *tsɛzi* is given also to his brothers, own and classificatory, when they visit his relatives-in-law.

While a bridegroom is accorded great honour by his relatives-in-law, he has many obligations towards them. When they bring beer, he must slaughter a goat for them and wish them godspeed with another 10s. after the feast. If they ask him to help them plough or weed, he must do so. Batamedi, for instance, every year ploughs the field of his wife's grandmother—but they will always entertain him with beer for his trouble. If they have to pay a heavy fine, but have not the wherewithal, they will approach the 'bridegroom', and, if they need more cattle or goats for the marriage of their son, it is again to the daughter's husband that they look for help. A friend of ours, a Christian, is even paying for the schooling of his wife's brother. Hence it is that, in spite of the fact that bride-price is more or less fixed within certain limits, it is always said 'bride-price never ends', for a bridegroom can never refuse to help his wife's relatives. He may not even suggest that they are demanding too much, for this would be a breach of good manners reparable only by the handing over of a pardon goat. His only policy is to remain respectful, promise to 'look for' what they require, then later to send a message that he has been unsuccessful, even if he has many goats and they know it.

The Lovedu do not have that strict system of lasting avoidances between certain relatives-in-law that is to be found among Nguni, where it involves the use of separate paths by the married women of the village and even proscribes the use of words with syllables contained in the names of the husband or his relatives. Avoidances associated with marriage are, among the Lovedu, found also on other occasions. When a girl comes from her puberty ceremony or a boy from circumcision, he will respectfully greet all his relatives and neither rise nor speak till they *nosa* him by giving him a small gift (6d. or soap or a leg or arm ring). Similarly, when a woman has a new baby, she will cover its face from inmates of the village till they *nosa* her to see it. Similar avoidances, ended by means of a gift, are associated with marriage.

As soon as a marriage has been agreed upon, prospective bride and groom avoid each other. They may not be together nor speak to each other and, if by chance they should meet, the bride will cover her face with one of the cloths she wears and turn half aside. Often several courting visits are paid by the boy without seeing the girl at all. He is entertained by the bridesmaids. After a few such visits, the boy will give 10s. or £1 to 'see the girl', to remove this taboo. The bride and her sisters similarly avoid all brothers of the groom till they *nosa* her by means of a small gift after the marriage. One often sees such boys teasing these girls to try to get an answer to some question, but they keep resolutely silent. Owing to the ramifications of the classificatory system, there are areas such as the queen's district, where most of the inhabitants are related in some way. Here many men and women cannot speak to each other because the men cannot afford to *nosa* all the brides of the family. After some years the women will tire of the avoidance and begin to speak to these men.

On arrival at the village of the husband, a bride avoids every one (by not speaking) till given a small gift. Her mother-in-law gives her a gift during the first week while she is still secluded, but the father-in-law usually waits longer. On the arrival of any visitor, the bride will lie down on her side in respectful salutation till given some small gift. As soon as a boy begins to avoid his prospective bride, he avoids also her mother. They may not be together in the same hut, the mother may not serve food to the boy, and, should they happen to come near each other, the woman will avert or partially cover her head. But whereas avoidance between groom and bride ends before marriage, that between a man and his mother-in-law ends usually about a year after the marriage, when the woman is given 10s. or a blanket. Andreas gave 15s. after the birth of his first child. Nevertheless, a man will always take care never to talk loudly or angrily in the company of his mother-in-law. If he does, she will walk away and if a man were to have words with his mother-in-law or scold her in a bout of drunkenness, he would have to pay a pardon goat to her family.

The most lasting form of avoidance is that between a man and his wife's brother's wife, especially the one who has been obtained with the cattle he handed over for his wife and who will bear the future wife of his son. Frieda always covers her face when meeting her husband's sister's husband. If he is in a hut, she may not enter it. Beyond exchanging greetings, she does not sit with him or talk directly to him and she may not herself serve him with food. The uterine sister of the husband of Madinji married Nagambi and so, according to all the rules, she should avoid him; but in reality she is his lover. He, Madinji, is known to be the father of one of her, Nagambi's, children, yet they are not socially ostracized nor have their actions been publicly condemned.

That this sort of breach of accepted standards is neither directly punished nor actively disapproved, unless forcibly brought before the public eye in a case, is in keeping with the haphazard nature of Lovedu social arrangements. Leṭavula, who, on the death of his parents, came to live with his grandfather (mother's mother's brother), has had four children by the wife of his mother's brother, the son of his grandfather, though he himself is a married man. We were at first inclined to attribute this state of affairs partly to culture contact conditions, which have kept the woman's husband in town, though not determining her choice of lovers. But we have revised our opinion, for many irregularities cannot be related to disturbances caused by culture contact and appear always to have existed. We came across other examples of intercourse with the wife's brother's wife, while a friend of ours, an important *induna*, was even publicly accused at a beer-drink of having had a child by incestuous relations with the wife of his father's younger brother, a woman much older than himself. But nothing further was done in the matter. Sometimes, however, such cases do appear before the courts. One of the most dramatic cases we ever heard was one in which a man was accused by the husband of his 'daughter' (the daughter of his own elder brother) of having a liaison with her. The affair was taken to a smeller-out, who decided he was guilty, but the case dragged on and we never saw the end of it. There has been, within the knowledge of informants, a case of incest between uterine brother and sister, and we were told also of a case in which a married man was brought to court by his own mother, who accused him of incest with her. He was tied in court, an unheard-of humiliation, and public indignation made his position so intolerable that on the pretext of wishing to go and relieve himself, he asked to be unloosened and then tried to cut his throat. This put an end to the case. He did not die, but since that time 'his head has not been right'. He still lives in his mother's village.

The different social duties and obligations between relatives must be thought of more as group links than purely individual ties, important in social structure rather than in the purely personal relationship between people. They are not always translated into behaviour: important as are the social obligations that mark off a father's sister from, say, a mother's brother's wife, it would be impossible to detect any differences in individual behaviour towards these two relatives. Similarly, a man respects both his father's brothers and his mother's brothers and the fact that decides him to go to his mother's brother for advice may be no reflection of any intimacy in their personal relationships. The social obligations towards a father's sister would and should be carried out just the same whether she is a stern, formidable woman or whether she is soft-hearted and motherly in her attitude towards her brother's relatives. Nevertheless, character and personality do enter into personal relationships between different relatives, so much so that the socially enjoined relationship at times breaks down altogether. Sons do not always respect and care for their fathers in their old age, and in a district head's court we once saw a young man fined one head of cattle and a goat and severely reprimanded for having beaten his father in a quarrel. Nor do all grandmothers pet and spoil their daughters' children. Mukhadi, a selfish, quarrelsome woman, made no effort to adopt her deceased daughter's children, who, in spite of accepted social standards, had to remain on in their father's village in the care of their father's mother.

All the obligations and duties associated with different relatives are, in the Native mind, subject to the qualification, 'if we agree'. Normally, one should and does agree with one's father's sister or with one's wife's relations; but if one does not, then obviously one will neither visit nor send beer, and sooner or later there will be an open quarrel. If a sister

G

were to go to court for a return of the cattle her brother used or if a brother were to accuse his cattle-linked sister of witchcraft, they could no longer be on friendly terms; it would then be said, '*vushaka vu file*', their relationship is dead. But since life in Lovedu society can hardly be lived without the social usages and mutual obligations associated with kin, a man will always find some one among his large number of sisters to take her place. The manner in which close alliances with relatives is built up is shown in the case of Eliah and Thagu. Eliah has moved into an area ten miles from his nearest relations. Thagu, who lives in a large kraal near him, has a sister who married a far-off father's brother of Eliah. Eliah, therefore, stands in the relationship of a remote *tsɛzi*—that is, son-in-law—to Thagu, for, since Thagu's daughters should marry sons of their father's sister (i.e. sons of Eliah's father's brother and therefore his brothers), these daughters regard the whole of that family and therefore Eliah and his sons too as possible husbands. Therefore, when the last child of Eliah was born, Thagu sent beer 'to see the child', as Eliah's wife's parents would do, even though they had never known each other before. Because they live close together and get on fairly well, steps have been taken to tighten the kinship bond between them. Mabulani is another example. Mabulani's fellow wife is the one married with her husband's sister's (Munyamani's) cattle, and her daughter should therefore marry Munyamani's son. But the fellow wife is old and all her children already married. Now Mabulani, in spite of the fact that she is disliked by Munyamani for having been instrumental in alienating her fellow wife from her husband's affections, is assiduously trying to build up good relations with Munyamani's household. She sends beer and pays visits because, as it is believed, she has two daughters, one of whom she would like to be married there.

A factor that completely nullifies traditional patterns of behaviour between relatives is that of age. Obviously the respect due to a father's sister, with all the prestige of a generation older than oneself, must fall to the ground in a case where the father's sister is younger than oneself. In this manner, polygyny plays the strangest tricks with kinship relationships. Since the youngest wife of a man may be considerably junior to his eldest children, some mother's brothers and father's sisters may be very much younger than oneself. Bilowi, aged about twenty-three, and Badama, aged five, live in one village. When Badama cries or fights with Bilowi's youngest brother, she pacifies and mothers them both. Yet Bilowi is Badama's 'child', since Bilowi's father's mother and Badama's mother are fellow wives.

Kinship is the greatest bond between people; beside it, taken all in all, any other single tie fades into insignificance. Even a fictitious bond of kinship established between ourselves and the head of an area in which we stayed served as a basis for the removal of suspicion and the building up of a better understanding between ourselves and the people with whom we came into contact. We were never admitted to the ceremonies connected with birth and early babyhood till our 'sister's' child had a baby. Then as a grandmother with a natural interest, which all could understand, in the welfare of our grandchild, we were permitted to be present. Here was a legitimate human interest—not merely the idle curiosity of a European or the recording of customs that might end in police intervention.

The kin share your joys and sorrows, give support in your hour of need and advice in the affairs of life. When you are in trouble and have to pay a fine which you do not possess, it is your brothers who will come to your aid. On the marriage of your children, your brothers are called to hear the matter and to give their advice; when there is death your kin rally to your side. A widow is never faced with destitution; her husband's brother will care for her, and to-day, when, as among Christians, this sometimes entails help in training the children for a career, it is often a heavy liability. In working parties or when meal has to be stamped for beer-making, it is the relatives living near who are most relied upon for their help. A woman whose husband is in town depends on her male kin to help her in the yearly renewal of storage receptacles, hut-building and ploughing. She will, where possible, reward them with beer, but this is by no means always done. People like living near their kin. An elder and a younger brother, one living near Tzaneen, the other in Ŭulovedu, both died. Then the grown-up son of the younger brother called the wife and family of the elder brother to come and build near them, saying that the children of his *ramuhulu* would not know him if they lived so far away. Kinship, as we point out elsewhere, knits together the political system. But it is worth repeating that the kin are the core of the district and the bonds between districts; that, in general, the father's relatives live largely in the same district, the mother's or the wife's in some other area and visits and gifts of beer serve as an introduction to the districts in which they live; and that all the heads of districts, by virtue of having to send a daughter to 'marry' the queen, are linked to the capital by a kinship bond.

One would expect that, in a society like that of the Lovedu, with a strong sense of kinship obligations, the position of orphans would not be very different from that of other children. Yet the Lovedu feel the position of an orphan, any one wholly dependent on relatives for food and shelter, to be a peculiarly sad one. Hence the riddle, 'Little fountain full of muck', and its answer, 'The heart of an orphan'; hence also the proverb, 'It takes a woman with a generous heart to keep an orphan well'. The smoky side of a fire is called 'the side where orphans sit', and if you sit chin in hand, people always say, 'Why are you so sad? Are you an orphan?' Even old women, those skilled and inveterate beggars, think that a sure way of enlisting your sympathy is to plead that they are orphans with no one to give them things.

It is said that orphans have to do harder work than other children and have many a time to hear complaints that they eat too much. When the children of the house receive clothes as presents from relatives, the orphan gets little or nothing; and nowadays, while the children of the house may be sent to school, the orphan remains at home herding. None of our own personal contacts with orphans bore out these tales, and when we cited them as examples contradicting their statements, informants admitted that those cases did not bear out the general principle. Indeed, what impressed us most were the conscious efforts made, and the universal approval of these efforts, to be kind to orphans. The chief trouble, it would appear, comes from the other children, who tend to lay the blame for all their wrongdoings on the orphan, who has no mother to champion him; they will quarrel with and tease him, goading him into fighting till even a well-disposed mother finds him a source of trouble in her home. It is significant that in a story much liked by children it is an orphan boy who succeeds in making rain when the rest of the country has dried up, and who receives many hundreds of cattle as a reward.

The concepts associated with orphans, the sad intonation that creeps into the very pronunciation of the word *tsiwana*, indicate that, though there may be little basis in fact for the ill-treatment associated with them, just as in our own society few stepmothers really ill-treat their stepchildren, on the whole the Lovedu feel as we do that not even the best treatment at the hands of relatives can make up for the loss of father or mother. We well remember how, one day at a strange village, a small boy burst into tears because we asked him which of the men of the village was his father. He was an orphan.

That on the whole it is only the closest relatives who are willing to undertake kinship obligations which offer no reciprocal advantages is shown by the fact that it is looked upon as the duty of the queen to look after orphans who have no near relations. They are brought to the royal village (as they were to a far greater extent in the last reign), where they are looked after and, in the case of boys, given cattle to obtain a bride. Similarly, when an old man or woman without near kin dies it is the queen who undertakes the responsibility and defilement of burial.

CHAPTER VI

SOME SOCIAL GROUPINGS

Groups in the tribe—analysis of the groups of a district—character, divisions, and subdivisions of groups—the patrilineal lineage as the core of co-residence—marriage groups, age sets, and regimentation.

THE Lovedu tribe is not, in the main, a body of kinsmen tracing descent from a single far-off ancestor. The nuclear or royal group are the Lovedu proper. They are, strictly speaking, *kwɛvo*, though you will very rarely hear this word, because it and its praise-title are associated with *hu kwɛva*, to elongate the *labia minora*. Ignoring popular usage and Lovedu sensitiveness, we may still call them *kwɛvo*, leaving to posterity to decide whether the name will survive or be lost in oblivion. This nuclear group, the *kwɛvo*, constitutes no more than 10 per cent. of the tribe; or, in other words, only one person in every ten bears the nuclear group name, *kwɛvo*, which we must think of as a patrilineal descent name, not unlike such oft-recurring surnames as Jones or Smith among us. There are numerous other group names and people bearing different names of this kind may be regarded as having originally been unrelated. They constitute over 90 per cent. of the tribe.

It is obvious that in these circumstances very strong bonds must exist to maintain the allegiance of the non-related groups, just as, among us, a vast network of institutions, of interlinked organizational systems, ramifying throughout the society, exists side by side with common sentiments of loyalty and of solidarity. But the interlinking machinery is very different from ours, and neither nationalism nor ideology is important as unifying sentiments or principles. There are important structural links which, on the one hand, form part of the social system and on the other are intimately bound up with the political system; and in this way both kinship and *munywalo*, or bride-price, are used to strengthen the solidarity of the tribe as a unit. These links are discussed elsewhere. They make good the absence of the bonds between the nuclear ruling group and the other groups. There are, for instance, the fundamental reliance upon the rain-making powers of the queen, the periodical tribute to the queen by the districts, and the national organization of some of the 'schools'. In this chapter we are concerned to point out some of the social groupings in relation to one another and to the solidarity of the tribe. The great work they have to do in the society will be realized when we remember how complicated and all-pervasive in our society are the links which unite us to one another and to the state. The work is all the greater in a society in which the language is the language of a group larger than the tribe, the historical background and traditions are not uniform, but diverse, governmental machinery is incipient and hardly impinges upon the subject, and there cannot be said to be much organization of common interests and ideals.

The first thing that strikes us is the large number of constituent groups in the tribe. Some of these groups are totemic, others are not, they come from all points of the compass. They are not clans in the accepted sense of the word and have no functions as such. They are so interwoven with the nuclear group, the Lovedu, and with one another, that it is not easy to disentangle them; they are usually interspersed with the general population, but, for one reason here and another there, they may be more or less concentrated in some part of the country. It is chiefly through the district organization that they become linked, upon the pattern of kinship, of marriage and bride-price, with the nuclear group. These groups are not arranged in any definite hierarchy of rank, though rank is of very great importance in the society. Yet there are distinctions between them: some are as honoured as the Lovedu themselves; some are regarded as rather of lower status, though intermarriage with them is not disapproved; others, mostly of non-Sotho origin, are despised and intermarriage with them is frowned upon.

This does not mean that there are institutionalized classes; there are no rigid lines cutting across the society, just as there are no definite functions that may be said to hold together these constituent groups. Functions of a political nature are bound up with the districts, not with the constituent groups as such; some religious and ritual functions are also bound up with the districts, but most of them (except those of national importance) are connected with kin groups, and this never means the whole constituent group and, indeed, usually not the lineage, but people from both sides of the family. Yet the lineage as a descent group has at least legal significance and to it are attached certain rights. On the whole, however, the lineages pale into significance beside the marriage or the bilateral kin groups. There is structural tension between the group which gives the brides and the group which gives the cattle; but one notices in ordinary life not so much the tension as the elaborate measures for maintaining good relations. Not only do the relations between these two groups obtrude themselves more prominently than those within the patrilineal lineages, but it is the main concern of judicial proceedings in the *khɔrɔ*, the most impressive feature of public life, to preserve harmony between them. There is ample reason for this emphasis because the whole social structure and, through it, the whole tribal system and the strongest bonds with the queen, depend upon the proper functioning of these groups. And these are again a part of, and supported by, the bilateral kin, who, with the cattle, the one relying on the other, constitute the ultimate basis of the social structure.

There are also age-groupings in the society. They have some wide integrating functions, but on the whole the organization into regiments is unimpressive and for national purposes of little value. The hierarchy of age plays a part of importance, however, as a regulative device; but it is not coincident with the hierarchy of rank and thus often occasions serious tensions in the social structure. Finally, we should remind the reader, though we cannot deal with them here, of groupings brought about by modern conditions. There is the more or less compact Christian group, with its divergent interests and loyalties, and the very scattered group of sophisticated men who, influenced by their experiences of European town life, have acquired values and needs disruptive of the old alinements. They have already come to our notice. But if we deal with them, we must also discuss the disturbances in the old settled spheres of men as distinguished from women. For this and for any elaboration of the manifold aspects of the various social groupings touched upon in this chapter we have no room. It will be sufficient to draw attention to a few points only.

Let us look briefly at the tribe as a whole. We shall obtain some impression of its constituent elements by merely listing the group names of the various district heads. For the moment it is sufficient to accept this name as a kind of distinctive designation; it may be the name of a totem or a place, of a dynasty or a tribe. Within the effective jurisdiction of the queen, which extends considerably beyond the reserve and the tribal farms, the following group names of district heads are found: thirty-four district heads bearing the name *kwεvo Muhale*, or the name of the royal group; sixteen Elephants, mostly of very different ancestries and very divergent places of origin; nine *kwεvo raudigwa* or *vamudiga*; fifteen *kwεvo rathɔle* or *vamahasha*, both spoken of as 'brothers' of the royal group, and also four *kwεvo mutshazi* or *vamavulana* not originally related but now the great maternal uncles of the queen's group; eleven Crocodiles, mostly from the west, but some with secondary designations indicating probable diverse ancestries; thirteen Venda, some with, some without totems, some from as near as Tswale, others from as far as Mpefu; five Lions whose interrelations, if they exist at all (coming as they do from such different directions and at such different times), are wholly obscure and lost in oblivion; and besides these, smaller numbers of Leba, those curious kosher-killing, exclusive wanderers with their moon ritual from the north, of Wild Dogs from the highveld, Khalaga and Dibanyika from Rhodesia, of Shangana-Ṭonga of various branches of that great group of peoples whose tenure of headship is only half recognized, of Koni who, in proportion to their numbers, hold very few districts, not to mention Ramafalo, who is a Pig of Luɔdε, one *kwεvo madavele*, a few Sia of Levia, and several sub-heads under the *vamamadeba* who are descended from Mugɔdɔ, the last of the Lovedu kings.

It is not to be thought that the relative number of heads of this or that constituent group in any way reflects the number of people of that group in the tribe. There is, for instance, a considerable population of Porcupines, of Impalas, of Mbεzi, of Goats, but there are no district heads of these groups or clusters. Nor must we conceive of these groups as entities having something more in common than their name and, where it has not been lost in oblivion, a background of history and tradition. There is no solidarity between their members. Where some of them live together in a district, it is their relationship to the head or the emphasis upon the common life of the territorial unit that holds them together rather than any conception of a link with a far-off ancestor or of a mystical bond with their totem. They are said to swear (*hu ana*) by their totem, which is sometimes called *muyano* (what is sworn by), sometimes *mutupo* (what is grouped together)—these two words are occasionally sharply distinguished, but more often, especially among the common people, they are identified or hopelessly confused. But if to swear by one's totem means something in some cases and among some groups, it usually signifies as little as when we swear by Jupiter.

Before embarking upon a further elucidation of these names, let us look more closely at an area in Uuloυedu so as to obtain a better idea of the distribution and nature of these constituent groups. We select an area towards the south-west, of about four square miles, because if we go to the centre we shall obtain an exaggerated impression of the proportion of *kwɛvo*, the royal group, whereas in the extreme north we may well think that we are in a tribe of Shangana-Tonga.

In this area, which has a population of about 830 people, there are, counting the group names of both men and women, Elephants, Cattle, Crocodiles, Leopards, Porcupines, Goats, Lions, Pigs, Duikers, Impala, Wild Dogs, Khalaga and Sia without totem, besides a fair sprinkling of Shangana-Tonga and even people using the name Zimbabwe. There are two individuals calling themselves Oorlams, one Bush and one Kapa (Cape coloured), which is most unusual and does not reflect the position in the tribe as a whole. There are, finally, some whom we must merely designate Venda because, as they say, they swear by no animal or object and they do not know to what Venda group they belong. That is not the end of the matter, for in the Elephants (*ḍou*) cluster there are fifteen different groups. Some of them may be remotely related, but they distinguish themselves by different secondary names and know of no common ancestry or of any links in the past; indeed, as they come from very different parts, they positively deny a common origin. For instance, there are *ḍou* of Khalaga, recent-comers from Rhodesia, *ḍou* of Tsubye, far away to the south-east near Phalaʋorwa, *ḍou* of Thoʋolo in the Game Reserve to the north-east, *ḍou* of Raʋothata, the messengers, it is said, of the royal group when they migrated from Rhodesia, *ḍou* of Sefareni, whose nearest relatives are in Nareni (Mahlo) country. Similarly, there are ten different groups of Lions: some, like the Khiɔga, were the aboriginal inhabitants, who are said to have known no fire and no political organization, and were ousted by the Loʋedu; others, like those of Selowa, come from the far east with the cult of the possessed, which they might have adopted from the Ndau in Portuguese Moçambique, and still others hail from Vendaland and Uuḍɔkwa. There are likewise clusters of Crocodiles with four, of Duikers with four, of Pigs, Khalaga, Sia, Impala and Wild Dogs, each with two different secondary designations (division or group names). Among the Shangana-Tonga, though they are comparatively few in number, there are no less than four different totems and nine different other names (*shibɔngɔ*), such as Lɔyi, Khɔsa, Mavunda, Mathie and Ngoveni. Reckoning all the differently named groups as distinct, we have over sixty such groups in this area alone.

The following table gives a rough representation of the position in the area in question:

PEOPLE IN AN AREA OF FOUR SQUARE MILES, WITH A POPULATION OF *c*. 830

Cluster	Per cent. of Population	No of Groups	Remarks
1. Elephant	14	15	Groups very divergent as to tribe (including Sotho, Venda, Khalaga, Leba—Shangana-Ṭonga. Elephants are enumerated under 7, below), place of origin and time of immigration. Majority of groups reducible probably to common, very far back, but now forgotten ancestor. A fortuitous cluster.
2. Khalaga	14	2	No animal or object of reverence. Mostly recent-comers and directly from the north. Interrelations obscure, but some appear to be Sothoized Shangana-Ṭonga or Nyai.
3. Pig	11·8	2	One of the groups, the *kwɛvo*, is of the royal nucleus and has further subdivisions; the other is from Mamavolo, a tribe which split from the Lovedu about 250 years ago. The two groups no longer acknowledge relationship. A genetic cluster.
4. Lion	11·8	10	Groups very divergent as to tribe (Sotho, Venda, Khiɔga) and time of immigration. Some are aboriginal and were thinly scattered over a wide area, and their common ancestor, if any, has been forgotten; these aborigines cannot even remotely be linked with recent-comers from the north (Ʋirwa), from the east (Thɔvɔlɔ) and from the south (Pedi). A fortuitous cluster.
5. Porcupine	10·2	2	Said to be distinct from one another, coming at very different times from Phalavorwa and from Thavina; the connexion between them, if any, is obscure and is denied.
6. Duiker	8	4	These are all Koni and the secondary designation refers to four tribes (Khaha of Maupa, Maake, and Mamija, all of whom are Koni, and the Letswalo). A genetic cluster.
7. Shangana-Ṭonga	8·3	13	Four are totemic, totems being borrowed from the Sotho; the rest have retained their *shibɔngɔ*. Some came before the great migration, 1840–94; others as part of it. Still call themselves Ṭonga, but come from very different parts of Ṭongaland.

Cluster	Per cent. of Population	No. of Groups	Remarks
8. Crocodile	6·9	4	Groups are reducible probably to two genetic clusters, the Kwɛna of Ʋudupi, who are Ngwato from Bechuanaland, and the Kwɛna from Khimosa in the east near the Game Reserve.
9. Mbɛzi	3·5	1	People from East Vendaland, who are probably Nyai. All river animals are taboo to them.
10. Cattle	3·2	1	All from Nareni originally and largely as a result of the transportation of the Letswalo in 1894. But some came later.
11. Goat	3·0	1	All Venda, i.e. of the Kwindɛ group. Have lost the Venda observance of peeling the skin off the goat's tail before killing, which is still practised by the Tswale tribe near by.
12. Impala	2·4	2	Some of them are from the north, some from the east. The Loʋedu are sometimes also called *phala*, but the true significance of that is obscure. *Phala* in the east (Phalaʋorwa) are regarded as having had no fire, and were ousted by fire.
13. Sia	1·3	2	Appear to have been neighbours of the Loʋedu since very early times, living to the north of them. Some come from the Mashau (Venda); others from Molɛpo. Affinities obscure.
14. Venda	0·4	1	Venda who cannot trace their origin or ancestry to any definite group; not all related.
15. Zimbabwe	0·3	1	People from the north; they also call themselves Khalaga. Do not know the Zimbabwe ruins.
16. Wild Dog	0·2	2	Probably these two groups are related, but the relationship is not recognized; all we can say is that they are Sotho.
17. Leopard	0·2	1	Recent-comers from the highveld (Ḍɔkwa).

SOME SOCIAL GROUPINGS

Cluster	Per cent. of Population	No. of Groups	Remarks
18. Bush	0·2	1	Said to be Vaalpens; a mixture of Bush and Bantu. From the towns.
19. Kapa and Oorlam	0·2	1	Cape coloured. The word 'Oorlam' has a special connotation, implying sophistication. From town.
20. Springbok	0·1	1	Origin obscure; come from Phalauorwa.
Total	100·0	67	

This is the position in a single area. It is somewhat more complicated in the tribe as a whole; we certainly would not like to say how many clusters, groups, and sub-groups are to be found; and as for disentangling their origins and histories, and linking them up with common ancestors, that is a task which, if it can be successfully undertaken at all, will require infinite labour and extensive research. For our present purpose, it will be sufficient to indicate the nature of these groups. And let us first consider the nuclear group.

If you ask a Lovedu what his *mutupo* (group name) is, he might say *kwɛvo*; some, however, will say Wild Pig (*golovɛ*). But upon closer examination it will be found that *golovɛ* is really the *muyano*, though this is not a word that many of the other groups use. Certainly the name *golovɛ* includes, not only the royal group, but also groups in several other tribes: Mamaila, Sekhɔpɔ, and Rakwadu are also Pigs of Muhale. The Pigs of Luɔde, the Ramafalo, are associated with the Venda, though there are many in Uulovedu and since long ago some of the important national doctors assisting with the initiation 'schools' have come from this group. The Ramafalo are not regarded as being of the same group as the royal group, but they are nearer to it than the Mamavolo, Pigs of Maḑaji, who live on the highveld and with whom all, except the very oldest men and women, strenuously deny any relationship whatever. There is certainly nothing in common between the Pigs of Muhale and the Pigs of Maḑaji; even their customs and institutions differ more widely than those of the Lovedu do from such unrelated neighbours as the Khaha or the Nareni. There are quite a number of Pigs of Maḑaji, especially in the south-western districts of Uulovedu, and they are, of course, also scattered among many other tribes.

There are no all-pervasive bonds between these scattered *golovɛ* people; there are merely bonds within the families and lineages of which they are made up. With their relatives in Uulovedu, who are not Pigs at all, their bonds are much closer than with people of the group name who fall outside the kin. If, again, we consider the Pigs of Muhale, we shall find that the relationship between their branches Mamaila, Rakwadu, and Sekhɔpɔ, on the one hand, and the royal group in Uulovedu, on the other, is hardly a close one; it is certainly not as close as that between the groups, the Mudiga, the Mahasha, and the royal family, which came into existence long before the Rakwadu and Sekhɔpɔ broke away. The Mudiga and the Mahasha are not clans; they have the same *mutupo* and *muyano* as the royal group, but each has his own distinctive praise (*khirɛdo*), though there are also distinctive praises of still further sub-divisions, the sub-groups, especially when a member of such sub-group is a district head.

The process of division and subdivision can be traced back to the very earliest times; but there are specific periods when the tendency towards division was specially marked, often coinciding with national crises, the parcelling out of new districts to relatives of the royal group, or the emergence of outstanding personalities. To-day in the royal family it is curious to observe how some of the sons of the queen's deceased brother say they are Mulogwane, others that they are Mujaji. They have strenuous arguments about the matter, as they are not quite sure whether the new designation is in imitation of surnames among Christians or in accordance with precedents of the past.

To sum up the position and to clarify the confusion somewhat we may state the position as follows:

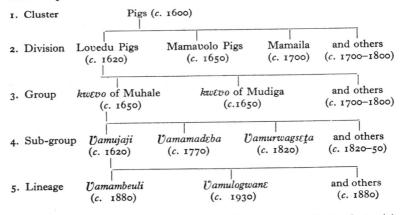

There is, first, the all-inclusive group which we may call the *cluster* (1) of the Pigs. This is a genetic cluster because, although it is not generally recognized that all the Pigs are related or descendants of a single ancestor, their group histories are interconnected. Clusters are not all genetic; nor are they all totemic. In a fortuitous cluster, such as that of the Elephants or Lions, the histories cannot be linked up and no genetic relationships can be established or are recognized in any sense at all. Within the fortuitous cluster there may be smaller genetic clusters—for instance, some Lions or Elephants who have a common ancestor. The genetic cluster has large *divisions* (2), sections that broke away completely very long ago—for instance, the Lovedu Pigs or *kwɛvo* and the Mamavolo Pigs, with whom relationship is only very faintly recognized as a matter of history and by a few of the oldest men, and also more recent segments, such as the Mamaila Pigs and the Pigs of Sekhɔpɔ, with whom relationship is recognized fairly generally, but as a matter of form. Two individuals of such divisions cannot, however, concretely trace relationship. Within the divisions there are *groups* (3), such as the *kwɛvo* of Muhale, of Mudiga and so on, some very old, some of more recent date. These are real groups, however, in which some bonds exist, such as a common praise, and a few specially placed individuals can trace relationship to one another. These groups, again, are divided into *sub-groups* (4) of various orders and arising at various times, such as the *vamujaji*, who came into existence 100 years ago. According as we go further and further back, less and less people can trace relationship, and the sub-group imperceptibly merges into the group. On the whole, however, in spite of infinite variations, distant lineal relationship is generally recognized, but it is not given concrete expression in kinship terminology or in behaviour patterns. Finally, we have a further sub-division, which we call the *lineage* (5), between the members of which kinship terms and behaviour patterns come into play, to a greater or lesser extent according to the operation of a large number of circumstances, such as family pride, contiguous residence, agreement among one another, and so on. There are lineages in the process of being formed to-day, such as the *vamulogwane*, the children of Mulogwane, who died in 1934; but at present they are still members of a family, acting in concert in domestic situations, with which the lineage is usually not concerned at all.

Each of these, from the cluster to the lineage, as we have defined them, is functionally distinct in some ways; but they do not have distinctive generic names. We must not make the mistake of thinking that they are sharply demarcated from one another. The patrilineal alinement is secondary; it is overshadowed by the territorial alinement, which may cut across and break up the solidarity of the comparatively small and closely linked lineage. The largest group or cluster, such as the *golovɛ*, has no cohesion whatsoever. This is evident among the *golovɛ*; but it is much clearer among such clusters as the Elephants and the Lions, in which the groups bearing the names Elephant or Lion with a secondary designation may not be segments of a single original group at all. It is quite evident that a Shangana-Ṭonga Elephant cannot have any common ancestor with a Sotho Elephant; it is equally clear that there can hardly be any relationship between Elephants of Selowa, of Sia, and of Sefareni, for the Selowa people are from the north-east and the Sia and Sefareni, though local, have entirely different histories and ultimate origins.

The names by which people designate themselves cannot be relied upon to establish relationship. A man may designate his group or ancestry or tribe by a totem or chief or dynasty or place or other name or a combination of these. Tradition records several unaccountable or arbitrary changes in these designating names, even in totems; often a non-totemic group adopts a totem of another group or a totemic group adds to its existing totems with subsequent loss of some. And this process occurs, not only in respect of totems or primary names, but also in respect of secondary names. There is a word (*phodemulɔgɔ* or *khaga-mutupo*) for a person who, not merely when he has no legal father, takes the totem or secondary name of another group. We can, therefore, make no off-hand deductions from the names. Identity or similarity of name may or may not imply similar ancestry. A positive assertion of similarity or identity based upon the similarity or identity of the descriptive name is not conclusive; it may merely reflect a present sense of being related, important in itself, but with no basis in history or fact. It is by no means easy to deal with a situation of such infinite complexity; and from our present point of view there is no need to do so. Except where the name is significant for some other purpose, not that of reckoning relationship as such, and except within the functioning unit, little attention is given to these names. For the purposes of rank within the tribe, against other tribal units, it is important to designate oneself, not Elephant or Lion, but Lovedu. But when we have said this as regards the general position, we have also, as in everything else, to begin pointing out exceptions.

An Elephant of Ravothaṭa has as such nothing in common with an Elephant, say, of Selowa. Their backgrounds, their origins, even their customs, are conceived to be different. The Elephant of Ravothaṭa have come in recent years to tolerate the Elephant of Selowa; intermarriage is beginning to establish bonds, and common allegiance to the queen is breaking down the old barriers; yet on the whole an Elephant of Selowa is a *murska*, a person of the low country, not fit to aspire to such high positions in the tribe as the Elephants of Ravothaṭa. The *murska* is, however, much closer to the Ravothaṭa than the Shangana-Ṭonga Elephants; the latter are not unlike the lower classes, the dwellers in the slums, as compared with the aristocracy, among us. Through sagacity and some forms of achievement, they can rise in the scale, but as yet intermarriage is frowned upon and there are some strong barriers between them. What we wish to point out is that the Elephants of Ravothaṭa are far more closely associated with their immediate blood relatives and their relatives-in-law, whether they be Elephants or Lions or Pigs or what not, than with Elephants of Selowa or other Elephants, including far-off *varavothata*; and by far off we mean not merely any one of the sub-group within which kinship terms and behaviour obtain, but also any one of this lineage who lives far away or with whom there is no agreement. And yet there is something more to the matter. The history of the Ravothaṭa, their very early association with the royal group as messengers on the way from Rhodesia, the fact that since the earliest times their heads held an extensive district and still do, their prestige as makers of the skin of the sacred drums, all this and more places them in a special position. These things distinguish the Ravothaṭa as a group; they are like the crest of a noble family or like its traditions. They are scattered all over the tribe, it is true, and any ordinary member of the group would not presume to give himself airs because of the achievements of the past. They never act together, except within the limits of the interested family or lineage, just as happens anywhere else; yet there is some consciousness of belonging together, as indeed there is among families among us.

The same may be said of any other groups in Vulovedu. There are, for instance, the *vamavulana*, so closely linked to the royal group to-day that they are called the *kwɛvo* of Tshazi. Their history also dates back to the earliest times, when they were Tshazi quite unrelated to the *kwɛvo*. They are now and have been since the time of Khiali (*c.* 1740) the great maternal uncles of the royal group. They have their distinctive praise-titles and also a distinctive laudatory response. If one of the Maʋulana is called by his superior he answers by prefixing his words with the praise *moni*. These laudatory responses (for which there is no generic name) are found only among a few groups. The Raʋothaṭa say *zemula*, the Crocodiles of Ʋudupi *myagani*, the *kwɛvo mulemyazi*, the Dipanyika *nɛpya*, some Venda (those from Twsale) *sigo*, the Khaḍa *khɛnɛlo*, and the Lions of Magwale *maan*. This laudatory response honours both the speaker and the person addressed; and it occurs sometimes in the great praises of the group—for instance, 'Maʋulana of Ʋutshazi! At Makhifaja, the place of pasturing, we pasture our cattle in autumn; at Ḍaja it is that the cattle graze in spring. We are *moni*.' A specific response does not, however, belong to the whole group. You may hear a *kwɛvo* say *mulemyazi*, but, after all, the Tswale also call themselves *kwɛvo*, and they say *sigo*, while the Mahasha, who are *kwɛvo rathɔle*, may answer *muloʋedu rathɔle*, and a Crocodile of Ʋudupi, *ʋudupi ʋya mamyaka*.

The cluster, such as all the Pigs or all the Elephants, never has one common praise-title. One does not even find a common praise for many groups or sub-groups, such as the Crocodiles, say, of Ʋudupi; and the same is true of most of the groups. The members of some of the groups and sub-groups use common praise-titles, but the really live praises, those that stir people and stand as a symbol of their unity, are the district praises. They are taught in the *ʋyali* initiation and are sung when beer is brought by the district to the queen. The district praise may or may not coincide with the praise of the sub-group or lineage of the head of the district. The Mudiga of Madumani, for instance, one of the sub-groups of the Mudiga, identify themselves closely with the royal group, but their distinctive praise-title refers to the mountain of their district, just as the distinctive praise of the Mudiga of Mareroni, another district, refers to the place name as well as to a forebear to whom the district was originally given. In addition, both Madumani and Mareroni have the old Mudiga praise, 'You are hemmed in [by lions]' (*le a digwa*). The local district praise is far more alive than the group or sub-group praise, if it exists at all, in the case of people living in the district who are not Mudiga, but Crocodiles or Elephants or Lions and so on. It is thus far more usually a locality than a group praise, though, with regard to the people of the lineage of the head, it often is both. The exquisite poetry of these praise-names cannot easily be rendered in English, '*Ʋuuga ʋya uuga bula ea na*', the praise of Leʋibi, we may translate as 'When it thunders at Ʋuuga, the rain rains', but we cannot recapture the rumbling of the *u*'s nor the pattering of the *a*'s.

Let us look more closely at the Crocodiles. They are by no means a real group at all. At Matsui, where one of them is a district head, they are very closely linked to the royal nucleus; the mother of Matsui was a relative of Mamujaji the mother of the first Mujaji, and it is at Matsui that the cow Mamujaji, belonging to the head of the district, is dedicated to the spirit of Mamujaji. These Matsui Crocodiles, though they can trace their ancestry to the Ngwato of Bechuanaland, are, firstly, a closely linked lineage in their district and, secondly, they are relatives-in-law of the royal group as well as of several other groups, including Mavulana; but the other Crocodile groups never so much as obtrude themselves in their interests or consideration. There are the Crocodiles of Maunadala, who also answer *myagani*; yet they have a distinctive praise in which they refer to themselves as the 'outcasts of the rain' (*murɔka wa metsi a bula*), because they are unable to make rain. They also are Crocodiles of Vudupi, but they are quite distinctive. They have a long history; they lived on the furthermost southern boundaries of Vulovedu relatively independent even for these parts; they held their national 'schools', as they still do to-day, with scant deference to the precedence that should be accorded to the queen; and among them are celebrated doctors of the *vuhwera*, *vyali*, and *gomana* complex of institutions. They owe their solidarity not so much to their common ancestry as to their concentration in a district in which they have been able to rule themselves and to build up their own traditions; but it is the solidarity of the people of Maunadala, whatever their totem or ancestry, not that of the Crocodiles. And much the same applies to Khaḍa, the Elephants of Sefareni, also called *ḍou Khalaga*. Their genetic relationship with the Leba, though, by way of derogation, affirmed by their neighbours, cannot be credited; there is no association, no intermarriage, no acknowledged relationship with the Leba. Their immediate alliance is to Khaḍa and the district; their ultimate alliance is with the royal nuclear group; with other Elephants they have nothing in common. And so we may go through all the constituent groups.

We have said enough to dispel the idea that the tie of real or supposed common ancestry in itself is of importance. In the larger groups the union that exists is due to other factors. The bonds within them do not even necessarily imply an informal feeling of preferential comradeship. The groups and sub-groups are not as such charged with specific functions, though, as we have seen, individuals in them may have special functions. For some time now one of the families of the Mudiga has been responsible for distributing the rain medicine (*mufugo*), but it would be a conception foreign to the Lovedu that the Mudiga only could be entrusted with this work. Not only Ramafalo, a Pig of Luɔdɛ, but many others of different groups are doctors of rain; and the same applies to other special positions.

It is not difficult to see how these things work. One may still observe the process of the introduction of a new cult in neighbouring tribes. Rasekwalo, a Crocodile, recently brought the *gomana* to the Tswale tribe, just as another Crocodile brought it to the Virwa of Makhatho. By running the 'school', these foreigners pocket some of the fees and naturally try to safeguard their rights. Their children follow them and the special function or privilege appears to be attached to the group of Crocodiles. But in time the drums of the cult become the drums, not of the Rasekwalo, but of the chief; his descendants may still take a prominent part, not because they are Crocodiles, but because some of the secrets

V. THE LOUEDU BABY

(a) FEEDING BABY   (b) BATHING BABY

VI. HOUSEWIVES, YOUNG AND OLD
(a) THE WATCHED POT
(b) WATER AND VEGETABLES FOR HER HOME

and medicines are in their hands, or rather in the hands, not of the group, but of the specific family. That family may be honoured by being given a district to rule, and, as marriage is patrilocal, the area gradually may contain a fair percentage of the lineage of Crocodiles of Rasekwalo. They may be lucky and retain the privilege, but there need be no necessary continued association between the *varasekwalo* and the *gomana*. All depends on the circumstances.

No one thinks of a certain group as having certain functions, from which other groups are excluded. Yet only some district heads may, for instance, hold the great national 'schools'; it is rather the privilege of those heads whose people have traditionally held them. But this is not considered to be a privilege of the groups; it is the privilege of a lineage if that lineage happens also to be in charge of a district, for the organization is territorial. The Lovedu, indeed, use the word *khɔrɔ*, but, as applied to groups of people, it does not mean a segment of any kin group. One speaks of the *khɔrɔ* of Mavulana, for instance; but the term refers to the people that live in the district of Mavulana, not the *vamavulana* who are scattered over many districts. One may even speak of the *khɔrɔ* of Mulogwane, meaning a section of the capital which was in charge of Mulogwane. Equally, one hears of the groups, the Mudiga, the Mahasha, the Crocodiles of Uudupi and so on spoken of as the *dikhɔrɔ* of the tribe. The connotation of the term is quite indefinite; it is as likely to refer to a group or sub-group of people as to a district; the word is not commonly used and is considered to be foreign.

The patrilineal groups or sub-groups have as such no functions. They do not regulate marriage, nor do they imply co-operation and mutual helpfulness. They are not at the basis of solidarity in legal and political situations. It is not unilateral grouping which unites people in their common interests or common activities, except when we come to the smaller sub-divisions, in which close relationship is acknowledged. If there was any real cohesion within them, the groups or sub-groups would cut across both tribes and districts; they would constitute a challenge to the principle of local contiguity, and the culture would be as diverse as the groups are numerous. Lack of group cohesion helps the diffusion of the fundamental values and institutions. There is great diversity in details, but the broad pattern of the culture stands out boldly. Unilateral grouping of a smaller kind, such as the core of a lineage, is not disruptive, for, on the one hand, the lineages which give tone to the remarkably autonomous districts are intimately linked with the queen and the tribal structure and, on the other hand, they harmonize admirably with that local unit which is a great political unit. Co-residence tends to be limited to the immediately effective lineage, the regulative principle being patrilocal marriage. The sentiments developing about co-residence are strengthened by inheritance and succession in the male line; the core of the lineage has common property and other interests. The segregation of this core is promoted by the tendency to take a name which, according to the circumstances, is the name of a grandfather or a father. It is the lineage, or, rather, the operative segment of a lineage, that may be regarded as an important institution in the society.

H

The patrilineal lineage, however, is a formal rather than a friendly group, at least when one goes beyond the brothers' sons of one father who, as the phrase goes, 'share even the head of a locust'. There is nothing, however, apart from the name of its members which divides it from sub-groups or groups. It has no generic name and no observances such as special milk or other taboos; but marriage within the patrilineal lineage is incest, at least outside the royal family. It is the group which exercises certain kinds of control; though it must be remembered that the head of a lineage is head only of his, not of his brother's or even his son's village. Within the lineage there is more often than not considerable friction. The conflict is a conflict about legal precedences, for if seniority is emphasized in the society, if the influence and status of a man or a woman depends largely upon his or her age or seniority in a certain position, it is the chief son or daughter, the issue of a man's mother's brother's daughter, however young he may be, who steps into the shoes of his father. A younger brother, whatever his legal status by this reckoning, calls his elder brothers 'great one' (*muhulu*) and later in life, when the chief brother becomes district head or councillor, there is at least the 'war of the eyes' between them. You will see struggles for influence and position everywhere within the lineage for this reason. The enormous weight of the social structure is massed behind the chief son; but seniority is given precedence in the 'schools' and in the kinship terminology.

It is not our intention to give more than a glimpse of the patrilineal lineage. But it is necessary to insist, on the one hand, that it is the *mulɔgɔ* relatives, both on the father's and on the mother's side, that the Lovedu have constantly in mind, and, on the other hand, that the groups with the most impressive reciprocal rights and obligations are the *vaḍuhulu* and the *vamakhulu*. In the most general sense and whenever these groupings are spoken of as linked groups of people, the *vaḍuhulu* are the people where one gets bridegrooms—that is, it gives *munywalo* cattle and receives brides. The *vamakhulu* in this context are the people who supply the brides and in return receive cattle. These two terms, in other contexts, have other connotations; for instance, the *vaḍuhulu* include all one's grandchildren, own and classificatory, but the term also refers to children of one's sister (man speaking). The pivot of the alinement of the two groupings is the cattle-linking of brother and sister and its co-ordination with cross-cousin marriage. The primary linking of brother and sister, described elsewhere, is immensely strong; and this strength is transmitted to the further linking of the two groups. The *vaḍuhulu* and the *vamakhulu* are not so much separate groups as interlinked people, and the bonds between them are partly kinship bonds, for they both are part of the *mulɔgɔ*; but the specially emphasized link is the link forged by the cattle. The linkage must, in its widest application, be regarded as binding together people who do not live together.

The patrilineal lineage is the core of co-residence units, such as the village and the districts. But the strongest links between these units are the links binding together the *vaḍuhulu* and the *vamakhulu*; they are the cattle links. The cattle forge links within the *mulɔgɔ*, a much wider group, ramifying both through males and females throughout the society. But kinship terminology and behaviour patterns, because they effectively operate only within narrow limits and are unsupported by tangible reciprocities beyond these limits—though distant relationship is spoken of as a 'flavour that is familiar' (*ledugɛla*, literally, a salty taste)—cannot hold together widely spread groups without assistance from other social arrangements. And this is precisely where the complex of kin segregated out by the cattle plays its decisive part. In generation after generation the links are renewed as grandfathers, fathers, sons, and grandsons all take their chief wives from and send their cattle to the same group. The bridegrooms not only give the cattle, they are perpetually giving all their lives, assisting the group of the brides in paying their debts and helping its male members with *munywalo* and in a hundred other ways; on the other hand, the brides or parents-in-law must always honour the bridegrooms and must maintain relationship with them by periodically bringing beer. These reciprocal obligations are at the very basis of the social system, of the interrelations between villages, of the bonds between the districts, and, finally, of the vast and intricate system that binds the nuclear group to the other groups and to the districts. If the lineages are the bricks out of which the society is constructed, the *mulɔgɔ* and particularly the cattle-relatives (*mulɔgɔ wa dikhomu*) constitute the straw and the mortar, even the steel framework. It is also within the grouping brought about by these cattle that the fiercest conflicts occur. The price that is paid for a system, without which the fundamental structure and interrelations of the society might crumble to the ground, is certainly great; but in view of the functions of this system, it is perhaps not too great.

The *munywalo* system is also closely associated with the hierarchy of rank within the household. For the chief house of a polygynist is the house established by the cattle he received from the marriage of his sister; and at the same time the mistress of this house is his cattle-linked cross-cousin. The rewards of rank thus support the *munywalo* system. But rank reckoned in this way is not completely co-ordinated with seniority and other arrangements in the society. Some of the conflicts that arise are mentioned elsewhere. Here we shall refer briefly to social groupings based upon age. Firstly, there are age-mates (*thaga*). Girls, on the one hand, and boys, on the other, from an early age club together in their games and their activities. The group is a very loose one, wholly unorganized from without; it is not unlike our play gangs. Techniques of co-operation and group cohesion are well developed, especially among herdboys. They have their games, their heroes, and their bullies; their loyalties are, in a sense, in conflict with adults, but they are not antisocial. They may not tell tales out of school; if they do, adults will dismiss the matter as nonsense. Girls bathe together, get firewood together, play and stamp mealies together. They know one another's love affairs, they share one another's troubles. This group of age-mates is purely localized; it does not extend beyond the district and is often confined to a few neighbouring villages. In later life these age-mates continue to be on friendly, even intimate and joking terms—that is, as far as such is possible when they are also relatives. Among girls especially, a whole group of age-mates may be punished for the delinquency of one of the group, but it is not strictly the same group as played together; it might be young mothers only, because one of them had insulted an old woman.

Besides the *thaga* there is the *murɔle*, the age-set brought into existence by the great national initiations, the *vudiga* for boys and the *vyali* for girls. (The word *murɔle* is also applied to cattle born in the same year.) But these age-sets have much less significance than in other tribes. Their chief function is to grade men and women into groups to which a distinctive name is given and by which they can readily reckon their relative ages. In the very old days the age-sets had some military function, but the queens relied less and less upon their fighting unit and to-day nothing is left of the old basis, if it was such, of the age-set. There is hardly a bond of mutual help and fellowship within the group. It does not constitute the unit that is usually called to perform communal duties for chief or tribe. This work is done by districts rather than by regiments, though it is said that in the old days there was some sort of division of labour as between the different sets, and to-day occasionally in the district of the capital the youngest age-set is called upon to weed the field of the queen. Certainly there is still the conception that each regiment is entitled to some particular portion of a beast that is slaughtered, but in practice there is no evidence of the observance of this rule. It is as if, with the breakdown of their military functions, their other specific functions also fell into disuse. What remains are the privileges attached to seniority and to age. The enclosure of the queen's *khɔrɔ* is built by men of all ages, called up by districts; this applies equally to labour on the roads, brick-making, and building. If young men are sometimes given a specific piece of work, it is primarily because they are young men or the young men of such and such a district, and never in our experience as the whole age-set in the tribe.

But the function of marking relative ages, seniority in respect of important activities in the tribe, is of very great importance. A young man who has gone through one initiation may have advanced one important stage towards adulthood, but he is still very far from being a complete man or from being initiated into the inner secrets of the 'school'. In the second initiation he becomes a shepherd (*mudabi*), in the third he may be one stage higher up (one of the *medidi*), and, if he is lucky, he may reach the fourth stage, that of the old men or of one of the officials of the initiation. Girls have to go through even more stages before full initiation in the puberty ceremonial. And in the *vyali*, as we saw in 1939, only men who were initiated as far back as 1894 were allowed in the enclosure for men. The beer and the food and delicacies which were brought by the girl initiates were for these old men, though occasionally they relented and passed on a pot of beer to their juniors watching the proceedings from outside the enclosure. And there is a similar hierarchy in the *gomana* cult. Only gradually are men introduced to the innermost secrets; only the old men play the part of the weird whistling spirits (*zwiḍajani*), until they become too old to play the part and are replaced by younger men.

Generally speaking, a man's prestige increases as he grows older; but, on the one hand, as his age disables him, practical control gradually passes out of his hands, and, on the other, there is the conflict for position, mentioned elsewhere, between the old and the middle-aged in the royal family. A grand old man like Mavulana is more genuinely respected than the greatest of the royal councillors, and people humble themselves more graciously before him than before even royalty itself. But he lives far from the capital, some five miles over stony places and up a difficult hill, and it is not he, but his sons, who conduct the business of the district with the queen; and of them it is not the chief, but the eldest son, who started earliest on this business and is gradually establishing himself as the next head after the death of the father. In every walk of life, in the supreme councils of the queen, in the struggles for succession to headship of districts, among the wives of a polygynous household, among siblings in a village, the same phenomenon repeats itself. The society values age and experience, sagacity and diplomacy; the claims of age and seniority are validated in kinship terminology, in the precedences accorded the elder brother or sister with regard to priority of marriage or in the initiation ceremonies; but on the whole it is the values of the society rather than its institutionalizations which emphasize the importance of seniority. The society also stresses the hierarchy of rank, such as the status and rights of the chief son, the position of the great wife, and the pre-eminence of the cattle-linked sister, though she be the younger sister. But at the very core of the society there is uncertainty: the heir to the throne is not determined by rigid rules, based upon seniority or legal precedences, and the councillors are involved in a conflict which throws into confusion, at least, the principle of seniority. The total configuration of the society cannot wholly rely upon these devices without damaging the foundations of the sacred kingship. The uncertainty of the succession is the guarantee that the queens are queens by divine decree.

CHAPTER VII

EARLY TRAINING

Nursing and growing up—herdboy gang life and the learning of veld-lore—an institutionalized play-school—'crossing' rites and the significance of ordeals and obscene language—opportunities and satisfactions of old age—the task of the modern school.

W E have not yet dealt with all the values and arrangements of Lovedu society to which the individual must be adjusted if he is to become a co-operating member. But it will not be premature to give a short review of the moulding process, as we shall thereby be led to consider some striking institutions of the tribe. The moulding of the individual is a lifelong process; yet some of the main characteristics appear early.

To the Lovedu the aggressiveness of young European children of two or three years old and their inability to play amicably later on with other children, characteristics natural in a competitive, non-co-operative, individualistic society like ours, are a source of surprise and often also amusement. 'European children are not like ours,' they say. 'They like very much to fight.' The Lovedu child is from early infancy treated with great lenience and kindness. 'Care for it,' they say even of an uterine child, 'for to-morrow it will care for you' (*khi lɛle, ga matso khi lɛla wɛna*). There are no struggles for food, no strict rules of feeding. Whenever an infant cries, it is put to the breast. If its mother is away, its grandmother or even the young girl nursing it may put it to their breast to comfort it; but it is strictly forbidden for a suckling mother to allow any but her own child to drink of her milk. A woman who allowed a baby to cry without attending to it and trying to hush it would be severely reprimanded by the older women of the village. A baby is never left alone. Indeed, it is almost an appendix of its mother, at night sleeping against her naked breast, by day being carried on her back in its skin cradle. A woman, it is said, may forget all manner of things, but never the skin cradle of her child. When a mother wants to go out, there is never any problem as to what to do with baby. He is simply strapped to her back to accompany her, and should she choose to dance at a ceremony, even the most violent jumping movements would leave him unperturbed. So accustomed does a Lovedu baby become to his position on his mother's back that, when picked up, he quite naturally stretches out his feet at right angles to his body. While his mother stamps or hoes, the baby will be nursed by his grandmother or a nurse girl a little older than himself. This mode of life and treatment gives the child a sense of security, safety, and warmth. His wants are immediately attended to and the absence of cloth spares him even such small discomforts as wet napkins.

Before the long suckling period is over, the child is already walking and forms part of a group of toddlers, who give him his first lessons in independence. If he falls and hurts himself while playing with them, there is no one to fuss over him; if another child hits him, he will hit back or sit down and cry, but, beyond a few sympathetic words from his friends and the injunction to be quiet, nothing is done which may enhance his sense of his own importance. In competition with the growing interests of the toddler, who is able also to partake of the ordinary food of adults, suckling becomes of less and less importance, indulged in only at night or when he feels in need of being fondled. His companions, too, many of them a little older than himself, begin to tell him there are worms in his mother's breast and perhaps even tease him a little. If there is no younger brother or sister, a child may continue drinking at his mother's breast until about four or five years of age and it is not at all an unusual sight to see a boy of five stealing a drink at his mother's breast before running off in the morning to herd goats with the others. Most children leave off drinking quite naturally; sometimes, however, the mother puts some chili on her breast or a bitter herb to deter the child. It is said that boys generally like to drink from the breast much longer than do girls, and certainly it was little boys from three to seven years of age, not little girls, who used to nestle up to and stealthily fondle one of us.

There is no necessary connexion between weaning and the resumption of sexual intercourse by the parents, which may take place at any time after teething and depends largely upon the number of wives there are. It is, however, believed that normal sex relations should not be resumed till after weaning. If they are resumed before the child is able to walk, the old women who control such relations between husband and wife will warn the parents to be careful: 'For who will carry both children?' Sex intercourse on the part of its mother is believed to harm the suckling child. That is why, when husband and wife resume such relations, some of the semen of the husband must be smeared all over the child 'that it may know its father' and not take ill. Often the semen is mixed with powdered medicine as well as with the vaginal secretions of its mother. A suckling woman is seldom accused of adultery; it is thought that she would not wilfully do a thing that is harmful to her child. Christians resume intercourse after the child is a few months old; such external intercourse is said by them to 'make the child grow'. The sending of children to the mother's mother for a few years is likewise not definitely associated with the weaning, though naturally it cannot take place before.

Grown-ups try to teach children to greet (lɔsha) at an early age or they clap their hands to make the toddlers dance, however unsteadily. When a child is able to go on an errand to the next courtyard, this is considered a great advance. It is then said, 'The child is able to hear.' Bodily control is not expected of small children; but by the time a child is about three years old its mother will take it outside the village near the ash heap and smack it if it messes in the hut or courtyard. At five or six a child will go out into the bush.

There are few restrictions in the life of a small child: no elders run after him with injunctions not to touch this or that; if he chooses to roll in the ash heap, he may do so without getting into any greater trouble than a mild rebuke from his mother, who will tell him she objects to suckling so dirty a boy. One may see a child playing with a sharp knife without a word of admonition from his parents. There are no regular hours. A child will sleep when it feels sleepy or run about when it is not. Up to the age of about six it will be called to bed by its mother at night, but older children go to bed when they feel inclined, often long after their parents have retired. The only form of washing that may be insisted upon is that of the child's face before eating. In comparison with the life of a European child, constantly under the vigilant eye of a grown-up parent or nurse, surrounded by dangerous or valuable objects which he must not touch, dressed in clothes which he is expected to keep clean, and forced to keep regular hours, Bantu childhood is a wonderfully care-free existence with plenty of good companionship. Constant comradeship with those of his own age tends to make a Lovedu child shy in the presence of grown-ups, especially after the age of about six. But independence of its parents and of adults in general is developed to a marked degree. Small boys of seven will disappear from home to go and visit some relative miles away. Their parents will be unperturbed, though, if they do not return within a few days, they will set out to look for them. Boys of ten or eleven may run away to work with European farmers (though this is infrequent) and prove themselves well able to withstand the unsympathetic treatment they sometimes receive.

The attitude of parents to children is one of indulgence, but there is little spoiling, because parents are busy and a child spends most of his time with those of his own age-group. Punishment of children is infrequent, though threats are common. A child who is disobedient to his father 'will be eaten by the vultures'; and a situation which one sees enacted over and over again is an adult, stick in hand and with many imprecations, chasing away a group of toddlers and young children from the courtyard where a case is being held. The children, screaming and laughing, run away, only to return again within ten minutes, when the same performance has to be repeated. Beatings are relatively infrequent and children are never dealt with by stinting them as regards food or clothes. Small children may be smacked if they steal monkey nuts from their mother's stores; we have seen a child of four beaten on the legs with its mother's string necklace because it was crying for a second mealie when it had already been given one, and herdboys are beaten if they let the cattle stray into the gardens. On the whole, however, beatings are seldom administered, praising of children for their good actions being far more common. Discipline in a Lovedu child's life comes, not from parents, but from children older than himself. When a child gets into tantrums the attitude of adults and older children is one of forbearance; disciplinary action is never thought necessary. Maḍarabani, in a fit of temper because his sister had upset his tin of grasshopper stew, ran amok, hitting out at his elder brother and treading in the mealie meal put out to dry in the courtyard. Instead of punishing him, as he might have been in a European household, those around him merely tried to calm him: his elder brother humoured him and tried to distract his attention by showing him a double-bladed knife, while his sister tried to make amends by offering him a sweet potato. His mother, busy with her cooking, took no notice.

The personality of a child, his likes and dislikes, are respected by adults, as are also any rights of ownership he may have. A child, who has been given a piece of land of his own to cultivate, will dispose of its produce as he pleases, and he may sell it for clothes or allow it to be used by the household. If he has been given fowls and the father wishes to kill one, he will mention it to the child and promise him another. Among parents one does not find the competitive jealousies that are apt to arise between European mothers about the relative size, weight, or health of their children, and there is little or no comparison of babies or boasting of their ability or cleverness. But a very precocious child is not liked; people may suspect that he is being taught to be a witch; and 'he outwits you obliquely [by way of witchcraft]'. Frightening of children by adults is of common occurrence. Not only are children told when naughty that a Shangana-Tonga or European will come and catch them or that a big elephant stalks about the village at night killing small children who will not go to bed, but mothers take pleasure in frightening them even when they are not naughty. Often a mother would try to force her child to come near us when she saw it was afraid or would tell it that we were about to carry it away in our suitcase. When it ran away crying, she would laugh with great merriment. If a small child refuses to greet a relative in the correct manner, his mother might take a knife and threaten to cut him or take hold of a pot and threaten to cook him unless he obeys. But fear of bogies is not excessive and fear is certainly not the only or most effective means of control.

Children learn the tasks required of adults simply by doing them. They are anxious to imitate their elders, and there is never any compulsory element in the teaching of these skills. Moreover, in their education they have this advantage, that it is not carried on in an institution divorced from everyday adult activities. The child feels that he is an essential part of society; all he does is a direct contribution to the domestic economy. If a small girl of five accompanies her mother to the fountain and returns solemnly carrying a diminutive calabash of water on her head, she feels she is doing important work, for her contribution will be used with that of her mother. 'The stick even of a child helps the adult across' and, in fact, a girl of six is able to fill quite large pot of water for a busy mother by going to and fro with small quantities at a time from the fountain. One night, while sitting in a hut, we watched a girl of seven learning to cook. Fermented porridge was needed for the baby and this the girl set out to make in a small pot in the presence of her mother and several other girls somewhat older than herself who happened to be there. When the water boiled, she put in some ground grain, twirling the porridge twirler between the palms as she had seen her mother do. She took the comments and criticisms of the company with good grace, even when they smiled at her awkwardness. Meanwhile, her mother mentioned to us how useful it would be to have some one who could cook the evening meal on days when she came home late or tired from fetching wood. To a helpful toddler, its mother might say, 'Thank you, my lady' (*Ahee Khɔba ya ga*), praising her by implying that she has already reached the maturity and usefulness of a mature young woman; or she may quote the maxim, 'Bearing children is not the same as gathering greens' (*hu bɛ ba hasi hu ka murɔhɔ*), meaning that children are always of value, unlike relish, which can be used once only.

It is not so much technical skill as usefulness and willingness to help that are the great virtues. There is great tolerance of mediocre achievement and no one is made to suffer humiliation on account of it. Whenever she gets the chance, a small girl will, when her mother is stamping, try to follow suit, often with a play stamper specially made for her, and it is surprising how quickly a child will learn to winnow. Girls of from eight to ten are able to do almost every kind of housework, including the preparation of a meal. Beer-making, which requires considerable skill, is, however, not learnt till after puberty, and heavy work, such as carrying wood, is not done by young children. At the age of ten or eleven, a girl may be given a small portion of her grandmother's field to cultivate for herself. She will plant the crops she likes—lots of sugar-cane and also mealies and groundnuts—and in the disposal of these she acts as she pleases. Girls also learn the art of collecting leaves for relish: which plants can be used, which leaves are the most tasty and at what time of the year they should be picked.

Most children are pleased to help a little in the household tasks, for there are not very many outside diversions. They have, however, plenty of time also for play and are gloriously free to romp on moonlight nights long after their parents have retired to bed. As with us, play among the Lovedu is largely directed to the learning of skills useful in later life. A popular pastime of children is dancing, usually among small girls, to the accompaniment of drumming on paraffin tins. At adult dances young girls seize every opportunity in between dances to practise on the drums and, when the dance is in full swing and the men in a ring round the drums are bursting their cheeks as they blow their reed pipes, it is not unusual to see five or six small boys of from three to six years old going round on the outside, reed in mouth, imitating every movement of the adults. In the games of girls (those of boys will be discussed later), imitation of adult activities, such as a game resembling initiation mummeries and play-cooking, loom large. Sometimes they build miniature villages, mould small clay pots, and pretend to cook, but often their play takes a more real form. We have seen a group of small girls collect ripe morula fruits to make their own cider in pots borrowed from home. Next day, when it was ready, they all sat down solemnly to drink it, passing round the clay dish with great dignity, as they had seen grown-ups do. A group of small boys hung around in the hope of being invited to join in and they were not disappointed. The cider was perhaps a little dirty (small girls are not particular about washing hands before pressing out the juice), but the boys found it wonderfully good.

The education of a boy is received largely through the institution of herding. His first introduction to herding is pleasant enough. At the age of four or five he sets out with one of the bigger boys, who carries food for him, since he is as yet too young to remain long without a meal. Now he has his first taste of goat's milk, the food of herdboys, who do not notice the smell that nauseates adults. The goats are milked into hollows scooped out in rocks, into which juice of various kinds of acid fruits, such as *ditshidi*, may be squeezed to cause curds, eaten by means of a certain kinds of grass or leaves. At this stage the boy goes out with his protector to herd or stays at home with his nurse just as he pleases. Soon, however, he must begin seriously to herd goats and donkeys near home with other boys of his age. He finds this irksome at first and whenever he can he tries to remain at home with the girls. But his father will tell him that always being in women's company will make him grow up to be a coward; visitors coming to the village will ask, 'Are you herding yet?' and boys older than himself may begin to beat him if he does not accompany them, so that in the end he finds himself going out day after day to herd, whether his own father has goats and cattle or not. In the old days, when cattle raids were feared, full-grown men herded cattle; to-day this is not seen, except sometimes when on a rainy day an adult will go out with the cattle to prevent his children from getting coughs and colds. On wet days rough shelters are made, in which the herdboys sit round a fire. Just as the work of girls in the home as nursemaids and helpers forms an integral part of the whole economic structure of society, so herding is an important and essential activity. This the herdboy knows and feels.

Herding is a form of gang life in which a boy and his age-mates are very strictly controlled by those just older than themselves. It is the only discipline to which he is subjected outside the circumcision lodge, and it is characteristic of the society, that boys and girls both in and out of the formal initiation 'schools' are disciplined, not by adults, but by the group just older than themselves. It is the adults, more especially old people, who sometimes intervene on their behalf, lightening their burden. Much of what they are taught in the 'schools' likewise comes from the next age-set. As an educational principle, this is of considerable value: children learn more easily and more willingly from other children than from adults, and every boy knows that soon he too will enjoy the privilege of authority over those younger than he is. In herding, the smaller boys are made to do most of the unpleasant work. They are left to herd on hot afternoons while those older than themselves indulge in games and amusements; they have to fetch and carry for older boys and are often bullied into fighting one another. Constant fear of being made to fight decided a boy of eight to run away to his mother's brother's place. But there he had also to herd and, instead of escaping the fights he found so distasteful, he was again pitted against and worsted by boys stronger than himself. Every group of herdboys has its leader (*shɔlwɛ*), usually the strongest of the group. He and the other elder boys have many privileges. The younger boys have to do the fagging and, if they find a tree with ripe fruit, they may neither climb it nor pick fruit till they have called the older boys, who, after eating their fill, will allow them to have their turn. One branch must, however, be left untouched for the leader of the group. When cattle have strayed, the men beat only the bigger boys, knowing that the smaller ones will already have been punished by their seniors. Herdboys have their own standards, not always in accord with that of the rest of society. They steal sugar-cane, nuts, mealies from other people's fields; sometimes they collect honey from hives in the bush surrounding graves, a practice that is strictly taboo; they may even steal fowls to kill and eat, but in this they are invariably discovered and severely beaten. Among girls the emphasis upon the rights of seniority is in abeyance until initiation at puberty.

Herding and its concomitant activities afford an excellent education to the growing boy, one designed to fit him for the sort of life led by adults in the old days and which, even in the changed circumstances of to-day, gives him much of value that it would be impossible to get in any school. A good deal of time is spent in hunting and trapping birds, cane-rats, squirrels, rabbits, and, near the forests, domestic cats that have become wild. Boys become experts in the use of the bow and bulb-headed arrow and in hunting learn much that is useful about the habits of animals. But this is of small importance beside other aspects of their training while herding. Everything a boy uses in hunting or in play he has to make himself. He fashions his own bow and arrows, his own traps. If boys wish to play a game of khɔrɔrɔ, which somewhat resembles hockey, they must cut out and shape their own clubs. They have no toys but those they have made themselves, and toy-making gives them a wonderful training in handicrafts. Herdboys mould clay oxen and manufacture toy wagons, motor cars, guns, sleds in a number of different mediums—wood, clay, mealie pith, prickly pear leaves. One day the herdboys near us would all make watches (one boy even had a locust inside his to move the hands!); on another they all came home wearing spectacles made of mealie pith, exact replicas, cleverly constructed, of those they had seen us wear. In February and March, when the grass is long, they weave grass arm bands and hats and caps of various shapes and sizes. They make a humming top of a hard-shelled fruit, muṭuzi (*Oncoba spinosa*) and ropes to put through the nostrils of riding oxen for reins; they make their own musical instruments and cut reed pipes for their own play-dances. In this manner herdboys learn to know a vast number of useful things about their environment—the uses and quality of the wood of various trees, which are hard and strong and which soft or pliable, those useful for carving platters, and those used in basketry, the kinds of trees that yield bird-lime, the kinds of bark that can be used for making string. In their constant quest for food, they learn to know every edible fruit, berry, and root in the veld. A herdboy walking along with you will give you the name and uses of almost every tree or shrub you pass in that rich bushveld environment, and once a boy of fifteen astonished us by being able to name over 200 specimens of plants from that area.

Besides riding oxen and donkeys, boys play games, some of which resemble European games, such as hide-and-seek, cat-and-mouse, twos-and-threes. One game, that of hurling at a rolling tuber a stick furnished with a circle of points at one end, is recognized as a training in hunting and exactness of aim. Bands of herdboys from neighbouring districts are keen rivals, but sometimes the rivalry is between pagans and Christians. Frequently fights take place. The winners will then milk the goats and ride the oxen of the vanquished, who may be made to undergo the disgrace of driving home the cattle of their conquerors.

Even if blood flows, no case can be brought against a herdboy, for he is still uncircumcised, irresponsible.

Training for both boys and girls in home-making is embodied in the institution known as *manḍwane*, which, while being little more than a game, is nevertheless accorded adult recognition. Utilization by the children of the harvest gleanings after reaping, which may be regarded as its practical economic aspect, is to-day not much in evidence, but while it lasts women whose sons are taking part are saved the trouble of cooking the evening meal. After the reaping, when the cattle graze in the mealie lands near home, *manḍwane* is begun by the girls calling the boys to come and be chosen. They stand in a row while each girl chooses a 'husband' by kneeling before and greeting the boy of her choice. He signifies his consent by answering the greeting. After the parents have been told of their intention to hold *manḍwane*, the boys begin to build rough huts in the fields, while the girls smear the floors and courtyards. Each couple may have its own establishment with very often also a small child chosen as their 'child', or one large house for all may be made. With pots, baskets, spoons, and other utensils borrowed from home, the girls stamp mealie meal and cook dishes of porridge, nuts, and pumpkin, while the boys, if they can, bring home birds as relish. The game begins about eleven o'clock in the morning and ends in dancing and singing after dark; this lasts for about ten days or more till, at the end, the miniature village is burnt. Each 'wife', in addition to serving food to her 'husband' in the proper manner, must also take food every evening to her 'mother-in-law' in the boy's home. This is eaten, not by the mother-in-law herself, but by children of the household who are not taking part in the game. Occasionally the elders walk over to watch activities in the play-village and give a word of advice. That the institution is taken seriously by adults is shown by the fact that, though *manḍwane* partners never marry, the mother of the girl will very often after the *manḍwane* take a gift of beer (usually five calabashes or so) to the parents of her small daughter's 'husband', who will slaughter a goat in recognition of the gift just as though the relationship were real. There is nothing to prevent relatives from being *manḍwane* partners. To-day the 'husband' is usually much younger than the 'wife' and the game is confined to children under the age of puberty. Not more than a few years ago, however, boys and girls of marriageable age used to take part, the institution being considered as primarily for them. One of the reasons for the change is the absence of many of the older boys at work in town, while the failure of young men to keep the rules against impregnation in the play sexual intercourse that often forms part of the game makes mothers loath to allow elder girls to join in.

General behaviour, attitudes, and values are not taught by any formal training. These are inextricably bound up with life in the society and become unconsciously adopted by any one fully partaking in social life. Even a European, when speaking the language and trying to enter into their social activities, finds himself unconsciously taking for granted values that he never had before and which are certainly not to be found in European life. They seem to follow naturally from the social situation and to be bound up with language itself. A group of small girls were playing house in the sand with twigs and pebbles and tiny pots moulded in clay. 'What have you got in those pots?' we asked. '*Vyalwa*' (beer), came the reply, but the intonation and meaning they put into the word, the expression on their faces as they said it, implied a whole social situation. It was clear that, young as they were, the word 'beer' meant to them, not just a drink or food like porridge, but something prized and valuable, yet a source of pleasure and joy, something important in life. In short, they had a Lovedu attitude to beer, an attitude that has no parallel in European society. Certainly no European child could have conveyed what they did in that single word.

Where the standards of the society are apt to conflict to some extent with personal desires, as in the inculcation of good manners, censure and praise become important. If a child does not accept a gift with both hands he is told to do so with some remark, if he is big enough and should know better, calculated to rebuke him. Good manners in eating consists in avoiding noisy or hurried swallowing (one can smack one's lips to one's heart's content) and in sitting flat on the buttocks, not standing or squatting. Great importance is attached to the sharing of food: if any one approaches while you eat, he is automatically invited to share it by the words, 'We are eating.' His reply is either a refusal or consists in his sitting down to join you. Even small children are made to share tit-bits with their companions. If you give some sweets to good-mannered children such as you find in parts unaffected by the modern self-seeking spirit, you will still see how an elder girl calls all the children to sit down round the sweets. They eat slowly and decorously, each taking a second sweet when the first is finished with no sign of greed or hurry, in spite of the fact that they rarely see sweets. This does not mean that Lovedu children do not on occasion try to hide their sweets from others; but greater stress is laid on sharing food by them than by us and, what is more important, there are always half a dozen other children on the spot to share whatever is given. A child is taught to respect those older than himself, especially adults in whose presence there must be no swearing or bad language. When sent on errands, he must obey gracefully without grumbling. A child who observes these rules will be praised by adults to other children. They will say, 'The child of So-and-so is very polite, has good manners.'

The qualities that are most admired in adults and that therefore are most insisted upon in children are generosity and unselfishness and ability to live in peace with others. Quarrelsomeness is one of the worst faults. Thus it is that, when children fight or quarrel, there is never any inquiry into who began the trouble; both are beaten, so that next time, even when in the right, the child will be afraid to fight. There is a proverb that 'it is the child that cries who is given to eat' (*muyana hu la ye a ilaho*) and in later life misplaced modesty as regards asking for the things one needs is deprecated. A man who as a guest diffidently nibbles at instead of enjoying the food lavished upon him by his host or who timidly passes by instead of begging for beer, even if it is the beer-party of the chief, suffers a loss for which only his over-sensitiveness is to blame, for as they phrase it, 'If you are ashamed of gnawing a bone, you will presently throw it away, meat and all.' Closely associated with that irritating characteristic of the Lovedu, especially Lovedu women, which the European terms shameless, unblushing beggary, is the aversion to theft. A child is told a thousand times, 'Always just ask (*hobɛla*) for anything you may want; never steal.' And whenever there has been a theft it is said, 'People should beg (*hobɛla*), not steal.' It is only when you get great differences in wealth, as when a European comes among Natives, that this custom becomes irritating. In this begging from Europeans, Natives do exceed the canons of politeness even of their own society, but many consider it of little consequence in dealings with the European, who, after all, is notoriously ill-mannered in his dealings with Natives.

Correct use of terms of relationship or address is not expected till after puberty and the young child, only gradually learning not to call people older than itself by their everyday names, makes many mistakes. One would think that the formal behaviour required in such complicated ceremonial as that of marriage visits would require some form of special instruction. This is, however, not the case. A young man learns these things simply by hearing others talk, while a girl, by forming part of bridal parties when others in her village are married, comes to learn what is required of her. These facts bear out what experience shows, viz. that formalities are not so rigid as one is apt to imagine. Proper respect, politeness, and correct behaviour, involving use of the right terms of address to those older than yourself, are not insisted upon till after the puberty initiation in the case of a girl and circumcision in the case of a boy. Before this you are regarded as irresponsible, without proper knowledge of how to behave, lacking judgement and that wisdom in personal relationships associated with adults. You are a *leshovoro*.

It is significant, however, that, especially in the case of girls, a single ceremony is not considered sufficient to effect this great transformation to responsibility and adult status. In addition to her own puberty ceremony (*khɔba*), every girl has to attend and take part in a number of subsequent puberty ceremonies in the area—six in the royal area, four of five in other areas. At the first ceremony after her own she is a *thɔvyana*, who sits in seclusion with the *khɔba*, eats of the same food and, like her, is allowed no relish, is beaten hard and takes no part in the dancing at night. Instead, however, of having to go early each morning to the river with the initiate, she fetches water and helps with the cooking. The other *dithɔvyana* are responsible for all the work: they fetch wood and water, stamp, and cook; they run errands for the elder girls who have finished their course of initiation and wait on them; they carry the drums to the river and may be made to sit in the water with the initiate.

In control of the ceremony are the elder girls who have been fully initiated (*dishɔlwɛ*). They walk about with a great sense of their own importance and have to be royally entertained. It is essential that there be plenty of good food at an initiation ceremony. Mealie meal is cooked twice a day, much light beer is made, and monkey nuts and other delicacies are abundantly supplied. At one ceremony, lasting six days, a whole bag of mealie meal was consumed by the girls—that is, more than twice as much as would normally be consumed by the same number of people; and in addition they had large quantities of nuts, only exceptionally provided in ordinary life. For purposes of economy, the mother of the initiate usually makes porridge for her household of the bran of the stampings of the girls. Sometimes, in times of scarcity, a girl's puberty ceremony will be postponed, and it is noticeable that in the ploughing season, when the people are busy all day in the fields, there are few or no initiation ceremonies. Though in charge of the ceremony, the elder girls are subject to an old woman, 'mother of the *khɔba*', who has been chosen by the initiate herself and who, ever after, will be called 'mother' by her. For her own mother may have nothing to do with the ceremony and, even though it is held in her courtyard, may not enter the hut of seclusion. The girl's mother feels very sympathetic towards her daughter and often grumbles that the girls are 'killing' her daughter when she hears them beating her. But she has no say. If a girl is unpopular, her parents sometimes arrange for the ceremony to be held at a relative's village in another area, lest she be too badly treated.

The Lovedu girl does not approach her own mother about such an intimate and personal matter as her first menstruation, but confides in a friend, who will inform the mother by means of the metaphorical phrase, 'So-and-so has scolded the women.' The other girls of the area are thereupon called to come and the ceremonial opens with their carrying the novice on their backs from a spot outside the village, where they have forgathered, into the hut of seclusion, usually the cooking hut of the mother. Some girls keep the fact of their menstruation hidden for months before divulging the secret. Mabula waited for three months. It will not be possible here to do more than indicate the main incidents of a girl's puberty ceremony. It must, however, be borne in mind that there is considerable variation in detail between one ceremony and another and that no mere analysis can give the atmosphere prevailing in such ceremonies. On the arrival in her hut of seclusion the girl is 'strengthened' (*hu thuswa*) by the old women. Ground herbs mixed with ochre and some of the girl's own menstrual blood are smeared on various parts of the body—in a circle round the wrist, on the head, nose, mouth, neck, arms, etc. The medicine is *ya hu rɔrwa bidzi mavala* (to give the zebra its stripes) and is said to prevent the girl from becoming ill (*hu khuma*) when entering the villages of other people. That night towards sunset the women of the area forgather at the village of the initiate, trilling and shouting, '*E a luma*' (it bites), on the way; they come to drum and dance, as they do almost every evening of the six days' seclusion.

While in seclusion the initiate and her companion sit to one side of the doorway of the hut without any covering except the loincloth. They talk in whispers only. When a stranger approaches the hut, she wails in a thin voice to warn him off (for she can see through the crevices of the doorway), and when the elder girls enter she must wail loudly lest she be beaten. When she wishes to relieve herself, she walks out completely covered in a blanket. Early each morning the initiate is taken to the river. She walks in a stooping attitude, covered in a blanket and surrounded by girls uttering a high-pitched wail as she goes. In the stream

VII. ADOLESCENCE
(a) REALISTIC PLAY-COOKING IN THE MAN̩D̩WANE
(b) A TROUPE OF YOUTHFUL DANCERS

VIII. GIRLS' INITIATION INTO WOMANHOOD

(a) COMING FORTH FROM HER PUBERTY SECLUSION (b) GIRLS IN THE DYALI

a hole is hollowed out so as to be deep enough for her to sit in (if possible the water should reach the neck) while a fire is kindled for the other girls, at whose pleasure she remains in the water, uttering her wail. If the girl has a good friend among the old women, she may free the initiate from going to the river after the first morning by a gift of snuff to the elder girls. This is called 'lifting the weight' from the girl (*hu rula*). They return home about eleven o'clock in the morning, when they have their meal. After this the elder girls return to their homes or do as they please, while the novice and her friend remain in their hut. They sleep if they can, for at night they get little chance to do so. During the initiation the girl undergoes harsh treatment at the hands of the older girls. She 'pays', by being beaten, for going to sleep, for waking up and on the slightest pretext. At night her blankets are taken away and used by the older girls, while she lies exposed with no fire to warm her. Not only is she allowed no relish with her porridge, but she may also be given filth to eat. One girl's menstrual blood was put in her porridge, which she immediately vomited up; sometimes a frog is given them to eat and one of us has seen initiates made to eat sand as relish. If she asks for water, the elder girls may clear the nose into it before it is given. All this harsh treatment is looked upon as good discipline.

Initiation at puberty includes instruction in rules connected with the new stage of life the girl is entering upon. She is warned that she has reached maturity and must be careful, in sex play with boys, to avoid becoming pregnant. She is advised also not to have more than one lover at a time, lest there be difficulty in establishing the paternity of her child should she have one. In the old days she was at this stage given a calabash doll which at her marriage was carried in a basket by the wedding party. If she was not virgin, the calabash was pierced. This custom has, however, fallen into disuse. The girl is taught the rules connected with menstruation: not to enter a sick-room while menstruating, not to enter a cattle kraal, not to sleep with men during her menses. If she has not enlarged her *labia minora* properly, she is severely scolded or punished by having hot, roasted sesamum put on them. In one case the elder girls inserted a mealie cob in an initiate to show her the dangers of intercourse, hurting her so badly that she was unable to walk properly. Her parents complained to the queen, who imposed a heavy fine on each of the elder girls responsible. There is no teaching connected with marriage. An initiate must be respectful to her elders: she is told that if people older than herself are in a hut she must greet (*lɔsha*) on entering. She is taught in a song to honour and obey her mother. Most of the teaching is in the form of songs or mummeries. The dancing that takes place every night when the women come consists largely of movements in a bent position on the haunches, with arms held above the head for better balance. Some of the dances are associated with the lessons of the initiation: two girls, one with a cloth passed between the legs to represent the loin covering of a man, dance facing each other; the 'man' dances with a lighted firebrand between the legs, the girl wears a cloth which makes her look pregnant. Another dance consists of movements in which legs are held close together, and sometimes crossed, symbolic of the manner in which male advances can be prevented from becoming dangerous. These are *digɔma*, secret things or mummeries.

The last night of the ceremony is devoted to dancing and the showing of many *digɔma*. It is *khilalawemi*, the night when one sleeps standing—that is, does not sleep at all, though, since people just take a nap any time they feel tired, the name is somewhat exaggerated. All the women of the area who wish to attend gather either in the village, from which men will be debarred, or at a secluded spot somewhere near, bringing with them mealies and nuts to roast and eat while there. There is a great deal of dancing and singing. The greatest *digɔma* are shown at about 3 a.m., after a period of comparative quiet that sets in towards midnight, when most of the people begin to doze around the fires, and these continue until dawn, when disguised figures come dancing in. Each mummery has its own meaning, but this is not clear to the initiate, who does not even see many of them. In the morning, while the girls are at the river, the hut of seclusion is swept and freshly smeared. On her return, after having her head shaved along the sides and back, leaving a circular top, which is a form of hairdress much liked by girls and associated with ritual occasions, the girl is anointed with fat and, except when she is of the royal family, also with ochre. She is given three skins to wear, a frontal covering, a rear covering, and a skin to wear over the shoulders like a cloak. Round her neck is a thick collarette of beads. When dressed, the girl has respectfully to salute the assembled company of women in the courtyard by lying down on one side, palms held together. Now follows a few days during which the novice speaks to no one and walks with bent head, fists clenched and held to the breast. She is taken by the elder girls to greet various relations, who must *nosa* her by means of a small gift before she can rise. A month or more after the ceremony a grand beer-party is given by the girl's parents for the women of the area, who, at a spot near which men are not allowed, have a dance of *digɔma*, specially disguised figures. When the novice has been through the requisite number of ceremonies, she is taken to the queen or the wife of the district head to be beaten with a stick as a sign of her graduation.

Boys' initiation (*vudiga*) is much more spectacular than the *khɔba*. Typically it is held by the whole tribe every twelve to fifteen years, but some district heads occasionally do not wait for the authority of the queen. The last *vudiga* upon a national scale was in 1919, but since then there have been local lodges, such as the one held by the district head Maunadala in 1937. The interval of more than twenty years is not considered extraordinary. Sometimes in the past there were delays, especially in the latter half of the reigns of queens, because, so it is said, they wished to postpone their ritual end, which coincided with the fourth initiation after their accession. In 1938–9 the *vyali*, or girls' initiation, was revived after thirty-five years, partly as a preliminary to the next boys' initiation; and if within a year or so there is a *vudiga*, it will be the third of a reign that has already lasted forty-three years. There are other reasons for the present delay. The *vudiga* involves an immense organization, brings all public activities, such as the courts, to a standstill, upsets the economic routine, and concentrates energies upon one supreme object. In modern conditions it is not easy to cope with such a situation. On the one hand, many men work in the towns and some boys attend mission schools, and on the other the mobilization of the necessary organization and incentives is difficult in the face of discouragement and opposition. Many people realize that for practical purposes the payment of tax marks the introduction to manhood. The Christian mission cannot countenance interference with its schools. Adjustments are necessary, and in some tribes they are being successfully made; for instance, among the Koni of Maṭala, we saw an experiment whereby the whole *vudiga* was crowded into the month's holiday of the school in June–July, the purpose being to avoid conflicts with the Church and the educational authorities.

We cannot in this brief and generalized account do more than refer cursorily to a few aspects of the institution. It involves circumcision, but has nothing to do with biological puberty. Side by side with toddlers still drinking at their mother's breast, such as Khiɛbɛ in the 1919 initiation, married men of thirty or forty go to be circumcised. They will all one day belong to the same regiment. Moreover, there used to be an attenuated puberty rite, *hu fura khirugulu* (chewing the herb *khirugulu*), which is also chewed by doctors in order to give them power and insight to interpret the bones. The puberty rite took place after the first nocturnal emission; the boy went down to the river to wash; he was made to dig up a root, chew it and rub it between his legs in order to prevent the danger of *makhuma* (illness associated with crises in life); and he advanced from being a *musinaba* (child) to being a *muṭaŋga* (adolescent or young man).

The *vudiga* is quite different: it is a circumcision rite which invests the adolescent with the beginnings of social adulthood. But the investiture is imperfect, for manhood is not attained at a single bound; one grows into it by imperceptible stages. There is no single criterion of adulthood and the maturity that is required cannot be given merely by a ritual act. For that reason also, the *vudiga* teaches, not any single virtue, but impresses upon the boy all the values of the society and the necessity of a new outlook. From the almost outlaw play-gang, he must be conducted to the fringes of responsible society or be placed in a position from which he can gradually make his way into society. It would be an exaggeration to say that the *vudiga* is designed to cope with the turbulence of youth; for even the circumcised are still wild.

The general pattern of the *vudiga* has often been described and is not difficult to understand. After some preliminary practice of songs, which are the life-blood of the institution, the would-be novices undergo a series of rites culminating in the circumcision at the river and are taken into a lodge hidden somewhere in the bush. This cuts them off completely from the outside world. In their seclusion, emphasized by all manner of taboos and restrictions which mark the difference of their lives from that of ordinary people, they learn strange songs and unintelligible formulae. The spirit of this period is difficult to recapture and the obscure symbolism and secret rites seem unrelated to any cultural realities; yet we must think of them as having their roots deep in the past, while they have become overgrown with the meanings and purposes of the present culture. Then follows a stage, for about a month, of even stranger events, and it is heralded by a re-orientation of life within the lodge. At their singing performances the novices begin to sit facing the east, not the west, as in the previous three months. This re-orientation gradually affects more and more activities and issues in tentative contacts with the outside world. At last the lodge is burnt down and the initiates go home, where for a further week they remain on the fringes of ordinary life, to be drawn closer and closer by gradual ritual steps into the society and its everyday activities. But if these broad stages are intelligible enough, it is very different when we examine the details. They obviously have an immense background, both in a past that is lost in oblivion and in a present that owes many of its values to that past, but has at the same time added to and modified these values. Fortunately, however, as it is beyond the scope of this book to deal with those details, we may content ourselves with a few general observations.

The first stage among the Lovedu is *hu huva*, when the heads of districts are told to arrange that the novices be taken into the veld to learn songs. The teaching is quite informal; it is a preparatory class, so that the proceedings in the lodge two weeks later may go with a swing. The teaching is done, not by the real shepherds (*medabi*), but by their juniors, those who were very young in the previous lodge. They were the large-bellied toddlers (*dimbana*, literally 'little stomachs') who ran away from their mothers to enjoy the excitement of the lodge. It could hardly be expected that they would have absorbed much and so they learn now by teaching the novices. At this preliminary and informal training, the boys may attend if they like; there are no taboos and no restrictions; the teachers may not chastise their pupils. There is as yet no seclusion. Nor are the novices given any special work to do for the chief. The fence of the *khɔrɔ* at the capital has to be rebuilt, but the novices do no more than they, as youngsters living at the capital, would do on other occasions when the *khɔrɔ* has to be repaired. When they come home they, as well as other young boys, bring light branches used to fill in the interstices between the poles. From areas beyond the capital it is only the older men who, as is customary whenever the *khɔrɔ* is built, give their assistance. At last the new moon appears, and Copernicus heralds the approach of winter. The shepherds have their hair shaved, district heads come to 'take the firebrand', the symbol that authorizes them to hold the initiation, and the *vudiga* officially opens at the capital. It is a ritual occasion: the older men beat the younger, sometimes black porridge without relish is eaten in the cattle kraal, there is an alarm, and the boys are conducted to the river to be circumcised.

For the circumcision the boys go to the valley which is appropriately called 'the place where things are forgotten'. They are being separated from ordinary life; they 'get lost'. The '*gɔma* first bites its owners', for in this as in other acts regard is had to certain precedences. It is the hierarchy of rank, as at a formal dinner among us, that is emphasized; but the precedence extends only, so to speak, to the three people sitting at the head table; the others take their place anywhere. As the operator proceeds, the old men chant, 'Sever, sever with the knife, [the foreskins] let the fishes take' (*tshikhi-tshikhi ga mufaga, khɔvɛ jia*). It is the shepherds who are chastised as they drive the novices, called cane-rats (*magwɛlɛle*) at this stage, to the circumcision; they run the gauntlet through the ranks of singing men. It is enough that the novices should suffer the painful operation. Some bleed profusely, but it is their own fault (so it is thought); the medicine they are given can only alleviate the penalty for pre-circumcision promiscuity. Much else is enacted, but we must pass on to the next stage, the three months of intensive training in the lodge. It is the period, *par excellence*, of seclusion. The novices learn songs and formulae; they make a dancing costume and practise dances; their eating is a hurried ritual, for, as they phrase it, 'We are going to the medicines, the medicines of the veld to which there is no end.' By this they mean they have to go out to hunt, but clearly it is more than hunting that is intended; the outside world is full of wonderful things, shrubs and trees and animals which require their urgent attention; and there is so much to be done and to be learnt, that they should not spend all their time filling their bellies.

If that is the meaning of the ritual at the sacred tables, great *digɔma* which shepherds, polluted by contact with women, approach at the peril of causing the novices to vomit, the ritual of the boys when they sit by the side of the fire 'stabbing the elephant' is inscrutably obscure. In other tribes the fire is undying and is called 'the elephant'. The Lovedu call the fire *khisibe* (meaning 'unknown', but probably from Kharanga *zimbe*, a coal of fire) not *ḍou* (elephant); they do not conceive it to be undying and they know nothing of the conception of 'stabbing the elephant'. Yet some of these conceptions are clearly present in the ritual: the ritual singing is *hu fɛfa ḍou*, merely one of the special phrases of the lodge; the song is *ḍo' vetsi*, an obvious contraction of *ḍou etsela* (elephant lie down); but not even the old men could suggest the derivation of the one from the other; the boys swing their arms in imitation of a stabbing action, but it is not thought of as such and, as they sing, the old men chant, 'Stab the elephant with arrows; next moon we return to those who have stayed at home.' Even this last is interpreted to mean that the boys by their action push on the moon to accelerate their return home. At a later stage, after the 'change', the *ḍo' vetsi* song becomes '*Mamaṭo u ile ḍou sala shagoni*' (mother-of-eyes said, 'elephant remain in the country'—because the boys are going home). We give this brief reconstruction to show how, despite obvious suggestions in this central ritual of the lodge, the Lovedu have reinterpreted the whole situation. This is one of the details to which we have referred, but with which we cannot here deal. The whole *vudiga* ritual is full of them and as often as not the original words of songs or formulae have become distorted out of recognition. Indeed, the diffusion of a culture element is far from being a simple matter.

The three months' seclusion is marked by taboos and restrictions and a régime which, for the Lovedu, is exceptionally strict. But, by comparison with other tribes, the taboos are not stringent and a great deal of latitude is allowed. The large-bellied toddlers are tenderly cared for by the old men. By day they play about in the lodge enclosure and by night they sleep by the 'mother' of the lodge (*maḍala*) near the fire. Those a little older set their traps and catch mice, which they roast by the *khisibe* fire; but relish and wild fruit is usually forbidden to them and they may not, though they often do, drink water. Sick boys, elsewhere subjected to hardships and taunts, are nursed and given soft food, not the hard *khivonɛlo* of the novices. The novices who go out to hunt certainly resent the malingering of the lazy ones (*magɔtha*), who are strong enough, but stay at home on this or that pretext. But the true spirit of the *vudiga* is seen, not so much in the beatings that the shepherds (*medabi*) administer, for they are beaten as much as if not more than, the novices, but in the actions and attitude of the older men. There are *medidi*, one regiment senior to the *medabi*, who are never beaten, but may be fined; and older than they are the old men (*vakhalabye*). They are kindly greybeards, some of them officials of the lodge and some who do no work (*vuralizita*). Some of them constantly intercede for the young and weak boys who are threatened with punishment or trials beyond their strength or endurance, or 'stand for' those deserving novices who had been obedient or generous or respectful in their childhood. Above all, these old men, mellow with age and mature in wisdom, conditioned to a culture founded upon compromise and easy relations, not only restrain excesses, but add to the beauty of the performances by chanting their refrain of sayings and proverbs, encouragements and admonitions. It is they, not the shepherds with their whips, that give the tone to the proceedings.

The stage after this period of seclusion is called the 'change' (*hu fedulɛlwa*). The boys sit by the fire facing the rising, not the setting, sun, as was the case in the previous three months. Of course, we must not expect precision: the 1919 fire ran north-south, not east-west; the ideal always gives way to the practical, for the east-west disposition was rendered difficult, though not impossible, by the slope of the ground. In other respects also it was the spirit not the letter of the law that determined various arrangements. After the 'change' life is somewhat different in the lodge. The boys used to do homage (*lɔsha*) to a *morula* tree near the fire as if it were their ancestor (grandparent). But the tree mysteriously withers and, after the change, is replaced by a pole (*murakadu*). No teaching is done from either tree or pole as is the case in other tribes, but it is associated with a whole series of ritual acts. After the 'change' no longer shepherds but women bring the food; boys perform within sight of women; some of the food taboos are raised, but relish, though always brought, is forbidden and still thrown into the refuse heap. Apart from these and many other changes, we must also mention the visit by the novices to the village in order to 'beg for salt'. Then they sing the praises of salt, the seasoning virtues of which they now fully appreciate, having gone without it for so long. But on their return the pole has gone; their grandparent has died.

And now we press on to a day of great doings. The novices go out to 'scratch [as fowls do] for food', only this means a spectacular dance before the women. That night, the last night in the lodge, it is *khilalawemi*, the night of standing, though many quietly doze off or escape to rest in the bush near by; there is none of the concentration we expect on occasions of importance. The boys are shown several sacred objects (*digɔma*), each with its own meaning; and the proceedings end with the naming of the lodge and the new regiment that has been created. Next morning the boys remove the clay that 'disguised' them during their seclusion. They are given a loin cloth, which they wear back to front, their hair, except for a circular crown, is shaved and they are smeared with fat (not ochre among the royal Lovedu). They are 'people from the refuse heap' (*zwigwamathukhu*), a name they discard only when, a week later, their heads are completely shaved. As they leave, the lodge, with all in it, is burnt down.

The *vudiga* is not at an end yet; it has merely entered a new stage in which the discipline is further relaxed. The novices leave the lodge with double-pointed sticks, covering with their hands the two ends, which are fashioned like the *glans penis*. In that manner they go about whenever they are in public; the action is said to impress upon them the necessity of concealing the object and meaning of circumcision. When they arrive at the village their mothers appear dancing with joy and choose out their sons, not always correctly, because their heads are bent down and their bodies have grown a good deal in the lodge. A goat is killed for them; it is the goat 'of vomiting the rats', for as men they must cast out the things of their childhood. Then for the next week they are in a state of semi-seclusion, but there are still many observances. They appear in public only in the bent, humble attitude, they carry their sticks, and they wear their loin cloths the wrong way round. Nevertheless, the 'gathering up' (*hu aluha*) into the society proceeds apace. They have a special enclosure made for them in the veld, the *khikhudɔ* (hiding place or secluded spot), in which they spend some time of the day. But they are scattered, as each group of villages has its own secluded spot; and their separateness and solidarity is further broken up by sleeping at home and herding for their own people. They do not speak, especially not to women, but at night at home they have contests of riddles (*nyebo*) with the old women who come to visit them, exactly as after a marriage ceremony. This stage ends with the 'seizing of the lion' (*hu tswara dau*). One night the shepherds go out with bullroarers, the whirling of which produces the roar of the lion. The boys give chase and he who catches the 'lion' is praised by the old men.

Finally come the last ritual acts. The boys are taken down to the river to lift the 'stomach of the cow', a log tied to a stone in a pool, and then to 'kindle a fire on the river' (done on a log in the water), for a man must be both strong and clever; he must be able even to make fire in the water. After these tests there is the final ordeal at the cave to which the boys are taken one by one, are beaten and given their last admonitions. At the cave the double-pointed stick is discarded, the fat removed from their heads and, if two brothers have attended the same lodge, the elder beats the younger on the way home to remove the presumption of belonging to the same regiment. At home the initiate's mother must *nosa* him by a gift to 'open his mouth', and next day each of the boys, accompanied by a shepherd, goes to visit some relative, who will feast him with meat and beer.

That in the briefest possible outline is the procedure followed in the *vudiga*. To recapture the whole atmosphere, to present the details of a four months' ceremonial full of incident and meaning, is not possible. All we can do is to single out one or two special features of the educational aspect. Let us first dispel the idea that the régime is a rigid one. How can it be when there are toddlers of six or seven years of age nestling up to the 'mother' of the lodge where he sleeps by the fire? The boys are beaten, it is true, and they have to undergo various kinds of punishment, but the old men are there to 'stand for them'; and when the novices are tired, one of these kindly old men or a visitor will *rula* them, take off the weight from their heads, so that they can go to bed early. The little ones do not go out to hunt, they play about in the lodge. If one of them cries, the 'mother' of the lodge will inquire the cause from the *washe* (the head of the initiates), and if the *washe* has been negligent, it is he who will be punished. The cold is never severe nor are the boys attacked by worms or ants (for the floor is covered with ash); there is no rule that they must sleep on their backs with head or feet toward the fire, so that they will suffer more from the cold. Boys do not talk as if the *vudiga* is a terrible ordeal; it is the shepherds as much as the initiates who are punished. The food is not nauseating, but what is mentioned as particularly trying is the stench issuing from the healing wounds. The stomach contents of a buck killed in the hunt is sprinkled over their porridge, but they like it and it is used in ordinary life as food. They may not drink water, but the lodge is quite near the river and it is not difficult to steal a drink now and then. Meat is never wholly taboo. They can always trap mice and rats and sometimes they are given meat, though it must not be openly displayed. Sometimes, when they are out hunting, the command '*Zapi*' is given; it is a signal for the boys to make an onslaught upon a sweet sorghum field or on wild fruits. It is said that a clever boy is very seldom beaten. The silence that is enjoined upon them, for theoretically they may communicate only by whistling, is not absolute; they may whisper to one another and only loud speaking is punished. They are not driven into cold pools every day to remove the scab of their wounds. On the contrary, the old men examine the wounds every day; and the doctor who has operated badly may be disgraced, as one was during the 1919 school; he was ignominiously chased away from the lodge. In short, despite the trials and restrictions, the régime is on the whole a mild one.

Obscene language does not loom large; it plays its part, not as obscenity, but as ritual, but it is not an imposing part. After the 'change', when women start bringing the food, it is the shepherds who may swear at them. 'Go and eat,' they say; 'your pubes are torn'; or 'The red inside of your private parts, oho'; but they add, 'Do not feel hurt, women. We are not swearing at you. We are praising you.' But wilful swearing is an offence, as we saw in the *vyali* (girls' initiation), when even one of the important officials of the school, the attendant of the Bird, swore at a girl who had made a mistake and was promptly fined a goat. When the boys sit eating by the tables, it is at the command 'Let them defecate' (*A vu-le nyɔ*) that they stop, but in the circumstances it means no more than 'Dismiss'. Indeed, the word *musadi* (women) and any word associated with women is not to be used within the lodge at all. There is a rounded ball of porridge set upon a stick which is stuck into the food brought to the boys and it is called *khigɔgɔnɔnɔ* (clitoris); when the boys sit down by the tables or fire they are ordered to 'close the anus' and have to press one heel into the anus as they sit; and undoubtedly many of the formulae appear to have obscene references. But it would be a very great surprise to a Lovedu boy to learn that the *vudiga* teaches anything about sex or that there is anything obscene in it. Indeed, they know but disapprove of the delight in obscenity at the Shangana-Tonga lodges.

There is little direct teaching. One of the trials, that of hopping along with a stick, sharpened at both ends and pressed between the knees, is said to remind the boys that they must not defecate on the road, but should go into the bush. But note that little Mulati was too young to undergo it, Khiɛbɛ escaped it because his uncle 'stood for him', and Mudiva was sleeping in the hedge on the night it was undergone. The boys are all told they should avoid women since for a long time the wound will be liable to reopen and become bad. They are also warned not to divulge the secrets of the lodge. But that is practically the sum total of the direct admonitions. The laws and songs and formulae do not contain any precepts that the initiates understand or can bring into relation with virtues. And the same may be said of the punishments and ordeals. These things have nothing to do with moral standards or the inculcation of knowledge of facts. But they contribute to the general atmosphere, and their effect, in the context of the whole, is tremendous. The initiation is something different from ordinary life. Its genius lies, not in direct teaching, but in the manner in which the values of the society are emphasized. The final effect is to transform the boys into men; and certainly the situation is manipulated with consummate skill to attain this end. To us everything may appear meaningless. But we hardly realize how small is the life-adjustment value of mere verbal knowledge of facts and how important is the inculcation of a new set of standards. We know of these things from such religious experiences as conversion. The *vudiga* performs the same function; it is a turning away from the things of childhood and a turning towards the things of adulthood. Our pedagogical techniques might be tenfold more effective if they relied more upon the methods of the soap-box orator, of commercial advertising, and even of the yellow Press. Symbols and slogans, skilful manipulation of psychological situations, the play upon sentiments rooted in the cultural background—these are the methods of the *vudiga* as they are also the methods of our most skilful propaganda and our most effective advertisements. Who can deny that they contribute more to the moulding of our values and of our behaviour than do the science and history and mathematics in our schools? Perhaps it is fortunate that our pedagogical techniques are impotent, for the somewhat unrealistic world of our schools would otherwise wholly unfit us for life. But the technique of the lodge, though it teaches no verbal knowledge of facts, is effective and there is nothing in the *vudiga* which is out of harmony with the realities of life.

Consider for a moment the situation as the boys 'stab the elephant'.

As they do so, the old men, mature in their wisdom, kindly guardians of the initiates, slowly and solemnly 'sing with signs' (*va rɛma zwega*). These *zwega* are often also an accompaniment of the songs of the boys, in themselves most exquisite poetry. Many of the 'signs' are unintelligible, e.g. 'You may bring me a skin cradle. I am carrying an infant, my little children'; or 'The guinea fowls are crying; they are scratching for food, my children.' The old men always greet the novices, *vana va ga* (my little ones), though to one another and to the shepherds they are *valɔi* (witches). The old men also chant proverbs and sayings, warnings and advice, all manner of admonitions and encouragement, some stereotyped, some extempore. To enumerate them would be to enumerate the virtues that are esteemed and the vices that are condemned in the society. 'I told you, O novice, but you plugged your ears with plugs of wood' is a general admonition, reminding the boys that, when they were young, they often were disobedient and now their errors are being expiated. Young boys are often told that, when they go to the *vudiga*, their impudence and disobedience will make their trials harder. 'Beware', a man might say to a youngster who is unwilling to help him or an elder. 'The *vudiga* is not far off; you will find no one to lift the weight from your head.' The virtues that are inculcated in this way are merely those the boys have heard of a thousand times in their ordinary lives. Again, one must not imagine that the boys take more note of the words of the old men in the lodge than we do when we sing a hymn in church, but they know that those *zwega* and admonitions express the fundamental values and ideals in the society: generosity, respectfulness and obedience to the elders, helpfulness, and so on. 'Give your seat up to an old man, carry his bundle for him on the road, go with him further than he asks you, do not mock at the blind or cripple'—these are some of the things one old man may say, whereas another will condemn theft and adultery and extol mutuality and modesty, almost impersonally, it is true, but always beautifully, solemnly, and effectively. These things sink into the minds of the novices, not as so many individual precepts, but as part of the ritual of the lodge, all indivisibly united into one whole concretion of values and sentiments. A man will say that the *vudiga* is a wonderful thing, but he will be at a loss to tell you anything concrete that it teaches. For you cannot dissect out a precept here and an example there—it is all one, like life itself.

We may now, before proceeding to adult education, touch upon a few aspects of the *vudiga* and the *khɔba*. Besides breaking the girl's attachment to the things of her childhood, the *khɔba* stresses the importance and dangers of sexual maturity. But it can hardly be said that the *vudiga* is much concerned with the sudden emergence of a capacity for true sexual experience. Both institutions help us to understand the meaning and methods of attaining social adulthood; but they belong to different cultural backgrounds and are derived from different cultural sources. They are not counterparts of one another. The *khɔba* is indigenous, the *vudiga* is foreign. We cannot here study the manner in which these two institutions, as well as the *vyali* and *vuhwera* (two further initiations for boys and girls), have merged with the different cultures in neighbouring tribes though the varying acceptance or rejection or remoulding of culture elements provides important clues to understanding the Lovedu. The *vudiga*, despite its admirable integration into Lovedu culture, still overstresses national regimentation and military virtues; it makes too much of the repudiation of association with women (a tendency rectified in the *vyali*); and the conception in it of an ordeal or revenge inflicted by adults, who have suffered circumcision, upon novices whose turn to suffer has come is too pronounced for a culture that abhors vengeance. It is curious, also, that in a society in which mates are born for one another the problem of harmonizing romantic love with the limited range of socially approved choices is not dealt with in the *khɔba* or the *vudiga*. Pre-marital sexual experiment is excluded at least as a means of avoiding individual incompatibilities; but such incompatibilities are not phrased as a difficulty in marriage, the sexual aspect of which is one of the least important in Lovedu society, and the institution of *vuḍavu* (of having lovers), with whom married much more than unmarried men or women form liaisons, gives an outlet to romanticism and supports the long suckling period. The chastity that is stressed in the *khɔba* is the pre-marital chastity that leads to no complications in the social structure, such as would be caused by the birth of a child to an unmarried girl; it does not preclude those satisfactions the desire for which is inevitably aroused by the great value that is placed upon fertility.

The rites of the *vudiga* and *khɔba* do not, as we have seen, change boys and girls from youth to full-fledged manhood. The transition is a gradual one. The *khɔba* becomes a bride; the bride after the birth of her first child is a *mudwana*; and she in turn, when her children marry, is a venerable old woman (*mukhegulu*). The bride is of small consequence even in her own home; for long she serves an apprenticeship under the control of her mother-in-law, who also takes her child out of her hands, baths it and feeds it. Only as an old woman does she reach the peak of her life. With a man the position is no different. After the *vudiga* he has a kind of legal status. After marriage he advances a further stage, but in his marital relations and as a father he is a child dependent upon advice from his elders. In public activities, such as in the courts, he still sits and listens, but the old men may entrust a case to him and his agemates to teach them a sense of responsibility. His helplessness is strikingly in evidence when a child is born to him: he does not see it at first, knows little of its progress, is ordered by the old women to seek this or that root, for what purpose he cannot tell, and, when the child is taken out of the hut, he is merely called, given medicine and told what to do with it. Finally, he must seek the advice of the old women as to when he may resume sexual intercourse with his wife. In other spheres of life also, the education of the man or the woman gradually advances. Craftsmanship, for instance, is the province of the old. Young men and women may learn from their fathers or mothers, but more usually the leisure and inclination come in their old age. A bride, fully occupied with housework and cultivation under the eye of her mother-in-law, has no time for pottery and mat-making; a young man's life is too unsettled to allow him quietly to sit down to make a basket or a stamping-block. The Lovedu are not at all anxious that their children should be taught craftsmanship in the mission schools.

In contrast to our customs, education never ends. As the physiological capacities vary, so new activities are undertaken. The culture always provides a place for the aptitudes of every stage of life, and neither men nor women become redundant in their old age, unless, indeed, they are utterly decrepit. With their physical decline, the culture provides new avenues and interests, to which they are continuously adjusting themselves. They suffer no sense of frustration, because their adjustments are dynamic. With us old age may be tragic: among women, the menopause may precipitate a crisis; among men, retiring from work often causes loss of interest in life and mental decay. But old Lovedu men and women always have something more to learn and to do. Women are not perturbed about external signs of age and complacently accept the end of their childbearing years, for these years bring increased influence, a fuller life, and greater rewards. If physical disability excludes old men from active political life, they receive ample compensation in reduced responsibilities and added prestige. There is no sense of impotence that upsets their balance. Instead, the changing sphere of their roles and their interests both keeps them stable and makes them precious to the society. The distress of old age among us is seldom seen, for rewards always stimulate the new adjustments that have to be made. Utter decrepitude is, however, a tragedy, fortunately ended by the neglect that we may regard as pitiless, but which realistically eliminates those who cannot attain even the mediocre level of achievement that the society calls for. He who cannot attain this level cannot make simple adjustments. But he who can still use his faculties in his old age may become a doctor of note, or a recognized authority on tribal legends or history. Finally, the psychological effect of beliefs attaching to the very old is to provide them with new incentives and renewed opportunities. The widespread suspicion that they have personal contacts with the world of darkness enhances their power, while their elevation, in anticipation, to godhead, for they are already so near death that they may be referred to as gods (*vadimo*), invests their dignity and their wishes with a supernatural halo.

Beside this all-pervasive system of tribal education, the modern school, with its three R's, is as yet of small importance. It reaches, and only in an attenuated form, no more than 3 to 5 per cent. of the children. Its methods are foreign, divorced from life; its teachers are immature, handicapped by inadequate equipment and by being uprooted from the soil of tribal culture. Yet the modern school is the force of the future. Education is passionately desired by the young, and the old would welcome it if they did not feel that it was subversive. There is no compulsion upon a scholar to become a Christian; but the belief persists that education and Christianity are inseparable. It is a belief that raises an awkward dilemma: must the school, which at the same time is the gateway to Christianity, give up its task of breaking down, or can it compromise with superstition? Can it work from within, integrated into the culture, without defeating its purpose? The answer cannot be given here. The task of the school and the Church is no less prodigious and delicate than the difficulties of the young boy or girl are great and the conflicts within him irreconcilable. He is ragged by other scholars unless he also attends church; he is discouraged from playing with his friends, the pagans who do not attend school; he is deprived of the joys of dancing and drumming. The *khɔba* and play-housekeeping are taboo to him. Tensions and maladjustments arise: Christian girls disgrace themselves and outrage Christian sentiment by having more illegitimate children than pagans; people laugh when they see Christian men attending beer-drinks and scornfully remark upon the bad manners of pretentious school-children.

The school, nevertheless, has made a notable contribution. Its teachings have some immediate life-adjustment value. Reading and writing, a training for a profession, a knowledge of English or Afrikaans are valuable aids in the economic struggle. But more important in the modern world is the long-run adjustment value of the outlook engendered in the schools. In the culture-contact situation, with the scales weighted in favour of a capacity to accommodate oneself to European thought and methods, the training of the school prepares the way to some measure of co-operation with agricultural demonstrators, European health officers, and those who are concerned with the reclamation of the reserves. The idea of progress takes root and, though it is a perverted idea, it provides new incentives and counteracts the sense of frustration before the march of an overwhelming force, the force of Western culture.

Unfortunately, the gains are counterbalanced by the losses. It may be that the losses are temporary, because, on the one hand, they are losses from the point of view of the old culture and, on the other, in a period of transition there must inevitably be tensions and conflicts. Men are guided by vast systems of values and sentiments, built up laboriously by centuries of tradition; these cannot be replaced by a new set of standards inculcated by a single institution, such as the modern school, especially when that institution uses ineffective techniques and is external to the main trends of the culture. Some of the losses are not inevitable: it is not the school as such which disables educated young men from accepting manual labour and housework. It might even be possible to avoid the loss of that valuable body of veldlore which the herdboys learn during the years of herding. Boys and girls need the three R's; they need to understand and trust the ways of the white man; but they also need the knowledge and the standards that make life worth while in the society of which they are part. It is the task of the school to take account, not of one, but of all these needs.

CHAPTER VIII

FERTILITY AND THE DRUM CULT

The setting of the sacred drums in a mystical cult—initiation into the secrets of the whistling ancestors—calendric observances connected with fecundity, masks, and mummeries.

BESIDES the girls' puberty ceremony and the circumcision of boys, there are other initiation ceremonies among the Lovedu. One is the *vyali* (often looked upon as the women's counterpart of circumcision because of its regimentation), contemporaneous with which is the boys' *vuhwera*, consisting largely of masked dancing; another is the *gomana* for men. These are closely interwoven with a fertility and rain cult which, because of its association with sacred drums, one may call the drum cult. Their educational object, never very strongly marked in Bantu initiation schools, pales into insignificance before the ceremonial. Indeed the *gomana* as a 'school' is only an aspect of *gomana* ceremonial as a whole, the primary function of which is to secure rain. The *vyali-vuhwera-gomana* complex is characterized by esoteric masks, mummeries, and mysteries and by a category of values which we may term the 'mystical philosophy' of the Lovedu. We shall give merely a brief picture of the complex, because, at the time of writing, the first *vyali-vuhwera* held for thirty-five years is still in progress and our ideas as to its true meaning are far from being settled.

The sacred drum cult has many ramifications. The *zwiḍajani*, supposed to be ancestral spirits coming to earth to take part in *gomana* singing and drumming of the sacred drums, have become incorporated into other aspects of the culture. They appear in the bush near the village whenever a harvest offering has been made in the families of royal relatives; they come at the installation of a new district head and at the death of close relatives of the queen. On these occasions they join in the singing and dancing of *lesugu* songs, songs associated with the *vyali* of men and which, in addition to the above-mentioned occasions, are employed also when women dance for rain. The type of instrument by means of which the *zwiḍajani* whistle or bleat out their songs and messages is used also by the Bird, the ruling spirit of the *vyali*.

Drums are much used in Lovedu life; they are played in the *gɔsha* dance to the accompaniment of reed pipes, they are important in all initiations except circumcision, they are beaten for days at the dancing of possessed people, and it is significant that the public recognition by the queen of a new district head at his installation consists in the handing over of a drumstick (*khiɔba kha gɔma*). Drums are of two types: the long cylindrical drum played with the hands as it lies on its side and the *gɔma*, a rounded drum with handles, played by means of a drumstick as it stands in an upright position. The sacred drums (*digomana*) of the tribe are of the *gɔma* type, but, unlike ordinary *gɔma* drums, are played by hand, not with a drumstick. They are four in number, each with its special name, and are kept at present in a village beside the bush in which the last three rulers lie buried. Their keeper is a descendant of Malegudu, eldest son of Mugɔdɔ, who fought with Mujaji for the throne. These drums are not to be seen by the public, nor are people, except inmates of the royal district, supposed to pass anywhere near there. In appearance and decoration they are no different from ordinary drums, but they are made in a special way and it is said that the maker 'will see them with his eyes but never hear them with his ears' (i.e. he will be put to death when his work is done). The largest is *phaṭaṭɛ*, which stands about 4 ft. high; next in size is *ṭaŋga*; then comes *pekahare*; while the smallest and most important of all is *raŋwedi*, to which is attributed powers even of locomotion, because in 1892, when Albasini set fire to the royal village, it was the only one of the *gomana* drums that was not burnt. While all four *gomana* drums are said to contain a human skull instead of the stone that one usually finds inside it, *raŋwedi*, the smallest, has the facial skin of a human being placed (in strips, it is said) under the resonator of ox hide and has, smeared on the outside, the body dirt of the person (said to be always a chief councillor or other important person of royal blood) killed for its manufacture. This drum is thought to be closely associated with the welfare of the tribe. Should the chief have occasion to escape from enemies, she should take with her this drum, and it is said that, when the heir to the throne receives instruction in the use of rain medicines just prior to the death of the ruling chief, she must be sitting upon it. In some of the neighbouring tribes the sacred drums are pierced on the death of the chief.

The care of these sacred drums, involving periodic smearing with fat and ochre to keep out weevils and moths, renewal of the skin resonators, building and repair of the hut in which they are kept, is the work of a special section of people, those of Ravothata, whose totem is *ḍou* of Uulɛbye. Uulɛbye is in Phalavorwa, where this drum cult is much stronger than among the Lovedu. These Ravothata are also responsible for closing the *vyali* initiation at the capital when they come at its end with their weird-costumed dancing performers, the *magɔgɔbya*. Thus once again the *gomana* and the *vyali-vuhwera* are linked into a common complex. The sacred drums, played only on special ceremonial occasions and by men, not women, who are usually responsible for drumming, are looked upon as gods (*vadimo*). The praise of *phaṭaṭɛ*, the largest, is 'Leg of *phaṭaṭɛ* of Muhale [the old chief]; if it is not a god we can throw it away rattling to the pool' (*Goto la phaṭaṭɛ a Muhale hɛ ŋga ve a se mudimo re ga laṭa re khogolosa ra isa madiveni*). The Thavina and Nareni, tribes to the south of the Lovedu, offer to the sacred drums the first-fruits, and everywhere their beating is associated with rain and the agricultural year. Not only are the drums gods, but their sound is thought to be very pleasing to the *zwiḍajani*, those ancestral spirits who, when the drums are sounded, come and sing and dance. The knowledge that their part is played by initiated men does not appear to detract from their importance in the eyes of those who are in the secret. The instrument used consisted in the old days of the tibia of a human being with a feather inserted (and there is reason to believe that some of these are still extant) but to-day they use mostly two pieces of wood slightly concave on the inside in which a piece of sinew or reed is temporarily inserted. The language being tone-bound, messages and songs can be understood when whistled. Not all ancestral spirits, but only those of the Lovedu proper and of some of the important groups, such as the Khaha and Nareni, are thought to be able to visit the earth as *zwiḍajani*.

The most important feature of the drum cult was the beating of the sacred drums in an enclosure near the village, usually in the afternoon and evening on six successive days twice every year: in the spring just before the sowing and in winter after the harvest thanksgiving. The spring drumming was preceded by propitiation of the royal ancestors by means of a libation on their graves in Ḍaja Forest, where the earlier chiefs lie buried. There was a special procession which no one was to see on pain of death, the Mulodozi River had to be crossed at a special spot called *Khiṭaba-vakɔlɔlɔ* (washing place of great people) and it is maintained by some that a black ox was also slaughtered. The district head at Ḍaja, who was responsible for clearing a way to the graves, had to plant near the royal graves a little of every seed cultivated. The people would then see, it is said, which grew best and would plant much of that. The *gomana*, the beating of the sacred drums, 'was the chief thing that had the power of asking rain from the ancestors'. The sounding of the drums at harvest-time was a thanksgiving. The first harvest *gomana* after the circumcision took the form of an initiation, in which the neophytes were introduced into the drum ritual and the secret of *zwiḍajani*, and received cuts on their faces as a sign that they had passed through it.

Though the sacred drums are still kept and the Ravothaṭa people are still called to repair the hut in which they are placed, the regular beating of *gomana* drums has fallen into disuse. The last *gomana* initiation held officially by the queen in the tribe was in 1892, just before the accession of the present queen. It is difficult to account for this lapse when among neighbouring tribes the cult is still fully carried out. Some say the reason lies in the ritual murders that are associated with the drums, but since it is an accepted principle that a sheep may satisfactorily take the place of a human being and, moreover, this difficulty must somehow have been overcome in other tribes, this reason does not appear good enough. Possibly the cult was introduced from the south and had not become sufficiently assimilated or taken deep enough root to survive the lethargy induced by European contact. Perhaps the rain-making powers of the queen herself made it largely unnecessary. It is not impossible that it will suddenly spring back to life, as did the *vyali* in 1938-9 after a lapse of over thirty years.

Though the queen herself now holds no *gomana*, the institution is not dead. Elements such as *zwiḍajani* have taken permanent root and the queen has allowed a stranger, Rasekwalo, a rain doctor of the *kwɛna* totem who came to live on European-owned land under her jurisdiction, to hold a *gomana* with, of course, his own drums, and in 1929, when he came to ask that boys from the royal village should be allowed to attend the initiation, she gave her consent. He holds one *gomana* a year, receiving

IX. MASKED DANCERS OF RAUOTHATA

X. MASQUERADE OF THE UUAHWERA
(a) STRUTTING OF THE UUAHWERA DANCE
(b) DANCE OF THE DUIKER

special permission from the queen on each occasion, and initiates circumcised and uncircumcised alike.

Gomana initiation to-day as held by Rasekwalo does not differ from the ceremonial in the queen's own *gomana* of old, though it is regarded as a 'business', a source of revenue to Rasekwalo, without the great power of the old Maulwi ceremony. Madume relates his experiences in 1929. He and about twenty others from the royal village, some of them over forty years of age because there had been no initiation for so long, set out for the scene of the initiation some twelve miles away in the charge of some men (*medabi* or shepherds) who had been through the *gomana* initiation. They walked at a very fast pace, almost running, because they 'were anxious to be initiated'. As members of the royal village, they did not, like the others, pay 5s. entrance fee, but on arrival in the evening were offered two huts to sleep in and given a meal. At sunrise next morning, when the *gomana* drums began to sound in the enclosure kept permanently for *gomana* purposes, the initiates gathered in the courtyard to be ceremonially beaten. This beating with sticks that have been medicated is said to *thusa* (help) the neophytes just as the *hu thusa* ceremony of a baby on the day it is first taken out of the hut strengthens it to withstand evil influences of the outside world. This beating is thus conceived to give health to the neophyte. The head of the school (Rasekwalo) himself stood at the gate holding two canes, a bent one in the left hand, a straight one in the right. As each boy passed with bent head and bare back, Rasekwalo, while pretending to beat with the left hand, really beat on the back with his right. The boys then put on the shirts they had had to doff for the beating and were conducted, filled with fearful anticipation, to the lodge by shepherds, who surrounded them and told them to look straight ahead.

On their arrival in the enclosure, they were made to kneel in two rows facing each other with bent heads for the operation. First some one blowing a spirit whistle brushed a handful of *muhulani* grass (*Rhynchelytrum repens*) over their heads, then two operators, one for each row, came with awl and knife. Four semicircular cuts are made on either cheek from mouth to cheekbone, the awl being used for lifting up the flesh. The process is very painful, but no importance is attached to manliness and the drumming and whistling drown all cries. Immediately after the operation, a piece of cloth (of any colour), bought by each boy for 6*d*. at the store, is put over the head, with loose ends hanging over the face and tucked in at the back under the shirt. This cloth must be worn when the initiates walk about, so that the cuts are not seen by the uninitiated, who are told that the boys are bitten by the *gɔma*. To Madume it came as a great surprise to find that the crying of the spirits was caused by whistles. After the operation the men whistled the song, 'Whoever reveals a *gɔma* brings about his own death or that of his father or mother', which was interpreted for the benefit of those who found it difficult to follow the whistling. They set out for home again almost immediately after the operation, for the formulae of the *gomana* are taught them at home.

The journey home was slow. The initiates, accompanied by five shepherds, walked, whistling as they went and holding sticks they had cut. Soon they met a man and were ordered by the shepherds to whistle '*mulao wa ga*' (my law). The stranger in reply recited a *gomana* law for them. A little further on they came upon three women and a man, all of whom fled on their approach, for, should they meet any one unable to give them a law, he is beaten unmercifully. The next initiated man they met asked the initiates to give him a law after he had recited one and, when they could not, he demanded 'his leg', i.e. each boy was to sit down holding up the left leg to be seized and beaten. As, however, they had not yet had an opportunity of learning any formulae, their shepherds procured exemption for them by giving the man snuff instead. That night they asked for food at a village, for they had had nothing all day, but the man insisted on their sleeping there and killed a goat in their honour. They set out again long before dawn so as not to be seen by women.

At home an enclosure of branches was made for them very near the village where they had to spend their time for the next few weeks. Here their food was brought from home by the shepherds, but they slept in the village in huts set aside for this purpose, coming in late at night and leaving again before dawn when women began to stamp. There were no food regulations. By day the smallest boys went out to herd goats, but the old initiates remained in the lodge, going out every afternoon either to fetch wood, each one log only, for the evening fires, or sometimes to hunt birds. When outside the lodge, they have to whistle as a warning to the uninitiated not to approach too near. They may not talk to each other except when out of sight. During this time many formulae, most of which are quite meaningless to the initiates as well as to older people, are taught by the shepherds, who beat them when they are unable to remember them; but there are no songs. The laws are passwords which indicate that you have been initiated. On the day after their arrival home, powdered medicine was given the initiates to put in their wounds, but for the rest one day was much like another. By the fifth week, when they were all thoroughly bored and tired, the order was given that they must go and wash at a place near Maulwi called *vuṭaba-mavoha* (where the *gomana* initiates wash). While they washed, the *zwiḍajani* were crying in the bush and the big sacred drum at Maulwi was beaten a few times. Then they went home where, on kneeling to greet, each one received 1s. from his parents (*hu noswa*). The lodge is merely broken down and the cloths taken home to be used. The *gomana* initiation is an initiation into a cult rather than a 'school', for, beside the formulae, the boys receive no instruction beyond the warning not to divulge what they have seen in the *gomana* lodge. The main purpose of their seclusion is to enable their wounds to heal before they can take part in ordinary life.

The *vyali*, generally looked upon as an initiation for girls, is to a great extent also the concern of old and mature men, who from a certain stage take part in it as fully as, if not more so than, the older women. Further, in many districts, though not at the royal village where they do not have *vuhwera* (their boys undergoing a kind of attenuated form of this initiation for a few days only at Maunadala's), the *vuhwera* for boys is held simultaneously with the *vyali*, but beginning rather later when the grass is sufficiently long to be used for the elaborate costumes worn. As in the case of circumcision, the *vyali*, though of national importance, is held locally by various district heads. Only those heads whose ancestors traditionally have held the *vyali* are allowed to hold it, and control is exercised by the fact that permission (literally, *khiso kha mullo*, or firebrand) has to be obtained from the queen by all those wishing to hold a *vyali* by payment of £1. One finds considerable variation from one district to another. In some the *vyali* only is held, their boys having to go elsewhere for initiation into *vuhwera*; in others *vuhwera* is held simultaneously with the *vyali*, while everywhere there are variations in detail according to the doctor responsible for the initiation or the religious habits and desires of the headman holding the initiation. Hence it is that, while at the royal village men of the last regiment (*maŋgwɛ*—Leopards) were in 1939 considered too young to be allowed to enter the enclosure of the girls or the place where the old men sit with their wonderful Bird, in many of the districts they were not debarred at all. At the great opening ceremony, when the gods of whoever holds the school are approached for their blessings, those of the royal *vyali* were merely 'cooled' by the spurting of water and a prayer, whereas those of Relɛla were propitiated with beer brought to the family graves in the depths of the forest. And while at the royal village the initiates were smeared with the stomach contents of a head of cattle killed by being shot, for those of Relɛla the tail fat of a sheep ritually killed with a medicated knife was used, the stomach contents being mixed with medicine for strengthening the enclosure. The doctor at the royal ceremony carried all the meat of the slaughtered beasts away on donkeys for his own private use, but at Relɛla the assembled company, including men, ate the meat with medicine. The institution is sufficiently flexible to allow for changes in keeping with modern needs and modern ideas: six European nails were allowed in the construction of the hut of the Bird, a stipulation being made that they should not be visible, loin cloths of material took the place of hide in many areas and other, more far-reaching innovations differentiated the 1939 ceremony from those in olden days. All the 'schools' do not open simultaneously: months after the queen's *vyali* had begun in 1939, district heads were sending to ask permission to hold theirs, while even in the queen's own *vyali* new initiates were joining as much as five months after the opening. In a society where time is unimportant this is not unexpected.

It is not possible here to give a detailed account of *vyali* ceremonial. Only a few of its most important aspects and main functions will be touched upon. Considerable emphasis is laid in the *vyali* on age and rank. The initiates have to be very respectful towards old men and women, greeting them in a special manner (kneeling and clapping with hollowed hands) whenever they pass them. This general pattern is exactly the same as that found in the *vudiga*, the boys' circumcision. The last initiated regiment is to some extent in authority over the novices. Yet the initiates themselves vary in age from small girls of seven or eight to married women. Indeed, in the 1939 *vyali*, held after a lapse of thirty-five years, it was found necessary to divide the initiates into two distinct regiments. Each local *vyali* has its office-bearers, whose rank above that of the rest is emphasized in a number of ways. Chief among all initiates is the *muluvɛ*, the nearest relative of the chief or district head. She represents all the initiates, just as the queen represents the whole tribe, and so intimate is the bond between the *muluvɛ* and the others thought to be that witches wishing to harm the whole 'school' may do so through her, and in 1939, when a snake appeared in the courtyard of initiates at the royal village, the chief initiate only was 'doctored' and the snake disappeared. She is distinguished from the rest by a special kind of dress and is always given good things to eat by another office-bearer, her 'dog', whose duty it is also to run before her, barking, when the rest are given work to do or are taken to the veld. Another office-bearer is the 'shade' of the chief initiate; towards the end of the initiation, she holds a branch above the latter's head to keep off the sun. There are some half a dozen office-bearers among initiates, as well as among the women in charge; they sit at specially prepared fireplaces and their precedence is recognized in all ceremonial.

The *vyali* is of such importance that during the year that it lasts it overshadows everything else. All men's attention, all men's energies, are taken up by the *vyali*, to which everything else becomes subsidiary. Even in the *khɔrɔ*, the forum of the men, only essential cases are dealt with. All marriages are held up: any one having the temerity to take a bride to his home during the *vyali* must pay a fine of one head of cattle and a goat. To such an extent are the attention and interest of the whole country focused on the *vyali* that no rival ceremonial is tolerated. There may be no dancing other than *vyali* dancing, no singing of songs other than those sung in the *vyali*. Even the dancing of possessed people is prohibited, a taboo communicated to the various possessing spirits at a large farewell dance of all the possessed in the area just prior to the opening of the *vyali*, when they are ordered not to manifest themselves and told that none of the usual taboos of the cult will be observed for the next year. It is customary, too, before the opening of the *vyali* for each district head to bring a farewell *gɔsha* dance to the royal village, but this was omitted in 1938 owing to the length of time it would require. The flexibility of Lovedu rules is illustrated also in the permission which the queen gave in 1938 to people on a European farm who wanted to hold a *gɔsha* for Christmas, to do so, though for one day only. These rules bind even the spirits who, during the *vyali*, never come to sing and whistle when there is a harvest offering.

There is a period of preparation lasting about a month or six weeks in which the initiates are taught some of the songs they are to sing, the manner in which they have to greet their elders, and the way in which debarked wood will have to be collected. Only after this preparatory schooling does the official opening take place. On this occasion the doctor in control of the 'school' strengthens the girls for the initiation by means of special medical treatment and reinforces the courtyard of the chief or district head, where the initiation is held, against the entry of witches who may wish to harm the girls. The initiates are ritually beaten with medicated sticks as at the *gomana*, precedence being given to the office-bearers of the *vyali*. It is significant that medical treatment is not confined to initiates, but includes, not only the 'owners' or holders of the 'school', but in many instances also all the older men and women present. It is done to make the ceremony a success. After their treatment, the initiates may not wash until about ten days have elapsed, when the 'mother' of the 'school' takes them to the river. From this time the novices, except in the case of pregnant women, are allowed no covering over the shoulder or body. Their loin-coverings should consist of hard, unworked skins, but in the 1939 *vyali*, owing to the difficulty of obtaining skins, European cloth was allowed.

From now the *vyali*, held in the *khɔrɔ* of the district head or chief, will continue for a period of a full year. Except on a few special occasions, however, all the activities are confined to the evenings and early mornings, leaving the initiates free to carry on their ordinary work at home for the greater part of the day. Most of the initiates sleep at home and married women become pregnant and have their babies during the year of their initiation without any inconvenience.

One of the most important activities of the *vyali* is the singing and drumming every morning and evening during the whole period of the initiation. Some of the songs are related to the stage of the initiation, different stages being characterized by different songs: thus after the medical treatment marking the official opening in about September a new song that has not been practised previously is begun, and later, when summer fruits are plentiful, a song is sung in which this abundance is mentioned. There is a cluster of songs associated with bringing the singing to a close each evening, when the *khɔrɔ* has to be closed by the girls, and again in the early morning, when the gate is opened. Most of the songs consist of a simple phrase repeated over and over again, the words of which are meaningless to the singers, and frequently, even where the song is long, only a small portion of it is repeated. There are songs consisting of praises of the queen, well-known district heads, and their areas, and a very important one in praise of the chief girl of the *vyali*. One song sung by the 'shepherds' refers to girls who enter only towards the end of the initiation, pointing out how inferior this is to full initiation, while another exhorts initiates to pinch and otherwise torment such girls. *Musɛvɛthɔ* songs, which are accompanied by dancing and begun in about December, are the main feature of the singing after the Bird, the pivot of the ceremony, has arrived (April). They are very similar to *lesugu* songs sung for rain, associated with the *zwiḍajani* spirits, and are believed to be identical in function. There are also *lesugu* songs in the *vyali*, and it is significant that among the Nareni there is each year a woman's counterpart of the *gomana* drumming in which *lesugu* songs are sung. If any initiate is seduced during the period of initiation, special songs of derision are sung in which she and her family are mentioned by name. Where the songs have no dancing accompaniment, they are sung to the clapping of hands until the arrival of the Bird, when two flat pieces of wood are used.

Initiation is considered to be a time of hardship for those who undergo it. The singing every evening, sometimes as late as eleven o'clock and every morning from about five o'clock till after sunrise, is looked upon as a burden that has each time to be 'lifted' (*hu rula*) by the order of some old woman or man until the arrival of the Bird, when it will *rula* the girls at its own pleasure. Only on rare occasions, when an important visitor comes and presents the older women with a gift of snuff or money, can initiates be excused altogether for an evening. It is a hardship, too, to go all through the winter, mild though it is in the lowveld, with no covering over the upper part of the body—so much so that one married woman in the 1939 initiation pretended she was pregnant in order that she might cover her body. When she was discovered, however, she was severely beaten. The discipline of the *vyali* is not so strict that initiates are not able occasionally to absent themselves unnoticed from the singing. If discovered, they are beaten, sometimes by the queen herself. More serious cases in which an initiate has been absent for several days are treated more drastically: a whole procession of women carrying the drums sets out to her village where they pull the thatch off the roofs of the houses and exact a fine of a goat, which is killed and eaten by women and initiates alike. Breaches of the rules in the *vyali* are punished in the 'school' itself: when a number of girls shaved their hair, an action strictly forbidden during the year of initiation, not only they but all their age-mates were beaten for the offence. As a result, the offenders were pinched and ill-treated by their fellow initiates, who had been punished on their behalf. Initiates who quarrel among themselves are beaten when they gather in the enclosure to sing. There are no hardships connected with food, but on various occasions, when the girls are taken out to be shown secret objects (*digɔma*), they are beaten—and one may see the marks of the sticks on their bare backs when they return. Sometimes there is an ordeal, such as being made to crawl along a path strewn with the velvet stinging-bean which causes intense irritation and itching over the whole body.

But such hardships occur only on special occasions and are by no means the order of the day. We should also be careful not to construe the beatings in terms of our conceptions. Where we have seen them, they were half serious, half playful—for instance, when the attendant of the Bird, amid merriment from the onlookers, chastised late-comers to the evening performance, the force of the blows being spent innocuously upon the skirts of the girls as they ran past him to take their places. The hardships and beatings certainly do not depress even the smallest of the girls. During the *morula* season they had to make a large quantity of cider which was consumed by initiated women, who gave a little also to the men, and, on one occasion, when the courtyard became overgrown with grass, the initiates were made to weed it. These tasks over a period of a whole year indicate clearly that work is not a major hardship.

A most essential aspect of the *vyali* is the showing of *digɔma*, usually in some secluded spot to which the initiates are taken, but also on occasion at home in the evening, when there will be dancing all night (*khilalawemi*—night of standing). The connotation of the word *gɔma* is difficult to grasp. A *gɔma* is something secret and wonderful, something which it is a privilege to see and which is usually shown to initiates during an initiation.

Though made by men or women, there is something almost supernatural about a *gɔma*: its manufacture is called 'giving birth to' (*hu dzwala digɔma*) and though, for example, in the case of a dancing *gɔma*, every one knows that some person is playing the part, this in no way detracts from its importance. Many of the *digɔma* are masked figures in costumes made of grass, reeds, or leaves. Some are mummeries with a meaning attached; others are simply interesting or wonderful objects. One *gɔma*, *dau* (lion), consists of a sound made by passing the hand down a stick on a piece of hide held over a pot. These *digmɔa* are traditional in initiations, but very often new ones are invented and, since different regiments or areas come on many ceremonial occasions with their own *digɔma*, there may be a mild competitive element in the showing of *digɔma*, especially in *khɔba* and *vyali*. Laws taught in initiation ceremonial are also referred to as *digɔma*. But the greatest of all *digɔma* are the *gomana* drums, which are looked upon as gods and are associated with the ancestors and religious ritual. *Digɔma* vary from laws or mummeries to semi-gods. The element of awe, so conspicuously absent in Lovedu religious practices, is found in their attitude towards *digɔma*—not that there is any display of awe towards them or in their presence, but that in referring to some of them people talk as though of something awesome or god-like. Even the *zwidajani*, ancestral spirits, who come to earth when *gomana* drums are played or at religious ceremonies, are thought of as *digɔma*, which in this manner become part of religion itself.

The greatest *gɔma* of the *vyali* is *khiudogani* or *khiudogala*, referred to also as the great Bird of Muhale or of Rhodesia who, like most *digɔma*, is believed to come from a pool in the river. It is a *gɔma* of the men and manifests itself only when there is moonlight, returning, it is said, to its pool when the moon is dark. But it is always there, secreted in its enclosure. The girls have to sing whether it is there or not, and often, though the moon is dark, it whistles its directions and commands. It consists of a light, semicircular framework about 4 ft. high, over which are put strings of the *muga* thorn tree (*Acacia rehmanniana*), which have been placed in water to become black. Surmounting it all is a small head crowned with an ostrich or other feather. It is seen only occasionally, when it comes dancing into the *vyali* courtyard at night, and, in spite of bright moonlight, its black colour makes it difficult to discern it clearly. It speaks and sings by whistling through an instrument similar to, but larger than, that used by *zwidajani*, made of the leg-bone of cattle.

This Bird is the ruling spirit of the *vyali*. It has many praises used by the girls in its honour. Coming as it does when the green foods of summer are being eaten and the grass is long, it is the embodiment of plenty and has daily to receive from each initiate summer foods and beer. All the time it is there every one in the area who makes beer has to bring one calabash to its enclosure. If this is not observed the person may be fined. The Bird regulates the whole procedure of the *vyali*, ordering which songs have to be sung, telling the girls when to dance, when to stop singing, what to do. At times it even gets angry and then, if it is dancing, it may stamp out the courtyard fires. Any infringement of the rules of the school are referred to as 'breaking the ribs' (*hu rɔva letagori*) of the Bird. One man was fined a goat for beating his wife. The Bird said, 'You've beaten my *muṭagani*' (married initiate); another, an important official in the *vyali*, was fined for swearing at an initiate who made a mistake in her answers to the Bird. From the time of its arrival, the women of the village may not get up and begin stamping in the early mornings before the Bird has made itself heard, and it is even said that *khiuḍogani* does not like cocks near the village, because they crow before he has begun to whistle and so disregard his precedence.

The arrival of *khiuḍogani* is a culminating point in the *vyali* and comes after long and elaborate preparations. For months before its arrival, men have been erecting various enclosures beside the village—one enclosure and hut to house the Bird itself, leading into a large courtyard in which the singing and drumming of the initiates is to take place once the Bird has arrived. At the far end of the courtyard is a row of de-barked poles set up in a specially medicated furrow, backing a carefully prepared platform on and around which the initiates stand when singing in the mornings and evenings. It is looked upon by the initiates as a kind of refuge from the Bird should he come too near. In front of this *levalɛlo* stands the *khulunoni* shrine of the *vyali*, a long medicated pole of *musoso* (*Terminalia sericea*) forking at the top end into a circlet of branches. Round this pole a circular mound has been built, containing a river stone like many religious shrines. Here it is that the initiates have to stand when conversing with the Bird. Besides the enclosure, there are other preparations for the arrival of the Bird. From February and March, when the grass is long enough, bandoliers of *leṭaṭe* rush (*Mariscus sp.*) to be worn by the initiates once the Bird has arrived, are woven, dancing skirts of a special kind of reed strung together in pieces about 1 in. long are made, and pointed, flat pieces of wood, two for each girl, are prepared for use while singing. No significance is attached to their manufacture.

A great deal of the ceremonial of the *vyali* centres on the Bird and, in the ritual conversations that take place morning and evening between the women and the Bird, special terms peculiar to the *vyali* are employed: mealies are 'teeth of Shangana-Ṭonga'; beer is 'fat of the crocodile'; native potatoes are 'fingers of the baboon'; firewood is 'bones of the giraffe'. Every day some girls and women are detailed to carry the drums at about four o'clock in the afternoon to the enclosure, there to await the pleasure of the Bird. Sooner or later the Bird whistles out '*muluvɛ a Khidigwe*', the opening phrase of the praise of the head of the initiates, whereupon one of the girls (any one—not necessarily the chief girl herself) mounts the shrine and replies in a loud voice, 'I've been waiting here a long while, Bird of Muhale', adding one of its many praises. 'Whose *myali* (initiate) are you?' asks the Bird. 'I am the *myali* of So-and-so' (giving the name of her father). The Bird will then, whistling metaphorical phrases, order the drums to be beaten, indicating what song is to be sung. The sounding of the drums is the signal for all the initiates to come to the enclosure, which gradually fills as they arrive in twos and threes. After much singing and drumming, the Bird may ask, 'What have you brought me?' to which the initiate, replying, answers, 'Crocodile's fat', or whatever she has brought. In the 1938–9 *vyali* there was at the royal village an arrangement whereby a certain number of girls brought beer every evening (six to eight calabashes), while in the mornings each initiate came with green mealies, nuts, or any appetizing dish. These are put down at a certain spot from where the *lumati* and *lumatyana*, men who act as go-betweens when the Bird is crying, interpreting if necessary what he says, carry it all into the Bird's enclosure, where it is consumed by old men. During the *vyali* these old men sleep in that enclosure if they like, and greatly enjoy the good food brought for the Bird. Sometimes, when too much for them has accumulated, they may send some to the queen or district head. Later the Bird orders the girls to eat their supper, which they have brought with them, and after a long time gives the order to stop, 'Kwaŋga'. After a while the Bird asks for his wood. Each initiate has brought one piece of wood, with bark removed, lest, it is said, scorpions which are apt to be found in the bark bite the Bird, and at the order of the Bird all proceed to a spot near the entrance to the Bird's enclosure. Here at a given signal they throw down their wood with a great noise and rush back to their platform of safety. If the moon is bright, the girls will be told to don their dancing skirts and do their whirling dance and, if it likes, the Bird itself will come dancing in, keeping to the shadows, and with one or two men always near to act as guides. They are given the order to stop by the Bird at about ten or eleven o'clock at night or eight o'clock in the morning.

Towards the end of the *vyali*, when *musɛvɛthɔ* songs are sung, the older men come and dance before the women, waving ox tails in their hands. They would, in the *vyali* of old, wave the tail over the head of a woman they liked and, if she acknowledged it by bowing the head and clapping with hollowed hands, she was giving her consent to be his lover during the initiation. For a remarkable feature of the *vyali* was promiscuous sexual intercourse between men and women in which initiates could take part only at the end. In the 1938–9 *vyali* there was no such intercourse: it was thought that the young married men were too 'wild' (owing to modern conditions) to tolerate a position in which the older men could have free access to their wives in the initiation, and it was said that the great preponderance of women over men might lead to great jealousies and conflicts between the women for the favours of the old men.

Towards the end of the initiation a number of important events takes place. There is, first of all, a ceremony in which the old men tie up the hair of initiates—which during the year has grown to a length of an inch or two—in tufts all over the head with strings of the bark of *mutswiriri* (*Bauhinia Galpinii*). After this the women belonging to the previously initiated regiment come into the enclosure one by one, dancing and shouting the praise titles of any area in the country. They are followed by the initiates, beginning with the office-bearers, and the ceremony therefore takes a full day or longer. While this is going on, one of the girl initiates, who is addressed by the praise-title of a wife (*muṭanoni*) of the queen, is taken to have her hair shaved and is dressed in a leopard skin with a collarette of beads round the neck. On her return a mat is spread for her to sit on and she does obeisance in the normal manner (not the manner of initiates). Another office-bearer (*muridi*) is given a standard of feathers to shade the head girl. After much dancing, cloths are tied round the initiates in the manner common to the possessed. This ceremony foreshadows the end of the initiation and indicates to the whole country that it is drawing to a close. The last month is devoted to dancing: every area that is holding a *vyali* sends its initiates to dance before the queen, some coming with *vuhwera*, others without. Last of all come the people of Rauothata with the *magɔgɔbya* and it is their performance that closes the 'school'. The *magɔgɔbya* have more imposing costumes even than the *vuhwera*, characterized by the stuffed baboon and duiker that surmount them. After a number of important *digɔma* have been shown, there is a grand finale one night (*khilalawemi*), when the Bird hangs its head sideways and says, 'My head aches and I know my end has come.' A *gɔma* of the women, the Butterfly (*khiruruvɛlɛ*), dressed in leaves, comes dancing in at the girls' entrance to tease and chase the Bird. Before sunrise, when the Bird has returned to its hut, some of the initiates (those who have come for a short time only) may be taken to 'touch the Bird', a terrible ordeal. Then next morning they are all taken to the river, where they are shaved and given new clothes to wear. They are now 'things from the rubbish heap' (*zwigwamathukhu*), like boys after circumcision: they walk in a bent position, may not speak freely, receive gifts, and at night ask riddles (*dinyɛbo*) specially associated with initiations. The enclosures are burnt. After a final washing in the river the initiates return to ordinary life and activities. A small operation is performed on initiates at the river on the last day. Among some tribes it consists of defloration, but among the Lovedu it is said to consist of a cut above the clitoris which is so small that it causes no pain or inconvenience.

At the time when the initiates make preparations for the arrival of the Bird (February–March), the boys of those areas that have the *vuhwera* as well are taken out into the bush every day to learn how to weave the elaborate costumes associated with this initiation. These are of two types: a light one, said to be for hunting, and a heavy one. Both costumes have skirts of loose-hanging grass, flung out in a circle by the gyrations of the dancer, as well as comely waist, arm, and leg bands and under-skirts of woven grass. The light costume has in addition broad shoulder bands crossing over chest and back and a mask resting upon the shoulders, veiling the face and open at the top. The heavy costume is far more imposing. Besides a woven waistcoat, there is an immense covering for head and shoulders, rising to a crested summit, flanked by what gives the impression of scales arranged in rows or projecting wings, and fronted by a snout like that of a crocodile. The dance reminds one, now of the prancings of a male bird courting its mate, now of a lizard convulsively shaking its whole body as it rests upon a rock. The lizard-bird suggests a weird dragon-like mythical monster, but its appearance belies its functions and qualities, though perhaps not the mystical meaning of the *digɔma* of the 'school'.

The enclosure for *vuhwera* boys is made beside that for the Bird. Here, after having being beaten with medicated sticks, the boys spend their time, except when out hunting or dancing, their food being brought to the *vyali* courtyard by their sisters. They are taught a few 'laws' or formulae associated with the *vuhwera*, but their main activities are learning to make the elaborately woven costumes and later to dance in the *vyali* courtyard. Towards the end of the initiation they spend most of their time going about to dance, accepting invitations from other district heads and paying their respects at the royal village. They do beautiful movements to the drumming of their own *vyali* girls. Only two dance at a time and, while they dance, attendants (*medabi*) stand near by supervising. The masked boys may whistle out the tune to which they wish to dance or may beg snuff by means of whistling (for this is their only means of conversation during their initiation). When they dance well, women and girls come to give them gifts of leg- or arm-rings. The *vuhwera* is a kind of finishing school, an initiation into the secret of what the Bird is and how the costumes are made. It is almost as though this is an esoteric art, the preservation of which has become the main function of the *vuhwera*. A person who enters the *vuhwera* enclosure may be required to display his skill at weaving and in 1939 a man who was unable to weave (and thus showed himself to be uninitiated) was heavily fined. The fact that there is no *vuhwera* held at the royal kraal, whose boys used in the old days to go for this initiation to Khaḍa or to the *Tzaneni*, a section of the Khaḍa, suggests that the institution is a more recent adoption than the *vyali*.

It is not easy for a European to appreciate the meaning and value of such institutions as *vyali* and *vuhwera*. Most of their features cannot be explained by the Lovedu themselves. They are the result of a long, historical development which, in the absence of all evidence, may never be unravelled. The *vyali* has many aspects. One of the most important is that of a crossing or initiation similar to circumcision. The initiates are often called *vawedi* (crossers) and initiation may be referred to as 'to cross over' (*hu uɛla*). It is conceived as a period of hardship, a crossing for which medical treatment and ancestral blessings are essential. Respect for those older than oneself is emphasized: the initiates must be humble; but older people, especially the old men who remain in the Bird's enclosure, live royally on the beer and delicacies brought daily by initiates. There is emphasis, too, on the importance of the rank of district heads and chief, and the learning of praises of all the areas, followed towards the end of the initiation by inter-district visits, is an important feature.

Intermingled with and overshadowing the *vyali* as an initiation is the *vyali* as a fertility and rain cult, related to the *gomana* drum cult and serving the same purpose. The *vyali* lasts a year, a full agricultural cycle, and some of its stages are associated with the seasons: the typical *vyali* dress of the girls cannot be plaited till the grass has grown long; the Bird arrives only when there is plenty of food. The singing of *vyali* songs is believed to bring rain. Even before the rains of the summer of 1938–9 had fallen, it was said in Uulovedu that the year would be one of plenty on account of the *vyali*. These expectations were more than realized, for not only was the summer rainy, but even the winter, which is normally dry, was exceptionally wet. Stress is laid in the *vyali* on grass and vegetation: the girls wear plaited bandoliers of grass which are said by some to render them fertile; the *digɔma* are almost all made of grasses, reeds, or leaves; the remarkable *vahwera* costumes are made of various special kinds of grass; and on one of the most important excursions made by the *vyali* girls, called *maiḍini* (at the locusts), they are made to collect the bark of various kinds of trees. The *vyali* as a fertility rite is most clearly seen in the sexual intercourse at the order of the Bird which used to be indulged in towards the end of the initiation on the approach of spring. The true meaning of the Bird is difficult to discover, though it is significant that it is associated with moonlight, comes from a pool, and declares on its departure that it will leave mists behind it. In one praise song of the Bird it appears to be referred to as *vaḍaja*, the ancestral spirits: 'I have heard you, Bird of ours and Rahufa of Muhale. The father of giving has gone, O *vaḍaja*. There remain only things for which one must pay' (*Gi hu phulaphudɛ noni yesu le vuRahufa a Muhale rahufa khi ile, vaḍaja, hu sadɛ kha muthɛgo fɛla*). This Bird, *gɔma* of the old men, is related to the *gomana* cult, using the same method of whistling through an instrument.

The Lovedu appear to have borrowed *vyali* and *vuhwera* and the *gomana* drum cult from neighbours. Some elements, like *zwiḍajani*, have become firmly embedded in a number of institutions; others, like *vuhwera*, are looked upon more as entertaining appurtenances without any very serious meaning beyond that of giving pleasure. But the sacred drum cult clashes to some extent with the rain cult of the queen and there is little doubt that to this fact one must partly attribute the failure to beat *gomana* drums in recent years.

CHAPTER IX

MARRIAGE AND THE SOCIAL STRUCTURE

Mate selection and marriage exchanges as reflections of the social structure—social and psychological aspects of nuptial rites—the handling of the themes of sex and concubinage, of barrenness and premature death in the marriage situation.

FROM mummeries and masks we turn to marriage and *munywalo* (bride-price). The secrecy of the *digɔma* contrasts strangely with the publicity of marriage ceremonial; but they are both cultural devices for dealing with cultural problems. The hidden forces in nature and man are intractable and can be brought under control only by rephrasing them as mysteries, the fear of which is overcome by man-made initiations and cults. Marriage is also an initiation, but its complicated ceremonial is concerned chiefly with laying the concrete foundations of the social structure. This is a gigantic and delicate task, almost beyond the capacity of the culture. Fortunately, we can see more clearly than in the case of the *digɔma* how this task has been accomplished, but unfortunately we shall have space merely to glance at the larger features instead of examining closely the exquisite workmanship and superlative ornamentation.

It is not easy to appreciate the immense implications of marriage among the Lovedu. For one thing, the concomitant cattle exchanges transform it into something wholly unlike the contract between two individuals of different sex among us. The fact that a Lovedu woman may, just like a man, marry a wife, warns us that we are in a world entirely different from our own. The elaborate ceremonial reflects the enormous importance of marriage and of the network of links that are forged by the cattle that pass. The bonds that are created in this manner can be put to all manner of uses. They form the basis of the *munywalo* ring of exchanges. They hold together the political system, incorporating as they do foreign elements in the tribe, and casting the net of relationship over the whole country. Marriage and *munywalo* provide the pattern even for dealing with homicide: the murder is not avenged; by handing over cattle or by giving his daughter, the murderer and his relatives become enmeshed in the network of exchanges; he is transformed from criminal to kinsman and a potential blood feud is turned into the reciprocal relations between the people of the bride and those of the groom. A man threatened with starvation when his crops have failed and his cattle have died can, by linking himself to the *munywalo* ring of another, save both himself and his family.

But the most startling proof of the importance of Lovedu marriage lies therein that the tribunals of the *khɔrɔ*—in other words, the organization that corresponds to our legal system—are mainly concerned with marriage and *munywalo* tangles; the *raison d'être* of the *khɔrɔ* and its law appear to be the preservation of the marriage system. The whole genius of *khɔrɔ* law and of *khɔrɔ* judicial proceedings is the genius of resolving tensions within the gigantic superstructure built upon marriage and its associated institutions. In these circumstances, it is patently absurd for us to orientate ourselves as if marriage affects only personal relationships between two individuals. To regard marriage as primarily a sexual partnership or even as an institution for promoting the procreation and rearing of children is to misunderstand completely its great role in the social organization.

As the main function of marriage is to create and perpetuate alliances between groups of people, sexual or temperamental compatibility between the prospective spouses is not regarded as an ideal. Emphasis on romantic love, and pre-marital sexual experimentation, with a view to testing out compatibility, would be incongruous with the prevailing type of marriage. Mate selection in its ideal form is socially regulated, and the ideal form is the basic pattern of all marriages. The social organization determines whom one shall marry, and the parents, not the individuals concerned, set the machinery of the organization into motion. The ideal marriage is marriage of a man with his mothers' brother's daughter or of a woman with her father's sister's son. This does not mean that all cross-cousins are preferred mates. It is, for instance, considered irregular for a man to marry his father's sister's daughter; that cases of such marriages are found should not surprise us. There are irregularities in every sphere of culture, and the rules of mate selection are particularly liable to be upset because of the complex interrelations that arise in the social system. The fundamental rule is that a man must marry, not the daughter of any brother of his mother, but the daughter of that brother who has used his mother's marriage cattle to obtain a wife for himself. His mother and his mother's brother are cattle-linked sister and brother because, when she married, the cattle that came in were handed to the brother for obtaining a wife: the cattle of the sister are said to 'build a hut for her brother'. We may thus say that a man must marry a daughter of his cattle-linked maternal uncle, and we may call her his 'cattle-linked cross-cousin'.

But the Lovedu phrase the matter rather differently and more significantly. They say that the sister has 'built the house of her brother' (the cattle-linked brother), that therefore she 'has a gate' by which she may enter his house, this gate being 'the gate which the cattle seek', and that it is her right to demand from the 'house built by her cattle' a daughter who must come to her as her daughter-in-law to stamp and cook for her. Note that the right is not phrased as the right of her son to obtain his wife from that house; note further that the right is in respect of the house—that is, of the wife of the cattle-linked brother, not in respect of the brother. That wife is the *muvoyi* (returner) of the sister, the person who is obliged to return her daughter to the place whence the cattle came; and it does not matter if in the house of the sister there is no son to marry this daughter. The *muvoyi* must send her daughter if requested, and, if cattle are offered, to be the daughter-in-law of her husband's cattle-linked sister, whether that sister has a son or not; for it is the sister's right to be served and helped, especially in her old age, by the daughter of the house which she has established. The ideal is that a girl should not be married to her father's sister's husband or, in other words, that a man should not marry his wife's brother's daughter. But one finds a suggestive number of cases of this marriage and, what is noteworthy is that even to-day a girl still jokingly calls her father's sister's husband *munna* (husband) and, it is said, not long ago regularly called him 'husband', while the girl's own husband was 'child' (*ŋwana*) to her. These vestiges may reflect a rather different system, not unknown in tribes further north which Lovedu *munywalo* arrangements have reshaped.

The sister may, as we have said, demand that her cattle-linked brother send his daughter either to be the wife of her son or, if she has no son, to be her daughter-in-law and, in the latter case, the sister 'marries' her cattle-linked brother's daughter on behalf of a supposititious son. If the demand is not acceded to, whether the reason be that the daughter refuses to go or her parents refuse to fulfil their obligation, the results may be disastrous. The sister (or her husband) may 'pull down the house she built at her brother's' by taking back her cattle, and she may give them to some one else who will establish a house that is prepared to fulfil its obligations; or, if the cattle have already passed on, in the chain of exchanges, from the wife of the cattle-linked brother to that wife's brother or, further still, the 'roots of the cattle' may be 'followed', perhaps involving the snapping of the chain at several points. The whole system of interrelations created by the cattle may, in such a case, be thrown out of gear and the repercussions may be so widespread that the whole country is said 'to be spoilt'. There are, however, many safety devices and the genius for effecting compromises ensures the isolation of the stresses and strains to manageable limits.

The ideal form of marriage, that of a man with his cattle-linked cross-cousin, turns out to be an inevitable consequence of the whole social system, the ground pattern of which is determined by kinship obligations though the detailed arrangements are regulated by the cattle-linking exchanges. It is conceived of not so much as a cross-cousin marriage as of a niece performing an obligation towards her cattle-linked aunt. The conception of a marriage is not wholly submerged, but it stands out far less boldly than the conception of the duty of a niece to love, cherish, and obey her cattle-linked aunt. The central feature, the pivot upon which the whole system is conceived to turn, is the passing of the cattle from a sister, by whose marriage they come in, to her uterine brother, to be used by him for the purpose of acquiring a wife; and from the wife of the brother they pass on to her uterine brother and so on *ad infinitum*. Brother and sister of the same house are cattle-linked, but each is also linked to a partner by the marriage validated by the cattle. The sister-brother cattle link and the husband-wife marriage-plus-cattle link form a continuous chain from sister to brother to wife of brother to brother of wife of brother and so on, which is doubled and redoubled in the second generation, when the same interlinking takes place and the son of the sister marries the daughter of the brother, the brother receiving cattle and the sister a daughter-in-law, while the son of the brother marries the daughter of the brother of his wife. It will be noticed that the three essential links are those between brother and sister, between husband and wife and between cattle-linked cross-cousins, and these links, as well as the whole network of subsidiary links, arise from the implications of marriage and cattle-linking. The brothers who receive the cattle from the sisters return daughters to them and again receive cattle; the brothers become the nucleus of a group providing brides, and hence, from the point of view of the sisters and their children, they are the brides or parents-in-law (*vamakhulu*), while the sister's husbands are, from the point of view of the brothers and their children, the group supplying bridegrooms (*vatsɛzi*) or sons-in-law (*vaḓuhulu*). The *vamakhulu* give brides and receive cattle; the *vaḓuhulu* give cattle and receive brides.

That is the complex network in which cross-cousin marriage is enmeshed. Cattle-linked cross-cousins are said to be 'born for' one another; a man is said to marry where his father has married, a woman is said to go to her father's sister (thus marrying where the latter has married). Actually over 60 per cent. of the men marry the cattle-linked cross-cousin 'born for them'; and she, whether married first or last, becomes the chief wife. This means that she bears the chief son. It may happen that she is not married at all during the lifetime of the man she was 'born for'; she may be too young or he may die prematurely; yet she will be the wife who must, for any important purpose, bear the chief son. If the husband 'born for her' has died or never comes into existence, and a successor to him is required in any position of importance, such as headship of a district, she will nevertheless be married to him; the cattle will pass and he who 'enters' will be some one else, chosen not by her, but by the group of the bridegrooms or, more precisely, the house of the non-existent bridegroom (which in practice more often than not means the mistress of that house). Of course, the system is not inflexible. When nothing of importance as regards status or position is at stake or, if the girl is headstrong and refuses to allow the chosen one to enter, she may 'pick up children in the bush'. But she has no right to marry any one else, though sometimes she is inherited by the brother of her supposititious spouse as if she were a widow; sometimes she merely goes to cook for her cattle-linked aunt and there bears children as if she were the chief wife of that aunt's son.

It is only a step from this situation to the further elaboration that allows a woman to marry a wife, not for her son, but for herself. If the system logically implies that a woman may have in her service a husbandless daughter-in-law doing all the work of a wife, by a slight extension of this conception she may actually marry a wife. There is ample precedent for this elaboration in the fact that the queen has wives; she is their 'husband' and to the children of her wives she is 'father' (*vubabe*). This model is followed by other women, especially women of importance and women who, as doctors and potters, have cattle of their own with which to obtain wives. In general, however, such women call their wife 'daughter-in-law', as though they had been married, not for themselves, but on behalf of a son.

It is not only these peculiar elaborations that result from the pivotal institutions of cattle-linked brother and sister and 'being born' for one

XI. DOMESTIC DUTIES
(a) DISHING UP REQUIRES GREAT SKILL
(b) STRAINING THE PRECIOUS BEER BREW

XII. THE BRIDE BECOMES A WIFE
(a) 'LITTLE BRIDE OF OCHRE, SEEK SHELTER'
(b) STILL IN HER FINERY, THE BRIDE BEGINS WORKING

another. On the one hand, the whole marriage ceremonial is based upon the assumption that it should subserve these primary arrangements; and, on the other hand, the range of permissible marriages (except marriage outside the kin) is circumscribed by their logical implications. We shall turn first to the preferential marriages. A marriage is obligatory or approved, or discouraged or strongly disapproved or absolutely interdicted, quite apart from considerations of incest, according as it strengthens and upholds or harmonizes with or strains or to a lesser or greater degree conflicts with the foundations and superstructure of the edifice erected by the cattle. We must conceive of the bonds of reciprocity between cattle-linked brothers and sisters extending eventually to the whole *munywalo* chain, which from one point of view is a chain of cattle and from another a chain of brides and bridegrooms. The cattle move in one direction, the brides in the opposite direction.

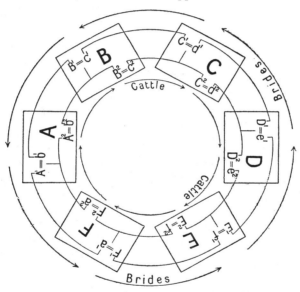

At the risk of over-simplification, we may represent the position by the diagram above, though it must be clearly understood that nothing so definite and regular will be found in the society, nor does the chain in practice form the complete ring represented for greater convenience in the diagram. The six rectangles represent, not complete patrilineal lineages, but nuclei in the patrilineal lineages of A, B, C, D, E and F. Thus A^2 is that son of the house A^1b^1 who marries where his father father A^1 married, viz. a daughter b^2 of the house B^1c^1 which has been built by the cattle coming in by the marriage of b^1 and passing to her brother B^2. If we may call the houses A^1b^1 and B^1c^1 cattle-linked, we may designate the houses A^1b^1 and A^2b^2 cattle-descent houses. The cattle-descent houses then constitute the nuclei of

L

the patrilineal rectangles, while the links between the cattle-linked houses are the primary links between these nuclei. Each nucleus, it will be observed, is linked to its immediate neighbours on the right as well as on the left. To the left it sends brides and in return receives cattle (e.g. a^2 goes to marry F^2 and the cattle for her are received by the house A^1b^1); to the right it sends the cattle so received and in return receives brides (i.e. the cattle coming in from the marriage of a^2 and received by the house A^1b^1 pass on to the house B^1c^1, whence a daughter b^2 is returned as a bride of A^2). Thus brides move continuously from the right to the left, but ordinarily only between two immediately adjacent nuclei, while cattle move right round in a clockwise manner, so that the same cattle or their offspring are in turn used by A, B, C, D, and so on. It will also be seen that each nucleus is both doubly obligated and doubly entitled. A is bride-obligated to F and cattle-obligated to B; but A is also bride-entitled in respect of B and cattle-entitled in respect of F. These are the primary reciprocal relations, but they are extended by the operation of kinship bonds beyond the nuclei of cattle-descent houses—that is, from the core of the lineage they extend to the whole lineage. The cattle-descent houses in the rectangle F, which is the group of bridegrooms in respect of A, are the core of A's sons-in-law (*vaḓuhulu*); while B similarly are the core of A's parents-in-law (*vamakhulu*) because the brides of A come from B. The core is segregated out from the larger groups by the arrangements implied in the *munywalo* system.

The vast implications of this system need not be further elaborated. But from the point of view of preferential marriages some points may be referred to. Difficulties obviously arise where in the cattle-descent houses there is an unequal number of daughters and sons. The primary cattle-linking of brother and sister, which is the pivot of the system and of the strongly institutionalized reciprocity pattern between uterine brother and sister, is necessarily thrown out of alinement by such an inequality. If in any house there are more sons than daughters, some of the sons may have to receive the cattle they need, not from their uterine sisters, but from elsewhere. Should the cattle be acquired by their own labours or the labours of their parents, there need be no upsets, for the sons may continue to marry into the group where their father married. But a new alliance may be dictated by a variety of circumstances and in that case new alinements are created: the son and his descendants become a new cattle-descent nucleus, cattle-obligated to the group whence the son's wife came. The cattle for the marriage of a son may, however, come from a relative, and in that case the simple primary arrangements of the whole system become greatly complicated.

To attempt an analysis of the complications is beyond our present purpose. All we need point out is that, provided the cattle come from the right direction (in the diagram from the left) the essential pattern is maintained and the marriages that logically follow upon the basic principle, that where a man receives cattle he must send brides, are approved. Suppose, for instance, that A^2 has no sister and hence is given the cattle that come in from the marriage of a^1, his father's sister; in that case A^2 must send his daughter to marry a^1's son F^1, and F^1 marries his cattle-linked cross-cousin-once-removed (*mudzwaladzwalani*)—that is, his mother's brother's son's daughter. This is a common and strongly approved arrangement, for the cattle-descent houses maintain their dispositions towards one another, brides from A still go to F, and cattle still move from F to A—in short, this is merely a variation upon the fundamental theme. Suppose the house A^1b^1 has only daughters, the most approved arrangement would be for b^1 to send some of the cattle to B^1, her brother, who establishes a second house from which daughters-in-law may come, and to use some to set up a house of a supposititious son through whom the cattle-descent nucleus may be continued. But if A^1 used the cattle to obtain a second wife for himself complications arise, both in the *munywalo* arrangements and in the relationship between A^1's daughter and his second wife, for, though this second wife is the daughter's *mmani* (small mother), the daughter has rights over that *mmani's* house, rights of authority incompatible with the status of a daughter. Yet the essential *munywalo* configuration, though greatly complicated, is maintained, and the arrangement is possible, though not approved. What is really surprising is an arrangement that, upon the pattern of cross-cousin marriage, appears legitimate, but turns out to be absolutely prohibited. It is said that 'two sisters cannot eat one another's property'—that is, the cattle accruing to the house of one sister though the marriage of her daughter cannot be used to provide a wife for the son of the other sister. The reason for this rule lies again in the *munywalo* configuration. If the two sisters have married into the same cattle-descent lineage, the one will be giving cattle to the other, who must return brides, and the same lineage will be both cattle- and bride-obligated to itself; if, on the other hand, they have married into different lineages, the reciprocities arising in respect of giving cattle or brides are incompatible with their possibly generations-old configuration.

Whether the system described in outline is the result of the merging of cattle exchanges and antecedent intermarrying lineages or of an elaboration of the arrangements implied in the cattle-linking of brothers and sisters superimposed upon cross-cousin marriage, it is unnecessary to determine. We are merely concerned to indicate how mate selection is regulated by its fundamental principles and thus harmonizes as completely as possible with the social organization. A man cannot marry his father's sister's daughter, because such marriage reverses cattle- and bride-giving reciprocities. But this type of marriage, though rare, does occur, and the irregularity illustrates the extreme complications in the system. Marriage with the wife's brother's daughter, which does not disturb the fundamental alinements, is quite regular; but marriage with the wife's brother's wife is impossible, as in Lovedu phraseology it is tantamount to taking back one's cattle. Seizure of this wife is a method, however, of vicariously bringing pressure to bear upon the lineage of the wife's brother, should one's wife desert. For by taking her, which is usually done only by order of court, one breaks the link between the wife's brother and the people of his wife. The wife's brother, having been deprived of his wife, can claim back his cattle from her people, and so is enabled to return the cattle to his sister's husband, thereby releasing his wife. The measure is a drastic means of getting back one's cattle, and negatives any conception of marrying the wife's brother's wife.

The *munywalo* configuration is, of course, incompatible with brother-sister exchange; the cattle cannot both come from and go into the same direction. So also does it exclude marriage of ortho-cousins, though complications introduced by reckoning relationship though the queen as if she were a male and the stress upon maintaining the purity of the royal blood lead to arrangements that appear to be based on such marriages. The children of all the queen's wives are brothers and sisters, but unless their natural fathers are identical, the formal relationship recedes before the physiological, and these brothers and sisters can and do intermarry. Moreover, in the society generally and especially among royal kin, a man may be related to another man or to a woman in many ways; what they will call one another depends upon status or rank or arrangements agreed upon between the families, and is often determined by personal choices and adjustments. A man who wishes to 'play with' his classificatory sister (reckoning relationship through, say, the father) will call her cross-cousin (reckoning relationship through, perhaps, the mother). How such a situation can arise is at once clear when we remember that a man may have a woman as his legal father, even taking her lineage name; but it arises in many other ways, such as the tremendous entanglements in the *munywalo* system. Among many neighbouring tribes a special ritual of 'cutting the kin' sometimes makes possible the marriage of incestuously related mates; among the Lovedu such a device is unknown. Many tribes have a highly developed technique of love charms; the Lovedu regard love charms as illegal, akin to sorcery and witchcraft, though there is one interesting exception, a rite based upon a religious pattern. Resort to love charms, except in the service of the arrangements of the social structure, would obviously strike at the basis of the conception that spouses are 'born for' one another.

We may now turn very briefly to the marriage ceremonial which, in harmony with the leading part played by the institution it supports, is one of the most impressive features of Lovedu life. Apart from its function of transferring the cattle and laying the foundations of a structure within which the greater part of human interrelations are enacted, the ceremonial stresses many values unconnected with marriage. The general plan of the ceremonial is patterned to the needs of the ideal form of marriage, that with the cattle-linked cross-cousin. In some neighbouring tribes, a man must bespeak his cross-cousin by paying a special beast; in others he must hand over an additional beast for her; but among the Lovedu all marriages are arranged on the one model, as if there were no other competing forms of marriage. Because the girl is said 'to be born' for the boy, his parents simply send the 'goat of the skin cradle' to intimate that he is coming. It is a most appropriate action for, as she is 'born for' him, his people must provide the wherewithal in which to carry her, the cradle symbolizing nursing, tender care, and upbringing. Marriages to strangers, nevertheless, are initiated in the same way, as if the conception of being 'born for' the boy and its implications were projected upon them. It is only in the case of cross-cousin marriage that one speaks of 'binding the kin'; but the ceremonial of all marriages significantly stresses this aim. The boy takes no prominent part in the proceedings; it is his mother who, as cattle-linked sister of his maternal uncle, is entitled to ask the uncle for a daughter and, as we have seen, he can refuse her only at the peril of having his house broken down. His sense of obligation, owing to the cattle he received, explains why the transaction must be in a ceremonial form.

There is no trace of hostility between the *vaḓuhulu* (sister's sons) and the *vamakhulu* (the people of the brother who gives the bride); they are always on the best of terms, even in the midst of the marriage negotiations. Structurally, the relationships between the two groups are liable to strains and tensions—so much so that *khɔrɔ* proceedings mainly turn upon, and have developed their special genius for effecting compromises in connexion with them. But equally the social system strives to set up reciprocities and to further smooth relations between them. An aggressive potentiality in the social system is converted into a co-operative actuality. We must expect no recriminations between the intermarrying groups, no bargaining for advantages, and no competitive displays; and indeed there are none.

All communications of a formal nature go through a *khivaga* (umpire, one who settles disputes) or *madizila* (one who goes on the road between the parties); and both sides have such an umpire. In a cattle-linked cross-cousin marriage these umpires appear on the stage, not when the 'cradle' is sent, but only later. Their main function is phrased as being official witnesses of the gifts that pass and, in actual fact, in the courts it is always upon the evidence of the *zwivaga* that reliance is placed; the *khɔrɔ* hardly ever decides what has to be returned upon divorce without calling them as witnesses. It is possible that their intervention between the parties in the marriage negotiations adds to the dignity and decorum of the situation; but they do not appear to be there to avoid the friction that in other tribes accompanies the hard bargaining. The gifts that may be asked are institutionalized and the idea that one party is trying to outwit the other is utterly foreign. The bride's people ask for what they want; the bridegroom's people do not always give it, but they never refuse: they say they will go and 'look for' it. It is a familiar formula—people are always 'looking for' the things they owe others; they may never find them, but that on the whole does not matter; what is important is the expression of their willingness. Bargaining and calculation are abhorrent; they cannot co-exist with the great reliance of the social structure upon mutuality and co-operation. And so in the marriage negotiations there is never any inquiry as to the resources of the boy's people, no tacit, much less express, agreement beforehand as to how much is to be handed over for the bride. The *munywalo* for a princess is no different from the *munywalo* for a commoner. The transactions move on slowly, perhaps over a period of many years. One may roughly distinguish certain stages, and here and there a stage, for some reason, not necessarily connected with the end result, is emphasized, marked by the delivery of a special beast or thrown into relief by a significant ceremony; but on the whole there is not the gradual unfolding of a plan such as in the initiations.

We may single out for brief consideration a few of the many aspects of the marriage ceremonial. First there is the *munywalo*, the things of marriage (*hu nywala*). Of about thirty institutionalized gifts, each with its special name and special function, some pass in connexion with a ceremony, others mark the beginning or the end of a stage in the proceedings. The average *munywalo* is eight cattle, seven goats, £11 cash and odds and ends of clothes and cloths, beads and leg-rings to the value of about £2. There are variations, but they are not determined by the rank of the bride or the affluence of the bridegroom's people; poverty of the boy's family or general scarcity of cattle in the tribe affects some individual cases or lowers the amount as a whole. The cattle, which constitute over 70 per cent. of the value of the *munywalo*, are the cattle which came in through the marriage of a girl in the family of the bridegroom. The actual average corresponds very closely to the socially approved norm to-day, which is eight cattle, eight goats, £10, and various odds and ends; yet we must not imagine that the theoretical norm weighs heavily with the people. One rather gets the impression of a muddling through, of wide latitude allowed to personal inclinations, of no one striving consciously towards absolute conformity, yet somehow attaining it.

Munywalo, above all, 'builds villages': from the point of view of a man, it 'builds a hut for his brother-in-law', because it is he who in turn uses the cattle to *nywala* (marry) a wife; from the point of view of a woman, it 'builds the house where she [as cattle-linked sister] may put her things' and which will produce a daughter-in-law for her. Her cattle are the 'cattle of the gate' which open the way for her to the house. When a wife dies, the husband reports to her people that 'the house has fallen' and they may, if they like, re-establish it with a girl who 're-opens the door'. Even underlying the names of the main gifts that pass there is the same idea; these gifts appear symbolically to build a complete village and a complete herd. The value placed upon erecting a village is intelligible, but the insignificance of the role of cattle as food is in strong contrast to the emphasis in the terminology upon building up a herd. Among the *munywalo* animals are: the 'cow-and-calf of the men's *khɔrɔ*' (*zwɛdɛ ya khoroni*), the 'cow-and-calf of the women's place', the 'axe of the *khɔrɔ*' or its 'branch', which refers to the instruments or materials with which it is built; the 'string to tie the cattle', so that they may be milked; the 'knife' that enables the recipients to exercise the supreme right of killing them and that symbolizes the acquisition of control over them; the 'manure of the cattle', which represents a commodity of value in keeping the hut tidy, and, to mention only one other, the 'beast for bartering' (*khiṯuḏɔ*), which is to be traded for the grain that will sustain the household. The names are all associated with the cattle, the courtyard, the things that go to make up a home.

There is no notion of compensation for the loss of the bride. The home which is built is linked up, through the girl, with other homes, and the same cattle continue to build homes in an endless, interlinked series which firmly holds them all together. But to build for an all-comprehensive ideal is not enough. The individual builders must be made to feel that they have a personal stake in the social investment; their desire for recognition cannot be ignored; to maintain their interest at the requisite intensity, they must be significantly rewarded. And so the 'cow-and-calf of the women's place' is conceived to be a personal reward to the bride's mother; it is her special property, not, indeed, to be detached from the chain of exchanges, for *munywalo* cattle must remain *munywalo* cattle and can never become unencumbered property of an individual, but to be preserved by her, if she so desires, in order that she may help her youngest son, who succours her in her old age. Often in the old days when the bride's chastity was an honour to be displayed, but rarely to-day, because absence of chastity is a disgrace to be concealed, the 'cow-and-calf of the woman's place' was withheld or claimed back if the bride proved not to be a virgin. As things are to-day, this gift mainly recognizes, as it also did in the old days, the special contribution of the mother to the health and strength and virtues of her daughter, the bride. The 'beast for bartering' is a contribution to help the mother of the bride, but not so much in her personal capacity as in her capacity as food-provider of the home; owing to the aversion to killing cattle, this beast passes to-day only in times of shortage when the bride's mother is really in need of grain.

The 'cow-and-calf of the courtyard' recognizes the special interest of the father and vicariously his male relatives; it is a gift that acknowledges their special services in bringing up the bride. The situation must be made acceptable also to the bride herself, for marriage is not an easy matter, involving new and heavy responsibilities and partially severing the bride from her home. In the old days the girl was usually given the *musubullo*, a cow, said to provide a change of clothing for her; to-day she is given £5 or £6 worth of clothes. But the rule that she forfeited this wedding outfit if she were found to be deflowered is in disuse to-day, since young men object to the public humiliation of their brides.

There are many other gifts which, apart from contributing to the main result, recognize particular aspects of the situation. The sending of the 'cradle', for instance, intimates that the sister lays her claim to the bride as her daughter-in-law and, when the goat is killed and members from both families partake of the meat, it is the tacit consent to the projected alliance to which the families, rather than the boy and girl, are the true parties. Or, again, the 'calabash of water', usually a goat, signifies that the boy is asking the girl to come and set up home with him, while the girl's people equally indicate with the 'goat of killing' their satisfaction that all they asked has been duly given and that, as far as they are concerned, the bride may now leave.

All too soon we must pass on to some other aspects of marriage ceremonial. The absence of strained relations between the parties makes unnecessary the subterfuges and displays of hostility often found elsewhere in marriage negotiations. The go-between, whatever message he brings from the boy's family, is well received, for 'The messenger sent to swear at a king must fulfil his mission and cannot be harmed'. His first announcement is direct and to the point: 'I am sent by So-and-so to ask whether you will *beba* them' (that is, carry the girl in the cradle). This applies to marriages between strangers, for in the case of marriages between persons 'born for' one another, there is no go-between at this stage. The girl may dislike the proposed alliance and, though there is great social pressure on her to accept a proposal coming from the father's cattle-linked sister, she is not quite powerless. The society dislikes resorting to any form of compulsion. A proverb warns people that an unwilling bride is liable to commit suicide or to suffer some misfortune, and it is legitimate to send back the answer, 'We have no power. Ask the girl.' This formula seems to contradict *munywalo* dispositions, but the culture is full of apparent contradictions testifying to its flexibility and to the subjection even of institutional arrangements to the desire for agreement and compromise. At the formal betrothal, involving a public exchange of gifts, it is quite often not the bridegroom, even if he is available, but his sister or even his daughter that acts for him. One often sees a man's daughter paying what we would call the formal courting visits, not merely on occasion, but from the beginning throughout all the years of negotiation until the end of the actual wedding. Indeed, the wedding itself may be by what we would call 'proxy'.

The courtship visits provide the prospective bridegroom with an opportunity for self-expression and contact with the age-mates of his bride, at least if he is not already an old man. Certainly, however, courtship is a conception very different from ours. The young man always takes a companion (if his sister or daughter goes, she also will take with her a girl friend) who serves as a link between him and the bride's friends. These are the affairs of the young people, which provide a whole side-show of their own, with its own rules, its observances, its entertainments and so on. There is no set number of visits and, except for the last visit, no development in the formal relations of the parties. The bride never reciprocates these visits. Restraint and caution characterize the bridegroom's, not his companion's, attitude, but he does not resist, or require any persuasion to accept the hospitality. Similarly, the bride maintains her distance, veiled in her blanket and inaccessible to her suitor, but her companions are not so reserved. The whole outward behaviour pattern is almost exactly that which is expected when a son-in-law or any member of his group visits his parents-in-law or any member of their group, with this addition that the bridegroom and bride are subject to special taboos, while by contrast, in private at least, their companions relax to an extent which we might regard as licentious.

In olden days there was a custom called *hu khatswa ditsɛzi*, whereby the leader of the group of girls placed cakes of porridge one on top of the other on her left hand and thus offered food to the visiting bridegroom and his companion, but the last cake, the one resting on her hand, could not be eaten by them. It had to be left, just as nowadays some of the food given by the girls to the visitors must be left in the basket, as a sign, they say, of their good manners. There are countless observances of this nature, designed to impress upon the visitors the importance of good manners and dignified behaviour, and upon the hosts the necessity of being hospitable to their future brother-in-law. These things are of supreme consequence in supporting the structure that the marriage will eventually build up. Courtship visits are concerned, not with courting, but with laying the foundations of the new pattern of reciprocity between the young people. They were cross-cousins before, free and easy in their relations with one another; after the marriage they are in-laws, between whom the delicate balance of adult privileges and responsibilities must be evenly maintained.

The courtship visits have other functions. They would hardly appeal to the young if there were no lighter side to the heavy burden of their serious purpose. All Lovedu ceremonial recognizes the need for diversity, for dramatic interest, for ringing the changes between the serious and the superficial, the purposeful and the playful, the grave and the comic. The bridegroom, unseen by his bride though he be, has a thrill in displaying his best clothes. He sometimes deliberately breaks taboos. In the old days the *musubullo* used to 'reveal' the bride, for only after it the bridegroom could see her and speak to her in private, a privilege he obtains to-day by a gift of a few shillings or more (*hu nosa*) long before the *musubullo* is given. Nevertheless, there is to-day adventure in going to the store, where, besides making her wishes felt by requiring this or that as part of her *musubullo* (change of clothes), the bride must be coaxed by gifts to look at one thing, to handle another, and at every step. After he brings the calabash of water, 'the beast of asking the bride to come home with him', the bridegroom and his companion come on the *hu sεla* visit. *Hu sεla* means that they will 'trouble' the girl and her companions. In other tribes the parents have to be 'begged' to release the bride; the Lovedu *hu sεla* is designed to irritate the parents so that they will be impatient of the bride's unwillingness to go and will bring pressure to bear upon her. For the *munywalo* has all passed and the will of the bride must not be allowed to cause them discomfort. The boy's companion especially makes things unpleasant. He interferes with the work of the girls, worries and annoys them at night when they want to sleep He tries to stir their hearts by playing a plaintive stringed instrument, pinches and beats them. But what is really effective is his interference with their cooking: he throws sticks and filth into the porridge pots, and the older people, always particular about the cleanliness of their food, complain bitterly and say that the bride had better go.

The drama ends usually with an exciting 'elopement' of the couple. It is not a true but an institutionalized elopement. Sometimes it does not occur and sometimes it occurs even after a religious ceremony with which, strictly speaking, it is incompatible. Indeed, theoretically the giving of the *musubullo* is supposed to exclude resort to an elopement. But the 'elopement' is so common that it is the only form usually described. One night the bridegroom, having left 1s., 'the thing resting under the mat', which in the old days was an arrow, surreptitiously escapes with the bride and her companions. The 'thing under the mat' explains the flight. The journey to the bridegroom's village is painfully slow: at each step the girls call a halt and have to be persuaded by gifts (*hu nosa*) to move on; they may even have to be pushed, threatened, carried. The bride is completely covered with a blanket amid the troop of girls as they walk in single file. The bride (and sometimes her companions too) weeps, fearful of the new life full of responsibilities. They visit the boy's cattle-linked sister to be offered a goat and as a reminder that it is that sister who with her cattle has erected the new home. There may be a dumb show as the girls, marching up and down, display their final reluctance to give up the bride and, by contrast, the old women humorously mock the girls. At the gate of the boy's village they have to be carried in, and at last, as they humbly crawl to enter the hut, some one pours water on the roof and you hear the song, 'Little bride of ochre, seek shelter, you are raining wet'.

This is merely the general plan; there are many embellishments and many variations. But of some significance and worth mentioning as illustrative of the comprehensive nature of the ceremonial are the last few gifts just before the bride leaves home. There is a goat or 10s. to 'lift' the bride from maiden to wife, for every important new step she takes may, in Lovedu phraseology, be made the occasion for asking something; another goat to 'take out the stamping block', symbolizing the transference of the bride's chief economically productive power; and still another to 'finish the complaints' of the bride's mother. Among neighbouring tribes there are similar gifts, but sometimes with different names and often, though having the same name, with different functions. A study of their reinterpretation by, and merging with the purposes of, each culture cannot be undertaken here. To two points we may, however, briefly refer. Occasionally among the Lovedu there are reciprocal feasts entailing the slaughter of a beast, first by the bride's and then by the bridegroom's family, and ending with an extra beast given by the latter to 'fill up the *munywalo*'. These feasts belong to a very different pattern, found, for instance, among the Virwa, where bride and bridegroom before the final acts are made to sit together on a mat, are offered advice and given presents. Secondly, and in strong contrast to many other tribes, the bride comes to her new home without any presents from her people. The troop of girls carry a waisted basket (*khirudwana*) in which there are certain grains from the bride's village, but everything else except the grains, even her clothes, have been given her by the bridegroom. Her people give her nothing whatever to set up a new home. Household utensils she does not need, for she cooks in the hut and uses the pots and furniture of her mother-in-law until, with the coming of a younger daughter-in-law, she becomes independent and has her own cooking hut.

In a really orthodox marriage among the Lovedu there is a religious ceremony. It is preceded by the slaughter of the 'goat of killing' brought by the bridegroom; a leg is given to him and from the skin the bride's *thevyana* (skirt) is made. Thereafter a prayer is offered to the gods on behalf of the girl: 'Here is the woman. We let you know that she is leaving us. She is going to the place where she is married. Let her be happy there; let all she does there be right; let her be smeared with fat [have children]. We have no complaint against her [i.e. we shall not cause illness through being angry and so also you should not]; we have given her beads to help her so that she may make a good home where she is going.' It is, of course, an extempore prayer, not bound to any set words. After this rite there is no need to elope; it is *hu vega*, to marry with proper rites, not *hu ṭala*, to run away surreptitiously. Yet the secret elopement by night is so interesting that it frequently follows, and in any case the slow journey of the troop of girls, who must be persuaded at every step, is always part of the ceremony.

The final stage of the marriage ceremonial consists of several successive steps lasting a month or longer. Again a whole series of new gifts (*manosa*) passes and new rites are enacted. From early morning until late at night the bride's companions are busy—cooking, stamping mealies, bringing water for the inmates of the village to wash in, and in other ways. At night there are contests of riddles between the visiting girls and the boys and girls of the village; they are ordinary riddles (*dithai*), not those curious *dinyɛbo* that end the initiations, but the pattern of the institution is the same. There is, for instance, the *hu nosa* of the girls at every turn and their exaggerated politeness. Then, after a week, having fetched wood and distributed among themselves the gifts received, the bride's companions go home, crawling out of the village and accompanied some way by the boys. The bride is now alone and, still in her finery, she begins to do the household work. When she menstruates for the first time, she secretly 'flees the moon' (*hu shava muɛdi*), running to an old woman, who takes her back with beer of 'shunning the moon' and a goat is killed for her. This shunning of the menses is a minor detail in marriage ceremonial, with rules and observances, however, in which the virginity of the bride, the part played by the go-between, the division of the beer and meat, the reciprocal duties of the *vamakhulu* and the *vaḍuhulu*, the one giving beer, the other returning a goat, are once more emphasized.

But all the rites and ceremonies are equally full of meaning, not only for the purpose in hand, but for the whole social structure. About three or four weeks after the marriage the bride goes to her home with the goat or 10s. of 'pouring out her bridehood' (*hu shulla vumyɛji*), and thereafter, according to ideal standards, the bridegroom may exercise full marital rights. This 'pouring out', with its associated observances, is still universally carried out, though the couple may already have received permission to cohabit. If the bridegroom migrates to town, as sometimes happens, before the home-bringing of the bride, the breach of orthodox rules, implied by the premature permission, is avoided. After a while the bride returns and brings the beer to 'open the way' for her mother. In the old days the boy's people then sent the *hu hobɛla* goat, the goat 'of asking permission' for the consummation of the marriage. At the stage when permission to cohabit is given, the couple are ritually mixed, the ceremony varying from mutual inoculation to common steaming under a blanket: it is a rite pregnant with meaning and with the associations it acquires as being a part of many other ritual occasions. The bride becomes an apprentice to her mother-in-law, there are avoidances and gifts (*manosa*) to remove them and so, at every stage, the marriage ceremonial is cut to the configuration of the social structure, fitted into its foundations and walls, and made to merge into the smallest details of its ornamentation.

There are scores of aspects we cannot even touch upon. There are rules as to the kind of cattle or other beasts that may properly be used as *munywalo*: the rules may seem curious to us, but they have their reason in social and other arrangements. The number seven is taboo, for the seventh finger 'points', as does a witch when he says, 'You'll *see*,' and it is wrong so to point at one's in-laws, with whom co-operation is essential. Similarly, as the size of the testicles of full-grown male animals is an insult, because it is a challenge, such uncastrated animals cannot be part of the *munywalo*. So also yellowish cattle presage jealousies between co-wives; they will cause the bride to run away. Marriage is patrilocal, otherwise a man is said 'to have been married by his wife'; it is good to live near, but not too near, one's wife's people; for, if proximity is an economic and social advantage, to live under the roof of the parents-in-law is to relinquish all authority in one's own home. Generally speaking, the bride's family do not call the bridegroom to help them with actual work, such as building huts or ploughing. But the idea of service instead of, or in addition to, *munywalo* is faintly reflected in the fact that men now still living were required towards the end of the ceremonial to build a hut for their parents-in-law. The rule was that, when a bridegroom had completed the hut, he climbed to the roof and refused to come down until the bride was immediately released to go home with him and she by greeting (*hu lɔsha*) signified her willingness to come. Such a hut in case of divorce counted as one head of cattle. And perhaps we should add, though it is clearly implied in all we have said, that no one except the boy's parents contributes and no one except the house of the girl's mother receives the *munywalo*. More than that, a man cannot help the son of one house by taking the cattle of another, for it is said, 'One house cannot eat the property of another,' though this, as everything else, is subject to the supreme principle that 'if they agree', the rigidity of the rule may be relaxed. It may involve difficult readjustments, but agreement is conceived as being able to overcome the difficulties. Sometimes also a relative who has brought up the bride is given one of the beasts of her *munywalo*, but it is not a custom as in many tribes, it is merely a matter of agreement.

The sexual aspect of marriage is treated with great moderation. Among us, where love looms large and represents a romantic ideal when we are young, it more often than not ends in disillusionment when we are old. The structure of Lovedu society lays no stress upon sexual compatibility, and marriage almost completely ignores sexual adjustments. Co-operation and agreement as regards its main purposes, both economic and structural, not companionship of husband and wife, is the ideal. Agreement is the watchword of the society, the guarantee of harmonious relations between spouses as well as co-wives. In describing the possible relations and dispositions within the family, no phrase is more frequently used than the phrase, 'if they agree'. No custom, no rule, no arrangement, decreed by the laws of the family, are absolute; and because the *khɔrɔ* judicial proceedings deal with difficulties in the family and in the social structure, they also are guided and controlled by agreement and compromises. And so it is agreement, not sexual compatibility, which is the foundation of happy marriage. It is an attitude inculcated by the immense marriage ceremonial, and it must be understood in its total complex within the social structure. Sexual adventures and compatibilities may be sought outside the marriage relationships. And so we have the *muḍavu* institution, a realistic concession to the impossibility of completely conditioning so primeval a force as sexual attraction to the purposes of the social structure; it also meets the difficulty of the long suckling period. As might be expected, it is married rather than unmarried people who have their lovers (*vaḍavu*). Nevertheless, a European finds it difficult to understand that old women so frequently have liaisons with young married men and that these men so frequently seek their adventures with women who might well be their mothers or grandmothers. But in the Lovedu system it is not unnatural that our preferences and our conceptions of sexual attraction should as often as not be completely reversed.

The ideal for girlhood is chastity, but the society is rather impatient of both men and women who spy upon the love affairs of their spouses. These affairs are not matters to be talked about; but, on the other hand, despite the mocking songs sung on special occasions (the *vyali*) about deflowered girls, the society has a humane outlook towards what we call illegitimacy. Unmarried girls among pagans rarely have illegitimate children; this is more frequent among Christians. The seducer is fined twice as much as in the case of adultery with a married woman, yet only one-third the amount that is customary among Shangana-Ṭonga. The fine is certainly not the main deterrent; nor is the disgrace of the girl. She maintains her position in society; she is congratulated by friends and relatives; even the queen herself may, as we have seen, pay a visit to see and praise the infant. The girl has been 'spoilt', but she proudly displays her baby. She will not have offers of marriage from young men, but older men are wiser. Great blame falls upon the guilty man. It is a curious mixture of values, for there is no doubt that virginity in a girl is highly esteemed. In the marriage ceremonial, as we have seen, virginity entitles both the bride's mother and herself to special rewards. There is even a symbolical reference to it in the calabash that the bride used to take with her to her husband's home: if it was whole, it occasioned joy and was proudly worn by her younger sister; if not, the girl's people had to make amends with beer.

New values and sensitiveness to-day insist that the absence of chastity be concealed, not that its presence be publicly applauded or rewarded. Girls are still examined, especially at the *khɔba*, but the matter is private; and the public display of a calabash has fallen into disuse. Yet the sins of the girl-mother are not visited on the innocent infant; it remains a thing of joy to every one. Abortions are said to be common, but the only evidence adduced is the high incidence of lung diseases (*ḍɛrɛ* or *vulwɛḍɛ vya vasadi*). A man gets *ḍɛrɛ* from intercourse with a woman who has had an abortion; it is not merely the most dreaded of all diseases, a death from *ḍɛrɛ* may prevent rain, and men are again and again in their lives warned against promiscuously consorting with women.

Sexual compatibility between husband and wife is a minor matter.

If a wife refuses cohabitation, there is usually a good reason, but a reason that has nothing to do with sexual incompatibility. The husband concerned will perhaps solicit the aid of the old women; but never will he dare say that he can go elsewhere for his pleasure, for she has equal power to retaliate in that manner. The Lovedu know of the belief of other tribes that continued sexual intercourse after pregnancy builds up the child forming in the womb. They also continue intercourse, but they do not stress, and even deny, that semen builds up the foetus. It is worth noting that sexual intercourse at a late stage of pregnancy (after the seventh month) is considered not quite correct, and this ideal is reflected in the anger of the midwives, who may reprimand the husband if they find signs, as they think, of his semen on the new-born infant. Nor is the sexual act brought into relation with so many special occasions as elsewhere; it has not to any extent been institutionalized in connexion with dangerous or new enterprises, as is the case among the Shangana-Tonga in their midst. Full coitus is taboo while a mother suckles her child; the milk of the new pregnancy will poison the child, but a child is not sent away when sexual relations are resumed. Even the theme of fertility is handled with moderation or submerged under a mass of ritual. A wife is not ochred on her first pregnancy and, in those ceremonies that are directed to fertility, this motive is kept far in the background. Likewise, barrenness in a woman is not regarded as entitling a man to nullify his marriage and, when a substitute is sent, the children are presumed to be, not the children of the barren wife, but of the substitute. The conception of 'buying a womb' is negatived by the fact that full *munywalo* is given for the substitute, who is not subservient to, but independent of, the barren wife. These arrangements also imply that barrenness is not a great humiliation. A married woman is theoretically denied the right of having children if her husband is impotent or absents himself for years. In practice, 'picking up children in the veld' is realistically tolerated, but it must be done surreptitiously, for the custom in other tribes, whereby the husband appoints a 'bull', is not approved. A wife can never be lent to another, for, as the proverb runs, 'About clothes you may say, "Lend them to me," but never about a woman' (*ŋg'adimeni gi a guvo, musadia a na ŋg'adime*).

Marital fidelity is not a matter of great importance; a father will reprimand his adulterous son, but only because in his pursuit of other women he fails in his duty to look after his wife—that is the main thing in marriage. Similarly a wife's adultery can never be the cause of divorce; but it must be judicious; it must not offend the proprieties. No doubt a man has greater opportunities than a woman and before marriage one may speak of a double standard of morality, but after marriage the differences are small. Both a husband and a wife can administer medicines to the other partner, making extra-marital irregularities very dangerous to health. A wife during pregnancy by a lover is also a grave danger to her husband. On the whole, the remarkable thing is, not that there is marital infidelity, but that there is so little of it. After all, a man may not 'mix' his wives; he cannot go from the one to the other; he cannot bring home a second wife until his first has had a child or, more usually to-day, until she is pregnant; and he has to avoid his wife to some extent until the baby is weaned, a period of three years or even more.

If a wife is barren, a substitute may, as we have seen, be sent. The whole subject of substitution is too large for adequate treatment here, but some aspects of it may be mentioned. Among the Lovedu a man may marry two sisters in the ordinary course of events, quite irrespective of whether the first married has prematurely died or is barren, but the wife's sister is not specially reserved for the husband as if he had a prior right to her. The marriage is desirable, not enjoined by the society, when it is known that the sisters will co-operate and care for each other's children. In the case of barrenness, there is substitution, but the substitute wife is not a subservient wife. It is not a case of true substitution, but a strengthening of a weak link in the chain of bride and cattle exchanges. A barren wife cannot be discarded; on the contrary, the insistence upon treating her well, though it recognizes, also represses the tendency to regard her position with misgivings. Men make a great effort, by treating a barren wife well, to elicit the praise of others, especially the queen, whose continuous interest is a guarantee that the virtue will be idealized. There are other considerations that reinforce the great concern of a female ruler for peacefulness and good relations. A man who ill-treats his barren wife need expect no reciprocity from her parents, and he has no weapons against them. He cannot demand back his cattle, for failure to have children does not vitiate the cattle exchanges. He cannot even initiate the procedure whereby his parents-in-law will send him a substitute. On the contrary, he must await their pleasure and if they do decide to send a substitute, he must *nywala* (give cattle), and he may be asked more *munywalo* than for her sister. But if he has been a good husband and is poor, less may be asked. A man realizes that the virtue of treating a barren wife well is richly rewarded.

Similarly, a husband whose wife has died prematurely without issue is in the same position: he has no right to demand a substitute or, in default, the return of the *munywalo*. When he is offered his wife's sister or other suitable substitute, he must hand over cattle for her. It is true that the substitute sets up the house that 'has fallen', but the really important point is that the relationship created by the cattle exchanges should be maintained. A husband must report the death of his wife with an ox; he must call her people to the ceremony ending the mourning period; he must continue his visits as son-in-law; he must always be prepared to help his parents-in-law. All this will not necessarily induce them to give him a substitute; and if he neglects these things, the potential right to such substitute is not effaced. On the other hand, his parents-in-law must continue to honour him when he visits, they must still send him beer, they must acknowledge relationship with him. If they do not do these things, if they spread tales that he has been the cause of the death of their daughter, the relationship may be broken; and consequently the claim to a substitute, non-existent before, now is given recognition. If they value the link broken by their conduct they must reforge it by sending a substitute; if they do not, their action has already caused it to snap and the *munywalo* must be returned. But it is only at the stage where interrelations have become intolerably strained that the widower can demand back his cattle. The law thus is that a man who has lost his wife has no right to demand a substitute; but if it appears that his parents-in-law maliciously refuse to give him one, in circumstances that break the bonds established by the *munywalo*, he may do so.

Substitutions have to be distinguished from inheritances of spouses, for the latter is not spoken of as marriage at all; it is '*hu khɔva*', to hand over or allocate, and implies looking after. Among some of the neighbouring tribes, a man may, on the death of the brother, inherit the wife of his brother, both of his elder or his younger brother. Among the Lovedu the theoretical rule is that only a younger brother may inherit an elder brother's wife; but sometimes, if the parties agree, it is the elder brother who inherits. Among some tribes a man cannot inherit his father's wives, unless they are wives that have not yet actually been married. Among them the supreme vice, the sin that disqualifies even the heir to the throne, is to 'spoil' the wives of their father. Among the Lovedu the two things are not interconnected, and a man may inherit any of his deceased father's wives, if he calls them *mmani* (little mother), which inplies that they are wives junior to his mother. A woman may inherit wives just as she may marry them, especially the widow of her cattle-linked brother, but also the widow of her elder or of her younger brother. There are no rigid rules as regards inheritance of wives; if a man's younger brothers are preferred to his sons and the latter are preferred to the sons of the younger brothers, the actual arrangements are in essence determined by the deceased's cattle-linked sister, who officiates but acts upon the advice of her father's brother or her own brothers and sisters. It is all a matter of agreement. There is no institutionalized method whereby the inherited wives may signify their approval or disapproval, but in practice they are exceedingly independent, almost invariably remain in their own village wherever the man who inherits them may be, and not infrequently become everybody's prey. They sometimes marry wives of their own, which releases them from undue dependence upon their inheritors, who are, however, obliged to assist them in the things that men do. Sometimes their gardens and houses, just as their beer drinks and entertainments, are markedly superior to those of married women; for they are able to accept favours from numerous admirers. And on the whole the lot of a widow is not an unenviable one.

A man cannot inherit his mother's sister, nor can he inherit the wife of a son of his mother's sister. Such arrangements would be incongruous with the *munywalo* complex, for 'two sisters cannot eat one another's property'. Nor may a father inherit his son's wife; it would upset the hierarchical arrangement of the society. Again, a man cannot inherit his mother's brother's wife, even if she is not the mother of his own wife. It is also curious that the Lovedu do not attach great importance to seed-raising. They speak of 'raising seed to the family' (*hu dzosa mulɔgɔ*) when a girl marries at her cattle-linked aunt's, and that is the primary meaning of the phrase. A younger brother who takes his elder brother's widow is not primarily conceived of as raising seed; his main duty is to care for her and to maintain intact the *munywalo* scheme.

The economic aspect of marriage is more important than the sexual. The duty of a niece to marry at her cattle-linked aunt's is phrased as an economic obligation. A wife has power because she is the provider of food. There are many other sources of the influence of an old woman, both over her son and her son's wife, and they have economic implications. Nagambi, a man of thirty-five, scorned to bow to his wife's wishes except when she was possessed; yet the wishes of his mother dictated when he should go to town or return home, what land he should plough and when, what medicines or doctors he should get for his baby. The apparent helplessness of women when a stranger calls and asks for information or wishes to do business is not wholly assumed, for theoretically business and politics are the affairs of the men; but often enough it is convenient to defer to the men and to exercise a woman's influence behind the scenes. Thrift and industry are the virtues valued in a wife; it is the hard-working girl who is coveted as a bride. For that reason also, a faithful concubine (*mugaula*) has in practice a high status.

Madume's brother had both a wife and a *mugaula*, and when he died the *mugaula* took all his property for her son. Madume, who denied her right to do this, brought an action and the case eventually came to the capital. The court wholly ignored the issue as to whether a *mugaula* had legal rights. It contented itself with urging the *mugaula* to give Madume control of the assets which had accrued from the work of his brother's son, warning Madume not to press his case. 'Did not the *mugaula* cook and work long for your brother?' it asked. 'And was it not due to her thrift that there are goods? You are wrong to worry her.' Unions with concubines are often stable and economically satisfactory. Quarrels, even jealousies, between a man and his *mugaula* sometimes come before the courts, just as if they were disturbances within a family. Muhale complained, not that his son was living with a *mugaula*, but that the *mugaula's* laziness had prevented him from giving a beer-drink for a whole year. When the jealousy of the *mugaula* threatened domestic trouble, the queen considered the matter important enough to send a messenger, who, with the district head, came to settle the dispute; the court dealt with the matter exactly as if the parties were married, urging mutual forbearance and co-operation. A man who illicitly lives upon a woman, eating from her porridge bowls (*madilo*), acquires no rights over her or her children, and is derisively called 'father of the porridge bowls' (*ramadilo*).

Instead of attempting to deal with the conflicts and tangles in *munywalo* and marriage, we shall refer to a few of their aspects merely. The conditioning of cross-cousins for their obligations as marital partners does not eliminate temperamental differences, and in modern conditions, which emphasize individual acquisitiveness as against reciprocity, the burden of obligations in the *munywalo* ring becomes too heavy. A father, more intent upon the polygynous circle of huts than upon maintaining the chain of *munywalo* exchanges, may use the cattle coming in from his daughter's marriage to acquire a wife for himself; and an almost unmanageable complication arises, unless there is agreement between all the persons interested: the son to whom the cattle should have been allotted, the daughter from whose marriage they came, the house established by these cattle, and the father himself. Tensions arise in many other ways: neglect of one wife and favouritism of another in respect of economic services, interference with the independence of the houses, and so on. Unwillingness to co-operate in the home and in fulfilling the wider group obligations is a more potent cause of trouble than adultery; and witchcraft, except as a symptom of tensions otherwise created, takes a minor place; and neither adultery nor witchcraft as such can snap the *munywalo* bonds.

The character of these tensions may be briefly illustrated by the case of Muʋirwa and Mara. Faced with starvation, Mara obtained cattle from Muʋirwa (who was a friend, not a relative), promising, in accordance with the 'mud-stamper' institution, a daughter in exchange. In fact, this daughter, the little 'mud-stamper', as she is called, because she is too young to stamp mealies, was not yet in existence. That is not unusual in these transactions, which require that the 'mud-stamper' shall in due course be given gratuitously to the benefactor; and thereby the two lineages become cattle-linked, so that, for instance, Mara and his descendants would have to offer brides and receive cattle and Muʋirwa and his descendants would offer cattle and receive brides. If Mara had no brides to offer, Muʋirwa would still have to give cattle; otherwise the link might be broken. The 'mud-stamper', after reaching years of discretion, may dislike the benefactor, who is usually already old and decrepit, and that may lead to conflicts. In this instance, when Mara's daughter entered her *khɔba* initiation, Muʋirwa, as is customary, paid the *levala* goat, for a bridegroom for whom a bride is 'born' must, so to speak, nurse her and 'grow' her. Not long afterwards the 'mud-stamper' died. Mara offered another daughter and, as the girl had died before actual marriage, no further *munywalo* was required from Muʋirwa. But the substitute, having grown up, married and then deserted Muʋirwa, who was already very old; she ran away to a lover, Mara himself conniving at the desertion. Mara returned some cattle to Muʋirwa, thereby severing the relationship, and promised the balance when the lover had paid *munywalo*.

Years passed and nothing happened. Muʋirwa eventually brought an action, which Magaebia, Mara's wife, contested. She said that on the death of the 'mud-stamper' she had offered to return the cattle, but this was refused, that the substitute was forced to marry Muʋirwa against her will, and that the religious ceremony was omitted. Muʋirwa replied that he had already received seventeen of the twenty-four cattle (the number to which the original eight had increased), that it was thus not he who had broken the relationship, and that the religious ceremony, which for various reasons could not be held in Mara's village, had taken place at the village of Magaebia's brother. The court could not but side with Mara, but it tried hard to reduce his claim, for twenty-four cattle, it said, were an enormous number. Then recriminations broke out between Mara and his wife, which revealed a many-sided conflict in the family. 'That woman,' said Mara, indicating his wife, 'took her daughter from Muvirwa and gave her to the lover because I had eaten four of Muvirwa's cattle. Two of them I gave to a son of another house to help him marry and two I sold for food. My wife disagreed and deserted me. Now the lover has given seven cattle to my wife. She can pay Muvirwa with them. As for me, I wash my hands of the whole matter, because my wife has deserted me.' But Magaebia replied, 'It is you who, seeing the seven cattle arrive, urged me and my daughters to marry a wife with them. They refused and the cattle have died.' The court, realizing the nature of the conflict, said, 'We see that you, Mara, were planning things to your own advantage. But you have already paid many cattle. It will be enough, if Muvirwa agrees, that you give him four more cattle, to show that you are weeping with him, for he has lost a wife (the 'mud-stamper' who died). If you do so, we shall know that you are not bad people. As for the disagreement between you and your wife, the discussion where to get the four cattle may bring you together again. Go home and decide the matter between yourselves.' The court was right. Mara had another daughter from whose marriage he was receiving cattle and he had thought of using the cattle for himself, as the daughter, siding with her mother, had also deserted him. That would have led to further complications. It was better to give way and arrange amicably with his wife how the future claims of her house should be settled. And once this was done, the cause of the conflict disappeared.

CHAPTER X

COGS IN THE POLITICAL MACHINERY

Ritual suicide, divine selection, the fire rite, and celibacy as aspects of the royal complex of institutions—links in the political system forged by the wives of the queen—the part women play in politics—structure and individuality of the districts.

THE political system is not a thing apart, standing aloof from marriage and social structure. These and other institutions are closely interwoven. The political scheme is effective largely because it is patterned upon the arrangements and relies upon the genius of the social system. Its most emphasized aspects are the elaboration of institutions which centre in the queen and the highly developed local administration in the hands of the district heads. The districts form a federation rather than a union, but their autonomy is counterbalanced by subtle devices holding them closely together in the meshes of a web radiating from the capital. The district and the tribe itself may, from certain points of view, be regarded as the village writ large, but the village is not a political unit, and the approach from its organization is not comprehensive enough for fruitful examination.

The district, with its distinctive community life, is linked to the capital upon the pattern of reciprocities created by marriage and *munywalo*, the system thus harmonizing with the most powerfully supported institutions. The reliance upon the queen as a rain-making divinity further stimulates the growth of a common tribal consciousness. Elsewhere chiefs are also rain magicians, but failure to produce rain is not a fatal defect. The Lovedu queen, however, suffers deposition if she fails, and it is upon her rain-making divinity that are based the structure of the royal institutions and much of the political system. And the two systems, centring apparently poles apart, the one in marriage and *munywalo* and the other in rain-making, have been interlocked as skilfully as the most intricate piece of machinery.

The complexity of the tribe as regards constituent groups, and the submergence of the royal group amid the other groups create a problem which, from the point of view of tribal solidarity, could conceivably be solved in many ways. The Lovedu solution stresses local autonomy side by side with social links. Many functions elsewhere reserved to chiefs are exercised by district heads, and the theoretical authority of the queen is seldom interposed in practice. Yet they are powers of persuasion, not of coercion. Her authority is congruent with the main emphases of the society: the reliance on compromise, the aversion from military institutions, and the subtlety of feminine persuasion. These characteristics promoted the willing allegiance of the many foreigners drawn to the sanctuary of Uulovedu, where they were safeguarded, not only against their foes, but also against the uncertainties of nature. In return for protection and security, they sent their daughters and sisters to be the wives of the queen. And in the system these wives, after a period of training at the royal court, were re-allocated to district heads and royal relatives.

The system is not unknown elsewhere. Among the Shona, so we are told by Bullock, when one tribe conquered another, the survivors were incorporated by being given wives; in time of famine, tribes sometimes exchanged their daughters for food; and some of the Mambo handed their wives to their bodyguard, who gave in return, not bride-price, but faithful service. The Rozwi appear to have maintained their dominance over subjected chiefs, not by deposing them, but by assisting in their ceremonial appointment and the superimposition of the cult of Mwari, the high god, which had its priesthood and could withhold rain. This cluster of institutions is interesting to us because the Lovedu came from those parts and have retained some of their features. Lovedu district heads give 'tributary' wives to the queen in exchange for rain and these wives are re-allocated to important men. But the form and setting of the institution has changed; the circulation of wives, drawn into the network of the political and social scheme, subserves the purposes of the Lovedu cultural configuration.

By singling out for brief consideration the complex of royal institutions and of districts, we are giving prominence to certain aspects of the political structure. That is unavoidable in a generalized account, which must largely ignore the variations among the 140 districts (of which fifty are on European-owned land). We have often referred to cultural divergences and the tolerance towards them. In the autonomous districts they are very much in evidence. You may be told over and over again there is no such thing as ancestors represented by snakes, except among the possessed and in their cult; and the conception seems alien to a religion in which ancestors are not reincarnated in an animal, but animals may be dedicated to ancestors. Yet suddenly one day you may find that the sacred object (*thugula*) of a head of a district, such as Relela, is a snake. The lack of uniformity and the tolerance of almost contradictory customs may give the impression of ineffective political institutions. Conformity there must be in the interests of economy and solidarity, but the conformity need not be that of a regimented society such as ours. As to the royal cluster of institutions, we shall consider those maintaining the confidence of the people in the powers of the queen, and those converting tribute of wives into the visible links of the social organization. The elaboration of the royal institutions must not, however, obscure the essential humanity of the queen; we do not deal with the latter, but we must remember that it is a factor of great importance in the dynamics of these institutions.

In 140 years there have been only three queens, and Mujaji III, after having already ruled for over forty-three years, is still physically strong and is said never to have had a day's illness. The Lovedu attach little importance to the longevity of their queens, who in other tribes have been immortalized. In the north, whence the Lovedu came, kings ruled only for brief periods; they were not allowed to become old or decrepit, lest the kingdom suffer; and either they committed suicide or they were killed. Don Santos, writing in 1607, records that the kings of

Sofala had formerly to take poison when disaster or a natural defect fell upon them. Among the Lovedu, tradition decrees that the queen shall have no physical defect and must poison herself, not when she is old, but at the end of the fourth initiation (*vudiga*) of her reign. The emergence of physical imperfections and the holding of the fourth *vudiga* cannot both determine the date of suicide. In fact, no reign has been cut short because of bodily defects, though the conception of the relation survives. The queen is believed to be immune from disease and it is thought that her first will be her last illness; it is even said that Mujaji III's elder uterine brother was excluded from the throne because of his weak ankles. At the same time, not kings, but queens are wanted, there are no tests of physical fitness as are recorded for tribes in the north, and in the legends of the Lovedu and of tribes which, following the Lovedu, have ritual suicide, physical defects do not figure as a theme. In this complex, heirs to the throne have been disqualified or chiefs have been deposed because of inability to make rain, disobedience to their sovereign, or adultery with his wives. Among the Mamaila, a branch of the Lovedu, one chief is said to have become a cripple because he forced open the door which magically yields to the touch of the true heir, and the Nemesis that overtook him is attributed to his sin, not to his defect. Impotence disqualifies in the north, but Mujaji II was barren and, in the pattern as adopted in some tribes, such as the Khaha of Maakɛ, barrenness of the queen is expected; for, as the queen may have no official husband, it is a virtue to have no children. That conception is not accepted by the Lovedu, for Mujaji II's barrenness was a source of sadness and strife and every effort was made to cure her. Physical fitness is an aspect of the perfection and divinity of the queen, but it has no practical relation to the right of succession.

The relation between the length of a reign and the initiations is far more obscure. In many tribes where ritual suicide is enjoined (Thavina, Khaha, Uirwa), the number of 'schools' is said to be seven. The 'schools' are there held more frequently, and possibly there is some connexion with the number of sacred drums (*digɔma*), for the Khaha have seven and the Lovedu four. The chief's life, as we have seen, is intimately bound up with the drums; both drums and 'schools' are great *dogɔma*, objects or activities in which power is concentrated. Power is also concentrated in *dithugula*, a category of objects chiefly associated with the gods. The distinction is not that between magic and religion; the *digɔma* and *dithugula* appear to belong to different cultural complexes. The one was characterized, we may suppose, by 'schools', drums, and cults linked up with national calendric observances, dramatization of the crises in life, and the sanctity and power of the chief; the other, by sacred beads, shrines, reincarnation of ancestors in dedicated animals, and ritual suicide of the chief. In the process of merging, the great *digɔma* were, we suggest, grafted on to the royal institutions and brought into relation with the life as well as the death of the chief. This is little more than speculation, for it is difficult to isolate the oldest cultural substrata and their distinctive patterns.

The rule about physical fitness is now merely an ideal and, similarly, ritual suicide is not conceived to have any relation to the welfare of the country. People do not say that the country will suffer if the physical powers of the queen fail. But ritual suicide does elevate the queen to a divinity; only by her act, not because of susceptibility to the weaknesses of man, can she die. Age neither increases nor decreases her powers. She is the 'soil'; her death 'heals' or 'dries up' the soil in the double sense of defiling it (as twins do) and scorching it (as the sun does); and as they phrase it, the 'country dies with its owner'. Consequently, after the queen's death, famines come, cattle and people succumb, and many flee the country. When Mujaji II committed suicide in 1894, there followed the *matshɔna*, the three years of unprecedented drought and pests, during which, according to contemporary European observers, practically all the cattle and a third of the population died. After the death of Mugɔdɔ, likewise, there was a great famine. The only other famine vividly recorded by tradition was during the reign of a chief who, being a usurper, was unable to make rain. Though the death of a chief presages death of the country, there is no great hurry to appoint a new queen. To the unfolding of a plan that guarantees abundance, immediate needs, even the need for the life-giving rain, must be subordinated.

For an account of succession to the throne we have to rely upon the memories of men who were adults forty-five years ago. The practical and the ideal are confused in their minds. The generalized account we give is thus not specifically related to the death of Mujaji II unless otherwise indicated. Shortly before her death, the queen calls together her great men, sits silently looking at them for a while, and then retires to her hut. She will not see again the young boys who have gone to the *vudiga*. Long before this, Mujaji II and her inner 'council' had named the daughter of Leakhali, who was her 'sister' and great wife, as successor; she had driven both mother and daughter with their brothers from the country, but was secretly receiving and instructing the daughter. None but a small circle of close relatives knew of these arrangements; and a little later she took poison (*khitaba*) in which the fatal ingredients are said to be the brain and spinal cord of the crocodile. There is a rule that the killer of a crocodile is for ever debarred from entering the capital, a prohibition patterned upon the taboos against bringing into a village the wood of trees with which shrines and protective charms (*dithugula*) are made, for these trees 'reveal', and so render useless, what they create. The poison is not conceived to kill instantaneously; the queen dies in the presence of those who know the secrets, but the death is not made public. Those who pass the royal hut still greet her; even cases are still submitted as if for her final decision. Deception of the people is the aim emphasized in descriptions and in phraseology. In the old days many cattle were killed 'to deceive the people', but neither this killing, which provided at least for the funeral feast and the skin for the dead body, nor the other arrangements, had this function only. The spirit of the deceased continues, as it were, to preside over the country and no one could take over the reins of government.

The body decomposes, it is ritually rubbed (*hu fɔrɔla*) to remove skin and dirt for the vital ingredient of the rain medicine, and after a while close relatives secretly dig a grave at Maulwi, the place where to-day the sacred drums are also kept. The grave is deep, for the queen must stand upright, 'taking care' of her country, and facing to the north, whence her ancestors came. The body is wrapped in a greenish-black cloth, a portion still of what was brought from the north, and over it is wound the skin of an ox. The hearse proceeds from the village secretly at night, and, as the great must rest, the bearers stop every few yards. Sacred beads, a calabash of water, a firebrand, the grains upon which people live and (in the old days) the body of a man, the 'mat' of the chief, are interred with the queen. The calabash and firebrand, used also to expel a usurper, provide the essentials for the 'journey' to be undertaken. A slab of stone covers the mouth of the grave and facilitates the re-opening whenever rain medicine (*mufugo*) is to be poured into it. The grave is not all at once filled up with soil; it is guarded against enemies, who might destroy the country with the medicine the body provides; and it is said that a wooden structure, on which the watchers sleep, is built over the grave. The soil at last reaches the neck, but the head must be left uncovered for perhaps six months, until it has completely decomposed.

A year later the district heads are assembled at the capital, the death is announced and the drum beaten, and people shave their heads. It is said that foreigners entered the country at the peril of life and belongings. When the hair has grown and the mourning period ends, all fires in the country are put out. This same fire-rite figures, as far as a district is concerned, at the installation of its head, and as far as the whole country is concerned, when all-pervasive impediments to rain are removed. It essentially consists—we have described it briefly in Chapter XV—of putting out fires with medicine (*mufugo*) by boys who receive the medicine at the capital, and of a chain of payments, by the women to the married men for the firebrand obtained from the *khɔrɔ* to re-light their fires, by the men to the boys for their services in the rite, and by the boys to the official keeper of the *mufugo* at the capital. Two distinctive patterns are explicit in this rite: fire in its aspect of a valuable commodity and as almost the prerogative of the chief, to whom his subjects must pay a royal 'fire tax'; and fire in its aspect of giving out deleterious 'heat', which must be counteracted by 'cooling' with *mufugo* (*hu fuga*, to blow upon by a cool breeze, to sprinkle with 'cooling' medicine).

Fire also belongs to a third pattern which links it up with crises or great changes, ritualizes its value, and uses it to extinguish an evil or to purify a state of defilement. In their present cultural connotation among the Lovedu, these three patterns are implicit in the nature of fire, but they do not always merge in ritual situations, and, as far as the evidence of the cultures of the Northern Transvaal go, they belong to different cultural configurations. This evidence seems to indicate that the 'royal tax', through which authority is asserted and acknowledged, came from the Karanga, that the association with purification and 'transitions' was borrowed from the old Sotho, and that the conception of 'heat' as the antithesis of health of body and well-being of the country, was contributed by a wider and less easily determinable culture substratum. The significance of the fire rite at the accession of a queen can be understood only in the context of the three patterns as they have been integrated into Lovedu culture and become merged in the rite.

Firstly, fire figures in the borrowed 'transition' rites, but not in the girls' puberty rite (*khɔba*). Midway in the sacred fire of the boys' circumcision (*vudiga*) is its central shrine at the place where the chief initiate (*washe*) sits. In the sanctum of the Bird of the *vyali* there is an undying fire. The end of these 'schools' is spoken of as 'a burning down' (*hu swa*): the fire destroys all the distinctive things of the 'school', the lodge, the tables, the tiniest bits of grass that fell from the dancing performers, and, as the lodge burns, the initiates, turning their backs upon it, may not look round and are irrevocably severed from their past. Again, when 'the country is not right' and has to be re-established or purified of its pollution with 'cooling' medicine (*mufugo*), a transition is implied, for it is said, 'The fires are put out to usher in a new year'. The same conception reappears when *mufugo* is used before the accession of a new queen.

Secondly, the firebrand, as the symbol of authority, figures in the warrant (*khiso*, i.e. firebrand) given by the queen which authorizes district heads to hold 'schools'. This warrant of authority is most strikingly evident in the firebrand and calabash handed to a disaffected noble or would-be usurper as an intimation that he is expelled from the country. It has merged with the *mufugo* rite enacted to render the earth receptive to the power of rain magic or to herald the accession of a queen; and here it takes the form of a 'royal tax' vicariously exacted through the women, their husbands, the boys sprinkling the medicine, and the keeper of the *mufugo* at the capital.

Thirdly, 'beating out' of fires with 'cooling' medicine belongs to a complex of rites for counteracting the harmful effects of 'heat', a conception explained in Chapter XII. 'Heat' not only arises from the contamination of death, but is the concomitant of disease, weakens the charms (*dithugula*), impedes rain, and defiles the earth. In all these cases it is combated with 'cooling' medicine, as we describe elsewhere. In addition, the *gɔma* drums are prevented from losing their concentrated power by the 'cool' river stones in them, witches are thwarted by protective charms (*diphaba*) in which the products of the sea are the most powerful elements, and the 'heat' of the ancestors' anger is 'cooled' with *mufugo*. The death of a queen 'dries up' or 'heats' the whole country, which has to be cooled as a preparation for the new ruler.

Thus in the fire rite at a queen's accession, the culture is handling complicated and all-important conceptions. The pervasive evil corrupting the country must be neutralized; the relationship of ruler and ruled, superior and inferior, must be visibly reasserted; and there must be enacted a momentous new start marking the inception of a new destiny and preparing the universe for the reception of the next rain-maker. The fire rite on this occasion symbolizes a mighty purification and 'transition', epitomizes the allegiance of subjects and the authority of the queen, and inaugurates a cosmic order in which the magic of a new rain-maker may be auspiciously manifested. That, in the Lovedu cultural context, is the meaning of the fire rite.

After the fire rite there follows the rite of opening the door, which will determine the identity of the heir. No one knows for certain who will succeed. Some nobles, availing themselves of the interregnum, mobilize their supporters, and all come fully armed, for there is sure to be some display of hostility. Even in 1896, at the accession of Mujaji III, a son of a wife of Mujaji II and great councillor marched upon the capital supported by the Mahasha, but there was no strife, as Mujaji III's followers were prepared. The rival claimants, in the presence of the assembled people, go one by one to the hut in which the queen died and which (like one of the queen's huts even to-day) has two doors. They approach the door one by one, address the spirit of the deceased, saying who they are, and lightly touch the door. It is arranged that the most ambitious claimants go first, and those who are indifferent as regards their prospects last, the true heir to whom the door will open taking his place between them.

The spirit of the deceased, by opening the door, chooses the successor. The new queen, taking the axe, spear, and shield of her royal predecessors, escapes by the other door. She may have to flee, if the party of a rival is too strong, but in time she will be formally presented by a great councillor to the people. There is doubt as to the fate of the person who held the door from within: some say he must die, others that he is given a wife and sent out of the country. There is much uncertainty and secrecy about what happened in 1896; it is even doubted whether the door was opened. The reason lay in the fear of European intervention, for just previously the Boer General had been deceived and the lowveld tribes conquered, as described in Chapter I. Cowed by disaster, the Lovedu wisely decided to emphasize, not their own ritual, but the formal confirmation of the accession by the European.

The opening of the door, as known among neighbouring tribes, serves chiefly to resolve conflicts between rivals to the throne. It sometimes co-exists with institutional predetermination of the heir—for instance, where he must be the chief son of a wife married with special ceremonies and with cattle contributed by the whole tribe, the issue of a house in which the tribesmen all have a stake. In such circumstances conflicts arise, and European authority throws its weight on the side of 'constitutional arrangements' rather than 'coincidence'. In some tribes the opening of the door serves to strengthen the claim of the institutional heir; that is the case where there is no great massing of institutions behind the chief heir and conflicts are liable to break out if there are several claimants of standing. Among the Lovedu, succession was quite uncertain, the personal choice of the chief, not primogeniture, being stressed. The great son seldom succeeded, it is said, because the second child was favoured; and that is one explanation of the origin of the Mamaila, Sekhopɔ, and Rakhwadu tribes, for the great son was driven out of the country. In traditional history the 'Filler of the Rivers', who was chief son and seized the throne, had to make way for the 'Drainer of the Rivers', who proved to be the choice of his father and to whom the rain secrets had been imparted. Khashani, the great son, was expelled by Mugɔdɔ, his younger brother (we do not know whether he was the second son), of whom it is said that his father treated him as an outcast in order to deceive the people. Khashani was, however, given ritual precedence and in this as well as in the fact that it was the line of Malegugu, great son of Mugɔdɔ, which provided the 'husbands' of the last two queens, we may see perhaps an attempt to compensate the great son and retain his allegiance. The pattern of antagonism to the true heir continued to be followed by the queens. Mugɔdɔ was outcast from the capital, Mujaji I was born in despised Lekhwareni, and Mujaji II and III were expelled from the country.

The choice of the heir among the kings is represented as exercised by them personally; he who must raise the heir to the queens is chosen by an inner, secret 'council' of relatives. We cannot describe its membership by saying that one is a sister, the other a brother, and so on; each is related to the chief in a dozen ways and their pre-eminence in the royal 'councils' derives from complicated inter-relationships, prestige, sagacity, and loyalty as well as institutionalized arrangements.

The accession of queens has raised new problems of succession. The heir apparent is theoretically prohibited from having children before she ascends, and, when she ascends, her powers of bearing children may be exhausted. This is a simple statement of a much more complicated situation, but suffice it to add that, ideally, should the queen or, if she is barren, her wife who is chosen to bear the heir, have male issue, the child has either to be killed or to be excluded by a mechanism with strong social or ritual sanctions—namely, the opening of the door. Mujaji I's son was killed, so it is said; but the uterine brother of Mujaji III was allowed to live and become a great councillor. Another problem is the exclusion from power of the 'husband' of the queen. Queens may not marry, but the physiological father of their children may be a councillor, as he was in the reign of Mujaji III, and it is essential that he should be a close relative. To support such arrangements in a patrilineal society is one of the functions of the 'opening of the door'. It also confirms choices made by the inner 'council', visibly and publicly demonstrates the will of the ancestors, enforces loyalty to all relatives of the royal house any one of whom may become chief, and unmistakably points out to whose hands the rain secrets have been entrusted.

The quarrels and conflicts leading to the flight of the heir are much stressed in tradition; they are nothing if not realistic, and one is often in doubt whether they are genuine or merely staged conflicts. Leakhali and her brother, together with Leakhali's daughter, Mujaji III, were genuinely expelled. Leakhali had her own village and her own wives and was proud and independent; she and her brother objected to the influence of a doctor who had come to cure Mujaji II of her barrenness, but stayed to be her lover. After a public insult to this doctor in the presence of the queen at a beer-party at Leakhali's village, the queen sent her wife the calabash and firebrand. Leakhali and her brother fled, and in exile Mujaji III was taught by her mother's brother, thus fulfilling, it is said, the law that the heir must be taught by her maternal uncle. The situation appears to be re-enacted to-day, with this difference, that it is the queen's own daughter who, after her lover's quarrel with a great councillor, fled to join him in exile. The conflict was so serious that the tribe seethed with disaffection, though the queen seemed to be torn between love for her daughter and disapproval of the whole episode. The present conflict is in many respects typical. There is, as there used to be in the past, strife between the old councillors, who lose their power when the old queen dies, and the new councillors, who side with the new queen. The latter gradually supplant the former, but regard with fear the day when the friends of the heir in turn will oust them. This struggle is very real, and seems to reflect a more fundamental conflict; for the exalted purpose of the royal institutions exacts an unnatural sacrifice by the queen in order to make way for the heir she naturally loves.

The whole royal complex is perfectly logical once it is granted that there must be queens, that succession is uncertain, and that ritual suicide is the guarantee of the chief's divinity. In a society in which the 'sister' (*khadi*) is priestess, her great religious role, still seen to-day among neighbouring tribes where chiefs are males, falls to the queen among the Lovedu. The ideal, imperfectly actualized since queens replaced kings, still persists that the *khadi* of the chief should have power and be given a large district to rule. In theory the brother of the chief is the great councillor, general, and judge. But in practice the complications set up by having queens throws these arrangements out of gear. True to pattern, the greatest district head is to-day a woman, who is a 'sister' to the queen and, though a 'sister' threefold (through mother, legal father, and paternal uncle), she is not the uterine or ritual 'sister'. At present the relatives through the queen's mother, not through Mujaji II her legal father, are important councillors, but it is not unlikely that in the next reign the great councillors will be the present heir's relatives through her legal father, the queen, who is also her physiological mother.

Owing to the inapplicability of the term 'council' to Lovedu arrangements, we need say only a few words on this subject. There is no need of a visible organization to support Lovedu court life, which is ceremonious, but not politically oriented. Power and authority derive from the queen's divine appointment, her exclusive secret of rain-making, and her strategic position in the social web. She is neither a military nor a political leader; she does not even have a priesthood organization to assist her in her function as high-priest. There are confidential advisers, but they neither constitute the more or less definite secret council (*sephiri*) of some neighbouring tribes nor necessarily function as political councillors; on the contrary the former, having assisted in the accession of the queen, are in institutional conflict with the latter, who later gain political control. The councillors represent the assertion of power by the rising generation of men in the sphere of law and politics as against women and the older generation in ritual, religion, and the social system. They are part mainly of the court (*khɔrɔ*) and the tribal gathering (*khivijɔ*), two indeterminate bodies.

Confidential advisers are mainly important district heads; councillors are always residents in the capital. Both are relatives, but, in the case of the confidants, not necessarily close relatives of the queen. In the inner royal circle, the closest kin are necessarily those reckoned through the queen's mother—that is, either the queen's predecessor on the throne or, if she has borne no children, the queen's physiological mother. The unofficial husbands of the queens are brothers chosen from the line of Malegudu (elder brother of Mujaji I), but relationship is not reckoned through them as fathers. Closeness of relationship is important, but personality and opportunity count as much. The most influential councillor is often said to be the queen's mother's brother—in other words, the brother of the deceased queen or, if she has no issue, the brother of the wife of the queen who bore the queen. In fact, however, other relatives rise to equally influential positions. To take a concrete instance, the councillors of Mujaji III have been relatives either through Leakhali, chief wife and 'sister' of Mujaji II and physiological mother of Mujaji III, or through Mujaji II, her mother, Mujaji I, and the latter's brothers, such as Malegudu. Muneri, the chief councillor to-day, is Leakhali's uterine brother's son, and before him there were Mulogwane, uterine brother of the queen, and also Leakhali's uterine brother. Earlier still, but in the present queen's time, the greatest councillors were others tracing descent from Malegudu. There is no precise rule either as to the number or identity of the councillors. The *duna* of the queen should not be a relative; he is merely a messenger, and, unlike the *induna* elsewhere, is of no account, having no special legal or other status or function.

The *khivijɔ* is neither the more or less determinate body of private advisers (*kxotla*), nor even the tribal gathering (*pitshɔ*), of the Sotho. It is mainly constituted by district heads, or their representatives, and the men of the capital, but any one attends; and it is never conceived of as a general assembly of all the initiated men of the tribe. It has little power and less initiative; it is summoned mostly to discuss European matters, and there is now a tendency to place some decisions of the men of the capital before it for confirmation; but it is hardly a means of gauging popular feeling or of expressing the royal will. The co-operation of the tribe is secured and its desires made known, not through the *khivijɔ*, but through other social arrangements, which we shall describe at greater length.

These arrangements run parallel with a distinctive system of wives of the queen, called *vaṭanoni*, a term also applied to the wives of all nobles, and women other than the queen may have *vaṭanoni*. The majority of the queen's wives are given to her by her district heads. In a sense, these wives are tribute (*va hu lova*), but the queen always gives some *munywalo*. She also receives wives from foreign chiefs who supplicate for rain or for peace, and from headmen who settle in her country and send their daughters or sisters; in these cases no *munywalo* is given. Finally, she is sent wives by the nobles, by those to whom she has given wives or cattle with which to secure wives, and by those who promise their little 'mud-stampers' as repayment for the assistance they ask. Sometimes also the queen takes a liking to a girl and asks her in marriage and sometimes commoners send their daughters. It will be impracticable to deal with all these cases; and, from the point of view of the political organization, we are mainly concerned with the wives sent by district heads. They send their daughters for purposes of *hu lova*, a word used in a wide connotation, including the conceptions of showing allegiance, doing homage, paying tribute, honouring, but, above all, supplicating for rain. District heads *lova* in this way, it is said, in recognition of the land which the queen has given them to rule; but what is really important is their dependence, as holders of land of the queen, upon the protection and security of her rain-making powers. Uulovedu, her country, is the land where persons (i.e. wives) and other possessions are utterly lost (*hu lova*), because they are given in exchange for the rain that the queen makes. The queen has accepted wives even from the Shangana-Tonga, with whom marriage is not permitted, but in that case she hands them to her nobles, not as wives, but as daughters; and after a time they become sufficiently Loveduized to be given in marriage to commoners. These wives usually stay at the capital for a limited time; only a few of them, some six to nine to-day, remain permanently; the others are handed chiefly to district heads and nobles.

While the wives are at the capital they do the work that wives ordinarily do: they hoe for their husband, the queen, who sometimes accompanies them to the fields, they attend to domestic duties, they stamp and brew beer, but only two or three of them are sufficiently noble and trusted to cook for the queen. The queen is bridegroom to their people and they are her relatives-in-law; and even the details of the marriage ceremony are maintained. There are variations upon the ordinary pattern of marriage and *munywalo*; the *munywalo*, for instance, is less, but what is particularly stressed is the virginity of the bride. For a time she wears only a loin cloth as evidence that she is not pregnant and a substitute must be sent for a girl who has been 'spoilt' before marriage with the queen. The first daughter of the district head of Mulloni was 'engaged' to the queen, the second to her cross-cousin, a nobleman. The fiancée of the queen became pregnant and was rejected, the queen arranging an exchange with the nobleman. The same nobleman years ago had been 'given' a wife by the queen and recently in return, as is obligatory, he sent his daughter as wife to the queen. This daughter became pregnant, was allotted to another nobleman, whom she deserted, and now stays with her father nursing an infant of two years of age. Such complications merely throw into relief the ramifications of the system.

The queen does not accept 'spoilt' brides and she equally expects that her wives shall remain chaste, at least for a time. Theoretical insistence upon chastity co-exists with a realistic attitude to the weaknesses of human nature. Seduction of a wife of the queen is penalized as if she were still unmarried and the daughter of the queen. Pregnant wives, unless the queen has authorized the liaison, are disgraced, sent home, and returned with beer to wipe out the disgrace, and sometimes an ox is slaughtered for the returned wife, the peritoneum being hung round her neck to indicate that she is the queen's wife. According to the standards of the society, the seducer, as in any ordinary case of seduction, may not marry the woman he has seduced; he may not even see his infant child. Few of the wives of the queen permanently remain chaste, though it is a great honour often very specially rewarded. The great wives, if they remain chaste, may be given areas to rule or special villages of their own.

If favoured by one of the great councillors, they could be given their own hut (and in the old days a cow into the bargain) and be allowed to cohabit there with the councillor. This gains for them an honourable place in the capital, where they exercise great influence in the private councils of the queen, intercede for others with the queen and are her companions. *Vaṯanoni* of high rank may, as mistresses of their own villages, aspire to the great circle of huts drawn by the establishments of their wives, and they may even attain the pinnacle of prestige where, as happens when the queen is barren, they are chosen to bear the heir to the throne. The lesser *vaṯanoni*, who have remained chaste, may be released from their vows and allowed 'to go about in the bush', and eventually they may be handed out to nobles or district heads.

It is, however, contrary to the ideals expressed for a virgin *muṯanoni* to be given away, though the ideal recedes before other considerations, such as the poverty of a noble or sympathy in a loss he has sustained. Only some of the *vaṯanoni* who have illicit children continue to remain at the capital—for instance, there is an old woman who has a married son about forty years old. She had her lapse when she went on a visit to her home, but no one knows who her lover was. The son still lives with his mother at the capital; as a son of the queen, he is not without influence, but his influence is resented. He and his mother are regarded as witches, and he has many enemies and for long periods has to escape to town to allow threatening storms to blow over. Councillors can hardly afford to allow wives of the queen who have sons to remain permanently: the honour is too great and the opportunities of exploiting their position too numerous. The institutional arrangement of sending *vaṯanoni* with children away to be married to others avoids this danger. The children may, if they are proud, call themselves Mujaji and they are described as 'the heads of Muhale', but legally they are no longer children of the queen and they lose their opportunities for intriguing.

Through her wives, the queen becomes 'son-in-law' to all her district heads, and by allocating these wives to other district heads and to noblemen she becomes parent-in-law to them. The system thus uses the mechanism of the social system to forge a great network of chains radiating from the queen like a web to all strategic points in the society. The link with the queen theoretically never breaks, as a wife handed out must, when she has a daughter, send her in turn to be married by the queen. An important wife, even after allocation, may still enter the queen's hut. The queen remains interested in the welfare of her erstwhile wives and takes them back if the husband ill-treats them or their children. A new link, that of marriage, is created between the people of the wife allocated and of the husband to whom she is given. A man pays no *munywalo* for such a wife, yet the link is a true *munywalo* link; for, if the wife deserts, the husband may, though he has given nothing, demand back *munywalo* from her people (that which the queen gave them). He may complain to the queen, who can, if she wishes, urge his case, but she usually says, 'I can freely give. I cannot return by force.'

How district heads become linked with the queen and with one another may be shown by an illustration which we have greatly simplified for

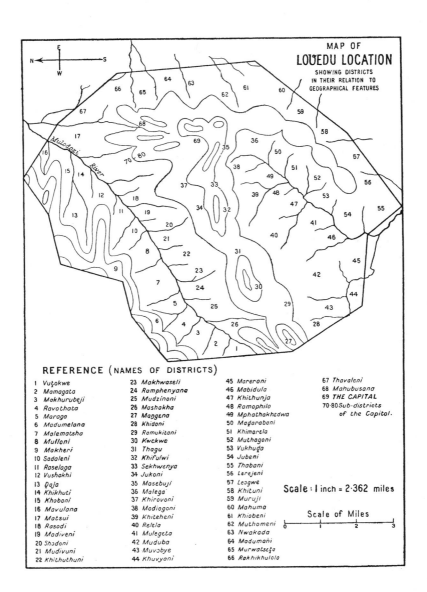

ease of presentation. Mavetha, district head of Mareroni, some thirty-eight years ago gave his daughter, Muthatso, to the queen. Muthatso after a time was allotted to Khidima, the queen's maternal uncle. Later Khidima sent a daughter to be one of the wives of the queen and this girl in turn was given by the queen to Nagambi, district head of Maulwi. Meanwhile Mavetha's son, Muhale, succeeded at Mareroni and sent the only issue of his wife, the daughter Makwajo, to the queen (1936). The next ruler at Mareroni will be either Makwajo or an heir raised by the wife acquired with the cattle given by the queen as *munywalo* for Mukwajo. Already these arrangements link the district heads of Mareroni and of Maulwi with the queen and one of her nobles, and also with one another. The network is indefinitely continued in all directions, and though its ends appear to diverge, they centre in the queen and become interlinked at many points. For instance, to Rasodi, a younger brother of Nagambi, the queen gave Makwada, her wife, who came from Malematsha, an important district head, and as a result Rasodi's son must marry at Malematsha's. Once these interrelations are established, they set into motion the whole social system and the reciprocities which double the links and perpetuate the interrelations. In the district of the capital the ramifications of exchanges and re-exchanges are so complex as to defy analysis.

Broadly speaking, districts may be divided into those given to one of the old *kwεvo* or royal groups (of Muhale, of Mudiga and of Mahasha), those originating from *vaṭanoni*, and those held by heads of foreign groups. The so-called *vaṭanoni* districts constitute a composite group, because women do not normally succeed to one another. We have already mentioned elsewhere how the district Matsui was given by Mujaji I to her wife, who, marrying a Crocodile, was succeeded by her son Matsui and his line of Crocodiles. In 34 per cent. of the 100 districts we know well enough to trace their origin, the position has not been very different. To-day sixty of these 100 districts are held by the royal groups and forty by foreign groups, and of those held by foreigners sixteen were acquired, as Matsui was, through *vaṭanoni*. Thus 40 per cent. of the foreign and 30 per cent. of the *kwεvo* districts, as far as we know, were originally handed to wives of the chiefs. Districts may originate in many other ways. It was customary for the kings to place their districts under sisters and brothers and temporarily also under their wives. Their wives could not as easily as among the queens consolidate their position, as they were unable to send their daughters as wives to the king, whereas now they can and do send such wives to the queens. Districts were also given to the great messengers (*diduna*) of the chiefs; to foreigners, who, though they came with no large following, were renowned doctors of the national 'schools', some of which they introduced; to men who gave the queen cattle and a wife, and occasionally to those who had rendered services of value.

It does not much matter how a district originates from the point of view of the links that are gradually established with the queen and with one another. If foreigners come with a large, compact body of followers, they are often given an area and in return send their daughters as wives to the queen. A Talɛrwa group came from the west in Khiali's reign (c. 1740), had a *mutanoni* at the capital and were given a large district. Malematsha, a son of the *mutanoni*, having married a daughter of Mugɔdɔ, the next chief, was given half the district, the other half being ruled by the Talɛrwa head. By these arrangements the Talɛrwa line became *vamakhulu* of Malematsha, whose son succeeded to the whole area in 1895, when the Talɛrwa ruling family left as the result of famine. The Malematsha are *vaḍuhulu* of the royal Lovedu. At Bagoni, which was originally given by Mujaji I to her younger brother, Murwatsɛta, there now rules Mukupi, daughter of Murwatsɛta's son. Mukupi had been the wife of Mujaji II, but, as there was no living male heir, she was released by the queen so as to enable her to rule the area. The true heir, son of the girl whom Mukupi's brother, had he lived, would have married (for the girl was the brother's cattle-linked cross-cousin), is now about forty-five years of age. It is doubtful whether he will ever succeed, for Mukupi is an ambitious and important woman, a district head who, like the queen, has no legal husband, but several wives; she is related to the queen and her councillors in a dozen ways, the most important being that she is *mukhadi* of the queen and was wife of Mujaji II. Relɛla has a long history, but we need go no further back than the time when it was entrusted by Mujaji I to Mathogani, daughter of Mugɔdɔ, the chief, and *mutanoni* of Mujaji I. Mathogani married first Rampi and, after his death, Muhotɛla, Rampi's brother. Kwathi, son of the latter, who was given a *mutanoni* by Mujaji II, for reasons we need not here consider, usurped the headship. Segɛte is a district given by Mujaji II to her wife Makhivasɛ, who was daughter of a Venda chief, and, as Makhivasɛ had no issue, she was succeeded by her sister's son, the sister having married a direct male descendant of the elder brother of Mujaji I. This elder brother, Malegudu, had a daughter, Magɔvo, who became *mutanoni* of Mujaji II. Mujaji III made Magɔvo head of Maulwi, and Magɔvo's son, Mugɔdɔ, was the man who was chosen to raise the next heir to the throne. A son of Mugɔdɔ by his chief wife (not the queen) is now district head at Maulwi. These are but some of the cases, much simplified, that give us an idea of the manner in which districts originate and become linked up with the queen and the royal group.

The district is a political and a territorial unit, often very small in size, and usually having a distinctive praise. The size varies from half a square mile to nine square miles, the average in the congested reserve being under one square mile. Originally the districts were larger, but, as European occupation advanced, the old districts were divided and sub-divided to make room for the heads that were ousted. The praises, already mentioned elsewhere, are generally praises of the group or sub-group of the head. At Maunadala, though he migrated from Naji, near Tzaneen in the south, to the tribal farm Khinobɛlwa to the north of Uulovedu, they still sing, 'Crocodile of Mugazi, outcast (*murɔka*) of the rain water,' because his people had no rain-making magic; when Mahubusana brings beer, the praise runs, 'At the kitchen-hut of Magwala of Khodini, where potatoes are eaten,' though Mahubusana now rules near the capital, having long ago left Khodini, to the south of Uulovedu;

and at Khimarela one may hear, 'You are drunk, you of Maleakhotho, you who are habitual smokers of hemp.' Not only have sub-groups and even lineages distinctive variations upon perhaps a common praise of the group, but there are different praises appropriate to different occasions.

Owing to patrilocal marriage, the patrilineal kin tend to form the core of a district. These cores were perhaps more distinct in the distant past, for it is quite clear that, for instance, the districts of the Mudiga lay towards the east, while those of the Mahasha clustered together in the north-west. But members of the Mudiga and Mahasha were always scattered throughout the tribe and never co-operated as groups in any political situation. We must not think of co-operating patrilineal groups, for 'A man has influence and fortune where he has relatives-in-law'. The core of the district may be the brothers, father's brothers, and their sons in the district, but generally the mother is a link with one outside district and sisters and daughters marry into others. There is seldom a numerical preponderance of the lineage of the district head in the territorial unit, their number and solidarity depending upon a large number of factors: length of residence or of headship, the homogeneity of diversity, size, dispersion or concentration of the group that immigrated and was given a district, agreement within the group, and so on.

We may take Matsui as an example. The head, a Crocodile, and his male forebears have ruled the area for over a century. Matsui is at one point immediately adjacent to the capital, but it is also near a whole chain of old Crocodile settlements, which 150 years ago extended from Mamaila in the north to Uudupi in the south. The district is largely a valley area and thus avoided by the Lovedu royal group, but extensively occupied by the Shangana-Tonga since about 1840. The population is 22 per cent. Crocodile and 14 per cent. Lovedu; 47 per cent. of the people belong to foreign groups or sub-groups, with whom intermarriage is not wholly disapproved, and 17 per cent. Shangana-Tonga. The Crocodiles are patrilineal kin and the Lovedu are relatives-in-law of the head, but the links with the Shangana-Tonga are those of neighbourliness, some friendship, and some economic interdependence. Of the intermarriageable foreigners, 20 per cent. are related in some way to the head, being mostly relatives of the line of 'messengers' (*diduna*) of the district head. It is generally felt that the messengers should not be patrilineally related to the head because of possible conflicts, but their alliance with the head is usually a close and long-established one. In the case of Matsui, the links are not only through the capital where the group of the 'messenger' used to be officials, but also through the district head's brother, who is the *muḍuhulu* (cattle-linked sister's son) of the 'messenger'. In other districts, of course, the dispositions are different: on the hills, for instance, there are no Shangana-Tonga and few of the more or less outcast *varɔka*. The diversity of the groups is very great, as we have indicated elsewhere, but the manner in which they have been interwoven into the royal group, chiefly through the districts, is even more impressive.

The patrilineal core of the district is no more important than the link through the bilateral kin, especially through mothers and sisters and daughters and the cattle-chains forged by them with other areas and with the capital. These links emphasize the part played by women in the political system. The intermediaries or registrars at the capital, through whom political and legal matters are taken from the district to the queen, are called, not fathers or councillors, as is very usual in other tribes, but 'mothers' of the district heads (*mma vɔna*), a very appropriate name in the light of the fact that one usually approaches the paternal authority through one's mother. 'Mothers' of districts may be women as well as men, and quite often a male 'mother' is succeeded by his widow. The position opens large avenues of political opportunity for women. Again, at present 14 per cent. of the acting district heads are women, some holding in their own right, some on behalf of a male heir, who perhaps, as in the case of Mukupi, will never have much influence during the lifetime of the deputy. If we reckon cases in which a son is ruling in consultation with his mother, the percentage is much higher.

Let us take a few examples. Mukoko, the jester (*khidada*) at the capital, is nominally head at Ravothata; but until her death it was his mother, daughter of the brother of Mujaji II and a wife of the queen, who was in charge, and it is now his wife, also an ex-wife of the queen, who has remained behind and rules, though Mukoko has appointed a deputy. At Madumani, the heir has quarrelled with and was expelled by the sister of his deceased father; she installed another son, Khobi, as nominal head; and when Khobi died, his sister took over control, feathering the nest of her son, against whom the chances of the rightful heir seem at present to be small. At Muthomeni the mother's influential relatives secured the succession of Mudzwalo against that of his younger brother, the legal heir. Matsɛre's sister's daughter is head at Khiobeni and her husband does the court work. Khimarɛla, an old Mudiga district, was consistently given to wives of the queen; and in its recent history, Mathagu, a wife of the queen who married a Mudiga, was head until her son, Thagu, took over. The mother of a district head at Khithunja rules because the son has paralysis. At Lerejini, Bogi, who is now head, entrusted the district to his elder sister, who, in order to rule, as she did until her death, left her husband, who lived in another area. Rapada at Mashakha had only one daughter in the great house and she was a wife of the queen when he died; his wife is now head and, if the ideal pattern is followed, she will be succeeded by the heir of the daughter-in-law, supposititious wife of her son, who comes to cook for her; but this daughter-in-law, as experience shows, is likely to overshadow her son, the true heir. Magovo, sister of Mugɔdɔ, the chief, was the first ruler at Mudzinoni; as she had no issue, her sister succeeded her, the next head was daughter of the sister (because the son expelled the true heir and then died prematurely), and this daughter was followed by her own choice, the son of her brother.

Cases of this nature, where a woman plays the decisive role, may be multiplied. They may give the impression that there are no strongly institutionalized rules of succession; yet these rules exist. They are patrilineally patterned, but they recognize the claims of the sister's son (*muḓuhulu*). The weight of the social structure, in all complicated cases, balances unevenly between the cattle-descent and the cattle-linked houses—that is, between the heir raised in the chief house of the head and the head's cattle-linked sister. The daughter of the cattle-linked brother comes as daughter-in-law to the mistress of the chief house, her cattle-linked aunt, to bear the heir, whether that house has a son or not; and legal precedences support this arrangement and succession. This emphasizes the power of the mother and her lineage. But the position of the cattle-linked sister is also strong, as we have indicated elsewhere, and in cases of succession to the headship of a district is further strengthened if she has been a wife of the queen. Conflicts do often arise and it is not strange that the queen usually leaves them to settle themselves. It is seldom that she interferes or interposes her authority, though she does so when the balance of convenience or interest strongly inclines one way. Tenure of headship is tolerably secure. The queen would only exceptionally and for very good reasons favour the displacement of a district head of one of the old groups; and in that case the district itself must strongly desire it while, not a stranger, but the nearest acceptable relative of the lineage will be substituted. If, however, the links with the royal family are not close, tenure by the lineage is less secure and it occasions no surprise that a man, coming to the queen with a few pounds, may be given a district where there has been trouble. We have seen a few such cases and it seemed incomprehensible to those with whom we discussed them that we suspected bribery and corruption.

The district is singularly autonomous in its political arrangements. Land is allotted by the district head not, as in many neighbouring tribes, by the chief. The district head, if he wishes, gives land to people living in other districts; at Mawa, for instance, non-residents hold over 300 fields. The district head reports the settlement of a stranger from another tribe by taking £1 to the queen, but it is to him as district owner that landholders annually bring beer. A non-resident also nowadays cultivates the district head with beer, clothes, and even money before asking for land. The land given to a non-resident is not very securely held; the tenure is so imperfectly institutionalized that practice varies from one district to another and definite rights and obligations cannot easily be deduced; on the whole, it is not unlike lending, though the culture does not recognize lending of land for a consideration. A non-resident holding land in a district, unlike a resident, cannot, generally speaking, interchange it with or lend it to others without the consent of the head; but at the capital he can, even without reporting to the queen; and there also a resident may break new land without any one's permission.

Land tenure is too complicated for treatment here, but we may note that where a district head takes back the land of a resident, the queen's court may, but does not usually, interfere in the interests not so much of security of land tenure as of peace. If a resident quarrels with the district head, he cannot beg pardon with beer, highly though that method of reconciliation is appraised, because he would be 'humbling himself with the mealies of the land' or, as it is sometimes phrased, 'paying a fine with the calf of the cattle of the district head'. A resident migrating from the district should bid its head farewell with 'the beer of greeting'; application for land would then be regarded more favourably should he one day return. The fruits of the soil are dealt with in much the same manner. A man may graze his cattle inside or outside the district, but the cattle posts of the old days were within the district only. We have mentioned the rivalries of herdboys of different districts; we may add that some district heads, because of traditional values and limited grazing land, object to fencing. District heads sometimes reserve valuable trees for themselves, and it is they who give permission for the cutting down of large and shady trees or indigenous fruit-trees (though they be on the landowner's land). Honey found in trees, but not that found in the ground allotted, belongs to the district head. Some heads allow only residents to cut grass, making others pay. Hunting and water rights are not so regulated, but digging of clay is sometimes, if illegally. The preservation of large forests, a national asset, as places of the gods or of refuge in time of war is the concern of the queen, so that, for instance, Mujaji II had her cattle driven into the gardens of some people, including a district head, who had cleared part of the Levyeni forest and had not begged pardon by sending a *muṭanoni* to her.

Some distinctive cultural and administrative arrangements of the districts have already been mentioned. There are many others. All district heads used to have, and many still have, certain fields cultivated for them. The queen also has such fields in her districts, and since 1927 each district head has had to cultivate a field (*muremo*) in his district for the queen, an innovation suggested by the European to enable the queen to help her people during famines. The experiment has turned out very differently. These fields are badly cultivated, for years some district heads bring no mealies, the failure only sporadically leading to the penalization of the head and his district, and the mealies are always converted into beer for entertainments at the capital that benefit only the local residents. The storage of mealies is impracticable and a system of distribution is not implied in cultural arrangements. A district head unwillingly surrenders land and sometimes expropriates first one then another landowner, so that there is much dissatisfaction and even refusal to cultivate the *muremo*.

In many respects district heads are like chiefs. They are often called 'chief' (*khosi*) and, like the queen, have medicines to safeguard them in their position of authority. A district head is not only the most important person in the district, the centre of its political and legal life, the man who is responsible for the welfare of his people, but the obligations of district residents towards him emphasize both his position and the reciprocities between ruler and subject. It is expected that his subjects shall bring him beer periodically, and sometimes it is held that he should be invited to every beer party held in his area, partly because he is responsible for order at the beer drink and partly because it is his due. All his subjects must make *morula* cider for him in the proper season, and similarly, when at certain ceremonies, held by him for the well-being of the district, beer is required, every resident must contribute. The most important occasion is at the harvest thanksgiving and the beer brought is regarded as being in return for the land given by the head to his people. On the pattern of services to a chief, residents must also build his village and mend his huts. These privileges and obligations are not merely theoretical; they are very much in evidence and can be observed to-day in the districts as much as, if not more than, at the capital. The first edible termites found in the district must, in the case of some of the more important heads, be brought to the district head; these ants are ritually associated with rain-making and are put into the rain pots which these heads have.

The national 'schools' are sometimes held independently by district heads; in 'biting' the first fruits (*hu luma*) and in turning the first soil, the precedence of the queen is hardly recognized. The head at Ḍaja and the senior male line of the royal family have theoretical precedence in *hu luma* and, in contrast to many neighbouring tribes, there is little stress upon having the queen's field hoed first; in practice to-day her field is never ploughed first. Maunadala, it is said, in the old days paid an ox to anticipate the queen's hoeing and thus avoided threatening starvation; but dispensations of this nature, while recognizing a theoretical rule, throw into relief the much greater autonomy of the district here than elsewhere. The district head is solely responsible for *hu upa*, the rite that drives away destructive birds and monkeys when crops are ripe; to him the death of every resident is reported (the report being transmitted to the queen only when a relative of hers dies) and the resulting 'holiday' is held only in the district. Each district head has his own drums through which he controls dancing (*gɔsha*), religious observances, and some of the 'schools'. The girls' puberty rite (*khɔba*) is entirely district-controlled.

The individuality of some districts is seen in esoteric customs; elsewhere by taboo, succession ceremonial, and a distinctive community life. At Khiobeni people may construct on the edge of the village a rain-shelter (*kwado*) in which fire is made; in neighbouring areas this is taboo. Work on the day following the new moon is said to have been taboo in the old days at Matsui, though the rule is never observed to-day; in neighbouring areas there never was such a holiday. The Thɔʊɔla in one district have a special dance with a special ritual. As regards succession, the queen usually merely confirms, though she maintains touch through an elaborate ceremony: she is notified of the death of the head, sends the 'mother' of the district to take part in the ceremony of installation and, in the case of heads of the royal group, the *zwiḍajani* appear. The ceremonial, however, more intimately concerns the district: there is a local 'holiday' after the death, the *gɔsha* dance is taboo for a year, girls undergo puberty initiation elsewhere, beer is made by the district to 'open the drums', and each head of a family sends a goat or 10*s*., 'the eye of the chief', to acknowledge their new head. The life of the district is often distinctive. Matsui is said to be wasteful and, according to one of their praises, people there, instead of stamping, for which they are too lazy, 'burn their finger-nails roasting green mealies'. Everything is rather slack and happy-go-lucky, beer drinks are apt to be unruly, the district head is at loggerheads with his uncles, and his subjects talk disparagingly of 'this district-head business of going about and drinking beer'. Bacchanalian orgies after the harvest, slack morals, and other irregularities at Matsui contrast strikingly with conditions at Bagoni, an adjacent district. At Bagoni there is a tradition of thrift, strict control of beer-drinks, interest in national affairs, of pride and independence. Of course, a great deal depends upon the personality of the district head, but traditions in the district are not unimportant.

Districts are not always left to go their own way. In the last resort, as in legal matters, the authority of the capital may be invoked, and it may be invoked even against a whole district. Just as a district may collectively take action against a threat to its well-being, as occurred in the small-pox epidemic in 1938, when one district assembled and collected funds to have the witch who was causing the deaths smelt out, so it may be held collectively responsible by the capital for failure to cultivate the chief's field. This is the more striking because there is no kraal responsibility and the so-called 'spoor law' (whereby a kraal head, unwilling or unable to explain why the track of stolen cattle leads to but does not leave his kraal is held responsible, whoever the thief in his kraal might be) is not known. We have seen a district fined, never a kraal. The queen has theoretically to confirm the expulsion of a subject; in cases referred to a diviner, the 'ears' or official witness should be, but is not always, appointed at the queen's court. In practice, however, the queen seldom interposes her authority. For years now no one knows who is head at Dithejine, the balance swinging unevenly between three claimants. At Maḍarabani, Muteze, who persistently refused to do homage (*hu lova*) to the queen with beer, was deposed; but that there were other considerations at issue appears from the fact that immediately afterwards he was installed at Uukhuda. When Thagu at Khimarela in 1936 expelled his paternal uncle's son for whom he was deputizing, nothing was done. At Ralselaga when the head died, the messenger (*duna*) took over, ruled for years without confirmation from the capital and in 1938 was recognized (because his son became valuable as driver of the councillor's newly acquired motor car), the real heir being quietly overlooked. Not long ago the nobles at a tribal gathering carried their point that only royal relatives should be appointed as district heads on the farms that were being purchased, but the rule remained a dead letter and of the ten heads appointed in these areas eight are foreigners.

In its visible structure, the political organization may appear unimpressive and in its dynamics chaotic. Its efficiency certainly is and always was—for it is not culture contact that is responsible for the irregularities—of an order different from ours. Efficiency is relative to the purposes of the culture. The aim has never been power or empire, but holding subjects together on the model of the social organization. The slight regimentation of the 'schools' subserves no political or military purpose, and court life is not concerned with displays, nor is it characterized by differentiated officials and courtiers controlling a great central organization. Unlike the Shangana-Ṭonga, the Lovedu cannot deal with large gatherings of men such as collected on Coronation Day in 1937. The genius of the society is in organizing relationships between people, and as long as the reciprocity and compromise and the sentiments built up by interdependencies are reasonably maintained, it does not much matter that irregularities occur here and there. The influence of the queen, always on the side of peace and harmony, is characteristically exercised to keep alive these relationships. Important disputes—domestic, administrative, or political—are discussed with the queen and kept out of the courts, the object being to minimize animosities and to prevent public recriminations. Not external sanctions, but values internalized by the culture, are emphasized and upheld.

In the modern world the bonds of the social organization are liable to become burdens and the absence of a differentiated centralized political system a grave defect. But the old values are still the great dynamic forces. Nowhere else have we seen court etiquette so well preserved. People still remove their shoes when they enter the capital; the queen is still relatively inaccessible and may not leave her country. Mujaji was the only chief in the Union who, because of her ritual position, could not exercise her vote on behalf of the tribe when in 1937 the Native Representative Council was elected. Chiefs still come to supplicate for rain and, such is the queen's prestige and reputation for sagacity, a few years ago she adjudicated upon a succession dispute among the Dɔkwa Yet Mujaji is accorded no precedence by the European administration, in whose eyes she is completely overshadowed by her erstwhile subject, Muhlava of the Nkuna.

CHAPTER XI

THE GENIUS OF JURIDICAL ADJUSTMENTS

Conciliation machinery at the capital—quasi-judicial systems of appeasement—reliance in full-dress trials and sanctions upon agreement and compromise—procedure in 'blood' cases—appeals to ordeals and diviners.

THE genius of the Lovedu political system is its network of reciprocities; the genius of the legal system is its procedure of reconciliations and compromises; and both the political and legal systems reflect the main emphases and purposes of the culture. *Khɔrɔ* proceedings, the full-dress trials of the Lovedu, stand out conspicuously amid the various judicial arrangements, some of which we may be inclined to call quasi-judicial, but in reality none of our legal terms are appropriate. Their *khɔrɔ* is court-like, but it is not a court in our sense of the term; their law is law-like, not the equivalent of our law. All the procedures aim, not at settling legal issues, but at effecting compromises and reconciliations. The *khɔrɔ* itself, the most imposing feature of public life and the pinnacle of the cultural edifice, relies, not on force, but on friendly adjustments. It is the courtyard of compromises, not the arena of casuistic contests. It disposes of no sanction of execution: coercion is incongruous with its purposes. Culture contact has weakened the effectiveness of compromise and thereby has rendered necessary what it denies to the *khɔrɔ*—namely, the sanction of force.

In this chapter we deal briefly with the organization of the *khɔrɔ* and then touch lightly upon certain quasi-judical processes. These lead us to cast a passing glance first at *khɔrɔ* procedure and thereafter at various other types of procedure which centre, not in the *khɔrɔ*, but in other arrangements such as those involved in settling 'blood' cases and in dealing with the deeds of darkness by divination and the ordeal. All these procedures are part of the legal machinery, but they can be understood only as part also of the whole social structure. A comprehensive account of them is out of the question; we have no time even for a glimpse at substantive law.

The queen is at the head of the *khɔrɔ* organization. She never sits in the *khɔrɔ*, for it is the courtyard of the men. But she is always in the background, and in theory all decisions at the capital should be reported to, and confirmed by her. Five years ago, when the queen's uterine brother still lived and was a councillor, this was no formality, but to-day only very serious cases or decisions are submitted for her verdict or confirmation. This divergence from the ideal is due to conflicts, fear of involving the queen with European authorities, and a growing desire to reserve *khɔrɔ* affairs to the men. The queen's approval is still sought, always when the dispute involves the position or status of a royal relative, often when a district head expels a subject, and sometimes when a recalcitrant party is to be sent to the Native Commissioner or when one of the parties objects to the decision of the khɔrɔ. It is the queen's prerogative to settle disputes between royal relatives, but she also privately settles differences which, for reasons of public policy or of the prestige of the parties, should not be publicly discussed, and sometimes, to avoid the hardening of transient differences into permanent hostility, even withdraws cases, especially witchcraft cases, from the jurisdiction of the khɔrɔ. The queen has an unshakable reputation for integrity, and acts independently, if she likes, though often she consults trusted advisers, some of whom at present are not her councillors.

The role of the queen is not unconnected with the institution of 'mothers' of districts. 'Mothers' are appointed by the queen or with her approval, and are usually her relatives, living at the capital and having direct access to her. Generally they report in the first instance to the councillors, especially to the son of the queen's mother's brother, who is the greatest councillor. The office of 'mothers', though hereditary, often changes hands because of its responsibilities and inadequate rewards, the opportunities of favourably placed persons and the requirement of residence at or near the capital. Often a widow, familiar with her husband's arrangements, takes over the position, enlisting the help of a relative, who at her death naturally steps into her shoes. Since the fees received cannot meet the needs of taxpayers, usually only old people are 'mothers', but inability to cope with long journeys forces them to entrust some of their work to available sons or relatives, who in turn may succeed to the position. 'Mothers' are often related to, but may be only fortuitously linked with, the heads of districts under their charge. A foreign chief or headman may be introduced at the capital by a friend or relative or stranger, who thereupon becomes his 'mother'. In 1912, when a colony of settlers from Basutoland came, Mashaveli, who had no previous association with them, took the message of their arrival to the queen and henceforth acted as their 'mother'. Independent foreign chiefs also have their 'mothers', who sometimes live far from the capital.

'Mothers' have politico-legal and other functions. They receive their 'children', the district heads or foreign chiefs, and act as intermediaries whenever formal relations with the queen or great councillors are involved. When it is impracticable for a district head to bring beer to the queen, he may send mealies, which are deposited at the 'mother's' and there converted into the tributary beer. The arrival of beer from a district is always reported to the 'mother', who receives one calabash. 'Mothers' are the messengers or ambassadors of the queen sent to settle disputes among their 'children' or to represent her, for instance, at the formal installation of a district head. Important links in politics, they are the master links in the legal system. Some 'mothers' supervise the legal interrelations of many districts with the capital. As some districts are far off, eight to ten miles, they may delegate the work, in respect of some districts or of some of its aspects, to others, such as sons, wives, sister's sons, or wife's brothers. Thus Khidima, 'mother' of Mavulana, Maraga, Madumani, Gabiani, Musugududzi, and a European-owned farm, sometimes puts cases coming from the first three districts in the hands of his sister's son, but, since Khidima's own son has reached years of discretion—he is now forty years of age—it is to him that the court work has been entrusted. Quite recently (1938) Khidima, too old to walk far, deputed his son to settle a serious dispute at Dithejeni, a sub-district of Maʋulana; but the conflict which involved the interests of Maʋulana, the maternal uncle of the queen, and Khashani, direct descendant in the senior royal line, 'overcame' the son as it subsequently 'overcame' even the queen's *khɔrɔ*. It is thus apparent that 'mothers' have responsible duties and must be men of tact and experience.

'Mothers' often act as arbitrators in district courts. In some districts they regularly preside when important cases are decided, in others they hardly ever appear: recently established districts whose heads are foreigners need some supervision and linking up with the capital, while in old districts much depends upon the pride or prestige or ability of the district head. 'Mothers' are sent to investigate or try cases which are reported directly to the capital without reference to the district head (an irregular procedure which he resents) or which have 'overcome' him either in a *khɔrɔ* trial or in his attempt to effect a private reconciliation (*hu khumɛlwa*). The district head may accompany a deserting wife to beg pardon of her husband, but if the overture fails, she may present her case to her 'mother' or to the queen who usually arranges for a 'mother' or messenger to arbitrate, often quite informally, between husband and wife. Messengers become versed in handling compromises from an early age, at first as envoys (*maharula*) merely registering consents, later as true arbitrators. They accompany the district head to the home of the disputant or sit in the *khɔrɔ* of the district, reporting the result to the 'mother', who in turn reports to the queen or councillors. Or if 'overcome', they summon the parties to the *khɔrɔ* of the capital. The procedure economizes effort and promotes amicable settlements; it induces a uniform outlook towards disputes, but not uniformity of substantive law, throughout the country. Thus Shangana-Ṭonga law, where it differs from Loʋedu law, remains intact; the 'mother' or messenger or the *khɔrɔ* itself is concerned, not with differences of law, but with reaching agreements acceptable to the parties.

As an officer of the *khɔrɔ* at the capital, the 'mother' presents cases, summons defendants to appear, is usually present in court and may, if called upon or on his own initiative, explain the antecedents of the case. But these activities are so unostentatious, so alien to our conceptions, that it is very rare that you will notice a 'mother' in the *khɔrɔ*. To avoid being suspected of favouring his 'children', he remains discreetly in the background, his presentation of the case is unnecessary as he has already privately reported to the councillors, and the arrangements of the *khɔrɔ* are so flexible and its spirit so homely that formally introducing cases or calling witnesses to come nearer is quite out of place. In the midst of a defendant's oration or the 'chewing' of the case by the *khɔrɔ*, you may see a 'mother' intervene to say that the defendant has neglected to pay him the goat that is the 'fee of the feet' (messenger's fee) and the case is abruptly stopped, 'hung up' in the *khɔrɔ*, until the fee is paid. Loʋedu judicial processes are so unlike ours that it is wholly misleading to picture the 'mother' as an officer of the court arranging the roll, marshalling witnesses introducing cases like a prosecutor, or advising parties as to the case to be met or the witnesses to be called.

The two great councillors are in a pivotal position, since 'mothers' report to them. But in the first place they are not the officials who in other tribes head the panel of assessors or 'remembrancers'. It is not necessary, though it is usual, for one of them to be present or to preside at the regular sessions which are nowadays held for convenience on Sunday morning. On week days, if the other men at the capital feel unequal to the task, the absence of the great councillors sometimes holds up a case; but many cases are tried without them. Their position enables them to do the bulk of the work, but they have no specialized functions. All cases are not reported to or through them, as many 'mothers' have direct access to the queen. Checks and balances of the system even counteract that strengthening of their powers which results from the practice of European officials to deal exclusively with them. Secondly, there are no specially appointed assessors or advisers or 'remembrancers'. Compromises within a broad pattern, not details of law and precedents, are important. The oldest men at the capital are rarely consulted, in our experience only twice in many hundreds of cases; they are the victims of the conflict within the complex of royal institutions. The queen's *khɔrɔ* consists of men, generally speaking, drawn from the capital and neighbouring villages. But any one may attend; there is no special privilege and no special appointment. Some are more welcome, some have a higher reputation for integrity or sagacity, than others, some are friends, some enemies of the councillors. The *khɔrɔ* is a fortuitous rather than a fixed body of men.

A glance at some of the personalities of the queen's *khɔrɔ*, as it was in 1937, will make our general observations more concrete. Muneri, the queen's physiological mother's brother and called 'mother's brother', more often presided than his fellow councillor, Murwatsɛṭa, the queen's uterine brother's eldest but not chief son. They were both middle-aged men, lived at the capital and were rivals. R., a man in his prime, usually attended, though some years before he had been expelled as a murderer and witch from the district of the capital in which he still lives; he also befriended S., the would-be traitor, and was so much hated that he was once assaulted in the *khɔrɔ* by a son of the queen's brother. R. often sat in the centre of the *khɔrɔ*, eloquently using his commanding voice to reprimand, cajole, moralize, and even skilfully to guide contestants towards a compromise. Maduludi, in 1937 only about fifty-five years old, but now dead, came from the valley to enjoy the *khɔrɔ* discussions. An excitable extrovert, he used to rise from his seat in order to enforce an *ad hoc* argument or to shake his fist in the face of a recalcitrant defendant, and often he prematurely rushed to conclusions, imposing a fine even before the evidence was led, but he was tolerated and gently restrained by the others. B. frequently almost slunk into the *khɔrɔ*: emaciated and consumptive, nervous and suspicious, hated and feared by the councillors, suspected of having murdered a royal relative with his witchcraft, he was wholly inaccessible to us, yet in the *khɔrɔ* his hoarse, screeching voice, as he now and then interjected a high-pitched but incisive remark, carried great weight. There was also muddled-headed old Mabungwani, who, as judgement creditor, regularly for two years came from a far-off district fruitlessly to complain that Maake, the debtor, had not yet paid him, but was still 'looking for' the fine; he took a prominent part, muddling the issues, but humouring the men; and it was a real joy to listen to him These were but some of the striking personalities of the fifty men or more who habitually came to the *khɔrɔ*. They attended, some for one reason, some for another, as we would attend a function which is partly an entertainment and partly a responsibility. The *khɔrɔ* is not wholly a casual assembly, since men living in the neighbourhood are expected to give their assistance at the sessions every Sunday morning.

Not the men of the *khɔrɔ*, but only 'mothers' and messengers, are specially rewarded. A plaintiff, resident, say, in the district of Madumani, taking his case to the capital, should go accompanied by a messenger from Madumani to report his complaint to his 'mother', Khidima, to whom he gives three goats or their equivalent, usually £1 and a goat. By this formal complaint (*hu ḍalia*) he becomes the plaintiff (*muḍalii*): the £1 is *hu ḍalia*, serves to 'open' the *khɔrɔ*, and is handed by the 'mother' to the queen; the goat or 10s. is to 'break down the *khɔrɔ*' and will be retained by Khidima if the defendant lives in one of his districts, for then Khidima must summon him; but if he resides in, say, Matsui, Khidima must give the goat to Muneri, 'mother' of Matsui, who is responsible for calling his own 'children'. The 'mother' himself, as was usual in the old days, or a messenger of the 'mother', as is common to-day, receives from the defendant he summons a goat called *budi va bija* (goat of the pot) or *leudu la mudzeḍa* (fee of the feet). In cases of 'blood', of witchcraft, and of offences against the tribal authorities, when they come before the *khɔrɔ*, the procedure is different and these fees are not paid.

All the young men in the district of the capital are *maharula*, envoys of *khɔrɔ* or queen. The usual work of a *leharula* is to call district heads to tribal gatherings (*khivijɔ*), though much of this is now done by herdboys, who every fortnight drive the cattle to the dipping tanks. The *maharula* also represent the queen at *morula* cider drinks, given to the queen by districts other than the capital, for, except on special and very rare religious occasions (say once in every few years), she does not move beyond her own district. But for our present purpose we shall consider the *maharula* as a kind of police force, though without its powers. Police, prisons, process for executing judgements are alien to the culture, but situations akin to contempt occasionally arise in the *khɔrɔ*, and, if it is a young man or woman who despises the authority of the old men, a *leharula* may be detailed to supervise the execution of a patently absurd piece of work by the offender. The object is to humiliate, the onlookers are amused, no force is used, and usually the prisoner submits before he has started the work. *Maharula* do not specially attend the *khɔrɔ* for this purpose; the *khɔrɔ* usually ignores indignities; and submission, even if merely assumed, is accepted as sufficient.

Another duty of *maharula* is to collect fines, imposed by custom, not by trial, upon a whole district that has offended. When, for instance, in 1937 none of the young boys and girls of the district of the capital responded to the order to weed the queen's field, *maharula* went to collect a fowl from each 'rebel'. They collected seven fowls, because most of the delinquents could offer excuses which showed, to the satisfaction of the *maharula*, that they had repented. In 1938 Mahubusana complained that the residents of his district despised him. They had successively ignored his order to make *morula* cider first for himself and then for the queen and also to bring the 'money for the petrol of the queen's car'. *Maharula*, the councillors said, would be sent to exact one goat from every household. Nothing happened. Later Mahubusana brought the five main culprits to the capital and there they were told to pay 5*s*. each to their district head and to leave the district after having gathered in their harvest. 'You have despised the district head and the queen,' it was said. 'Go, then, and live where there is no chief, for here you worry the queen.' There was no trial; and a year after the 1938 harvest the rebels were still living in the district. *Maharula* are also sent to exact the fine due in those 'blood' cases that are reported to the queen. Despite apparent exceptions, *maharula* are not and never were deputed to execute upon a decision of the *khɔrɔ*, for the *khɔrɔ* is concerned with private delicts, wrongs between individuals who, in the last resort, are left to arrange restitution among themselves.

At the village of each district head there is also a *khɔrɔ*, the arrangements of which resemble those at the capital; but, of course, there are many variations. Its competence is in practice determined by the presumptions of the district head; and the law it applies is not necessarily the law of the capital. Some district heads, having sub-districts under them, attach 'mothers' and *maharula* to the *khɔrɔ*, but usually these are only messengers for calling defendants. *Khɔrɔ* trials are usually held in the district of the defendant, and the messenger or 'mother' is entitled to the 'fee of the feet', but not all district heads charge for 'opening' the *khɔrɔ*. The district head may have a special *duna*, often his elder brother, who is entrusted with legal matters and 'presides' in his absence; women who are heads do not appear in the *khɔrɔ*, but confirm decisions. Sometimes the district *khɔrɔ* is better organized and controlled than that at the capital, there may be regular judges and assessors, the word is 'passed' (*hu suma*) from the junior to the senior members, contempt is strictly dealt with, and so on. But this is unusual, the organization being much more haphazard and the procedure much less regularized. Mostly the district head intervenes at the request of one party to see whether he can effect a reconciliation: he sets out with the plaintiff to the village of the defendant rather than summons the defendant to his *khɔrɔ*, or he goes as an intermediary (*mukhumedi*) of the one party to persuade the other to accept the settlement offered. Full-dress *khɔrɔ* trials are often like heated family consultations. *Khɔrɔ* cases in which the fine of restitution is a head of cattle must theoretically be reported to the capital, not for confirmation, but for directions as to the disposal of the fine; but in practice this rule is often not observed. 'Blood' cases not reported to the capital are dealt with by the district head, whose function is something between that of an intercessor and a judge. In theory 'blood' cases are not tried, and in practice district heads do inquire into and often finally settle such cases.

The procedure to-day involved in witchcraft cases can be set into motion and these cases may be settled by district heads. In short, set rules as to competence do not exist and district heads are left to cope with as much as they can manage.

A brief discussion of some quasi-judicial processes will enable us to appreciate better, as it will introduce us to the procedure and spirit of the *khɔrɔ*. Firstly, there is the method by which especially old women deal with disrespectful or insulting behaviour of younger women. Should one or more young women play a practical joke upon or be disrespectful to an old woman, or playfully 'dance' an infant child, even their own, or prematurely try to make it sit up or walk or scold or beat it, in the presence of the grandmother or of an old woman, their behaviour is regarded as insulting. The conception is that old women in their role as midwives, rather than young mothers, have brought children into the world and the old, not the young, are the guardians of the babes. If one young woman arrogates to herself rights and privileges which belong to the old women, the latter are entitled to take suitable action. The insulted old woman reports to a few of her age-mates and in consultation they decide to punish the age-mates of the young woman resident in the same territorial unit—for example, a district. There is neither 'trial' nor tribunal. The punishment consists of three elements: the age-mates of the young women (say all those who have one baby) must brew beer with which to effect a reconciliation with the older women; in a rite accompanying the beer drink and resembling that used at initiations, the oldest woman canes her immediate junior, who in turn canes the next, and so on, including the culprits; and, finally, the culprits are read a lesson as to the iniquity of being disrespectful to their elders.

One day three young married women, in circumstances that implied disrespect, sent three old women a tiny quantity of snuff. The older women immediately fined the younger and vicariously all their age-mates living in the Christian settlement, for they were all residents there. They were told to grind snuff and restitute their wrong with beer. Five days later the twelve young married women of the settlement came to the house of the oldest woman, bringing large quantities of nuts, light beer, pumpkins, and other food; their husbands, in addition, sent a large tin of snuff and these 'gifts' were divided among the old women. Then followed the rite and the warning. On another occasion all the young mothers of a district were fined because one of them had 'danced' its baby in the presence of its grandmother. Likewise, it is said, though we have not seen a case, that the old women may fine a young father and his age-mates, if he forgets their privileges in regard to babies. But we cannot speak of regimental courts, the age-grades are not determined by the 'schools', the responsibility is territorial, and the punishment is 'beer of reconciliation' (largely replaced by food among Christians).

The second procedure, that called *hu khumɛlwa* (to beg pardon, to reconcile), has an enormous province and a profound significance, not only for legal arrangements, but in the whole culture. The procedure uses a *mukhumedi*, the emissary who intervenes on behalf of one of the parties to beg the pardon of the other. Its essence is not humiliation of the one, but bilateral reconciliation: thus people often talk of *hu khumɛjana*, to beg pardon of one another, to become reconciled. If A., to whom B. has lent her pot, breaks it, A. should send an old woman as conciliator (*mukhumedi*) to express regret and to ask forgiveness. But the *mukhumedi* figures in every conceivable kind of case, whether or not amenable to the courts: in homicide and adultery settled out of the *khɔrɔ*; in breaches of etiquette, such as bad behaviour of a bridegroom on his courtship visits, which cannot be submitted to the *khɔrɔ*; in disputes already before the *khɔrɔ*. It is not necessarily the wrongdoer, objectively considered, who should initiate the procedure: an illtreated wife who runs away to her parents must be sent back with a *mukhumedi*. Nor will the *khɔrɔ* necessarily order the guilty party to *khumɛlwa*: he who must beg pardon is the junior, or the person of inferior rank.

The great province of *hu khumɛlwa* is in family and kinship disputes, only a small proportion of which ever reach the *khɔrɔ*. The group of people concerned as a family council is determined by cultural arrangements. A quarrel between a father and son of one of his wives is the immediate concern of that house alone; no one else, not even the father's brother or a co-wife, may intervene; but the cattle-linked sister who built the house with her cattle presides and 'cuts' the case. A brother of that sister may be called in, but it is not necessary, and in any case he may only advise if his opinion is asked. If the matter concerns a wider circle, others may be called in; it is impossible to lay down general rules, since on the one hand, each cultural complex (e.g. marriage or inheritance) implies a different set of interested persons and, on the other, each case has its peculiar aspects. The marriage of the daughter of a house is, as regards its obligation to a cattle-linked house, the concern primarily of that house, but if the daughter is to be married to a stranger the mistress of the cattle-linked house must be consulted. If co-wives quarrel, their differences are the concern of the houses concerned, but if one of the wives has bewitched the other, the husband is a mere spectator as regards the arrangements that may be made between the parents of the co-wives; and even in a *khɔrɔ* case, it is not the husband, but the parents who are the parties who may be ordered to *khumɛjana*.

Hu khumɛjana may be likened to compounding a wrong, but it clearly has much deeper significance: it may be ordered by the *khɔrɔ*, alone or in addition to restitution; and it is quite irrelevant whether the wrong is amenable to the court. There is no wrong that cannot be submitted to this procedure. Though theoretically 'A dog which eats another cannot grow fat' (i.e. a murderer must always be killed), *hu khumɛlwa* is in practice always possible, for 'He who kills another kills his brother-in-law' (i.e. if the victim's kin agree, the homicide may be made good by a full *munywalo* or a daughter or sister). In modern practice, most interesting cases have arisen. In one case some years ago the murderer, who had killed his victim for medicine, a heinous crime, offered his sister in marriage to the victim's elder brother; the investigation by the European authorities failed; and to-day there is a child of the marriage, and permanent links between victim and murderer because, on the pattern of bride and cattle exchanges, they have become cattle-linked kin. The handing over of a bride or of *munywalo* may supplement the supposedly inadequate punishment meted out by European courts, or be in substitution for the penalty such courts would have imposed if the parties had given away the facts. There is no payment to the queen, no trial, only *hu khumɛlwa*. The bride is not returned, as is reported in the case of other tribes, when she has borne a child in the lineage of the victim. In 1938, when the sons of A. and B. were herding together, A.'s son pushed a large rock which rolled over and accidentally killed B.'s son. A. sent a *mukhumedi*, but B. refused to accept a mere apology; he wanted 'something to wipe away his tears'. Eventually he accepted four head of cattle, which were brought to the *khɔrɔ* of the district head and there handed to him. A little later A. demanded back his cattle, saying that he had lost too much and hoping that publicity would frighten B.; but A.'s object was defeated by a device which we cannot describe here except to say that it was as cunning as it was effective.

Hu khumɛlwa is the predominant procedure in the districts, and everywhere it is considered especially appropriate to adultery, damage to crops, and 'blood' cases or bodily assaults; it is often the only permissible procedure in family disputes; and it is praiseworthy in theft cases. It may involve an elaborate series of acts, to some features of which we may refer. In one case a wife had committed adultery, and when the husband, after the birth of the child, had discovered the identity of the adulterer, he sent his wife to him. The adulterer, as is customary when he admits his wrong, sent the wife back with the 'goat of [illicitly] meeting one another', which he had borrowed from a neighbour. The goat was killed and the husband gave his erring wife the back leg, the portion that really belonged to him, which was an unusual humiliation. The wife went to an old woman, who took her back to beg pardon on behalf of the wife and to say that the adulterer would later send a cow with his own *mukhumedi*. The procedure in adultery or seduction is not rigid, but essentially the injured husband or the father sends a messenger to adulterer or seducer, who, if he admits the accusation, sends back his *mukhumedi* with an offer of settlement; negotiations may continue for some time and the culprit may be let off lightly, in many cases only a goat being exacted, though, to avoid publicity, more than the usual compensation may be paid. In 'blood' cases *hu khumɛlwa* strikingly benefits both assaulter and victim. In theft, the offender must offer the thing stolen plus a goat or even a head of cattle 'of causing [the thing] to come back'. Mudiwa, living at the capital, one day found that some of his pumpkins had been stolen in a field at Khikhudini. A little later he met a woman who, caught with some pumpkin leaves as she came from the field, admitted her guilt. Mudiwa reported to the district head at Khikhudini, who arranged that the parties met him at the woman's home to discuss the matter. There she offered a pig as pardon. Mudiwa accepted, told her to sell the pig and give him 10s. The proceedings were more or less private, those present being only Mudiwa, the woman and a relative or two, and the district head, in the role technically as judge, but really as *mukhumedi*. If the matter had been between residents of the same district, the intervention of the district head would have been unnecessary; but very frequently he acts as *mukhumedi* in these cases.

Hu khumɛlwa is the only proper initial procedure in cases of damage to crops. The owner of the cattle is called to see the damage, begs pardon with a goat, and is told to strengthen his cattle kraal. If depredations continue, he may be taken to the *khɔrɔ*. To omit the preliminary procedure of *hu khumɛlwa* is not necessarily fatal, but is regarded as being revengeful and nothing is abhorred more than revenge. If the man whose crops are damaged refuses reconciliation and makes the owner of the cattle 'pay' instead of allowing *hu khumɛlwa*, the owner will, it is said, seek an opportunity to revenge himself, and the saying that applies is: 'It is the blow that follows, not the first blow, that hurts.' The saying is, however, of general application and is invoked in regard to any injury or wrong. Practice differs in the various districts as regards *hu khumelwa* for damage to crops, and when a man is resident in one district and has his fields in another, very interesting conflicts of jurisdiction and law sometimes occur, but we cannot stop to consider them.

After formal complaint—that is, after a case is 'in the *khɔrɔ*'—*hu khumɛlwa* may, according to the circumstances, either end the matter or be treated as a confession of guilt (*duma muladu*) by plaintiff or *khɔrɔ*. *Duma muladu* is a term used also outside the *khɔrɔ*. If the owner of cattle continues to be careless after several warnings, he may find that his goat of reconciliation will be regarded, not as a goat of begging pardon, but as a confession of guilt, and the victim will exact what he considers to be the real damage. To accept pardon stops *khɔrɔ* proceedings, and if after *duma muladu* the culprit makes good what the victim demands there also can be no *khɔrɔ* trial; but if he does not, the offer of pardon is a confession, not conceived as having been made without prejudice, but admissible in evidence. More often *duma muladu* refers to a goat which the defendant offers in the *khɔrɔ* in settlement and apology. The circumstances, especially the attitude of the plaintiff and the previous history of the case, will then determine whether the matter ends there. The *khɔrɔ* may say, 'This is your *duma muladu*; now pay the ox which in our [or the plaintiff's] opinion fits the offence.'

Examples of *duma muladu* are difficult to give as a long history is involved and, to understand them, we should have to refer to details of the culture which are not dealt with in this book. But it may be possible to simplify for presentation here the case of *Mabula* v. *Magɔsha*, though it lasted six months in the *khɔrɔ* of the capital alone. These two women were co-wives of Khidai and were entangled in one of those polygons of jealousies arising in polygyny which are the counterpart of the eternal triangles of our monogamy. The co-wives quarrelled and fought about their extra-marital lovers, and Magɔsha bit Mabula on the lip. When the wound refused to yield to treatment it was said to be due to the 'bad teeth' of Magɔsha, who, it was suspected, must be a *leshɛga*, a person who had been allowed to live though her upper teeth had appeared before the lower. Having vainly appealed to her husband to order Magɔsha's teeth to be scraped for medicine, Mabula complained to her parents. After much manœuvring in order to avoid being drawn into the conflict, the mother and the brother of Mabula went to the parents of Magɔsha, who, however, refused to allow the scraping of their daughter's teeth on the grounds that it implied that they were witches.

When the matter came before the *khɔrɔ*, the view was taken that, 'If a dog bites you and the wound festers, it is not wrong to ask the owner for a hair from its tail': you are not imputing witchcraft and it does not matter that the hair or scrapings may have no healing virtues, the important matter being willingness to help. Many side issues emerged, especially as to whose responsibility was the scraping of the teeth: the husband's or the parent's. Once Mukugoloi, Magɔsha's father, by escaping from his village, evaded the attempt made by Mabula's elder sister to scrape Magɔsha's teeth. There were at times recriminations in the *khɔrɔ*, which showed that the *munywalo* links were about to be broken. 'If you no longer care for us,' said Mukugoloi, 'I shall pay Mabula's parents'; but Khidai replied, 'What kind of ill-bred woman is that daughter of yours, who is pregnant by a lover, and swears at me by the things inside my trousers. My cattle have provided wives for two of your sons and only I of all your sons-in-law have "gates" in your village.' An old man interjected, 'The jealousies of the child are settled by its parents. Khidai is not responsible. You, Mukugoloi, must *khumɛlwa*.' A week later Mukugoloi offered a goat of reconciliation. But the *khɔrɔ* said, 'No. This goat is *duma muladu*. We now want you to bring an ox, because the father of Mabula has come to you often to ask you to *khumɛlwa* and you refused.' And the father added, 'Yes, I came also to the *khɔrɔ* (a distance of eight miles) for eighteen weeks, but you did not turn up. Can I "work" eighteen weeks for merely a goat?'

Mukugoloi consented to pay, but urged that he had a case against Khidai, who should have prevented the drawn-out proceedings by settling it. That was another matter, said the court, for 'The kidneys of an elephant cannot be harnessed together' (they are, like two cases, too weighty to be dealt with at the same time). We may doubt whether it was wise, in view of the polygon of conflicts, to treat as *duma muladu* the goat offered in reconciliation, but in these matters the *khɔrɔ* is generally wiser than we are.

Hu khumɛlwa and its elaborations lead us to consider the procedure in the *khɔrɔ*. The conceptions are interwoven, but a *khɔrɔ* trial is regarded as essentially different from the quasi-judicial procedures. It is public, unlike *hu khumelwa*, and it starts with *hu ḍalia* (a formal complaint to an officer of the court); there are 'opening' and 'closing' fees and compensation or restitution (*mulefo*); and the constitution of the *khɔrɔ* is not based on alinements of interested parties. Before *hu ḍalia*, there is no *khɔrɔ* case; the matter is private. *Hu vela*, privately to ask a debtor to pay, precedes but does not necessarily lead to *hu ḍalia*; it may end in *hu khumɛlwa*. But *khɔrɔ* trials and settlement in the family or by reconciliation out of court do not differ from one another as regards the sanction of force; both rely upon consent. Because the *khɔrɔ* is public, contempt of its authority may be punished, but the humiliation of the offender is a means rather of inducing him to consent than of enforcing a judgement; we have never seen it applied as an alternative to paying the fine or making the restitution. The great feature of the *khɔrɔ* is its publicity. It constitutes a large part of the public life of the men and, while it lives as an institution, it will powerfully counteract the sense of frustration resulting from the intervention of the white man.

The *khɔrɔ* is the final safeguard of the *munywalo* system and, through that system, of the intricate social structure. It also deals with witchcraft, theft, assault, adultery, and other disputes; but its province in witchcraft and sorcery is limited and has only recently developed, theft and adultery do not lend themselves to its genius, and other cases are primarily to be settled by *hu khumɛlwa*. Of all disputes coming before the *khɔrɔ*, 76 per cent. are *munywalo* cases, but if we consider only the disputes that are really submitted to trial and not merely for confirmation or registration of a decision otherwise reached, the percentage rises to 88. Yet the chief subject of litigation is *munywalo* only if we ignore completely the conflicts that are settled by *hu khumɛlwa* or in the family. In our opinion, though by the nature of the case the evidence can never be complete, these latter cases outnumber *khɔrɔ* cases to the same extent as *munywalo* cases outnumber all other cases of the *khɔrɔ*.

Of the many implications of these facts, we shall refer merely to two First of all, contrary to what is often stated concerning the Bantu, it is not that most conflicts in the society arise from *munywalo*, but that, of the disputes having, as we phrase it, legal consequences, none are more in evidence than *munywalo* tangles. But as the *khɔrɔ* is really a *munywalo* court, we cannot argue from the litigation we find in it to the general nature of the conflicts in the society. The error is somewhat like concluding from cases coming before special divorce courts among us, that marital disputes are the main causes of dissension in our society. *Khɔrɔ* proceedings are essentially *munywalo* proceedings because the complex *munywalo* system, and the safeguarding of its intricate reciprocities, can adequately be entrusted, not to private arrangements, but to an imposing public organization. The stresses and strains in the system are not only of a personal but of an institutional nature, involving the integration of diverse elements in the social structure. Compromises affect individuals as well as larger groups and their interrelations, and, for the solutions required, the society needs the wide perspective and wisdom of a trained body of men. They have to adjust personal difficulties, but in the context of an intricate system that is easily thrown out of gear. Herein also lies the special genius of the *khɔrɔ*.

Secondly, legal arrangements appear to be made and controlled by men, but that is because we identify law with the *khɔrɔ*, the place of the men. In *hu khumɛlwa* women are at least as important as men, and in family disputes no one occupies so pivotal a position as the cattle-linked sister, the legal 'builder' of most houses in the country, she who 'cuts' cases arising within the house and regulates the inheritance of goods and of widows. These 'judicial'-like activities cover vast provinces of the total culture, and they are fully recognized in *khɔrɔ* proceedings in which neither in arriving at a decision nor in safeguarding its execution can the men ignore the wishes, authority, or influence of the sister. In complicated cases, they often postpone their decision again and again until she appears, and they rely upon her to suggest a solution and to guarantee its being put into effect. Old women, sitting on the fringes of the court, are sometimes heard to mumble, as if impersonally, about the tortuous ways of the men when such-and-such is the simple solution; a man within earshot overhears the remark and applies it to the case; and more often than not, as you see the men 'jump upon' the happy phrase or formula suggested, you realize that men do not have the monopoly of wisdom. Women are the strongest pillars of the social structure and without their support there can be no guarantee that the adjustments in the superstructure will be lasting or effective; and, in a society that relies on compromise and not on coercion, this role becomes even more important. Women appear as plaintiffs or defendants as frequently as men; we have never heard either the *khɔrɔ* or a party object that an opponent was a woman unassisted by her guardian; but we have heard an old woman, the defendant, refuse to proceed in a case where the plaintiff was a young man of twenty-five years. It was a divorce case, in which the young man presumptuously had handed *munywalo* cattle, not to the mother of the bride, but to the bride's husband. The mother took back her daughter and the young man sued for the return of his goods. The mother said in the *khɔrɔ*, 'I scorn to discuss the matter with you, a mere child. You know nothing about cases. Bring your father. I do not understand your complaint.' The *khɔrɔ* agreed. Of course, the *khɔrɔ* is the province of the men, and their place and function in it have been institutionalized; by contrast, only a few women have an institutional hold upon the *khɔrɔ*, but they are firmly entrenched in the social structure, which is the *raison d'être* of the *khɔrɔ*.

We cannot do more than give a general picture of a few aspects of the practice and procedure of the *khɔrɔ*. There are the usual preliminary processes. A creditor, going alone directly to the debtor, complains (*hu vela*) once, twice, perhaps many times; the complaint is not made through the village head. The debtor may ask his district head or another to intercede as his *mukhumedi*. But if nothing happens, the creditor warns the debtor that he will proceed to *hu ḍalia*, the formal complaint to the district head, not the village head, which begins the case. The dispute may still be settled privately with the district head appearing in the role of an intercessor rather than a judge, probably at the defendant's village. If this fails, the assistance of the 'mother' of the district may be called in, as already described, or there may be a full-dress *khɔrɔ* trial, with its 'opening' fees and 'fees of the feet'. Should the district head be 'overcome', the case may go to the capital. The parties are summoned to appear on a certain Sunday and there are present some fifty men, all of them potential arbitrators. It is difficult to distinguish judges, litigants, and visitors, and, though there is some one presiding, now one, now another of the men, even though they have been found guilty in a previous case the same day, may take the lead and decide the case.

The *khɔrɔ* is not unlike a family council: there are no set forms or formulas or procedures, no precise order in which cases are called or matters are discussed. While the parties to one case, unable to reach agreement, retire to the 'dung of the dogs' along the fence of the courtyard, where they may more freely advance personal considerations, the *khɔrɔ* goes on to the next case. After plaintiff and defendant have spoken, the discussion may become general and heated, or it may peter out or degenerate to *ad hoc* arguments in various quarters, and no crisp decision may be given. There are many interruptions. Yet the men say that *khɔrɔ* work is arduous and requires much concentration—clearly their conceptions are very different from ours. They attach great importance to impartial justice, and bribery in our sense is rare. The danger of partiality arises from relationship and friendship; arbitrators do not recuse themselves, but often show their embarrassment by silence or slipping out of the *khɔrɔ*. We have seen cases in which a district head was fined by his own *khɔrɔ* for assaulting one of the residents of his district. Even the queen may be judged (in private) by her retinue, the nobles (*Ʋaramuhaṭulwa gi valada*).

The problem of the *khɔrɔ* lies, not in sifting evidence or dispensing justice according to law, but in adjusting personal differences within the general framework of the social structure. Success is achieved when personality compromises can be harmonized with the implications of the social system. The *khɔrɔ* is not much concerned with strict law or the details of law. They do not rely upon judicial precedents for authoritative legal material. If precedents are quoted, and that is exceedingly rare, their purpose is to suggest arrangements and adjustments that are effective, not to determine a legal rule. The law is not the law of the courts; it is the 'law' of the institutions and is embedded in the institutions; and the harmony of different institutions and their 'laws' results from the total cultural configuration, not the judgements of the *khɔrɔ*. If the arrangements or 'laws' of two institutions conflict in a case, as they sometimes do, the *khɔrɔ* is powerless to resolve the conflict; for law is not of an autonomous order.

We cannot speak of examination, much less of cross-examination, of witnesses. All the parties are present when evidence is given, for 'Only Europeans conceal what one says from another and allow secret manipulations of evidence behind the backs of others'. The foreknowledge of the *khɔrɔ*, the availability of the weapons of confrontation and publicity, reduces direct perjury to a minimum. Litigants know the art of presenting their cases and of skilfully twisting a story, but a man caught out in telling an untruth readily confesses the truth. Falsehood is dealt with by ridicule and laughter; it is not punished as perjury. There are no rules as to what may be admitted as evidence, but the probative value of different kinds of evidence is well understood. The evidence need not bear upon the issue presented to the court, for that issue may merely reflect a more fundamental conflict, and it is with this conflict and its resolution that the *khɔrɔ* is concerned. Hearsay and irrelevancies may furnish important clues as to the origin or nature of the dispute. Rigid proof is necessary when elementary facts are in issue, as when the sole question is how many cattle have to be returned upon divorce, and then reliance is placed upon the evidence of the two marriage intermediaries. In theft and adultery cases, despite presumptions that supplement the evidence of the senses, the *khɔrɔ* is peculiarly helpless and extra-*khɔrɔ* procedures must be invoked.

Besides the *khɔrɔ* fees already mentioned, there is a 'closing' fee, required only where *munywalo* is returned. Theoretically, one of the cattle is slaughtered and eaten by the *khɔrɔ*, but in practice this is rarely done. Much more usually does one see, when plaintiff is paid some goats or some cattle and goats as the result of a judgement, that the *khɔrɔ* orders one of the goats to be set aside as the 'goat of the shaking of the beards', which is killed for those attending the session, in recognition of all the talking they have done. The queen receives only the £1 exacted as 'opening' fee—required always in *munywalo* suits, rarely in theft, and never in other cases—and the head of cattle paid in 'blood cases' that come before the *khɔrɔ* of the capital. What she receives in this way can never enrich her, though it helps her to provide the *munywalo* of her many wives.

Fees and fines or restitution raise questions of execution. The *khɔrɔ* never levied execution in the past and it cannot do so to-day, but self-help is absolutely forbidden. The *khɔrɔ* reluctantly and rarely calls in the aid of the Native Commissioner, and for a litigant to place his case in the hands of a solicitor is an abomination which, whatever his rights, will turn the *khɔrɔ* against him. Execution is frowned upon almost as much as intervention by the European authorities; it is so alien that few things in the society arouse such indignation as seizure by the European sheriff. People hate to be coerced, not only in *khɔrɔ* proceedings, but in every sphere of activities, including their labour for the queen; just as differences must be settled by consent, so also the queen must solicit labour with entertainments. There are exceptions, some apparent, some real: a disloyal district head may be deposed; a subject who disobeys and does not pay the fine imposed may be expelled; a witch's cattle used to be confiscated. But these are not *khɔrɔ* cases and, except in the case of the witch, there is no execution upon property or person.

The enforcement of *khɔrɔ* decisions is left entirely to the parties. But they must agree; they cannot resort to force. This does not mean that the values of the society have been irresistibly internalized or that men are supersensitive to conscience and shame. It is the continuous pressure of institutionalized obligations, the impossibility of doing without the tangible day-by-day mutualities, and the disorganization caused by failure of the long-run reciprocities, not a sense of guilt or shame, which slowly but surely force a man to carry out the compromise reached in the *khɔrɔ*. A judgement creditor may receive no satisfaction for years; he may complain again and again to the *khɔrɔ* that no restitution has been made; yet if the debtor, appearing in the court, says that he is still 'looking for' the payment, it will usually be sufficient. 'Looking for' implies willingness to pay and it rehabilitates the wrongdoer; the *khɔrɔ* may even reprimand an impatient judgement creditor, at least if he has no grounds for casting aspersions upon the honesty or sincerity of the debtor. 'The law', in their phraseology, 'does not eat the man-who-says-I-shall-pay'. Culture contact has struck a severe blow at settlement by consent; the *khɔrɔ*, in an attempt to regain prestige, clamours for the power to punish; and the parties, reluctant to invoke European aid, bolster up the crumbling reciprocities with supernatural sanctions. Most men still have great confidence in the *khɔrɔ* and its methods, but some men increasingly resort to a mixture of the supernatural, the 'sending back' of the evil, and the processes of the European courts.

'Blood' cases and disobedience to tribal authorities, as well as witchcraft, are dealt with by procedures essentially different from those so far described. Homicide, especially accidental killing (*gozi*), is usually restituted by *hu khumɛlwa* and by converting the criminal to a kinsman, without the intervention of the *khɔrɔ* or payment to the queen. But other procedures were also used: a murderer might be killed in the heat of the moment by a relative of the victim, and in such a case that ended the matter; or he might be executed by order of the queen unless he could escape to one of the recognized sanctuaries in the country; or he might be dealt with as a witch. Homicide in its manifold aspects is too large a subject for treatment here, but since it is, in regard to aspects of law dealt with in this book, adequately illuminated by our next subject, viz. procedure in 'blood' cases, we may content ourselves with the remark that homicide apparently did not involve a *khɔrɔ* trial.

'Blood' cases to-day present a curious mixture of different procedures of the past. One old element of the procedure, being incongruous with the disapproval of self-help, has completely disappeared. Old men told us that 'blood' cases were settled by the kin, not submitted to the *khɔrɔ*. That, but no doubt also the reluctance to appeal to the European, to-day explains the emphasis on reconciliation and the encouragement of *hu khumɛlwa* in these cases. If a 'blood' case comes to the *khɔrɔ*, the victim gets nothing and the assaulter pays heavily; if the matter is privately settled, the victim gets something and the assaulter pays less. In the old days, if private settlement failed, the kin of the victim went to attack the assaulter's village: they reported to the queen, but she exacted no fine if in the attack a man was killed. Though this method of execution is unknown to-day, it is still said that a man who kills an aggressor pays nothing, not even to the queen, for 'He who dies on the road is not to be cried for. Let the aggressor kill himself' (*mufa-dzileni a u lɛlwi, mulala u ibolaɛlɛ*). This precept is also invoked to justify 'revenge' by means of medicines, but here, as in the case of aggression, it is regarded as self-defence, not self-help, just as killing an adulterer caught in the act—in which case also no blood-money is paid, even to the queen—is thought of as killing a thieving dog. These conceptions leave intact the aversion from vengeance: there is no blood revenge, no vendetta, no trace of the *lex talionis*, though a limb for a limb is known not very far off. Self-help, even in cases where it is admitted among tribes with more highly developed legal institutions, is frowned upon: one may neither kill a pig of another that damages one's crops nor drive cattle that have entered one's gardens into the fields of their owner. A man, provoked or assaulted by another, has no right to retaliate; and it is doubted whether the provocation will mitigate his offence, for no man may take the law in his own hands. Pheduli's relative had been killed by Magwale's sorcery, and in anger Pheduli struck Magwale's cow, which subsequently went lame; yet he was ordered by the *khɔrɔ* to pay the usual compensation.

How has the old procedure merged with the new conceptions? We can give only part of the answer. The exaggerated abhorrence of self-help and the insistence upon *hu khumɛlwa*, side by side with the tendency to regard blood as belonging to the queen (phrased as 'the head belongs to the chief'), has not driven the old procedures wholly out of the field. Old men say that 'blood' cases cannot be submitted to the *khɔrɔ*, yet they are second in number to *munywalo* cases. In theory, the procedure is that the victim, having notified his district head, runs to show his blood at the capital, messengers (*maharula*) of the queen are sent, not to institute an inquiry or conduct a trial, but to collect one goat from every married man in the district of the victim; and each *leharula* takes two goats for himself and gives the rest to the queen. We have never seen this procedure applied in practice; the danger of European intervention makes it wholly impracticable. Instead, the wounded person reports immediately to the district head, sometimes to the queen, or if the wound is not serious the parties settle the matter by *hu khumɛlwa*. The district head often arbitrates successfully; but he can neither try nor fine nor exact court fees. If the victim goes to the queen, she sends a *leharula* (and often more than one) who exacts one goat (the 'fee of the feet') from the assaulter and one from the victim (the 'stick for roasting meat') and should he settle the matter informally, for he cannot conduct a full-dress trial, he receives one further beast (the fine) from the wrong-doer. The latter is given to the queen; the goat given by the victim is killed for the *leharula*, who takes a hind leg to the queen's *khɔrɔ*, where it is eaten chiefly by the councillors; and the victim gets nothing. But if the *leharula* fails in his mission, which in practice means that the assaulter refuses to submit to him or denies his guilt, he is summoned to the *khɔrɔ* at the capital. There is no 'opening' fee, for 'blood' opens the *khɔrɔ*; sometimes the parties are ordered to settle the matter between themselves and sometimes the offender is fined one head of cattle, which goes to the queen, and one goat, which is killed for the *khɔrɔ*. Sometimes, however, a victim reports to the queen merely to obtain a letter to the Native Commissioner.

These general principles are subject in individual cases to many variations which reflect the transitional nature of the procedure and the adjustments that are being made by the society. We have been able to observe the cases that came before the *khɔrɔ* far more closely than those settled privately. In one case where a father intervened in a fight between his son and his son's wife, the son in anger stabbed the father; the *khɔrɔ* ordered the parties to become reconciled by *hu khumɛlwa*, the son to beg pardon with a goat. In similar circumstances, where a stranger intervened, the husband was ordered to clear the grass in the queen's garage. In another case the husband wounded the mother of a youth whom he found with his wife, because the mother interfered in the ensuing quarrel between the husband and the youth; the *khɔrɔ* told the youth to beg pardon with three goats but fined the husband one head of cattle and one goat. While the *zwiḓajani* (whistling ancestors) were performing at a religious ceremony, one of them, very much intoxicated, blew his whistle in public and tried to drag one of the women away to the bush. A district head, an initiated man, forcibly ejected the offender, who next morning assaulted him, but was worsted; the offender then reported his wound at the capital. A *leharula* was sent to collect the blood fine from the district head, but, not finding him, left a message summoning him to the *khɔrɔ*. There the case was discussed with only initiates of the *gomana* present. The men could not decide upon their course of action. They said, 'Let no one be angry. The district head did right, but we cannot carry out the law of the "school" (the man who reveals the *digɔma* secrets must die). We cannot even impose a fine; no one knows what the fine should be. Let the matter rest.'

Khashani, working on a European farm, called his wife, whose baby was ill, to come to him. The baby died and Khashani, seeing 'medicine' on the fireplace, suspected and severely beat his sister's daughter as well as his sister. The case came to the *khɔrɔ* of the queen, which pointed out that if, as Khashani thought, his sister was a witch, he also probably was one. This did not satisfy Khashani, but his sister demanded back her cattle, and the *khɔrɔ*, attempting to isolate the struggle, said, 'We are discussing the "blood". You, Khashani, must pay your sister one head of cattle.' Khashani replied, 'That I agree to do. I shall even drive away my wife, so that I can return my sister's cattle.' The *khɔrɔ* was not much perturbed, since it thought that Khashani's threat was either bluff or the raving of a madman.

In the last case it was the victim, not the queen, who was awarded the head of cattle. The argument sometimes used by Lovedu men against such an award is better known in other tribes: it is that, if the victim is benefited, all he need do to become rich is to provoke others to fight him. And the theory held by those advancing this argument is that to spill blood is 'to break the queen's calabash', and therefore 'blood' cases must be submitted to the *khɔrɔ*. This is the view gaining ground, so that *maharula*, going to collect the blood fine, become messengers summoning the parties to the queen's *khɔrɔ*, without, however, ignoring the position of the district heads. The whole procedure is in a state of flux, but we can see in outline how the blood feud has gradually receded as the kin groups become submerged by the district organization and how, as a consequence, the procedure of reconciliation gained so firm a hold that it maintains its stand against the forces making for centralization.

Not long ago the procedure appropriate to cases of witchcraft and sorcery was the ordeal (*mureu*); and though the *mureu* has given way in Uulovedu to smelling out by the diviner (*mugɔme*), it can still be seen further east among the Phalavorwa. The test takes various forms; drinking poison, usually an extract of *zavazava* (*Datura stramonium*), licking a medicated stick or a heated hoe, removing a stone from boiling water, floating the kernels of *muṭuzi* (*Oncoba spinosa*) in water and observing whether they separate or come together, sometimes accompanied by an oath or followed by the washing of hands or the squirting of water (*hu phasa*). All these are well-known in the lowveld, though the Lovedu used only or chiefly the first; but on the highveld, where witchcraft and sorcery are treated as private matters, there is no legal but only a magical method of dealing with them: the evil is sent back by a doctor privately employed by the victim. The Lovedu no longer rely upon the *mureu*, because it involves too great publicity and danger of European intervention, though they say, perhaps by way of rationalization, that the doctor of the ordeal could manipulate the test. As this procedure is merely of theoretical interest, we need refer only to its salient features.

The victim or his relative privately consulted a bone-throwing doctor, whose verdict he had confirmed by perhaps two or more other doctors before he or an intermediary on his behalf made a public accusation. The ordeal or test took place at the capital and was public. Lineal relatives of accuser and accused or, according to some, two strong men chosen by them, were given an intoxicating drink by the official 'doctor of the ordeal', the spectators watching to ensure that equal quantities were administered. Those who had drunk were put in the sun and he who began moving about or became dizzy, drunken, or incoherent was in the wrong. The witch was usually executed at once, at the orders of the queen, being strangled at the river; but if she was a woman, one of the executioners first had sexual intercourse with her; and the body, tied to a weight, was sunk into the water to be eaten by animals. But the witch was sometimes delivered to the victim to undo his evil work (*hu mu lɔulla*), and if the illness left the victim the witch was released. Sometimes, also, suspected witches were beaten, tied up (nowadays, as we have seen, handcuffed and submitted to ridicule and abuse), and left without food or tortured with velvet stinging-beans until they confessed; this was sometimes done privately, and it was possible also to kill them without the public ordeal, the killing being reported to the queen; but usually they were merely banished.

The property of a witch who was killed was not all confiscated, but *baza*, consisting chiefly of his cattle, was taken by the queen for division between herself and her nobles. No one else could appropriate *baza*; even the village head, if he did so, was regarded as a thief. The witch's gardens reverted to the district head, the crops were taken, not by the queen, because she could not eat the 'dirt of the witch', but by the messengers of the queen, for they were so busy in her service that they could hardly cultivate their fields. Residents in the district surreptitiously during the night took the witch's crops, but it was regarded as disgraceful to do so openly during the day. The wife of a witch was taken by a classificatory brother, and his children were adopted by the queen, who received *munywalo* when she married the girls to her nobles (in more recent times, to commoners, because the girls often deserted). In the days of the kings, all the relatives, or, as some say, only those on the mother's side—the mother's uterine brothers and sisters especially—were killed. The queens had only a uterine brother or sister killed if they failed to leave the country. The witch, unlike a murderer, could not find sanctuary in the forest of Ḍaja; and only a witch's, not a murderer's, property was *baza*—confiscable property.

Since the beginning of this century submission of issues to ordeal has been replaced by their submission to the smelling-out diviner (*mugɔme*). The institution of the *mugɔme* has been borrowed from the Shangana-Ṭonga and its whole complicated legal procedure is still in a state of flux, adjustments being constantly made especially to avoid European intervention. The procedure involves, first, private consultations of a doctor, followed by an accusation directly or through an intermediary, a wager by the parties, publicly made often in the *khɔrɔ*, then a journey in the company of the 'ears' (official witness) of the chief to a distant smeller-out, the actual smelling out, at which the victor may be given a buck's horn to blow on his way home, and, finally the report to chief or district head and the adjudication of the *khɔrɔ*. We are here concerned only with the legal aspects, but we must at the outset remark that the procedure, primarily used in witchcraft cases, is relied upon whenever there are evidential difficulties, and, paradoxically, it has rendered theft, adultery, and other wrongs, not less, but more amenable to some form of *khɔrɔ* control. Publicity and centralized control in the phenomenal, periodical *mureu* proceedings at the capital in the old days guaranteed their effectiveness, but men could privately execute self-confessed witches. To-day, amid conflicting tendencies, *mugɔme* proceedings are less public and hardly the prerogative of the queen. Witchcraft is not conceived necessarily to strike at the whole society; it is often dealt with privately; and even, after resort to the *mugɔme*, agreement by the parties in the district courts may end the matter.

The *mugɔme* procedure lends itself to fixing responsibility when a whole district feels threatened, just as in the old days the *mureu* was used whenever the whole country wished to ward off danger. When, at a certain district gathering, it was decided to send delegates to a *mugɔme* concerning the occurrence of many deaths in the district, one young woman objected, saying, 'It is nonsense; we know the sickness is not "sent". If you go to the *mugɔme* and he "beats" (points out) members of your family, the whole district will be quarrelling.' The *mugɔme* pointed out the young woman who had objected, but she demanded that, if any one accused her, he should go with her to another *mugɔme*, and when she appealed to the capital for appointment there of the official witness, no one came forward as a direct accuser and for that reason the case broke down. Subsequent cases in which the young woman was involved reflected how the proceedings had not relieved, but aggravated, the sense of insecurity in the district. Shall we conclude that the remedy is worse than the disease? We cannot do so, because where there are no *mugɔme* proceedings, as on the highveld, the incidence of witchcraft and sorcery is not less. Moreover, *mugɔme* proceedings are believed to, and do often, remove grave threats to the community. In 1938 the tributary *morula* cider was being made at the village of the head of a sub-district. On the second day the cider frothed suspiciously and after a meeting of the sub-district, money was collected and representatives of every family went to the *mugɔme*, who found that the headman had poisoned the cider, and in truth everything pointed to the use of cattle-dip or locust poison. The matter was reported to the capital, where, without formal trial, the headman was ordered to leave the district. In our opinion a dangerous criminal had been successfully dealt with, but, what is more important, the feeling of security of the people had been restored.

We may now shortly examine some aspects of *khɔrɔ* control over *mugɔme* proceedings. The challenge, supported by a wager to submit the truth of an accusation to the *mugɔme*, is made before, during, or even after *khɔrɔ* proceedings, but if the dispute is dealt with by the *khɔrɔ*, the findings of the *mugɔme* can be accorded recognition only if the official witness, the 'ears', has been previously appointed by the *khɔrɔ*; the results of a private consultation cannot be given in evidence before the *khɔrɔ*. The 'ears' is sometimes appointed by the district head of the person challenged, but the theory is sometimes advanced that only the capital has jurisdiction to do so. His integrity is an important factor, for he must relate to the *khɔrɔ* the details of the wager, the competence of the *mugɔme*, the method by which the decision was reached and its nature, and whether or not the parties consented to the decision. The 'ears' must be a disinterested person, to avoid accusations of corruption and favouritism, as well as to guarantee that there is no manipulation of the fees entrusted to him by the parties for defraying the expenses of the expedition. Integrity and impartiality are best guaranteed where the capital appoints the 'ears'.

Often enough the findings of the *mugɔme* are accorded no recognition at the capital when the parties have gone forth from a district *khɔrɔ*. This does not mean that the parties cannot agree to the verdict of the *mugɔme* at the district *khɔrɔ* where the 'ears' has been appointed; nor is there any great desire to centralize control, which is sometimes encouraged, sometimes feared, and sometimes more or less an inevitable consequence of the need to obtain passes at the capital for the journey to a distant *mugɔme*. The practice of appointing 'ears' in the districts is not unconnected with the danger of implicating the capital with the European authorities. It sometimes happens, when the parties come for a pass and a report is made at the capital, that the queen's councillors disclaim any interest or concern in the matter. Wherever the 'ears' may be appointed, he is given the *phitho* (thing to be hidden), any small article such as a snuff box or coin which is concealed and must be named and found by the *mugɔme* as a test of his competence before the divination begins.

Khɔrɔ control is evident also in the manner in which it may refuse its assistance or dissuade the parties from going to the *mugɔme*, even though it can come to no decision in the dispute. The attitude of the *khɔrɔ* may be manifested in many ways, and its aim in refusing assistance is much the same as that of the queen when she intervenes behind the scenes in the interests of reconciliation by forbidding the publicity of *mugɔme* proceedings. We shall refer to a few only of the cases we have witnessed. A recruiter used to pay all labourers recruited £2, which had to be paid into the tribal fund before the tribal 'secretary' issued a pass to the labourer. For reasons we need not detail, the 'secretary' gave the labourer no receipt and the recruiter sued the 'secretary'. This is precisely the kind of case that the *khɔrɔ* finds very difficult to handle and, as the 'secretary' was a Christian, not amenable to *mugɔme* proceedings, the recruiter challenged the labourer to go to a *mugɔme*. But the *khɔrɔ* disallowed the challenge on the ground that the transaction had occurred in daylight, and instead ordered recruiter and 'secretary' jointly to pay the £2.

The *khɔrɔ*, by refusing to appoint 'ears', can prevent submission of a dispute to the *mugɔme* or it may send back the parties to their district head for him to appoint the 'ears', the purpose often being to tire them out or to exhaust their resources, so that they will more easily come to an agreement. But the opposite often happens: the *khɔrɔ*, tired of the obstinacy of the parties, may tell them to submit their differences to a *mugɔme*. Mudali complained that Uumme, mother of Muloi, was spreading rumours that he had caused Muloi's illness. Muloi was known to be a witch who had killed two of her brothers-in-law, sons of Makhulu, and Makhulu had with the aid of a great specialist 'sent back' a terrible illness which was rotting great holes in Muloi's body. But Uumme could not proceed against this legitimate revenge and, as it was rumoured that Mudali was a lover of Muloi, Uumme attempted to inculpate Mudali. These facts were generally known, but were not disclosed in the *khɔrɔ*. Mudali said that his accusers knew that he had no medicines and to clear his name he challenged Uumme to go to a *mugɔme* with him. Uumme retorted that she resented the insult from an adulterer, and the *khɔrɔ*, fearing that the conflict would spread, advised the disputants to go back to their district head and there arrange to go to the *mugɔme*. 'Ears' was appointed and early one morning we all stood ready at Mudali's village, with food for a long journey, perhaps 100 miles; messages and counter-messages passed to and fro between the villages of Mudali and Uumme, but nothing happened; and the following Sunday the case was again in the *khɔrɔ* of the capital. Uumme's people said that, as they had made no direct accusation, they refused to go to the *mugɔme*, but the *khɔrɔ* retorted, 'If Muloi dies, you must not blame Mudali. Now pay him the "cutter of the tongue" (which silences the mouth), for if Muloi dies the Europeans will come.' Uumme refused, and Mudali, satisfied that his name had been cleared, allowed the matter to be dropped.

The *khɔrɔ* or the queen may dissuade the parties from resorting to the *mugɔme*. Siga accused Maidi—they were co-wives—of having removed a tooth from Siga's child, who died, and of inserting it into the mouth of Maidi's baby. Maidi's relatives advised her to challenge Siga, but the queen, calling Maidi to her, said, 'I cannot support you. The witchcraft may be that even of your mother. Let the matter be.' And her advice was accepted. Similarly the *khɔrɔ* discourages unfounded accusations among members of the family, curbs the inclination to squabble, and in various ways attempts to prevent the challenge which so readily rises to the lips of angry relatives. A young married woman, accusing her mother-in-law of harassing her with familiars, fled to her parents, who, when the mother-in-law came to call her back, imputed to her the death of the children of a relative of theirs. The mother-in-law brought an action, but, as is usual when there is danger of *munywalo* and family entanglements, the *khɔrɔ* quashed the case as nonsense (*zwitshɛle*) and sent the parties home to compose their differences by *hu khumɛlwa*. Tsezi, instigated by his mother-in-law, who had a family quarrel with Dali, accused the latter of sending the lightning which had struck down a tree near his village, but the district head stopped the challenge from being submitted to a *mugɔme* by dismissing the case as unfounded gossip. Sagani, whose adultery with his father's young wife was exposed by her, accused her of causing his son's death; but the khɔrɔ told him to beg pardon with a goat, which would also serve as the 'cutter of the tongue'. When uterine sisters challenged one another before the khɔrɔ the men ridiculed them, saying, 'Who has ever heard of uterine sisters bewitching one another'— not a very conclusive argument, but sufficient for the purpose in hand. When Mabula, the cattle-linked sister, was called to squirt water (*hu phasa*) for the sick child of her brother, she construed the summons as an accusation of witchcraft, for to call another (not a close relative) to perform this rite is one method of imputing witchcraft; but Mabula's husband intervened in the khɔrɔ, explained how his wife and her brother by their quarrels were breaking up his home, and suggested that they beg pardon of one another. The khɔrɔ agreed and averted the challenge.

Even if the parties had been to the *mugɔme* with the official witness the khɔrɔ is not absolutely bound. In the old days, it is said, the khɔrɔ allowed argument as if the divination of the *mugɔme* was not infallible and if the parties were not satisfied the khɔrɔ could on the initiative of one of them send them to a second *mugɔme*. To-day, despite the theory that the *mugɔme* is infallible, the old practice persists. We have seen many arguments on the merits and many reversals of the findings of the *mugɔme*. These findings may be attacked on the grounds of irregularities in the procedure, such as separation of the parties when they were on the journey, corruption of the 'ears', incompetence of the *mugɔme* who failed to find the *phitho* or to indicate correctly the group or totem names of all the parties, dissatisfaction of the one party with the findings at the séance, confusion of the bones by medicines 'thrown' at home, and many others. When there is a conflict between the evidence or a presumption (such as, in adultery cases, the presumption that a woman's evidence is almost as reliable as the bones) and the findings of the *mugɔme*, there is no telling which way the ultimate verdict will go. The cases in which these conflicts have occurred are too complicated for adequate handling here, largely because the primary object of the khɔrɔ is appeasement of the parties and reconciliation of what appear to be incongruous institutions.

There are other aspects of the procedure that have great legal interest— for example, the principles governing vicarious representation of challenger and challenged before the *mugɔme* and the right of the person vicariously smelt out to appeal for a second expedition of which he is a party, the rule as to the conduct of the parties on the journey, the requirement of the khɔrɔ that it can take cognizance, not of gossip or general rumour, but only a specific accusation by a specific challenger, and many others. We shall touch upon two further points only.

Firstly the *mugɔme* is always a Shangana-Tonga and lives far away. Litigants from other tribes come to Uulovedu, but the Lovedu generally say that they are going to Phafuli, on the borders of Portuguese East Africa. The theory is that the more distant the *mugɔme* the more reliable his verdict will be. But distance also safeguards the diviner from the vengeance that neighbours might take, shifts the incidence of distasteful responsibilities from the khɔrɔ and eliminates strife between the two

XIII. AT THE CAPITAL
(a) RE-BUILDING THE COURTYARD OF THE CAPITAL
(b) THE COURTYARD (KHƆRƆ), WITH A CASE IN PROGRESS

XIV. THE PURSUIT OF HEALTH
(a) DIAGNOSING THE CAUSE OF ILLNESS
(b) THE KHADI POURS BEER TO APPEASE THE ANCESTORS

powerful jurisdictions, the *khɔrɔ* and the *mugɔme*. The *mugɔme*, great though his powers be, holds a precarious position in the modern world. His fees are not fixed, but the usual amount is £1 2s. 6d., though it may be 5s. or more for each person of the party. Much of his technique is directed towards preventing the consultants from giving him away to the European authorities. 'If you say I am a liar,' declared one *mugɔme* to the parties, 'take back your money and go elsewhere. I even challenge you to take me to the Europeans; they will agree with me, as I have a licence to divine.' In another case a *mugɔme* refused to find any one guilty. 'You force me,' he said, 'to smell out the witch, but you have left him at home. The other diviners who smelt out this man [the challenged person] are all wrong. And you [the challenger], if you wish to settle the dispute, must place a head of cattle as a sacred beast to wake up your grandfather.' But this finding did not persuade the parties to withdraw their case from the *khɔrɔ*, and the *khɔrɔ*, ignoring the finding, settled the matter in its own way.

Secondly, the wager is not made by way of an oath, but it is sometimes reduced to writing: 'They bet four head of cattle' (*va bɛjije khomu je nne*); that is all. The tiny slip of paper is kept by the 'ears'. The use of the term *hu bɛja* shows, as the people say, that the wager is a new conception. But we cannot be certain that the wager has been borrowed from Europeans. It fits the whole complex of judicial process: its essence is consent of the parties to be bound by their wager and by the findings of the *mugɔme*. If one of the parties disagrees with these findings, he is entitled to demand back the money paid to the *mugɔme* and ask the party to go further to another *mugɔme*. The *khɔrɔ* may, however, vary the bet. The victor comes to the *khɔrɔ* and blows his horn; and the women ululate and dance (*hu pɛbɛla*, which by extension also means to be acquitted or declared innocent by ordeal or *mugɔme*). Meanwhile the vanquished party goes home and, if he is contrite, he says that he could not help doing wrong. Next day he might appear in the *khɔrɔ*, ask for time to pay or *khumɛlwa* or send an old man to plead for a reduction of the bet. The victor pretends to refuse, but in the end, if the *khɔrɔ* presses him, he will agree. Or the *khɔrɔ* may, on its own initiative, reduce the bet. Everything depends on the circumstances. Where the mother of a man was alleged to have killed the wife of his elder brother (the challenger), the *mugɔme*'s verdict was against the mother, but as he had said that she was not a born witch, but had only purchased the medicine from another, the *khɔrɔ* awarded the challenger two head of cattle instead of the six actually wagered. The bet is often not paid in full, while sometimes nothing at all is exacted as the 'cutter of the tongue' of the slanderer. But we have seen cases in which the *khɔrɔ* has, at the suggestion of one party, raised a wager from four to six head of cattle.

This is not the place to discuss the interrelations of the tribal and the European systems. For one thing, the subject requires a volume to itself. But it is necessary to insist that in criminal matters the system of Native courts is by European law essentially an integral part of the European structure. In 1934 Mujaji was given criminal jurisdiction in respect of offences punishable under Native law, but fines are limited to two head of cattle or £5; and so many offences, including grievous and indecent assaults, arson, and pretended witchcraft, are excluded that, when the queen received the letter granting jurisdiction, she exclaimed, 'Is there anything left to us?' In practice, as we have seen, a good deal is not so much left as quietly taken. Moreover, fines imposed can be enforced only by the process-in-aid also available in civil cases. Civil jurisdiction, as granted by the European, is more generous; it includes civil claims arising out of Native law brought before the chief by Natives against Natives resident within the area of jurisdiction. But, it need hardly be said, the alien conceptions of civil law and criminal law and their distinctions are only faintly understood. The chief has no power to proceed to execution against the wishes of the judgement debtor, for where the judgement debtor (or others at his instigation) resists execution, and seizure in the opinion of the messenger might lead to a breach of the peace, the messenger must report to the judgement creditor and it is he, not the chief, who if he so desires may apply to the Native Commissioner for process-in-aid. The *khɔrɔ* is not a court of record, but there are provisions as to appeal to the Native Commissioner, whose functions in hearing the case, as if it were a case of first instance, are not merely to determine the appeal, but also to act as a court of first instance for purposes of recording evidence.

This is a bare outline of the formal aspects of the situation. The sociological implications are fortunately infinitesimal compared with what they might have been if Native Commissioners had not been wiser than the law they administered. Their policy has been not to interfere. Moreover, the procedure of the *khɔrɔ*, by its insistence upon agreement and compromise, not only does not rely upon, but is inconsistent with, execution or the sanction of force. Compromise and physical coercion are contradictory principles which cannot co-exist. Litigants sometimes reluctantly resort to European courts and their processes-in-aid, not because European law has castrated the *khɔrɔ*, but because culture contact has cut some of the sinews of reciprocity.

CHAPTER XII

THE PURSUIT OF HEALTH

Anatomical conceptions in relation to the science of drugs and of healing—cardinal categories of the causation of disease—training for the medical profession—divinatory dice as a method of diagnosis.

LOʋEDU therapy is linked, on the one hand with law, and on the other with medicine, magic, witchcraft, sorcery, and religion, but it is more closely interwoven with these last than with the first. If disease and death are the main objective of witchcraft and sorcery, disease is also the occasion of most religious rites, medicine the means of restoring the health of the human body and law the guarantee of the well-being of the social organism. Law and medicine are both largely concerned with the results of dissension between men. Open strife, which leads to social evils, is examined by the *khɔrɔ* and resolved under the guidance of its wisdom; secret malice, which causes death and disease, is diagnosed by the bones and treated by the doctor; but for the detection of the deeds of darkness the *khɔrɔ* calls in the aid of the doctor. The *khɔrɔ* relies upon public discussion and its genius effects contact and reconciliation between one litigant and another, while the doctor uses private divination and his art inspires the consultant with confidence against his secret enemy. The social psychology of the one is the counterpart of the psycho-therapy of the other. But we must not think of them as essentially different worlds, the one primarily natural and the other primarily supernatural. The medico-magico-religious is to the Loʋedu rather a tangible world of mundane arrangements and subject to 'natural' forces than a cosmos, inscrutable in its configuration and governed by 'supernatural' destinies. In truth, Loʋedu healing is based to some extent upon observed relations between cause and effect though more largely upon practices and beliefs which, though they will not stand the tests of our science, constitute the psychological therapy of the society. We are far too apt to discount the value of their empirical body of knowledge, instead of using it to construct a sound scientific approach to medicine. We can also do better than scorn as superstitious absurdities those indispensable techniques of medicine which, because our medical profession takes little account of them, enable the charlatan and quack to flourish among us.

To understand Loʋedu conceptions of the causation of disease, we must orientate ourselves from their knowledge of human anatomy. It is indeed very meagre. All they know has been gleaned indirectly from the slaughter of cattle and goats, for they practise neither embalming nor dissection of corpses. As a result, though they have names for all the more important organs of the body, they are not always sure of their correct location. Nor have they much idea of physiological function. They know that the stomach and intestines are digestive organs and that the bladder contains urine, but lungs and the diaphragm are vaguely connected with breathing. The womb, ovaries, and testicles are definitely reproductive organs, but in medical practice this function is obscured by the role of an internal snake believed to be intimately bound up with fecundity and childbirth. Every one is said to have a snake in his stomach. It is not a real snake, yet it is conceived of as having a head and of being able to crawl up to a man's neck (causing what we call indigestion) and running back again when he coughs. When a person has stomach-ache it is often said, 'The snake is biting,' while dysentery is referred to as 'red' or 'white snake', according to the stage of the disease. The most important function of this snake, and one that forms a common subject of conversation in connection with barrenness, is, however, its reproductive one. It is believed that semen comes from a man's snake; if his snake is 'no good', a child will not be born. The snake of a woman is sometimes identified with the womb and for conception it is necessary that this snake should accept the semen. There are two possibilities which prevent conception: either the snake's head may be wrongly oriented or it may catch up the semen, but spit it out again. In the first case the remedy is to 'turn round' its head by medical treatment, in which very often the womb of a scapegoat is used. In the second case, since the snake rejects the semen unless the bloods of husband and wife agree and the snake of the man may be as much at fault as that of the woman, it is usual to include both husband and wife in treatment for barrenness. If six to nine months elapse after marriage without conception having taken place, steps are at once taken to set the matter right.

Though the Lovedu have no knowledge of the circulation of the blood, they assign to it properties which lie at the basis of their medical theory. Blood is so generally believed to be the root of most ills that a Native describing his symptoms always says, 'I am pierced by blood.' Rheumatism, stiffness after exercise, a pain or swelling in any part of the body, is attributed to blood that has collected there or blood which is 'boiling', making the body hot and feverish. Swellings of all kinds, including goitre, are therefore always cupped to get rid of surplus blood, and bloodletting as a cure for headache and other ills is as popular with the Lovedu as it was in Europe not so long ago. The beating of the heart is not believed to be continuous: it is associated with sudden fright and with illness; but, though it is known that often the heart beats loudly when one is not ill, they have no idea why it should do so. Veins contain blood, but go by the same name as sinews and muscles, all of which are believed to give strength to the body. Occasionally, though infrequently, individuals are to be found who have other ideas. Thus David, a Christian who has often worked in towns and has a mind of his own, has his own theory as to the function of the heart, a deduction from his observations on dying fowls. He believes that the heart beats, not to circulate, but to exclude the blood, and the moment the heart stops beating the blood enters it, causing death to the fowl or person.

A considerable list of terms for different diseases indicates that distinctions are recognized, but it is easy to be misled into believing that the Natives' knowledge is greater than it really is. Some terms are peculiarly Native without any corresponding category among us, but many, like smallpox, measles, mumps, fever, consumption, migraine, syphilis, epilepsy, show appreciation of causes or symptoms which fit into our scheme of classification. Practice is characterized by vagueness and a very wide and loose, instead of a specific, use of many of these terms. The term *khitshipidi* denotes primarily a swelling or tumour containing white matter. In practice we have found it applied to scrofula or glandular swellings below the ear, which were cut open and squeezed, to slime coughed up and said to be internal *khitshipidi*, and to general aching of all the teeth or tenderness of the gums with no sign of matter. Similarly the term *ŋɔbɛ*, bleeding of the nose, is often applied when there is no bleeding, but general debility, in which case the trouble is thought to be caused by blood in the body that should, but has not, come out. Such false correlations are due not merely to wrong conceptions of cause and effect—any evidence suggesting the presence of blood suffices to incriminate that arch enemy of health—but also to careless observation and loose reasoning. This laxity in medical conceptions is in marked contrast to the logic and coherence of other arrangements of the society. Inaccurate observation and undeveloped symptomatology must be attributed to the extensive reliance, firstly, for diagnosis of all but the most everyday illness upon the divining dice, and, secondly, for curing upon what in the last resort is the psychological rather than the physical.

Lovedu therapeutics includes a number of treatments that have undoubted curative value, but many more are based on purely magical assumptions. On the whole, those which we should consider to be of some medical value are chiefly home remedies of the humble non-divining herbalist. The higher one goes in the medical scale, the more divorced from scientific principles become the treatments. Simple ailments are dealt with very much as among Europeans: sniffing up water is used for colds, the milk of a certain euphorbia is supplied to draw out deep-lying thorns; splints of strips of wood are used for broken limbs or sprains; teeth are extracted by being levered up by means of an instrument like a poker, which is inserted between the roots, a method said to be no more painful than the clumsy use of European forceps. Very detrimental to the speedy recovery of wounds is, however, the practice of scraping or washing off all matter before each application of healing powders. This destroys the new young tissues, delaying for months the healing of sores that normally takes weeks or even days. Use of enemas is unknown and emetics are not nearly as common as among the Zulu. With the Lovedu as with us the commonest treatment is the drinking of medicines. Instead, however, of the bottle of medicine we receive, a Native is given a small bundle of roots or twigs cut into even lengths to take home and boil in water which is drunk or used for making a soft porridge. Sometimes the medicine is bruised and a cold infusion made. There is none of the careful measurement of quantities characteristic of the mediaeval apothecary or of prescriptions found on Egyptian papyri, but the amounts used are not wholly undetermined, for in practice the smallest pot is used and 1 to $2\frac{1}{2}$ pints of water are added; the dose seldom exceeds a few mouthfuls taken once or twice a day for a few days only. If this is not effective, something else will be tried. Wet cupping is a common home remedy, as the numerous scars on head and shoulders of people testify. After scarification, a cupping horn is applied, the narrow end of the horn being closed by a piece of beeswax, in which a small hole can be made when the mouth is applied for suction. Vein-cutting, however, requires greater skill, though even this operation is outside the province of the diviner. A vein on the back of the hand or on the instep is lifted with an awl and cut with a piece of iron or a razor blade. When enough blood has run out, cold water is applied and the cut held tightly with the fingers to stop the bleeding. This is a common treatment for illness believed to be due to unwanted blood in the body.

Scarification, except in the mutual inoculation and blood mixing of husband and wife prior to their first sexual intercourse after marriage and after the death or miscarriage of a child, is a treatment that is directed less at the evils of blood than towards a strengthening of the body or part of the body by the insertion of medicine. It is used in curing headache, for sprains and broken limbs, and for all 'strengthenings', such as that prior to taking a child out of the hut for the first time or the 'fixing' of one's body against witches. For general strengthenings, incisions are made on all the joints and on other parts of the body, such as head and neck depression, which are considered important. Scarification is, with the drinking of medicine or eating of powders, quite the most common form of medical treatment; it is used in the home as much as by diviners and forms part of many other treatments, such as the vapour bath. By far the most interesting form of scarification is, however, '*hu thɛmɛla*' (vaccination) against smallpox in which matter from the pustules of affected persons, mixed with other medicines, is inoculated to introduce the disease in a mild form. It is done on the dorsal side of the wrist or on the forehead, a pattern which supports the claim that it was known prior to the advent of the European; moreover, the ingredients of the serum used by Europeans are not known. Possibly the treatment was borrowed from Arabs, who were the first to study smallpox and measles. The old method was still widely practised in the 1938 smallpox epidemic, for, though it was realized that it 'called' the disease instead of curing it, people noted that, despite European vaccination, there was still much illness.

Steaming and the vapour bath also form part of the practical elements in Lovedu medicine. There are various forms of steaming and smoking, all of which go by the same term. To 'loosen' a cough, chips of a certain root may be placed in a pipe with a live coal and smoked; to purify a person after a death, chips are charred on a potsherd and the smoke inhaled through a reed; before being taken out of the hut, a new-born child is held naked in the smoke of burning chips or root and bark; boils and other swellings are brought to a head by the application of the steam of boiling roots. To cure fever or general weakness of the body after an illness and for purification of husband and wife after the death of a child the procedure is more complicated. Red-hot stones are put into a large pot of medicated water and when it bubbles and boils the patient, naked except for a cloth passed between the legs, is covered with a blanket and steamed. After much spluttering and shouting, he is taken out, sprinkled or washed down with cold water and then either scarified on the joints or subjected to *hu hata*—that is, a river stone is pressed on the joints and is later taken back to the river. This treatment is considered too drastic for a really weak patient. Sprinkling and *hu hata*, combined very often with other treatments, are also used alone. When there is an epidemic of coughing or dysentery, it is said 'a wind has come' and a doctor is called to sprinkle the people to ward it off. *Hu hata*, pressing a counter-irritant to the affected part, is used for toothache, when large pieces of heated bark are held to the cheek; for bruises, which are treated by the application of hot boiled leaves of certain trees; after childbirth, when hot porridge placed in a small flat basket is pressed daily to the stomach to ward off pains, and for many other purposes. But the hot poultice or emollient is not known.

Characteristically, the above-mentioned treatments are used both on occasions where they might be of real therapeutic value and for purifications and strengthenings where they could not. The principle of inoculation, which immunizes in diseases such as smallpox, is widely applied to effect cures and to further magical ends with which an empirical relation in our sense is wholly obscure. The relation must be sought, not in the objective link between cause and effect as we see it, but in the Lovedu conceptions of disease, their causes and symptoms, and in the cultural pattern of the methods by which evil may be cast out or symbolically laid upon a scapegoat. This is by no means as foreign to European thought as might at first be supposed, being used to this day among the more backward peasants both in Europe and in South Africa. A cure for headache among the Lovedu is to tie a piece of medicated string or sinew round the head for a day, after which it is cut and allowed to fall with the evil it has absorbed into a hole. To cure gout you scarify the leg to insert medicine, wiping off the blood with the leaves of a growing *muṭagola* bush (*Euclea sp.*) to leave the disease on it. The frog is a common scapegoat. We once witnessed how, in the case of pulsating fontanelle of a baby, considered to be a grave danger, some of the medicine inserted into the scarifications, made around the throbbing spot and on other parts of the body, was placed on a green-and-white frog. The frog was stood on the fontanelle, where it puffed itself up by rhythmic inhalations not unlike the beating of the fontanelle and finally, as a scapefrog, to which the evil had been transmitted, it was taken back to the river. One method of curing convulsions is to shave the hair in two 'paths' which cross in the centre of the child's head and to make a bark cockroach, smeared with medicine, run along each path till it drops off. In curing barrenness and in initiation into the cult of possession, a goat, after being made to lie beside the patient or having its nostrils blown into, is killed and used in the treatment.

Lovedu medicines appear to us to be a jumble of science and magic. Fully 80 per cent. are of vegetable origin. There is hardly a plant in that rich lowveld vegetation which is not used in the pharmacopoeia of some herbalist or doctor and it is significant that new plants are constantly tried out. The pattern of supposed relations that are believed to exist between symptoms and diseases, of the unscientific analogies which we call sympathetic magic, and the use of roots and barks more frequently than leaves or flowers and fruits, limits the value of this testing out of medicines. Nevertheless, many drugs have effects which either obscure or cure the symptoms, and whether for that reason and its psychological effect or because of a truly curative value, men have great faith in the medicines. There are undoubtedly ingredients in Lovedu medicines which cannot be empirically related to either symptom or cure, since they operate mainly by a technique of analogies which we relegate to the magical world. Such are animal products like hair, skin, excrement, and ovaries used in a variety of ways—for instance, for barrenness and indigestion; minerals like ironstone used for strengthening babies; and sea or river products, sand and shells, indispensable for keeping witches out of the village. But to Lovedu men and women the use of such ingredients in no way differs from the use of a herb: both are thought to have curative value and for them our distinction between magical and scientific treatments, between cause and effect and false analogy, does not exist. Just as a herb may have properties for curing disease, so, for example, the backbone of a python is effective in curing general debility or backache. The bone is pounded and the powder inoculated into scarifications along the back, by which means the immense power of the python is thus imparted to the patient. But note the sequel. So powerful is this medicine that the patient, when his time has come, will have difficulty in dying. His eyes will remain alive though the body is dead until once more the python powder is applied by being burned under his nose that he may inhale the smoke. This strengthening and the reversal of its influence are like injection and desensitization in our medical practice.

When we pursue Lovedu conceptions as regards the nursing and treatment of patients, we have once more to regard them from their point of view. Cleanliness and hygiene are very remotely related to health. Flies are freely tolerated because it is unlucky to kill them, not because, as is held in some other tribes, abundance of flies means riches in cattle. Invalids are not given a special diet, so that instructions by European doctors that a mother should feed her ailing baby on vitamin-containing foods or fruits are ignored unless medicine is given to be mixed with the food. It is equally fatal to appeal to the curative powers of nature: an invalid will impute unwillingness to help, ignorance or even sinister designs, if you tell him that nature will heal him and give no medicine. It is medicine and medicine alone that is thought to heal. But even medicine is never allowed much time in which to do its curative work. If one drug is not effective within a week it will be changed for another. Often a number of medicines are used at the same time, so that if one is ineffectual the other may heal. In every case we attended we found Native treatment was being given at the same time as, and often to the detriment of, our own. Nor would our protests be of any avail. Even in hospitals there are secret chewings of herbs and surreptitious steamings. Though it is admitted that certain medicines may not 'agree' when used together, use of the wrong medicine is not thought to have any harmful effects. At the most, a medicine merely does not heal; it never definitely harms the patient. Inexactness in the quantity of medicine taken is accompanied by a laxity in the carrying out of doctors' instructions which, though of no consequence where Native medicines are used, may do immense harm if the medicines are European. A careful comparison between the instructions of Native doctors at consultations and the actual manner in which these were carried out showed great discrepancies between the two. There are certain general principles known to all and on the whole people trust to their knowledge of these and the powers of the medicines themselves rather than slavishly following instructions.

The sick like to be in the open or in the sun, but it is for comfort and warmth, not because the curative power of nature or the need for nursing is recognized. An invalid generally spends the day lying wrapped up in his blanket in or near the courtyard or in the sheltered storage enclosure. This open-air sick-room, sunny or shady as the needs of the body dictate and protected from wind, is, in the absence of light, well-ventilated rooms, the best possible place for the health of the patient. At night, however, or when the patient is too ill to move, the sick-room is the kitchen hut, where the evening meal is cooked, and it is generally foul with smoke and full of people. A patient suffering from a bad cough is given a potsherd of sand to spit into. If at all possible, a patient goes outside to relieve himself, but if he is too weak to walk a broken pot is provided as a commode. Very sick people are given soft porridge without meat or relish, and great pains are taken to persuade patients to eat lest they lose strength and waste away. The treatment in diseases such as smallpox, measles, and chickenpox, which one generally gets once only, is peculiar and shows how values and procedures used in other spheres of culture may become interwoven with medical practices. The illness is dealt with as if it were a stage in life like puberty or circumcision. When the first symptoms appear, the patient is isolated and a stick, placed across the hut door, warns people off, for *muridi* (shadow) will aggravate the illness if the patient comes into contact with certain people. After some days, when the rash has disappeared or the pustules no longer contain white matter, he is smeared with fat and ochre, whether he feels better or not, and allowed out. The treatment is called *hu ɛba*, the term used for going through the circumcision initiation. But there is another aspect of the treatment. The pox pustules are scraped daily with soaked bark of *mutsɛre* (*Bridelia sp.*), the purpose as phrased being to cause the white matter to come out and to prevent the pustules from going deeply into the endodermis, thus leaving pock marks.

'Transition' diseases, as we may call those dealt with upon the pattern of *hu ɛba*, lead us to consider some general conceptions underlying Lovedu medical practice and causation of disease. These conceptions remind us of the Greek theory of humours which long dominated European medicine and were at the basis of mediaeval physiology. Physical and mental qualities and dispositions were attributed to the four chief fluids or cardinal humours of the body, viz. blood, phlegm, choler, and melancholy or black choler. Choler, probably derived from the Greek word for bile and from which we get our word 'cholera', was, for instance, the humour causing irascibility of temper. The Lovedu attach less importance to temperament and have based their cardinal categories, not upon physiological fluids, but upon conceptions associated with shadow (*muridi*), mingling (*makhuma*), heat (*hu fɛsa*), and sex. These do not constitute an exhaustive list, and their application extends over a wide field, which we might call the magico-religious.

Murudi (shadow) is conceived of as an evil power, but of its many properties the most emphasized is the property of aggravating disease. It is as if certain real evils cast a shadow which may infect those upon which it falls. If they are normal, healthy people, generally speaking they suffer no discomfort themselves, but they may act as carriers of the shadow, and by contact with others, especially those who are ill, they may transmit the evil as if they were intermediary hosts, weakening the patient and aggravating his illness. The host may transmit the shadow to both persons and things. A person who has attended a funeral or who has lost a close relative is infected by the shadow of death. Twins have such great shadow that if they come near a sick person he will die: hence twins must be killed and are still generally killed, despite European law and the example of Christians to whose grown-up twins no specific evil can be attributed. A woman who has had a miscarriage has *muridi*. Pregnancy up to but not after the end of the third month infects a woman with *muridi*, for a clear distinction is drawn between the two stages of pregnancy: before the end of the third month the foetus is amorphous, not a human being; after it, the foetus takes human form, the woman 'has grown', and a miscarriage is regarded as a death, so that people come to condole and there is a mourning period ended by the [removal of] 'dirt' rite (*khitshila*), just as for the most important adult. After childbirth a woman has *muridi*, but this is not the reason for her isolation. She remains in the hut till her child is strengthened, lest she bring to it shadows from outside. Girls over puberty and non-suckling, childbearing women, though having no definite *muridi*, are a potential source of danger to the sick, and men have not infrequently refused to allow us to wash their wounds with water drawn by such women. It is not at all clear, however, whether it is menstruation that is feared or the danger of possible early pregnancy. Sexual intercourse between husband and wife brings about a mild form of *muridi*; hence, if a very young child is ill, husband and wife sometimes abstain from intercourse. *Muridi* from sexual intercourse is believed to affect the meat of slaughtered cattle or goats unless certain precautions are taken, and causes stomach trouble to those who partake of it. Men who are sleeping with their wives are therefore not allowed to approach a slaughtered animal before its stomach has been pierced or to help skin it without first smearing their hands with leaves of *thɛɛbɛ* (*Amaranthus Thunbergi*) or other medicine. Here again, so it seems, the danger is not the actual intercourse, but the possibility of an unformed foetus in the womb. Thus, in the early stages of his wife's pregnancy, Nagambi was forbidden to approach slaughtered animals, but later, when pregnancy was advanced, the restriction fell away, even though he was still cohabiting with his wife.

A person whose upper teeth appear before the lower or whose molars appear first is full of *muridi* and should be killed. In the area surrounding the royal village every child is brought to the queen for examination on the appearance of its first teeth. The mother carries with her a small basket of eleusine and, if all is well, it is said that the child has 'danced with joy' (*u pɛbɛdɛ*); if not, there are no ululations of joy and, though to-day the child is allowed to live, it must be treated by a doctor. When several children have been brought, beer must be made by their mothers for the older women, the queen attends, and there is much joy. If a person whose teeth have appeared in the wrong order is not killed, he is called a *leshɛga*. He must be most careful never to bite any one, for the wound will not respond to healing treatment. But it is believed that matter taken from the teeth of the *leshɛga* may be applied as an antidote. It will be remembered that in the case of *Mabula* v. *Magɔsha* the parents of a *leshɛga* who had bitten her co-wife were ordered to beg pardon and to allow the 'scraping' of the teeth of their daughter. They had denied that she was a *leshɛga*, but the court decided that, *leshɛga* or not, neither she nor they could refuse something that might help the wound.

Muridi is, on the whole, dangerous, not to its primary intermediary host, but to others. Its source is conceived to be usually a person, but it may also be places, such as cross-roads and large rivers which become infected owing to the number of people crossing them. Nor is all *muridi* equally dangerous. Precautions are taken to protect the sick against its influence; a sick person is smeared with medicine or a stick is placed to bar entrance to his hut, its warning against entering without permission being a function also of the stick barring the door of the hut of a new-born child. Allied to but not the same as *muridi* are *leridi* (monstrous shadow) and *letala* (sinister spoor, the word for an ordinary track being *mutala*). A warrior who has killed an enemy has *leridi* and, unless purified, he stands in grave danger of becoming mad or extremely quarrelsome (one of the worst social sins). If two men have had sexual relations with the same woman and one of them is ill, the other must on no account come near lest his track (*letala*) cause him to die. Similarly, the husband's mistress should take care to remain away from the hut of his wife when she is ill or in childbirth.

Makhuma, from *hu khuma*, to mix together, is a conception similar to *muridi*, but the evil, a kind of illness, infects the immediate host, who cannot transmit it to others. Critical changes especially constitute the source of the evil which mingles with or contaminates or infects the person who has just undergone the change or who, in the case of death, comes into contact with its baleful emanations. In all the initiations strengthening medicine is given the novices as an antidote to the *makhuma* to which they are subject after the initiation: for instance, the initiates in the boys' circumcision lodge are given black medicine just before the change from west to east to protect them from being injured (*hu khuma*) after entering the ordinary world. One may *khuma* if, after an absence from home during which a death has occurred, one eats food without some precautionary measure, such as chewing a piece of ant heap (*khithoni*). The treatment given after a death is chiefly to prevent the onset of *hu khuma* among relatives. A woman who has lost a child will cause her next child to *khuma* if she allows it to drink before her breasts have been doctored. Cattle may *khuma* after a death in the village or if women enter the kraal, and measures to fortify them are always taken after the funeral. *Makhuma* also affects possessed people who fail to use their powdered medicine with the first-fruits.

Though usually associated with the stomach, the symptoms of *makhuma* are not very definite, diagnosis being chiefly *ex post facto*. If one child has died, any illness its successor might have, even beating of the fontanelle, is liable to be attributed to *makhuma*. After the miscarriage of Madume's wife, Ḍwagu, a non-related inmate of the same village, did not trouble to be purified when the doctor came; but when, shortly afterwards, his stomach became upset, he immediately attributed it to *makhuma* and hastened to take medicine for its removal.

The conception of *khuma* has been extended into other fields. Divining bones *khuma* at the end of each month as well as when used to divine about a death, and must be washed in medicine before being used again. Similarly the rain charms of the queen are liable to *khuma* (or *figɛhɛla*) unless given the first-fruits and the first termites of the year to 'bite' (*luma*) before any one else in the royal area eats them, as also when certain people neglect certain observances, such as burial in wet soil of infants dying before their teeth have appeared. *Hu khuma* of the rain charms has serious consequences, causing drought throughout the country. That Christians do not observe these regulations has as little effect on the rain as when Europeans do not conform.

Hu fesa, or the state of being 'hot', is a conception far wider than *muridi* or *makhuma* and is the antithesis of the condition of coolness which is conceived of as healthy, propitious, or right. The properties of this 'heat', which may be caused in a variety of ways, are not unlike physical heat. Bodily illness, even *muridi*, causes the blood to be 'hot' or to be 'boiling' and may be treated by 'cooling' the body: thus the *khitshila* ceremony, which removes the 'dirt' of death, also 'cools' people. The hair of near relatives is shaved with medicine and put in a wet place or in certain kinds of drought-resisting plants. But it is usually the source of the 'heat', not the 'heat' itself, the symptom of the disease, that is treated, though both may be dealt with. The blood of a woman in certain conditions—for example, after an abortion—is said to 'burn', she has (or is) *lesua* (great burning), and the man who has sexual intercourse with her also 'burns', but whether it is because the 'heat' is conducted to him or because of the disease, *ḍɛre* (coughing illness) or urethritis, which he contracts, is by no means clear. The treatment is directed at the disease in him, not towards counteracting the 'heat'. Often after steaming a patient, a river stone is pressed against all joints of the body and then taken back to the river, a treatment in which we may discern an attempt to 'cool', though it also contains the conception of 'throwing out'.

Since heat withers the vegetation and causes drought, it is opposed to rain. Precautions must therefore be taken against whatever is thought to cause the country to be hot and dry. A man succumbing to *ḍɛre*, a person struck by lightning, a woman dying in childbirth, and the foetus of a miscarriage—all these must be buried in wet soil or with rain medicine if the country is to be kept 'cool' and the rains are to fall. Coolness connotes rightness. Charms protecting the village against witches are sometimes called *mashɔthɔjɔ*, because they *rɔthɔja* (cause to be cool, calm, or soothe) the village. Cooling is an effective weapon against sorcery: when the doctor made Nagambi vomit the foreign object introduced into his stomach by a sorcerer and causing the illness *khileso* (thing caused to be eaten) he ordered it to be buried in a wet place and water to be squirted (*hu phasa*) over it with an injunction to the disease to return to its sender. Even the gods must be kept cool, for if hot they stand up (*va ɛmɛ*), are discontented, and make trouble; hence the black river stone in many shrines and perhaps also the river stones in the drums. 'To cool' might be translated by our phrases, to calm, to free from agitation, to soothe, to appease, or, more generally, to put right.

The great role of sex in medical practice can only be briefly dealt with. Many illnesses and even death are attributed to sexual intercourse in certain circumstances or to some supposed abnormality in the sexual organs. Some men and women are believed to have a small thick hair (*levoya*) in their genitals which enters the stomach of any one with whom they cohabit and there pecks (*hu gɔba*). The *levoya* from a man will cause the woman he impregnates to die in childbirth, and the *levoya* of a woman kills all her lovers. Pheduli, whose wife's death was attributed to *levoya*, found some difficulty in re-marrying, and the parents of the girl whose love overcame her fear insisted on his submitting to curative treatment before the marriage. But usually there is merely rumour that So-and-so has *levoya* and no definite precautions are taken. Men avoid intercourse with a menstruating woman, not because of danger to her, but because, as even educated men in the towns believe, they are liable to become afflicted with swollen penis or urethritis. *Mafa*, swelling of the whole body, is contracted if one, without previous steaming and mutual inoculation, cohabits with one's deceased brother's wife; but a stranger, though liable to get ill, does not contract *mafa*, because it is chiefly due to the 'dirt' of one's brother.

To *ɖɛre* or *vulwɛdɛ vya vasadi*, the woman's disease, and the most dreaded of all diseases, more than 30 per cent. of the deaths of men during our stay among the Lovedu was attributed. It is believed to be contracted by a man if, without previous precautionary treatment, he has sexual intercourse with a woman who has had a miscarriage or abortion or whose child has died before weaning. So fatal is it regarded to be that, unless cured immediately, the patient's chances of getting well are seriously impaired by the weight of subtle mass suggestion and his complete surrender to the inevitable. One illustration, the death of an educated man and a close friend of ours, will suffice. He had an irritating cough which every one believed to be *ɖɛre*, but one European doctor found nothing wrong, while another, to whom we explained our anxiety, diagnosed miocardiosis, which would readily respond to hospital treatment. Our friend had no faith in the diagnosis and refused to go to hospital; he resorted to one Native doctor after another and vainly endeavoured to get 'medicine' from the girl he suspected. He became more and more emaciated, resigned himself to his fate and within a month after examination by the second European doctor he was dead.

Ɖɛre is not syphilis nor a sexual disease. Its main symptom is coughing, but any illness, even if there is hardly any cough, may be diagnosed as dɛre if the circumstances of the personal relations of the patient justify such a diagnosis. People thought that Maḍaradani's cough was dɛre, but when he insisted that he had no lovers it was diagnosed as khileso; Mulada's debility was probably due to chronic malaria, but his friends suspected that he had taken no precautionary measures before resuming co-habitation with his wife, who had miscarried after seven months. Ḍɛre is distinguished from lefiha (consumption) by its rapid course and the fact that lefiha (hu fiha, to breathe) is not caused by women. Ḍɛre can be cured only in its earliest stages, an ingredient of the medicine being a portion of the abortion or, in the case of intercourse with a woman who has lost a child, can be prevented by steaming and mutual inoculation. The prevalence of dɛre suggests that abortions are common and that effective abortifacients are in general use. In reality, however, innocent women are accused as soon as a lover falls ill, and rather than be thought murderers, they often give him medicine purporting to be a portion of the abortion mixed with sand to be used as a cure.

Disease and healing are in the last resort connected with the guardianship of the ancestors. If they are annoyed and relax their vigilance, their descendants may be rendered susceptible to disease, or medicines used cannot have their full effect. Ancestors, however, do not merely ward off disease or assist cure; they also actively cause illness. The crying all day of a baby may be due to the spirit of a grandfather pinching it in order that it should be given his name; sore eyes in children are often, and in adults sometimes, attributed to ancestors; barrenness or difficult birth is laid at their door, and sometimes they seize the whole body of a person because they wish to 'possess' him. But ancestors never cause death: even if at first an illness is said to be due to them, should death supervene, it is attributed to witches. Complaints of living relatives, especially of the father's sister, may also cause illness.

By far the most important of all causes of ill-health, however, is the evil work of witches and sorcerers. Certain illnesses, such as khileso, are characteristic of sorcery and can be contracted in no other manner. But any disease may be caused by witchcraft and witches may avail themselves of the opportunity offered by any minor illness to enter and aggravate it. Diagnosis depends on the course of the illness. Dysentery is regarded as due to natural causes; but should it not respond to treatment or should the patient suspect an enemy, a witch will be implicated. During the 1938 smallpox epidemic, the head of a district which was more hardly hit than its neighbours called a meeting of residents. Men declared, 'Smallpox kills people here; they merely get ill and recover elsewhere. There is a witch in our midst.' Money was collected, three men sent to a diviner, and, in the end, two women were accused. A specialized cause of illness is legitimate vengeance-magic used against theft and called khidɔba, which makes the finger of the thief swell up or the stolen goat bleat in his belly.

It must not be imagined that the Lovedu do not recognize a large number of diseases as natural. Many illnesses 'just come'. Such are all minor ailments like coughs, colds, stomach disorders, and also other more serious diseases like dysentery and malaria. Too much beer is known to affect the stomach, many kinds of spinach to cause diarrhoea. Epidemics of smallpox, measles, coughs are thought to be brought by 'wind' (*phεfo e ḍile*) and steps may be taken to combat them by sprinkling with medicines the inmates of the village. Usually an epidemic 'just comes', but on occasion one hears that a witch has 'sent' the wind. Ancestors, too, are thought to exercise some controlling influence over wind; in most libations they are asked, 'Prevent for us these winds'— that is, as we might phrase it in our prayers, 'Guard us from disease.' Diseases are never classified as natural or non-natural solely according to their nature or symptoms. Any natural illness may also be 'sent' and, though natural death is recognized as possible, in practice those closely affected always attribute death to witchcraft or sorcery, though outsiders may give other reasons and some even say of an old man dying, 'The gods have called him to rest.' Of the thirty deaths, including a number of old people, that came to our notice, none were, however, thought to be natural. Contagiousness (*hu fεdεla*) of certain diseases, such as venereal diseases, leprosy, whooping cough, measles, is recognized, and it is known that consumption may be transmitted by parents to their children, as one of its names, *lehɔṭɔla la tata-mulɔgɔ* (cough of the family father) signifies.

There must, of course, be a body of professional men and women trained in and practising the art and science of medicine, but there are also many who have an extensive knowledge of home remedies. This is not unexpected in a society in which ordinary mortals live close to, and know a great deal about, nature. Every one is familiar with plants and their properties, which is one of the bases of pharmacology, with the meagre conceptions of anatomy and physiological relations, and with much of the intricate system of causation of disease. There are many men and women who know some special medicines or types of treatment, inherited usually from father, mother, or spouse, and kept secret, not because the knowledge is a source of material benefit, for the remedies are generally given free, but because it lends some recognition and prestige. Mamutho, despite all our efforts, divulged her medicine for inflamed eyes to us only as a parting gift. Madinji treats sprains and fractures; Khiεbε specializes in mutual inoculation of the newly wed; and Khapani knows roots for dysentery. These are herbalists, not doctors, but some herbalists are so well-known for the efficacy of a medicine they have that even diviners send patients to them. Knowledge of these remedies, however important, does not make one a doctor (*Ḍaga*): that appellation is accorded only to those who are initiated bone-throwers or as herbalists have achieved general recognition as dispensers of many medicines and treatments. Muhale's wife, though no bone-thrower, is a good midwife and wields expertly a blood-letting awl. But a herbalist, even if called *Ḍaga*, remains *Ḍaga-tshubya*, a doctor without horns (power), because he does not divine; he can prescribe for recognized diseases, but he cannot diagnose in other cases for which the divining dice are necessary. From our point of view, the herbalist diagnoses and prescribes along scientific lines; to the Native he is a novice unable to deal with witches or the more serious diseases.

The distinctive characteristic of the doctor with 'power' is that he is a diviner. That must necessarily be so in a society in which pathology is the science of diseases, the nature and causes of which lie so largely in magico-witchcraft conceptions. Special techniques are called for in place of what we call diagnosis and bedside manner. The diviner's function is, however, more than that: he must be called in about the details of every religious ceremony to discover the wishes of the ancestors; he decides where, in order to avoid the danger of the witch, every village must be built; he makes the witch-proof fence. Besides the bone-thrower, to whom we shall refer as doctor and who is consulted at every turn, there are two other classes of diviner, the *lelɔpɔ* doctor and the *mugɔme*, both foreign introductions from the East. The *lelɔpɔ* doctor is often a tribesman, the *mugɔme* always a Shangana-Ṭonga, preferably living outside Ṿulovedu. The spheres of these classes of diviner are different: the doctor heals disease and is the general medical practitioner in its wide Lovedu sense; the *lelɔpɔ* doctor, almost always a woman, initiates the 'possessed', and often is also a general practitioner, divining with bones and healing disease, especially barrenness and ailments of children; and the *mugɔme* is, as we have seen, the forensic physician, and if he is famous he keeps no medicines, though otherwise he combines smelling out of the guilty with a general medical practice. Both *mugɔme* and *lelɔpɔ* doctors claim direct inspiration from the ancestors, but the doctor reads his bones by rule.

As it is difficult to persuade outsiders to divulge their knowledge, the profession of doctor, in theory open to all, is in practice more often than not handed down in the family, from father to son or daughter, maternal uncle to nephew, husband to wife, or even wife to husband. Interest and inclination determine who the pupil will be. To acquire a working knowledge of the bones, with which people are generally familiar to some extent, may take only a few months, but it is useless knowledge unless one has medicines and experience, which may take years to acquire. Ambitious doctors spend their lives gaining these perquisites, buying from one, begging from another, colleague; many travel from tribe to tribe or go periodically to Johannesburg, where good money is to be made. There are many specialists: Ramavulana, like his father before him, is a noted rain-maker; Mambye is a master of *madabi*, by which he changes people into animals or hangs organs of the victim of his vengeance-magic on pegs in the hut; Mashao makes the hedge of the *vyali* lodge witch-proof; Rathavala strengthens the queen for office; Mulebye doctors the boys' circumcision lodge. A doctor who has not inherited cannot easily acquire such specialized knowledge: the price is high and the secrets not readily given away. The greatest doctors are said to use human remains in their most potent medicines, and to satisfy this need there are *zwigevɛgwa*, murderers who waylay and kill people at night. During our stay, people, even at public gatherings, discussed and warned against the activities and haunts of these murderers. The wife of Thagu, the doctor, one night came home very drunk and next morning discovered part of her genitals excised. She accused her husband in the district *khɔrɔ* and, though he denied the crime, he paid the fine. As

Thagu is not a great doctor, people surmised that he wanted the flesh, not for himself, but as the price of a medicine he bought from a renowned doctor.

A good doctor, unless, as is most common, he grows up in the profession, undergoes a long period of *ad hoc* training of 'walking about' with doctors. Maḍarabani, who hoped by becoming a doctor to save his family the expense of constantly calling in medical aid, began by going about with doctors he knew, from time to time persuading them to show him a few medicines; he put his knowledge to successful use in his family and started collecting a set of bones, buying those he could not pick up himself. Gradually he acquired the elements of divining, finishing up his training at the feet of a Shangana-Ṭonga *mugɔme*. Tuition in divining teaches one the various combinations of the dice; really to 'know' the bones one must drink their soup in a ceremony called 'cooking the bones'. It is the only cooking the dice undergo, so that it is taboo to use bones that have been cooked as food; it completes a diviner's training, and it not only creates a bond between dice and diviner, but gives him insight to see what is obscure to others. The ceremony varies from doctor to doctor, but consists in essence of three main features. Firstly, a young cockerel or, according to older custom, a goat is killed, its flesh is cooked with the dice and the broth is drunk by the pupil. The cock quickens perception both of bones and diviner, for it heralds the dawn before man perceives its approach. Secondly, the novice is given medicine (by inoculation or as a drink) containing *inter alia* the heart and nose of the vulture and wild dog, as well as sometimes the heart of the cooked fowl, so that he may sense things from afar. And, thirdly, the bones are buried at the cross-roads overnight 'to gather the news' and next morning are unearthed. When a male passes, a bone representing a male, when a female passes one representing a female, is taken out, and a beer drink is given so as to ensure many passers-by. Thereafter the novice can tell, in a test to which he is submitted, how the bones have fallen without looking at them.

Possession, in the ordinary manner of the cult, but by a spirit who in life was a doctor, constitutes the initiation of a *lelɔpɔ* doctor. He may divine during possession when the possessing spirit speaks or chants, or he may throw the dice when not possessed like an ordinary doctor. If during possession the dice are thrown, it is merely for effect, for they are hardly looked at. It is claimed that *lelɔpɔ* doctors read dice without training, being guided by their spirit; but in practice we found that either they had for months attached themselves to another doctor or, as members of a divining family, had become familiar with the bones prior to possession. The *mugɔme*, like the *lelɔpɔ* doctor, is guided by a spirit which manifests its desire that he should become a diviner by making him ill, but, unlike the *lelɔpɔ* doctor, he is not actually possessed. The *mugɔme* is the master diviner, but in fact he seldom throws the dice more than once or twice before proceeding to divine 'by the heart'. His initiation comprises the curing of his illness, apprenticeship to another *mugɔme* and the cooking of the bones. *Lelɔpɔ* doctor or *mugɔme* and guiding spirit are closely associated. A *lelɔpɔ* doctor never uses a goat in healing, without setting aside pieces of meat for his spirit, and a *mugɔme* always has his special shrine where he reports all money professionally earned. An ordinary doctor sometimes has a shrine where he places horns of goats received or hangs medicine bags when he prays to the spirits, but many do not have these things. To a doctor his divination is like a craft that he has learnt, and he gives offerings only when scarcity of clients is attributed to the displeasure of the gods. When about to divine, he begs the bones to tell him the truth, not the ancestors for guidance.

The divinatory dice constitute the chief diagnostic method. The Lovedu set is fairly stereotyped, consisting of about forty pieces, most but not all of which are bones; the bones and *hakati* shells (oval-shaped stones of a fruit) of the Shangana-Ṭonga *mugɔme* are somewhat different. Dominating the usual Lovedu set are four flat pieces of ivory or bone, two male and two female, which fall in sixteen different combinations, the cardinal positions. Each position has its own name and its own praise referring, though vaguely, to its meaning; and it is these four pieces from which the general configuration of influences or prognostications is read. There are other sets of four: pieces from the ventral surface of a tortoise, each with two easily distinguishable sides, and shells, two Oliva standing for males and two Cyraea standing for females. Having thrown the dice, the diviner looks first at the ivory pieces and gives the praise of their disposition, which indicates the general situation, say, dissension, loss, or complaints of the father's sister. But this general situation must be related to the lie of certain other bones, particularly *malope*, the knuckle-bone of the steenbuck (*Raphiceros campestus*), from which, as representing the chief, the diviner next orientates the situation. The procedure thereafter involves linking this situation, on the one hand, with events or specific prognostications of good or evil and, on the other, with people playing a part in these events. *Thakadu* or *mudimo*, the talus of the antbear, represents the ancestors, who, like the antbear, live underground, shows whether they are angry or not, and is diagnostic of the health or life of a person which in the last resort lies in ancestral hands. *Dau*, the phalanx of the lion (or in some sets *ŋgwɛ*, the phalanx of the tiger) which is also a pointing bone showing direction, *phiri*, the knee-bone of the hyena, of which there may be two, male and female, and *tshweni*, male and female kneebones of the baboon, all stand for the evil power of witches and their familiars. The baboon bones, in addition, indicate, by the side on which they fall, danger or illness on a journey, suitability of the spot for building upon and, in case of barrenness, whether or not a child will be born. Every set contains two morula pips with functions less specific, depending as they do upon the whole configuration of forces or events, and a river pebble, *lemɛja la gwɛna*, the thing swallowed by a crocodile, which is diagnostic of *khileso*, the illness caused by foreign substances which sorcerers cause their victims to swallow with food or drink.

To bring these evil or good influences into relation with specific people, to determine who is ill or who is bewitching the consultants, the diviner turns to certain astralagus bones, capable of falling on four sides and representing people. Two or three sheep bones stand for important or respected persons, such as district or village heads, and goat bones, numbering two to six, for mere commoners—a real separation of sheep and goats. If there are two goat bones, they represent male and female; a third represents a child; four bones extends the range to male and female children, and the further two bones differentiate widow and bachelor. Different totems are shown by bones of the animals revered. Lovedu sets have two (male and female) *maḓavu* (rietbuck) bones standing for the Crocodile totemic group; two *phala* (rooibuck) bones for Khalaga and sometimes also Lovedu; two *golove* (wild boar) for Lovedu, two *phudi* (duiker) for Khaha and Koni; two *shɔshɔ* (bushbuck) for the Tshadzi of Mavulana; and in areas in which there are Phalavorwa and Thavina also two *nogo* (porcupine). Elephants and lions are represented by the bones of these animals. These totem-indicating bones vary greatly according to the people with whom the diviner comes into most contact. Many diviners have one or two extra pieces, such as a shell or a stone found in a strange place. Malematsha, for instance, has a piece of chalk from France, where he served in the labour battalion during the Great War.

The detailed rules of divination are far too complicated for treatment in a general ethnographical study, but a few general principles, common knowledge to all in the society, may be mentioned. Firstly, it is the side on which the bones fall rather than their disposition to one another that is important. All the pieces can fall in two ways, either positive, dorsal, or negative, ventral surface up, while in addition the astralagi have two narrower surfaces, one, the concave side, with a deeper cleft than the other, the convex side. In the normal position, with dorsal side up, the power the bone stands for is said to be active, the person it represents well or walking in the direction it is lying; in the reverse position, with ventral side up, it is sleeping, powerless or dead and hence, when the people represented are witches, a good sign, for they are then on their backs and harmless. An astralagus lying on its convex side with the cleft up shows laughing, happiness, talking, or even quarrelling (much talking), and with convex side up, anger, complaints, sadness. Secondly, the significance of these positions and particularly of the combinations of the sets of four bones varies according to the purpose of the divination: a particular position means one thing when it is illness, another when it is a building site that is in question. Thirdly, despite intricate rules, divination is in the last resort not an exact science, but an interpretation in which the diviner's ingenuity, his knowledge of human nature and his estimate of the interplay of motives in the society play an important part. In this connexion, the praises of each bone and of various positions have an unsuspected function. These praises are not trade secrets and are fairly generally known; to be word-perfect is unnecessary and parts may be recited or omitted, while half may be uttered at one moment and the remainder much later. This occupies the mind of the client and gives the diviner time to think and orientate himself. Moreover, interpretation abounds with metaphorical expressions, as does the parlance of European fortune-tellers with club-men and diamond-girls. Many Lovedu diviners, imitating the *mugɔme*, use a peculiar chant, half Shangana-Ṭonga, half

Sotho, a jargon difficult to understand and reinterpreted by the doctor or by some one of the party more conversant than the client with the procedure.

The procedure in divination is a subtle process combining suggestion, free association of ideas, and techniques of leading the client and inspiring confidence in the diviner. On opening the bags, the doctor pours out the dice and watches how they fall, but he does not always vouchsafe anything at this stage. Before casting his dice, he chews a piece of root (*khirugulu*), which he blows out on to the bones: both he and the bones are thereby given insight and power. Then, taking them in both hands and uttering a praise by way of encouragement, he casts them on to the floor or on the mat provided. At this stage he reads the cardinal positions, perhaps elaborating on the general trend indicated, and suggests what the client has come to consult him about, often in so doing eliciting some information. Thereafter the client himself throws the bones, speaking to them as dictated by the doctor; the practice of bringing a piece of rag breathed upon by the patient is not known, but the consultant may be directed to mention the patient's name. The client will have to cast many times till the trouble has been thrashed out. The next step is for the doctor, after suggesting a remedy, to cast the bones and interpret their reply to the suggestion. Whatever the cause of the illness, the first suggestion is always placation of the ancestors and thereafter medicines and treatments. At each throw only some of the dice are studied, the position of the others being irrelevant to the immediate purpose. Sometimes it takes long (often as we have seen, over two hours or a whole afternoon) for the bones to give a clear indication and, if they fall in unreadable combinations, various causes may be assigned: the bones may not have been properly 'washed'; or a condition precedent to effective divination may have been omitted, such as in one case we witnessed, when the consultant's people had not yet held the removal of 'dirt' (*khitshila*) ceremony after the death of a child; or the bones may unaccountably 'refuse'.

To illustrate the procedure, we give an actual case of divination simplified by the omission of the praises. Ramatiti, the doctor, had just finished divining for Dumedi when Dwagu, Dumedi's friend who lived some ten miles away, came upon the scene and, handing over his 1*s*. to the doctor, asked that the dice be thrown for him. Ramatiti poured out the bones, looked at them, but remained silent. He then chewed a piece of *khirugulu*, took the bones in both hands, spat on them and, mumbling a praise, cast them. 'They have fallen *muferegere*' (a position meaning dissension), he said, uttering the relevant praise. 'You have been greatly troubled,' he continued, enlarging upon the greatness of the trouble. 'The tortoise bones lie *mutagola*' (indicating long illness), he added. 'You suffer from "blood" and intestinal trouble. Do you have dreams?' 'Yes,' replied Dwagu, 'chiefly about dead people.' '*Tshweni*' (the baboon bones), went on the doctor, 'are full [lie on their convex side]; your sickness is on the chest.' Thereupon Dwagu was given the bones to throw and told to repeat after the doctor a praise of the bones: 'Tell us you spy with eyes that see, tell us why we are afflicted; whether it be a god or whether it be a witch, tell us.' When the bones had fallen, Ramatiti asked, 'Do you know any *gwɛna* [man of the Crocodile totem]? Are your in-laws Crocodile?' 'No,' replied Ɖwagu, 'I know only neighbours, not relatives, who are Crocodile.' After Ɖwagu had denied that he had quarrelled with these people, the doctor warned him not to drink beer with them, and when he objected, 'But we are always drinking together', the doctor said. 'It is they who have given you *khileso*.' Ɖwagu was doubtful, but replied, 'I remember that once, when I came out of the *gomana* "school", a son of those neighbours gave me monkey nuts and afterwards my stomach was upset.'

Ɖwagu threw the bones again and the doctor asked him if he were troubled by matter in the ears. Ɖwagu admitted that both his ears were affected and added, 'That is how the trouble began, and I have tried many remedies in vain.' The doctor now had a substantial clue. 'The ears are causing blood on the chest', he said. 'Has a *lelɔpɔ* doctor tried to cure you?' 'No,' Ɖwagu replied. 'Only a woman who was one day called for my mother.' The bones were once more thrown to determine whether the woman would succeed if she were called again. The *malope* bone lay on its back and with *dau* and *phiri* upside down, showing the power of the witches to be broken, and *golovɛ* (wild boar) in its normal position, the doctor declared that Ɖwagu would recover. But, though it was silently passed over, the diviner was mistaken in thinking that his client was of the *golovɛ* totem. Again Ɖwagu threw the dice and the question asked, viz. whether he should offer to (*suma*) his dead father, was answered in the negative; but though *phiri* (hyena) and *tshweni* (baboon) lay powerless, the positive position of the lion (*dau*), associated with witches, indicated that the stomach-ache would remain. 'Have you bilharzia?' inquired the doctor. 'No.' 'Well, then, do you enjoy your beer?' 'No,' was the reply. 'But one calabash fills my stomach; I can't drink much.' Another throw, this time by the doctor, was favourable to the medicine mentioned as a cure. 'But,' asked the doctor, as he scrutinized the bones, 'what child at home is ill?' When Ɖwagu said it was his, the doctor congratulated himself on his perspicacity and could not resist following up his success.

Ɖwagu thus had to cast the dice about his child. The doctor diagnosed *zwiso* (sores), a vague term covering external rashes or sores of all kinds, as well as internal trouble, and a common complaint of children. 'Yes,' replied Ɖwagu. 'The sores are in its mouth,' adding a full account of the complaint. The *khilumɛ* goat bone (indicating a young male person) was lying positive, so the doctor said, 'It is a boy,' but again he was wrong. Unperturbed, the doctor now threw the dice, having suggested the cure, 'Dung of witches (metaphorical for the insectivorous bat) and mice and moss hanging from trees. Burn one portion holding the child in the smoke and smear its body with the other portion. Tell us, you spy with eyes that see. I say let the fowl (child) be well.' But the bone standing for a small girl fell on its back: the medicine would not succeed. Again the doctor threw, mentioning different ingredients, but similar treatment, and this time the bones were propitious.

The doctor is an important person in the society, not because his practice brings him wealth, but because disease is a matter of ever-present interest. He is paid chiefly in beer, which provides entertainment for friends and neighbours, payer and payee, and enhances his prestige. The family doctor usually receives nothing at all, but is called to beer that is drunk in the family. Diviners receive the 1s. or fowl for divination and perhaps, if they are mercenary or have taken great pains about the medicine, 5s. for opening the medicine bags; but payment for treatment is made only for successful cures. A patient should on recovery not shave his head before bringing beer to the doctor, when the 'hair of his illness' is shaved, perhaps with medicine by the doctor and taken to a hollow tree, where it is left with the words 'Sickness remain there'; but this rule is, as often as not, observed in the breach. The correct charge for curing barrenness or epilepsy is £1 or £1 10s., yet we have seen many cures of barrenness for which only beer was given. The means of the patient and his relationship to the doctor are material factors. *Lelɔpɔ* doctors are usually mercenary, requiring a goat for most of their treatments and fining patients who shave their heads without permission. *Mugɔme* are the wealthiest doctors, receiving anything from £1 to £7 at one sitting. Many set up temporary villages along the roads to catch clients, and one living in Portuguese East Africa has a lorry for transporting clients from the Transvaal lowveld to his home. The *mugɔme* exacts full payment before he divines; other doctors have to wait until the cure is effected. A doctor never goes to court about his fees, but he sometimes threatens to cover up the holes where he dug the medicines to call back illness upon the patient.

When medicines are not effective, it is etiquette to acquaint the doctor with the fact before going to a second doctor, but this etiquette is not always observed. Health is the quest of every one at all times, and disease is the most persistent and dangerous enemy of the individual; for the causes of illness are incalculable and even the most harmless disease may let in the witch to strike at his victim. The office of the doctor is both important and honourable, for he is the guardian of the people's welfare. There is no oath that binds him to loyalty and integrity, but these things are expected of him; he even preserves the secrets of his clients and, though the *mugɔme* advertises himself, such action by a doctor is regarded as derogatory.

CHAPTER XIII

THE ROLE OF THE ANCESTORS

Ancestral caprices and complaints and rites to appease them—the universe of the ancestors a replica of the everyday world—relations of magic, morality, and religion—possession by spirits as a religion and socio-psychological phenomenon.

NATURE spirits and hero-gods have no place in the Lovedu scheme of things. There is, however, Khuzwane, the creator, who made all things, including men, and left his footprints on certain rocks in the north when these rocks were new and soft. But no one knows what has happened to him and no one ever thinks of him. The gods of the Lovedu are their ancestors, deceased fathers and mothers who guard one in death as they did in life. Each family has its own ancestors, and religious observances are thus peculiarly a family concern.

Ancestors have various attributes. They are one's protectors and no harm can befall one unless they, the ancestors, are neglectful. Witches, powerful as they are, can neither enter the village nor cause sickness without their connivance; hence the procedure in divination, even in the clearest case of witchcraft, of inquiring whether the spirits should be appeased. Disease cannot enter nor epidemics break out if only the ancestors are watchful enough and well-disposed. Again and again one finds this idea expressed in prayers; 'Protect us from epidemics [winds]', they say; while the queen in a prayer at her harvest ceremony put it even more positively: 'As regards life, we have been very well, but now we are being killed by that epidemic which you have allowed to come', referring to smallpox. There can be no success without the co-operation of the ancestors. Medicine cannot help nor doctors heal if the ancestors are not with one. This idea, reminiscent of our 'By the will of God', is expressed in the phrase, 'We do not say our doctor, [will heal]; we say our doctor and the ancestors'. It appears also in a prayer we heard on behalf of an absent son working in town, when a goat, dedicated to his grandmother (father's mother), who had made him ill two years before, was being given the new corn: 'Here is the child; here he is, mother. We ask that you let him be happy and cool (give him health). Tell all the other spirits [certain names mentioned], and we who remain, *we say our thing with the gods.*'

The phrase '*vadimo lalane*' (spirits, sleep) which rounds off so many prayers, and the constant fear of waking up (*hu dzosa*) the ancestors, causing them to stand (*hu ɛma*) and cause trouble, appear at first as a peculiar contradiction, as though people do not wish their gods to be watchful. The term *lala* is, however, idiomatic, expressing peace, things being as they should be, as in the phrase, '*Ha va mulao; shago la lala*' (There was order; the country slept), implying that the rains were good and all was well; while *hu dzosa* in this sense means stirring to anger rather than waking up from sleep.

The ancestors are responsible for the fertility of the crops. True, nothing could grow without rain, for which the queen is responsible and which royal ancestors only can withhold; differences in the harvest between one area and another are often attributed to fights between the witches of the two areas, and even variations in yield between one man's field and his neighbour's may be due to witchcraft. Yet one finds in prayers many a request for a good harvest, even though there are no special ceremonies devoted to this end. A man pouring a libation for a sick child said among other things, 'Give us corn; when we plough let us also reap. Why are you stinting us?' And it is significant that the only regular religious observance is the harvest offering of beer made of each year's new corn in villages where there are shrines or dedicated animals. When any one dies, there is thought to be danger that the fertility of the crops will depart with him or her. Hence, when a gourd of seeds of every kind is placed in the grave together with a firebrand and calabash of water for the journey, some of the seeds are scattered over the body with the words, 'Do not depart with all the corn and seeds,' and very often the grain belonging to the deceased is treated with medicine in order that it may remain fertile.

Above all, the ancestors complain, a fact which lies at the basis of Lovedu religion, for by far the greater proportion of religious rites are those performed in response to ancestral complaints. One might at first think it strange that the gods, in life just ordinary, well-disposed people, should in death be so liable to bring trouble upon their kin. Sometimes it is thought to be a sign of love: when Masilu's grandmother had made him ill because she wanted a goat dedicated to her, his mother said, 'No wonder his *gogo* seized him. She was always so fond of him.' But chiefly it is the nature of ancestors to complain; as the Lovedu phrase it, 'When people sleep (i.e. are dead), they ought to complain' (*Hɛ vathu va khi lala fase va swanɛdɛ hu velɛala*). When there is illness, they are, as it is phrased, 'seen in the divining bones'; it is they who sometimes 'hold' the woman experiencing difficult childbirth, and sometimes, but far less than among the Nguni, their complaints cause dreams. Our close friend Walter, coming to seek work in Johannesburg, dreamt disturbing dreams of his dead father, who appeared to say that he was needed at home. He thereupon returned home and, when he arrived, his mother took him to a doctor, whose bones declared that the dead father was annoyed at not having been told of the journey to town and had to be appeased (*hu phasa*). Walter was well educated, but he had failed in his last examination and felt doubly frustrated. He had great ambitions of reforming the political system of the tribe, from which his education had divorced him, and in town he was dissatisfied that nothing was open to him but the unskilled work of his uneducated compatriots.

An ancestor may complain about the way he has been buried, and if he has died far from home, may demand to be 'brought back home' in a ceremony in which, besides the dedication of a beast or goat, a goat is killed and eaten, its bones being buried as though it were a person. But this 'bringing home', involving the making of a shrine, applies only to those dying at a distance and does not resemble the 'bringing home' of the Zulu, among whom it is part of death ceremonial. At times the gods complain of neglect. But in the majority of cases no definite reason for the complaint is either given or required; and frequently no special spirit is mentioned. It is enough to know the cause of the trouble and what rite is necessary to placate the gods. Even complaints of neglect are usually put positively: 'He complains that you should give him (his shrine) a libation'. The ancestors desire mainly to be remembered: they want their beads worn, their name revived, a beast or goat dedicated to and named after them. They also like to be told about journeys undertaken or marriages, in much the same way as the living, and to be approached with a libation. Yet, unlike the Nguni, they never complain of being hungry; nor are the gods said to drink the libation or even its spiritual counterpart, but are merely pleased to be given their due. There is no such thing as resting secure because you have done all that is necessary for the gods; there is always some ancestor who can cause trouble, and it is best to wait and see what is wanted. Moreover, the ancestors are wayward; there is no knowing what they may desire. Mambeuli asked to be buried at Khikhuti, but after his death he caused sickness, saying, 'Why did you bury me in the valley in the sun' (instead of in the ancestral grove), and a black sheep had to be sacrificed on his grave. Similarly, Mulogwane, brother of the queen, who in 1934 became a Christian on his death-bed, withheld rain in 1935 because they had buried him in a Christian cemetery. Religious rites among the Lovedu tend, therefore, to be addressed to those spirits that cause trouble and in the absence of illness there may be no rites at all.

Certain objects which were once in the possession of the ancestors are used in religious ceremonial and are thought to have special powers of protection and healing. These objects, consisting of ancient beads of glass or native-worked iron or copper, native-wrought assegais, hoes, axes, iron rods with spiked heads, are handed down in the family and carefully cherished. Very often when a daughter leaves to be married, she is given a few beads to take with her for use when she is ill. Such charms are called *thugula*. Illness caused by an ancestor can generally be cured by a ceremony known as *hu phasa*: a mixture of ground grain and water is poured over beads or other *thugula* objects in the presence of the patient while a prayer, scolding the spirits and asking for health, is made. The beads are then worn by the patient till he recovers. After *hu phasa* on beads for any one, he may wear them at any time with protective results, and small children generally wear many old beads. Maseriba called hers 'my hospital' (*spitele aa ga*) to illustrate their powers to us in European idiom. Patzere says, if he does not wear the crocodile bone that was his father's, he gets ill or dreams much of dead people. Association with the ancestors, not anything inherent in these objects, gives them their powers, for we have seen an old Boer gun brought out as a *thugula* at an offering. Yet for a charm to heal it is not essential that it should have been in the possession either of the complaining ancestor himself or of his family. Sometimes the gods, through the dice, mention beads or other objects not known in the family at all. It is then concluded that they have been lost and steps are taken to procure them from some one else or from the queen, who has many. Then when they pray, it will be mentioned: 'We are replacing the lost bead.'

Offerings may be poured on the ground or on *thugula* objects. Sometimes, however, the ancestors desire a shrine or a dedicated animal. The queen herself and some others have dedicated cattle, male or female, according to the spirit represented; a few families have sheep, while the majority have goats. Fowls are neither dedicated nor killed for the gods. But we have one instance of a dedicated snake, that in the Relɛla family, to which in 1939, at their burial grounds in the depths of the forest, libations were offered when the *vyali* initiation began in that district; the conception is wholly alien to the Lovedu, though the Relɛla have been so long linked with, as to be indistinguishable from, them; and the snake, said to whistle, is described as like that dreaded monster, the 'mountain snake' which is often thought of as a mamba but strikes terror like the omen it is. The use of these different animals is traditional in, and bears no relation to the wealth of, the families concerned; some have a dedicated animal, others merely a shrine, while many have both. The dedicated animal receives the name of an ancestor, father or grandfather in the case of the head of the lineage, or of any complaining spirit that has demanded such *thugula*, and it is believed that his spirit (*muya*) has entered into it. Some dedicated animals are credited with abnormal powers: Mamujaji's agitation one day, while being driven to the dip, correctly presaged unpleasantness with the dip inspector; Malegudu is the fiercest bull in the land, like the warrior whom he represents. Though some people unceremoniously pour beer-offerings down the throat of dedicated animals, it is generally claimed that, unlike ordinary animals, they readily drink beer, but the claim is contradicted by the mealie leaves put over the beer to coax the animal to drink. In 1938, when Malegudu, called from the herd to drink the harvest beer, remained immovable, every one was afraid to approach him, but it was considered sufficient to throw the beer over him from a distance, so that by licking himself he might partake of the offering.

Shrines, which are to be found generally on the left-hand side of the entrance to the sleeping hut of the chief wife, vary in appearance and contents. A shrine may consist of a small mound of earth, containing the bones of a sacrificial goat; it may be a sacred plant or tree, usually *ṭiṭigwani* (*Hypoxis villosa*) or *leɔmɛ* (*Hæmanthus sp.*) and *muṭabu* (*Ficus capensis*), a black river stone, a long stick, or even a piece of a certain kind of ant heap (*khiṭhoni*). The queen's own shrine is a mound under which are buried the bones of a goat slaughtered some twenty years ago when it was set up. Mashishimali's shrine contains no bones, but consists of a *ṭiṭigwani* lily and a river stone, both visible above ground. Ramatiti has three shrines and one dedicated goat, all of which have arisen out of illness caused by ancestral complaints. Of the first, the shrine of his father, nothing is visible above ground; it consists of a buried piece of ant-heap, used instead of a goat because Ramatiti is not the chief son, who should have the dedicated animal, and a black river stone which keeps the spirit cool and appeased (lying down), as well as the three plant substances *mufɛra*, *lesogo* (*Alipedia sp.?*), *vulevaja*, which are placed in most shrines to make the ancestors 'forget'. The other two are mounds containing the bones and heads of goats, one representing his mother, the other, like the live goat, his mother's brother, his wife's father.

In the actual working religion of the Lovedu the commonest and most conspicuous rite is *hu phasa*, consisting of a prayer and the pouring on to earth or *thugula* of a mixture of ground, sprouted grain and water, a mixture colloquially referred to as *muṭazwa lesɛlo* (the rinser of the winnowing basket). More rarely *hu phasa* is merely spitting out water in the courtyard to the accompaniment of such prayer. There is no formulated distinction in principle between the two forms; the Lovedu say that the dice decide which is to be used. We found water squirted in illness caused by complaints of the living; in some cases of difficult birth; where in the initiation of a possessed woman the spirit was begged to manifest itself; and in one exceptional instance water was squirted on the face of a corpse addressed in prayer before it was buried (usually the corpse is merely addressed when the grains are put into the grave). The efficacy of *hu phasa*, which is also used magically to render witchcraft ineffectual, appears to lie in its 'cooling' effect. *Hu phasa* is performed in connexion with a large number of cases of illness and bad luck and is the recognized approach in asking for blessings on a journey or an undertaking. Hardly a week passes without some one in the neighbourhood having to *phasa*, and generally the prayer in these cases takes the form of a 'scolding' (*hu rohana*), in which the spirits are asked why they are causing illness and told to be satisfied. One does not *phasa* without also using charms in the mixture to make the spirits forget, and the officiator may be male or female, whomsoever the dice have indicated. Rites of thanksgiving, except for the customary harvest beer, are almost unknown. We came upon such a rite only once when the bachelor brother of Madinji returned home after an absence in town of thirty years and she performed *hu phasa* in the presence of the family, saying, 'Spirits of Mambeuli, this is one of your fowls. We thought he was lost; now he is back. Keep him as you have kept the rest of us. If he goes away, let him soon remember and long for his home.'

The only regular offering is the annual harvest beer given to dedicated animals and shrines, though even this may be neglected: the village may be moved without the shrine, or the dedicated animal die without being replaced. We ourselves witnessed the setting up of a shrine and dedicated sheep after twenty years' neglect in the chief house of Sedena. Much more formal than ordinary rites of *hu phasa* is the harvest offering, which may take place any time between July and November, for there is here no rule that the queen should take precedence. The officiator is a woman where possible, the *khadi*, who is specially called to come, and real beer, called *muphaba* and made of eleusine, is prepared for the ceremony. If eleusine is not available, red kaffir corn (*makhaha*) may be used, but no other grain is acceptable to the spirits. In its preparation, which is in the hands of old women or girls below the age of puberty, care must be taken that the eleusine is stamped, not ground on the grindstone, and that none of it is tasted before the gods have been given some. Ordinary beer is tasted to see if it is ready, but *muphaba* is smelt or tested by stirring with a twirler. Though the married women of the village play no part in the religious rites on such occasions, it is the duty of the chief wife in whose courtyard the ceremony will take place to smear with dung the place where they will pour and to carry the beer in the *khirudwana* basket used in honour of the gods. The occasion is one of joy. The women have already in all likelihood sung *lesugu* songs special to the occasion amid joyous trillings while preparing the beer and, since in addition to the special beer of the gods much ordinary beer will have been prepared, a wide circle of relatives, including those of the wives, will have been invited.

When the queen held her *thugula* ceremony in August, 1938, Ḍiḍi was despatched at eight o'clock in the morning to fetch home Magoʋo, the cow dedicated to the queen's mother, for the harvest giving should take place fairly early in the day, though in practice the rule is often observed in the breach and we have seen ceremonies take place after midday. As it is not easy to drive home one cow of a herd, all were driven and put into the *khɔrɔ* where every one had gathered. When Magoʋo's hind legs had been tied, the chief wife of Mulogwane, deceased brother of the chief to whose family the queen is *khadi*, appeared carrying in a basket a calabash of beer and the queen's mother's beads (*mudala*, the well-known 'beads of the water'). Pouring some of the beer in a wooden platter, she handed it to the queen, who, holding the beads in her hands, placed it before Magoʋo with the words, 'Here is beer, Magoʋo of Muhale (one of the earliest kings), beer of the new corn. We say, Stop this epidemic (winds) to which you have exposed us. Here, too, are your beads. We see neither people (subjects) nor riches; we see only that poverty which you have left for us.' The cow sipped a little of the beer, whereupon all prostrated themselves in greeting (*hu lɔsha*), while one or two women rent the air with their joyous trillings. Sometimes (but it was omitted on this occasion) the beads are placed round the neck of the cow and left there for the whole day.

The dedicated cow having been untied, all now repaired to the courtyard of the chief wife of Mulogwane, where they sat round the shrine, the queen and sons and daughters near by, wives further away, while the small children were made to kneel on the lower side of the shrine, hands together and palms up. Pouring out beer on the mound, the queen said a prayer similar to the previous one, adding that the gods must tell one another and not leave any one out. Then, drinking a little herself, she placed the calabash on the ground for the next person to take up and drink. Each one in turn placed the gourd on the ground for the next to take up, till all the relatives had drunk, when it was returned to the queen. She drank once more, saying, 'He who gives to the gods must not remain hungry,' and laid the calabash upside down on the mound. The small children lapped up the beer from the ground, and trilling and *hu lɔsha* marked the end of the ceremony.

Now pots of beer for the crowd that had gathered were brought out and general drinking began. After a while the men took out the drums and began dancing an old dance, the *matagwa*. Thereafter the women began the sacred *lesugu* songs, to which men and women danced in a ring in the courtyard of the chief wife. The queen herself beat the big drum. It was now near sunset. Suddenly a wail like the bleating of a sheep was heard; another, then another, in the direction of the bush behind the village. It was the *zwiḍajani*, ancestral spirits come to join in the joy and revelry of the living. They opened the next song and joined in the singing of the women, all in the whistling language which people make out by its tone. Later more beer was brought out and when the *zwiḍajani* began a new song no one took any notice. 'If you are drinking beer, what are we to drink', came the wails of the *zwiḍajani* and a pot of beer was brought to the bush by councillors. Dancing and singing continued till the small hours of the morning, when the sounds of the *zwiḍajani* disappeared in the direction of Maulwi, the burial grove of the dead queens, and the revellers, happy and drunk from beer of the *thugula*, retired to bed. The spirits visit only important members of the royal group and a few other families, but beyond this there are no differences between the harvest giving of the queen and that of other people.

Ritual killings of all kinds are insignificant by contrast with the beer offering. There are, first, killings specially for the ancestors, but they are so rare that many people have never seen them. Secondly, there are occasions when the killings, clearly ritual, are not thought of as an offering or sacrifice, because nothing is given to the ancestors. And, thirdly, there are killings, not associated with ancestors or religion, in which small pieces of meat may nevertheless be set aside to 'tell' (*hu suma*) the gods of some event or to propitiate them. *Hu suma* is a conception somewhat different from our 'offer' or 'give'; it has two connotations as used in ordinary life: it is either merely to inform a superior or, by extension of this idea, to send him a share of something good one has, such as a leg of an animal slaughtered or a calabash of the beer one has brewed. In approaching the gods, sometimes one and sometimes the other conception is uppermost.

The killing which most clearly contains the conception of an offering and the primary purpose of which is propitiation of the gods is the slaughter of a black sheep for rain at the grave of a royal ancestor: the victim is immolated, small pieces of meat cut from all parts of it are set aside for the gods, and all the bones are collected and buried in the grave, together with the stomach contents. Equally stressed, however, is the eating of the meat without salt by the assembled crowd. At the installation of a district head, a beast, referred to as a *thugula*, is killed and, in so far as it is killed in a special manner and morsels of meat set aside for the gods to be cooked and later eaten without salt by children below the age of puberty, it is the vicarious submission of a gift to the ancestors. But the major portion of meat is not ritually eaten nor are the bones collected, for a hind leg is sent to the queen. So little is the 'goat of killing' in marriage ceremonial regarded as an offering or sacrifice that we sought for it in vain in the context of a killing for the ancestors. Yet pieces of meat are laid on the shrine and a prayer offered, though the rest of the meat is not ritually eaten nor are the bones kept. Still further removed from an offering is the goat killed on a death to provide a skin for covering the body: its meat is eaten without salt, and all who partake of it must sleep in the hut of the deceased, but nothing is given to the ancestors and no prayer is offered. On the other hand, though the *lelɔpɔ* doctor, when killing a goat to treat a patient, sets aside pieces of meat for his ancestors, this killing, primarily medical in purpose, is not to propitiate and has no religious significance.

An interesting though unusual killing among the Lovedu is the 'bringing home' of a spirit. Mabɔrɔmɔ, an uninherited widow living with her three children in a village of relatives, had had much illness in the family which, after consultation with many doctors, was attributed to her husband's brother Pheduli. Pheduli had been stabbed to death in a Johannesburg compound and was now complaining, 'I want to be brought home with a head of cattle.' All his relatives were asked to be present and contribute their share of corn, because 'We are placing a beast to be Pheduli'. On the day of the ceremony a young black and white bull-calf was caught and held, and, when beer (*muphaba*) was poured down its throat, the *khadi* uttered a prayer, saying, 'Drink and tell all the other spirits these matters.' Then they repaired with the same calabash to the courtyard, where all the children were called to sit near: the *khadi*, praying for health, poured the beer on a spear, battle-axe, and horn which had belonged to Pheduli, and the children drank what was left in the calabash, each one placing it in turn on the ground. The doctor, who, supervising his side of the ceremony, had been busy in a hut preparing his medicines, now came out and asked that the dedicated calf again be caught. Mixing a powder, said to consist of *mufɛra* and other medicines to make spirits forget, he told the *khadi* to smear it on some of the hairs at the end of the tail and to tie a knot. He himself then smeared the whole tail and body. Repairing to the courtyard where the *thugula* objects still lay, the doctor took out a bag of powder, which he shook up to 'smoke' the objects in its dust. Then he dug a hole where the beer had been poured.

Meanwhile the meat of a goat which had been killed was cooking in a pot. Before the killing (which we did not witness), medicine, we were told, had been smeared on the goat while the doctor uttered the words, 'Sleep, sleep here, and look after your people.' The meat was eaten without salt by the relatives as well as a few others who were present and the bones carefully collected. A dog seized hold of one and was chased by all till the bone was retrieved. Having placed the bones in the hole, the doctor inquired, 'In which direction do the Lovedu look when buried?' The *khadi* pointed to the north. Then, taking the head of the goat, he placed it facing north on top of the bones and said, 'We people all look in that direction.' He took out medicine, which he gave to the *khadi* to pour on the bones, smoked them with his powder, and ordered that the hole be filled with the stomach contents mixed with earth. The *khadi* then beat down the earth and made a small mound. Dancing and the singing of *lesugu* songs now began and continued all night till at dawn the *khadi* took some water and squirted (*hu phasa*) thrice, saying, 'As for us, we are going, we are returning home. And you, may you remain in peace.' In the beer that was provided for this festive occasion was put some medicine, 'the powder of death', generally used after a death, lest people khuma; for the burial of the goat symbolizes the burial and bringing home of their ancestor, just as the dedicated goat symbolizes the immortality of his spirit.

The immortality of Lovedu spirits is of practical importance in their working religion only for two or three generations back; beyond this they are hardly remembered. The spirits that cause most trouble are one's grandparents, and in religious practices these tend to be the most important. Both sides of the family, that of one's father and that of one's mother, are equally important; both cause trouble and both must be placated; and this is an accurate reflection of the social structure, of relationship reckoned bilaterally, and of the cattle links. The configuration of the ancestral world is no different from that of the ordinary world. It is therefore not surprising that all four lines of grandparents are recognized. Even when a spirit in the line of the father's father is being placated, the line of the father's mother may also be mentioned: thus we have heard an officiator in a *phasa* ceremony calling, not only upon his father's younger brother, the spirit troubling its granddaughter, but also upon his father, father's father, elder brother, mother, and elder sister. Dedicated goats to male ancestors tend to, but do not always, run in the male line. As in social or political arrangements, the male line may recede before the female; it may even, as far as ancestors are concerned, become almost completely obliterated. In the Matsui family, for instance, the father's father's line is neglected, except for *hu phasa*, when they cause illness, but the father's mother's line is all important. It is to the latter that the beast Mamujaji is dedicated and it is to this beast that the new corn is given every year. This emphasis reflects the links with the queen which the family wishes to emphasize, for Mamujaji, the ancestor of the father's mother, was mother of Mujaji I.

The coherence of the social and the ancestral worlds is seen even in regard to the implications of the *munywalo* system. Biological relationship not socially recognized is of no importance in religion, and not only can the biological father of an illegitimate child or his relatives never cause illness, for the 'gods follow the cattle' (*medimo e tɔvɛla dikhomu*), but the queen's ancestors cause illness in children of any of her wives, whoever their father may be, and it is the queen who is often required to *phasa* for them. In the gathering together in worship of all relatives the social system is similarly reflected. When after many deaths or much illness in a family the dice order a *mukhovo*, a religious gathering of all relatives, not only the lineage but relatives on both sides (*mulɔgɔ*), including those by marriage, meet. Each brings a basket of corn as a contribution towards the beer for the occasion, but a relative who is on bad terms with the others will, of course, simply stay away.

Not only the scheme of institutionalized social relations, but the nature of these relations in ordinary life is reflected in religion. The fact that the gods were known in life is largely responsible for many of the outstanding characteristics of Lovedu worship. We must not expect a behaviour pattern of humble worshipper to omnipotent god. Awe and trepidation characterize the attitude to the mysterical secrets of great *digɔma*, but they constitute a category poles apart from the ancestors and *dithugula*. People pray to ancestors as man to man, scolding them or reminding them of their duties to their children. The following prayer, uttered when Pheduli was brought home, is typical: 'We say, here is your corn, Pheduli.

What sort of person are you who do not live happily with your people? To-day all your children have gathered here. They have come to see you given corn. And to-morrow, when they depart, don't let there be a single one who remains troubled. Don't seize them, they are your children.' The difference between a spirit and the very old is not great, for an aged person is sometimes even referred to as 'our god' (*mudimo wɛsu*) and his displeasure during life may be 'seen in the dice' as the cause of illness or, after death, be avenged upon those who have angered him. An old wife of the queen, who had long been ailing, sent her a message saying, 'Unless you give me ox liver, I'll never die, but keep on troubling people.' The queen, notoriously averse from slaughtering cattle for meat, nevertheless complied with this request, because it came from so old a woman.

Living relatives, even if not old, but because of the social implications of their close relationship, may by conscious or even unconscious (repressed) displeasure in their hearts cause illness. When Ramatiti's daughter was about to set out for her new home, her mother, quite unexpectedly and without the previous knowledge of any one, took some water and squirted (*hu phasa*) it on the ground near the shrine, saying, 'You people of ours, I myself, mother of the girl, *phasa* lest they say I remained with a dissatisfied heart.' By intimating that she had no grievance, she tried to safeguard herself from being, at some future date, found in the dice as the cause of her daughter's barrenness. Unconscious grievances are recognized as working like our so-called repressed complexes. If the dice assign an illness, say barrenness, to a person who has no conscious complaint, he must nevertheless *phasa*, but his prayer will be, 'Don't say when you [the ancestors] seize her womb that it is I' (meaning, do not attribute your being 'stirred up' to dissatisfaction in my heart); or he may say, 'If it is I, let the child be well' (meaning, as I am unaware that I am the cause and do not wish to be, let the child recover). *Hu phasa* in these circumstances recognizes psychological principles that have been clearly formulated only in the twentieth century. If one has a grievance one prays, 'Why is it that you rise up on my account? If it is I, I say, let them give me such-and-such a thing [e.g. beer of reconciliation] and you gods do not "be after" it' (cause further trouble about it).

As the gods have human attributes, 'worship' is not characterized by humility or formality. Even at the most important offerings you may find it difficult to catch the words of the officiator amid the talking and laughter of the onlookers. But you will probably hear him say, 'It is not water; truly it is beer', or 'It is not just *mabudu* (light beer); it is real beer', when he pours out flour and water and, you may see, as we once did, how he winks at his friends who smile at the deception. The asking of a favour from the gods with beer is patterned on everyday conceptions of reciprocity. You sometimes definitely state in your prayer, 'We give to you that you may give her [the patient] life.' Religion is cheerful; at the harvest offering the gods come to drink and be merry with you, and the idea of solemn communion with the gods for the uplifting of the soul, found in higher religions, is absent.

The relation of religion and morality is too large a subject for discussion here, for both concepts are different from ours. Their relation is not immediate and usually not consciously phrased, yet in the total complex of the culture all things are interconnected, albeit in ways that are not easy to see clearly. The gods help good and bad men alike, they send illness whether one is careful or neglectful of the observances due to them, and the after-life is the same for all. But we should be careful not to deduce too much from this. The position of a sister and her privileges are sanctioned by the gods, as is also the respect due to old people. In general the gods are not upholders of custom, yet on one occasion in 1937 two *zwiḓajani* cried all day in the bush at Maulwi because some women had broken the taboo against cutting wood there. The chief concern of the gods appears to be to look after their own interests. They complain when they dislike the manner of their burial, but they are undisturbed when twins are not buried in wet soil, even though this has a disastrous effect on the whole country. If they were disturbed about custom in general, instead of things directly affecting them, they would complain of many disturbing changes in these days of culture contact; instead, one only finds that possessing spirits dislike European things and that at offerings European utensils are generally not used.

Another outstanding characteristic is the almost entire absence of any speculative element. The Lovedu are not concerned with such things as the life hereafter and the mode of life of the gods; theirs is essentially a practical religion in which rites are of far greater importance than attitude of mind, action than belief. Its rites are directed to practical ends, such as recovery from illness and the procuring of rain. In vain does one inquire into the meaning or reason of a rite, for the reply always is, 'The bones tell us to do these things,' and the practical end is phrased as determined by the bones. There are considerable differences from one family to another in the conduct of religious rites and the nature of shrines and, since religion is primarily a family concern, few people know what their neighbours do. Not uncommonly one finds a practice said to be impossible by some people accepted as normal by their neighbours.

Lovedu religion is not distinct from magic. The very terminology of the two is identical: *thugula* is a shrine, dedicated animal, or a sacred object once in the possession of the ancestors, but it is also any charm of bone or herbs concocted by a doctor. *Diphaba* are used in shrines or offerings to make the ancestors forget, as well as to ward off witches from the village. *Hu rerelela* means both to pray and to utter a spell. *Hu phasa* is used both to approach the gods and with medicines when sending back disease to a witch; one may also *phasa* on the charms in the village gate on the arrival of beer in order that more may come to the village. In a sacrifice for rain, the magical rites are of as great importance as the purely religious; and *hu phasa* in case of illness is thought to have a compelling force. It cannot fail; if it does, there must be some other cause, for an ancestor can never refuse to be placated by the *phasa* rite.

The merging of religion with magic and medicine is everywhere evident, but nowhere is it more prominent than in the cult of possession. This cult is not indigenous; it came with the Thovɔlɔ and, since its first reception some thirty years ago, has gained considerable popularity.

The form in which it is found is different from that among Shangana-Ṭonga and lent itself to ready incorporation into Lovedu religion. Among Shangana-Ṭonga, the possessing spirit is regarded as a foreign spirit from some outside tribe; among the Lovedu it is an ancestor who may, like any ancestor, demand the usual shrine or dedicated animal. The cult is not accepted by all and the royal family deprecate it as foreign and as detracting from their prestige. Its noisiness and showiness, though incongruous with the traditional reserve and lack of display, makes a popular appeal in these more insecure days.

A spirit entering a person causes illness and the first object of the cult is directed at curing the illness, so that initiation is regarded as therapeutic. Long-continued illness of a patient, which will yield to no curative treatment, will be diagnosed as due to an ancestral spirit 'pressing him down', because it wants to manifest itself in him. The symptoms are never very definite: Mashishimali was 'ill all over the body' and suffered from swollen legs which five different doctors had tried unsuccessfully to cure; Mamolatɛla was weak and ailing after the birth of her first child. The symptoms are neither violent, like the running amuck which accompanies *ukuthwasa* among the Nguni, nor of a specifically nervous nature. Epilepsy, which is common, bears no relation to possession, and any peculiar behaviour is more liable to be attributed to witchcraft than to the spirits. It is believed that a possessed person after death likes in turn to manifest itself in some descendant and there is a tendency for possession to run in families. In one family three sisters and their mother were all possessed. Sometimes, especially where others in the family are possessed, a person does not even get ill; he just becomes possessed when people are singing or dancing in the manner of the cult. Contact with certain localities or people associated with possession is often sufficient. Thus it is said that, should one be among the Sekhwasha in Portuguese East Africa, who become possessed in a manner different from the Lovedu, one risks becoming possessed by merely picking up something dropped by a member of that tribe or eating the fruit of the fig, *mudomma* (*Diospyros mespiliformis*), or *munɛbɛbɛbɛ* (*Cassia petersiana*).

Once it is known that a person is being 'pressed down' by some spirit wishing to manifest itself, a *lelɔpɔ* doctor, himself possessed and skilled in dealing with the possessed, is called to cure the patient. This is done, not by exorcism, but by rites designed to enable the spirit to come and make known its wishes along legitimate channels, known in the cult. For the spirits that possess people are not evil spirits to be expelled; they are the ancestors whom one worships, and their desire occasionally to manifest themselves through some living relative is comparable to that impulse towards life that makes them desire shrines, dedicated animals, and the perpetuation of their names in their descendants. The method by which a spirit is enabled to 'come out' and disclose its identity and the possessed person to become the host (*ledala*) of the spirit without being ill consists largely of dancing; and on all subsequent occasions when the spirits manifest themselves they signify their desire to dance.

Dancing is the central feature of the cult. The spirits are thought to enjoy this dancing; when manifesting themselves at festivities of the possessed, they often say they have come to 'play' with the others and they may even cause slight ill-health on this account. Hence quite often when a possessed person does not feel well, he will ask for the drums, saying he must dance. *Lelɔpɔ* dancing consists of fast movements of the foot to the accompaniment of drums or tambourines and rattles. At a seance of *malɔpɔ a zwikwe*, those who speak *Thɔvɔlɔ*, the large hemispherical *gɔma* drum is used in addition to the conical drums. All are, however, beaten with the hands, the elbows being placed on the drumskin in a peculiar manner. *Malɔpɔ*, who speak Sotho or Lovedu, use only the conical drums in the ordinary manner.

If the dance has a great fascination—after a seance one finds even small children practising the steps—the dress worn by the possessed adds to the attraction. Cloths of different colours are worn round the waist and tied at the back; round the legs are usually leggings of the outer shell of the *dit̯uzi* (*Oncoba spinosa*) fruit filled with pebbles to rattle as one dances; on the head is a cap of fur or brightly coloured wool or a head-gear of black feathers, while very often a spear, battle-axe, or stick is brandished in the hand. These are the *zwit̯hamo* of the spirit, worn only during possession. The nature of the dress of each possessed person has been indicated by the spirit itself, and people do their best to comply, lest the possessed person dies. Once at a seance the spirit of a woman asked that a beast or, failing that, a goat be 'placed' for him. 'We'll do our best,' the relatives replied, 'but remember we are poor and it is a matter that will take time.' The spirit, angry at this unwillingness, retorted, 'If you don't comply, I'll take away my person [in whom I manifest myself] and go and sleep with her. Tell Makhade (elder brother of the possessed who learnt the profession of doctor from the spirit) I'll take away my profession from him.' 'We'll do our best,' urged the relatives, 'but don't go away in anger.' In spite of this power, possessing spirits have nevertheless to take cognizance of public opinion and the desires of royalty. The spirit of the wife of a royal relative asked for a man's loin-cloth, which women possessed by male spirits occasionally wear, but he refused to allow it on the grounds that for a woman to wear man's attire is unbecoming. An old woman therefore addressed the spirit, saying, 'People here don't like it,' and the spirit was satisfied.

A short description of an institution which contains all the elements of an ordinary seance must suffice to illustrate some of the main features of the cult. When the doctor, called to conduct the initiation, has arrived with his or her attendants, drums are fetched from the district head, and other disciples of the doctor invited to be present. Nothing can, however, be done before the spirit of the doctor descends upon her. To allow this, they retire to a hut and lie down as if to sleep, while an old woman puts down some pinches of snuff on the ground and calls upon the spirits to come. In a few minutes the doctor groans and quivers and the spirit signifies its arrival by a song of greeting. It calls for its *lelɔpɔ* clothes and the doctor is dressed. Soon the spirits of her attendants also arrive and treatment, which consists in making the novitiate dance, is begun.

When Betty was being initiated, we arrived early one Saturday evening, attracted by the noise, to find a picturesque scene. It was winter and five little fires had been lit in the vicinity of the courtyard of Betty's hut. In the centre were three women dancing to the music of drums and rattles. We sat down by the nearest fire and found ourselves with a group of old women. For people had arranged themselves, naturally as is their manner, in age-groups round the various fires; young married women at one, small boys at another, girls above the age of puberty at a third. The dust rose high; what had sounded pleasant enough at a distance became, as one sat in its midst, an almost unbearable din; while in the flickering and uncertain light of the fires the dancing took on a frenzied effect that lent to the scene a wildness and weirdness seldom met with except in travellers' tales of darkest Africa. Never again in our frequent attendances at *malɔpɔ* dancing did we recapture that first sense of weirdness so largely due to its novelty and our own ignorance. That night the dancing stopped at 1.30 a.m. but by dawn it had begun again, continuing with intervals of rest during the whole of Sunday and Sunday night. Betty danced most of the time; if she rested too long, the women urged her on, saying, 'How do you expect the spirit to come out if you don't dance?' All this time she was being treated with medicines: black powder mixed with butter fat was smeared on her legs, white froth of medicine churned with a porridge stirrer was applied on various parts of the body, some being administered also internally, and infusions were given her to drink. No food was eaten either by Betty or by the women whose spirits were upon them; the very sight of porridge makes some *malɔpɔ* vomit and the only sustenance allowed while dancing is beer, if there happens to be any.

Late on Sunday afternoon they called her mother's brother to try to induce the spirit to manifest itself, for doctors had indicated that the troubling spirit was on the mother's side. Taking a calabash of water in his hand, the mother's brother knelt near the dancing girl and spat mouthfuls of water out on the ground, saying, 'Come out, spirit, that this person also may be well. She remains ailing, and when we go to doctors they tell us it is a spirit. Come outside that this person can be well [cool].' Sometimes, instead of *hu phasa* with water, mixed grains of all kinds are thrown over the dancer and the words used are, 'We are giving you everything to come.' It may even be that something, which can be overcome only by magical means, is holding back the spirit, as when, on one occasion, the spirit was said to be bewildered at the cross-roads, not knowing which to take. All the roads except that leading into the village were magically 'barred' and the spirit, thus guided, came straight in and manifested itself. Difficult as it is for a spirit to come on the first occasion, once initiation has taken place, it becomes a simple matter. To make a spirit manifest itself, a person has only to dance in the manner of the cult or to lie down while some one calls on it to come. The spirit may also come of its own accord at any time without being induced.

Early on the Monday morning Betty, showing signs of exhaustion, began to stagger in her dancing, and people knew the spirit must be near. Her movements became more frenzied, she put up her hands to her head and dragged her feet uncertainly, and then fell to the ground. Several women who had been expecting this, caught and carried her, still quivering and groaning, into the hut. 'Good day, grandparent. Come nicely, grandparent,' they kept saying. After a few moments Betty began a song, one usually sung on the arrival of a spirit, giving the name of the spirit upon her—namely, Mamaile, her mother's mother. Those present sang the refrain to the accompaniment of rattles. Staggerings and fallings, groanings or growlings are always signs of an approaching spirit; sometimes the possessed person runs away for a short distance. A goat was now brought into the hut. Its body was smeared with medicine, some was poured down its throat and, after the patient had breathed hard into its mouth, it was taken out and killed. Under supervision of the doctor, small pieces were cut from all parts and placed in a bowl, while the stomach contents and portion of the liver were set aside to be used in curing the patient. The experts say that the sickness from which the ancestor suffered before its death and which presumably causes the patient to suffer, goes into the goat. Before proceeding further, the doctor took the bowl of meat to the hut entrance, where, after setting aside half of it, she placed it with a little snuff on the ground, praying to her spirit. Later this meat was roasted and eaten by small boys. The stomach contents were smeared on various parts of the body of the patient; the small pieces of meat were roasted, mixed with a black powder, and administered on the end of a stick to all four of the possessed people present.

The doctor now busied herself charring chips of various kinds of bark in a basin in which some of the goat's liver had also been put. With this the patient was smoked three times under a blanket till she coughed and spluttered. This took a considerable time, during which the other possessed women sang songs in turn. Mabelowa, who is possessed by a man, called for her pipe in which some hemp was put and evinced great astonishment when her fellow wife, her attendant when she is possessed, struck a match to light it. This was a European innovation unknown in the days of her spirit. Similarly, when a potato was brought, all the possessed women examined it with wonder, asking each other whether it was edible. While the meat of the goat was being cooked with medicine in three pots for those present, the possessed women sat outside on a mat, an honour accorded to their spirits. They sat, silent and dignified, saying nothing. A fowl was killed in order that its leg might afford a medicine bag for the patient and the chips of bark used in smoking were ground to a powder to be used by the patient when eating of the first-fruits. It might be mentioned that the doctor carried home with her the hind leg, shoulder, and breast of the goat as her share, while the other meat was regarded as a reward to the crowd for its share in dancing and singing.

For some time people sat and talked to their friends while the doctor worked with her medicines and the possessed women sat quietly in the shade. Suddenly we became aware of a kind of pantomime in which the initiate, directed in song by the doctor, was made to play-act all the work of women. She went to fetch water and wood about 20 yards from home, swept the courtyard, imitated hoeing, the stamping and winnowing of mealies, cooking and dishing up, finally serving food in the correct manner to the small boy whose mother she had married (Betty had married her father's sister). Last of all she was taken to the drums and shown how to dance in possessed fashion, all, it was said, lest when her spirit left her she should be lazy and not know how to work. Betty walked as in a dream with a wooden, expressionless look and at times appeared so exhausted that we feared she would not be able to lift the stamper when imitating stamping. This mime-show is not performed in all initiations, nor is a goat always killed, for the methods of doctors differ considerably and the patient's relatives may have no goat. Often the patient is set to dance and treated with medicines till she falls down with the spirit upon her.

It was now three o'clock in the afternoon, and, the initiation being complete, the doctor thought it time that the spirits departed. She ushered the possessed into the hut, where they all sat down, offered them each a pinch of snuff, took a rattle and began her farewell song, the whole company (for the hut had filled with spectators) joining in the refrain. Next the initiate sang her farewell song, mentioning what she wanted as her accessories—several white cloths, a woollen cap, and a spear to hold when dancing. When all had finished singing, they took off their *zwiṭhamo* (clothes), which their attendants (for each possessed person has some one to help him when his spirit appears) put into bundles to take away, and lay down to sleep. After three minutes the doctor grunted and groaned as departing spirits are apt to do, sat up and began dressing in everyday clothes. The others followed her example and went outside. The patient, but a short while before so exhausted, came smiling out of the hut and scolded the people for letting her oversleep in this shocking manner (appearing to have no knowledge of her initiation). Then all washed their faces and urinated in the hedge, as women do on rising in the mornings.

Initiation into the cult is said to make the person well again, and all into whose history one inquires claim to have been cured. Betty herself had no further trouble. If, however, they become ill again, it may be a second spirit, for many people have three or four. There is, however, no further initiation; the second spirit is merely called upon to manifest itself. A second or third spirit may take possession without causing any illness, merely announcing its arrival and making known its wants when the person is possessed. After initiation the spirit manifests itself when it has some complaint or desire, when the person has broken some taboo, or when specially induced by dancing or prayer. A possessed person has to keep certain taboos: he may never eat such firstfruits as pumpkin leaves or green mealies, *morula* fruits or beer made of the newly-harvested corn without medicine given him at his initiation and renewable every year or every two years; any new thing undertaken, as when a possessed woman becomes pregnant, must be reported to the spirit. Some *malɔpɔ* may not be beaten with a green stick, lest the spirit descend upon them; others may not touch European medicine. Many of them run away from Europeans even when not actually possessed, and one man had to keep his books securely locked in a suit-case lest his wife should see them and become troubled by her spirit. The very mention of the word *lelɔpɔ* in the presence of some may cause the spirit to come. Observances are not the same for all and taboos to be observed depend largely on the doctor who does the initiation. There are no special burial rites associated with the cult. There is, however, a vague belief that injury to a snake in the village may in some cases harm a possessed person, an interesting belief in view of the fact that there is so little trace in Lovedu religion of the Zulu idea that ancestral spirits manifest themselves in snakes.

There is a special relationship between a possessed person and the doctor who initiated him: every year when the medicine needs renewal, beer or *morula* cider is prepared, the doctor, who comes with a number of disciples and attendants, is called and there is a great dance of the possessed often lasting several days. This is 'dancing for medicine' (*hu vinɛla tshidi*). Some possessed people have to be specially doctored before drinking the first *morula* cider and the *morula* season is always a time of *lelɔpɔ* gatherings; others are required to contribute corn at harvest time for a large *lelɔpɔ* dance at the home of the doctor. These gatherings, at which a goat may be slaughtered in addition to the cider provided, add greatly to the prestige of the doctor. There is sometimes considerable jealousy between *malɔpɔ* doctors, who, with those initiated by them, may form rival schools. Some doctors refuse to allow their followers to dance with those initiated by other doctors without special permission. At one seance, at which there had been some unpleasantness, the doctor smeared some powder into incisions on the neck, tongue, crown, and sides of the heads of her disciples. Then, taking some medicated water in her mouth, she squirted (*hu phasa*), saying, 'I "place" you. Don't you dance any more. I don't like dancing every day without my special permission. Any *lelɔpɔ* who dances where you are dancing will break her leg or be badly hurt.' The remainder of the water was given them to drink.

An interesting feature of the cult of possession is that many people when the spirit is upon them speak in a foreign tongue, said to be Thɔvɔlɔ or Kharanga. Investigation into this matter, however, shows that this is not as startling a phenomenon as it might appear. When possessed, a person for the most part sits silent unless he is a doctor. If he speaks at all, this is in monosyllables, for all his wants and messages are conveyed in song. *Lelɔpɔ* songs are stereotyped and known to many because the uninitiated have to join in the refrain when rattling the accompaniment. In these songs there is usually a number of foreign words, though many consist purely of meaningless sounds, such as '*We le wee eva o wee wee wee wana wee*'. Often peculiarities in the pronunciation of vowels are interpreted as Thɔvɔlɔ. When the refrain begun (*hu suma*) by the possessed person has been taken up by the chorus, he continues with the song or interpolates his own words, usually Sotho with a few foreign words interspersed, till he wishes to stop. In this way he makes known his wishes. It quite frequently happens that no one understands the gibberish of the possessed person, and doctors generally have an attendant who interprets what they wish to convey. There are, however, numerous well-known words in general use by people when their spirit is upon them—for instance, *mufoto* or *movoto* for *lefɔla* (snuff), *bula* or *mvula* for *meetse* (water), *va ga mbaya* for *va ga ntiya* (they may beat me), *kaya* for *hae* (home). But many possessed people speak pure Sotho, and it is recognized that a newly initiated person may not know Thɔvɔlɔ. The Lovedu themselves are not critical, and the usual reply when one expresses any doubt about the genuineness of the possessed or the possibility of fraud is, 'If they were not really possessed how could they speak a strange tongue?'

It is not our purpose to discuss the psychology of possession among the Lovedu. We should, however, point out that it is in no way associated with abnormalities of character or with crises in the life of the individual. Its symptoms are not of a nervous nature, such as indicate *ukuthwasa* among Nguni; there are, except when the spirit descends upon them, no twitchings; uncontrollable hiccups are unknown; members of the cult are not hysterical or mentally unbalanced nor can they be distinguished in their daily activities from others. There is no change in the personality of the individual when his spirit is upon him, although some of them sing in a low voice when possessed by a man and others dance in a peculiar way. Nor is there any difference to be seen between one possessing spirit and another in the same individual: when his second spirit comes upon a possessed person, it often continues the conversation where the first spirit left off, and the only indication of its arrival may be its own announcement in a song or perhaps gulping movements and a gentle falling back of the patient. Finally, of interest psychologically was the farewell dance of all *malɔpɔ* just before the *vyali* initiation for girls in September, 1938. Their songs and dances were taboo during the period of the 'school' as they were not allowed to compete with those of the *vyali* which had not yet ended in October, 1939. We must not conclude from this or from the fact that Christians do not become *malɔpɔ* that possession is imposture. There are wide avenues for fraud, but most *malɔpɔ* are genuine victims of mass-suggestion. The cult, though open to men, is confined largely to women. It is not associated with gifts of prophecy or the finding of lost objects, and there are no revelations concerning the Beyond.

The bearing of the possessed when not dancing is quiet and dignified and detached in contrast to the diabolical manifestations of the possessed in Europe in the Middle Ages. It appears to be neither a paranoic nor a compensatory phenomenon. We dare not relate trance experience with neuroses or psychoses, for we need to orientate ourselves, not from our own, but from a wider relativistic psychology or psychopathology; the mental reflects the cultural configuration and the disposition of drives in the mind must be viewed relatively to the disposition of forces in the culture. The whole cult among the Lovedu is remarkably stereotyped; behaviour under the influence of the spirit, the songs, the things demanded by spirits, conform to a type. Even the possessing spirits themselves are stereotyped, being almost always grandparents.

It is our impression that if any one in the least degree suggestible were made to dance without sustenance for several days in the noise and excitement of seances, he would be liable to fall down exhausted and respond in the traditional manner to the attentions of the women. But not all initiations are successful. In one case witnessed by us, the young woman quite obviously did not want to become possessed: she danced in a half-hearted manner and, under the pretext of tending her baby, kept away as much as possible from the doctor. In another, the patient began to stagger towards the end of the second day, but, though every one expected the spirit to arrive, nothing happened and so the doctor left. The reason for failure in this case may have been (but we are not sure) the loud complaints of her brother that no one in the family had ever been possessed before.

CHAPTER XIV

WITCHCRAFT AND SORCERY

Techniques and manifestations of day and night witchcraft—distinctions between witchcraft and magic—smelling out of witches by the forensic physician—social incidence and psychological aspects of witchcraft.

ULƆI, as the Lovedu use the word, comprises both witchcraft and sorcery, but the distinction between them, as accepted by many modern ethnographical writers, diverges considerably from the distinctions made by the Lovedu. In order, therefore, to preserve Lovedu conceptions and terminology, it is necessary, firstly, to use a single word—namely, witchcraft (*vulɔi*), and, secondly, to distinguish night-witchcraft (*vulɔi vya vusiu*) and day-witchcraft (*vulɔi vya matsiare*). *Vulɔi* is distinguished from other forms of what we should call magic, not so much by the methods employed, though some of them are confined to witches, as by intent and results. *Vulɔi* is anti-social; it is illegal and aims at harming people from motives of jealousy, revenge, frustration, or anger. Though witches are believed to have a kind of compulsion to do evil—their fingers burn to bewitch—they are never unconscious of their own evil deeds and powers, as has been reported by Junod for Shangana-Tonga and Stayt for the Venda. The witch knows his own powers and uses them to obtain his own ends. Knowledge of witchcraft does not inevitably involve its practice; the child of a witch may refuse to kill people while using his powers to increase his crops, and it is even possible for a witch to protect some one he likes against the machinations of others.

There are important distinctions between night-witches or night-witchcraft, on the one hand, and day-witches or day-witchcraft, on the other. The night-witch is a 'born' witch, taught in early infancy by his mother. He works chiefly by night, but can also work by day. The day-witch is any ordinary individual who, by means of medicine obtained from some doctor or witch, tries to kill his enemies. He has no knowledge of witchcraft beyond the medicine obtained for some definite end. There is a certain amount of vagueness about the distinction between day and night witches, and in practice, when any one is accused of witchcraft, there is never any inquiry into which type of witchcraft has been used. Nevertheless, the distinction is essential for an understanding of Lovedu witchcraft.

The night-witch is able directly, and without the aid of any medicine, to effect his evil purposes. He can enter a hut through the smallest crevice. But his absence from home will never be missed, because he will throw his slumbering companions into a deep sleep or even leave a hyena in his own image; but the soul is never sent out to do the work, as among the Azande. When one wakes up from a dream in a sweat or fright, it is a sign that night-witches are near, and in consultations with doctors such symptoms are often described by patients as very relevant to the diagnosis of their illness. Night-witches are not often seen by people, but there is certain medicine which can be put in the village fence to keep a night-witch rooted to the spot, unable to move till you come and find him. As soon as he is addressed, he will scurry away. Those who have seen witches, always describe them as naked, perhaps because people always sleep naked wrapped in their blankets. The most effective way of keeping witches at bay is the placing of medicine (*diphaba*) round the village fence, which either makes them forget their errand or makes the village appear like water or a forest.

Night-witches cause all manner of illness in ways unknown to ordinary people. They may pour blood over you, then next day you are ill; your blood is not right and soon you die. They may cut off portions of your body to insert millet or sand, which causes intense pain. If your bones ache and you feel tired without knowing why, it may be that a night-witch has made you hoe in his garden all night or beaten you all over your body with sticks. Sometimes he even makes you ride a bicycle all night. Besides killing, night-witches are fond of causing barrenness in their enemies. They are great destroyers of crops. After you have ploughed, they go into your field and pick up all the seeds so that nothing grows, or they rob your field of its fertility to increase that of their own fields. They also send their familiars at night to milk your cows or let them out of their kraal to cause damage that may bring you to court. Night-witches form a sort of fraternity: they all know one another and meet at night to drum and dance for amusement. They also fight one another: those of an area in which the crops have failed will send wind to break mealies and trees in another area or worms to destroy the crop. The destructiveness of such contests is a reality to some, for in one district in which many worms appeared in the mealies, so we heard, a public meeting was held and one man accused Shangana-Tonga witches, whom he said he had seen the previous night. Often a real battle against foreign witches takes place in which wounds are received that the witch does his best to hide during the day. Witches have even been known to die from wounds received in battle at night, as sometimes admitted by themselves.

Night-witches employ familiars (*dithomya*) such as the hyena, the snake, the *muishond* (*Pœcilogale albinucha*), and, to a lesser extent, owls and the striped *muishond* (*Ictonyx capensis*): both kinds of *muishond* are polecats or skunks. How the witch tames these animals is not known, but they become so intimate that they come at night to ask for food and call the witch their mother, but there is no sex relationship between witch and familiar as is reported for the Pondo. Two actual cases were reported to the queen while we were in the field in which 'sent' snakes had been killed; one of these had been found to contain porridge and relish, certain proof of its association with a witch. The difference between an ordinary snake which also bites and a 'sent' snake appears from the circumstances: if, for example, others walk along a path before you and escape, but you get bitten, then the snake must be 'sent'. For 'sent' snakes are real snakes; the Zulu practice of smearing medicine on sticks to turn them into snakes when your enemy passes is not known to the Lovedu. The most fearful of all familiars is, however, the *khidudwane*, a human being who has been killed by a witch to be his slave. The *khiḓuḓwane* is not an ordinary corpse, though witches do call corpses out of their graves in order to cut off portions of their body for medicine, a procedure that can be prevented by magical protection of the grave. Only a person specially killed for the purpose can be a *khiḓuḓwane*; when they bury him, it is only his shadow that goes into the grave; the real person has been enslaved and put in a large earthen pot or in a cave. At night he hoes for his master, cuts poles for building, or goes on nefarious errands. If you meet a *khiḓuḓwane*, you faint at the sight, and even after medical treatment your body may feel dried up, as though it has no blood.

That the fear of *zwiḓuḓwane* is very real to the Native, and backed by what is to him convincing evidence, is shown in the case of Madume. In November, 1937, Madume, a man residing near us, died. Ever since his wife's death he had lived with (*hu gaula*) a woman whom he had never properly married and, after his death, it was rumoured that he had been killed by the mother of his son's wife for the sake of her daughter, who was jealous that her husband's father should be fonder of, and show more favours to, a concubine than to his legitimate daughter-in-law. The mother of the girl had first, so it was said, wanted to kill Madume's wife, but her daughter had argued that it would be better to kill Madume himself, since he might pick up some other woman and they would have the same trouble over again. How much of this story had actually been given by the diviner and how much was sheer surmise we were never able to discover, but a month after the death people began to be afraid to go near his village at night, as he had been seen standing at his gate. The concubine, afraid to remain at home at night, went to sleep with neighbours, whence she would return at dawn to do her household duties. One morning when it was just getting light, she rose to go home. On her way she suddenly ran shouting into the nearest village and fell in a faint at the entrance. People rushed to help her and called in Madume's sister to revive her in the manner usual in such circumstances: by holding smoking chips under the nose to cause sneezing (*hu ɛtsemudisa*). She told them she had seen three *zwiḓuḓwane*, a man called Khishweni who had died long ago in the neighbourhood, and two children, dancing and singing on the road. From this evidence the conclusion was immediately come to that Khishweni must have been killed by the same witch as Madume, since both were walking about, and so great was the fear of going out at night that the women of the neighbourhood could not be persuaded to attend a girl's initiation ceremony which had begun before this episode.

Contact with Europeans has led to the conception of *khipogo* (spook) which must not be confused with *khiḓuḓwane*. A *khipogo* is the ghost of a dead person, but the sight of a *khipogo* does not, like that of a *khiḓuḓwane*, make one faint or dry up; it only makes one's heart jump in fright. Such a ghost can be laid by means of medicine (*diphaba*) on the grave. Children often run to their mothers with scared faces and bated breath to say they have seen a *khipogo*, sometimes even in broad daylight.

Night-witches can be male or female, but the great majority are female.

There is nothing corresponding to the witch-substance found in the stomachs of Zande witches. A witch is said to imbibe witchcraft with its mother's milk, yet it involves learning, a process begun on the second or third day after birth, when its mother throws it up against the wall, to which it clings like a bat. On one occasion the anger of a grandmother that her grandchild had been 'taken out' of the hut (*hu thusa*) without her presence or knowledge was construed as due to a sense of frustration because this had prevented her from teaching the child witchcraft. The dullness at school of a certain girl whose mother was said to be a witch was ascribed to the difficulty of simultaneously learning two things: witchcraft and books. Since witchcraft is learnt from the mother (though one sometimes hears that the mother teaches her daughter, a father his sons), brothers and sisters of one mother cannot accuse each other of witchcraft without involving themselves; that such accusations do occur shows how theory often gives way to practical considerations. In one such case, where a woman brought her son to court for beating her and her daughter, the son accused his own mother and sister of killing his child. His sister asked, 'If I and my mother are witches, what about you?' When he replied, 'My mother stinted me, giving only you the knowledge,' the court laughed, saying, 'Boy, you're mad. Where have you ever heard of a man accusing his own mother of witchcraft?' But the boy insisted on going to a *mugɔme*, though the court warned him of the consequences of breaking his relationship with his cattle-linked sister, whose cattle, if called back because of the imputation, could no longer serve as a bond for future marriages. Night-witchcraft is learnt, but unlike day-witchcraft it can neither be learnt from an outsider nor be bought. Yet one hears of such transactions, more especially among Christians, who aver that payment consists of the blood of a close relative, usually your own child. Jeremiah associated the beginnings of his stepmother's witchcraft with the death of her own child, followed shortly afterwards by that of her step-daughter.

The day-witch is almost always a man, since women cannot easily buy medicines. He is distinguished from the night-witch by his use of medicine and spells. Spells have no fixed phraseology, but consist in telling the medicine what to do, mentioning the name of the person. Very often the medicine works as well without the spell as with it. The day-witch employs no familiars, belongs to no fraternity, does not inherit his knowledge. He is called a day-witch, not so much because he works by day, for he may work at night too, but because of the technique he uses. Whereas the night-witch himself goes out and steals your mealie seeds, the day-witch puts medicine on the soles of his feet and walks through your field; and while the day-witch introduces substances into your body by means of medicine, the night-witch employs a stoat to take up its abode in you and eat all your food. Certain techniques are associated with day-witchcraft, though it is possible for any night-witch to use also all the methods of the day-witch, simply by getting the right medicine.

The day-witch can cause illness or death by *hu lega*. *Hu lega* means to try, to tempt, and hence, by extension of meaning, to challenge or to send misfortune by means of medicine. The witch may mix your footprint with medicine or put a medicated thorn in the path you usually take, to cause pain in the leg, which gradually passes into the rest of the body and kills you. He may cause your death by pointing a medicated finger at you, or using water you have washed in or clothes you have worn. Hair and nails are, however, not much used in witchcraft and only a few people, more especially women, are careful about their disposal. To point at a man in a menacing way, or to say the words, 'You will see' (*u ḍɔ vɔna*), suffices, should evil befall him, as ground for an imputation of witchcraft. In a violent quarrel between a woman who had a child by her lover and the lover whom she had jilted because the liaison was causing trouble with her husband, the angry lover flung out the challenge. 'You've got a daughter who is my blood, yet you love me no longer. You will see!' A few weeks later the child became ill and died. The mother, overcome with grief and fury, carried her dead to the lover's house and threw it down, saying, 'Here is your meat. Cook it and eat it.' This phraseology suggests, though no one believes, that witches eat human flesh; it was construed merely as a dramatic accusation and created quite a stir; but it was considered justifiable in view of his threat. The *mugɔme* to whom the matter was taken pointed out, not the lover, but the woman's own husband as the culprit. When the latter, refusing to accept the verdict and to pay his bet, was required to leave the area, his wife, a staunch believer in his innocence, accompanied him. Use of *malego* by ordinary people is witchcraft, but its use by doctors against one another is legitimate. Doctors often 'try' their skill against one another: one doctor, we were told, turned himself into an elephant for the purpose of attacking his rival; not to be outdone, the latter became a bird and flew away.

Sending lightning, to cause lightning to strike (*hu tiisa ḍadi*), is a common means of harming one's enemies employed by day-witches. To say of a person, 'He knows lightning', is tantamount to calling him a witch, for, unlike the Zulu, the Lovedu have no socially recognized lightning doctors. The Lovedu distinguish two kinds of lightning—natural or 'lightning of the bird' and 'sent' lightning. The former comes with rain and is caused by the lightning bird, which has blue feathers and looks somewhat like a goose with large feet. These birds get no food unless there is lightning and then their food is the *zuhululu*, the blue-headed tree lizard. When the bird strikes a tree, it leaves its urine as a white substance at the root; then doctors come and take the soil into which it has soaked to be used as medicine to cause lightning or for curing burns. Natural lightning, in theory and according to the diagnosis of the dice, is believed to strike only trees or rocks far from villages, never animals or people; but some say that it is dangerous to men in autumn, when it follows the sweet sorghum spat out on the road. 'Sent' lightning, on the other hand, strikes near the village, killing cattle or people. It comes with little or no rain and is more terrifying than that of the lightning bird. Lightning is judged almost solely by its results: if it does no harm it is natural; if it strikes any one or destroys anything in the village it is *ḍadi ya vathu* or *khiḍadi muthwana*, 'sent' by people.

Doctors frequently 'try' one another by sending lightning. A lightning witch may either fly himself or may smear medicine on a dove or a red-winged locust which, when it thunders, is able to 'go with the lightning' and strike where its owner wishes. Use of the lightning bird itself for this purpose is impossible. A man who himself strikes as lightning must be scarified with medicine containing some portion of the lightning bird, and when learning to strike may be taken to a high desolate place where he is taught accuracy by being required to strike one of a number of aloes in a row. An informant once saw a man with black-and-white stripes all over his body and two branches tied to his hips; he concluded that this must be a lightning witch (*cf.* the striped hyena with its mane of upright hair on neck or along back, or the striped polecat, which bristles up its tail in anger). One who controls lightning is able to prevent it from striking him by cutting or piercing the flash with a medicated axe or spear, telling it to go elsewhere. Lightning frequently strikes villages and people in Uulovedu and in many instances some accusation is brought before the court. Huts may be magically protected against lightning. If a witch strikes a protected village, it is believed that he will 'fall', change into a person, and can then be caught. There are no taboos against milking or working during lightning, but the day after it has struck the whole district has a holiday.

Day-witches use several other techniques. A very common form of day-witchcraft is *hu lesa* (to cause to eat), the introduction of medicine into beer or food, which on being swallowed turns into an indigestible piece of meat or other object that makes one ill. Most people one meets have at some time or other suffered from *khileso*. To pour real poison into food (*hu shɛla khitaba*) is a modern though still very uncommon method of killing. *Hu fahɛlɛja* (*hu fa*, to die, *hu ɛlɛja*, to cause to go for) is to cause a person to leave home, e.g. for European employment, and die far away. This is done chiefly by day-witches, but also sometimes by night-witches; it is, however, neither common nor well-known. Modern conditions, with increased tribal contacts in European towns, have led to a tremendous increase in day witchcraft. New methods and medicines for *hu lega*, unknown in the tribe before, are being introduced. Some even go so far as to say that the sending of lightning is a relatively recent thing from Nareni.

There are many practices bordering on witchcraft, indistinguishable from day-witchcraft in technique and method of procedure, but considered legitimate and therefore not witchcraft in the true sense. Some of these are so close to, that they are sometimes looked upon as witchcraft. The deciding factor in such cases is always the result: if it causes death it is witchcraft; if it does not, or if it is done with an object that is recognized as legitimate, it is not witchcraft. *Hu dabɔka* is essentially legitimate. Its technique consists in changing the nature of things, making medicated pieces of the skin of an animal turn into the animal itself, changing a person's sex, and one of the best-known doctors in Lovedu-land is skilled in *madabi*. It is a technique confined to men, employed to make a woman marry you or to frighten her into coming back to you when she has run away. No one has ever heard of a woman sending *madabi*.[1] A woman ran away from her husband to live with another. Whenever she was cooking or doing her household duties at her new home, monkeys and other animals appeared at the village till, frightened out of her wits, she ran back to her first husband. *Madabi* are often sent in connexion with childbirth. Sometimes the sending of *madabi* is looked upon as witchcraft. Malaji changed the sex of Muhale's daughter so as to make the birth difficult each time she was about to bear a child, because the child was his, but the girl no longer loved him. We were not allowed into the hut, but the midwives, whom we knew well, testified to a real change, though probably because certain types of difficult birth are conventionally so explained. Eventually the birth took place, but shortly afterwards the baby was dead. This was considered to be witchcraft, the case was brought to court, and a large fine imposed. Only the doctor who used *madabi* can undo or reverse its power by *hu dabekulla*, but other doctors may, if there has been any injury, heal it with medicines.

A practice similar to *madabi*, but differing from it in object is *madilebɔ*. At the time of the Swazi raids, Raŋwagu, instead of hiding in the forests, put his faith in *madilebɔ* (marvel, wonder). When the enemy came, his village turned into water and they could not find his cattle, though they heard their lowing. Masia, who was wanted by the police during the whole period of our investigation, was able, when chased by them, to disappear even in the open; he would hang like a bat on a plough to look just like a spanner. When eventually he was arrested, he averred, and many people agreed, that it was because he was tired.

Khidɔba is a technique used against thieves and it is both public and legitimate. Some kinds of *khidɔba* are known as a home remedy; some are obtained from doctors. By means of medicine used on *ledzigɛri* grass (*Hyparrhenia Tamba*), one can cause a severe and painful itching in the finger of the thief which may compel him to confess. Likewise, by *hu dɔba*, a stolen goat may be made to cry out in the thief's belly, as happened in a recent case, probably of compulsion neurosis, in which bleating was taken as conclusive proof of his guilt. Another method of *hu dɔba* causes the eyes of the thief to protrude till they fall out on to his stomach; if his mother then cries on seeing him, he may die. *Khidɔba* strikes the thief even when he hides or sells the stolen goods. Besides these measures, taken to bring a thief to book after the theft, one may by anticipation protect one's property by means of a piece of *letate* rush (*Mariscus sp.*) split at one end to resemble the mouth of a snake and smeared with coloured medicines. When placed at the hut entrance or on the border of your field, it turns into a snake and bars the entry or exit of a thief. A doctor we knew used to have serious talks with his son about the fortune he would make if he knew this medicine, especially in Johannesburg, where theft is common and victims pay high prices. The only recognized cure

---

[1] The word comes from *dalo* plus *inbi*; *dalo* (well being), is a noun from *hu lala* (to lie down, to be peaceful), and *inbi* means bad. *Dabi* should be calamity, but it is used only in the sense of excessive rain (causing evil). The plural, *madabi*, means misfortune or pain or disease legitimately 'sent'. The verb is *hu dabeka*, legitimately to send misfortune, and its converse, *hu dabekulla*, means to neutralize or remove the effects of *madabi*.

of the power and effect of *hu dɔba* is by asking for pardon, when the doctor who gave or used the *khidɔba* will be asked to *dɔbulla*, i.e. reverse the effects of his medicine. He will usually charge a large fee (even an ox), which he shares with his client.

Use of medicine on a grave which causes the death, not only of the witch who killed the deceased, but also of other members of his family is not considered to be witchcraft. This is called *hu tsikɛla* or *hu diɛla leviḍa* (to work on the grave) and is done in various ways: the corpse may be smeared before burial, or the seed of a certain plant from Rhodesia sown on the grave, and when it grows the witch will die, or medicine and the stomach contents of a goat may be poured down a hole to reach the body in its grave. This is the usual sense in which *hu tsikɛla* is used, but sometimes it is conceived of as a kind of *hu dɔba*, against a thief with the purpose of wreaking vengeance, not only on him, but also on all those who have eaten of the thing stolen, whether they are innocent strangers or guilty accomplices. It kills, unlike *hu dɔba*, which merely injures. As in *khidbɔa*, this form of *hu tsikɛla* is more or less public, for the villagers and neighbours must be previously informed, so that they will have an opportunity to confess. The other and more usual form of *hu tsikɛla* is directed against witches who are murderers and for that reason it is not public, for it is conceived that the witch might take counter measures or bribe a bad doctor to 'call back' the medicine. It may be sent to a definite person discovered by consultation with the bones, but the name of the person will not be mentioned in the spell lest the witch take counter measures. The spell is not in set terms, but it usually runs as follows: 'You Mufuba (the deceased in the grave whose death is to be avenged), we are to-day working on your grave. We call all those who killed you to follow you to the grave. We do not say only one of them. We mean all who are of them [the whole family]. Do you also call them, so that all of them should follow you.'

A death is sometimes ascribed by the bones to *hu tsikɛla*; and in one case the suicide of a girl, who was said to have bewitched her husband's people, was found to have been caused by such medicine. Paradoxical as it may seem, it is possible for a witch, who gets a doctor to *tsikɛla* for him, to be struck down by the medicine intended for another. It is curious that, though he knows that the medicine seeks out the true witch, he will risk such a procedure, but the explanation is that, though a doctor might be deceived—his bones confused by the witch's medicine (*khiŋalaŋaga*)—the medicine cannot be, and that the fatal effect of *hu tsikɛla* is diagnosed *ex post facto*. Thus in one case where a woman died, her sister went to a *tsikɛla* specialist; but subsequently the sister herself and some of her relatives died. When a great *mugɔme* was consulted, he said that the sister had sent *mutsikɛla* to people whom she hated and that, not finding the murderer there, it returned and struck down the sender. *Mutsikɛla* will continue its deadly effects unless 'stopped' by the doctor who sent it, though there is a medicine (*lesɛlo*) which may be eaten by all those who think they are in danger of vengeance-magic to neutralize its effects. It is recognized that the witch may retaliate in the case of vengeance-magic, though this is considered unusual and almost always ineffectual.

There are many other specialized techniques, but for our purposes it will suffice to refer briefly to love-magic. Love-medicine was not known to the Lovedu, and its use is generally said by the older people to be witchcraft. Nevertheless, this magic, introduced from the towns, where, especially among Zulu and Xhosa, it is common, is used by many young men in Uulovedu to-day. One method, scarification of the forehead or use of medicine in your snuff, makes all the girls love you; blowing a medicated pipe of the *mukhure* shrub (*Ricinus sp.*) morning and evening, while calling the name of a certain girl, will make her come to you soon; and there are various other medicines. Love-magic to cause hysteria in girls is known as a Zulu practice, but is not used in Uulovedu. It would be looked upon as witchcraft.

These borderline methods, sometimes called witchcraft, sometimes not, and often referred to as 'good' *vulɔi*, bring us to a consideration of what constitutes *vulɔi*. All witchcraft is socially disapproved, anti-social, but this criterion is not always sufficient to distinguish between witchcraft proper and practices bordering on witchcraft. Swearing at people, or scolding them violently, when the cause hardly justifies it, is liable to call down upon them forces which lead to death or misfortune to them or their family. It is called *lesola* and is reprehensible; but it is not *vulɔi*; nor is *mahava*, illness caused by the ill-feeling of a father's sister or other relative. The conduct of a woman who, having had an abortion, causes her husband's death through neglecting to give him the medicine necessary to ward off such disaster is strongly disapproved of, but it is not witchcraft, even though it causes death.

Since many borderline practices are judged by their result and become witchcraft when they cause death, it might be argued that this criterion must be distinctive. It is, however, not enough; causing death to a husband by abortion is, as we have seen, not considered to be witchcraft, nor is the murderous *khigevɛgwa* a witch, even though he secretly kills people at night and sells parts of their body to doctors. Furthermore, many accusations of witchcraft have arisen where there has been no death, but only sickness or loss by lightning. The only difference between the killing by a *khigevɛgwa* and that by a witch lies in the method employed. The killer uses ordinary weapons; the witch kills by means of medicine or some peculiar powers not known to ordinary people. The distinguishing feature of all cases of witchcraft is the use or supposed use of medicine or witch-power. Intent is another feature by which one judges an action. Where a woman causes the death of a husband through abortion, her conduct is anti-social and the act is done in secret, but it differs from witchcraft proper in the absence of intent to kill. Fear of the consequences of adultery is the main force deterring her from correct behaviour; and it is argued that, if she really wishes to kill she need not employ so roundabout a method.

The conclusion we may draw is that, for an action to be witchcraft, it must satisfy, not one, but all the following three requirements: it must be disapproved of, anti-social; there must be an intent to kill or to harm; and it must be thought that either medicine or the mysterious forces of night-witchcraft have been used. Secrecy is not peculiar to witchcraft; it is not a distinguishing feature, because it is characteristic also of most magic: one does not want witches to know the steps taken to counteract them.

Only a very small proportion of cases of witchcraft lead to an open accusation and legal procedure; for going to a *mugɔme* involves a long, expensive journey, and *khɔrɔ* proceedings do not stop the witch, who may indeed redouble his efforts. In many cases of illness diagnosed as due to witchcraft there is nothing definite said about the person responsible; the disease is cured, the cure itself usually involving magic to 'send back' the illness to its owner. The verdict of the dice is necessarily vague. Usually only the totem and sex are given and the client himself, with his knowledge of his own friends and enemies, decides which of them is meant. The dice may indicate a totem to which none of the client's friends or enemies belong; but even if he thinks he can place the witch, one illness would hardly end in an accusation. Even death need not necessarily lead to an accusation; the grave may be treated to 'send back' death to the witch, but there are many cases in which there is neither accusation nor treatment of the grave.

To cause a witch to desist, the victim or some one on his behalf more often, after consulting a doctor privately for instructions, may resort to *hu ɛbɛla*—that is, shout out an indefinite warning from his courtyard, if possible within earshot of the suspected witch. There is no fixed formula, but usually the gist of the warning is as follows: 'People of this village, I want you to know that you must leave my "person" alone; you must not kill him. If you kill him, I shall get a doctor to kill all your relatives. If my "person" has done any harm to you, I will pay for him; if he has done no harm, you have no right to make him ill. To-morrow I want my "person" to walk. If he dies, you will see.' In one case a girl suffered from epilepsy and her father, standing in the courtyard, shouted, 'The person who bewitched my daughter, I know him. I shall kill him with an axe. I speak not to the villages of Pheduli, Muŋgadani, and Ratshegu. I mean this village of ours.' In another case, when a snake appeared at the *vyali* initiation and a diviner had indicated two men as the culprits, an old woman, the herald at the capital, in the presence of the women in the courtyard, called out, 'The person who has sent these snakes will feel pain. The *gɔma* of the queen is not to be "tried" (*hu lega*).' Very often there is a threat that, if the sick person is not cured, the injured person will go to a *mugɔme*. The procedure is said to shame (*nyɔɛlwa*) the witch, or he may take fright and withdraw the witchcraft he has sent.

Sometimes, when you have a witch in the village, so that strengthening of the fence would be of no avail, you *fɛra* him, i.e. cause him to forget to act and be 'cool', just as you *fɛra* the spirits to keep them satisfied. More usually, however, you just move away and establish your own village somewhere else. Thus, when Rasodi's daughter lost her baby and the doctors all agreed that the husband's people were responsible (some said the husband's mother, others mentioned another relative), they quietly moved away, having been warned not to talk much about the removal, lest the witch got to know.

Accusation of a specific person may lead to *khɔrɔ* proceedings, which involve, as described elsewhere, the appointment of the 'ears', who receives a goat or 10s. from each party as well as provisions, a wager of a head of cattle, or £1 10s. or more, and payment, the vanquished eventually to reimburse the victor, of £1 10s. or more, as the fee of the *mugɔme*. Occasionally in practice, if accused does not demand to have his innocence proved, the accuser does not go to court and the matter is left. All victims of witchcraft do not act in the same manner. One man proceeds to a specific accusation the very first time he is harmed, another only if the same witch has been responsible for many evils; if the witch is a great rival or personal enemy, the victim more readily resorts to action, but a commoner, unless he is prepared to leave the district, will be careful to avoid accusing his district head or a relative of the queen. A victim never makes an accusation without previous private consultation with a number of doctors and often even a *mugɔme* as well, and the accusation is conveyed to the witch, either directly by the victim or indirectly by his intermediary, and usually in metaphorical language. In case of illness, the witch may be invited to 'come and *phasa* for our patient' or, in case of death, to 'come and shave us', duties which only special relatives can perform; or, more directly, he may be asked 'to come with us to consult the bones'. The accused will then demand to go to a *mugɔme* to clear his name; if he does nothing, but merely remains inactive, his accuser may proceed further and take the case to the *khɔrɔ*.

When proceeding to a smeller-out, the parties have no definite destination. They set out in a north-easterly direction, where *megɔme* abound, usually with the intention of going somewhere very far away. After a day or two, however, they grow tired, or the official witness complains of the heat, and they find some one nearer. The witness has on his person an object called *phitho* that has been given to him by the court or at the royal village. This the smeller-out has to name and find, and it is said that, unless, in addition, he is able to give the totem of every one in the party and clearly to distinguish between accuser, accused, and official witness, they will pass on to some one else. How far this is carried out in practice we shall see later. It is sometimes said by Europeans that smellers-out have spies who bring them the information necessary for their divining. This would, however, be impossible: not only do people come from all directions or tribes, sometimes as far distant as Mapulaneng beyond the Olifants River, but it would require an elaborate system of espionage that could hardly be kept secret from the people in the conditions that obtain in Bantu society. Moreover, the methods employed by smellers-out make such a system unnecessary. There is no doubt that *megɔme* are clever, and we have ourselves been amazed at the manner in which, under test conditions, a *mugɔme* was able to name and find an object hidden on our person. But it must be borne in mind that they use a trial-and-error technique based upon the responses of the audience. Of course, the presence of a European is always a disturbing factor, but in our experience, after the first few responses, the *mugɔme* begins to speak more and more loudly and quickly and a situation of free association of ideas and great suggestiveness arises. The consultants become less guarded and the *mugɔme*, skilled in his art, is able to draw conclusions from their reactions. A good deal of vagueness is permissible: the term *mukhalaga*, for example, can refer to a number of different totems: *mukhalaga* proper, *mukhalaga munyai*, *mukhalaga ḍou* (elephant), and this applies also to other aspects of their divination. An actual example, albeit a case of theft, not witchcraft, will elucidate the methods employed.

Mudana accused Bodile, his half-brother's son, of stealing £9. The case had been tried first at home, and then at the Native Commissioner's, where it had been dismissed owing to insufficient evidence. The parties decided to go to a smeller-out. On the second day of their journey, when they were resting under a tree to enable the official witness to take off his jacket, a small boy standing some way off said to them, 'There is a *mugɔme* over there.' He was a decoy watching the road to direct people to a diviner who had lately arrived and set up a temporary village of rough huts. Deciding that it was too hot to go further, the party followed the boy and sat down outside the village fence. A man approached them and, after ascertaining how much money they had to offer, showed them into an enclosure of old sacks. At the entrance stood the diviner himself, holding a stick under which the four of them were made to pass in single file. Diviners are said quite frequently to test their clients in some such manner; sometimes they are made to jump over a furrow and it is said the guilty man usually falls in.

When they had seated themselves on the ground, the diviner asked first of all for his money. The official witness handed him £1 5s., but he insisted on 10s. more, because, he said, it was a difficult case—one that had been much tried in other courts. Stick in hand, but without the use of any divining bones, the diviner began asking the party to respond (*hu vuma*). '*Ya vuma*,' they replied, and he proceeded with his chanting in a mixture of Sotho and Shangana-Ṭonga in sing-song phrases, at the end of which the clients had to assent. 'You have come from home on a matter', he began. Pointing to the official witness, he said, 'You have accused this boy (pointing to Bodile) of witchcraft. No. I'm making a mistake on purpose. You have not come for this reason.' Looking into a large shell, he continued, 'You have come on a different errand. You have come about money. The sum concerned is £30. No. It is £15. No. It is £10. The owner of the money sells hemp.' Continuing in this manner in short phrases, to which the party responded '*Ya vuma*,' and, suggesting first this, then that, he eventually said, 'I don't like to cause brothers by the same father to fight. Your quarrel is a vain one. The money was stolen by a woman of the Crocodile totem living near your village. She has not yet used the money.' Pointing to Bodile, he said, '*You*, why do you want to kill *him* [Mudana], and you [Mudana] be careful. They may kill you with medicines they have just bought.' Turning to the official witness, he demanded, 'Give me my *phitho* (hidden object). What kind of thing is this which is hidden from me? It is a snuff-box. No. It is a half-crown. No. It is a penny. No. It is European iron. If you think I am telling lies, take out of your left-hand pocket the thing which you have been given.' The official witness took out of his pocket the battery of a torch. He doubted the competence of a diviner who had been so vague about the nature of the object—'European iron' can be any metal object—but the main thing was that Bodile and Mudana were satisfied and so the party went home, relieved that it was an outsider who was found to be the culprit.

Objectively considered, this seance may appear naïve, but the parties, and even an outsider who was present, did not think so. There was no initial and formal identification of accuser, accused, and 'ears' which one expects from theoretical accounts; but forms and procedures are never set, and it is not unusual for these identifications to emerge later as the divination proceeds. It is by theoretical standards necessary that the *mugɔme*, as a test of his competence, should name the totem or other groups of the consultants, but in this case the parties did not even notice the omission, as they were satisfied on the main issue. The *mugɔme* erred somewhat as regards both the sum involved and the relationship of Mudana and Bodile; but the parties were impressed that he was only £1 out and, although they were not brothers, they were related through brothers. The wide connotation of terms and indefiniteness of conceptions lend themselves, as meanings and rigid categories in a European language cannot do, to manipulation by the *mugɔme* and ready acceptance by the parties of suggestions. In the *khɔrɔ*, the vanquished party often complains of the vague or incorrect indications as to totems and of other unsatisfactory features, but unless the 'ears' agrees, the *khɔrɔ* usually dismisses these objections, since, if he had really been dissatisfied, he would have demanded back the money from the *mugɔme* and proceeded to another. But it is necessary to add that the *mugɔme* often backs up his art with a very high-handed manner or behaviour. Some even beat witches that they have smelt out. It is usual for the diviner to shave one side of the head of the witch and to take from him his jacket or any other object of clothing he would like to have. To the accuser is given a buck's horn to blow on his way home as proof of his success and, when he enters the royal village to report, he is met with joyful trillings of women.

The attitude of people towards convicted witches depends largely upon the nature of the crime, but also upon the number of relatives of the injured party living in the neighbourhood. If he has harmed a number of people in the area, or if the injured party has many relatives to side with him, the witch may be forced by public opinion to leave the area. Malaji, who had caused the difficult birth and the death of the child of his lover, became very unpopular when the witchcraft had finally been attributed to him; from being one of the cheerful young bloods in the district, he became reserved and restrained, and shortly afterwards he left to work in town. But he was not ostracized by any one except the relatives of the injured woman and, when he returns, if we may judge from other cases, the whole matter will have blown over. On the whole, the attitude of the general public to a convicted witch is one of unconcern as long as his efforts have not been directed against them personally. People are accustomed to living in an atmosphere in which any one of their friends or relatives may turn out to be a witch. The atmosphere is illustrated in a proverb the sense of which is that you may be the unsuspecting victim of the witchcraft of your closest friend, or, more literally, Bɛlɛgwane, the enemy, does not care; [so intimate with him are you that] you eat with him, [yet] he is the foe that eats you (*Bɛlɛgwane mulala a khi vone; u la nayɔ, gi mulala was hu la wɛna*). And people chased away as witches from one area or tribe never have any difficulty in being accepted into another.

Considerations such as the return of cattle are often strong enough to deter a man from chasing away a wife who has bewitched some one in the village (he would never chase away a wife merely for bewitching outsiders). When once we asked a man why he kept a wife who had been found guilty of bewitching her fellow wife, he replied, 'She is my witch' (*gi mulɔi wa ga*). Being fond of her, he merely built her a separate village. Some people who have never been publicly accused of witchcraft are nevertheless known to be bad witches. In such cases, people may fear them and try to keep on good terms with them in order to avoid evil consequences.

One of the most fruitful studies in regard to witchcraft is the investigation of the relationship of the people who bewitch one another. Two main categories must be distinguished, viz. cases in which relatives bewitch one another and cases in which the evil is sent by non-relatives. The Lovedu maintain, and the opinion is borne out both by one's general impressions and by the facts, that witches injure mainly those with whom they are in close contact—that is, relatives and neighbours—and that it is difficult to bewitch a stranger. And it is remarkable that of fifty cases of witchcraft observed by us as they came before the *khɔrɔ* and given in the table below, 70 per cent. involve close relatives. Not all relatives are apt to bewitch one, but both men and women are equally liable to harm either men or women. A mother never, it is believed, bewitches her own children, and there is even a saying to the effect that a *mugɔme* who points out one's mother is not able to divine (*mugɔme u a tia vummahu a u khɔni hu laula*); and, although brother and cattle-linked sister sometimes hate one another, openly as well as secretly, they cannot harm one another, it is said, because they would use 'the medicine bag of the [same] mother'. Similarly neither a son nor a daughter can bewitch the mother.

The most prolific single source of witchcraft is the conflict of co-wives (24 per cent. of all cases). Their relationship in the polygynous family is a difficult one; the houses are independent, not subservient to one another, yet they are in close contact, and the insistence upon compromises occasions many mental conflicts. Spouses also bewitch one another, but wives kill or injure their husbands more frequently than husbands kill their wives; it is said that a husband who has only one wife will never bewitch her, except perhaps among Christians, who can have only one wife. The conflict of spouses is an aspect of a wider institutional conflict, that between relatives-in-law. If they have irksome obligations towards one another, the society insists that their relationship shall be characterized by mutual respect and helpfulness and that their difficulties, especially *munywalo* difficulties, are to be resolved as far as possible by the methods and procedure of the *khɔrɔ*. These factors explain why, despite the many sources of tension between them, the cases are not, as one might expect, overwhelmingly predominant: only 20 per cent. of the total given in our table are cases of wives or their relatives bewitching husbands or their relatives, and only 16 per cent. husbands or their relatives bewitching wives or their relatives.

What is even more arresting is the fact that easily aggrieved relatives who, as it is phrased, are 'very sensitive' and readily nurse grievances, never or rarely bewitch: such are cattle-linked brothers or sisters, father's sisters, fathers, father's brothers and grandparents. It is even clear from what we have already said that they are believed to have repressed complaints, but they cannot project as witchcraft the displeasures or misfortunes or failures upon those who must, but do not, respect and humour them. They can and do cause illness, but it is not by way of witchcraft, and the resolution of the conflict is by pardon and *hu phasa*, through the gods, not through *vulɔi*. In other words, witchcraft is a reflection, not of tensions as such, whether open or repressed, but of tensions within the framework of cultural mechanisms for avoiding their being projected as witchcraft. They must be studied in the whole configuration of institutions and social values: the permissible or approved remedies, the interposition of the hierarchy of age and rank between competing individuals, the compromises and reconciliations that are insisted upon, and the extent to which mental drives are conditioned to the cultural pattern or allowed outlets or are blocked by culturally stressed values.

The incidence of witchcraft between strangers is much more intelligible to us, because it arises in situations of conflict that are not very different from our own. But the percentage of these cases (30 per cent.), even when we include the 10 per cent. of cases between distant kin who are neighbours rather than relatives, shows how largely the social structure is built upon the kin.

The following table represents a very broad analysis of fifty cases of witchcraft that we observed as they came before the *khɔrɔ* and that may be simplified for statistical presentation:

Category of conflict	Witch(es)	Victim(s)	No. of cases	Remarks as to nature of conflict	Percentage of cases
I. *Relatives* (a) House or co-wife against house or co-wife	Co-wife	Co-wife	1	Jealousy about lovers; neglect by husband	
	Co-wife	Co-wife and child of co-wife	2	Jealousy about children and husband's attention	
	Co-wife	Child of co-wife	2	Disagreements about *munywalo*	

Category of conflict	Witch(es)	Victim(s)	No. of cases	Remarks as to nature of conflict	Percentage of cases
I. *Relatives* (*a*) House or co-wife against house or co-wife—*cont.*	Co-wife and her mother	Co-wife's child	2	Favouritism of husband and other mixed motives	
	Inherited wife	Co-wife and her children	2	Use of cattle of one house by another and questions of prestige	
	Widow	Fellow widow's child	1	Property arrangements	
	Wife of brother	Wife of another brother	1	Complex jealousies	
	Son of co-wife	Chief son and his wife	1	Status and position	24
(*b*) Wife against husband	Wife	Husband	2	Friction, favouritism of other wives, position	
	Wife and/or wife's mother	Husband's adulterine child or lover	4	Sexual jealousy and neglect of wife	
	Wife	Husband's sister's child	1	Disagreement about marriage of children and *munywalo*	
	Wife	Husband's brother, his wife, or his child	2	Position, jealousy	
	Wife's mother	Husband's child	1	Disagreements	20

Category of conflict	Witch(es)	Victim(s)	No. of cases	Remarks as to nature of conflict	Percentage of cases
(c) Husband against wife	Husband	Wife	1	Pre-marital seduction and *munywalo* trouble	
	Husband	Wife's adulterine child	2	Husband impotent; sexual jealousy	
	Husband	Wife's sister	1	Husband jilted	
	Husband	Brother's son's wife and her mother	1	Revenge for misfortune (illness)	
	Husband	Wife's brother's daughter's husband	1	Wife's brother refused his daughter as wife to witch's son	
	Husband's mother	Wife		Unfaithfulness of wife	
	Husband's mother	Wife's sister	1	Wife's sister jilted witch	16
(d) Parent and own child	Son	Father	1	Son wished to oust father from position as district head	
	Father	Son	1	Son cohabited with young wife of father	6
	Father	Son's wife	1	Son cohabited with inherited wife of father	
(e) Uterine brothers and sisters	Elder sister	Younger sister	1	Younger sister jilted elder sister's husband	
	Sister (and mother)	Brother's child	1	Brother resents power of sister, and *munywalo* trouble	4
Total relatives					70

WITCHCRAFT AND SORCERY

Category of conflict	Witch(es)	Victim(s)	No. of cases	Remarks as to nature of conflict	Percentage of cases
II. *Strangers* (a) Sexual conflicts	Girl	Lover	1	Lover jilted girl	
	Boy	Lover	1	Lover engaged to her cross-cousin	
	Adulterer	Married woman's child	2	Loss of fine and right to woman or child	
	Commoner (orphan)	Girl of noble birth	1	Refusal of marriage by parents who had adopted orphan	10
(b) Various conflicts	Man and his mother	Whole village	1	Status, loss of prestige and amenities	
	Woman	Distant male relative	1	Refusal to implement economic arrangement *re* partner-ploughing	
	Widow	Distant male relative	1	Indirect economic rivalries	
	Man	Male neighbour	1	Stranger held cattle that came from witch as *munywalo*	
	Man	Male neighbour	1	Envy of sewing machine acquired in town by neighbour	
	Man	Driver of car	1	Jealousy *re* privileges secured because he could drive car	
	Male friends	Man	1	Man's popularity with girls, owing to dancing ability, resented	
	Woman	Rival	1	Rivals for councillor's attention, sexual and otherwise	
	'Mother' of khɔba	Khɔba initiate	1	Initiate who is to marry cross-cousin wanted by witch as daughter-in-law	
	Shangana-Tonga	Lovedu man	1	Competition for job in town	20
Total strangers					30

It will take us too far afield to discuss the nature of the conflicts in detail in the various cases. But a few observations are perhaps necessary.

Firstly, the cause of the conflict is not necessarily the one assigned by the parties, though the objective situation is often seen by others. Sometimes very trivial causes are given, but they have to be interpreted in their total setting. Secondly, as regards non-relatives, it is said that nobles are sometimes 'seen in the dice', but they are never publicly accused by mere commoners; it will be noticed that, on the other hand, there is one case of a noble accusing a commoner. Rich people who are not nobles enjoy no special immunity; unpleasant people, especially those who are quarrelsome, ambitious, or competitive, are often accused. Conflicts arise owing to close contacts, but may continue after the parties are separated, and witchcraft may be sent any distance, even as far as Johannesburg. Thirdly, the table does not give a number of types of cases; they are merely the cases that came before the court, many of them being dismissed as nonsense. Finally, although the motives are complicated in most of the cases, it is possible to say that jilted love or refusal of sexual advances is an important factor in about 32 per cent. of the cases recorded.

But we must not think of Freudian repressions, for sexual affairs are given recognition in the institution of *vuḑabu*. We must consider lovers' conflicts in the cultural setting. The sexual urge is not repressed, but the lover whose advances are rejected, though he has opportunities elsewhere, feels aggrieved. The girl, whose choice of a marital partner is limited, seeks extra-marital adventure, but it must be clandestine and occasions difficulties, and the situation between lover, husband, and wife is an uneasy one in which ill-feeling readily arises. The man who has a child by a lover has no institutional claim on that child, and he may be given away by the woman and have to pay a heavy fine, with the result that he is angered. There are also dangers in sexual intercourse and, if a man or woman suffers as a result, he may take revenge. In other words, the conflict situation must be ascribed, not to repressions, but to the incidents of the whole cultural system. Similar considerations apply whenever we analyse any of the other situations of conflict. It is far beyond the purpose of this book to undertake an analysis of the psychological aspects of these conflicts, but we would say that witchcraft is to be explained mainly, not by psycho-pathology, but by a relativistic psychology, arising out of the values and institutional configuration of the culture.

When a man is ill he will immediately, if he has an enemy or has had a quarrel, think of the possibility of witchcraft. This impulse is encouraged by the technique of the dice, which, while indicating the totem or sex of the witch, leaves the client to decide to whom among his friends, enemies, or relatives these must apply. A person with a grievance or an unpopular person is more likely than others to be thought responsible for harm. When some cattle of the queen, usually used by Mudumi for ploughing, were traded to a European, he complained most bitterly. A week later when lightning struck a storage enclosure in the royal village Mudumi was immediately suspect. Some of the cattle belonging to Setemane's inherited wife had been taken by the police, together with those of her husband, in settlement of a debt. She grumbled continuously about her loss. A year and a half later, on the death of a child of her fellow wife, she was suspected at once and, after consultation of the bones, her husband chased her away. A person with an unpleasant face very often earns the reputation of being a witch, even though nothing has been definitely attributed to him. A very old person, too, is apt to be thought a witch; his long life is attributed to his bartering the lives of younger relatives for his own. Just as people with grievances are suspected of witchcraft, so successful ones are thought to be specially liable to being bewitched—those who reap better crops than others, successful hunters, those favoured by their European masters. On the other hand, their success is also liable to be attributed to witchcraft on their part.

It has been said that witchcraft is a reflection of the intense hatreds of which the Bantu mind is capable. True, the European is appalled at the seriousness of the crimes attributed to witches for the most trivial reasons. The mother's brother's wife kills the child of her husband's sister who is living with them because he eats too much: 'he finishes our corn'; because a woman no longer loves him, a man not only causes intense suffering to her during a prolonged birth, but also kills the child; jealous of the large crop reaped by his neighbour, a man sends lightning to destroy his whole harvest. These things do not, however, present themselves in this way to the mind of the Lovedu. A Lovedu argues, not from real cause to effect in such matters, but from effect to cause, which makes it all appear in a somewhat different light. A child dies and he looks around him for a possible cause. He thinks of possible motives and enemies, but can find none. He consults the dice, which point to a woman of such-and-such a totem. The only one to answer this description is the mother's brother's wife. She happens to be known as ungenerous, perhaps she was one day heard to comment on having an extra mouth to feed. The misfortune is thus projected upon her: but it is not a psychopathic, it is an approved cultural escape technique or compensation. In cases of illness or death, people tend to seek the cause in the direction of traditional jealousies. A wife of the queen dies in childbirth. The cause cannot be a jilted lover, because she and the father of the child were on the best of terms. But he is a married man, and women are known through jealousy to cause difficult childbirth to the lovers of husbands. The death must have been caused by his wife (even though she lives miles away). Nothing is done in the matter; moreover, there is no general agreement in the verdicts of different doctors. Six months later a young girl in the village dies suddenly of blood poisoning; her mother is known to have had quarrels with the deceased wife of the queen. It is therefore generally rumoured that the grave must have been treated to 'send back' death and the death of the child indicates that her mother was the witch responsible. Nothing more is said of the lover's wife.

Witchcraft provides an explanation of the worst evils, such as sickness and death, that befall man; it is the principle of evil, the Bantu Satan. Illness caused naturally or by ancestors is generally curable; it is only witchcraft that really kills. It was at first a source of great amazement to us that a man could find it possible to live on socially good terms with some one who had killed his father, attending the same beer-parties and able to converse in friendly fashion. But unless the case has been publicly dealt with and the witch smelt out, the evidence is considered incomplete, in spite of one's own convictions. Moreover, it does not follow that the witch has any evil designs upon one, though he has killed some one else. Personal adjustments with the witch are more easily achieved than we might imagine; they are even imperative, partly because witchcraft is so universal a cause of death that in this respect the witch is almost part of the inevitable order of things, partly because, unless a confirmed witch, he is not regarded with horror by the whole society, and partly because he may be an influential and respected man.

Witchcraft serves also to explain the differential incidence of misfortune or death which we generally leave unexplained; but it is not often invoked in this respect. An old, dried-up tree stands in a field. People often rest beneath it at hoeing time. One day, while two children are sitting in its shade, it falls down and kills one of them. The Lovedu realize that dead trees are liable to fall down. But it has long been standing there. Why has it fallen just on that day and, moreover, at that particular time when the children were there? Further, what made it kill one, leaving the other unhurt? This combination of circumstances must, they feel, be due to some malignant controlling force directed against the child. Or, when people recover from a disease such as smallpox in one district, but succumb to it in another, the differential effect in the latter is ascribed to the work of a witch. The occasion for evoking witchcraft as an explanation in certain circumstances is an aspect of witchcraft, but it is not an explanation of its nature and psychological basis and only part of the explanation of its function.

Witchcraft is employed to account for unusual or anti-social behaviour. Hysteria might be attributed either to witchcraft or possession. A girl ran away from her own puberty ceremony, an unheard-of and reprehensible action. Her relatives said she must have been bewitched into doing it, so, instead of being punished, she was given treatment to remove the baleful influence. Attributing certain types of anti-social action or the breaking of some customs to witchcraft makes it possible for the society to withstand successfully many blows; an issue is avoided and the transgressor made to feel himself incapable of such actions but for the witchcraft. We must also remember that abnormalities need not necessarily evoke comment. A person may be born an imbecile, but it may be considered quite normal. This is so because there is a place in the society for the weak-minded, sometimes even as jesters of the court. Personal defects or limitations do not, to the same extent as among us, disable a man from performance markedly below the standards required in spheres in which he can be useful; and thus there need not arise an intolerable situation from which escape is sought by psycho-pathological devices or the projection of one's misfortune as witchcraft upon others. Finally, to attribute death to witchcraft, and to set about taking steps to send it back to its owner, probably provides greater emotional satisfaction to the bereaved than the feeling of impotence in the face of an uncontrollable, natural force. The same kind of emotional need is answered when a man with a grievance feels that he can, in the last resort, employ medicine to gain his ends, and people not infrequently indirectly hint to their enemies the possibility of their doing so.

CHAPTER XV

THE RAIN CULT

The rain-queen in her sphere of safeguarding the seasons—technique of transforming the clouds—evils that cause 'heat' and act as impediments to rain—'cooling' rites counteracting the 'heat' of the earth.

As the centre of the agricultural cycle, rain is the focus of many human interests; as the elixir of life, it is one of the ultimate bases of man's sense of security; and as a manifestation of celestial grace, it is the supreme justification of the divine right of the queen to rule. The queen is primarily not a ruler, but a rain-maker, and men rely for their security, not on regimentation, armies, and organization, but on the queen's power to make rain for the tribe and to withhold rain from its enemies. All ultimate reliances are based upon the magico-religious world, and rain-making and its cult are an important part of that world. The rain cult is not composed of a few magical passes made by the queen; it is a whole complex of institutions with ramifications through many aspects of tribal life. The cult is not confined to measures taken to secure rain in times of drought; its observances must be kept at all times and a good year involves as much care on the part of the queen as a bad one.

The chief actor in the rain cult is the queen. During life, she is not merely the Transformer of the Clouds, but she is regarded as the changer of the seasons and guarantor of their cyclic regularity; when she dies, the seasons are out of joint and drought is inevitable. Her very emotions affect the rain: if she is dissatisfied, angry, or sad, she cannot work well, and in 1934-5, when the first rains did not come till December, the drought was attributed to her being upset at her daughter's liaison with a commoner. Her rain-making is not confined to dramatic ceremonies in time of severe drought; it is conceived of as continuous care throughout the summer. Furthermore, the Lovedu do not attribute every fall of rain to some special activity or volition on the part of their queen, but rather believe that the queen exercises some general control or care which ensures a good season.

Such being the powers of the queen, she is the person to be approached when there is no rain, not only at the beginning of the season, but any time during the summer in a country in which three weeks' drought might ruin the maize crop. There are various ways of doing this. Great councillors or important relatives may approach the queen in person, saying, 'The people are crying,' and asking her to help them. When there was no rain, Mugwena, related to the queen through his mother, used to walk near the queen's hut complaining, in a voice calculated to reach the royal ears, that it was a bad thing for the chief to kill his people by withholding rain. When the first summer storm of 1937 opened with much lightning and thunder, the two chief councillors mentioned informally to the queen at beer that they hoped she would ward off wind and thunder and give them a good year. Heads of districts approach the queen (*hu lova*) with a gift, usually nowadays of £1 or £1 10s., and very often bring with them in addition dancing performers (gɔsha) to please her and to evoke her pity at the sorrowful sight of people dancing in summer when they ought to be ploughing. The movements of this dancing do not differ from those of ordinary dancing, but the music consists of *lesugu* songs sung also at the annual harvest ceremony, on the death of important royal people, and at the girls' initiation 'school'.

The most renowned of all dancing for rain is the *legɔbathɛle*, a special kind of *gɔsha*, the mourning dance of a section of Thʊʋɔlɔ people living under one of the district heads, Maʋulana. It is more dignified, its movements slower and more stately, and its drumming more subdued than in an ordinary *gɔsha*. So lightly are the drums struck that the clear, silvery, varied tones of the reed pipes ring out like the peal of bells. Only two drums are used, and none but those who have lost at least one parent may perform, and it is begun in the dim light of the dawn before sunrise, when, after a short spell, it stops and is resumed later in the day. When some one person has greatly angered the queen, and drought is believed to be due to her displeasure on this account, the married women from all the villages in the royal neighbourhood assemble every morning after cooking to dance, singing, 'We are being killed on account of a bogyman in skins' (*re vulaiswa gi Madikadyana di vɛlɛvɛḍana*). Grandmothers nurse the babies and encourage the younger women with their trillings and dancing movements. The dust rises high and by sunset they are black with dirt and sweat; but next day and the next they come again, sometimes for as long as a week, till rain falls or continued drought makes it clear that some other cause is operating as well. The great hardship this dancing entails (for nursing mothers who perform have no time to feed their babies) is thought to melt the heart of the queen. Too much rain, as well as too little, is laid at the door of the queen. On one occasion, when it had rained almost incessantly for six weeks, the chief councillor said in the presence of the queen, 'Fat does not fill the pot' (*makhura a a ḍale bija*), meaning that there can be too much of a good thing—a hint to the queen to regulate things better.

There is no belief that is stronger in the tribe even to-day than that in the power of the queen to transform the clouds. This does not, however, mean that they do not recognize the regularity of the seasons. People know that the month of February is generally the rainiest in the year; that the month *Morenane* (October), when the Southern Cross sets just before bedtime, is the time when the first rains are approaching, and no one would *lova* rain in winter any more than Europeans would organize a day of prayer for rain in that season. Yet if rain does not come at its proper time or the season is generally bad, it may be said, 'The queen has not changed the hoeing season [i.e. the year] nicely' (*a va fedula ledzema ha vutse*); for if the cycle of seasons is considered inevitable, whether the new year is brought in propitiously or otherwise is in the hands of the queen.

Though renowned as the greatest rain-maker in South Africa, Mujaji never works alone. She always has a rain-doctor, of whom there are many in the tribe, to work with her. She chooses any renowned doctor, but may change him for another if people complain that the rain is bad—

that is, insufficient or accompanied by too many thunderstorms. For these deficiencies, the queen herself is never blamed. The chief function of the doctor is to co-operate with the queen in some of the things she cannot do: he divines the causes of drought and discovers which forces are hindering the queen's power from taking effect; and, using his own medicines, he aids her in removing these causes and setting right what is wrong. The relation between rain-doctors and the queen is interesting. They are specialists in their art, which they have inherited from their fathers, and are even consulted independently by outside tribes. Khishidwa, the queen's own rain-doctor, is often called by Nwamitwa, the Shangana-Tonga chief, in time of drought, and Tshivulane, a Venda chief, comes, not to *lova* Mujaji, but to call Levea, a rain-doctor on a farm within her jurisdiction. Any payments they receive are their own. Yet these doctors themselves unreservedly state that in the last resort they are dependent on the queen: if she stays their hands, their powers will avail them nothing. It is said, 'If the chief holds the rain from falling, the doctor cannot cause rain' (*hɛ khosi a ga tswara bula hore e khi ne, Daga e ga se nese*). A rain-doctor sent by the queen to make rain for a Venda chief who came to *lova* once in our presence urged the chief councillor, 'Tell the queen not to hold my hands.' In addition to the chief's right-hand man in rain activities, there are certain lesser rain-doctors whom she employs as her messengers when outside tribes *lova* rain, for she would never dream of giving a suppliant medicine to take back with him. These messengers, though sent by the queen, are, strange as it seems to us, not given any medicine or charm to use in their rain-making. It is considered enough that they come from her, and their payment is the entertainment they receive at the foreign court.

What the queen does to transform the clouds and the exact nature of the objects and medicines associated with her work are enshrouded in the greatest secrecy. It is doubtful whether any one other than the queen herself is in possession of this secret, for it is bound up with the title and power to succeed to the throne. The secrets are always imparted to the successor just prior to the death of the chief, and on occasion in Lovedu traditional history the would-be usurper, to whom the secrets had not been entrusted, has been deposed in favour of the 'chosen' heir. The queen's rain medicines are kept in rough earthen pots (*mehago*) in a part of the village to which few have access. Some of their power is said to derive from a human skull in the rain-pot, and there are horns which are kept in a hut. When these rain-horns (*dinaga ja bula*) are placed on the ground, rain falls; when they are hung up, it clears up and is dry. The medicine in the rain-horns is said, when burnt, to produce smoke which rises up in the air to draw and to produce the clouds. The technique is not unlike *leshwava*, luck medicine, which when burnt draws customers to traders and touts. Associated with the rain cult are the *gomana* drums the beating of which in former times was believed to bring rain, but the true *gomana* ceremonies have not been held for about thirty years. The rain cult to-day is largely confined to observances connected with the queen and her medicines or charms (*dithugula*).

The chief ingredient of the rain-pots is the skin of the deceased chief and of important councillors who are her closest relatives: when a chief dies the body is left for some days in the hut, so that, when it is rubbed in a certain way (*hu fɔrɔlwa*), the skin easily comes away. Other ingredients are fat of the scaly ant-eater (*khwara*), a royal animal which, when found, has always to be brought alive to the royal village, and parts of the kudu (*thɔlɔ*). The queen's rain-doctor told us that essential ingredients were sea-water, because it foams and froths (*hu pukula*), feathers of the lightning bird, white and black sea shells, and various roots and barks, chief among which is the stem of the *khadi* (*Adenia gumnifera*), a tough forest creeper that contains much water. *Khadi* stems are also used for sprinkling 'cooling' medicines and for tying the bodies of dead people. Whether the queen uses these ingredients, we cannot say. From time to time a black sheep is killed to give strength to the queen's rain medicines; it has to be washed with water which is afterwards poured into the rain pots, but it is said that such a sheep is merely a present-day substitute for a human being, usually a child, whose brains were used. Important district heads related to the chief also have their rain-pots. Every year in about August, at the command of the queen, such a district head collects certain roots and barks, knowledge of which he has received from his father, places them in his rain-pot, mixed with water that has been drawn by girls below the age of puberty, and stirs them up so that rain may be good that year. Rain-pots are great secrets and only after years of friendship were we privileged to see one: it was well hidden in the cleft of a rock and partly buried at the foot of a tree on the upper slopes of a hill where the owner's father had dwelt. The rain-pots of the queen we have not seen, and what regular measures she takes are not known for certain; but, since it is said, when there are good rains, that the queen has firmly laid the foundations (*hu thea*) of the year, it is not unlikely that she also stirs her medicines.

Great care has to be taken lest the rain-pots 'weaken' (*hu figɛhɛla*). They have to be given (*hu lumiswa*, to cause to be bitten) the first green foods (*mutshatsha*) every year, kaffir water melon (*legwadzi*) mixed with other green foods being used for the purpose, and at the royal village no one cooks and eats the new summer relishes before this has been done. On this day possessed people or people who have epilepsy also eat medicine with the firstfruits, but ordinary people do not *luma*, and there are none of the public festivities of a semi-military character associated with the eating of the firstfruits among Swazi and Zulu. It is very important too that the first termites (*dinntwa*), which appear usually in December, just after the first good rains, should be given to the rain-pots. Termites are closely associated with rain: they always fly out of their nests just after the rain; in a dry year there are very few; and it is believed that sprinkling the antheap with rain medicine (*mufugo*) makes the ants come in great numbers. Termites for the rain-pots may not be gathered by married women or girls over the age of puberty, and in 1937, when some young girls carried the first termites to the queen, she gave the termites to the dogs, refusing to use ants that had been thus defiled. The giving of the first termites to the rain-pots is called *bulane*. An interesting case arose out of this practice in January, 1938, when certain people in Uuthudi area ate termites before the *bulane* of the head. An inquiry was held by the district head and four men were fined two goats each. They were told that, if their case had come before the queen herself, they would have had to pay a head of cattle. Only the few sub-areas under the immediate jurisdiction of the queen herself send termites to the queen; in other areas they send to their own head, and there is no rule that the queen's own rain-charms should be given before others.

The powers of the queen to make rain are not absolute. The queen can control rain only 'in agreement with her ancestors' who are able, if they wish, to stay her hand just as she herself is able to stay the hands of rain-doctors. There are also certain things that, by causing the rain charms to become 'weak' (*figɛhɛla*), have power to stop the rain unless proper measures are taken. It has already been shown how heat is associated with illness and things being wrong. If a person has been burned to death or struck by lightning, he must be buried in a wet place near the river or his grave 'cooled' with special medicine obtained from the chief, lest drought ensues. Similarly, abortions or miscarriages, women dying in pregnancy or childbirth, twins killed at birth, babies dying before cutting their teeth or cutting the upper teeth before the lower, initiates dying in the circumcision lodge—all must be buried in a wet place.

Since an electrical storm often means little or no rain, it is believed that 'sending' lightning to kill one's enemies, a common practice of witches, spoils the country by preventing rain. Hence at a tribal gathering (*khivijo*), held in the spring of 1937–8, the people were told among other things that the chief does not want to see 'lightning of people' (as opposed to natural lightning); any district head hearing of anything like this among his people was to report at once to the queen. A common phenomenon in time of drought is the banking up of heavy rain clouds with all the promise of a soaking rain, only to be dispersed by wind. Anything associated with winds is thus thought to prevent rain. That is why witches, by hanging *lefalaja-maru*—literally, 'disperser of the clouds' (*Asparagus plumosis*)—or an ordinary broom on a branch where it will sway in the air, can disperse the clouds; and any one dying of a coughing disease, such as *ḓɛre* or consumption, must be buried in wet soil or soil that has been sprinkled with *mufugo* medicine. If abortions or people dying of a coughing disease are buried without these precautions, the grave is called *pukudi* (from *hu pukula*, which perhaps is the opposite of *hu fuga*, to blow upon by a cool breeze, to sprinkle with cooling medicine). *Pukudi* contains the conception of wind issuing upwards or hot air quivering above a heated surface. As soon as the vapour-laden air reaches the grave, it stops or dissolves in the wind and it is even believed that the corpse, thrusting up an arm, waves it about to cause the wind that drives away the rain.

How dangerous wind is considered to be in setting at naught the efforts of the queen was well illustrated on November 15th, 1937. On that day, after propitious black clouds had been dispersed by a gale that lifted the thatch off many a hut, it was proclaimed that the following day had to be a holiday. People said, '*Gi khumɛla*' (it is a 'turning back' before the goal has been reached), and we were told that in the old days men of importance used to come and condole with (*hu ɛmɛla*) the chief on such a day, as though to sympathize with her in the frustration of her efforts. There are other holidays associated with rain. On the day after the first rain of the season has fallen no hoeing or fieldwork is to be done. Such a holiday is called *le-nkhi-nteme* (do not cut me), as if the earth, believed still to be hot, dislikes being broken up by the hoeing. Such a holiday is also observed after the rain charms have 'bitten' the new termites and first-fruits of the year and when, any time during the summer, rain falls after two of three weeks drought, it is called *muene* (guest or stranger) and the next day observed as a holiday, for one honours a guest.

Wrong burials which stop the rain are righted by the use of *mufugo* medicine and the water obtained by squeezing the undigested stomach contents (*muswane*) of a sheep down a hole made in the grave with a stick and reaching the body. This is thought to disperse the 'wind' and cool the grave. The flesh of the sheep is eaten without salt. The conception is thus of a grave agitated by ghostly heat and wind, which may be 'laid' by 'cooling', or, as we might say, calming, in the treble sense often of pacifying [the ghost], modifying [the heat], and causing [the wind] to subside. *Mufugo*, the medicine so important in the removal of impediments to rain, has to be obtained from the queen and a specially appointed person is responsible for doling it out in bottles when needed. The office is not conceived to be hereditary, but it has been held by a Mudiga family for some time, being handed down by father to son. When the last official in charge of *mufugo* died, his son was an unmarried man too young for the responsibility of office. Some five years later (1938), when the queen decided that he should assume charge, he protested his youth, though he then had two children, fearing that after contact with the medicine he might forget to wash his hands before eating and thus be rendered impotent. In this he had the full support of his mother, who prevailed upon the queen to allow an older relative to undertake the work provisionally; but the present position is that, should this old man be away, the heir to the office will have to act. Whether *mufugo* is identical with the rain medicine of the rain-pots is not quite clear; but, whatever its ingredients may be, it is considered extremely dangerous, liable to rob men and women of their fertility, and great care is thus necessary when working with it.

Sometimes it is said that 'the country is not right' (*naha a e loge*) and then there is a special ceremony in which all the fires in the country are put out with *mufugo*. No generally recognized set of circumstances lead up to such a line of action, nor is there any idea that the fires are defiled in any way. It is simply looked upon as a method of getting rain when there is drought, resorted to when the divining bones of the doctor declare it to be necessary. People sometimes say, 'Fires are put out to usher in a new year,' but this does not mean that putting out the fires is an annual ceremony, as it is, for instance, among the Pedi. The word 'year' must not be taken literally, just as it does not refer to an abstract period of time in the phrase, 'The year has been infected by *hu khuma*', when what is meant is that the rain charms have 'weakened' (*hu khoma*). In this ceremony girls below the age of puberty are sent to draw water for the *mufugo* which the queen's rain-doctor prepares for the occasion, and after a day or two, when the medicine froths up (*hu pukula*), boys are sent with a horn of *mufugo* and a brush of *khadi* creeper (*Adenia gumnifera*) to every village in the land. First they heat medicine on the fire of the men's courtyard and thereafter on the threshold and hearth of every hut. The ashes are cleared away by an old woman, for so dangerous is the medicine used that any man, woman, or child entering the hut before it has been smeared with dung will *khuma* and be unable to have children. A new fire is kindled in the men's courtyard, whence each woman fetches a brand for her own hut, for it is taboo to kindle a fire from any other. In return for her firebrand, each woman gives the men stamped mealies or groundnuts, which they eat in the *khɔrɔ*. Each married man in turn must give something to the boys who have brought *mufugo*, usually 1s. or a fowl (in the old days an arrow or mealies), but often also tobacco or other gifts for, as '*mufugo* does not choose' (*mufugo a u khɛthe*), anything may be given. Each boy must give 1s. or a fowl to the keeper of *mufugo*, keeping the rest as a reward for his labours. It is taboo to work in the fields on the day after *mufugo*. In 1927 some boys, too lazy to fetch the medicine, took matters into their own hands and made a mixture of ash and water, which they used in their rounds. They were discovered and made to pay five head of cattle each and the ceremony had to be performed again.

When the divining bones diagnose drought as due to ancestors, steps have to be taken for a sacrifice at an ancestral grave. Any one of the close relatives of the queen can cause drought: sometimes it is the queen's mother Leakhali, buried at Khaḍa; sometimes it is Mugɔdɔ's sister, buried at Mudzinoni; in 1925–6 it was Mulogwane, the queen's brother, who complained that he was buried in the Christian cemetery, instead of in the shade of the forest. A sacrifice for rain will take place only after it has become clear that, in spite of steps taken to *lova* the queen by means of money or dancing, she fails by her ordinary methods to cause the rain to fall.

January, 1938, was hot and dry. Several headmen had been to *lova*, but no rain fell. Important district heads and councillors thus began to 'travel about, having the bones thrown', to discover the cause, while the queen herself also sent messengers to various well-known diviners. The reply came, 'Seek ye a black sheep. Go with it to show your care for the spirits and you shall see that it will rain nicely.' As is so often the case, no indication was given of the cause of their complaint; the suggestion as to the practical measures to be taken and the identity of the troublesome spirits were quite sufficient. The queen, however, remained inactive; it was not for her to take the initiative till her people humbly begged her to do so. On February 11th three of the most important men at the capital approached her, saying, 'People are crying. Help us.' Thereupon she impatiently replied, 'People tire me. The year was well established, but they have "weakened" (*hu figɛhɛla*) it. They want me to be troubled.' She implied that she had safeguarded the year, but that the people themselves, by breaking rain taboos and by their evil works and witchcraft, had undermined that safeguard. When the councillors continued pleading, she relented and said, 'Find me a black sheep without blemish [colour].' The first messenger they sent returned without success, but two others were dispatched to scour the country and on the seventeenth one was found. Kheshidwa, the rain-doctor, was now called. Four days passed, but he did not come. Then the queen, angry at the delay, suggested that she should proceed with the ceremony alone. But this the councillors would not hear of; 'You might deviate from the procedure the bones indicate to be essential,' they said. On the fifth day, however, Kheshidwa arrived, explaining his delay as due to the number of medicines he had to find, and at dawn on February 23rd the ceremony took place.

A calabash containing *mufugo* was placed in a basket for the chief wife of the queen's brother to carry, and a procession of most of the inmates of the royal village set out with the sheep. They stopped first at a clump of trees near the village, where lies Moyavudupi, a female relative by marriage to the queen on the mother's brother's side. When the queen ordered her chief councillor, as direct representative of the mother's brother's side, to begin, he uncorked the calabash and poured some of its contents over the grave, saying, 'Stop for us these winds and tribulations, that it may rain nicely. They say it is you people whose murmurings are impeding the rain.' His younger sister next took the calabash, praying in almost identical words, followed by the queen herself, who said, 'Aye, we say, stop for us all these *pukudi* [winds from wrong burials] that rain may fall and people find corn.' The people now respectfully greeted (*hu lɔsha*), repeating the praise of Muhale, the king of old, and, during the trillings that followed, the rain-doctor said, 'The frogs do not cry, sire. I do not hear them'; he may have meant that it was so dry that even the frogs were silent, but we do not know for certain.

The procession now proceeded to Maulwi, the sacred grove where are buried members of the royal family and the two last queens. At the grave of Mathɛkha, mother's brother to the queen and father of the chief councillor, they all sat down while the same procedure was gone through as at the other grave. When it was the queen's turn to pray, she took a small horn wrapped up in rags and placed it on the grave. Then, pouring from the calabash, she prayed, 'Do not continue to hold my arms; leave me to do my things, that rain may fall and people have corn. Tell one another, tell every single one, also the old woman [meaning Leakhali, her mother] and Mujaji, "huckster in the hut", who "casts away some and shares others with the vultures" [Mujaji I]. Do not continue leaving us to be burnt by the sun. As for our health, we are reasonably well; we are merely troubled by the poverty you have left us.' She poured out all the *mufugo*, turning the calabash upside down beside the horn, while the assembled company did obeisance and ululated. The sheep was slaughtered and skinned and small pieces, cut from various parts of the body, were placed in an earthen bowl while the doctor, sitting some distance away, began squeezing the stomach contents to separate the liquid from the more solid part. When he had finished, the chief councillor, his sister, and the queen placed the meat on the grave, telling the gods, 'We approach (*hu suma*) you with this sheep.' The solid stomach contents were placed on the grave, the assembled people greeted and trilled as before, the queen took away her little horn from the grave, and they all departed, carrying the sheep to an open spot some distance from the grave. Here they kindled a large fire and began cooking the meat in two large pots, one containing the internal organs (*mala*) and head, which, on this occasion, are not to be eaten by women of child-bearing age. Normally *mala* of a slaughtered animal are the portion *par excellence* of the women. While the meat was cooking, the doctor took a potsherd containing the 'water' of the stomach contents, his medicine bags and a stick of *khadi* creeper, and proceeded alone to the grave. It is surmised that he must have made a hole in the grave to pour down the water and medicine.

Meanwhile the clouds which had been in the sky at dawn had thickened and, while the pots were still cooking, rain fell and extinguished the fires, which had to be rekindled. The meat was eaten on the spot by all present and just before they all departed the bones were collected, wrapped in the skin, and placed on the grave. Prior to this, however, the doctor had spoken seriously to the councillors to approach the chief about the *pukudi* in the valley below, where a woman who had died in childbirth had been buried 'in the open' without *mufugo*. Ten days later the doctor was called to set the matter right.

This sacrifice is exceedingly rare, but it illustrates well the significant and usual intermingling of religious with what we should call purely magical rites. Thus, as the prayer is offered, it is rain medicine, which works by magic, not beer, the food of the gods, that is poured. The royal grave is treated, not to propitiate the gods, but to constrain them, to keep them cool, so that they will be unable to stop the rain. The sheep is an offering to the gods, a tangible indication that men still 'care for' their ancestors, but the use of the stomach contents on the grave falls into the magical pattern. Another point worth mentioning is that the queen was only one of several officiators: even her divinity does not give her precedence over the nearest living descendants in approaching the complaining spirits.

It has been shown that a great variety of steps can be taken to procure rain, their nature depending upon what is believed to be causing the drought. If the queen herself is thought responsible, and this is usually believed to be the case in the first instance, then her subjects will *lova* her with gifts or dances to excite her pity and to please her. If there have been wrong burials and rain taboos have been broken, these must be righted, while if the trouble comes from the ancestors, they must be placated. Sometimes one finds a combination of causes, but always it is the divining bones which decide what steps are to be taken. There are rain rites throughout the season, for not only may there be good rain in one area and not in another, but an inopportune period of drought in the best of seasons may have drastic effects on the crops. As an indication of the type of action taken in connexion with the rain cult in any one season, the following has been taken from our diary for the season 1937–8, by no means a very bad year, but one in which the rainfall was below the average:

1937	
November 12th	A rain-doctor sent to make rain at Mtimkulu's village, a petty Shangana-Ṭonga chief to the north, who had sent messengers to *lova* a few days before.
November 14th	A thunderstorm, with very little rain, but a very strong wind, broke in the afternoon.
November 15th	Holiday observed to 'turn back' the rain which has been scattered by the wind.
November 23rd	Rain fell with much lightning, which struck at Khiobeni, one of the districts.
November 25th	There was a thunderstorm in which lightning struck at Khidommamathɛka, a sub-area of the capital. The place was treated with medicine and in the evening soft rain fell, but not enough for ploughing.
December 2nd	Real set-in rain fell till the 3rd.
December 4th	Hoeing began.
December 8th	First termites brought, but given to dogs, as carried by girls above the age of puberty.
December 12th	First termites given to rain charms.
December 13th	Holiday.
1938	
January	Period of drought.
January 23rd	Mukupi, an important woman district head, came to speak to the queen, as there had been no rain for three weeks. The sun beat down fiercely and the crops were beginning to shrivel up.
	Several other district heads came to *lova* with money.
February 11th	People were consulting doctors about the drought. Bones declared a sacrifice necessary.
	Councillors approached queen and messenger sent for a black sheep.
February 17th	Kheshidwa, the rain-doctor, called.
February 19th	District head at Muduveni (several farms, but an old area of tribe) came with £1 10s. to *lova*.
March 1st–4th	*Legɔbathɛle* dance for rain by the Thɔvɔlɔ.
February 22nd	Sacrifice at Maulwi. Some rain fell, but not very much.
March 2nd	Kheshidwa called to put right a grave. This was done on the 4th.
March 7th	Levaga, a district head from the north, came to *lova* with £2.
April 2nd	Rain fell.

Some beliefs associated with the cultivation of *njugo* beans are relevant to our present subject. Among the Lovedu this crop is not planted until the mealies, among which it grows, are 1 ft. high, but this is regarded as a practical measure to prevent injury to the mealies rather than as dictated by the belief, firmly rooted and still put into practice by tribes to the south and south-east of Uulovedu, that *njugo* beans planted too early impede the rain. Only some Lovedu have this belief and no one, as far as we know, acts upon it; nor do the Lovedu pull up the young plants when there is no rain, which the Phalavorwa do, as one Lovedu suggested, because the beans look like hailstones. The Lovedu also say, but again as if it were a foreign conception, that no *njugo* beans should be planted during the year following the death of a chief. The association of rain and *njugo* beans seem to belong to a culture complex coming from the south.

The insistence nowadays is upon studying culture change as if it were a phenomenon important only in its relation to European contacts, but there has always been and there still is culture change of a different and, as far as the Lovedu are concerned, more vital nature. Even in the rain cult there have been changes. In the reign of Mujaji II, when the father of Kheshidwa succeeded Ramafalo as rain-maker, he instituted *hu runa*, a new ceremony of medicating all hoes with *mufugo* before the hoeing of the queen's field of eleusine, a practice which has fallen into disuse with the recent abandonment of the queen's hillside field for one in the valley which can be ploughed. The breaking of taboos is not necessarily a reflection of the breakdown and decay of custom. Indeed, the technique of the rain cult was based on the assumption that taboos were broken. Breaches account for drought and the countervailing efficacy of the queen's measures explains her reputation and the confidence people have in her. Wrong burials are known to prevent rain, but, since people try to avoid the unpleasant publicity involved in getting *mufugo* for the burial of, say, an abortion or in burying it in a wet place, these wrong burials are always taking place.

Neither European contact nor Christianity has succeeded in breaking down the implicit belief of every member of the tribe in the power of the queen to make rain. True, no Christians take part in ceremonies for rain and some do not believe that such things as wrong burials affect rainfall; but they harmonize the new with the old faith by the rationalization that the queen makes rain with the help of God, for they have all seen and can cite corroborative evidence for the powers of the queen. That the queen herself is honest and genuinely believes not only in her own powers, but also in the outside influences that prevent her from achieving success, can be seen in the reply she gave to the messengers who came on February 19th, 1938, with £1 10s. from a one-time district head in her kingdom to beg for rain. 'Go,' she said, 'and tell the master of Muduveni that we are trying, but things will just not come right' (arrangements were being made for a sacrifice to the ancestors for rain). The money, however, was kept.

CHAPTER XVI

TRIBAL TRAITS AND ATTITUDES

Harmonizing the bases of social security with outlets for personal expression—the role of beer—moderation as an ideal and in the spheres of sex and authority—preoccupation with the quest for health—attitudinal reaction to the Western world.

WE have drawn a rough outline of Lovedu culture and have lightly sketched in some of the forms of its institutions. From this has emerged the shape and structure of the society. The picture is, of course, incomplete, but we may perhaps give it tone by filling into the forms the shades of movement and motivation, and character by adding the colour of traits and attitudes. We have to undertake this task without the many forms which we have not sketched at all and, far more serious, without the wider background of surrounding cultures which would throw our picture into true perspective. To make good these omissions at this stage is impossible; all we can do is to orientate ourselves from a few familiar principles which will guide us in presenting our picture of the traits and interests of the Lovedu. These are the principles of man's wish for security, for achievement and for recreation.

Man must feel free to act without undue fear and uncertainty, and society must so order its arrangements that its members feel safeguarded against threats to their welfare; hence we in European society have our insurance systems which reduce the risks of our ventures, our legal sanctions which ensure the fulfilment of our expectations, and our conception of a righteous providence which consoles us in the face of a ruthless fate. Man's striving towards self-expression and recognition must also be satisfied, and society cannot neglect to demarcate spheres for, and to reward, individual achievement, though this is no simple matter because the opportunities that stimulate must be co-ordinated with the stability and security by which men may calculate the probability of the success of their ventures. Man also craves for recreation, adventure, and change from the monotony of those activities that are necessary to keep body and soul together; and here again the avenues that society provides must be integrated with the requirements of security and self-expression. Each society handles and co-ordinates these themes in a different manner; in one society, for instance, achievement is defined in terms of wealth or of ousting a rival; in another, in terms of wisdom or co-operation with others. The manner in which any particular society defines or handles these themes determines the interests, aims, values, and attitudes of its members; and it is from this point of view that we shall attempt to portray the Lovedu.

Lovedu culture is diversified: it is not like a man motivated by a one-track mind, or a fanatic obsessed by a single overpowering mania. But among its many interests, agriculture takes the first place. More time and energy are given to agricultural than to any other activities; no competing interest will move man to neglect ploughing and reaping, and no other way of life can oust it from its general pre-eminent position. The man or woman who is in need of a pot or other article in the busy agricultural season vainly places an order with a craftsman, and 'He who takes a journey in spring must transact all his affairs' (i.e. not only where he goes, but also on the way), for he will not be able to pass by again during that season.

Agriculture provides the immediate security of the people, but in turn it relies upon the life-giving rain, the power to make which has been projected upon the queen. The queen is thus the foundation stone of the security of the cultural structure. Her rain-making powers safeguard not only agriculture against the caprices of nature, but the whole country against the attacks of its enemies. The queen is more than that: the method of supplicating for rain has merged with the mechanisms of the social structure and has constructed the bonds with the districts, thus, despite political decentralization, securing the unity of the tribe. And, finally, the elevation of a woman to this exalted position has strengthened the status of women and their important role in the society and has emphasized the virtue of feminine qualities. But the queen is not conceived to be intimately linked with everything in the culture: her position in the *khɔrɔ* of the men is weakly institutionalized, she has no immediate contact with the European administration to the interferences of which her powers are doubly vulnerable, and the welfare of the cattle elsewhere, as among the Maḓala and Xananwa, ritually brought into relation with the chief, is outside her province.

As rain-maker, the queen controls half the great cosmic forces. Magic may be invoked, the gods propitiated, in the interests and for the ends of individuals, but ultimately these interests and ends and the destiny of the society depend upon the mediation and will of the queen. Man's sense of security in the face of personal misfortunes can be re-established by magic or religion, but the orderliness of cosmic laws is guaranteed only by the relationship of the queen with the supernatural. These laws are inscrutable, but the procedures for arousing pity in the heart of a human queen or for appeasing her anger are intelligible; and thus man can have confidence in undertaking his tasks. Moreover, he need not and must not resort to magic in his major economic activities, for he can and must rely upon the queen. Since the final justification of the pivotal position of the queen is her divinity, garden magic is conceived to be disruptive, like witchcraft: it competes with the power of the queen. One consequence of this conception is that success or failure in subsistence activities is regarded as immediately dependent upon industry, the application of practical knowledge and suitable materials, and that he who uses garden magic is a thief or a witch.

In most neighbouring tribes there is some public treatment of the seeds before they are sown, or the hoes and ploughs are smeared with medicine obtained from the chief: among highveld Sotho such as the Xananwa and Moletshe, there is even a special hut for storing the sacred seed, a few grains of which are handed to each householder at sowing time, and in this hut, which is associated with the *gɔma* drums and with fertility in man, girls reaching puberty are isolated and newly married couples sleep for the first few nights. Among the Lovedu these practices have no counterpart. Given rain, what is necessary to make the crops prosper is work and good soil, not medicine, and as a result one receives the impression of a practical attitude, not only to agriculture, but, by extension, also to most economic activities. But success both in hunting and in pastoral activities to some extent depends upon the use of magic, although by comparison with the Nguni and Tswana the cattle cult is very much attenuated.

Thrift and industry are regarded as virtues. It is the hard-working bride who is sought after, while the most eligible bridegrooms are the *dibuḍu*, those who by industry have filled their grain pits. But what is valued is not just work; it is work to attain self-sufficiency, that will make one independent, rather than work which places one in a subservient position. Even, as they phrase it, 'In work for the chief, it is only the fool who kills himself'. Hard work must not be thought of in terms of our conceptions, for the outlook of the Lovedu is far less dominated by intensive striving and deep concentration and more by care-free, easy-going standards than ours. Work has dignity, for the maxim, 'It is not the gift-pumpkin [but the produce of one's own garden] that is juicy', is meant, not to deprecate the gift, but to foster pride in the products of one's labour; it is a tenet appropriately urged when the clothes which a youth displays have been acquired, not by his own efforts, but as a present from his parents. Work is accorded recognition: the child who begins herding is said also to begin to deserve the food he gets. Work excuses failures and losses, for as they say, 'The one who loses cattle is the one who herds them', or, more generally, 'The one who breaks is the one who works'. On the other hand, there is scorn of indolence in the proverb, 'The sluggard has no locusts even if they sleep in his courtyard', and a warning in 'He who sits with staring eye-balls [idly] will die, but he who scratches for food [cultivates assiduously] will live'. Considering the craving for beer, it is almost heroic for a man, when refused this elixir of life, to console himself with the thought that 'He who stints me is he who helps me' [because I shall better be able to attend to my work]. But the work that is honoured and considered most congenial is work in situations in which, as in the work party, the reciprocities are fundamental.

The weakness of the queen as a woman is also her strength and the source of the prestige of the tribe. Her foreign policy is appeasement, not war; for, as they phrase it, 'The queen does not fight'. Reciprocity is the basis of her relations with her district heads, reconciliation the method of settling difficulties. Appeasement, one of the great values in the society, harmonizes with, supports, and is in turn supported by the reliance of the whole social structure upon compromise. This value and the traits corresponding to it interpenetrate every aspect of culture and of life. The hard régime of the initiation 'school' has been softened: there is no need to direct its procedures towards hardening the youth or instilling manly courage, and military discipline and regimentation are of little or no importance. Diplomacy works hand in hand with the methods of the *khɔrɔ* and of reconciliation (*hu khumɛlwa*), but it also strengthens the tendency towards cunning and duplicity (which safeguard the secrecy of the rain charms) and has given rise to the impression among Europeans that the Lovedu are cowardly and deceitful, lacking the manly qualities of their neighbours, the Shangana-Tonga. Foolish valour is discredited, for 'It is at the home of the coward that the porridge bowl is not thrown away': he lives to eat another day. The prestige of a queen as ruler also maintains the high status of women in a patrilineal society. Nowhere else are so many women heads of districts or in such important political positions. Women own cattle, have wives and may aspire to headship of large villages; and in the social system the main forces are oriented from the pivotal position of the cattle-linked sister. A wife or mother is queen of her establishment, as its old Khilovedu name, *mulago*, indicates: *hu laga* means to control like a leader, while *le lago* describes the excessive control of some overwatchful kraal heads.

Agriculture is not important as a field of achievement, for stores cannot be accumulated; immoderate success is suspect and a man cannot establish or alter his status by economic means. 'Yours is what you eat; what you set aside is another's', means both that expending energy upon accumulating goods is lack of balance and that the 'haves' cannot be ungenerous to the 'have-nots'. Nor is the royal complex of institutions, except in so far as it interpenetrates the social system, a field of achievement for ordinary men. It is the social system which, besides being one of the great pillars of security, provides the scheme in which man seeks self-expression and recognition. There are wide avenues of achievement for men, especially in the *khɔrɔ*, and women may aspire to influence within the *munywalo* complex and its 'houses'. There are other fields of achievement: men may find satisfaction in the circle of the huts of their wives, women in spirit possession, and both men and women may become doctors, district heads, craftsmen, or story-tellers, while the adventurous may seek expression in the fantasy of manipulating the forces of witchcraft.

But all these avenues are available only within the arrangements of the social structure, which on the whole are designed to eliminate competition and to reward co-operation. The activities of the *khɔrɔ*, in which men seek and display their highest self-expression, throw into bold relief the qualities and traits that are most esteemed in the society: mature wisdom, appeasement, reliance, not on force, but on agreement, and confidence in the effective operation of the long-run reciprocities of the social system. The task of the *khɔrɔ*, the most honourable and most arduous of all tasks, is successfully achieved only if the disputants can be guided towards reconciliation and acceptable compromises. Certainty—the idol of security set up by our aggressive society, the fetish worshipped by legalistic practitioners and the obsession impelling our courts to adjudicate upon conflicting rights according to strict law—is not a feature of the *khɔrɔ*. The *khɔrɔ* is oblivious of the fear that hard cases will make bad law, for it need not, as we do, steel itself against tenderness for the hardship of the unwitting offender, lest exceptions upset the certainty of the law and that elegant symmetry which, as we conceive, guarantees security. In the *khɔrɔ* the exigencies of personal adjustments may overrule the decrees of the law. In the setting of the *khɔrɔ* we thus see emphasis upon compromise and informality, faith in muddling through rather than in meticulous certainty, and reliance upon the pressure of the social reciprocities, not upon the sanctions of force. We may, in the context of European society, call them care-free standards, but that is to fail to see their place among the Lovedu.

These characteristics are faithful reflections of what one finds in the society and what is proper to the social structure as a whole. This structure provides the pattern of long-run reciprocities which, without the support of sanctions of force, ensures mutuality and co-operation. The reciprocities are motivated by inevitable necessity: 'The well-doer does well unto the well-doer; it is only his despoiler that the despoiler despoils'. Side by side with insistence upon give and take, the society provides in such a manner for the place and achievement of individuals that competitiveness is limited and aggressive traits are outlawed. The immediate goals of individuals are divergent, and men are not conceived as strenuously striving against one another for the attainment of the same end. Co-operation is essential to life and its tasks, for, says the proverb, 'One leg cannot dance a *gɔsha*'.

It is striking how the culture by re-interpretation prevents the struggle apparently inherent in the objective situation, such as when there are limited prizes or resources. The Reserve is overcrowded, the population presses hard upon the natural resources, and land is scarce; yet the people act as if the old abundance of land still prevails. They attribute ordinary shortages, not to scarcity of land, but to the indolence of the modern generation, thus rephrasing their difficulties in a manner which is congruous with social values, reduces the possibility of competition and permits of the resolution of the difficulties by human effort. And, generally speaking, economic resources and especially the *munywalo* cattle exchanges cannot be manipulated to acquire wealth or status or position. There is no special prestige attached to possessions and no socio-economic stratification of classes; for a great man, whether he be poor or rich, is first and foremost a royal relative, and the purpose of economic activities is self-sufficiency and independence. What particularly struck us was the absence of competition in craftsmanship: we have often seen one potter appraising the pots of another; we have always found it useless to urge expedition upon one worker by hinting that otherwise we would place our order with another; and it seemed to make little difference that the money was badly needed for tax purposes. Lucrative trade, calculation instead of mutuality in the work party, and display, both of possessions and of personality, are intensely disliked.

To the same pattern of values as non-competitiveness belong the disinclination to make comparisons and the aspiration towards equality with others. The role of these attitudes is not merely economic. The former reflects lack of interest in analysis as well as the absence of graduated yardsticks for comparing quantities and performances. Linguistic devices for expressing comparison—adjectives have no comparative or superlative forms—can hardly cope with our distinctions. It is very difficult to obtain any expression of opinion concerning the relative merits of things we quite naturally compare, such as objects of craftsmanship, achievements of individuals, or other elements of culture. They do not share our interest in analysing out parts of a culture complex in order to compare them, and they generally regard the complexes—for instance, two different types of dance—as wholes incommensurable with one another. Of course, they do compare things, but as regards economic goods they are chiefly concerned to be favoured equally with others. 'What are you stinting me of?' is a common phrase implying, 'Am I not, equally with others, entitled to share in your generosity?' A child, asking us for sweets, often says, 'Give me *also*', for he is begging for what others may receive, not a special advantage for himself. When favours are asked from the ancestors, the prayer is quite often phrased in such terms as 'Give us *also*' or 'Let us have health *like others*'. When a son had just been initiated as a doctor, his father prayed simply, 'Let him also be able to heal nicely,' and when a son was ill in town, the words, despite the competitiveness of town conditions, were 'We say, let him be "cool", Mother, and in his work let him be like others.' To stress, before the ancestors, a desire for personal achievement in competition with, or greater than that of, others is evidently improper.

Competition is not always eliminated. Doctors are not conceived to be rivals for a limited clientele, but they are said to 'try' one another: cultural definition diverts attention from the objective social situation of a limited number of customers, in which competition is discouraged, to the magical sphere, in which the fantasy of competitive strife is permitted. But the most striking arrangement that limits competition is the socially recognized, albeit not rigidly prescribed, hierarchy which defines men's status according to seniority or rank. 'Robes may be passed on [to strangers], never royal rank'; or, again, 'What becomes worn by age is clothes, not noble rank', because a nobleman can never lose caste or position. Younger brothers are taught to defer to their elder brothers, and in spite of displacements of district heads, it is hardly conceivable that commoners can oust royal relatives. Where the rivalry is fiercest, as among councillors at the capital, it is part of an institutional conflict and may not be openly displayed.

Dancing and music relieve the monotony of life, there is adventure in illegitimate sex relations and in the outlawed activity of witchcraft, but it is beer which provides the predominant recreation. Both beer and dancing belong to the co-operative, reciprocity pattern, whereas witchcraft is essentially competitive and anti-social. Unlike the Shangana-Tonga, the Lovedu dislike display in dancing, except in the esoteric dancing of initiation and the individualistic dancing of adherents of the alien cult of possession. Dancing, like beer, has other than recreational significance, and it is the manner in which beer has been integrated with diverse aspects of the culture that we may profitably consider.

Beer is the humanly satisfying element, even the justification of many actions; it is a recognized means of maintaining prestige and hence of achievement; and, as the medium of goodwill exchanges, it also subserves security. No occasion, whether social or ritual or religious or economic, is complete without beer. During some seasons of the year, people are in a perpetual state of exhilaration: some are singing or gossiping near the beer pots; some are expectantly watching their concoctions mature; and the rest are recovering from the last beer drink. Drunkenness is deprecated, but drink induces a state in which behaviour otherwise frowned upon is tolerantly regarded. Beer parties should be orderly, for they are occasions when some of the restraints of life may be relaxed and when jealousies and dissensions, normally under control, may rise to the surface. Though ostentation, even self-praise, is allowed in states of exhilaration, beer must be drunk with decorum; it should be lingered over, not bolted in haste.

A multitude of values centre round beer. It is a nourishing food, taking the place of meat feasts elsewhere; it is also the food of the gods. Beer is so great an attraction that it would be sheer lack of balance to keep one's appointments, to attend to other business, or to be worried by the passage of time if a beer party is imminent or in progress. A man's reputation for generosity depends upon his giving a beer party occasionally, although the entertainment is invariably in connexion with some definite purpose, economic, ritual, or religious. Beer is the medium of goodwill exchanges between relatives-in-law and between neighbours; and, as belonging to this context, the tributary beer from the districts to the queen is transformed from a burden to a pleasure. Beer is at the basis of the group of *valejana* (literally, those who eat together), composed largely of kin and neighbours who often co-operate in economic activities; this group cuts across the lines of the district and includes even such alien elements as Shangana-Tonga; and the main obligation of its members is to call fellow members to any beer that is available. Reconciliations are effected by beer, which also 'opens the way for the mother-in-law'. All the essential reciprocities are maintained by beer: a man returns a borrowed article with beer; a family doctor, instead of being paid for his services, expects to be called to the family beer; and in the work party beer removes labour from the category of subservience to that of mutuality. With beer one thanks, but with money one pays.

None of the interests that we have considered are intensive, and none of the striving, whether for security, achievement, or recreation, is concentrated. The diverse ideals and achievements that are permitted in social arrangements enrich personality and encourage the qualities of balance and wisdom; and the insistence upon a reciprocity which is not motivated by distrust, conditions mutual helpfulness and suppresses aggressiveness and display. An important clue to Lovedu *Weltanschauung* is their attitude to what may be considered to be ultimate power, the power through which the final goals of life and security can be attained. Such power is sought, not in privations, tortures, visions, and self-oblivion, but in normality, equanimity and maturity; it is derived, not from breaking the ordinary bounds of experience to escape to another world and from transcending the limits of the senses, but from manipulating mundane forces and from identification with nature. The Lovedu do not compel cosmic laws by the power of ecstatic states or trances; they bend these laws to their purposes by supplicating the queen and

XV. BEER AS A SOCIAL STIMULANT
(a) BEER BEING CARRIED TO THE QUEEN
(b) A BEER PARTY

XVI. RELIGIOUS PRACTICES
(a) AT THE LILY SHRINE
(b) A TYPICAL LOUEDU SHRINE

moving her to pity and by 'cooling' the heat of the earth and the anger of the ancestors. Frenzy and excess are outlawed, moderation and balance are honoured. They have little conception of the Buddhistic Nirvana or annihilation of human existence, of the fanaticism and fatalism of the soldiers of Allah, or even of Western concentration and intensive striving. From the point of view of our values, the Lovedu are Laodicean, 'lukewarm, neither hot nor cold', happy-go-lucky. They are always saying that they will 'try', never that they must succeed. But there is nothing intensive about their striving. A man faced with a difficulty is always advised to 'persevere', but that does not imply our grim determination, being more like the leisurely manner in which they set about all their tasks.

This theme permeates every aspect of the culture. In the boys' circumcision the object is to break the child of his wildness and lack of balance, and the purpose is achieved, not by excessive tortures and privations, but by the mature guidance of the old men. Neither strength nor stoicism are much made of, and the virtues inculcated are balance and self-sufficiency. The Lovedu tolerate ostentation only on occasions appropriate to exhilaration, quite unlike even such nearly related tribes as the Maḍala and Phalavorwa, who have institutionalized boasting displays by those famed as hunters or warriors. In the field of the magico-religious, fastings and visions do not figure, except among the possessed and the smellers-out, the latter always foreigners, the former a recent introduction. Possession in its Lovedu context has been shorn of its paranoic elements, its exaggerated trances, and its inception in a mental cataclysm. Cataleptic seizures do not serve as inductions to the supernatural as among the Nguni, for fits are due to witchcraft, and, unlike the smeller-out, who is a Shangana-Ṭonga and works by insight and exaggerated procedures, the Lovedu doctor divines by his craft and acquires power by learning and experience. Prayer is not an emotional outpouring of the heart, but a communication as between man and man. Dissension in her country upsets, and anger in her heart inhibits, the power of the queen. Spells are not characterized by intensity or malevolence; they are often merely directions to the medicine to bring about justice or to restore the balance. Even at a death or burial, there must be no display of distress, no undue weeping; both the dying and the survivors resign themselves with a calmness that is the admiration of Europeans who know the Lovedu well. Too much weeping by a mother is believed to injure her next child; Mputa, now thirty years of age, was born a cripple, it is said, because his mother, Makwada, wept bitterly at the death of her first son. We have never seen weeping at a funeral, and the property of the deceased is not so contaminated that it has to be destroyed, though in the midst of the Lovedu the Shangana–Ṭonga phrase death as a terror situation, even pulling down the hut of the deceased and removing from his village. Suicide is an escape, intelligible enough when a man is insane or (in the old days) has been condemned to death as a witch; but otherwise it is attributed to witchcraft, not to frustration.

In the method by which the themes of both sex and authority are handled there is the same aversion from excess or ostentation. The Lovedu

U

are not sex-ridden; it is we who, by outlawing the impulses, which we subtly stimulate in our romantic ideals, our literature, music, and art in general, create for ourselves neuroses and psychoses, maladjustments and perversions. The Lovedu have no problems of sexual adjustment or compatibility: their attitude is a matter-of-fact one. Sex is handled with moderation: men are warned against the dangers of excessive promiscuity, they learn from their proverb that 'A woman's pubes may break up the family', but passion is not esteemed and sex techniques are wholly undeveloped. In ritual, sex is symbolized to some extent, but only as an aspect of fertility, not as a sensual pleasure, while obscenity is inconspicuous and must sometimes be rationalized, as if it were questionable even under the auspices of the ritual. The fertility theme is itself pushed far back, so that it is unrecognizable in the symbolic background.

The Lovedu are innocent of Lesbian practices. They are also revolted by what they believe the Shangana-Ṯonga in their midst tolerate—namely, the marriage of immature girls to old men, who they say sometimes manually enlarge the vagina of these girls; and they regard as disgusting that extreme measure of Shangana-Ṯonga women, who in impotent rage against a man may display their genitalia. Yet the Lovedu are not unsexed; modern conditions are making nubile girls breast-conscious, so that they are beginning to wear attenuated bodices; young men admit to being aroused by the sight of the inner, smooth surfaces of women's thighs; and significantly the common word for the female sexual organs is *vadimoni* (place of the gods) or, among old women, *khitugulɔ* (a charm or object made sacred by association with the gods), and for the penis, *baḓa ya mutse* (staff of the village). In the one case of exhibitionism we saw tried before the *khɔrɔ*, the culprit, a man, was dealt with tolerantly as if he were an irresponsible madman; masturbation among children is looked upon as 'playing with' the sexual organs, and among boys it is indulged in less for its sexual satisfaction than to prove to their mates that they have reached maturity. The Lovedu do not suffer from guilt complexes because sex is not a temptation to be resisted by painful effort of will.

Again, within the family there is little of that assertion of authority that among us leads to the development of an Oedipus complex. One finds neither stern paternal authority nor fierce resentments and compensatory day-dreaming among children. In the *khɔrɔ* authority is distributed, in the work party dominance is resented. There are no institutions that foster the development of strong personalities. Recognition is not given to supermen, and there are no great heroes in Lovedu history. The precocious child is a potential witch and the authoritative councillor is liable to be regarded as intoxicated. One day the great councillor of the queen conducted the proceedings of the *khɔrɔ* in what appeared to us to be an expeditious manner, taking command of them, silencing irrelevancies, and crisply announcing his decisions. We could not help remarking upon the masterful exhibition, the order and efficiency, but our remarks caused great surprise and we were told that only a drunken man could have been guilty of the ignominious display. Modesty, not arrogance, and dignity, not assertion, are great virtues.

In the Lovedu configuration of values, moderation is allied to toleration of differences. The Lovedu do not attach much importance to precision and punctuality, rigid procedures and meticulous fulfilment of promises. Time is not valued and the word for slowness or absence of hurry is the same as that for goodness or moral virtue (*vuya*); the only way to ask a man to go slowly is to ask him to go in a good manner (*ga vuya*). Time is not the first consideration, for most actions can, within certain limits, be performed to-morrow as well as to-day. 'The far-off well causes thirst', they say, implying that one should drink [beer] where one can and not rigidly pursue some distant goal; the saying is an appraisal of opportunism as against inflexible purposes. Interest very rarely centres in exact forms, word-perfect formulas, or the precise execution of a rite. Prayers and spells are extempore, communications with the ancestors are often disturbed by gossip and intrusions, and consultation of a doctor about questions of life and death may be interrupted by all manner of irrelevancies. In the *khɔrɔ* the procedure does not rely upon set forms; there is toleration even of the differences of customs and laws in the districts; and great deviations from the norm are possible if people agree. An actual performance of a rite differs widely from the ideal description given by an informant. The important thing is always the broad pattern, the underlying spirit, not the exact form, the letter of the law; and magical power is hardly ever derived from a precise unfolding of a rite or adherence to meticulous details. The most highly formalized aspect of the culture is the *digɔma* complex, where we seem to see the remnants of a highly ceremonious outlook upon life, which was characterized by secret societies, masked gods, and symbolic objects, and by esoteric mysteries enmeshed in fixed forms and calendric observances. The obscure symbolism of the drum cult is inscrutable, but its dramatic interest keeps it alive, even if the power of its mysteries and mummeries appears to challenge the prerogatives of the queen.

Toleration of variations is necessary among the Lovedu to effect the incorporation and willing co-operation of so many divergent elements, especially in view of the fact that the ruling group has neither the means nor the inclination to impose its will by force; it is also implied in the autonomy of the districts and necessitates the elaboration of the links which overcome the weaknesses of decentralization. Variability adds to the scope of individual expression, permitting of the realization of very different temperaments and avoiding the dangers of repression. This is so because individuality will have, within the limits of the pattern, great play, not only in specific situations, such as rites and ceremonies in which the forms are not rigid, the roles of persons not fixed, and the precedences and procedures not invariable, but also in whole societies in which wide expanses of culture are not externalized in conventions or ceremonial. This is true of specific Lovedu rites, ceremonies, and institutions, as well as of Lovedu culture as a whole. Another aspect of the idea that man has many potentialities and many ways of realizing them is expressed in the saying, 'Man is an elephant; he does not eat one [kind of] plant only'—that is, he should try many things.

The socially stressed Lovedu values and the social arrangements are, of course, not congenial to every one, and frustrations occur; but the society provides for procedures whereby serious frustration is minimized. Thus the loss to one family of a murdered man is solaced by replacing him from the family of the murderer and building up permanent marriage and *munywalo* links between the two families. Tolerance of variations harmonizes with the insistence upon compromises, and in the setting of the culture it does not create serious problems of instability and insecurity. Security is provided by the integration and coherence of the dominant motivations and interests, the long-run reciprocities of the social system, and the unshakable confidence in the powers of the queen. At the same time the predictability necessary for stability is of a different order from that of our social arrangements; and it is measured very largely by the spirit and the willingness and attitude of people.

Conformity is not secured by external sanctions of force and only to a remarkably small degree by the ancestors. Nor are people so delicately conditioned to the values of the society that they spontaneously react to conscience. The internal sanctions are only moderately developed and there is no undue sensitiveness to shame or guilt, ridicule or abuse. An offender is not cast out; and a witch, generally speaking, is not ostracized. Over-sensitiveness to rebuffs, even in delicate situations such as when a man begs the favour of joining a beer drink, is deprecated, for, as they say, 'To chase a guinea-fowl [the beggar] is to cause it to go where it can scratch for food', so that it is foolish to feel crestfallen when the remedy is to pass on and seek beer where you will be well received. Nor should a man be sensitively timid or unnecessarily diffident: 'He who feels cold need not be shown the fire'; one may ask for favours and should not feel injured if refused; and there is no disgrace in begging for whatever one needs. Indeed, just as 'An ant bearing a burden cannot crawl under dry wood' (that is, things that will conceal him), so a man who has of the good things of life cannot hope to escape sharing with others who may legitimately beg some of them. Europeans often interpret these traits as obtuseness, shameless beggary, insensitiveness to high ideals, and even insolence.

The Lovedu are sensitive mainly to the intangible forces of the social system, and these forces are set into motion against a man when he disregards the reciprocities upon which the system relies. Since there are few repressed fears the pressure of which on the mind can be removed by confession and atonement, the sense of guilt seldom moves men; offenders very rarely repent merely at the dictate of conscience. The sense of shame is more delicately internalized, but it drives men to make restitution only when the misdeed has been exposed and brought into relation with the reciprocity system. The ego, in other words, is not highly vulnerable, for it is well-balanced, so that frustration of one purpose does not prostrate the individual, and there are many opportunities of escape from an antagonistic to a better disposed group or environment; as they phrase it, 'There is no madman but he has a friend'. Participation in the benefits of the culture depends upon not offending against the reciprocities; but the positive aspect, pride and self-realization in mutuality, is far more important than the negative aspect, fear of being deprived of the reciprocities.

It need hardly be said that the reciprocities are not precisely calculated equivalences, nor a series of exactly balanced obligations. People do not consciously think of the long-run result of their behaviour, and they know that social duty done is not always sure of its reward. 'Hard as the axe chops, it cannot eat the honey it extracts', they say to warn those who expect that their efforts will inevitably be rewarded.

The traits, motivations, and attitudes of the Lovedu become more and more intelligible in the context of the culture as a whole. Whether they are so delicately integrated that we can speak of the culture as an articulated whole, is not a question we shall try to answer. The tribal boundaries are certainly not the boundaries of the culture, which both in its forms and in its attitudes very gradually merges into the culture of a larger area, the limits of which cannot be exactly determined. In view of the increasingly great variations as one goes further and further from the nucleus, the degree of integration can be regarded relatively only to the area one chooses. Lack of integration is often more apparent than real. With regard both to recently introduced elements and to old elements which in their forms or purposes lag behind the changes of the whole culture, the process of integration is proceeding apace, but can never be complete. Thus the cult of possession is shedding those elements that are incongruous with the culture. There are also apparent inconsistencies in the divergent forms allowed in the districts and in principles of behaviour which are contradictory. Thus, for instance, revenge is permitted in the magico-witchcraft sphere, but is outlawed in the legal sphere. We may compare this contradiction to our approval of killing an enemy in war, which is conceived to be in the interests of national security, and our condemnation of killing a fellow man in peace, which is a crime against the security of life. Cultures often segregate contradictory aspects of social experience into logic-tight compartments, and there is no conflict as long as the contradictions can either be kept distinct or be reconciled. If they are embodied in the cultural system, no pressure is brought to compare them, and there is no lack of integration either in the mind of the individual or in the culture.

Men feel insecure chiefly in the face of disease and death, dissension, drought, and the disruptive danger of European intervention. The Lovedu attribute their fears to witchcraft, aggressiveness and quarrelsomeness, wrong burials, and the 'spoiling' of the country by the white man. We shall deal briefly only with two of these sources of insecurity: disease, which is one of the most constant preoccupations of the Lovedu mind, and the European, whose meddling has changed the shape and meaning of life and has upset the standards of right and wrong.

There is abundant reason for the perpetual anxiety about health, for disease is rife and even minor illnesses provide the occasion for the entry of the witch. Read against the background of their imperfect knowledge of anatomy and of the causation of disease, experience warns men that almost anything, from a simple scratch to the dreaded 'coughing disease', may cause death; in every case, not germs and poisons, but witches and sorcerers, may enter the body and take advantage of the weakness of the patient. Disease is combated, and susceptibility to disease is guarded against, at every step in a man's life. The infant is saturated with medicine: he is made to grow by means of medicine, he is steamed and strengthened, and every upset of the stomach, every sign of disorder, every major change in his life is treated as if it were a grave danger. The child is often inoculated against the 'poisoned shaft', the 'last, fatal arrow' that a malicious enemy might 'hurl' at him. Medicines by anticipation protect those who after their initiation ceremony might be weakened (*hu khuma*) when they resume contact with the world. Even adults in perfect health periodically consult their doctors to discover whether, unknown to them, some one is not planning an attack upon them.

To a European nothing is more amazing than the number of medicines that are tried, rejected, and changed when a man is or supposes that he is ill, unless indeed it is the contradiction that is implied in their preoccupation with their ailments as contrasted with their care-free attitude to life. The Lovedu are always telling of their illnesses, yet they seem to worry as little about them as the Englishman about the weather, although he can hardly converse without complaining about it. It must, therefore, not be imagined that life is weighed down by this interest in ailments; the Lovedu are seldom really depressed. They do not feel at the mercy of a capricious power, for their safety is ultimately in strong hands. They can use medicine to combat witchcraft and, though death is inevitable, their faith in the superiority of the good forces that they can invoke to control evil remains unshaken; for death is only the occasional triumph of evil, which time and again throughout life is defeated by the power of medicine. The outlook which supports security presupposes an ordered universe in which witchcraft is not merely outlawed, but can be overcome by employing well-recognized techniques.

In the face of the danger of the European, the position is entirely different. The white man is conceived to be part of a world which is antagonistic and incomprehensible; its forces are both disruptive, striking at the very significance of life, and capricious, not amenable to control by any known magical techniques. The projection of the danger upon the supernatural is but one aspect of a far wider conflict between European and Native, conqueror and conquered, perpetuated by divergent outlooks and different cultural configurations.

The conflict is an exceedingly complicated one. There is, firstly, the threat to the security of the Lovedu tribe, a threat that strikes particularly at the position of the queen and at the effectiveness of social mechanisms, causing criminals to multiply, encouraging disrespect for parents and for elders, and weakening the force of the reciprocities. Secondly, in the wider contact of Europeans and Natives attitudes have become vitiated by the antipathies that develop between the group of fellow men and the aliens outside it. The loyalties and trust between those within the group become transformed into hatred and suspicion towards those outside it; in the one case the human capacity for self-sacrifice, in the other case the capacity for selfishness, comes into play. Where the whole value system of the one group clashes with that of the other, antipathies are intensified. Moreover, the differences between the groups coincide with pronounced biological distinctions, such as colour, and with intense economic competition leading to poor-whiteism, and, as a result, an all-comprehensive theory of innate racial differences becomes a necessary philosophy to the European, while, to the Native, treachery and cunning towards the European become the ethical ideal and anything that he can get away with is thought to be legitimate.

These extremes are not always found, but even where a situation, such as that between farmer and labourer, is not vitiated by a sense of insecurity or the traditional antipathies, it may still give rise to misunderstandings. This is so because the Native is not trained in or conditioned to the European standards of concentration, industry, devotion to a single end, precision, and attention to detail, nor to the European conception of responsiveness to conscience. Many forms of Lovedu self-expression ill fit the contact situation, and often their behaviour is resented as the insolence of an inferior. Europeans may escape the feeling that they are treating the Native inhumanly by devising a theory of racial inferiority; the Natives, often accepting the reality, ascribe their status and misfortunes to the evil motives and systematic persecution of the European. It will not be possible to elaborate this theme, but a few of its aspects may be touched upon.

The vulnerability of the powers of the queen to European interference is one of the reasons for the all-pervading attitude of secrecy towards white men. There is a certain amount of untruthfulness and evasion towards fellow tribesmen: children are warned never to divulge the happenings in their homes or the possessions of their parents. But, as regards the European, deliberate lying is a positive virtue, for the inscrutability of the queen's powers is the essence of their preservation and of men's faith in them and in the queen, and secrecy is the only effective weapon against the European. Since disclosures to Europeans, even of the most commonplace activities or customs, might have unforeseen consequences, threatening the society, secrecy and its concomitants, hypocrisy and duplicity, have become ends in themselves. In our experience, despite our efforts to help people (which they often shamelessly exploited) and to justify the value to the tribe of our work (which made us only more distrusted), threats were often made against those who were our close associates and suspicion rested even on those whom we casually visited, unless, indeed, they could give an assurance that they had deceived us. At last, after incorporating ourselves as *khadi* (father's sister), foster father, and co-wife in various families, we became accepted, made some close friends, and overcame some of the suspicion. But, generally speaking, the good man is he who can circumvent the European and, conversely sometimes, the comprehensible European is he who has cheated the Native. In this context, it is not surprising that the European has an unflattering opinion of the Lovedu. And it is also intelligible that, to an essentially generous and easy-going people and in informal situations, the burden of secrecy imposes too great a strain and from time to time breaks down under cover of privileged confidences and the relaxation of drunkenness, or upon a sudden compulsive frankness. But in formal situations, such as in European courts, the Lovedu rely upon falsehood, and they believe that any lie is good enough to deceive a European.

Legal relations with Europeans have been tragically misrepresented, for the procedures and sanctions of the European legal drama are not very intelligible. The villains of the piece are the solicitors, who, in their eyes, plot to put an end to reciprocal obligations, and safeguard criminals. These villains appear to be the main actors on the stage, and their victims, baffled by the awesomeness and incomprehensibility of the situation, see the solicitors in the role of conspirators laying schemes behind the scenes, where corruption arbitrarily decides the fate of the victims, or of impostors displaying deceitfully purchased loquacity before the footlights. They see the victim at the mercy of forces that inspire a dread not unlike the dread of being assailed by witchcraft, with this difference—that against witchcraft the sense of security can be regained by invoking magic, while nothing will avail against the awful incomprehensibility of European justice.

The purpose of the whole drama is inscrutable. Should the dock prove to be a trap to the innocent victim, all he can do is to resign himself to the inevitable. Should the offender be acquitted or inadequately punished, he becomes the luckless victim of a new tragedy; his enemies in the society by *hu niɛlɛla* magically render him subject to an obsessive compulsion to relapse into crime, so that he may once more re-enact his part as victim in the court and so eventually expiate his original offence. Not only recidivism, but also imbecility, may be the result, for the victim 'will remain laughing at the passing flies'. *Hu niɛlɛla* is some kind of answer to the feeling of insecurity before European law, but it is a very inadequate answer: it is not much invoked, it cannot prevent the multiplication of criminals and the growing aggressiveness of witches who escape the clutches of European justice, and it tries to reinstate confidence by relying upon a recidivism which undermines security. To the European, the Native offender is a difficult problem. He will not confide his defence and he wastes time with rambling statements; policemen regard him as insolent and as having gangster proclivities; and the only way to deal with him, it is thought, is by repressive regulations, pick-up vans, and punitive raids.

In the wide expanse of the employment situation there are other difficulties. The sanctions of the reciprocities of Lovedu society are lacking, and the appeal to these sentiments that the European values has little effect, except when the mutualities, the give and take, of Native society can be simulated and the group antipathy or negative identification can be converted into a measure of sympathy or positive identification. Historical factors, proximity, and many other considerations cause the degree of vicarious identification of the hostility with situations and localities to vary, and likewise the difficulties of overcoming the hostility vary. In a locality where, with the best intentions, farmers have ejected Lovedu squatters from their ancestral lands in order to re-employ them as wage-earners, the hostility is fierce and cannot be overcome in the first generation, whatever means are adopted. Of the Government, which they think is always deceiving them, they say, 'Sire of I-come-I-come, the child is already born and has begun to walk', to denote how readily promises are made to come and help, but how dilatory the fulfilment is; and as the result there is a profound distrust which vitiates relations. In the situation of a European-owned mission station, both because of the threat attributed to an iconoclastic creed and of the supposed capitalistic exploitation, the services and sacrifices of a missionary are liable to be rewarded with ingratitude and suspicion.

But however favourable the conditions, the difficulties must not be underestimated. It is the sensitive ego that is easily controlled; if a man cannot ordinarily be moved by an appeal to a sense of honour, conscience, or cupidity, moral pressure cannot easily be brought to bear upon him. Not only is the Lovedu ego not vulnerable, but the resort to kindness and the appeal to high motives are liable to be construed as cunning and an attempt to overreach. 'An ingratiating person', such as a European who comes with pleasant words, the Lovedu say, 'lacks not ulterior motive; if he lacks it, he is doomed' (for in any case he will be suspected). No wonder that the European so often believes that firmness and coercion are the only means of controlling the Native.

The different views held by the Lovedu and the European with regard to certainty and precision lead to many conflicts. The lack of Lovedu insistence upon these traits gives an appearance of irresponsibility and disregard of obligations against the background of European society; and the white man readily believes that Natives are innately like children and always need supervision. As employers, masters, and administrators, Europeans have, in the setting of a competitive, calculating society, no alternative but to stress punctuality and precise regulation; but they are wrong in supposing that the essence of every society must be its regulative aspect and that anarchy must follow if irregularities and disregard of rigid procedures are allowed. The meticulous fulfilment of obligations, upon which the Western commercial structure depends, is not necessary in the timeless Lovedu culture, with its reliance upon long-run reciprocities. The Lovedu would easily understand the parable in which the people who worked for an hour in the vineyard in the cool of the evening received as much reward as those who had toiled there all day long in the hot sun, for they have little patience with the dull, mechanical systems that measure merit, work, and time by a highly graduated yardstick. In the hierarchy of Lovedu interests and necessities, time and punctual fulfilment of promises are secondary; but this does not mean that in the setting of the culture people are irresponsible and unreliable.

The beer-drinking of Natives is the bugbear of the European employer; it is a real problem to the farmer. Even in the Reserve its social function is gradually giving way to its pathological one. There are many reasons for the change: the greater abundance of grain, the increasing monotony of life, the sense of frustration, and the recognition in the society that relief and excess may be displayed in states of exhilaration. Farmers legitimately complain of the demoralizing effect of beer. Beer can never be used in its full cultural context on the farms, and its prior claims to time and interest can never be harmonized with the requirements of labour service. The problem that is raised is apparently insoluble, for total prohibition of beer leads to the surreptitious drinking of injurious, rapidly maturing concoctions, to a sense of grievance on the part of the Native, to his increased hostility to greater police activities, to evasions of and disrespect towards the law, and to irritation and loss of time by the farmer in prosecuting offenders. In the contact situation, the food becomes a drug and the vehicle of social intercommunication becomes the means of dipsomaniacal escape.

Similarly, it would be possible to show the inevitability of other attitudes of European and Lovedu to one another; but here as elsewhere in this book we must frankly admit that volumes will have to be written before the situation has been fully described. The opinions of the Lovedu held by Europeans are, however, not based upon unrealities. It is true that the Lovedu in the contact situation are liable to be indolent, irresponsible, unreliable, ungrateful, untruthful and irrational. Traders have reason to be exasperated by conduct and by the operation of motives which run counter to all their reasonable expectations. The farmer does not, without reasons which are very real to him, call them 'creatures' or regard them as drunkards who, incapacitated week-end after week-end, justify their existence by work in the intervals between bacchanalian feasts. Those who labour to elevate the 'barbarian', to give him the blessings of a new culture or religion, or to promote his material advancement do in fact find their sacrifices rewarded with ingratitude and advantage taken of their labour of love. These Europeans, as well as the Native, are the victims, sometimes of their personal prejudices, but more often of the whole background of the contact situation. Yet the Lovedu proverb, 'A person is a person; it is a stump that has no ears', encourages the hope that with skilful handling and sympathy the situation may be made to yield to reason.

The anthropologist, who ascribes the practical man's views solely to prejudice and ignorance and, worse still, to inaccurate observation, not only uselessly antagonizes those in closest contact with the Native, thus rendering a disservice to better relations and co-operation, but also brings discredit upon his field methods and science and condemns them to ineptitude and distrust. Judgements upon motives and attitudes are always liable to grave error, for valuations are subjective and the personality of the observer is as important as the behaviour he observes: two men, one frustrated and the other successful, may come to very different conclusions, though they observe the same behaviour. We must beware lest practical men, familiar with the Native, ascribe our judgements to our preconceptions, especially to a facile toleration of traits to which not we, the observers from without, but they, the employers and administrators, have themselves to adjust realistically. 'Wisdom', say the Lovedu, 'comes from the scar' [of experience]; and it is the practical man, not the anthropologist, who has suffered the wound. There is great need for co-operation and for resolving differences by open discussion, for, to quote another Lovedu saying, 'Quarrels have no hiding place'—that is to say, if people desire amicably to compose their differences.

CHAPTER XVII

CULTURE CONTACT AND CULTURE CHANGE

The relativistic approach: value of comparative and historical study—*interpenetration of the tribes*: ethnogenesis of the Lovedu and evolution of some of their cultural patterns—*the iconoclasm of Christianity*: breaking down and building up among converts, repercussions among pagans—*the challenge of Western conquest*: the indirect responses of the culture and its undisturbed foundations.

THE RELATIVISTIC APPROACH

FOR the past half-century Western conquest and civilization have been challenging Lovedu culture. For centuries before that various Bantu cultures had percolated into the Lovedu lowveld. As a result, there has been cultural change, not only in the past few years, but throughout all the ages. Change is inescapable, continuous, ever-present, and there is no evidence that in the European period it has been revolutionary, while in the pre-European period it was merely evolutionary. There is a distinction, but to present the contrast as that between disruptive change and gradual development is unwarranted. The greatest disturbances brought about by contact with Western culture cannot, in their effect upon institutions and cultural patterns, be compared with the major cultural evolution, not only of the Lovedu, but of many other tribes, within measurable periods of time.

The evidence of great changes afforded by an historical and comparative study of the tribes of the Northern Transvaal is overwhelming. Thus, for instance, the cultures of the Lovedu and of their kinsmen, the Mamavolo, have widely diverged since their separation from one another 250 years ago. The Mamavolo are like their immediate neighbours, the highveld Sotho, and unlike the Lovedu, not only in their handling of the major cultural complexes, such as the royal institutions, the 'schools', marriages, agricultural ritual, and village structure, but also in countless details of culture. They tolerate no female rulers, have given up ritual suicide of the chief, no longer appeal to the rite of the door to determine succession to the throne, and neither accept wives as tribute nor redistribute them in order to link up the political system. In minor details, such as their material culture and methods of threshing, and the absence among the Mamavolo of *thugula* (dedicated) cattle and of the practice of elongating the *labia minora*, their differences from the Lovedu are equally striking. The total impression of their culture and of their methods of expressing hostility to the European differs so greatly from that of the Lovedu that it is difficult to credit the common ancestry of these two tribes. Yet the evidence of history and of remembered, but no longer practised, custom is decisive.

Moreover, misgivings soon disappear in the light of further historical and comparative investigation. The Shai, immigrants since *c.* 1790 into the lowveld from amid Pedi and Transvaal Ndebele in the south, resemble the Lovedu far more closely than do their kinsmen, the Mamavolo. The

Sekhɔpɔ, splitting off from the Loʋedu royal group (c. 1800) and subjected to Pedi-highveld-Sotho influences, though only twenty miles from Ʋuloʋedu, are less like their present-day Loʋedu royal relatives than are the Tswale. But the Tswale are foreigners, tracing descent from the Venda royal house of Thɔhɔ-ya-Ndou; they entered the Loʋedu sphere of influence (c. 1730), and they lost close touch with the main body of the Venda (c. 1840). In language and almost all major aspects of culture the Tswale have been Loʋeduized. They have not adopted the specialized Loʋedu royal complex of institutions, but equally they have lost their characteristically Venda elements. Thus, of Venda elements, they have given up the *dɔmbɔ* and *thɔndɔ* 'schools' and the attribution of extensive powers to a high god; even the peculiar Venda disposition of forces and persons in the political organization is little more than a memory; and differences in detail from the Loʋedu, such as peeling the skin off a goat's tail before killing it ritually, which is a royal Venda feature, are no greater than the differences found between one district and another in Ʋuloʋedu itself. These are not isolated instances of divergent cultural evolution in response to divergent environments and contacts. Dozens of examples emerge from an historical and comparative investigation of the Northern Transvaal alone.

In the whole of our field investigation, nothing has been more fruitful and stimulating than our visits to twenty-six Northern Transvaal tribes. There can be no doubt that, had there been time to study ten times that number of tribes over a much wider area, the value and suggestiveness of the comparative and historical background would have been correspondingly enhanced, against which the direction, nature, and magnitude of cultural changes might be evaluated. There arise problems of method, even of the legitimacy of making inferences from one tribe to another. We shall not deal with them here except to say that breadth and depth of observation and fertility of interpretation largely depend upon the range of one's knowledge and experience. If inferences from variations within the tribe are legitimate—nay, absolutely necessary —for the most elementary presentation or generalization, by the same reasoning they must be legitimate across the boundaries of tribes. Culture elements, culture patterns, and the major cultural configurations do not stop short upon the borders of districts, nor of tribes, nor even of culture areas.

Comparative study has enabled us to see in actual being the diffusion of culture elements across the boundaries of districts, tribes, and culture areas. The different handling by different cultures of the same cultural material, according to the needs of their environment or the genius or emphases of their patterns, can be observed and its results established without any doubt by comparative investigation. Once it can be determined that the raw cultural material is the same, deductions from variations in forms and functions or in purposes and goals are far from being illegitimate, but illuminate the distinctive trends of the cultures in which they occur. Inferences from incommensurable variations are illegitimate; but the wider the range of comparison and the more intensive the functional investigation, the easier it is to eliminate this error and the more precisely can be estimated, not only the nature, direction, and magnitude of change, but also the relation of the change to the forms and purposes of the culture in which it is found.

Comparative study, as a technique of interpreting culture and its evolution, must go hand in hand with historical investigation. Both the past that survives in the memory of the carriers of the culture and the present are functionally important. They give us some of the clues to the psychological forces that cause or resist change and they provide data upon the nature of institutional evolution. But man is more than his memory and the living past is far more than the remembered past. So much is self-evident to a carrier of the culture that it will never be mentioned by an informant and will wholly escape the investigator's attention unless, with the aid of sustained comparative and historical study, he discovers the key that unlocks the memory and opens the way to the socially unconscious, that system of codes and standards which, without being conscious, condition experience and behaviour and are themselves conditioned by the social, psychological determinants of the past. Historical study is important for understanding the attitudes and reactions of the present, for estimating the evolution of forms and institutions, and for evaluating the relation to and reaction upon one another, not only of attitudes and forms, but also of the psychology of the people and the material content of the culture.

Culture change, according to this approach, must be investigated and interpreted, not merely functionally, but also relatively to the past and to reactions in other tribes. The method may be called relativistic functionalism. It implies observation and interpretation, not merely of the forms and functions of institutions within tribes, but also of the differential process of incorporation or rejection, under different conditions and in different tribes, of new culture elements.

This is not the place to justify this approach or to examine its theoretical and practical implications. All we need say is that, among the Lovedu, exceptionally good material exists for applying this method. Various sections of the Lovedu, as well as of numerous other tribes, of diverse origin and culture, have been subjected to diverse cultural influences for different but determinable periods of time; and their interpenetration can be studied in relation to both time and space. Particularly instructive are the differential responses to such patterns as the Venda royal complex of institutions and the transformations and modifications impressed upon such cultural material as the 'schools'. Thus, for instance, the royal pattern of the Kwindɛ (Venda royal group) can be studied in a chain of tribes of Kwindɛ ancestry extending into Ʋulovedu, some of whom have been subjected to intimate and long continued, others to less intimate and shorter, Lovedu contact. But this royal pattern has also interpenetrated other cultures, imposing itself upon the heterogeneous peoples incorporated by the Kwindɛ, like Koni, Karanga, Nyai, and Laudi, and leaving diverse impressions upon politically independent tribes such as the Ḍokwa, Ʋirwa, Nareni, and Lovedu. The differential interpenetration, especially of the various branches of the Lovedu, enables us to arrive at important conclusions.

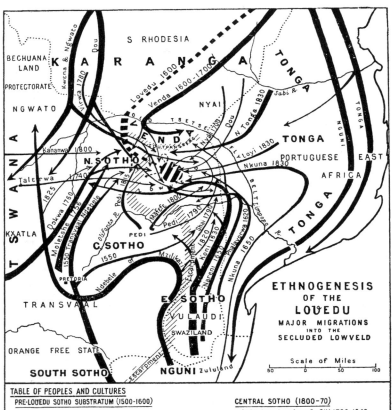

Oral traditions of the past, it is said, are unreliable and unverifiable. Accounts by informants about the present are also unreliable and often, unless one lives a lifetime in the society, unverifiable. Even the most elementary facts observed do not speak for themselves and have to be interpreted, and the verification of objective facts becomes a complicated process not unlike verification of historical material from such circumstantial evidence as is provided by comparative study. Certainly, in our experience, what was impressive was the substantial agreement among all the tribes upon the main events and migrations, which also provided useful clues to diffusions of culture in the past. The lack of discrimination as regards place and time and the dramatizations and justifications were difficulties which gradually disappeared as the background of comparison was enlarged. Even the discrepancies, seen against the total background, illuminated the local trends and motivations, and proved to be more apparent than real.

Most men of the Lovedu royal group to-day deny their Karanga ancestry, although ten years ago they admitted it. You will tap their memories in vain to discover either the truth or the reason for the change of attitude. But in the light of comparative investigation—for this phenomenon is not unique among the tribes—and of a study of reactions between 1926 and 1936, the change is intelligible. The suspicion that the releasing of land to the Native under the Land Act, in pursuance of a segregation policy, might be a device to dispossess the tribe engendered a profound disturbance to men's sense of security, which could be re-established only by affirming the title of immemorial occupation of Uulovedu. The method of relativistic functionalism ensures, not merely perspective, but also balanced and comprehensive interpretations.

INTERPENETRATION OF THE TRIBES

Lovedu culture as it is to-day is the result of a complicated historical process. For some indication of the genesis of the tribe and of its culture, the reader is referred to the accompanying map; we cannot discuss the evidence in this book.

More than 300 years ago there were tribes sparsely scattered over the whole of the Northern Transvaal. This area lay outside the main migratory currents: Nguni and Tonga coming down on the east, Sotho-Tswana circling the curve of the Limpopo on the west, and Karanga halting between these two to the north of the tsetse-fly belt along the Limpopo. The date of these migrations and their relation to one another is lost in oblivion, but trickles from these currents and backwater eddying from them, particularly from the Sotho-Tswana current, penetrated into the Lovedu lowveld. There were, however, Kwena and Ngwato who descended the escarpment in force only after arrival on the highveld of invaders from the east (Koni, *c.* 1700), the south or south-west (Dɔkwa, *c.* 1760, and Moletshe, *c.* 1750), and the north (Uirwa, *c.* 1780). Some of these Kwɛna and Ngwato form a chain of peoples, no longer independent, from the north, round the west and to the south of Uulovedu, into the political and cultural structure of which many have been incorporated.

In pre-Lovedu times there were also the famous *ḍou*, Elephants who are everywhere a dependent substratum, except for a small group, the Masoma, living among the Mahlo or Nareni of Segɔrɔrɔ. This cluster is very old, was interpenetrated with a culture evolved at the junction of Karanga and Sotho streams in the north-west near the home of the Uirwa, and scattered sparsely over the whole of the lowveld. Lovedu tradition asserts that the Lovedu, migrating southwards, found them on their way and incorporated them as messengers; and there is no doubt that at various periods many of them, owing to pressure elsewhere, settled in Uulovedu. There were other pre-Lovedu peoples in the lowveld, such as the Khiɔga, Ɗgɔna, Sɛja-Phala, mostly offshoots of mixed Sotho and Karanga, and a few so-called Transvaal Ndebele emanating from the far south.

Despite slight intrusions of Tonga, the ethnic and cultural composition of the pre-Lovedu lowveld was predominantly Sotho, considerably influenced, however, by the culture and peoples that had evolved on the borders of the Karanga. This pre-Lovedu culture, or people of Sotho-Tswana-Karanga we shall call the 'Sotho substratum'.

Into this geographically isolated area, penetrated only by small groups of people migrating under pressure, there came (*c.* 1600) the Lovedu royal group, descendants of Mambo, one of the sons of Monomotapa and chief of one of the provinces into which the empire of the Karanga had split up. Lovedu tradition as to the disruption of Monomotapa's kingdom is confirmed by Portuguese writers; it was the disintegration that enabled the Portuguese to extend their settlement inland as far as Sena (1609). There is much other evidence, but the relationship between the Karanga, Lozwi (two names used by the Lovedu in their praise songs), and Monomotapa (which some authorities say is a myth) is lamentably obscure. 'Judging from the customs, history and language', writes E. G. Howman,[1] 'these people [Vakaranga] were the tribe mentioned in all the Portuguese records of three hundred years ago as being the people of Monomotapa, though unfortunately no trace of this name can be found as surviving nowadays.' It is significant that in Lovedu tradition this name is known.

After the advent of the Lovedu, the history of the lowveld becomes more decipherable, for the tribes that rule to-day have more or less detailed traditions of their past which may be interrelated, while the peoples of the Sotho substratum either have no history or it is vague or starts somewhere in Lovedu times. Some of the histories are nothing short of amazing in their comprehensiveness. Muhlava, chief of the Nkuna, for instance, gave us a history covering a century during which the Nkuna were subjects of five different Sotho tribes, and every detail in it, whether of time-sequences or events or movements of people, was corroborated by the accounts given us in these tribes.

It is clear that in their early period the Lovedu for long remained undisturbed in their secluded environment. There were minor infiltrations, for there were movements of peoples on the far-off boundaries of the lowveld; but the first considerable body of people that came within

[1] *South African Journal of Science*, vol. xv, 384.

striking distance was the Venda. They crossed the Limpopo from the north in many successive waves, culminating in the arrival of the royal Kwindε group (c. 1700). The histories of Loυedu and Venda do not converge in Rhodesia, but both peoples had early contacts with Karanga, Lozwi, and Nyai and both have traditions of the Mambo. There is also the legend among the Venda of having conquered fireless aborigines with fire. But it is in the post-migratory period, and especially between c. 1750 and 1820, that contacts multiplied through trade, migrations, royal marriages, and the Venda practice of seeking their rain, not only from their high god Mwari at Mbvumεla in the Rhodesian Matopo Hills, but also from Mujaji, whom they sometimes call 'the wife who brings us water to wash our face'. When the kwεvo of Tswale and Moila, two Venda tribes, came to settle on the borders of Ʋuloυedu (c. 1730) a complex interpenetration started; they were Loυeduized, while the Mamaila section of the Loυedu, moving northwards, first became Vendaized, so that thirty or forty years ago the court language was still Venda, and subsequently, owing to historical factors, fell under influences from the south and south-west, and reverted to Khiloυedu and Loυedu-like cultural patterns.

The channel of inter-communication between Venda and Loυedu was so wide in c. 1780 that Mashau, a Venda chief, came personally to aid Mugɔdɔ to suppress the rebels in Ʋuloυedu; but it gradually narrowed from c. 1790 onwards, owing to the intrusion from the south-west and north-west of Ḍɔkwa and Ʋirwa respectively; and it was all but blocked since c. 1840 by the Shangana-Ṭonga invasion from the east. This invasion also drove southwards into Ʋuloυedu many Venda refugees, some of whom still speak Venda. Swelling the Venda or Venda-Karanga influences were the Nyai, whose northern manners and dress are still remembered, Ʋirwa, whose history appears to link them with the southern Zimbabwe at Mapungubwe, and the Thɔυɔlɔ. These Thɔυɔlɔ say they are from Ʋukhalaga, but it is clear that they had migrated southwards long ago and later became Sothoized to the east of Ʋuloυedu, mixing there with the Sotho substratum, especially the ubiquitous ḍou. About 1800 they fled before the Mafεfε invasion from the south and, settling in Ʋuloυedu, brought with them the cult of spirit possession

Great as has been the influx and influence of the Venda, it is eclipsed by that of the Laudi, a name under which we include the Phalaυorwa, Nareni (both Mahlo and Letswalo), and Koni. All of them, including large sections of the Venda, such as Mphaphuli, Lwamɔndɔ, and Masia, came either from Ʋulaudi or Phalaυorwa, in the south-east, near Swaziland. It is there that large bodies of the two original migrations of Sotho and Nguni from the far north converged upon and merged with one another. All Laudi tradition, even that of the Koni of Maḍala on the highveld, speaks of a settlement in Phalaυorwa (c. 1620–1720). The Phalaυorwa remained in the unfavourable environment between the Olifants and Letaba Rivers, some of them periodically breaking away from it and settling in Ʋuloυedu. The Nareni, having left Phalaυorwa, split into the Mahlo and the Letswalo, and the latter, scattering along the foothills of the Drakensberg, penetrated into Ʋuloυedu (c. 1750). At one

W

time, when Bodile ruled (1825-50), there was close contact between the Letswalo and the Lovedu, the chiefs of the two tribes exchanging rain medicines. The Koni also left Phalavorwa and eventually gave rise in the area we are considering to a great chain of tribes: the Khaha of Maake (c. 1730) and of Maupa (c. 1800), and the Koni of Maḍala (c. 1720) and Dikxale (c. 1830). By 1750 the Laudi had completely invested the Lovedu on the east, south, and south-west. Their influx into Uulovedu, the inviolable country of the Rain-Queen, greatly increased as the result of disturbances in the south and south-east, from 1820 to 1870. The turmoil was caused by Moselekatse's spoliation, ravages by fugitive cannibals, Pedi and Mafɛfɛ raids, Shangana-Tonga invasions, and Swazi depredations. The accretions to the Lovedu enhanced the great influence of the Laudi, predominantly an old Sotho people.

Between 1800 and 1870 many Central Sotho or Pedi scaled the Drakensberg and spread their culture first among the Laudi and through them into Uulovedu. The Mafɛfɛ, carriers of this culture, for long ruled several lowveld tribes; and the Shai, from amid a Pedi and Transvaal Ndebele environment, crossed the Olifants River and many settled in Uulovedu (c. 1840). But the main Central Sotho infiltrations, coming from the west, were greatly modified in passing through the sieve of highveld Sotho. Among them were the Kwɛna, already mentioned, and the Talɛrwa (c. 1740), but the Talɛrwa as well as other scattered bands from the high veld at first represented rather Northern Sotho influences; and only later, after considerable admixture from the west and south Tswana and Central Sotho elements began to predominate. The upper layer of highveld tribes, such as the Ḍɔkwa and Moletshe, originated from the west and south-west (Tswana). They have been very receptive to Pedi influences, since the Pedi themselves were overlorded by the Kxatla, who were, if not Tswana, close relatives of the Tswana. Thus during the ascendancy of the Pedi under Thulare (1800-24) and the Tɛvɛlɛ raids, when many highveld tribes fled to Pediland, Central Sotho culture penetrated deeply into the highveld. It was the Ḍɔkwa who carried this mixed Sotho culture farthest into the lowveld, but among the Lovedu the intrusion was regarded as a challenge to be resisted, and it has left a heritage of hatred and antagonism, which, though no justification continues to exist for it, is still alive to-day.

Numerically the greatest single invasion of the lowveld was that of the Shangana-Tonga. Some few Tonga, who came long before the nineteenth century, were assimilated without leaving any perceptible marks on Lovedu culture. During the nineteenth century successive waves of Shangana-Tonga fell upon the lowveld: refugees fleeing before Manukuza, leader of the Nguni from Zululand (c. 1836-40); groups escaping from the clash between Mawewɛ and Mzila, rival claimants to the throne after the death of Manukuza (Soshangane) (1856-70); and fugitives seeking safety after Ngungunyame's defeat by the Portuguese (1894). These are the unassimilable Shangana-Tonga, originating from all parts of Tongaland, and in the country of Mujaji segregating themselves in the valleys, while the Lovedu cling to the hills. They have an exceedingly complicated history, but it is sufficient to note that, though many of them have broken away from Lovedu overlordship since the beginning of the twentieth century, Ʋulovedu has been crowded and its borders surrounded by Shangana-Ṭonga.

It is manifestly impossible to examine in detail the nature and magnitude of the changes in Lovedu culture that may be attributed to the Sotho substratum, Venda, Laudi, Shangana-Ṭonga, and other tribes. We may, however, as an illustration, cursorily trace the evolution, under these influences, of the Lovedu royal complex of institutions. The germs of this complex come from the ancestors of the royal group. The Portuguese record that only a man without physical imperfections could become chief and that the Mambo handed his daughters to his bodyguard, who gave in return, not bride-price, but faithful service. According to Dos Santos,[1] writing in 1601, it was formerly the custom of the kings of Sofala to commit suicide by poisoning when any disaster fell upon them or they were disfigured by a physical defect, and, further, though it was incest outside the royal circle, kings married their own sisters or daughters. Even to-day there is evidence among some Shona of the rite of the door, of women rulers, and of celibate female rain-makers.

This is the nucleus around which the Lovedu have elaborated their royal institutions. Its primary elements did not come in the post-migratory period, for they are, except for the vaguest indications, absent among the Venda, who have always constituted the buffer between Lovedu and Karanga; and their presence among Nareni and Khaha to the south is not a feature of the Laudi or Eastern Sotho, but can be historically traced to the Lovedu. Among the Ʋirwa an attenuated form of this complex may be attributed to Karanga influences. The accretions to and fallings away from the old nucleus were inevitable in the new setting of the Lovedu. The powers of the Karanga high god, who made rain and supported the sacred king, became projected upon the Lovedu queen; a mere vestige is left of the saturnalian licence accompanying the accession of a Karanga chief; and unsuccessful Lovedu claimants to the throne, who generally flee the country after the interregnum, are still referred to as *mambo* (sing. *lembo*). But there is among the Lovedu no sign of the resuscitation of the spirit of the deceased Karanga king in the maggots emerging from the decaying body as it lies sealed in a special hut before burial.

It is curious that among the Mamavolo, after 250 years of subjection to influences of the Sotho substratum and the Western and Central Sotho, this complex has been obliterated, while among the Lovedu it has been elaborated. The varying response is, however, intelligible in the light of their different histories. The Mamavolo, hiving off from the main body, were overwhelmed by the Sotho; even a cursory study shows how they lost their bearings and abandoned their faith in their heritage and, for security, remodelled their institutions upon those of their powerful neighbours. But the Lovedu maintained their dominance in their lowveld environment; they dealt with the challenges of invaders by elaborating the royal pattern so as to absorb them; and they responded to the prevailing belief that, not a priesthood, but the chief himself must

[1] Quoted in Theal, *Records of S.E. Africa*, vii. 191, 194.

mediate for rain by a new conception both of the high god and of the divinity of the queen.

The forces refashioning the old nucleus are the result of composite internal reactions to external influences. In Chapter I ('Pageants of the Past') we saw how, in the face of a feeling of insecurity, Khiali tried to safeguard the succession by casting out the heir, and how the innovation set into motion forces that precipitated the change from kings to queens. Simultaneously came the elevation of the queens to veritable rain-gods. The Lovedu rain-making technique is Sotho and constrains the forces of nature by magic; it is a fundamental departure from the Karanga technique, which uses an appeal to the high god through his priests on the mountain, where he manifests himself in clamour and flame. But there is still a faint connexion, for foreigners allege that Mujaji herself originally obtained her power from Levibi, where Mwari appeared in thunder and lightning to a chief of the Ṭavatsinde, a group among the Venda. *Uuuga ya uuga bula e a na*, thundering [on the mountain of] Uuuga [is followed by] pattering rain, is still the praise-title of the Levibi of Uulovedu. The Lovedu, we surmise, have replaced Mwari by Kuzwane, creator-god, divested of his rain-making and celestial powers, and the word 'Mwari' (or 'Mwali') suggests, even to the Lovedu mind, Muhale, the Lovedu chief who is founder of the tribe, the only semi-hero of legend, and is associated with ritual, as, for instance, the Bird of Muhale in the *vyali* initiation, which is also associated with rain.

But if this is conjecture, it is significant that power to effect the great change from kings to queens was sought in father-daughter incest, a pattern enjoined by the Karanga and considered as the source of fertility among the Shona. Not only did the traditional model sanctify the change, but the success of the experiment was guaranteed by the elaboration of values already existing in the society. Indeed, the change is represented merely as a reassertion of an ancient but fictitious cycle of kings and queens. The accession of a woman, in spite of the high position of women, was obviously a difficulty; but the rationalization provided by a supposed cycle satisfied misgivings, and the change lent itself to transforming the danger of foreign encirclement into an instrument for extending the network of political institutions. The complicated exchanges of the queen's wives constitute only an extension of the old pattern of the house of Mambo, who received daughters from his sub-chiefs in return for protection or food or as a result of conquest, and who handed out his daughters to his personal bodyguard.

In the elaboration of the Lovedu royal complex, the model and justification came from their Karanga ancestors, but the vital addition of a new association of the chief with rain, which is neither Karanga nor Venda, was inspired by Sotho culture. But, in the Sotho substratum, rain, agricultural rites, and the drum cult were inextricably merged and, in the context of the Lovedu pattern, they did not all find an equally firm place. We shall touch lightly upon this complex, noting here merely the extraordinary fact that, despite the long-continued pressure of Venda influences, the Venda contribution to the Lovedu royal pattern is to-day hardly perceptible. The reason lies partly in its incongruity with the conception of a female ruler who is also a divine rain-maker, but partly also in the obscuring of the borrowed elements by readjustments since the accession of a queen.

For a time the Lovedu kings followed the custom of the solitary dance (*u pembela*) of the Venda. It was under the inspiration of such a dance just before his death that Mugɔdɔ (*c.* 1790) made his famous prophecy. Venda chiefs perform this dance either shortly after accession, when it firmly establishes against all claims their divine title to the throne, or towards the end of their reign, when it symbolizes abjuration of earthly things and elevation to godhead. These conceptions are inconsistent with the Lovedu pattern, which prescribes the rite of the door as the title to succession, and safeguards the queen's inscrutability by making her the inaccessible 'huckster in her hut'.

The special Venda disposition of forces and persons in the organization of the royal court has left numerous marks in Lovedu culture and its reception facilitated the transition from kings to queens. The *khadi* (father's sister or the sister), as priestess, is in a favourable position to assume control during the minority of the heir, as is the case to-day among the Sekhɔpɔ and in many districts in Vulovedu. There is also the critical instance of the Mamaila, where between 1825 and 1895 sometimes men and sometimes women ascended the throne, and where the inter-action of the two patterns may be closely observed. The Venda emphasis on the virginity, for a time, of the chief's wives has had widespread repercussions even as far as the Nareni; and among the Lovedu it has become interlocked with the cogs of the political machinery, so that, while the permanently chaste are rewarded, the unchaste go out as wives of great men to strengthen their loyalty to the royal house. Nowhere else has such an ingenious solution or reinterpretation been evolved, though the differing readjustments among the various tribes show amazing inventiveness and resourcefulness.

The patterns and culture elements of the royal complex among the surrounding tribes, which have found no place in the Lovedu complex, are too numerous to mention; but what is rejected is just as important as what is adopted in the evaluation and interpretation of the forces determining change. Least has been taken from the modern Shangana-Tonga, but there are similarities in detail, though not in pattern, which may be ascribed to a common heritage of the distant past. It is, for instance, only the Tonga in these parts who have to any extent elaborated the idea of placing chiefs' wives as rulers in the provinces, a practice known among the Lovedu kings long before the arrival of the Shangana-Tonga. Among the Shangana-Tonga the accession of a brother to the throne admits of the progressive realization of aspirations fostered by a culture in which at one and the same time the hierarchy of age and the coincidence of maturity with the peak of life as well as display and competition are more emphasized than among the Lovedu. This pattern is quite unacceptable among the Lovedu.

There are many other suggestive contrasts, but what must surprise the observer is the small contribution (apart from the rain-making technique) of the Sotho from the south and west. The distribution of medicated seeds by the chief, as among the highveld Sotho, is thought to savour of witchcraft, as only witches use medicine to make the crops grow. The Pedi pattern of the 'tribal candle', the chief wife whose first son succeeds and whose bride-price is contributed by the tribe (who thereby obtain a stake in the succession) has penetrated far. It has been partially accepted by the Laudi as well as the Sekhɔpɔ; but the Lovedu have not been influenced. Of absorbing interest and immense interpretative value has been the conflict of Lovedu and Pedi patterns where their incongruity precipitated a crisis among the Nareni and Khaha.

Everywhere in the lowveld the transition from kings to queens caused disturbances, and the form of justification invariably reflects values in the cultures concerned. Among the Mamaila the change is justified by the sin of the male heir. When the change first occurred, the male heir was ousted because he had cohabited with his father's wives, which is a disqualification by Venda standards. Thereafter males again ruled. When the change occurred a second time, the male heir was driven off because he had broken open the door, which is a sin by Lovedu standards.

Among the Khaha of Maake and the Nareni, both Mahlo and Letswalo, the position is different and may be considered less cursorily, though unfortunately only in very broad outline. The Khaha, greatly disturbed by invasions from the south, sought stability by trying to imitate Mujaji I, the security of whose tribe they attributed to her feminine powers and longevity. In those days (1827) the Mafɛfɛ, following the Pedi pattern of royal marriage, politically dominated the Khaha as well as many other tribes. Nevertheless, among the Khaha, Mali, a woman, succeeded as chief against her brothers and was 'placed' by Mujaji. She was the first Khaha female ruler, modelled her court upon the Lovedu pattern, and even adopted ritual suicide as a means to power. The whole Lovedu pattern was not incorporated, for the traditional basis was lacking, especially as regards the ascendancy of women, the unquestioned acceptance of the caprices of the door, and the conception of receiving tributary wives and redistributing them. Thus men were not excluded from the throne. Mali herself, having failed to prevent the flight into exile of her people, was succeeded by a male chief; but in 1928 a woman, Mali II (or Maake, as she is sometimes called), was called upon to rule. Mali II was married, was asked to renounce her husband, as queens could have no official husbands, and when she refused she had to abdicate and now reigns merely as regent during the minority of her brother. The task of integrating the Lovedu with the Khaha pattern was never completed: the door is invoked to decide only between rivals with plausible claims, and no adequate solution has been found to harmonize the Pedi and Lovedu patterns of royal marriage. The chief wife even of the queen among the Khaha is the mother's brother's daughter, and it is for her marriage that in theory each district head must contribute cattle 'to seek their mother' (*hu nyagɛla mma vɔna*).

Among the Mahlo Nareni, sporadically dominated by the Mafɛfɛ until as late as 1901, the change came under conditions of European control (1923). The door entrusted the rain charms and chieftainship to Manjana, wife of the deceased chief, Segɔrɔrɔ. But when strife occurred, the

European intervened, construed the opening of the door as coincidence, and recognized a son of Segɔrɔrɔ's first wife. (Incidentally, the Pedi conception of the 'tribal candle', though accepted for a time, by 1923 was again receding before the old Laudi insistence that the mother's brother's daughter required no additional support to be chief wife.) To-day the tribe is split: Manjana's magic has power to call up the clouds, but the quackery of the recognized chief sweeps up gales which scatter the rain.

Among the Letswalo the change, motivated by a desire for security, aggravated a crisis which continued into the European period and was ended by the drastic intervention of the European. Ramadau, son of chief Bodile, defied his father by refusing to espouse his one-eyed cross-cousin, whom Bodile himself then married. But this wife turned out to be a witch who expiated her offence of stealing the rain charms by being mauled to death by a lion. Angered by his son's disobedience and his wife's treachery, Bodile then (c. 1850) prophesied the coming of the ants and the accession of a woman; but in the total setting of the drama the son's disobedience is condoned by representing his cross-cousin as a deformed witch and the treachery that threatens the welfare of the tribe is made the occasion for the accession of Magaepia, daughter of Bodile The whole theme is handled less skilfully than among the Louedu and indicates the existence of many conflicting motives. Before Magaepia succeeded there were wholesale assassinations of successive heirs; Magaepia, having replaced the lost rain charms, became, first, rain-maker to Ramadau and, after his death at the hands of the Swazi invaders, queen, but only of a portion of the tribe. The strife continued, the European intervened, and, when the tribes of the lowveld rose against the encroaching settlers (1894), the Letswalo joined them, but suffered a devastating defeat.

Changes can be traced in all aspects of Louedu culture, some greater, some smaller than those in their royal institutions. It will take us too far afield to deal with these changes, but a few remarks may be of interest. Almost nothing of the *gomana-vyali-vuhwera-vudiga* complex came with the royal group. Some of it can be attributed to the Sotho substratum: it is the ḍou of Rauothata who make the *gomana* drums and close the *vyali* with their weirdly costumed dancers, the *magɔgɔbya*; the Kwɛna likewise claim always to have had the *gomana*; and Louedu boys are allowed to become initiated at the *gomana* lodges of the ḍou of Khaḍa and of the Kwɛna of Maunadala, who also may accept royal boys to 'cross rapidly' (*hu ḍubunya*), or become initiated in a few days, at his *vuhwera*. The *magɔgɔbya* are unique, but are found also among the ḍou of Masoma and it is from Tsubye (the country of present-day Shai) that these costumes came over a century ago, having been brought by two men named Masehisa and Dinawe. The evidence may be indefinitely multiplied, but it is more interesting to examine for a moment the different manifestations of the complex over the Northern Transvaal, because what has been emphasized in it or muted or rejected illuminates the character of the incorporating culture.

We have no evidence of the occurrence beyond the Northern Transvaal of the sacred drums, considered as shrines consecrated by human sacrifice and as the focus of a 'school' for revealing the secrets of the whistling ancestors (*zwiḓajani*). Some Venda north of the Limpopo have drums of the *mɔndɔrɔ* (spirits of the chiefs) and *zwiḓajani* (familiars of Mnisi, the rain-god), and there is some evidence of drum ritual among Pedi, Venda, and even Ṯonga; but the elaborated drum cult belongs to the Northern Sotho. It has three characteristic elements: the supreme moments of the agricultural year are signalized by the sounding of the drums and the cult is intimately linked with rain or fertility; these calendric observances, as well as other great national occasions, are, by the interposition of the drums, brought under the surveillance of the tribal gods, represented by men masquerading as spirits who have come to earth; and in a special initiation novices are inducted into the secrets of the cult.

This constellation is most emphasized in three tribal groups: Laudi (especially Phalavorwa), Maḓala, and Xananwa-Ḓɔkwa-Moletshe. Among the Phalavorwa the striking emphasis is upon the link with rain-making, upon the *lesugu* or women's counterpart, and upon the exulting display before the drums which is permitted to those who have military and hunting exploits to their credit. These features become progressively attenuated westwards towards Ʋulovedu. The stress upon display reappears among the Maḓala, though in a different form, for there we find the esoteric *khidinkhi*, which is at once a dramatic dance inspired by the sacred drums glorifying the prowess of the chief and of warriors, and a rain and fertility rite, blessing cattle and crops and safeguarding the people against disease. In drawing into the complex the welfare of the cattle and in the absence of the *lesugu*, the Maḓala pattern differs from that of the Laudi, but approximates that of the Xananwa-Ḓɔkwa-Moletshe. These differences coincide with the emphases of the different cultures. The Laudi have an attenuated cattle-cult, though it is better developed than among the Lovedu; whereas the highveld Sotho, influenced from the west and south-west, have a fuller cattle-cult, though by no means as elaborate as that of the west (Tswana) with its seasonal migratory life, conditioned partly by pastoralism and partly by a desire for security in a difficult environment. Among the Laudi men's and women's initiations are often combined, but on the highveld they are markedly separated, for the *vyali* and *vuhwera* exist as distinct institutions and the Bird, guiding spirit of the *vyali*, is usually absent. In the third area, that of the Xananwa-Ḓɔkwa-Moletshe, the dispositions are in many respects quite distinctive. The drums become the focus of an elaborate fertility cult, rain-making stands outside the complex, and the chief *motif* is not display, but dramatization of obedience to the gods and loyalty to the chief. The supreme moment is when the manhood of the tribe, collected in the cattle kraal, receive the command of the gods communicated, under inspiration of the drums, by the *zwiḓajani*.

There is every possible variation in the patterns among the intervening tribes. In some, such as Tswale, Moila, Dikxale, Mamavolo, and Ʋirwa of Makhatho, the cult is often structurally unintegrated, standing outside the province of the chief and consisting merely of 'schools' managed by outsiders who have their own drums. The cult in these cases is practised merely for revenue purposes; it is a 'business' as the

Natives say; the alien drums are pierced and rendered useless at the death, not of the chief, but of their owners; and the *zwiḍajani* are often visitors from tribes where the cult is better developed. Among the Lovedu the cult has been only partially accepted; the pattern is the pattern of the focal area in the east. The features that have been attenuated or elaborated can be explained in the light of the emphasis of Lovedu culture: there is no display, no stress upon fertility, no linking with the welfare of the cattle, no elaboration in connexion with agricultural ritual, but the *zwiḍajani* command peace and agreement among men.

Elsewhere in this book we have given slight indications that the Lovedu interlocking *munywalo* exchanges and social structure can be traced to Karanga models; that the Lovedu have rejected the pattern of the wedding feast and wedding gifts which comes from the west; that Lovedu legal arrangements are the resultant of composite forces; that the smeller-out and the cult of spirit possession come from the Shangana-Ṭonga and Thɔvɔlɔ. These and many other borrowed culture elements may be followed up with advantage, and indicate the magnitude of culture change. But for our purposes, before proceeding to discuss the nature and effect of the impact of Western culture, a brief reference to Shangana-Ṭonga influences will suffice. Despite similarities in detail—an attenuated boys' puberty rite, the conception of *makhuma* (ritual defilement), the indirect warning to the witch by *hu ɛbɛla*, to mention a few features— and despite the extensive reception by the Lovedu of Shangana-Ṭonga elements of material culture—fowls, various crops, and methods of storing and threshing and stamping—the striking feature remains the great gulf between the two cultural configurations. They have, for instance, different views as regards sex morality, different marriage patterns, different conceptions of the hierarchy of age and the position of women; they deal differently with the situation of death, with rain-making, display, and regimentation, and, whereas the social groupings are totemic among the Lovedu, they are non-totemic among the Shangana-Ṭonga.

There are many other divergences, but one difference that calls for comment is the attitude to and reception of European culture. More adaptable, if brazen, than the Lovedu, at least in their new environment, the Shangana-Ṭonga have, as fugitives under Sotho domination, more complacently submitted themselves to European conquest. Disciplined by the military heritage of the Zulu, they made efficient police and soldiers, especially against their Sotho overlords. Their training in competition, trade, and display enabled them to respond better than the Lovedu to the stimuli of Western culture. Above all, European penetration benefited them, while it dispossessed the Sotho. The history of the contacts and reactions is the history of a century, which is far too complicated for treatment here. But this can be said: the Shangana-Ṭonga gained land and the right to be ruled by their own chiefs; the Lovedu lost land which was given to their erstwhile subjects; the prestige of Mujaji in the eyes of the white man waned while that of Shangana-Ṭonga chiefs waxed; and the Shangana-Ṭonga subservience to the European hardened Lovedu antagonism and resistance both to the European and to his protégés.

THE ICONOCLASM OF CHRISTIANITY

Effective European contact with the tribes of the lowveld began only in the decade 1880–90. At first Mujaji II hoped to play off Christianity and the secular authorities against one another, but they proved to be inseparable allies. Christianity in those days tolerated no compromise with pagan practices: it could not envisage the salvation of souls except through sweeping away heathen custom. It interceded on behalf of the Native against the encroachments of an acquisitive society, but conducted its crusade with the support of the civil arm of that society. When Mujaji was recalcitrant, she was reminded of the fate of Sekukuni (1877) and Cetewayo (1879); when she complained that the new creed was iconoclastic, Albasini replied that the Government also 'had the Book'; and when farms were parcelled out to settlers, the missionary became landlord of 4,856 acres and exacted labour and fees from his tenants. The Native was already angered by the raids of Buys, servant of the Republic, freebooter, and 'upperhead or great captain', and of Albasini, Native commissioner, Portuguese trader, and self-appointed chief of the Magwamba (Knobnose-Shangana-Tonga). Thus he could hardly have been expected to receive with open arms either the missionary or the settler.

The highest praise is due to the missionary for his superhuman efforts, his espousal of the cause of the Native, his intercession that gave the Lovedu their location, his unrewarded labour of love, and the inestimable gift of education and a new outlook on life that he brought. Too little has been made of these services, of the difficulties overcome and of the ingratitude he encountered. Khashani, first evangelist and royal kinsman, was martyred (1884); and so fierce was the resistance to Christianity that the drought of 1881–2 was attributed to those who were its apostles. But all this we must pass over, for it is with the reception of Christianity and Western culture into Lovedu culture and its response to the challenge that we are concerned.

The historical background of Christianity is a sharp differentiation of converts from pagans, in order to minimize the danger of relapsing and to ensure the growth of solidarity and communal interests in splendid Christian isolation. But the result was the ranging of Christians and pagans in opposite camps and fierce conflicts of loyalty. The history of Western culture is not distinct all along the line from Christianity, but it may be distinguished as distant and distasteful control rather than direct and deliberate disruption of custom, causing hindrances and frustrations and antagonism among all sections, not preaching a new way of life to the carefully segregated few.

The great changes effected by Christianity are those among converts. Half a century of evangelization has brought forth conversion among 3 to 5 per cent. of the Lovedu. Beyond this small insulated minority there have been repercussions, but, owing to the segregation of the Christians in mission settlements and the protective secrecy of the pagans, these repercussions have not been great.

By far the greatest concentration of Christians is upon Medingen, the mission-owned farm. In 1936 the total population of Medingen was 1,870, of whom 893, or just over 47 per cent., were Christians. In 1911 the population was 1,731, and, as nearly as can be determined, 780, or 45 per cent., were Christians; and the figures respectively for 1921 were 1,883 and 990, or 52 per cent. The striking fact is that, despite the many influences favouring an increase of numbers, the percentage of Christians has remained practically stationary. The most powerful missionizing agent is the school, which is attended by about 300 children, who tend to complete their school careers with confirmation; moreover, in the past, Christians from everywhere sought sanctuary on the mission station, while there are powerful evangelizing forces on the station as well as obstacles to the settlement there of pagans. Figures of increases or decreases are not available for the rest of Uulovedu, where one of the most significant phenomena is the relapse to paganism in the last decade of large numbers of the royal sons. Among those who have relapsed, however, an impression has been made, though often they are, like the sophisticated Native, the most implacable enemies of the faith in which they have been nurtured. It is the disruptive effect of Christianity upon custom as seen among converts living on mission stations that we propose first of all to examine, turning thereafter to positive contributions among these converts and ending with a brief consideration of the repercussion among the rest of the population.

The distinctive feature of Christianity is that it breaks down in order to build up. In the form in which it appears on the mission stations it is not merely hostile to repugnant custom, but also works against everything that can be recognized as custom. Converts and their teachers hold that, without complete and irrevocable severance from traditional values, the emotional background easily reasserts itself and undoes the work of Christianity. Participation even in innocent heathen life evokes disturbing associations. To outlaw merely the repugnant part of a custom is useless; the prohibition must be total. An attempt to differentiate is like an attempt to give reasons; the reasons for a thing are liable to be confused with its substance and explanations often merely obscure the issue. The old, even if only doubtfully incompatible with Christian practices or beliefs, must not be presented to conscious attention. Hence Christianity draws the individual away from all things tribal. Compromises are impossible upon such questions as the freedom of the sexes, beer-drinking, polygyny, and among the older population even *munywalo* (bride-price); there is no room for a liberal interpretation of our system of religion or morality. The policy in the past has never been to graft the new upon the old; it has been to destroy the cultural pattern and to substitute another, irrespective of whether it could be woven into the remainder of the social scheme or harmonized with existing beliefs and institutions.

This is not an indictment of missionary effort; it is the result of a considered policy conceived to be in the best interests of posterity. The mission had, from the earliest times, to contend with lack of discipline, slackness where there was no supervising foreman irritating habits of duplicity and ingratitude, suspicion, and attempts to take advantage of kindness. These were construed as barbaric traits that had to be uprooted. There appeared, in addition, to be an unusually large number of anti-Christian practices: the tribal justice, proceeding upon no fixed principles, seemed corrupt; there were periodical smellings-out of witches; people believed in the divinity of the queen. Dancing and drumming were obnoxious, not merely because they were 'heathenish din', but also because of their association with the idolatry of the *digɔma* and the 'schools', the sexual laxity at the *gɔsha* dances and possession by spirits. There were also mendicant minstrels who played the xylophone (*dibila*) and sang for their food and lodging, whose songs did not always express Christian sentiments. One, for instance, not long ago, used to sing, 'Christians are cheats who put us to sleep before we eat [referring to grace], so as to kill us unawares', and another's song rang more crudely: 'The husbandless woman climbs to the roof of the hut; she urinates and the rats fall down in a faint'.

Early Church policy laid down what should be outlawed on mission-owned farms; wife-purchase, shrines, *digɔma*, rain-making, witchcraft, divination, 'strengthenings with medicine', the consecration of weapons, and other repugnant customs. It stamped as particularly reprehensible theft, sexual offences, opposition to the Church, and, later, migration to seek employment in the sinful towns. The sanctions with which it can enforce obedience upon a self-governed estate include refusal of such privileges as baptism and confirmation, public denunciation in church, various penalties, such as road-making and catechism classes, and even expulsion from the mission station. Natives believe that the whole system is served by a network of espionage, and the intrinsic difficulties of the situation have been immensely increased by the fact that financially the mission station largely relies upon the contributions in fees and work of its tenants. On one occasion a self-constituted committee of disaffected tenants in Johannesburg, who were in arrears, accused the mission of capitalistic exploitation and of robbing the Natives of their country, and drastic action was necessary.

The Christian attack upon the marriage pattern and especially polygyny has led to many subtle reactions. Devout Christians of the old order still refuse to accept cattle, but surreptitiously pocket money payments which by the nature of the case can be used to subserve personal, not social, ends. The Church no longer sets its face against *munywalo*, but seeks to turn it into a kind of dowry, and Christians call it 'thanks'. The Christian's freedom of choice of a mate weakens the reciprocities and emphasizes independence and materialism at the price of the patterns of co-operation and long-range mutuality. A Christian often marries a non-relative, but cannot easily escape the complex net thrown over the whole social structure by the cattle exchanges. He may have to face the opposition of those relatives whose displeasure may cause illness to him or his family. If he marries a second wife, his cross-cousin, he is excommunicated, and he will be unable, even on his death-bed, to secure the final consolation and blessing of the Church unless he sets aside his pagan wife. Polygyny, the inheritance of wives, and beer are so deeply rooted in the culture that they constitute the gravest difficulties of the mission as well as the most formidable obstacles to embracing Christianity. Christians are required to build a house before marriage: this again tears them out of the context of parental influences. Wedding feasts and bridal gifts introduce the pattern of the highveld Sotho and of the towns, but without serious disruptive effects.

Christian marriage sets up community of property and strikes at the economic independence of women; it emphasizes patriliny, but, in compensation, introduces a conception of marital companionship. Families are larger, because the old spacing of children has broken down: monogamy, proscription of the institution of 'lovers' (vuḑavu), the opposition to anything pagan, the diminished control of the old women are some of the reasons. There is more illegitimacy because the marriage of girls is later, examination for virginity is considered un-Christian, the disciplinary influences of the initiation 'schools' and of parental authority have weakened, and there is no training in the rules of incomplete sexual intercourse. Among some of the other results, it may be said that Christians are less complaisant about the infidelity of their spouses and that the care of a brother's widow occasions serious conflicts.

The iconoclastic effect of Christianity may be illustrated in a few other spheres of culture. Christians often object to performing the services to the chief expected of every tribesman. At the capital they plough one of the queen's fields, but have largely withdrawn themselves or have been excluded from the political and legal organization. They do not submit themselves to procedures involving appeal to the smeller-out, regard as repugnant the duties of messengers in 'blood' cases and, by extension, those of all court messengers, and, since the regular court sessions are held on Sunday, they cannot attend them, nor indeed are they welcomed as members of the khɔrɔ. At Medingen the districts are not recognized and the majority of offences come before the council of elders or the missionary. Christians disregard traditional holidays and taboos, such as those after deaths and the first rains or when lightning strikes down to earth. They defiantly plough over sacred places to show the absurdity of superstitious fears. They neither kill twins nor observe the rules as to burial in wet places. They oppose the 'schools', avoid the dances and ignore the firstfruits rites.

It is un-Christian to become possessed or to have the 'dirt'-removing rite after death. Even important royal kinsmen who become Christians must be buried in the Christian cemetery, not where they will be contaminated by heathenish associations. The bearers are Christians, and pagan relatives follow the hearse in the rear, segregated from the Christians, for they do not know the hymns that are sung. The corpse is made to face west, towards the setting sun, not north, whence the Lovedu came. When the queen's brother, who became a Christian on his death-bed, was buried, the only concession permitted to custom was the placing of an ox skin upon the coffin; no wonder that his spirit did not long lie at rest and that subsequent drought was attributed to his complaints. Not only are pagans and Christians separated in the procession to the grave, but, after burial, relatives on each side have their separate rites.

All this is but a reflection of the attempt to make the segregation as complete as possible. Even the visible evidence of different styles of building, of dressing, and of living together was in the past more boldly thrown into relief by the geometrical villages, with their square houses fronted by flower gardens and straight streets crossing one another at right angles and ornamented with orange trees. But the Christians' efforts to differentiate themselves from pagans are limited by two main factors. Neither the Bible nor their limited experience of the world has suggested too many different ways of living and behaving. In large spheres of culture they know no more than is supplied by the traditional background; and limited resources often make impracticable the adoption of different standards and attitudes.

Christians tend to defer in everything, not to the tribal, but to the church authorities. Local problems and church matters, as well as relations with the European, are advised upon and guided by the church and its officials. Christians set themselves up as interpreters of and intermediaries with the European; they tend to assume command upon occasions of European festivities or of intervention, except that of official business with the chief or the councillors. They crowd round inquisitively when agricultural officials arrive, while pagans avoid them; they prepare the programme or draw up the illuminated address when there is a celebration, such as the Coronation in 1937 or an agricultural show. And they work out these plans and addresses in consultation, not with the tribal authorities, but with the evangelist. It is not unnatural, for they complain that the tribal authorities will never learn and never listen to their advice or accept their suggestions. All this occasions friction and divided allegiance, it weakens the authority of the queen, and it antagonizes the pagans.

In recent years there has been more co-operation. The old influential Christians have died and the educated young pagans have learnt to manage things for themselves. Agricultural officials, despite active resistance from pagans and co-operation from Christians, realize that their work is incomplete without sustained efforts to secure the interest of the pagans. Christians are vouchsafed no information from the capital and their opportunities of leadership and interference become limited. Jealousies among Christians have led to disunity and they have lost control of the postal arrangements. The secretarial duties of the chief are undertaken jointly by a Christian and several pagans. And young men who in the past found their major opportunities in identifying themselves with the Christians are beginning to find it more profitable to side with the pagans. This is but a reflection of more universal trends: the importance of the church has receded before the rapid expansion of the activities of the administration, industry, and commerce; these activities are no longer in active co-operation with Christianity, and differences in religious outlook between pagans and Christians tend to be over-shadowed by the feeling of common hostility to and distrust of the European. How far the new tendencies will lead to constructive co-operation and to bringing Christians into more realistic touch with the total tribal environment are questions too large for consideration here.

But Christianity has not destroyed only; it has also built up. Christians wholeheartedly embraced education; pagans, believing that education implies the acceptance of a foreign faith, are torn by conflicting loyalties, and their ardent desire to acquire the three R's expresses itself in the attempts made to set up a tribal school, which will be the agent, not of an alien creed, but of traditional values. Education and the outlook it has engendered have equipped Christians for meeting the impact of Western conquest and culture. Schoolchildren lose much of the lore of the veld and the training of the tribal initiations, but they gain new games, new skills, and new knowledge, implicit in which are assumptions regarding the nature of man and the purpose of existence. The church, through its preachings and schools, has been the channel of more than half the influences of Western ethics and culture in their positive effects. Its future lies in its control of education, for its religious mission has become submerged in a mass of technical and routine duties, entailing the preparation of pupils for examinations and the filling up of forms, with consequent loss of personal contacts and pastoral care. Its religious influence is evident in grace at meals, prayers for oneself, church services, Biblical Christian names, feasts, sacraments, and periodical visits of the women of one settlement to commune with and advise those of another. But on the whole the purely religious has been eclipsed by the educational effects. The two are inextricably interwoven; and their separation might well mean that Christianity will have no message for modern man and will be regarded as linked with the repressive, not the progressive, forces of Western civilization.

The valuable adjustments brought about by Christianity are the adjustments towards the modern world: receptivity to Western standards, less reluctance to co-operate with Europeans, and aspirations to seek self-realization amid the opportunities offered by them. Christians are less sceptical than pagans of European health services and of the innovations of the agricultural demonstrator; and they are better equipped and, until recently, were more eager to accept such Government posts as those of interpreters, policemen, and forest rangers. Only Christians can be teachers. Christians are driven to action by the idea of progress; they seek their future and achievement in change; and they attribute the disabilities under which the tribe suffers to the ignorance of their pagan rulers. Not much of what they have learnt intellectually has merged integrally with their lives, but they are less frustrated than the pagans.

Their outlook stands in close relation to the great extension of economic needs necessitated by Christianity, such as church and school fees, books and occasionally newspapers, better clothes and more European household articles, brick houses, wooden coffins, and burial societies. Their contributions, which help to support the widespread organization and institutions of the Church, constitute one of the main resistances to conversion; but the necessity to meet the new demands has made them keener agriculturalists than are the pagans. You sometimes hear a pagan derisively call out to Christian workers, not the friendly greeting '*Uashumi*' (workers), but 'Fools, why labour when others rest'; the Christian reply is, 'We are orphans and must work to satisfy our needs.' Christians are for ever planning new schemes and trying new methods; even their women-folk take in washing and, despite the church's discouragement, occasionally seek work in the towns. Christian men eagerly take to making irrigated gardens, and some become transport riders or itinerant hawkers; while it is Christian women who hire out their services to neighbours and make a business of pottery. It is chiefly among Christians that salt, meat, and cash take the place of beer in the work party. The total result is not merely a better economic sense, but also a growth of the spirit of competition and calculation; not merely greater industry and less improvidence, but also exploitation of their fellow tribesmen and self-seeking; and, instead of relying upon the roundabout reciprocities, Christians demand more immediate satisfactions and more precise and personal rewards. Aggressiveness and display, rivalries and suspicion, develop side by side with ideas of progress and a desire for advancement.

There are often fierce jealousies in the Christian settlements, and the tensions occasionally set into motion waves of accusations of witchcraft which break up the settlements. The classical example quoted as evidence of the great incidence of witchcraft among Christians is the disruption of the station at Moila. No one could be trusted, and witches were said to administer medicines to children, taking them out at night to crack their skulls upon the rocks. Christian boys are said to gossip more about witches than do their pagan brothers, and nowhere except in Christian settlements were we warned against accepting food from strangers. Witchcraft among Christians is difficult to observe, as it is driven underground; Christians do not publicly appeal to the smeller-out or seek the diviner to discover the cause of death, but they secretly consult the bones and slander the enemies that are thought to have sent the death. They tend to combat witchcraft, not by open accusation, but by privately 'sending back' the evil; and they firmly believe that the queen makes rain, albeit through the grace of the Christian God. The pollution that prevents rain is ascribed to sin—especially incest, rape, adultery, sexual offences, murder, and witchcraft—rather than to wrong burials. Tensions in the Christian settlements and the suspicion of espionage increase secretiveness about personal business, fields, and crops; but Christians are far more communicative than pagans about tribal matters and custom.

Amid conflicting tendencies, we find it difficult to say whether witchcraft is more prevalent among Christians than among pagans. The new outlook upon the nature of man and of his purposes increases tensions and rivalries, but also calls into question the assumptions of magic and witchcraft; and proscription leads to more underground activity and the development of new techniques, but also drives out of the field the visible reminders of the world of supernatural forces. In our opinion, the total situation may be summed up in the words of a Christian informant who has maintained intact his tribal background: 'Education gives men the power of witchcraft, and when we all are educated we shall all be witches, but, like Europeans, quite harmless to one another.'

The repercussions of the Christian outlook in the tribe as a whole may be referred to briefly. The tendencies are changing because of the recent re-absorption of Christians into the tribe, but the main results to-day are still those coming from the segregated Christians. Christian holidays have to some extent become part of the life of the tribe. Sunday is, as far as agriculture and building operations are concerned, a day of rest, but, for this reason, it is set aside specially for public business, such as tribal gatherings and *khɔrɔ* trials; and one result is that Christians, even if their moralizing and attempts to improve law and procedure were better tolerated, are excluded from participation. People occasionally have 'beer of Christmas' or 'New Year'. Twin murders can no longer be reported to the queen, as there is danger of implicating her, and Christian women, more interested in the pregnancy, legitimate or otherwise, of their friends, threaten to take action if they suspect a murder. But the effect is unsuspectedly complicated: a pagan mother who under pressure allows her twins to live may be refused assistance by her husband's mother, and often reacts by underfeeding them in order to starve them to death; and much greater secrecy is maintained. In 1923, after a few convictions in the European courts, the queen forbade the killing of twins and ordered births to be reported to the mission station; but the rule became a dead letter as soon as it could be safely circumvented.

Real or pretended sensitiveness among pagans to Christian values has had some effects. Not only do pagans ascribe their misfortunes to disregard of duties fostered by the example of the Christians, but they advance Christian values as excuses for not fulfilling their own obligations. They may condemn the Christian intrusion as causing drought or disobedience, but they may justify their own doubtful behaviour upon principles of Christian ethics. In 1937, for instance, Mashishimali refused to accept a *gɔsha* dance on the ground that his wife's brother, who lived in the village, was a Christian, but the real reason was self-interest and unwillingness to kill a beast and to burden himself with feeding the dancers. For a similar reason, an old woman, nominally a Christian, refused to allow her son to accommodate the dancers, but the reason she advanced was the pagan associations of the drums. Slackness in obeying the queen is ascribed to the example of the Christians, who break taboos with impunity and escape their obligations as messengers of the *khɔrɔ* by declaring that the work is un-Christian.

At one time Christians could terrify pagans by predicting eclipses and locust invasions, visitations which they ascribed to the obstinacy of the pagans in refusing to accept the gospel; this weapon is useless to-day, but the Christian hell causes some uneasiness of conscience and repressed fear, especially evident in dreams and during illness. There are death-bed conversions, and the evangelist is sometimes anxiously called to interpret alarming dreams. Masilu, a budding doctor still learning the bones, which had been discarded by a Christian relative, suffered from a persistent illness. While bed-ridden he dreamt that he had ascended a great ladder half-way to heaven and came to a luxuriant country. There he saw two roads, but he was stopped by the guardian of the gate to which one of these roads led, and told to take the left-hand road going to the west. He suspected that that road led to hell. The evangelist, called in for consultation, prayed for his soul, explaining that the dream clearly warned the pagan sinner to mend his way of life if he wished to be admitted to the road that led to salvation. Masilu was half-persuaded, but when his wife scorned the imposture and he had regained health, he let the matter slide. But sometimes conversion takes place in such circumstances, especially as the view is held that many people, after a dream of this nature, suddenly die. We may also associate with Christian ethics such phenomena as the growth of a sex-guilt complex, the wearing of blouses to cover the breasts, and the repression of virginity observances.

The persistence of a belief among Christians that the restrictions imposed upon the tribe may be attributed to backwardness and refusal to give up custom has not been without its effects. Sophisticated pagans share this belief with the Christians, but on the whole the assumption of enlightenment and superiority derives from the conception, fostered by Christianity, of the darkness of the pagan world. There is much that can be advanced in support of their contentions: the location allotted to the tribe, it is urged, would have been larger if the whole tribe, not merely a portion of it, had presented itself to General Joubert when, in the 1890s, after their defeat, he commanded their presence in order to enable him to give them land proportionate to their numbers; and, similarly, the stringency of the dipping laws, the absence of any benefits from the fund of the local tax, the ascendancy of the Shangana-Tonga are laid at the door of the ignorance of the councillors. Christians allege that in other tribes, where there has been enlightenment, disabilities have disappeared. Some pagans, half-accepting the impeachment, blame their leaders; others, and they are in the majority and the most influential, resent the imputation and fiercely resist every suggestion that comes from the Christians. On the whole, however, the obvious advantages of knowledge of the ways of the white man and of the outside world cannot be gainsaid: it is the educated Native who gets the best posts and secures exemption from carrying passes. But where enlightenment is paraded by Christians, it merely occasions more resistance and opposition.

THE CHALLENGE OF WESTERN CONQUEST

The influence of Western culture, as a force distinct from Christianity, can be fully interpreted only against a background that extends, as regards time, to the earliest contacts between Bantu and European and, as regards space, over the whole of South Africa. Attitudes and reactions observable in Uulovedu are often intelligible in the light, not of local misfortunes, but of experiences of tribes in other parts of South Africa. We cannot here discuss this question; indeed, the problems arising from the impact of Western culture within the tribe alone are too complex for summary treatment. On the whole, there has only been legislation against utterly repugnant custom and, until recently, the restrictions that have been efficiently enforced were few, and did not strike directly at the integrity of custom. The policy has been one of *laisser-faire*; and no active attempt has been made to graft new culture elements upon the old patterns. The integration that has taken place has been a response of the culture itself to the challenges of the new order. Therein lies the greatest difference from the manner in which Christianity has influenced the culture. Since 1938 the policy has changed somewhat, and there are more active though still not conscious interferences with custom; but among the Lovedu the effect as yet has been negligible.

The labour migration to towns and farms, necessitated by taxation, is reluctantly undertaken. The Lovedu are not easy prey to recruiters, who have to give assurances regarding, not only labour and other conditions, but also immunity from arrest for arrears of tax. The ideal is to return home, for 'The only place one never returns to is the womb'. The migration has not had the great effect that is reported in other parts of Africa: very little that is brought back is incorporated into the culture, even the accent men acquire in towns being rapidly discarded: marriage ceremonial does not require the presence of the man, his bridal visits being often undertaken by others; the pivotal position of women in the social structure minimizes disturbances; and, since during the whole suckling period a husband should partially avoid his wife, his absence for six months or so in town is not a serious problem as far as sexual adjustments are concerned. The absence of the men creates difficulties in holding the initiations and in economic dispositions. But the salient fact is that the energies liberated by the use of the plough exceed the drain caused by the labour migration. Old men, who no longer pay taxes, conduct the political and legal affairs of the tribe, and women, who do not migrate, control religion and ritual.

In legal arrangements there have been changes. But the deprivation of the power to enforce decisions means little to the old culture, which never relied upon force, though it may mean something when the sanction of reciprocity has become undermined. The force of the law is being destroyed, not by the limited jurisdiction allowed, but by the interference of solicitors and the multiplication, so it is believed, of criminals acquitted or protected by the European. Witches, they say, escape punishment by Europeans, because Europeans neither have witchcraft nor understand its workings. We have elsewhere noted some readjustments in legal procedure. Here we need add only a few further points The *khɔrɔ* must be careful lest dissatisfied litigants report procedures or decisions that are illegal by European standards; but, on the other hand, it sometimes threatens recalcitrant debtors with the dire consequences of being sent to the European, and such is the disinclination to be judged by the European that the threat is generally effective. The *khɔrɔ*, for instance, takes care not to order an expulsion (which is illegal) before the crops are reaped, as the victim is then more liable to appeal, while many cases may be quoted in which the threat to send a litigant to the Native Commissioner has led to a solution by agreement. The weakening of the sanctions of reciprocity has led to increasing resort, not to the European courts, but to 'sending back' the evil.

The *khɔrɔ* has more and more to deal with written evidence, such as cattle lists, letters between the parties and from farmers, and pieces of paper on which had been noted the marriage cattle that have passed.

The handling of this evidence is woefully unskilful, but important distinctions must be made. Where the writing takes the place of the notches that used to be cut on sticks to indicate the cattle that had passed, it tends to be accepted if there is other supporting evidence; statements in a letter of the amount of money sent with the letter are generally given credence; but sentiments expressed in letters and written accounts of the circumstances of a case are usually completely ignored or dismissed as unimportant. In one case where a husband wrote that he had definitely deserted his wife, the court ignored the letter on the ground that, unless the husband gave his evidence in person, he might well reverse his attitude and appeal to the Native Commissioner. The subject of the development in the handling of written evidence is a large one; but to what we have said we would merely add that the recording of evidence in writing has been attempted, since 1932, in only fifteen cases all told. The attempt has miserably failed. The usual record reads approximately as follows: 'Andrew Malopo v. £19. 5 Jim Malate 2/8/32', and to that cryptic statement nothing is added by way of such embellishment as the nature of the case, whether the date refers to the day of trial or retrial or payment, whether in fact there has been payment, and so on. Native Commissioners have sometimes tendered advice about how cases should be decided and recorded, but it is beyond their province, and the results have been precisely nil.

Political institutions have suffered no fundamental change. External relations are maintained through the wives the queen still receives from, and the rain she still gives to, foreign chiefs; the suppression of military exploits and cattle raids has not affected the Lovedu. Relations with European authorities have modified initiative and control over large spheres of policy, for the tribal authorities receive instructions rather than discuss suggestions, though consultation is nowadays a recognized preliminary to the introduction of an innovation. The tribal gathering (*khivijɔ*) never was important in Uulovedu; now it discusses perhaps more tribal matters than in the past, as well as European proposals and demands, but it has little power. The councillors, presenting European matters, sometimes give a distorted version, finding it difficult to justify either the measure proposed or their inability to bring about modifications or to circumvent it; and very often they do not mention important points at all. The widespread tendency to justify a desired action by saddling the European with responsibility for it reappears again and again. The people may be told by the councillors (who have a car) to mend the road, because, they say, an official who broke the spring of his car upon it has complained to the Native Commissioner; the administrative admonition to maintain better control over young boys going to work without their parents' consent was presented to the tribal meeting as a warning that boys not carrying tax receipts would be arrested if found at beer parties. (By traditional standards, now maintained with difficulty, beer parties are only for adults.) The justification or circumvention is upon the pattern that is known, and that pattern, despite the intervention of the European, remains intact.

Measures taken to protect national (South African) interests, such as cattle-dipping, quarantine regulations, and the reclamation of the reserves, have increased in recent years. Unless some compromise can be reached in regard to the prohibition of cutting down trees, all the Native industries will be stamped out. The change from wattle and daub to sun-dried bricks for constructing huts began before the forestry regulations and is now accelerated, fortunately without causing a major disturbance. Dipping is regarded as a sinister device for keeping down the number of cattle—the hurried driving to and from the dip and the lack of care of wounded cattle or of those in calf do in fact cause deaths, but the absence of milch cows, also attributed to dipping, is the result of overworking the cattle, their poor quality, and inadequate grazing land. Natives believe that dipping exists for the special benefit of dipping officials, who come as poor men, but are rich when they leave. Dipping and quarantine regulations, as well as grazing fees in the Crown Lands, have led to complications in transferring the cattle of the marriage exchanges, driven out customs incipiently accepted from the West, such as cattle posts and cattle racing on the day of the first fruits festival, and introduced the conception of fees for *hu fisa*, the care of cattle by others.

But one of the most unsuspected results is the growth of a reluctance, not merely to slaughter, but also to sell cattle. The evil of this tendency is incalculable, but it is an inevitable result of modern conditions. Sales are difficult, because of the restrictions on movement and the absence of markets; the need to sell or to slaughter is smaller than it was because money is available and agriculture less precarious; the emphasis upon material possessions and the liberation among Christians of cattle from the chain of cattle exchanges tends to imbue them with new values. The tendency is for them to become a standard of wealth rather than a means of subsistence or of facilitating marriage. There is a strong aversion even to slaughter the cattle that used to be killed in marriage negotiations, their place being taken by money and clothes. A strong incentive to slaughter cattle cannot easily be created, since it is not meat, but beer, with which one regales one's neighbours and maintains a reputation for liberality. Among the Lovedu the growing anti-economic conception of cattle has nothing to do with their alleged sacredness.

Western culture has presented itself with a formidable problem. Improvement of stock by way of pedigree bulls, the Lovedu have decisively rejected: they suspect that the Government will claim perhaps the calves, perhaps some other right of interference. They have also for similar reasons refused other aid, such as the introduction of a suitable grass.

Not all the great changes in agriculture have come from the European. The Shangana-Tonga introduced valley cultivation, which was subsequently stimulated by congestion on the hills and by the greater ease of manipulating the plough in the valleys than on the hillsides. With the plough, rejected in its early heavy form, but accepted later when it became lighter, a new set of reactions started. Crops and beer became more abundant, the old forms of co-operative work were transformed, and the effect of the absence in town of the men was minimized. But the plough is destroying the protective verges of fields, sweeping away the borders planted with sweet sorghum, and breaking down the contour walls of stone that stopped the rush of water on the slopes. The soil, taxed to its utmost by the mixed crops planted, is gradually becoming exhausted; it is being more easily washed away and the erosion has already silted up the lower stretches of rivers, so that old riverside gardens there have been destroyed. The introduction of donkeys added to the cumulative destructive effect, with which neither the combined forces of agricultural demonstrators and forest rangers, nor the stimulus of agricultural shows and competitions, nor the innate ingenuity of the Native can hope to contend. The fundamental evil is over-population, not over-stocking. In the old days a man hoed near grazing land at his own risk; to-day he must plough where he can.

A miscellaneous series of reactions may be briefly enumerated. Money subserves some purely economic purposes: it purchases various European articles, such as clothes and cloths, sewing machines and soap, candles, lanterns and paraffin, sieves and enamel dishes, iron objects, cycles, and wagons. But, compared with articles of local manufacture, these introductions are insignificant except among Christians. In the new forms of service and co-operation money also has a purely economic function and threatens the old reciprocities. But it is not always easy to say whether money economy is more rapidly transforming institutions than institutions are transforming money economy: often money becomes incorporated into the pattern of goodwill exchanges. The victory may lie with Western conceptions, but incalculable forces are massing against them, and there is a tendency among the best-educated Natives to revive the past in answer to the challenge of the European.

The result will be a subtle and unpredictable interpretation. The suspicion that motivates the reaction is both effect and cause: it is the result of a feeling of insecurity, but it leads to protective adjustments in all spheres of culture. A woman may refuse to don a newly bought European blanket until it has been soiled by being worn by some one else susceptible to its dangers or, as they say, until 'the European can no longer be seen in it'. This attitude is evidence both of an old pattern and of profound distrust of the European. Tropical ulcers are sometimes attributed to Nyasaland boys, who are hated for their sexual adventures with Lovedu women; but in fact tropical ulcers have always been there, though the serious lesions appeared for the first time only after the great famine of 1894–6. The psychological determinants of change are resultants of subtle combinations of objective facts and subjective errors.

Change of diet in recent years has contributed to the evil of malnutrition. Its causes are complex. On the one hand, the variety of old crops has been reduced by the plough and congestion destroys the vegetation that is used as relishes and fruits; on the other, the substitutions are inadequate and consist mostly of starches. Physical degeneration weakens the Native as an employee, lassitude adversely affects the incentives and the energy necessary for the tasks of subsistence, and a sense of insecurity fans the flames of suspicion. The difficulties of the dietician and the medical man increase immensely. This is what an intelligent and particularly unbiased young man feels: 'In European hospitals they plan to kill us by poisoning and starving us, because they dislike hearing the groaning of a sick man. They will not allow us to go into the sun when we are getting well. The nurses ill-treat us if we do what we think is right. We get no filling food and our only enjoyment, conversation with one another, is repressed by the command to "shut up".' So profound is the suspicion, that one of our good friends died rather than go to hospital, while another, who had sustained a compound fracture, was persuaded to accept our advice to be taken to a European doctor only at the very last moment.

Yet let us not forget that in 1939 a tribal 'Cabinet' was set up and one of its 'ministers' was the guardian of health. His last message to us was that, in accordance with a decision of the 'Cabinet', he 'was watching the diet of the capital and had decided upon strictly prohibiting the running about of fowls'. By old and still persisting custom, it should be mentioned, fowls are not allowed in the capital, because, it is said, they are dirty animals.

Western culture hardly undermines magic and witchcraft: police boys use magic to ward off 'the spears of their enemies', guns are 'doctored' to make them shoot straight and even the inadequacies of European justice are compensated by magic (*hu niɛlɛla*). In this respect the culture has met the challenge, however inappropriately from our point of view. But it has failed to handle successfully the spirit of modern inquiry found among those who have been to school or have been stimulated by their experiences in the towns. Young men do not understand the long process of growing into a culture and ask questions which the old men cannot or will not answer. These young men, who judge by the standards of the little learning which is a dangerous thing, tend to despise what is not made intelligible to them. In their eyes, for instance, the mysteries of the *digɔma* and the *zwiḍajani* are shams, and the fact that no knowledge is imparted in the circumcision 'schools' condemns them as nonsense. This attitude and the inadequate response to it lead to lack of respect both for traditional values and old people. But the total effect is minimized by the reassertion of the old values as the young men grow older and begin to become part of and have a stake in the culture. Moreover, inquisitiveness is stamped as the immaturity, almost imbecility, of youth, and the insinuation that the doubts are due to the white man's insidious influence goes far to repress them as unworthy and disloyal.

In this book we have described Lovedu culture as it is to-day, touching but cursorily in the present chapter upon the changes that have occurred or the trends that are apparent in some groups of people. We have seen that the interpenetration in the pre-European period has effected far greater institutional changes than in the European period. Even the incorporation of the cult of spirit possession, which came twenty years after the European, represents a far greater direct evolution than the changes in forms brought about by the Christian religion. The feature of pre-European merging has been incorporation, with modifications, of culture elements and the reciprocal effect upon existing institutions and culture elements. The feature of European penetration, except in material culture and in the small body of segregated Christians, has been indirect response in attitudes and in the old institutions rather than incorporation of culture elements. The purpose has been to circumvent, if direct resistance was impossible, rather than to accept or embody.

Among the vast majority of the people the long-range pressure of new needs and the indirect response in attitudes has left intact almost all the essential features of the culture. Lovedu religion remains a reality, showing few signs of being modified by Christianity. Ritual is practically untouched—even Christians believe in the magical power of the queen. Magic and witchcraft have become more rather than less elaborate and have been applied to every new introduction from the European. Among the most devout Christians the underlying conceptions of the causation of disease and of therapeutics still hold sway. The essential structure of the political, social and marriage systems is intact, though the reciprocities have weakened. The 'schools', which in 1938 we had thought dead, have been energetically revived, everything in the country during the whole of 1939 being made subservient to the supreme purposes of the *vyali*. The need for dramatizing social values, and for self-expression, which is served by the 'schools', becomes greater as frustration and the lassitude of under-nourishment increase. The bases of subsistence have deteriorated and Natives are not slow to point out that in the sphere of culture most affected by the European the evil effects, despite the gains, are most evident. They blame the plough for the destruction of riverside gardens and for soil-erosion, but they realize that it is impossible to go back to the hoe; and they dislike the new forms of employment, but are unable to see any way of doing without them.

The Lovedu are now entering a new phase, that of greater interference by the European and of increasing community of interest with other tribes. This will ultimately mean a more direct challenge to their institutions and a response in terms partly of their local, and partly of a more comprehensive cultural configuration. The necessity of studying culture contact and culture change comparatively and over large areas will thus be more imperative than ever.

GENERAL INDEX

ADULTERY, 194
Age-groupings, 86, 99, 100, 104, 107
 age-mates, 99, 192
 age-sets, 100
Agriculture, 24, 30 ff., 34 ff., 55, 282 ff., 325-6
 cultivation, original, 40
 difficulties, 39
 See also Crops; Hoeing; Husbandry; Ploughing.
Ancestors, 222, 223, 226, 231 ff., 277
 reincarnation, 165
 See also Spirits, ancestral.
Animals, 251
 dedicated, 234, 236, 238
 See also under specific names.
Anthropology, ix
 methods, xiv-xv
Authority, 289, 290. *See also* Sanctions.
Avoidances, 78, 79-80. *See also* Taboos.

BARRENNESS, 158, 159, 166, 212
Barter, 61-2
 gift-barter, 61, 62, 63
 money-barter, 61, 62, 67
 See also Exchange; Transactions, commercial.
Beer, 20, 23, 24, 25, 26-7, 30, 41, 44-5, 53, 55, 60, 62, 63, 64, 76, 77, 78, 79, 82, 83, 95, 99, 109, 110, 111, 135, 137, 155, 157, 159-60, 181, 182, 183, 187, 192, 230, 234, 238, 240, 284, 287-8
 beer-drinks, 26-7, 53-4, 72, 183, 184, 297
 beer offerings, 76, 77, 238
 beer parties, 26-7, 31, 32, 53-4, 114, 182, 288, pl. xv (*b*)
 harvest beer, 235-7
 khirula beer, 27, 63, 65
 tribute to queen, pl. xv (*a*)
 uses of, 288
Begging, 54, 68, 111, 292
Bird, the. *See under* Mummeries.
Blood, 212, 213, 214
'Blood' cases, 191, 194, 200, 201-3
Bones used in medicine. *See under* Medicine, bones used in.

Boys, 99, 106, 108
 fathers, relations with, 74
 mothers, relations with, 73-4
 See also Children; Herdboys.
Bride-price (*munywalo*), 42, 44, 62, 63, 64, 65 ff., 72, 74, 75, 76, 79, 98, 99, 141 ff., 156, 158, 159-60, 161, 175, 197, 200, 316
 gifts, average, 150, 151
 queen's bride-price for her wives, 173, 177
 See also Cattle, *munywalo*.
Brothers, relations between, 74-5
 relationship with sisters, 67, 73, 75-7, 142-5, 146, 197-8
Burials, 232, 233, 275, 276, 281, 289, 317-18
 wet soil, in, 220, 241, 275

CALENDAR. *See* Seasons.
Cattle, 19-20, 27, 32, 34, 41, 42-4, 57-8, 68, 72, 107, 167, 182, 191, 194, 195, 200, 209, 325
 cult, 44, 312
 dipping, 43, 44, 325
 herding of, 43
 kraals, 19, 43-4
 munywalo, 65-7, 68, 75, 76, 82, 98, 99, 141 ff.
 ownership, 42-3
Ceremonies and cults, 46, 47, 76, 77, 82, 117, 120, 139, 140, 153, 159, 165, 166, 182, 183, 192, 218, 225, 232, 233, 235 ff., 312
 fertility cult, 140, 158
 fire rite, 6, 168-9, 276
 hu phasa, 233, 235, 238, 240, 241, 244, 264
 hu runa, 281
 opening of the door, 5, 170, 171, 310-11
 ritual killing, 237-8
 spirit, bringing home of a, 238
 See also Burials; Dancing; Drums; Harvest offering; Initiation; Marriage; Possession; Rain-making; Religion; Songs; Spirits; Taboos.
Charms, 18, 148, 169, 220, 233
 rain charms, 5, 220, 311
 thugula, 233, 234, 235, 236, 241
 See also Magic.

329

GENERAL INDEX

Chastity, in women, 151, 157, 309
  in queen's wives, 174-5
Chiefs, 166, 187. *See also* District heads; Kings; Queens.
Children, 22, 24, 25, 29, 47, 73, 74, 77-8, 83-4, 111, 123, 148, 171, 294, pl. vi
  babies, 74, 102, 192, 220, pl. v
  handicrafts and, 108
  home-making, 109
  parents and, 73-4, 102 *ff*.
  play and games, 106, 108, 110
  praise and censure, 110
  suckling, 102, 103
  teeth of, 218-19
  training and daily life of, 102 *ff*.
  See also Boys; Girls.
Christianity and Christians, 46, 50, 54, 55, 56, 57, 58-9, 61, 68-9, 71, 79, 83, 103, 124-5, 157, 218, 248, 281
  culture contact and, 314 *ff*.
Cider, 18, 20, 24, 31, 46, 106, 134, 182, 190, 191, 205, 247
Circumcision, 115, 116-17, 289. *See also* Initiation.
Compromise, 186, 188, 189, 192 *ff*., 284, 285. *See also* Reconciliation.
Cooking, 22-4, 28, 31, 32
Costumes, 135, 138, 139, 140, 243, 311, pls. vii (*b*), ix, x
  dancing skirts, 136, 137
Councillors, 172-3, 189
Courtship, 152-3
  visits, 152-3
Crops, 30, 35 *ff*., 106, 183, 231, 232, 284
  damage to, 195, 251
  failure of, 39
  rotation of, 37
  uses of, 34 *ff*.
  See also Agriculture.
Cross-cousins, 77, 78, 99, 142
  marriage, 142, 143, 144, 148-9, 161
Culture, ix-xvi, 17 *ff*., 34 *ff*., 282 *ff*., 289 *ff*., 299 *et passim*
  changes, 33, 38, 43, 50-1, 54, 56, 60 *ff*., 281, 311 *ff*.
  characteristics and outlook, 52, 60, 68
  culture contact, xii, xiii, 58 *ff*., 80-1, 124-5, 186, 200, 209-10, 293, 294 *ff*., 313 *ff*.
  European culture, conflict and differences with Native culture, 34, 35, 39-40, 44, 58, 293, 294 *ff*., 314 *ff*.
  values of Lovedu, 291 *ff*.

Customs, 17, 24, 27, 32, 44-5, 57, 63, 110, 152, 153, 155. *See also* Ceremonies; and subjects by name.
Cycads, forest of, viii, 14, pl. i (*a*)

Ḍaja, forest of, 6, 128
Dancing, 9, 32, 106, 112, 113-14, 117, 118, 126, 132, 133, 134, 137, 138, 139, 236, 242-3, 244, 247, 248, 272, 287, 309, 312, pl. vii (*b*), ix, x
  gɔsha, 32, 63, 64-5, 132, 183, 321
  masked dancing, 126, 127, 135, 138, 139, 183, 311, pls. ix, x
  matangwa, 64
  Venda, 309
  See also Costumes.
Death, 219, 257, 258, 289. *See also* Burials.
Dicke, *The Bush Speaks*, 3
Diet, 36, 326. *See also* Food; Vegetation.
Digɔma. *See* Mummeries.
Diseases, 48, 157, 212 *ff*., 221-3, 242, 251, 255, 293-4
  dɛre, 221-2
  increase of, 38
  See also Medicines; Witchcraft.
District heads, 114, 116, 126, 132, 165, 172, 173-4, 175, 179, 180, 182 *ff*., 188, 190, 191, 192, 198, 199, 274, 310
  succession ceremonies of, 183
Districts, 177 *ff*., 188
  'mothers' of, 180, 187 *ff*.
Divination and diviners, 45, 203, 204 *ff*., 211, 224, 225, 277
  dice, use of ('knowing the bones'), 220, 224, 225 *ff*., 259, 268, 279
  procedure and rules of, 227 *ff*.
  smelling out, 203, 204 *ff*., 260 *ff*.
Doctors, 211, 223 *ff*., 242, 243, 254, 255, 256-7, pl. xiv (*a*)
  fees, 230, 257, 287
  mugɔme, 260 *ff*.
  See also Divination; Medicine.
Divorce, 149, 158, 198
Donkeys, 27, 45
Drums and drumming, 106, 111, 126-7, 133, 136, 183, 243, 272, 273
  drum cult, 126 *ff*., 135, 140, 166, 291, 312, 313
  gomana drums, 126 *ff*., 135, 166
Dzugudini, 5, 6, 9

'Ears', the (official witness), 206-7, 209, 260
Education, 124-5, 218-19, 319

GENERAL INDEX

Exchange, system and types of, 52, 61 ff.
  Goodwill exchanges, 27, 57, 61, 62, 63 ff., 288
  See also Barter.

FEES, 190, 191, 196, 198, 200, 209, 230, 257, 260
Fines, 74, 81, 120, 132, 134, 136, 157, 190–1, 192, 199, 200, 202, 209–10, 256, 275
Flora. See Vegetation.
Food, 19, 20, 22–4, 25, 28, 31, 32, 33, 36, 45 ff., 110, 111, 120, 135, 137, 152, 326
  beans, 35
  cereals, 35, 36
  customs, 17, 24, 110
  eleusine, 35, 37, 235
  fruits, 34, 46, 47
  grasshoppers, 25, 28, 47
  groundnuts, 37
  guests, serving of, 24
  honey, 47, 182
  kaffir corn, 25, 35, 235
  locusts, 47
  maize, 22
  mealies, 19, 20, 25, 28, 31, 32, 35, 37, 111, 182, pls. ii, iv
    stamping processes, 25, 30
  millet, 25, 35
  monkey nuts, 23, 24, 28
  morula, 31, 46
  njugo beans, 35, 36, 280–1
  peanuts, 35, 36
  porridge, 23, 25, 28, 31, 36, 112
  pumpkins, 20, 24, 28, 31, 35
  relishes, xi, 20, 22, 23, 24, 25, 31, 32, 33, 46, 47, 106
  sesamum, 36
  spinaches, wild, 46
  blackjacks, 31, 33
  vegetables, European, 33, 37
  vuswa, 22,
  vuthithi, 25
  See also Crops; Diet; Malnutrition; Vegetation.
Fowls, 45, 327

GIFTS, 61 ff., 79, 80, 109, 114, 119, 139, 149, 150, 151, 152, 153, 154, 155, 277, 281
  queen, to, 10, 18, 46, 58, 271–2
Girls, 26, 28, 29, 73, 99, 106, 110, pls. vii, viii
  mother, relations with, 112
  See also under Initiation; Work.

Goats, 19, 27, 34, 44–5, 57–8, 63, 72, 75, 79, 80, 106, 119, 130, 134, 150, 151, 154, 155, 162, 188, 190, 191, 194, 195, 196, 200, 202, 208, 215, 225, 232, 234, 237, 238, 245, 275
Grandmothers, 28, 74, 77–8
Grandparents, 239, 248
Grasshoppers. See under Food.
Graves, the royal, 6, 7, 128, 278–9
Greetings, 18, 19, 23, 103, 113, 131, 156, 236
Group, royal or nuclear (*kwɛvo*), 14, 15, 85, 87, 88, 91–2, 94–5, 96, 301, 303, 304, 305
Guests, customs concerning, 24, 27, 44

HAGGARD, Sir Rider, 'She-who-must be obeyed', 3
Handicrafts, 32, 47, 49, 50, 51, 108, 123–4, 286, pl. iii
Harvest offering, 76, 77, 182, 232, 235–7
'Heat' (*hu fesa*), 169, 220–1
Herbalism and herbalists, 47, 223
Herdboys, 17, 20, 24, 27, 28–9, 32, 42, 45, 46, 50, 57–8, 106–9, 190
  leader, 107
  See also Boys.
History, 1, 4 ff., 299 ff.
Hoeing, 30, 31, 40
Hoernlé, Mrs. A. W., xvi
Hunting, 45, 108, 120
Husbandry, animal, 42
Huts, 20 ff.
  cooking huts, 21, 22, 154
  plan of, 21
  reception huts, 21
  sleeping huts, 21–2

ILLEGITIMACY, 125, 157, 317
Incest, 81, 98, 310
  royal, 5, 6, 9–10, 12, 307, 308
Inheritance of spouses, 160
Initiation, 100, 111 ff., 115, 122, 126, 131, 166, 169, 219, 311, 312
  ceremonies, 111 ff., 115, 126, 131
  gomana, for men, 126, 128 ff., 140
  khɔba, for girls, 122, 123, 157, 169, 183
  old men, the, 116, 117, 118, 120, 122, 137
  'schools', 96, 107, 131, 132 ff., 166, 169, 328
  training value of, 121–2
  vudiga, for boys, 100, 114 ff., 169

GENERAL INDEX

Initiation—*continued*
  vuhwera, for boys, 126, 130–1, 138–9, 140, pl. x (*a*)
  vyali, for girls, 95, 100, 120, 126, 127, 128, 130 ff., 139, 140, 248, pl. viii
  muluvɛ, 132
Intermarriage, 15, 86, 94, 179

Khadi, 77, 172, 235, 238, 309, pl. xiv (*b*)
Khashani, 8, 11, 170–1, 203, 314
Khiali, King, 7–8
Khidima, 187–8, 190
Khidudwane, 251–2
Khilovedu (language), xv-xvi
Khivijɔ, 173
Khɔrɔ, 19, 28, 97, 116, 133, 141, 149, 186 ff., 211, 262, 285–6, 290, 323–4, pl. xiii (*b*)
  fees, 200
  proceedings, 186 ff.
Kings, 165–6
  cycle of, 4, 5–8
  heir, appointment of, 5, 171
  rain-making of, 1, 2
Kinship. *See* Relationships.
Krige, E. J. and J. D., methods and work, xiv-xv, 295
  Smuts, Field-Marshal J. C., on research of, viii-xii
Kwɛvo. *See* Group, royal.

LAND TENURE, 181–2
Language, xv-xvi
Leakhali, 171, 173
Lejema. *See under* Work.
Lightning, 254–5, 275
Lineage, 86, 93, 97. *See also* Group, royal.

MAḌAJI, King, 7
Magic, 18, 19, 48, 60, 75, 216, 222, 241, 283, 284, 327
  khidɔba, 256–7
  love-magic, 258
  madabi, 255–6
  maḍilebɔ, 256
  vengeance-magic, 257
  See also Medicines; Sorcerers; Spells; Witches
Maharula, 190–1
Mahasha, 6, 170, 179
Makaphimo, 5, 6
Makhuma (mingling), 219–20
Malaji, King, 6–7
Malegudu, 173
Mali I, Queen, 310
Mali II (Maake), Queen, 310
Malnutrition, 38, 326

Manḍwane (home-making), 109, pl. vii
Manjana, 310, 311
Marriage, 78, 98, 141 ff., 123, 193
  avoidances, 79–80
  bridegrooms, 79–80, 99, 152 ff.
  brides, 79–80, 99, 123, 144, 150–1, 152 ff., 194, pl. xii
  ceremonies, 141, 148, 150 ff., 155 ff., pl. xii
  Christianity, effects upon pattern of, 316–17
  elopement, 153–4, 155
  husbands, 71
  ideal, 142
  intermarriage, 15, 86, 94, 179
  party, 29
  patrilocal, 97, 156, 179
  sexual compatibility, 156–8
  spouses, inheritance of, 160
  woman-marriage, 83, 141, 143, 144, 160, 178, 245
  See also Bride-price; Cattle; Courtship; Cross-cousins; Polygyny; Queens, wives of; Relationships; Sex; Wives.
Matrilineality, 77
Mealies. *See under* Food.
Medicines, xi, 39, 48, 112, 127, 158, 168, 169, 211, 213 ff., 219, 221, 222, 223, 224, 225, 238, 244, 247, 250, 252, 253–4, 255, 256, 258, 275, 294
  bones used in, 204, 220, 224, 225 ff., 259, 268, 279, pl. xiv (*a*)
  conceptions, four categories, 217 ff.
  graves, use on, 257, 269
  magic, 18, 19, 45, 216
  protective, 18–19, 43–4, 45–6, 48, 182, 251
  See also Diseases; Divination; Herbalism; Rain-making; Therapeutics.
Menstruation, 112, 113, 155
Messengers, 179, 188, 190, 191, 202, 203, 204, 210, 273, 317
Migration, 58–60, 323
Milk, 20, 41, 45
Monomotapa, King, 5, 304
Mothers-in-law, 72, 74, 80, 123, 207
Mudiga, 6, 179
Mugɔdɔ, King, 8, 9, 12, 87, 170–1, 178
  death, 167
  incest of, 9–10
  prophecy of, 9, 12
Muhale, King, 6, 76, 161, 308
Mujaji I, 171, 173, 177, 178, 239, 310
  incest of, 9–10
  rain-making powers of, 10
  See also Queens.

GENERAL INDEX 333

Mujaji II, 2, 3, 10–11, 171, 173, 178, 182, 314
  barrenness of, 166
  suicide, ritual, of, 167
  See also Queens.
Mujaji III, viii-ix, xiii, 2, 11, 165, 170, 171, 173, 178, 185, 209–10, 236, 240, 272
  Smuts, Field-Marshal J. C., on, viii-ix
  thugula ceremony in 1938, 236–7
  See also Queens.
Mulada, 56–7
Mummeries (*digɔma*), 113–14, 117, 119, 134–5, 138, 140, 291
  Bird, the great, 126, 133, 134, 135–7, 138, 140
Muneri, 173, 189, 190
Munywalo. See Bride-price; *and under* Cattle.

NAMES, divisions, 92 *ff.*
  group, 85, 87 *ff.*
  district heads, 87

OLD AGE, 124, 240
Ordeal (*mureu*), 203–4, 205
Orphans, 83–4

PARENTS, children, relations with, 73–4, 102 *ff.*
Patients, nursing and treatment of, 216–17
Patrilinearity, 97, 98, 145, 179
Pigs, 45
Pheduli, King, 7, 201, 221, 238
Ploughing, 37, 40, 41, 55, 58
Political system, 164 *ff.*, 184–5
Polygyny, 67, 70–1, 82, 316. *See also* Wives.
Population, 13–14
Porridge. *See under* Food.
Possession, cult of, 30, 31, 132, 220, 222, 225, 241 *ff.*, 289, 313
Praises, 2, 9, 92, 95, 96, 127, 133, 136, 178–9, 227
  district praises, 95
  name praise, 28
  praise songs, 9, 18, 49, 140, 304
  praise-titles, 5, 23, 85, 95, 137, 308
Pregnancy, 158, 218
Proverbs and sayings, 77, 83, 105–6, 110, 111, 122, 152, 158, 193, 195, 201, 263, 273, 284, 285, 286, 287, 290, 291, 292, 293, 298, 323
Punishment, 74, 104, 107, 108, 120, 134, 192, 194

QUEENS, the, (Mujaji), 1, 2, 3, 47, 85, 87, 127, 128, 164, 165–6, 181, 183, 185, 190, 200, 202, 204, 283, 284
  accession, 169–70
  burial, 168
  claimants, 170
  cycle of, 4, 8–12
  divinity, xiii, 172
  fields, 100, 182, 281
  gifts to, 10, 18, 46, 58, 271–2
  heir of, 171
  incest of, 9–10
  legal proceedings, disputes and, 185, 186–7
  orphans, care for, 84
  rain-making, divine powers of, ix, 2, 7, 8, 10, 164, 165, 271 *ff.*, 283
  relations with her subjects and foreign policy, 284–5
  skin, fairness of, 2, 3
  suicide, ritual, of, 114, 166, 167, 169, 172
  wives of, 15, 137, 144, 164–5, 171, 173 *ff.*, 180, 187, 269, 308
  children of, 148, 171
  See also Mujaji I–III.

RAIN-MAKING AND RAIN-MAKERS, 1, 2, 7, 10, 139, 157, 183, 185, 220, 224, 231, 237, 241, 305, 308, 311, 320
  ancestors and, 277 *ff.*
  charms, 5, 220, 311
  cult, 126, 128, 133, 271 *ff.*, 283
  doctors, 96, 272–3, 278, 279, 280
  fire ceremony, 276
  medicines, 96, 127, 168, 273–4, 275, 276, 277, 278, 279, 281, 306
  powers, handing down of, 7, 8
  queen, divine powers of, ix, 2, 7, 8, 10, 164, 165, 271 *ff.*, 283
  sacrifices for, 277–9
Ramatiti, 228–9
Rank, 86, 101, 131, 132
Rasekwalo (rain doctor), 128–9
Raselaka (headman), 19, 21, 26–7
Reciprocity, xi, 63 ff., 99, 284 *ff. See also* Relationships.
Reconciliation, methods of, 181, 186, 188, 189, 192 *ff.*, 284 285, 288
  duma muladu, 195–6
  hu khumɛlwa, 192 *ff.*, 201, 202, 284
Relationships, 66 *ff.*, 70 *ff.*, 82–4, 98–9, 179–81, 239, 263
  bilateral kin groups, 86
  cattle-linked, 66–7, 77, 98–9, 142–5, 146, 197–8

GENERAL INDEX

Relationships—*continued*
  classificatory, 70, 71, 75, 76–7, 80, 148
  group links, 81 *ff.*
  joking relationships, 77, 78
  reciprocity between, xi, 63 *ff.*, 99, 284 *ff.*
  relatives-in-law, 27, 32, 44–5, 63, 64, 72, 78–9, 80, 123, 156, 159, 207
  tension in, 63, 86, 162–3, 193 *ff.*
  terms, correct use of, 111
  See also Bride-price; Brothers; Cross-cousins; Grandmothers; Marriage; Mothers-in-law; Parents; Wives.
Religion, 231 *ff.*, 328, pls. xiv (*b*), xvi
Reserve, the, 13–14, 17 *ff.*, pl. i
Riddles, 29, 79, 83, 119, 138, 155
Ritual. *See* Ceremonies.

SACRIFICES, 277–9
Salt, 118
Sanctions, xi, 292, 296, 323
Seasons, the, 30 *ff.*, 46, 139
  khilemo (hoeing time), 30–1
  leṭavula (summer), 30, 31–2
  maria (winter), 30, 32–3
Sephumulo, 8
Sex and sexual relationships, 103, 113, 123, 137, 157–8, 161, 220, 221–2, 268
  attitude towards, 289–90
  inoculation, mutual, 155, 214
  medicine and, 221–2
  extra-marital, 123, 157, 158
  See also Incest; Marriage; Wives.
Shadow (*muridi*), 217, 218–9
Sheep, 45, 237, 274, 276, 277, 278
'Shepherds' (*medabi*), 100, 116, 117, 118, 119, 120, 129, 130, 133
Shrines, 136, 232, 234, 235, pl. xvi
Sisters, 75, 159
  relationship with brothers, 67, 73, 75–7, 142–5, 146, 197–8
Slavery, 58
Smuts, Field-Marshal J. C., holiday in Mujaji's country, viii
  on Lovedu, ix–xii
  on Mujaji III, viii–ix
  on work of E. J. and J. D. Krige, viii–xii
Smuts, Mrs., Mujaji III and, viii–ix
Snake, belief of, in stomach, 212
Soil erosion, 41, 326
Songs, 29, 113, 115, 116, 117, 122, 126, 129, 132, 133–4, 136, 137, 157, 236, 237, 245, 246, 247, 272, 316

Sorcerers and sorcery, 10, 96, 203, 221, 222, 223, 226, 250 *ff.*
Spells, 253, 257, 289. *See also* Magic; Sorcerers; Witches.
Spirits, 76, 100, 126, 129, 132, 238
  ancestral (*zwiḍajani*), 126, 127, 128, 130, 135, 140, 202, 237, 241, 242 *ff.*, 312, 313
  See also Ancestors.
Story-telling, 29
Sugar-cane, 28, 36
Suicide, ritual, of the chief, 5, 114, 165 *ff.*, 172, 307, 310
  effects of, 167, 169
Superstition, 39

TABOOS, 43, 47, 48, 53, 77, 80, 108, 115, 117, 118, 132, 152, 153, 156, 158, 167, 183, 225, 241, 246, 277, 281, 317
Termites, 31, 46–7, 183, 220, 274–5
Theft, 111, 194, 222
  technique against, 256–7, 261
Therapeutics, 211 *ff.*
  scarification, 214
  steaming and smoking, 211 *ff.*
Totems, 87–8, 93, 127, 227
Trade, 61, 67–8
Transactions, commercial, 52, 56, 60, 65, 67, 68
Transvaal, Northern, tribes and their cultures, 299–300, 303, 311–12
Trees, cutting down of, 50–1, 182
Tribes, 87 *ff.*, 299–300, 311–12
  history and migrations, 303 *ff.*
  map, 302
Twins, 218, 241, 321

VEGETATION, 14, 34 *ff.*, 45 *ff.*, 108, 215
  kinds and uses of, 48–50
  knowledge of, 108
Villages, 17, 18 *ff.*, 70, 75, 150, pl. ii
  lay-out, 20
Uulovedu, 17 *ff.*, 88, 91. *See also* Reserve.

WITCHES AND WITCHCRAFT, 18, 19, 36, 38, 45, 75, 82, 105, 132, 169, 175, 184, 189, 192, 196, 203–4, 205, 207, 208, 214, 216, 220, 222, 223, 224, 227, 231, 232, 250 *ff.*, 289, 294, 310, 320
  cases of, 264–8
  day witchcraft, 250, 253–4
  methods used against, 259
  night witchcraft, 250–3
  See also Magic; Medicines; Spells.

Wives, 21, 36, 67, 70 *ff.*, 141 *ff.*, 156 *ff.*, 173
   chief wife, 21, 72-3, 99, 144, 204, 235, 236, 310
   fellow wives, 21, 72-3, 82, 193, 195-6, 263, 264-5
   mother-in-law, relations with, 72, 74, 123, 207
   polygyny, 67, 70-1, 82, 316
   substitutes for, 159-60
   wife-beating, 71
   See also Marriage; Queens, wives of.
Women, 27-8, 112, 113, 114, 123, 161, 180, 192, 198, pls. ii (*b*), v, vi, xi, xii
   beer carriers, 27
   old women, 192
   ornaments and clothing, 7
   position of, xi, 180, 283, 285
   work, 20, 22 *ff.*, 31, 32, 37, 41, 43
   See also Brides; Chastity; Grandmothers; Marriage; Sisters; Wives.

Work, 32, 41-2, 52 *ff.*, 83, 100, pls. ii (*b*), vi, vii
   attitude towards, 52, 284
   co-operation in, 52 *ff.*, pl. iv
   khilɛbɛ, 55-6
   lejema, 26-7, 52-4
   girls, 25-6, 105, 106
   labour, division of, 40-1
   men, 31, 32, 40-1, pls. iii, xiii
   organization, 52 *ff.*
   phɔdwa, 53
   services and implements, 56-8
   solitary occupations and services, 56-8
   training in, 105-6
   women, 20, 22 *ff.*, 31, 32, 37, 41, 43, pls. ii (*b*), xi
   See also Herdboys.

Zwidajani. *See under* Spirits, ancestral.

INDEX OF TRIBES, CLANS AND RACES

BANTU, x, xiii

DIKXALE, 312
Dokwa, 1, 185, 301, 303, 306

KARANGA, 168, 301, 303, 304, 305, 307, 308, 313
Khaha, 166, 306, 310
Khahi, 128
Khioga, 6, 12, 88, 89
Koni, 87, 89, 115, 301, 303, 305, 306
Kwɛna, 90, 303, 306, 311
Kxatla, 306

LAUDI, 301, 305, 306, 310, 311, 312
Letswalo, 305, 306, 310, 311
Lozwi, 305

MAPALA, 283, 289, 312
Mahlo, 305, 310
Mamaila, 14, 166, 170, 179, 305, 309, 310
Mamavolo, 299, 307, 312
Moila, 305, 312
Moletshe, 283, 303, 306

NARENI, 127, 128, 133, 255, 301, 305, 310
Ndebele, 304
Ngona, 6
Nguni, x, 79, 232, 233, 242, 248, 284, 289, 303, 305
Ngwato, 96, 303
Nkuni, 304
Nyai, 301, 305

PEDI, 1, 13, 276, 306, 310, 311, 312
Phalavorwa, 203, 280, 289, 305, 312
Pondo, 75, 251

RAKWADU (Rakhwadu), 8, 14, 170
Roka, 14, 36
Rozwi, 165

SEKHOPO, 8, 14, 61, 170, 300, 309, 310
Sekhwasha, 242
Shai, 299, 306
Shangana-Tonga, 13, 14, 15, 26, 36, 40, 45, 47, 58, 67, 68, 78, 87, 88, 89, 121, 157, 158, 174, 179, 188, 204, 208, 224, 242, 250, 251, 285, 288, 289, 290, 305, 306-7, 309, 313, 325
Shona, x, 165, 307, 308
Sotho, x, xv, xvi, 7, 14, 89, 168, 173, 283, 299, 303, 304, 305, 306, 309-10, 312

TALƐRWA, 306
Thavina, 127, 166
Thovolo, 183, 241, 272, 305, 313
Tonga, 303, 312
Tswale, 96, 300, 305
Tswana, 284, 303, 306, 312

VENDA, xv, xvi, 1, 13, 64, 87, 88, 89, 90, 95, 250, 300, 301, 305, 307, 308-9, 310, 312
Uirwa, 96, 154, 166, 301, 303, 305, 307, 312

XANANWA, 283
Xhosa, 258

ZANDE (Azande), 250, 253
Zulus, 1, 213, 232, 258

*Made and printed in Great Britain by
The Camelot Press Limited, London and Southampton*